FORD

MUSTANG/CAPRI
1979-88 REPAIR MANUAL

CHILTON'S

Covers all U.S. and Canadian models of
Ford Mustang and Mercury Capri

by Richard Schwartz, A.S.E.

CHILTON *Automotive Books*

PUBLISHED BY **HAYNES NORTH AMERICA. Inc.**

AUTOMOTIVE PARTS & ACCESSORIES ASSOCIATION MEMBER

Manufactured in USA
© 1995 Haynes North America, Inc.
ISBN 0-8019-8580-3
Library of Congress Catalog Card No. 94-071960
8901234567 9876543210

Haynes Publishing Group
Sparkford Nr Yeovil
Somerset BA22 7JJ England

Haynes North America, Inc
861 Lawrence Drive
Newbury Park
California 91320 USA

ABCDE
FGH

Contents

Contents

SAFETY NOTICE

Proper service and repair procedures are vital to the safe, reliable operation of all motor vehicles, as well as the personal safety of those performing repairs. This manual outlines procedures for servicing and repairing vehicles using safe, effective methods. The procedures contain many NOTES, CAUTIONS and WARNINGS which should be followed, along with standard procedures to eliminate the possibility of personal injury or improper service which could damage the vehicle or compromise its safety.

It is important to note that repair procedures and techniques, tools and parts for servicing motor vehicles, as well as the skill and experience of the individual performing the work vary widely. It is not possible to anticipate all of the conceivable ways or conditions under which vehicles may be serviced, or to provide cautions as to all possible hazards that may result. Standard and accepted safety precautions and equipment should be used when handling toxic or flammable fluids, and safety goggles or other protection should be used during cutting, grinding, chiseling, prying, or any other process that can cause material removal or projectiles.

Some procedures require the use of tools specially designed for a specific purpose. Before substituting another tool or procedure, you must be completely satisfied that neither your personal safety, nor the performance of the vehicle will be endangered.

Although information in this manual is based on industry sources and is complete as possible at the time of publication, the possibility exists that some car manufacturers made later changes which could not be included here. While striving for total accuracy, the authors or publishers cannot assume responsibility for any errors, changes or omissions that may occur in the compilation of this data.

PART NUMBERS

Part numbers listed in this reference are not recommendations by Haynes North America, Inc. for any product brand name. They are references that can be used with interchange manuals and aftermarket supplier catalogs to locate each brand supplier's discrete part number.

SPECIAL TOOLS

Special tools are recommended by the vehicle manufacturer to perform their specific job. Use has been kept to a minimum, but where absolutely necessary, they are referred to in the text by the part number of the tool manufacturer. These tools can be purchased, under the appropriate part number, from your local dealer or regional distributor, or an equivalent tool can be purchased locally from a tool supplier or parts outlet. Before substituting any tool for the one recommended, read the SAFETY NOTICE at the top of this page.

ACKNOWLEDGMENTS

This publication contains material that is reproduced and distributed under a license from Ford Motor Company. No further reproduction or distribution of the Ford Motor Company material is allowed without the express written permission from Ford Motor Company.

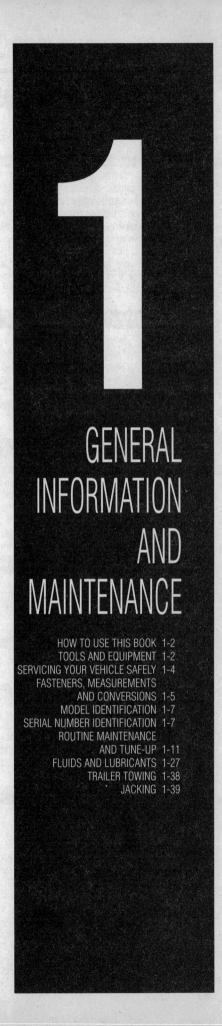

1

GENERAL INFORMATION AND MAINTENANCE

HOW TO USE THIS BOOK

This Chilton's Total Car Care manual is intended to help you learn more about the inner workings of your Mustang while saving you money on its upkeep and operation.

The beginning of the book will likely be referred to the most, since that is where you will find information for maintenance and tune-up. The other sections deal with the more complex systems of your vehicle. Systems (from engine through brakes) are covered to the extent that the average do-it-yourselfer can attempt. This book will not explain such things as rebuilding a differential because the expertise required and the special tools necessary make this uneconomical. It will, however, give you detailed instructions to help you change your own brake pads and shoes, replace spark plugs, and perform many more jobs that can save you money and help avoid expensive problems.

A secondary purpose of this book is a reference for owners who want to understand their vehicle and/or their mechanics better.

Where to Begin

Before removing any bolts, read through the entire procedure. This will give you the overall view of what tools and supplies will be required. So read ahead and plan ahead. Each operation should be approached logically and all procedures thoroughly understood before attempting any work.

If repair of a component is not considered practical, we tell you how to remove the part and then how to install the new or rebuilt replacement. In this way, you at least save labor costs.

Avoiding Trouble

Many procedures in this book require you to "label and disconnect . . ." a group of lines, hoses or wires. Don't be think you can remember where everything goes—you won't. If you hook up vacuum or fuel lines incorrectly, the vehicle may run poorly, if at all. If you hook up electrical wiring incorrectly, you may instantly learn a very expensive lesson.

You don't need to know the proper name for each hose or line. A piece of masking tape on the hose and a piece on its fitting will allow you to assign your own label. As long as you remember your own code, the lines can be reconnected by matching your tags. Remember that tape will dissolve in gasoline or solvents; if a part is to be washed or cleaned, use another method of identification. A permanent felt-tipped marker or a metal scribe can be very handy for marking metal parts. Remove any tape or paper labels after assembly.

Maintenance or Repair?

Maintenance includes routine inspections, adjustments, and replacement of parts which show signs of normal wear. Maintenance compensates for wear or deterioration. Repair implies that something has broken or is not working. A need for a repair is often caused by lack of maintenance. for example: draining and refilling automatic transmission fluid is maintenance recommended at specific intervals. Failure to do this can shorten the life of the transmission/transaxle, requiring very expensive repairs. While no maintenance program can prevent items from eventually breaking or wearing out, a general rule is true: MAINTENANCE IS CHEAPER THAN REPAIR.

Two basic mechanic's rules should be mentioned here. First, whenever the left side of the vehicle or engine is referred to, it means the driver's side. Conversely, the right side of the vehicle means the passenger's side. Second, screws and bolts are removed by turning counterclockwise, and tightened by turning clockwise unless specifically noted.

Safety is always the most important rule. Constantly be aware of the dangers involved in working on an automobile and take the proper precautions. Please refer to the information in this section regarding SERVICING YOUR VEHICLE SAFELY and the SAFETY NOTICE on the acknowledgment page.

Avoiding the Most Common Mistakes

Pay attention to the instructions provided. There are 3 common mistakes in mechanical work:

1. Incorrect order of assembly, disassembly or adjustment. When taking something apart or putting it together, performing steps in the wrong order usually just costs you extra time; however, it CAN break something. Read the entire procedure before beginning. Perform everything in the order in which the instructions say you should, even if you can't see a reason for it. When you're taking apart something that is very intricate, you might want to draw a picture of how it looks when assembled in order to make sure you get everything back in its proper position. When making adjustments, perform them in the proper order. One adjustment possibly will affect another.

2. Overtorquing (or undertorquing). While it is more common for overtorquing to cause damage, undertorquing may allow a fastener to vibrate loose causing serious damage. Especially when dealing with aluminum parts, pay attention to torque specifications and utilize a torque wrench in assembly. If a torque figure is not available, remember that if you are using the right tool to perform the job, you will probably not have to strain yourself to get a fastener tight enough. The pitch of most threads is so slight that the tension you put on the wrench will be multiplied many times in actual force on what you are tightening.

There are many commercial products available for ensuring that fasteners won't come loose, even if they are not torqued just right (a very common brand is Loctite®). If you're worried about getting something together tight enough to hold, but loose enough to avoid mechanical damage during assembly, one of these products might offer substantial insurance. Before choosing a threadlocking compound, read the label on the package and make sure the product is compatible with the materials, fluids, etc. involved.

3. Crossthreading. This occurs when a part such as a bolt is screwed into a nut or casting at the wrong angle and forced. Crossthreading is more likely to occur if access is difficult. It helps to clean and lubricate fasteners, then to start threading the bolt, spark plug, etc. with your fingers. If you encounter resistance, unscrew the part and start over again at a different angle until it can be inserted and turned several times without much effort. Keep in mind that many parts have tapered threads, so that gentle turning will automatically bring the part you're threading to the proper angle. Don't put a wrench on the part until it's been tightened a couple of turns by hand. If you suddenly encounter resistance, and the part has not seated fully, don't force it. Pull it back out to make sure it's clean and threading properly.

Be sure to take your time and be patient, and always plan ahead. Allow yourself ample time to perform repairs and maintenance.

TOOLS AND EQUIPMENT

▶ **See Figures 1 thru 15**

Without the proper tools and equipment it is impossible to properly service your vehicle. It would be virtually impossible to catalog every tool that you would need to perform all of the operations in this book. It would be unwise for the amateur to rush out and buy an expensive set of tools on the theory that he/she may need one or more of them at some time.

The best approach is to proceed slowly, gathering a good quality set of those tools that are used most frequently. Don't be misled by the low cost of bargain tools. It is far better to spend a little more for better quality. Forged wrenches, 6 or 12-point sockets and fine tooth ratchets are by far preferable to their less expensive counterparts. As any good mechanic can tell you, there are few worse experiences than trying to work on a vehicle with bad tools. Your monetary savings will be far outweighed by frustration and mangled knuckles.

Begin accumulating those tools that are used most frequently: those associated with routine maintenance and tune-up. In addition to the normal assortment of screwdrivers and pliers, you should have the following tools:

• Wrenches/sockets and combination open end/box end wrenches in sizes ⅛–¾ in. and/or 3mm–19mm ¹³⁄₁₆ in. or ⅝ in. spark plug socket (depending on plug type).

➡**If possible, buy various length socket drive extensions. Universal-joint and wobble extensions can be extremely useful, but be careful when using them, as they can change the amount of torque applied to the socket.**

• Jackstands for support.
• Oil filter wrench.
• Spout or funnel for pouring fluids.

• Grease gun for chassis lubrication (unless your vehicle is not equipped with any grease fittings)

• Hydrometer for checking the battery (unless equipped with a sealed, maintenance-free battery).

• A container for draining oil and other fluids.

• Rags for wiping up the inevitable mess.

In addition to the above items there are several others that are not absolutely necessary, but handy to have around. These include an equivalent oil absorbent gravel, like cat litter, and the usual supply of lubricants, antifreeze and fluids. This is a basic list for routine maintenance, but only your personal needs and desire can accurately determine your list of tools.

After performing a few projects on the vehicle, you'll be amazed at the other tools and non-tools on your workbench. Some useful household items are: a large turkey baster or siphon, empty coffee cans and ice trays (to store parts), a ball of twine, electrical tape for wiring, small rolls of colored tape for tagging lines or hoses, markers and pens, a note pad, golf tees (for plugging vacuum lines), metal coat hangers or a roll of mechanic's wire (to hold things out of the way), dental pick or similar long, pointed probe, a strong magnet, and a small mirror (to see into recesses and under manifolds).

A more advanced set of tools, suitable for tune-up work, can be drawn up easily. While the tools are slightly more sophisticated, they need not be outrageously expensive. There are several inexpensive tach/dwell meters on the market that are every bit as good for the average mechanic as a professional model. Just be sure that it goes to a least 1200–1500 rpm on the tach scale and that it works on 4, 6 and 8-cylinder engines. The key to these purchases is to make them with an eye towards adaptability and wide range. A basic list of tune-up tools could include:

• Tach/dwell meter.

• Spark plug wrench and gapping tool.

• Feeler gauges for valve adjustment.

• Timing light.

The choice of a timing light should be made carefully. A light which works on the DC current supplied by the vehicle's battery is the best choice; it should have a xenon tube for brightness. On any vehicle with an electronic ignition sys-

Fig. 1 All but the most basic procedures will require an assortment of ratchets and sockets

TCCS1200

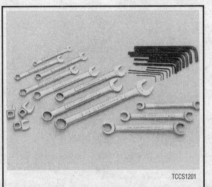

Fig. 2 In addition to ratchets, a good set of wrenches and hex keys will be necessary

TCCS1201

Fig. 3 A hydraulic floor jack and a set cf jackstands are essential for lifting and supporting the vehicle

TCCS1202

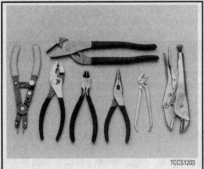

Fig. 4 An assortment of pliers, grippers and cutters will be handy for old rusted parts and stripped bolt heads

TCCS1203

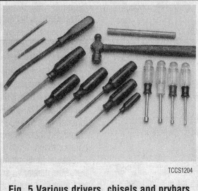

Fig. 5 Various drivers, chisels and prybars are great tools to have in your toolbox

TCCS1204

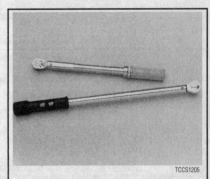

Fig. 6 Many repairs will require the use of a torque wrench to assure the components are properly fastened

TCCS1205

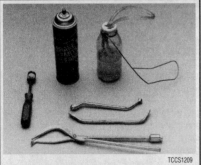

Fig. 7 Although not always necessary, using specialized brake tools will save time

TCCS1209

Fig. 8 A few inexpensive lubrication tools will make maintenance easier

TCCS1210

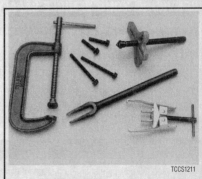

Fig. 9 Various pullers, clamps and separator tools are needed for many larger, more complicated repairs

TCCS1211

Fig. 10 A variety of tools and gauges should be used for spark plug gapping and installation

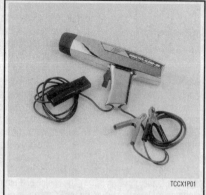

Fig. 11 Inductive type timing light

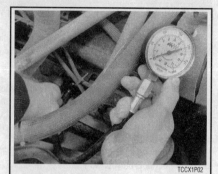

Fig. 12 A screw-in type compression gauge is recommended for compression testing

Fig. 13 A vacuum/pressure tester is necessary for many testing procedures

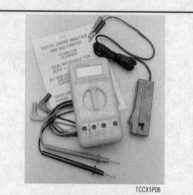

Fig. 14 Most modern automotive multimeters incorporate many helpful features

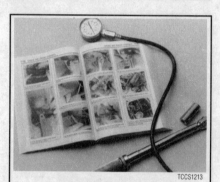

Fig. 15 Proper information is vital, so always have a Chilton Total Car Care manual handy

tem, a timing light with an inductive pickup that clamps around the No. 1 spark plug cable is preferred.

In addition to these basic tools, there are several other tools and gauges you may find useful. These include:

• Compression gauge. The screw-in type is slower to use, but eliminates the possibility of a faulty reading due to escaping pressure.

• Manifold vacuum gauge.

• 12V test light.

• A combination volt/ohmmeter

• Induction Ammeter. This is used for determining whether or not there is current in a wire. These are handy for use if a wire is broken somewhere in a wiring harness.

As a final note, you will probably find a torque wrench necessary for all but the most basic work. The beam type models are perfectly adequate, although the newer click types (breakaway) are easier to use. The click type torque wrenches tend to be more expensive. Also keep in mind that all types of torque wrenches should be periodically checked and/or recalibrated. You will have to decide for yourself which better fits your pocketbook, and purpose.

Special Tools

Normally, the use of special factory tools is avoided for repair procedures, since these are not readily available for the do-it-yourself mechanic. When it is possible to perform the job with more commonly available tools, it will be pointed out, but occasionally, a special tool was designed to perform a specific function and should be used. Before substituting another tool, you should be convinced that neither your safety nor the performance of the vehicle will be compromised.

Special tools can usually be purchased from an automotive parts store or from your dealer. In some cases special tools may be available directly from the tool manufacturer.

SERVICING YOUR VEHICLE SAFELY

▶ **See Figures 16, 17 and 18**

It is virtually impossible to anticipate all of the hazards involved with automotive maintenance and service, but care and common sense will prevent most accidents.

The rules of safety for mechanics range from "don't smoke around gasoline," to "use the proper tool(s) for the job." The trick to avoiding injuries is to develop safe work habits and to take every possible precaution.

Do's

• Do keep a fire extinguisher and first aid kit handy.

• Do wear safety glasses or goggles when cutting, drilling, grinding or prying, even if you have 20–20 vision. If you wear glasses for the sake of vision, wear safety goggles over your regular glasses.

• Do shield your eyes whenever you work around the battery. Batteries contain sulfuric acid. In case of contact with, flush the area with water or a mixture of water and baking soda, then seek immediate medical attention.

• Do use safety stands (jackstands) for any undervehicle service. Jacks are for raising vehicles; jackstands are for making sure the vehicle stays raised until you want it to come down.

• Do use adequate ventilation when working with any chemicals or hazardous materials. Like carbon monoxide, the asbestos dust resulting from some brake lining wear can be hazardous in sufficient quantities.

• Do disconnect the negative battery cable when working on the electrical system. The secondary ignition system contains EXTREMELY HIGH VOLTAGE. In some cases it can even exceed 50,000 volts.

• Do follow manufacturer's directions whenever working with potentially hazardous materials. Most chemicals and fluids are poisonous.

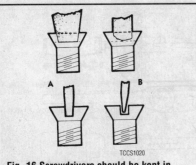

Fig. 16 Screwdrivers should be kept in good condition to prevent injury or damage which could result if the blade slips from the screw

Fig. 17 Using the correct size wrench will help prevent the possibility of rounding off a nut

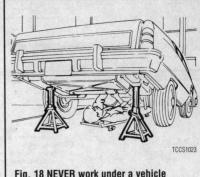

Fig. 18 NEVER work under a vehicle unless it is supported using safety stands (jackstands)

- Do properly maintain your tools. Loose hammerheads, mushroomed punches and chisels, frayed or poorly grounded electrical cords, excessively worn screwdrivers, spread wrenches (open end), cracked sockets, slipping ratchets, or faulty droplight sockets can cause accidents.
- Likewise, keep your tools clean; a greasy wrench can slip off a bolt head, ruining the bolt and often harming your knuckles in the process.
- Do use the proper size and type of tool for the job at hand. Do select a wrench or socket that fits the nut or bolt. The wrench or socket should sit straight, not cocked.
- Do, when possible, pull on a wrench handle rather than push on it, and adjust your stance to prevent a fall.
- Do be sure that adjustable wrenches are tightly closed on the nut or bolt and pulled so that the force is on the side of the fixed jaw.
- Do strike squarely with a hammer; avoid glancing blows.
- Do set the parking brake and block the drive wheels if the work requires a running engine.

Don'ts

- Don't run the engine in a garage or anywhere else without proper ventilation—EVER! Carbon monoxide is poisonous; it takes a long time to leave the human body and you can build up a deadly supply of it in your system by simply breathing in a little at a time. You may not realize you are slowly poisoning yourself. Always use power vents, windows, fans and/or open the garage door.
- Don't work around moving parts while wearing loose clothing. Short sleeves are much safer than long, loose sleeves. Hard-toed shoes with neoprene soles protect your toes and give a better grip on slippery surfaces. Watches and jewelry is not safe working around a vehicle. Long hair should be tied back under a hat or cap.
- Don't use pockets for toolboxes. A fall or bump can drive a screwdriver deep into your body. Even a rag hanging from your back pocket can wrap around a spinning shaft or fan.
- Don't smoke when working around gasoline, cleaning solvent or other flammable material.
- Don't smoke when working around the battery. When the battery is being charged, it gives off explosive hydrogen gas.
- Don't use gasoline to wash your hands; there are excellent soaps available. Gasoline contains dangerous additives which can enter the body through a cut or through your pores. Gasoline also removes all the natural oils from the skin so that bone dry hands will suck up oil and grease.
- Don't service the air conditioning system unless you are equipped with the necessary tools and training. When liquid or compressed gas refrigerant is released to atmospheric pressure it will absorb heat from whatever it contacts. This will chill or freeze anything it touches.
- Don't use screwdrivers for anything other than driving screws! A screwdriver used as an prying tool can snap when you least expect it, causing injuries. At the very least, you'll ruin a good screwdriver.
- Don't use an emergency jack (that little ratchet, scissors, or pantograph jack supplied with the vehicle) for anything other than changing a flat! These jacks are only intended for emergency use out on the road; they are NOT designed as a maintenance tool. If you are serious about maintaining your vehicle yourself, invest in a hydraulic floor jack of at least a 1½ ton capacity, and at least two sturdy jackstands.

FASTENERS, MEASUREMENTS AND CONVERSIONS

Bolts, Nuts and Other Threaded Retainers

▶ **See Figures 19 and 20**

Although there are a great variety of fasteners found in the modern car or truck, the most commonly used retainer is the threaded fastener (nuts, bolts, screws, studs, etc.). Most threaded retainers may be reused, provided that they are not damaged in use or during the repair. Some retainers (such as stretch bolts or torque prevailing nuts) are designed to deform when tightened or in use and should not be reinstalled.

Whenever possible, we will note any special retainers which should be replaced during a procedure. But you should always inspect the condition of a retainer when it is removed and replace any that show signs of damage. Check all threads for rust or corrosion which can increase the torque necessary to achieve the desired clamp load for which that fastener was originally selected. Additionally, be sure that the driver surface of the fastener has not been compromised by rounding or other damage. In some cases a driver surface may become only partially rounded, allowing the driver to catch in only one direction. In many of these occurrences, a fastener may be installed and tightened, but the driver would not be able to grip and loosen the fastener again.

If you must replace a fastener, whether due to design or damage, you must ALWAYS be sure to use the proper replacement. In all cases, a retainer of the

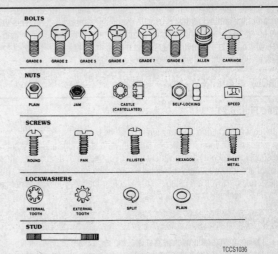

Fig. 19 There are many different types of threaded retainers found on vehicles

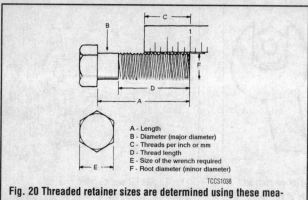

Fig. 20 Threaded retainer sizes are determined using these measurements

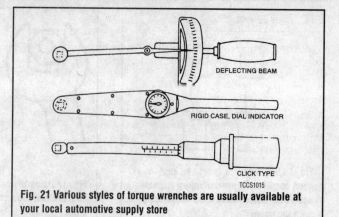

Fig. 21 Various styles of torque wrenches are usually available at your local automotive supply store

same design, material and strength should be used. Markings on the heads of most bolts will help determine the proper strength of the fastener. The same material, thread and pitch must be selected to assure proper installation and safe operation of the vehicle afterwards.

Thread gauges are available to help measure a bolt or stud's thread. Most automotive and hardware stores keep gauges available to help you select the proper size. In a pinch, you can use another nut or bolt for a thread gauge. If the bolt you are replacing is not too badly damaged, you can select a match by finding another bolt which will thread in its place. If you find a nut which threads properly onto the damaged bolt, then use that nut to help select the replacement bolt.

✳✳ WARNING

Be aware that when you find a bolt with damaged threads, you may also find the nut or drilled hole it was threaded into has also been damaged. If this is the case, you may have to drill and tap the hole, replace the nut or otherwise repair the threads. NEVER try to force a replacement bolt to fit into the damaged threads.

Torque

Torque is defined as the measurement of resistance to turning or rotating. It tends to twist a body about an axis of rotation. A common example of this would be tightening a threaded retainer such as a nut, bolt or screw. Measuring torque is one of the most common ways to help assure that a threaded retainer has been properly fastened.

When tightening a threaded fastener, torque is applied in three distinct areas, the head, the bearing surface and the clamp load. About 50 percent of the measured torque is used in overcoming bearing friction. This is the friction between the bearing surface of the bolt head, screw head or nut face and the base material or washer (the surface on which the fastener is rotating). Approximately 40 percent of the applied torque is used in overcoming thread friction. This leaves only about 10 percent of the applied torque to develop a useful clamp load (the force which holds a joint together). This means that friction can account for as much as 90 percent of the applied torque on a fastener.

TORQUE WRENCHES

▶ See Figure 21

In most applications, a torque wrench can be used to assure proper installation of a fastener. Torque wrenches come in various designs and most automotive supply stores will carry a variety to suit your needs. A torque wrench should be used any time we supply a specific torque value for a fastener. Again, the general rule of "if you are using the right tool for the job, you should not have to strain to tighten a fastener" applies here.

Beam Type

The beam type torque wrench is one of the most popular types. It consists of a pointer attached to the head that runs the length of the flexible beam (shaft) to a scale located near the handle. As the wrench is pulled, the beam bends and the pointer indicates the torque using the scale.

Click (Breakaway) Type

Another popular design of torque wrench is the click type. To use the click type wrench you pre-adjust it to a torque setting. Once the torque is reached, the wrench has a reflex signaling feature that causes a momentary breakaway of the torque wrench body, sending an impulse to the operator's hand.

Pivot Head Type

▶ See Figure 22

Some torque wrenches (usually of the click type) may be equipped with a pivot head which can allow it to be used in areas of limited access. BUT, it must be used properly. To hold a pivot head wrench, grasp the handle lightly, and as you pull on the handle, it should be floated on the pivot point. If the handle comes in contact with the yoke extension during the process of pulling, there is a very good chance the torque readings will be inaccurate because this could alter the wrench loading point. The design of the handle is usually such as to make it inconvenient to deliberately misuse the wrench.

➥ It should be mentioned that the use of any U-joint, wobble or extension will have an effect on the torque readings, no matter what type of wrench you are using. For the most accurate readings, install the socket directly on the wrench driver. If necessary, straight extensions (which hold a socket directly under the wrench driver) will have the least effect on the torque reading. Avoid any extension that alters the length of the wrench from the handle to the head/driving point (such as a crow's foot). U-joint or wobble extensions can greatly affect the readings; avoid their use at all times.

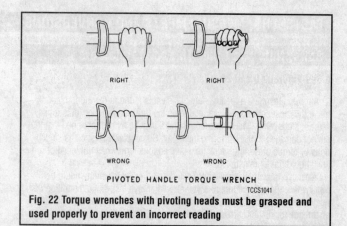

Fig. 22 Torque wrenches with pivoting heads must be grasped and used properly to prevent an incorrect reading

Rigid Case (Direct Reading)

A rigid case or direct reading torque wrench is equipped with a dial indicator to show torque values. One advantage of these wrenches is that they can be held at any position on the wrench without affecting accuracy. These wrenches are often preferred because they tend to be compact, easy to read and have a great degree of accuracy.

TORQUE ANGLE METERS

Because the frictional characteristics of each fastener or threaded hole will vary, clamp loads which are based strictly on torque will vary as well. In most applications, this variance is not significant enough to cause worry. But, in certain applications, a manufacturer's engineers may determine that more precise clamp loads are necessary (such is the case with many aluminum cylinder heads). In these cases, a torque angle method of installation would be specified. When installing fasteners which are torque angle tightened, a predetermined seating torque and standard torque wrench are usually used first to remove any compliance from the joint. The fastener is then tightened the specified additional portion of a turn measured in degrees. A torque angle gauge (mechanical protractor) is used for these applications.

Standard and Metric Measurements

▶ See Figure 23

Throughout this manual, specifications are given to help you determine the condition of various components on your vehicle, or to assist you in their installation. Some of the most common measurements include length (in. or cm/mm), torque (ft. lbs., inch lbs. or Nm) and pressure (psi, in. Hg, kPa or mm Hg). In most cases, we strive to provide the proper measurement as determined by the manufacturer's engineers.

Though, in some cases, that value may not be conveniently measured with what is available in your toolbox. Luckily, many of the measuring devices which are available today will have two scales so the Standard or Metric measurements may easily be taken. If any of the various measuring tools which are available to you do not contain the same scale as listed in the specifications, use the accompanying conversion factors to determine the proper value.

The conversion factor chart is used by taking the given specification and multiplying it by the necessary conversion factor. For instance, looking at the first line, if you have a measurement in inches such as "free-play should be 2 in." but your ruler reads only in millimeters, multiply 2 in. by the conversion factor of 25.4 to get the metric equivalent of 50.8mm. Likewise, if the specification was given only in a Metric measurement, for example in Newton Meters (Nm), then look at the center column first. If the measurement is 100 Nm, multiply it by the conversion factor of 0.738 to get 73.8 ft. lbs.

CONVERSION FACTORS

LENGTH–DISTANCE

Inches (in.)	x 25.4	= Millimeters (mm)	x .0394	= Inches
Feet (ft.)	x .305	= Meters (m)	x 3.281	= Feet
Miles	x 1.609	= Kilometers (km)	x .0621	= Miles

VOLUME

Cubic Inches (in3)	x 16.387	= Cubic Centimeters	x .061	= in3
IMP Pints (IMP pt.)	x .568	= Liters (L)	x 1.76	= IMP pt.
IMP Quarts (IMP qt.)	x 1.137	= Liters (L)	x .88	= IMP qt.
IMP Gallons (IMP gal.)	x 4.546	= Liters (L)	x .22	= IMP gal.
IMP Quarts (IMP qt.)	x 1.201	= US Quarts (US qt.)	x .833	= IMP qt.
IMP Gallons (IMP gal.)	x 1.201	= US Gallons (US gal.)	x .833	= IMP gal.
Fl. Ounces	x 29.573	= Milliliters	x .034	= Ounces
US Pints (US pt.)	x .473	= Liters (L)	x 2.113	= Pints
US Quarts (US qt.)	x .946	= Liters (L)	x 1.057	= Quarts
US Gallons (US gal.)	x 3.785	= Liters (L)	x .264	= Gallons

MASS–WEIGHT

Ounces (oz.)	x 28.35	= Grams (g)	x .035	= Ounces
Pounds (lb.)	x .454	= Kilograms (kg)	x 2.205	= Pounds

PRESSURE

Pounds Per Sq. In. (psi)	x 6.895	= Kilopascals (kPa)	x .145	= psi
Inches of Mercury (Hg)	x .4912	= psi	x 2.036	= Hg
Inches of Mercury (Hg)	x 3.377	= Kilopascals (kPa)	x .2961	= Hg
Inches of Water (H_2O)	x .07355	= Inches of Mercury	x 13.783	= H_2O
Inches of Water (H_2O)	x .03613	= psi	x 27.684	= H_2O
Inches of Water (H_2O)	x .248	= Kilopascals (kPa)	x 4.026	= H_2O

TORQUE

Pounds–Force Inches (in–lb)	x .113	= Newton Meters (N·m)	x 8.85	= in–lb
Pounds–Force Feet (ft–lb)	x 1.356	= Newton Meters (N·m)	x .738	= ft–lb

VELOCITY

Miles Per Hour (MPH)	x 1.609	= Kilometers Per Hour (KPH)	x .621	= MPH

POWER

Horsepower (Hp)	x .745	= Kilowatts	x 1.34	= Horsepower

FUEL CONSUMPTION*

Miles Per Gallon IMP (MPG)	x .354	= Kilometers Per Liter (Km/L)	
Kilometers Per Liter (Km/L)	x 2.352	= IMP MPG	
Miles Per Gallon US (MPG)	x .425	= Kilometers Per Liter (Km/L)	
Kilometers Per Liter (Km/L)	x 2.352	= US MPG	

*It is common to covert from miles per gallon (mpg) to liters/100 kilometers (1/100 km), where mpg (IMP) x 1/100 km = 282 and mpg (US) x 1/100 km = 235.

TEMPERATURE

Degree Fahrenheit (°F) = (°C x 1.8) + 32
Degree Celsius (°C) = (°F – 32) x .56

TCCS1044

Fig. 23 Standard and metric conversion factors chart

MODEL IDENTIFICATION

The vehicle can be identified by either the Body Serial Code or the Body Style Code:

Body Serial Code

This 2–digit number, found within the Vehicle Identification Number, is represented by the 3rd and 4th characters on 1979–80 vehicles, and by the 6th and 7th characters on 1981–88 vehicles.

Body Style Code

This 3–digit number/letter combination, found on the Vehicle Certification Label, likewise provides information on body type, series and line.

SERIAL NUMBER IDENTIFICATION

Vehicle

▶ See Figure 24

The official Vehicle Identification Number (for title and registration purposes) is stamped on a metal tab which is fastened to the instrument panel. It is close to the windshield on the driver's side and is visible from outside the vehicle. In addition to the aforementioned model identification, the Vehicle Identification Number also contains coded information regarding the assembly plant, model year, type of engine, and production sequence number. Beginning with the 1981 model year, the expanded Vehicle Identification Number also includes coding for the type of restraint system, as well as the identity of the vehicle's specific world manufacturer.

The Vehicle Certification Label is affixed to the left front door lock panel or door pillar. The upper half of the label contains the manufacturer's name, month and year of manufacture, Gross Vehicle Weight Rating (GVWR), Gross Axle Weight Rating (GAWR), and the certification statement. The lower half of the label contains the Vehicle Identification Number, as well as coded information regarding the vehicle's color, body type and interior trim, as well as axle ratio and transmission. Additional codes on the lower portion of the label pertain to the vehicle's air conditioning, radio, vinyl roof and sun roof (if applicable). Beginning

85801090

Fig. 24 The Vehicle Identification Number is visible through the windshield on the driver's side

with the 1981 model year, the Vehicle Certification Label also includes coding for body side moulding, front and rear springs and special order numbers.

1979–80

▶ See Figure 25

The first digit in the vehicle identification number is the model year of the car (9=1979, 0=1980). The second digit is the assembly plant code for the plant in which the vehicle was built. The third and fourth digits are the body serial code designations (2–dr sedan, 4–dr sedan, etc.). The fifth digit is the engine code which identifies the type of engine originally installed in the vehicle (see the Engine Codes chart). The last six digits are the consecutive unit numbers which start at 100,001 for the first car of a model year built in each assembly plant.

1981–88

▶ See Figure 26

Beginning in 1981, the serial number contains seventeen digits. The first three give the world manufacturer code. The fourth is the type of restraint system. The fifth will remain the letter **P**. The sixth and seventh are the car line, series and body type. The eighth is the engine type. The ninth is a check digit. The tenth is a letter representing the model year (B=1981, C=1982, D=1983, E=1984, F=1985, G=1986, H=1987, J=1988). The eleventh is the assembly plant. The remaining numbers are the production sequence.

Engine

A variety of 4–, 6–, and 8–cylinder engines, including carbureted and fuel injected versions, were available over the years. There was also a turbocharged version of the venerable 4–cylinder engine. Refer to the "'Engine Identification" chart in this section for specific applications.

Transmission

Several manual and automatic transmissions were available over the years. In order to properly identify a particular application, obtain the transmission code from the Vehicle Certification Label and refer to the following list:

Manual Transmission:
- 2 — Five speed overdrive
- 4 — Four speed (TREMEC)
- 5 — Four speed overdrive (1979 only)
- 5 — Five speed overdrive RAP model (1980–83)
- 5 — Five speed overdrive (Borg–Warner model T5OD) (1984–88)
- 6 — Four speed (Borg–Warner model RAD) (1979–82)
- 7 — Four speed ET model (1979–86)
- 7 — Four speed overdrive RUG model (1980–83)

Automatic Transmission:
- C — C5 automatic
- T — AOD (automatic overdrive)
- On some 1987–88 models, code T also represented the A4LD (automatic overdrive) transmission.
- V — C3 automatic
- W — C4 automatic

Drive Axle

A variety of differentials and rear axle ratios were available over the years. These included both integral carrier axles (conventional) and "Traction–Lok"

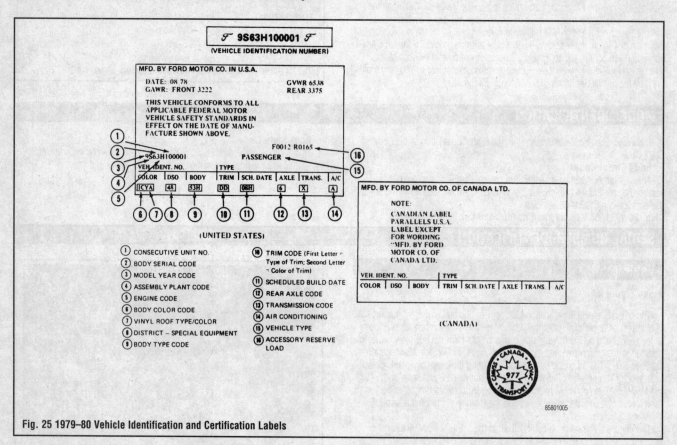

Fig. 25 1979–80 Vehicle Identification and Certification Labels

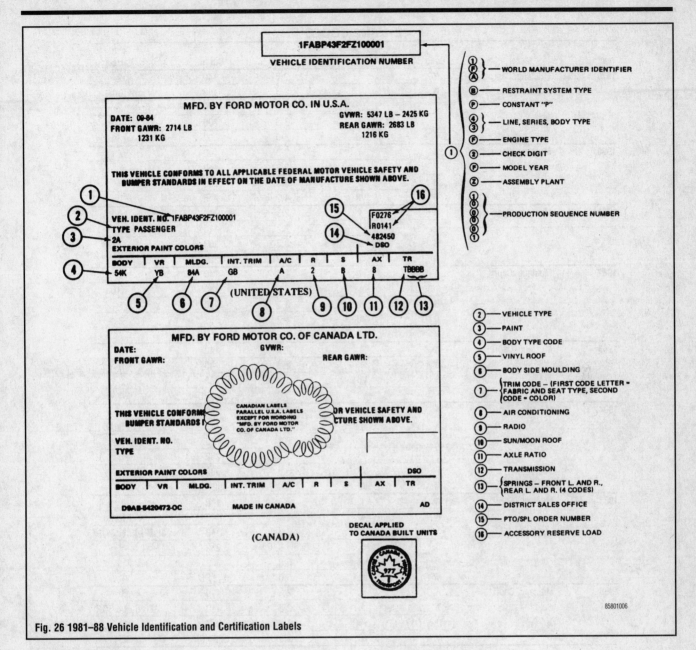

Fig. 26 1981–88 Vehicle Identification and Certification Labels

(limited slip) differentials. Refer to the Vehicle Certification Label and the following list for specific codes and their equivalents.

Conventional:
- Code B — 2.47 Ratio
- Code F — 3.45 Ratio
- Code G — 2.26 Ratio
- Code Y — 3.08 Ratio
- Code 3 — 2.79 Ratio
- Code 4 — 3.42 Ratio
- Code 5 — 3.27 Ratio
- Code 6 — 3.73 Ratio
- Code 8 — 2.73 Ratio

Limited Slip:
- Code C — 2.47 Ratio
- Code D — 3.42 Ratio
- Code E — 3.27 Ratio
- Code H — 2.73 Ratio
- Code L — 2.79 Ratio
- Code M — 2.73 Ratio
- Code O — 3.00 Ratio
- Code R — 3.45 Ratio
- Code W — 3.73 Ratio
- Code Z — 3.08 Ratio

ENGINE CODES

Year	Model	Code	Number of Cylinders	Litres	Cu. In.	Carb. Barrels
1979	Mustang, Capri	Y	4	2.3	140	2
		W	4	2.3	140	2-Turbo
		Z	V6	2.8	170	2
		T	6	3.3	200	1
		F	V8	5.0	302	2①
1980	Mustang, Capri	A	4	2.3	140	2
		T	4	2.3	140	⑦
		B	6	3.3	200	1
		D	V8	4.2	255	2①
1981	Mustang, Capri	A	4	2.3	140	2
		T	4	2.3	140	2-Turbo
		B	6	3.3	200	1
		D	V8	4.2	255	2①
1982	Mustang, Capri	A	4	2.3	140	2
		T②	4	2.3	140	2-Turbo
		B	6	3.3	200	1
		D	V8	4.2	255	2①
		F③	V8	5.0	302 HO	2①
1983	Mustang, Capri	A	4	2.3	140	1
		W	4	2.3	140	EFI-Turbo
		3	V6	3.8	232	2
		F③	V8	5.0	302 HO	4
1984	Mustang, Capri	A	4	2.3	140	1
		W	4	2.3	140	EFI-Turbo
		T	4	2.3	140	EFI-Turbo/IC④
		3	V6	3.8	232	⑤
		F	V8	5.0	302	⑥
		M	V8	5.0	302 HO	⑥
1985	Mustang, Capri	A	4	2.3	140	1
		W	4	2.3	140	EFI-Turbo
		T	4	2.3	140	EFI-Turbo/IC④
		3	V6	3.8	232	⑤
		F	V8	5.0	302	⑥⑧
		M	V8	5.0	302 HO	⑥
1986	Mustang, Capri	A	4	2.3	140	1
		T	4	2.3	140	EFI-Turbo/IC④
		3	V6	3.8	232	⑤
		M	V8	5.0	302 HO	SEFI
1987	Mustang	A	4	2.3	140	EFI
		E	V8	5.0	302 HO	SEFI
1988	Mustang	A	4	2.3	140	EFI
		E	V8	5.0	302 HO	SEFI

NOTE: Unless preceded by a ''V'', engines have all cylinders arranged in-line
CFI—Central Fuel Injection (single-point)
EFI—Electronic Fuel Injection (multi-point)
SEFI—Sequential Electronic Fuel Injection
MT—Manual Transmission
AT—Automatic Transmission
AOD—Automatic Overdrive Transmission
① A variable venturi (VV) carburetor was available in limited areas.
② Canada only
③ Code F only designated the HO version in 1982–83
④ Equipped with intercooler and boost control (SVO Mustang only)
⑤ CFI—50 states; 2 bbl.—Canada
⑥ CFI with AOD; 4 bbl. with MT
⑦ 2 bbl. Turbo with MT, CFI Turbo with AT
⑧ 2 bbl. with MT sold only in Canada

858010C1A

ROUTINE MAINTENANCE AND TUNE-UP

▶ **See Figure 27**

Proper maintenance and tune-up is the key to long and trouble-free vehicle life. Studies have shown that a properly tuned and maintained vehicle can achieve better gas mileage than an out-of-tune vehicle. As a conscientious owner and driver, set aside a Saturday morning, say once a month, to check or replace items which could cause major problems later. Keep your own personal log to jot down which services you performed, how much the parts cost you, the date, and the exact odometer reading at the time. Keep all receipts for such items as engine oil and filters, so that they may be referred to in case of related problems or to determine operating expenses. As a do-it-yourselfer, these receipts are the only proof you have that the required maintenance was performed. In the event of a warranty problem, these receipts will be invaluable.

The literature provided with your vehicle when it was originally delivered includes the factory recommended maintenance schedule. If you no longer have this literature, replacement copies are usually available from the dealer.

Air Cleaner

All engines are equipped with a dry type, replaceable air filter element. The element should be replaced at the recommended intervals shown in the "Maintenance Chart" located in this Section. If your vehicle is operated under extremely dusty or severe operating conditions, more frequent changes are necessary. Inspect the element at least twice a year. Early spring and the beginning of fall are good times for this inspection. Remove the element and check for holes in the filter. Check the cleaner housing for signs of dirt or dust that has leaked through the filter element. Place a light on the inside of the element and look through the filter at the light. If no glow of light can be seen through the element material, replace the filter. If holes in the filter are apparent, or if any sign of dirt leakage through the filter is noticed, replace the filter.

Fig. 27 Much of the routine maintenance is performed in the engine compartment

REMOVAL & INSTALLATION

Filter Element

▶ **See Figures 28 and 29**

The element can, in most cases, be replaced by simply removing the wing nut and cleaner assembly cover. If the inside of the housing is dirty, however, remove the assembly for cleaning to prevent dirt from entering the carburetor or intake assembly.

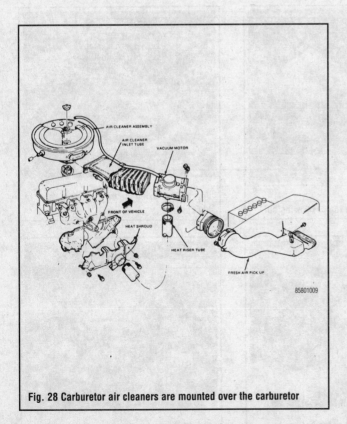

Fig. 28 Carburetor air cleaners are mounted over the carburetor

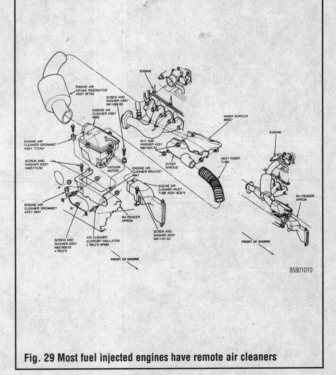

Fig. 29 Most fuel injected engines have remote air cleaners

Air Cleaner Housing

▶ **See Figures 30 thru 35**

1. Disconnect all hoses, ducts and vacuum lines from the air cleaner assembly.
2. On round or oval–shape air cleaners, remove the top cover wing nut and grommet (if equipped). Remove any side bracket mount retaining bolts (if equipped). Remove the air cleaner assembly from the top of the carburetor or intake assembly.

➡ **Air cleaner assemblies on electronically fuel injected vehicles have a different design and location. Instead of the traditional wing nut securing a flat–top cover above the carburetor or intake assembly, these irregularly shaped assemblies are typically attached to a resonator and are bolted to a fender apron. Filter elements within these types of assemblies may be accessed by removing the housing fasteners.**

3. Remove the cover and the element, if not already done. Wipe clean all inside surfaces of the air cleaner housing and cover. If so equipped, check the condition of the mounting gasket (between the air cleaner base and the carburetor or intake assembly) and replace the gasket if it is worn or broken.
4. Reposition the air cleaner housing, element, cover and grommet (if equipped) on the carburetor or intake assembly.
5. Reconnect all hoses, ducts and vacuum lines which were removed and finger–tighten the wing nut. On fuel injected vehicles, reinstall any fasteners which were removed or return the latches to their closed position.

Crankcase Ventilation Filter

▶ **See Figure 36**

Replace or inspect the air cleaner–mounted crankcase ventilation system filter (on models so–equipped) at the same time the air cleaner filter element is serviced. To replace the filter, simply remove the air cleaner cover and pull the filter from its housing. Push a new filter into the housing and install the air cleaner cover. If the filter and plastic holder need replacement, detach the PCV

hose elbow and remove the clip mounting the feed tube to the air cleaner housing. Remove the assembly from the air cleaner. Installation is the reverse of removal.

Fuel Filter

REMOVAL & INSTALLATION

✳✳ CAUTION

Never smoke when working around or near gasoline! Make sure that there is no ignition source near your work area!

Carbureted Engines

4–140 AND 6–200 ENGINES

▶ **See Figures 37, 38 and 39**

A carburetor mounted fuel filter is used. These filters screw into the float chamber. To replace one of these filters:
1. Wait until the engine is cold.
2. Remove the air cleaner assembly.
3. Place some absorbent rags under the fuel filter.
4. Remove the hose clamp and slide the rubber hose from the filter.

✳✳ CAUTION

It is possible for gasoline to spray in all directions when removing the hose! This rarely happens, but it is possible, so protect your eyes!

5. Move the fuel line out of the way and unscrew the filter from the carburetor.

Fig. 33 Removing the air filter element

Fig. 30 Disconnecting the air duct from the fender inlet

Fig. 35 Removing the air cleaner housing assembly

Fig. 31 Removing the top cover wing nut

Fig. 34 Label vacuum hoses before removal to avoid confusion

Fig. 32 Removing the air cleaner assembly cover

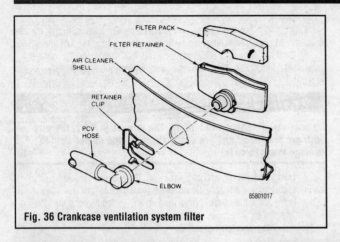

Fig. 36 Crankcase ventilation system filter

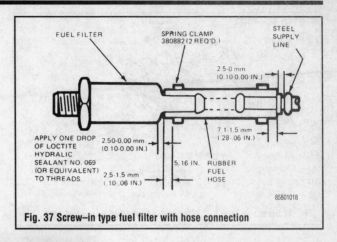

Fig. 37 Screw—in type fuel filter with hose connection

Fig. 38 Removing the hose clamp with pliers

Fig. 39 Unscrew the fuel filter from the carburetor

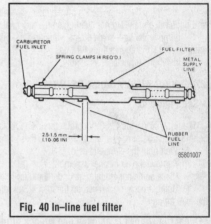

Fig. 40 In—line fuel filter

To install:

6. Coat the threads of the new filter with non—hardening, gasoline—proof sealer and screw it into place by hand. Tighten it snugly with a wrench.

✳✳ WARNING

Do not overtighten the filter! The threads in the carburetor bowl are soft metal and are easily stripped. You do not want to damage these threads!

7. Connect the hose to the new filter. Most replacement filters come with a new hose and clamps. If so, use them.
8. Remove the fuel—soaked rags, wipe up any spilled fuel and start the engine. Check the filter connections for leaks.
9. Install the air cleaner assembly.

V6 AND V8 ENGINES WITH IN—LINE FILTER

▶ See Figure 40

1. Wait until the engine is cold.
2. Remove the air cleaner assembly.
3. Place some absorbent rags under the fuel filter.
4. Remove the hose clamps. Slide the rubber hoses from the filter and remove the fuel filter.

✳✳ CAUTION

It is possible for gasoline to spray in all directions when removing the hose! This rarely happens, but it is possible, so protect your eyes!

To install:

5. Most replacement filters come with new hoses and clamps. If so, use them. Cut new rubber hoses to the proper length, if necessary, and position two new hose clamps at the middle of each fuel line.

6. Push one hose on the fuel filter inlet and the other on the outlet.
7. Push the inlet hose onto the metal supply line, and the outlet hose onto the carburetor inlet fitting.
8. Position and install the spring type clamps with pliers.
9. Remove the fuel—soaked rags, wipe up any spilled fuel and start the engine. Check the filter connections for leaks.
10. Install the air cleaner assembly.

V6 AND V8 ENGINES WITH SCREW—IN FILTER EXCEPT 2700VV AND 7200VV CARBS

▶ See Figure 41

1. Wait until the engine is cold.
2. Remove the air cleaner assembly.
3. Place some absorbent rags under the filter.
4. Using a back—up wrench on the filter, unscrew the fuel line from the filter.

✳✳ CAUTION

It is possible for gasoline to spray in all directions when unscrewing the line! This rarely happens, but it is possible, so protect your eyes!

5. Move the fuel line out of the way and unscrew the filter from the carburetor.

To install:

6. Coat the threads of the new filter with non—hardening, gasoline—proof sealer and screw it into place by hand. Tighten it snugly with the wrench.

✳✳ WARNING

Do not overtighten the filter! The threads in the carburetor bowl are soft metal and are easily stripped. You do not want to damage these threads!

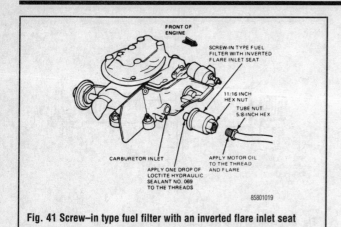

Fig. 41 Screw–in type fuel filter with an inverted flare inlet seat

7. Using the back–up wrench on the filter, screw the fuel line into the filter and tighten it snugly. Do not overtighten the fuel line!

8. Remove the fuel–soaked rags, wipe up any spilled fuel and start the engine. Check the connections for leaks.

9. Install the air cleaner assembly.

2700VV OR 7200VV CARBURETOR

▶ See Figure 42

Model 2700VV and 7200VV carburetors use a replaceable filter located behind the carburetor inlet fitting. To replace these filters:

1. Wait until the engine is cold.
2. Remove the air cleaner assembly.
3. Place some absorbent rags under the filter inlet fitting.
4. Using a back–up wrench on the inlet fitting, unscrew the fuel line from the inlet fitting.

➡A backup wrench is an open end wrench of the proper size used to hold a fuel filter or fitting in position while a fuel line is removed. A flared wrench is a special hex wrench with a narrow open end allowing the fuel line nut to be gripped tightly. A regular open end wrench may be substituted if used carefully, so that the fitting is not rounded.

✳✳ CAUTION

It is possible for gasoline to spray in all directions when unscrewing the line! This rarely happens, but it is possible, so protect your eyes!

5. Move the fuel line out of the way and unscrew the inlet fitting from the carburetor.

6. Pull out the filter. The spring behind the filter may come with it. Note the direction of the filter, so that the replacement can be installed in the same direction.

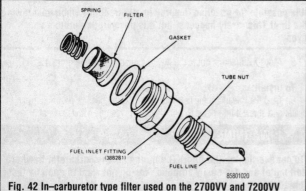

Fig. 42 In–carburetor type filter used on the 2700VV and 7200VV equipped engines

To install:

7. Install the new filter. Some new filters come with a new spring. If so, use it. Be sure to position the new filter so that its opening faces the fuel line.

8. Coat the threads of the inlet fitting with non–hardening, gasoline–proof sealer and screw it into place by hand. Tighten it snugly with the wrench.

✳✳ WARNING

Do not overtighten the inlet fitting! The threads in the carburetor bowl are soft metal and are easily stripped. You do not want to damage these threads!

9. Using the back–up wrench on the inlet fitting, screw the fuel line into the fitting and tighten it snugly. Do not overtighten the fuel line!

10. Remove the fuel–soaked rags, wipe up any spilled fuel and start the engine. Check the connections for leaks.

11. Install the air cleaner assembly.

Fuel Injected Gasoline Engines

The in–line fuel filter is located downstream of the electric fuel pump and is mounted on the underbody. On vehicles equipped with in–line fuel pumps, the fuel filter is part of a modular assembly which also houses the fuel pump.

IN–LINE FUEL PUMP

▶ See Figures 43 and 44

1. Disconnect the negative battery cable.
2. Raise and support the rear end on jackstands.
3. Depressurize the fuel system. See Section 5 in this manual.
4. Remove the quick–disconnect fittings at both ends of the filter. See Section 5.
5. Remove the retainer screws or bolts, and remove the fuel filter and retainer from the bracket.
6. Remove the rubber insulator ring from the filter.
7. Remove the filter from the retainer. Note the direction of the fuel flow arrow.

To install:

8. Install the new filter into the retainer. The arrow should point away from the fuel pump's connecting line.

9. Install a new rubber insulator ring.

10. Install the retainer and filter on the bracket, and tighten the retainer screws or bolts.

11. Install the fuel lines using new retainer clips.

12. Connect the negative battery cable.

13. Start the engine and check for leaks.

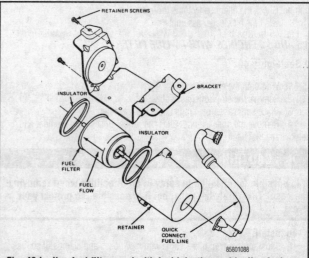

Fig. 43 In–line fuel filter used with fuel injection and in–line fuel pump

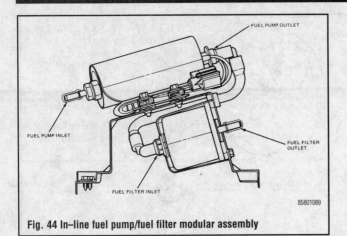

Fig. 44 In–line fuel pump/fuel filter modular assembly

IN–TANK FUEL PUMP

♦ **See Figure 45**

1. Disconnect the negative battery cable.
2. Raise and support the rear end on jackstands.
3. Depressurize the fuel system. See Section 5 in this manual.
4. Remove the quick–disconnect fittings at both ends of the filter. See Section 5.
5. Remove the fuel filter from the bracket by loosening the worm gear clamp. Note the direction of the fuel flow arrow.

To install:

6. Install the new filter into the bracket. The arrow should point towards the fuel line running to the engine. Tighten the worm gear clamp to 15–25 inch lbs.
7. Install the fuel lines using new retainer clips.
8. Connect the negative battery cable.
9. Start the engine and check for leaks.

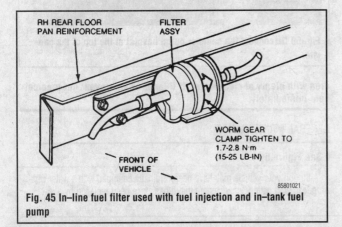

Fig. 45 In–line fuel filter used with fuel injection and in–tank fuel pump

Positive Crankcase Ventilation (PCV) Valve

All models use a closed ventilation system with a sealed breather cap connected to the air cleaner by a rubber hose. The PCV valve is usually mounted in the valve cover and connected to the intake manifold by a rubber hose. Its task is to regulate the amount of crankcase (blow–by) gases which are recycled.

REMOVAL & INSTALLATION

♦ **See Figures 46, 47 and 48**

Since the PCV valve works under severe load, it is very important that it be replaced at the interval specified in the maintenance chart. Replacement involves removing the valve from the grommet in the rocker arm cover, disconnecting the hose(s) and installing a new valve. Do not attempt to clean a used valve.

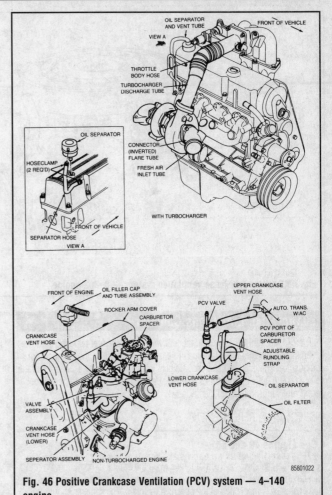

Fig. 46 Positive Crankcase Ventilation (PCV) system — 4–140 engine

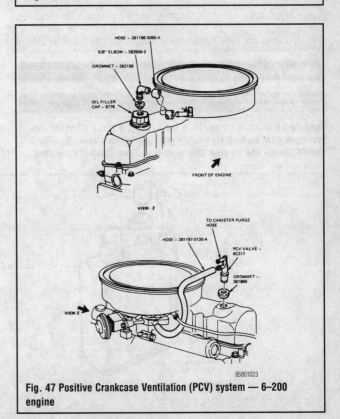

Fig. 47 Positive Crankcase Ventilation (PCV) system — 6–200 engine

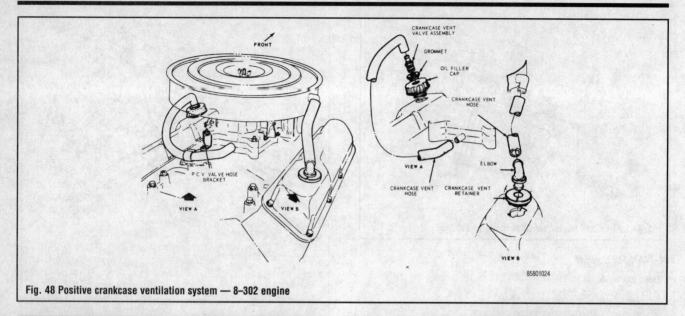

Fig. 48 Positive crankcase ventilation system — 8–302 engine

Evaporative Emissions Canister

The canister functions to cycle the fuel vapor from the fuel tank and carburetor float chamber into the intake manifold and eventually into the cylinders for combustion. The activated charcoal element within the canister acts as a storage device for the fuel vapor at times when the engine operating condition will not permit fuel vapor to burn efficiently.

INSPECTION & REPLACEMENT

▶ See Figures 49 and 50

Since the canister is purged of fumes when the engine is operating, no real maintenance is required. The only required service for the evaporative emissions canister is inspection at the specified intervals. The canister should be visually checked for cracks, loose connections, or other defects. If the charcoal element is gummed up, the entire canister should be replaced. To remove the canister, label and disconnect the canister purge hose(s), loosen the canister retaining bracket and lift out the canister. Installation is the reverse of removal.

Battery

❊❊ CAUTION

Keep flame or sparks away from the battery; it gives off explosive hydrogen gas. Battery electrolyte contains sulfuric acid. If you should splash any on your skin or in your eyes, flush the affected

Fig. 50 Disconnect the canister purge hose(s) at the top of the canister

area with plenty of clear water. If it lands in your eyes, get medical help immediately.

GENERAL MAINTENANCE

▶ See Figure 51

Although your vehicle may have been originally equipped with a water guzzling lead acid battery, chances are that it has since been replaced by a low

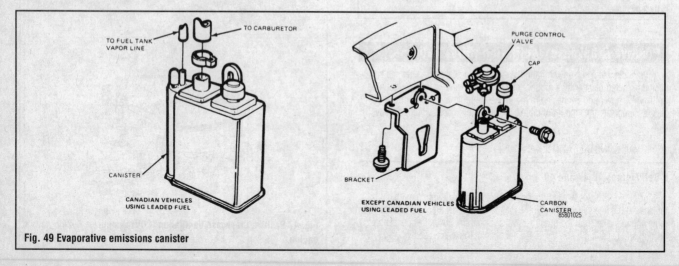

Fig. 49 Evaporative emissions canister

Fig. 51 Perform battery maintenance with household items, such as baking soda and water to neutralize acid, and with special tools, such as a post and terminal cleaner

maintenance or "maintenance–free" battery. Although these batteries significantly reduce or eliminate the need for checking and adding fluid, there are still several important steps which can be taken to ensure optimum performance and longer battery life.

1. Keep the battery top clean and dry.
2. If equipped with removable vent caps, be sure that they are snugly installed.
3. Keep the battery securely fastened in its tray. Be sure that the hold–down hardware is not loose or rusted away. If necessary, replace the hold–down hardware, preferably with the same size and style of parts.
4. Inspect the battery case for cracks or leakage.
5. Check the battery post–and–terminal connections for a clean, snug fit.
6. Monitor the battery's electrolyte level or charge condition.
7. Verify that the vehicle's charging system is operating normally, and correct any problems which occur. (See Section 3.)

FLUID LEVEL (EXCEPT MAINTENANCE FREE BATTERIES)

※※ WARNING

Do not remove the caps on a sealed maintenance free battery. Damage to the battery and vehicle may result. If the fluid is low in this type of battery, an overcharging problem or a defective battery may be at fault.

Check the battery electrolyte level at least once a month, or more often in hot weather or during periods of extended car operation. The level can be checked through the case on translucent polypropylene batteries; the cell caps must be removed on other models. The electrolyte level in each cell should be kept filled to the split ring inside, or the line marked on the outside of the case.

If the level is low, add only distilled water, or colorless, odorless drinking water through the opening until the level is correct. Each cell is completely separate from the others, so each must be checked and filled individually.

If water is added in freezing weather, the car should be driven several miles to allow the water to mix with the electrolyte. Otherwise, the battery could freeze.

CABLES AND CLAMPS

▶ **See Figures 52, 53, 54 and 55**

Once a year, the battery terminals and the cable clamps should be cleaned. Loosen the clamps and remove the cables, negative cable first. On batteries with posts on top, the use of a puller specially made for this purpose is recommended. These are inexpensive, and available in auto parts stores. Side terminal battery cables are secured with a bolt.

Clean the cable clamps and the battery terminal with a wire brush, until all corrosion, grease, etc., is removed and the metal is shiny. It is especially important to clean the inside of the clamp thoroughly, since a small deposit of foreign material or oxidation there will prevent a sound electrical connection and inhibit either starting or charging. Special tools are available for cleaning these parts, one type for conventional batteries and another type for side terminal batteries.

Before installing the cables, loosen the battery hold–down clamp or strap, remove the battery and check the battery tray. Clear it of any debris, and check it for soundness. Rust should be wire brushed away, and the metal given a coat of anti–rust paint. Replace the battery and tighten the hold–down clamp or strap securely, but be careful not to overtighten, which will crack the battery case.

After the clamps and terminals are clean, reinstall the cables, negative cable last; do not hammer on the clamps to install. Tighten the clamps securely, but do not distort them. Give the clamps and terminals a thin external coat of grease after installation, to retard corrosion.

Check the cables at the same time that the terminals are cleaned. If the cable insulation is cracked or broken, or if the ends are frayed, the cable should be replaced with a new cable of the same length and gauge.

TESTING

▶ **See Figures 56 and 57**

At least once a year, check the specific gravity of the battery. It should be between 1.20 in. Hg and 1.26 in. Hg at room temperature.

The specific gravity can be checked with the use of a hydrometer, an inexpensive instrument available from many sources, including auto parts stores. The hydrometer has a squeeze bulb at one end and a nozzle at the other. Battery electrolyte is sucked into the hydrometer until the float is lifted from its seat. The specific gravity is then read by noting the position of the float. Generally, if after charging, the specific gravity between any two cells varies more than 50 points (0.50), the battery is bad and should be replaced.

It is not possible to check the specific gravity in this manner on sealed (maintenance free) batteries. Instead, the indicator built into the top of the case must be relied on to display any signs of battery deterioration. If the indicator is dark, the battery can be assumed to be OK. If the indicator is light, the specific gravity is low, and the battery should be charged or replaced.

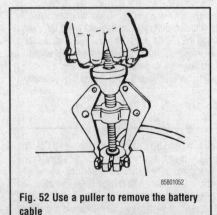

Fig. 52 Use a puller to remove the battery cable

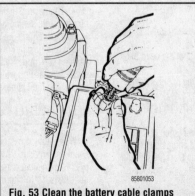

Fig. 53 Clean the battery cable clamps with a wire brush

Fig. 54 The underside of this special battery tool has a wire brush to clean post terminals

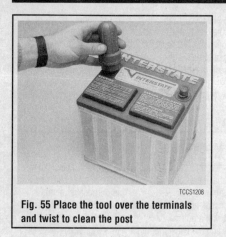

Fig. 55 Place the tool over the terminals and twist to clean the post

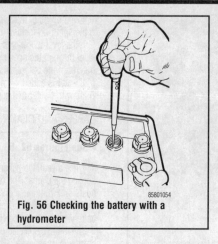

Fig. 56 Checking the battery with a hydrometer

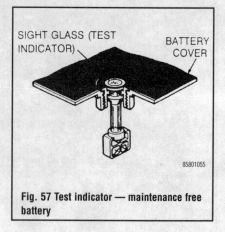

Fig. 57 Test indicator — maintenance free battery

JUMP STARTING

A vehicle with a dead battery may be jump started with the assistance of another vehicle and a set of jumper cables. Jumper cables are lengths of thick, insulated electrical wire of varying gauge and length, with insulated, spring–loaded clamps on each end. Connecting the cables between the two vehicles permits the vehicle with the discharged battery to receive a boost or "hot shot" which should, in the absence of some other problem, permit the vehicle to be started. When jump starting a dead battery, observe the following precautions:

- Be sure both batteries are of the same voltage.
- Be sure both batteries are of the same polarity (have the same grounded terminal).
- Be sure the vehicles are not touching.
- If the dead battery has removable vent caps, be sure the vent cap holes are not obstructed.
- Do not smoke or allow sparks around the batteries.
- In cold weather, check for frozen electrolyte in the battery. Do not jump start a frozen battery!
- Do not allow electrolyte on your skin or clothing.

✳✳ CAUTION

Make certain that the ignition key, in the vehicle with the dead battery, is in the OFF position. Connecting cables to vehicles with on–board computers will result in computer destruction if the key is not in the OFF position.

Jump Starting Procedure

1. Determine voltages of the two batteries; they must be the same.
2. Bring the running vehicle close enough to the disabled vehicle for jumper cables to be connected. Make certain, however, that the two vehicles do not touch.
3. Turn off the running engine, as well as all lights and accessories in both vehicles. Put both vehicles in Park or Neutral and set the parking brake.
4. If the terminals (or cable clamping areas) on either battery are heavily corroded, clean them.
5. Identify the positive and negative posts on both batteries and connect the cables in the proper order as follows:
  a. Connect one jumper cable to the positive (+) terminal of the dead battery.
  b. Connect the other end of the same jumper cable to the positive (+) terminal of the good battery.
  c. Connect a second jumper cable to the negative (−) terminal of the good battery.
  d. Connect the other end of this jumper cable to a good engine ground.
6. Be sure the jumper cables are not in the way of moving engine parts.
7. Start the operating vehicle and run it at a fast idle. Try to start the vehicle with the dead battery. Crank it for no more than 10 seconds at a time and let it cool for 20 seconds between attempts.
8. If it does not start within three attempts, there is something else wrong.
9. Disconnect the cables in the reverse order.

CHARGING

Before recharging a discharged battery installed in a vehicle, inspect and correct the following conditions, if they exist:
- Loose or broken alternator belt.
- Pinched or grounded alternator/voltage regulator wiring harness.
- Loose harness connections at the alternator and/or voltage regulator.
- Loose or corroded connections at the battery, starter relay and/or engine ground.
- Excessive battery drain with the ignition switch in the OFF position, caused, for example, by lamps remaining on.

In order to properly recharge conventional and maintenance free batteries, follow the instructions of the charger manufacturer. Since a cold battery will not readily accept a charge, it should first be allowed to warm up to approximately 5°C (41°F) before charging. This may require 4–8 hours at room temperature, depending upon the initial temperature and battery size.

A battery which has been completely discharged may be slow to accept a charge initially, and in some cases may not accept a charge at the normal charger setting. Batteries in this condition can be started to charge by use of the dead battery switch on chargers so equipped.

Completely discharged batteries which have been discharged for a prolonged period of time (over one month) or which have an open circuit voltage of less than two volts may show no indication of accepting a charge even with the use of the dead battery switch. The initial charge rate accepted by batteries in this condition is so low that the ammeter on some chargers will not show any indication of charge for up to 10 minutes.

Once it has been determined that the battery has begun to accept a charge, the battery can be charged to a serviceable state or to a full state of charge by one of two methods:

- The first method is to use the automatic setting on chargers so equipped. This setting maintains the charging rate within safe limits by adjusting the voltage and current to prevent excessive gassing and spewing of electrolyte. Approximately 2–4 hours will be required to charge a completely discharged battery to a serviceable state. If a full state of charge is desired, the charge can be completed by a slow trickle (low current rate) charge of 3–5 amps for several additional hours.
- The second method is to use the manual or constant setting on the charger. This setting typically utilizes a charging rate of 30–40 amps for approximately 30 minutes or as long as there is no excessive gassing and electrolyte spewing. If gassing results, the charge rate must be reduced to a level where gassing will stop. This is particularly true for maintenance free batteries, since excessive gassing would result in non–replaceable loss of electrolyte, thereby shortening the battery's life.

REPLACEMENT

When it becomes necessary to replace the battery, select one with a Cold Cranking Amps (CCA) rating equal to or greater than the original battery. Deterioration of system components and increased resistance in electrical wiring are good reasons to choose a replacement battery with at least 10%more CCA's than the original battery. Be sure to select a battery of the same group size as the original. This will ensure that the battery case's dimensions and post configuration will properly fit your vehicle. The use of another group size battery is unadvisable, since it could interfere with the battery's hold down hardware or cable routing.

Batteries in a particular group size are available with a variety of pro–rated warranties, usually ranging from 36 to 72 months. Generally, the warranty length is proportional to the amount of CCA's. Therefore, depending upon your vehicle's level of equipment and power requirements, an economy battery may not be practical, even for a short period of time.

Batteries are also rated in terms of their reserve capacity. This is the number of minutes that a fully charged battery could supply the electrical needs of your vehicle with its headlights and accessories operating, in the event of a charging system failure. This is also your potential protection against a dead battery when your headlights are accidentally left on. Battery reserve capacities also tend to be proportional to warranty lengths within a particular group size of battery. Although your vehicle carries no particular requirement, you may want to consider a higher reserve capacity for additional peace of mind.

Heat Riser

Some models are equipped with exhaust control (heat riser) valves located near the head pipe connection in the exhaust manifold. These valves aid initial warm–up in cold weather by restricting exhaust gas flow slightly. The heat generated by this restriction is transferred to the intake manifold, resulting in improved fuel vaporization.

SERVICING

The operation of the exhaust control valve should be checked every 6 months or 6,000 miles. Make sure that the thermostatic spring is hooked on the stop pin and that the tension holds the valve shut. Rotate the counterweight by hand and make sure that it moves freely through about 90° of rotation. A valve which is operating properly will open when light finger pressure is applied (cold engine). Lubricate the shaft bushings with a mixture of penetrating oil and graphite. Operate the valve manually a few times to work in the lubricant.

Belts

INSPECTION

♦ **See Figures 58 and 59**

Once a year or at 12,000 mile intervals, the tension and condition of the alternator, power steering, air conditioning, and Thermactor air pump drive belts should be checked and, if necessary, adjusted. Loose accessory drive belts can lead to poor engine cooling and diminish alternator, power steering pump, air conditioning compressor or Thermactor air pump output. A belt that is too tight places a severe strain on the water pump, alternator, power steering pump, compressor or air pump bearings.

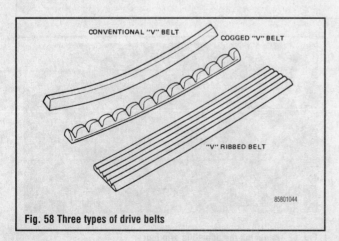

Fig. 58 Three types of drive belts

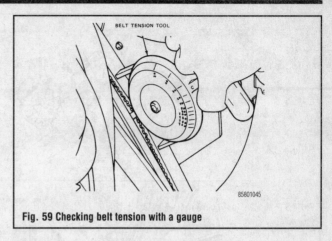

Fig. 59 Checking belt tension with a gauge

Replace any belt that is so glazed, worn or stretched that it cannot be tightened sufficiently.

➟**The material used in late model drive belts is such that the belts do not show wear. Replace belts at least every three years.**

On vehicles with matched belts, replace both belts at the same time. New ½ in., ⅜ in. and ¹⁵⁄₃₂ in. wide belts are to be adjusted to a tension of 140 lbs.; ¼ in. wide belts are adjusted to 80 lbs., measured on a belt tension gauge. Any belt that has been operating for a minimum of 10 minutes is considered a used belt. In the first 10 minutes, the belt should stretch to its maximum extent. After 10 minutes, stop the engine and recheck the belt tension. Belt tension for a used belt should be maintained at 110 lbs. (all except ¼ in. wide belts) or 60 lbs. (¼ in. wide belts). If a belt tension gauge is not available, the following procedures may be used.

ADJUSTMENT

✲✲ CAUTION

On models equipped with an electric cooling fan, disconnect the negative battery cable or fan motor wiring harness connector before replacing or adjusting drive belts. The fan may come on, under certain circumstances, even though the ignition is off.

Except Serpentine (Ribbed) Drive Belt

♦ **See Figure 60**

ALTERNATOR (FAN DRIVE) BELT

♦ **See Figures 61 and 62**

1. Position a ruler perpendicular to the drive belt at its longest straight run. Test the tightness of the belt by pressing it firmly with your thumb. The deflection should not exceed ¼ in..
2. If the deflection exceeds ¼ in., loosen the alternator mounting and adjusting arm bolts.
3. Place a 1 in. open–end or adjustable wrench on the adjusting ridge cast on the body, and pull on the wrench until the proper tension is achieved.
4. Holding the alternator in place to maintain tension, tighten the adjusting arm bolt. Recheck the belt tension. When the belt is properly tensioned, tighten the alternator mounting bolt.

POWER STEERING DRIVE BELT — 4–140 AND 6–200 ENGINES

1. Hold a ruler perpendicular to the drive belt at its longest straight run. Test the tightness of the belt by pressing it firmly with your thumb. The deflection should not exceed ¼ in..
2. To adjust the belt tension, loosen the adjusting and mounting bolts on the front face of the steering pump cover plate (hub side).
3. Using a pry bar or broom handle on the pump hub, move the power steering pump toward or away from the engine until the proper tension is reached. Do not pry against the reservoir as it is relatively soft and easily deformed.

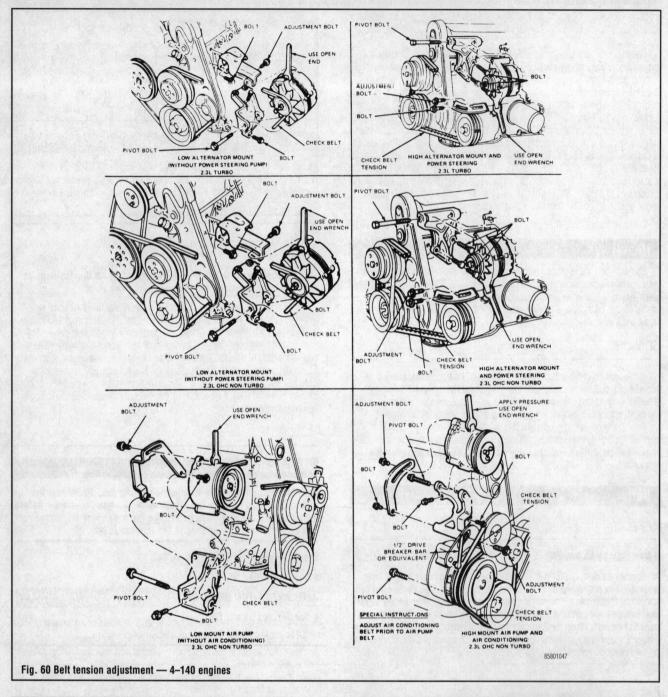

Fig. 60 Belt tension adjustment — 4–140 engines

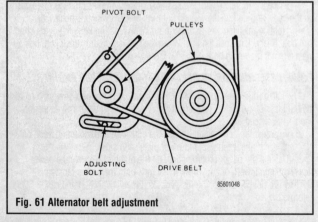

Fig. 61 Alternator belt adjustment

Fig. 62 Tightening the adjusting arm bolt

4. Holding the pump in place, tighten the adjusting arm bolt and then recheck the belt tension. When the belt is properly tensioned tighten the mounting bolts.

POWER STEERING DRIVE BELT — V6 AND V8 ENGINES

▶ See Figure 63

1. Position a ruler perpendicular to the drive belt at its longest straight run. Test the tightness of the belt by pressing it firmly with your thumb. The deflection should be about ¼ inch.
2. To adjust the belt tension, loosen the three bolts in the three elongated adjusting slots at the power steering pump attaching bracket.
3. Turn the steering pump drive belt adjusting nut as required until the proper deflection is obtained. Turning the adjusting nut clockwise will increase tension and decrease deflection; counterclockwise will decrease tension and increase deflection.
4. Without disturbing the pump, tighten the three attaching bolts.

AIR CONDITIONING COMPRESSOR DRIVE BELT

▶ See Figures 64 and 65

1. Position a ruler perpendicular to the drive belt at its longest straight run. Test the tightness of the belt by pressing it firmly with your thumb. The deflection should not exceed ¼ in..
2. If the engine is equipped with an idler pulley, loosen the idler pulley adjusting bolt, insert a pry bar between the pulley and the engine (or a breaker bar in the idler pulley adjusting slot), and adjust the tension accordingly. If the engine is not equipped with an idler pulley, the alternator may have to be moved to accomplish this adjustment. Refer to Alternator (Fan Drive) Belt Adjustment.
3. When the proper tension is reached, tighten the idler pulley adjusting bolt (if so equipped) or the alternator adjusting and mounting bolts.

THERMACTOR AIR PUMP DRIVE BELT

1. Position a ruler perpendicular to the drive belt at its longest straight run. Test the tightness of the belt by pressing it firmly with your thumb. The deflection should be about ¼ in..
2. To adjust the belt tension, slightly loosen the adjusting arm bolt and the mounting bolt.
3. Using a pry bar or broom handle, pry against the pump rear cover to move the pump toward or away from the engine as necessary.

✳✳ CAUTION

Do not pry against the pump housing itself, as damage to the housing may result.

4. Holding the pump in place, tighten the adjusting arm bolt and recheck the tension. When the belt is properly tensioned, tighten the mounting bolt.

Serpentine (Ribbed) Drive Belt

Many vehicles utilize a wide, ribbed V–belt that drives the water pump, alternator, air pump and, where applicable, the power steering pump and/or air conditioner compressor. This type of belt utilizes an automatic tensioner which eliminates the need for periodic adjustment.

REMOVAL & INSTALLATION

✳✳ CAUTION

On models equipped with an electric cooling fan, disconnect the negative battery cable or fan motor wiring harness connector before replacing or adjusting drive belts. The fan may come on, under certain circumstances, even though the ignition is off.

Except Serpentine Belt

1. Loosen the adjustment and pivot bolts on one or more components (alternator, air conditioner compressor, etc.) which are driven by the belt(s) to be replaced. Pivot the component(s) so that tension on the belt(s) is reduced.
2. Remove old belt(s).
To install:
3. Install new belt(s) over the components' pulleys.
4. Pivot the component(s) so that tension is restored to the belt(s).
5. Tighten the adjustment and pivot bolts which were loosened. Check for proper belt tension and adjust if necessary.

➡**When replacing more than one belt at a time, be sure to observe the correct routing and order of assembly.**

Serpentine Belt

▶ See Figures 66, 67, 68 and 69

1. Reduce belt tension by de–activating or moving the automatic tensioner. (For specific procedures, see the accompanying figures.) It may also be helpful to loosen the adjustment and pivot bolts, and pivot the alternator or other component driven by the belt.
2. Remove old belt.
To install:
3. Install new belt, being careful to ensure that all V–grooves make proper contact with the pulleys.
4. If the alternator or other component was moved in step 1, return it to its original position and tighten the adjustment and pivot bolts.
5. Re–activate or reposition the automatic tensioner.

✳✳ WARNING

Check to make sure that the ribbed V–belt is positioned properly in all drive pulleys before applying tensioner pressure.

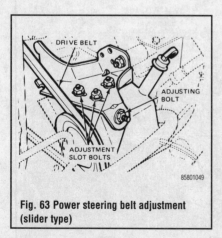

Fig. 63 Power steering belt adjustment (slider type)

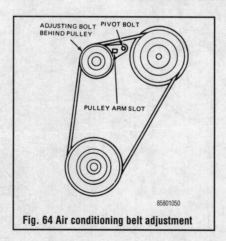

Fig. 64 Air conditioning belt adjustment

Fig. 65 Using a breaker bar and socket wrench for belt adjustment

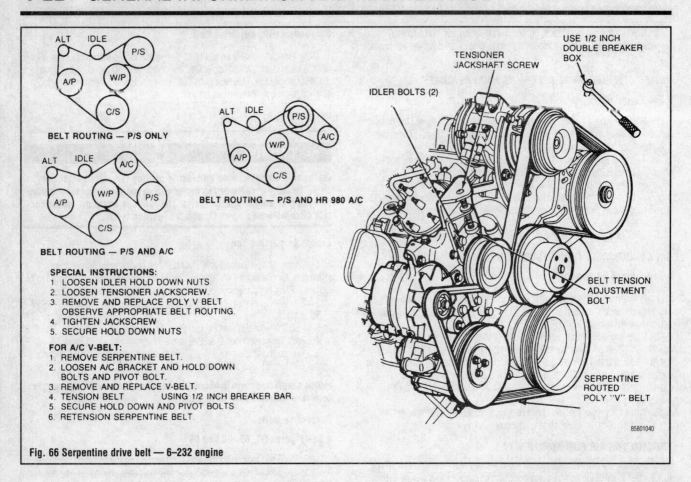

SPECIAL INSTRUCTIONS:
1. LOOSEN IDLER HOLD DOWN NUTS.
2. LOOSEN TENSIONER JACKSCREW.
3. REMOVE AND REPLACE POLY V BELT OBSERVE APPROPRIATE BELT ROUTING.
4. TIGHTEN JACKSCREW
5. SECURE HOLD DOWN NUTS

FOR A/C V-BELT:
1. REMOVE SERPENTINE BELT.
2. LOOSEN A/C BRACKET AND HOLD DOWN BOLTS AND PIVOT BOLT.
3. REMOVE AND REPLACE V-BELT.
4. TENSION BELT   USING 1/2 INCH BREAKER BAR.
5. SECURE HOLD DOWN AND PIVOT BOLTS
6. RETENSION SERPENTINE BELT.

Fig. 66 Serpentine drive belt — 6–232 engine

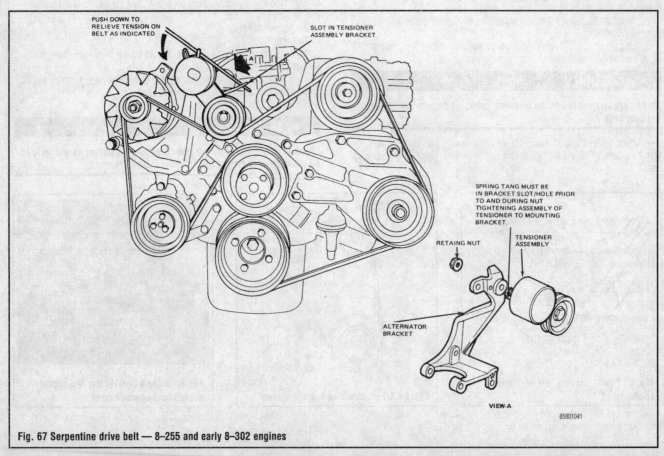

Fig. 67 Serpentine drive belt — 8–255 and early 8–302 engines

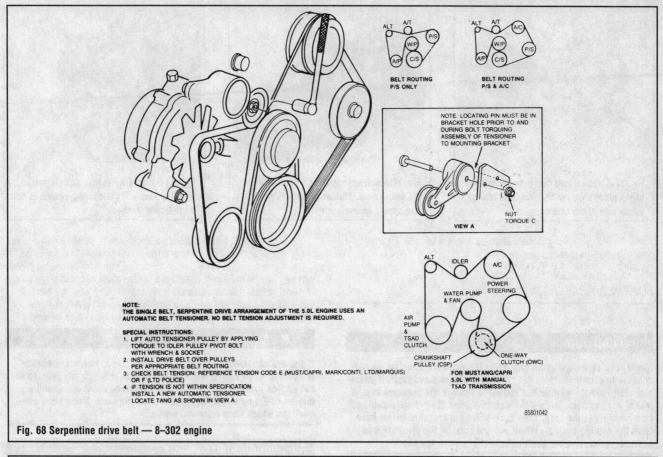

NOTE:
THE SINGLE BELT, SERPENTINE DRIVE ARRANGEMENT OF THE 5.0L ENGINE USES AN AUTOMATIC BELT TENSIONER. NO BELT TENSION ADJUSTMENT IS REQUIRED.

SPECIAL INSTRUCTIONS:
1. LIFT AUTO TENSIONER PULLEY BY APPLYING TORQUE TO IDLER PULLEY PIVOT BOLT WITH WRENCH & SOCKET
2. INSTALL DRIVE BELT OVER PULLEYS PER APPROPRIATE BELT ROUTING
3. CHECK BELT TENSION. REFERENCE TENSION CODE E (MUST/CAPRI, MARK/CONTI, LTD/MARQUIS) OR F (LTD POLICE)
4. IF TENSION IS NOT WITHIN SPECIFICATION INSTALL A NEW AUTOMATIC TENSIONER. LOCATE TANG AS SHOWN IN VIEW A.

85801042

Fig. 68 Serpentine drive belt — 8–302 engine

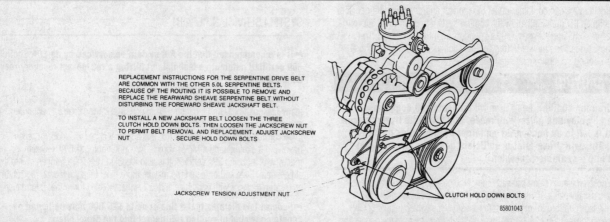

REPLACEMENT INSTRUCTIONS FOR THE SERPENTINE DRIVE BELT ARE COMMON WITH THE OTHER 5.0L SERPENTINE BELTS. BECAUSE OF THE ROUTING IT IS POSSIBLE TO REMOVE AND REPLACE THE REARWARD SHEAVE SERPENTINE BELT WITHOUT DISTURBING THE FORWARD SHEAVE JACKSHAFT BELT.

TO INSTALL A NEW JACKSHAFT BELT LOOSEN THE THREE CLUTCH HOLD DOWN BOLTS. THEN LOOSEN THE JACKSCREW NUT TO PERMIT BELT REMOVAL AND REPLACEMENT. ADJUST JACKSCREW NUT   . SECURE HOLD DOWN BOLTS

JACKSCREW TENSION ADJUSTMENT NUT

CLUTCH HOLD DOWN BOLTS

85801043

Fig. 69 Serpentine drive belt — 8–302 engine with manual transmission and two–speed accessory drive

Hoses

INSPECTION

▶ See Figures 70, 71, 72 and 73

Upper and lower radiator hoses, along with the heater hoses, should be checked for deterioration, leaks and loose hose clamps at least every 15,000 miles (24,000 km). It is also wise to check the hoses periodically in early spring and at the beginning of the fall or winter when you are performing other maintenance. A quick visual inspection could discover a weakened hose which might have left you stranded if it had remained unrepaired.

Whenever you are checking the hoses, make sure the engine and cooling system are cold. Visually inspect for cracking, rotting or collapsed hoses, and

TCCS1219

Fig. 70 The cracks developing along this hose are a result of age-related hardening

Fig. 71 A hose clamp that is too tight can cause older hoses to separate and tear on either side of the clamp

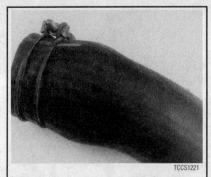

Fig. 72 A soft spongy hose (identifiable by the swollen section) will eventually burst and should be replaced

Fig. 73 Hoses are likely to deteriorate from the inside if the cooling system is not periodically flushed

replace as necessary. Run your hand along the length of the hose. If a weak or swollen spot is noted when squeezing the hose wall, the hose should be replaced.

REMOVAL & INSTALLATION

1. Remove the radiator pressure cap.

✳✳ CAUTION

Never remove the pressure cap while the engine is running, or personal injury from scalding hot coolant or steam may result. If possible, wait until the engine has cooled to remove the pressure cap. If this is not possible, wrap a thick cloth around the pressure cap and turn it slowly to the stop. Step back while the pressure is released from the cooling system. When you are sure all the pressure has been released, use the cloth to turn and remove the cap.

2. Position a clean container under the radiator and/or engine draincock or plug, then open the drain and allow the cooling system to drain to an appropriate level. For some upper hoses, only a little coolant must be drained. To remove hoses positioned lower on the engine, such as a lower radiator hose, the entire cooling system must be emptied.

✳✳ CAUTION

When draining coolant, keep in mind that cats and dogs are attracted by ethylene glycol antifreeze, and are quite likely to drink any that is left in an uncovered container or in puddles on the ground. This will prove fatal in sufficient quantity. Always drain coolant into a sealable container.

3. Loosen the hose clamps at each end of the hose requiring replacement. Clamps are usually either of the spring tension type (which require pliers to squeeze the tabs and loosen) or of the screw tension type (which require screw or hex drivers to loosen). Pull the clamps back on the hose away from the connection.

4. Twist, pull and slide the hose off the fitting, taking care not to damage the neck of the component from which the hose is being removed.

➡️If the hose is stuck at the connection, do not try to insert a screwdriver or other sharp tool under the hose end in an effort to free it, as the connection and/or hose may become damaged. Heater connections especially may be easily damaged by such a procedure. If the hose is to be replaced, use a single-edged razor blade to make a slice along the portion of the hose which is stuck on the connection, perpendicular to the end of the hose. Do not cut too deep so as to prevent damaging the connection. The hose can then be peeled from the connection and discarded.

5. Clean both hose mounting connections. Inspect the condition of the hose clamps and replace them, if necessary.
   To install:
6. Dip the ends of the new hose into clean engine coolant to ease installation.
7. Slide the clamps over the replacement hose, then slide the hose ends over the connections into position.

8. Position and secure the clamps at least ¼ in. (6.35mm) from the ends of the hose. Make sure they are located beyond the raised bead of the connector.

9. Close the radiator or engine drains and properly refill the cooling system with the clean drained engine coolant or a suitable mixture of coolant and water.

10. If available, install a pressure tester and check for leaks. If a pressure tester is not available, run the engine until normal operating temperature is reached (allowing the system to naturally pressurize), then check for leaks.

✳✳ CAUTION

If you are checking for leaks with the system at normal operating temperature, BE EXTREMELY CAREFUL not to touch any moving or hot engine parts. Once temperature has been reached, shut the engine OFF, and check for leaks around the hose fittings and connections which were removed earlier.

Air Conditioning System

SYSTEM SERVICE & REPAIR

➡️It is recommended that the A/C system be serviced by an EPA Section 609 certified automotive technician utilizing a refrigerant recovery/recycling machine.

The do-it-yourselfer should not service his/her own vehicle's A/C system for many reasons, including legal concerns, personal injury, environmental damage and cost.

According to the U.S. Clean Air Act, it is a federal crime to service or repair (involving the refrigerant) a Motor Vehicle Air Conditioning (MVAC) system for money without being EPA certified. It is also illegal to vent R-12 refrigerant into the atmosphere. State and/or local laws may be more strict than the federal regulations, so be sure to check with your state and/or local authorities for further information.

➡️Federal law dictates that a fine of up to $25,000 may be levied on people convicted of venting refrigerant into the atmosphere.

When servicing an A/C system you run the risk of handling or coming in contact with refrigerant, which may result in skin or eye irritation or frostbite. Although low in toxicity (due to chemical stability), inhalation of concentrated refrigerant fumes is dangerous and can result in death; cases of fatal cardiac arrhythmia have been reported in people accidentally subjected to high levels of refrigerant. Some early symptoms include loss of concentration and drowsiness.

Also, some refrigerants can decompose at high temperatures (near gas heaters or open flame), which may result in hydrofluoric acid, hydrochloric acid and phosgene (a fatal nerve gas).

It is usually more economically feasible to have a certified MVAC automotive technician perform A/C system service on your vehicle.

PREVENTIVE MAINTENANCE

Although the A/C system should not be serviced by the do-it-yourselfer, preventive maintenance should be practiced to help maintain the efficiency of the vehicle's A/C system. Be sure to perform the following:

• The easiest and most important preventive maintenance for your A/C system is to be sure that it is used on a regular basis. Running the system for five minutes each month (no matter what the season) will help ensure that the seals and all internal components remain lubricated.

→**Some vehicles automatically operate the A/C system compressor whenever the windshield defroster is activated. Therefore, the A/C system would not need to be operated each month if the defroster was used.**

• In order to prevent heater core freeze-up during A/C operation, it is necessary to maintain proper antifreeze protection. Be sure to properly maintain the engine cooling system.

• Any obstruction of or damage to the condenser configuration will restrict air flow which is essential to its efficient operation. Keep this unit clean and in proper physical shape.

→**Bug screens which are mounted in front of the condenser (unless they are original equipment) are regarded as obstructions.**

• The condensation drain tube expels any water which accumulates on the bottom of the evaporator housing into the engine compartment. If this tube is obstructed, the air conditioning performance can be restricted and condensation buildup can spill over onto the vehicle's floor.

SYSTEM INSPECTION

Although the A/C system should not be serviced by the do-it-yourselfer, system inspections should be performed to help maintain the efficiency of the vehicle's A/C system. Be sure to perform the following:

The easiest and often most important check for the air conditioning system consists of a visual inspection of the system components. Visually inspect the system for refrigerant leaks, damaged compressor clutch, abnormal compressor drive belt tension and/or condition, plugged evaporator drain tube, blocked condenser fins, disconnected or broken wires, blown fuses, corroded connections and poor insulation.

A refrigerant leak will usually appear as an oily residue at the leakage point in the system. The oily residue soon picks up dust or dirt particles from the surrounding air and appears greasy. Through time, this will build up and appear to be a heavy dirt impregnated grease.

For a thorough visual and operational inspection, check the following:
• Check the surface of the radiator and condenser for dirt, leaves or other material which might block air flow.
• Check for kinks in hoses and lines. Check the system for leaks.
• Make sure the drive belt is properly tensioned. During operation, make sure the belt is free of noise or slippage.
• Make sure the blower motor operates at all appropriate positions, then check for distribution of the air from all outlets.

→**Remember that in high humidity, air discharged from the vents may not feel as cold as expected, even if the system is working properly. This is because moisture in humid air retains heat more effectively than dry air, thereby making humid air more difficult to cool.**

Windshield Wipers

ELEMENT (REFILL) CARE & REPLACEMENT

♦ **See Figures 74, 75 and 76**

For maximum effectiveness and longest element life, the windshield and wiper blades should be kept clean. Dirt, tree sap, road tar and so on will cause streaking, smearing and blade deterioration if left on the glass. It is advisable to wash the windshield carefully with a commercial glass cleaner at least once a month. Wipe off the rubber blades with the wet rag afterwards. Do not attempt to move wipers across the windshield by hand; damage to the motor and drive mechanism will result.

To inspect and/or replace the wiper blade elements, place the wiper switch in the **LOW** speed position and the ignition switch in the **ACC** position. When the wiper blades are approximately vertical on the windshield, turn the ignition switch to **OFF**.

Examine the wiper blade elements. If they are found to be cracked, broken or torn, they should be replaced immediately. Replacement intervals will vary with usage, although ozone deterioration usually limits element life to about one year. If the wiper pattern is smeared or streaked, or if the blade chatters across the glass, the elements should be replaced. It is easiest and most sensible to replace the elements in pairs.

If your vehicle is equipped with aftermarket blades, there are several different types of refills and your vehicle might have any kind. Aftermarket blades and arms rarely use the exact same type blade or refill as the original equipment.

Regardless of the type of refill used, be sure to follow the part manufacturer's instructions closely. Make sure that all of the frame jaws are engaged as the refill is pushed into place and locked. If the metal blade holder and frame are allowed to touch the glass during wiper operation, the glass will be scratched.

Tires and Wheels

Common sense and good driving habits will afford maximum tire life. Make sure that you don't overload the vehicle or run with incorrect pressure in the tires. Either of these will increase tread wear. Fast starts, sudden stops and sharp cornering are hard on tires and will shorten their useful life span.

→**For optimum tire life, keep the tires properly inflated, rotate them often and have the wheel alignment checked periodically.**

Inspect your tires frequently. Be especially careful to watch for bubbles in the tread or sidewall, deep cuts or underinflation. Replace any tires with bubbles in the sidewall. If cuts are so deep that they penetrate to the cords, discard the tire. Any cut in the sidewall of a radial tire renders it unsafe. Also look for uneven tread wear patterns that may indicate the front end is out of alignment or that the tires are out of balance.

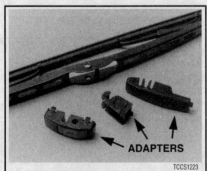

TCCS1223

Fig. 74 Most aftermarket blades are available with multiple adapters to fit different vehicles

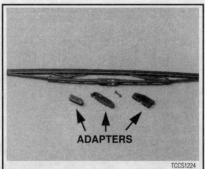

TCCS1224

Fig. 75 Choose a blade which will fit your vehicle, and that will be readily available next time you need blades

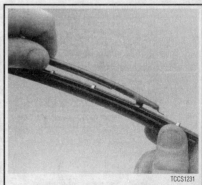

TCCS1231

Fig. 76 When installed, be certain the blade is fully inserted into the backing

TIRE ROTATION

▶ **See Figure 77**

Tires must be rotated periodically to equalize wear patterns that vary with a tire's position on the vehicle. Tires will also wear in an uneven way as the front steering/suspension system wears to the point where the alignment should be reset.

Rotating the tires will ensure maximum life for the tires as a set, so you will not have to discard a tire early due to wear on only part of the tread. Regular rotation is required to equalize wear.

When rotating "unidirectional tires," make sure that they always roll in the same direction. This means that a tire used on the left side of the vehicle must not be switched to the right side and vice-versa. Such tires should only be rotated front-to-rear or rear-to-front, while always remaining on the same side of the vehicle. These tires are marked on the sidewall as to the direction of rotation; observe the marks when reinstalling the tire(s).

Some styled or "mag" wheels may have different offsets front to rear. In these cases, the rear wheels must not be used up front and vice-versa. Furthermore, if these wheels are equipped with unidirectional tires, they cannot be rotated unless the tire is remounted for the proper direction of rotation.

➡ **The compact or space-saver spare is strictly for emergency use. It must never be included in the tire rotation or placed on the vehicle for everyday use.**

TIRE DESIGN

▶ **See Figure 78**

For maximum satisfaction, tires should be used in sets of four. Mixing of different brands or types (radial, bias-belted, fiberglass belted) should be avoided. In most cases, the vehicle manufacturer has designated a type of tire on which the vehicle will perform best. Your first choice when replacing tires should be to use the same type of tire that the manufacturer recommends.

When radial tires are used, tire sizes and wheel diameters should be selected to maintain ground clearance and tire load capacity equivalent to the original specified tire. Radial tires should always be used in sets of four.

Fig. 77 Common tire rotation patterns for 4 and 5-wheel rotations

TCCS1259

Radial tires should never be used on only the front axle.

When selecting tires, pay attention to the original size as marked on the tire. Most tires are described using an industry size code sometimes referred to as P-Metric. This allows the exact identification of the tire specifications, regardless of the manufacturer. If selecting a different tire size or brand, remember to check the installed tire for any sign of interference with the body or suspension while the vehicle is stopping, turning sharply or heavily loaded.

Snow Tires

Good radial tires can produce a big advantage in slippery weather, but in snow, a street radial tire does not have sufficient tread to provide traction and control. The small grooves of a street tire quickly pack with snow and the tire behaves like a billiard ball on a marble floor. The more open, chunky tread of a snow tire will self-clean as the tire turns, providing much better grip on snowy surfaces.

To satisfy municipalities requiring snow tires during weather emergencies, most snow tires carry either an M + S designation after the tire size stamped on the sidewall, or the designation "all-season." In general, no change in tire size is necessary when buying snow tires.

Most manufacturers strongly recommend the use of 4 snow tires on their vehicles for reasons of stability. If snow tires are fitted only to the drive wheels, the opposite end of the vehicle may become very unstable when braking or turning on slippery surfaces. This instability can lead to unpleasant endings if the driver can't counteract the slide in time.

Note that snow tires, whether 2 or 4, will affect vehicle handling in all non-snow situations. The stiffer, heavier snow tires will noticeably change the turning and braking characteristics of the vehicle. Once the snow tires are installed, you must re-learn the behavior of the vehicle and drive accordingly.

➡ **Consider buying extra wheels on which to mount the snow tires. Once done, the "snow wheels" can be installed and removed as needed. This eliminates the potential damage to tires or wheels from seasonal removal and installation. Even if your vehicle has styled wheels, see if inexpensive steel wheels are available. Although the look of the vehicle will change, the expensive wheels will be protected from salt, curb hits and pothole damage.**

TIRE STORAGE

If they are mounted on wheels, store the tires at proper inflation pressure. All tires should be kept in a cool, dry place. If they are stored in the garage or basement, do not let them stand on a concrete floor; set them on strips of wood, a mat or a large stack of newspaper. Keeping them away from direct moisture is of paramount importance. Tires should not be stored upright, but in a flat position.

INFLATION & INSPECTION

▶ **See Figures 79 thru 84**

The importance of proper tire inflation cannot be overemphasized. A tire employs air as part of its structure. It is designed around the supporting

---

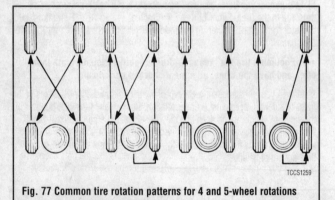

Fig. 78 P-Metric tire coding

TCCS1261

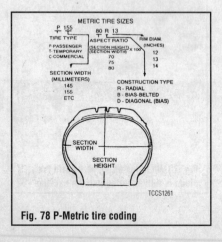

Fig. 79 Tires with deep cuts, or cuts which bulge, should be replaced immediately

TCCS1095

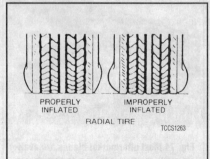

Fig. 80 Radial tires have a characteristic sidewall bulge; don't try to measure pressure by looking at the tire. Use a quality air pressure gauge

TCCS1263

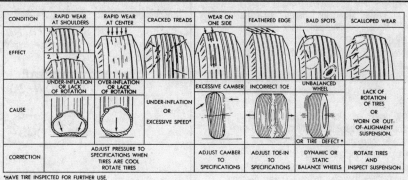

CONDITION	RAPID WEAR AT SHOULDERS	RAPID WEAR AT CENTER	CRACKED TREADS	WEAR ON ONE SIDE	FEATHERED EDGE	BALD SPOTS	SCALLOPED WEAR
EFFECT							
CAUSE	UNDER-INFLATION OR LACK OF ROTATION	OVER-INFLATION OR LACK OF ROTATION	UNDER-INFLATION OR EXCESSIVE SPEED*	EXCESSIVE CAMBER	INCORRECT TOE	UNBALANCED WHEEL OR TIRE DEFECT *	LACK OF ROTATION OF TIRES OR WORN OR OUT-OF-ALIGNMENT SUSPENSION.
CORRECTION		ADJUST PRESSURE TO SPECIFICATIONS WHEN TIRES ARE COOL ROTATE TIRES		ADJUST CAMBER TO SPECIFICATIONS	ADJUST TOE-IN TO SPECIFICATIONS	DYNAMIC OR STATIC BALANCE WHEELS	ROTATE TIRES AND INSPECT SUSPENSION

*HAVE TIRE INSPECTED FOR FURTHER USE.

TCCS1267

Fig. 81 Common tire wear patterns and causes

TCCS1265

Fig. 82 Tread wear indicators will appear when the tire is worn

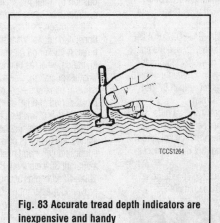

TCCS1264

Fig. 83 Accurate tread depth indicators are inexpensive and handy

TCCS1266

Fig. 84 A penny works well for a quick check of tread depth

strength of the air at a specified pressure. For this reason, improper inflation drastically reduces the tire's ability to perform as intended. A tire will lose some air in day-to-day use; having to add a few pounds of air periodically is not necessarily a sign of a leaking tire.

Two items should be a permanent fixture in every glove compartment: an accurate tire pressure gauge and a tread depth gauge. Check the tire pressure (including the spare) regularly with a pocket type gauge. Too often, the gauge on the end of the air hose at your corner garage is not accurate because it suffers too much abuse. Always check tire pressure when the tires are cold, as pressure increases with temperature. If you must move the vehicle to check the tire inflation, do not drive more than a mile before checking. A cold tire is generally one that has not been driven for more than three hours.

A plate or sticker is normally provided somewhere in the vehicle (door post, hood, tailgate or trunk lid) which shows the proper pressure for the tires. Never counteract excessive pressure build-up by bleeding off air pressure (letting some air out). This will cause the tire to run hotter and wear quicker.

❄❄ CAUTION

Never exceed the maximum tire pressure embossed on the tire! This is the pressure to be used when the tire is at maximum loading, but it is rarely the correct pressure for everyday driving. Con-sult the owner's manual or the tire pressure sticker for the correct tire pressure.

Once you've maintained the correct tire pressures for several weeks, you'll be familiar with the vehicle's braking and handling personality. Slight adjustments in tire pressures can fine-tune these characteristics, but never change the cold pressure specification by more than 2 psi. A slightly softer tire pressure will give a softer ride but also yield lower fuel mileage. A slightly harder tire will give crisper dry road handling but can cause skidding on wet surfaces. Unless you're fully attuned to the vehicle, stick to the recommended inflation pressures.

All automotive tires have built-in tread wear indicator bars that show up as 1/2 in. (13mm) wide smooth bands across the tire when 1/16 in. (1.5mm) of tread remains. The appearance of tread wear indicators means that the tires should be replaced. In fact, many states have laws prohibiting the use of tires with less than this amount of tread.

You can check your own tread depth with an inexpensive gauge or by using a Lincoln head penny. Slip the Lincoln penny (with Lincoln's head upside-down) into several tread grooves. If you can see the top of Lincoln's head in 2 adjacent grooves, the tire has less than 1/16 in. (1.5mm) tread left and should be replaced. You can measure snow tires in the same manner by using the "tails" side of the Lincoln penny. If you can see the top of the Lincoln memorial, it's time to replace the snow tire(s).

FLUIDS AND LUBRICANTS

Fluid Disposal

Used fluids such as engine oil, transmission fluid, coolant (antifreeze) and brake fluid are hazardous wastes and must be disposed of properly. Before draining any fluids, consult with the local authorities; in many areas, waste oil, coolant, etc. is being accepted as a part of recycling programs. A number of service stations and auto parts stores are also accepting waste fluids for recycling.

Be sure of the recycling center's policies before draining any fluids, as many will not accept different fluids that have been mixed together, such as engine oil and coolant.

Fuel Recommendations

It is important to use fuel of the proper octane rating in your car. Octane rating is based on the quantity of anti–knock compounds added to the fuel and it determines the speed at which the gas will burn. The lower the octane rating, the faster it burns. The higher the octane, the slower the fuel will burn and a greater percentage of compounds in the fuel prevent spark knock, detonation (pinging) and pre–ignition (dieseling).

As the temperature of the engine increases, the air/fuel mixture exhibits a tendency to ignite before the spark plug is fired. If fuel of an octane rating too low for the engine is used, this will allow combustion to occur before the piston has completed its compression stroke, thereby creating a very high pressure very rapidly.

Fuel of the proper octane rating, for the compression ratio and ignition timing of your car, will slow the combustion process sufficiently to allow the spark plug enough time to ignite the mixture completely and smoothly. Many non–catalyst models are designed to run on regular–grade fuel. The use of some super–premium fuel cannot hurt, but is no substitute for a properly tuned and maintained engine. It is a good practice, however, to use fuel with detergent additives that can help to prevent combustion chamber deposits. This is particularly important for vehicles with fuel injection. Chances are that if your engine exhibits steady signs of spark knock, detonation or pre–ignition when using regular, detergent fuel, the ignition timing should be checked against specifications or the cylinder head should be removed for decarbonizing.

Vehicles equipped with catalytic converters must use UNLEADED GASOLINE ONLY. Use of leaded fuel shortens the life of spark plugs, exhaust systems and EGR valves and can damage the catalytic converter. Most converter–equipped models are designed to operate using unleaded gasoline with a minimum rating of 87 octane. Use of unleaded gasoline with octane ratings lower than 87 can cause persistent spark knock which could lead to engine damage.

Light spark knock may be noticed when accelerating or driving up hills. The slight knocking may be considered normal (with 87 octane) because the maximum fuel economy is obtained under condition of occasional light spark knock. Gasoline with an octane rating higher than 87 may be used, but it is not necessary (in most cases) for proper operation.

If spark knock is constant, when using 87 octane, at cruising speeds on level ground, an ignition timing adjustment or other service may be required.

Engine Oil Recommendations

♦ See Figures 85 and 86

When adding oil to the crankcase or when changing the oil and filter, it is important that oil of an equal or higher quality than the original be used in your car. The use of inferior oils may void your warranty. Generally speaking, oil that has been rated **SF** by the American Petroleum Institute will prove satisfactory.

Oil of the SF variety performs a multitude of functions in addition to its basic job of reducing friction of the engine's moving parts. Through a balanced formula of polymeric dispersants and metallic detergents, the oil prevents high temperature and low temperature deposits and also keeps sludge and dirt particles in suspension. Acids, particularly sulfuric acid, as well as other products of com-

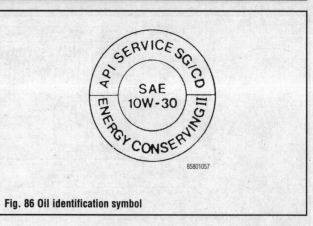

Fig. 86 Oil identification symbol

bustion of sulfur fuels, are neutralized by the oil. These acids, if permitted to concentrate, may cause corrosion and rapid wear of the internal parts of the engine.

It is important to choose an oil of the proper viscosity for climatic and operational conditions. Viscosity in an index of the oil's thickness at different temperatures. A thicker oil (higher numerical rating) is needed for high temperature operation, whereas thinner oil (lower numerical rating) is required for cold weather operation. Due to the need for an oil that embodies both these characteristics in parts of the country where there is wide temperature variation within a small period of time, multigrade oils have been developed. Basically a multigrade oil is thinner at low temperatures and thicker at high temperatures. For example, a 10W–40 oil exhibits the characteristics of a 10 weight oil when the car is first started and the oil is cold. Its lighter weight allows it to travel to the lubricating surfaces quicker and offer less resistance to starter motor cranking than, let's say, a straight 30 weight oil. But after the engine reaches operating temperature, the 10W–40 oil begins acting like a straight 40 weight oil, with its heavier weight providing greater lubricating protection and less susceptibility to foaming than a straight 30 weight oil. Whatever your driving needs, the oil viscosity/temperature chart should prove useful in selecting the proper grade. The SAE viscosity rating is printed or stamped on the top or side of every oil container.

Engine

OIL LEVEL CHECK

♦ See Figures 87, 88 and 89

The engine oil level should be checked frequently, particularly in older or high mileage engines. A good time to do so is at each refueling stop. Be sure that the vehicle is parked on a level surface with the engine off. Also, allow a few minutes after turning off the engine for the oil to drain into the pan, or an inaccurate reading will result.

1. Open the hood and remove the engine oil dipstick.
2. Wipe the dipstick with a clean, lint–free rag and reinsert it. Be sure to insert it all the way.
3. Pull out the dipstick and note the oil level. It should be between the SAFE (MAX) mark and the ADD (MIN) mark.
4. If the level is below the lower mark, replace the dipstick and add fresh oil to bring the level within the proper range. Do not overfill.
5. Recheck the oil level and close the hood.

➡**Use a multi–grade oil with API classification SG.**

OIL AND FILTER CHANGE

♦ See Figures 90, 91, 92, 93 and 94

The engine oil and oil filter should be changed at the same time, at the recommended intervals on the maintenance schedule chart. Because of their operating characteristics, it is extremely important to change the oil and oil filter on all 4–cylinder, turbocharged vehicles at 3,000 mile intervals.

1. Run the engine to normal operating temperature.
2. After the engine has reached operating temperature, shut it off, firmly apply the parking brake, and block the wheels.
3. Raise and safely support the front end on jackstands.

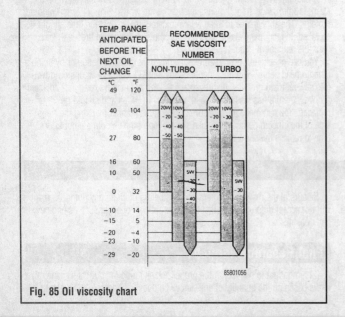

Fig. 85 Oil viscosity chart

Fig. 87 Removing the engine oil dipstick

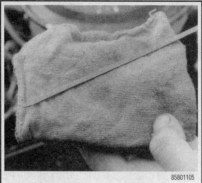

Fig. 88 Wipe the dipstick with a clean, lint–free rag

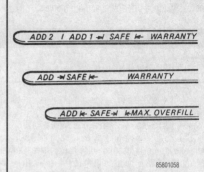

Fig. 89 Checking oil level with a dipstick. Oil should be within the SAFE range.

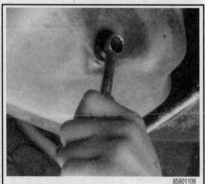

Fig. 90 Use the correct size wrench to remove the drain plug(s)

Fig. 91 Removing the used oil filter with an oil filter wrench

Fig. 92 Before installing a new oil filter, coat the rubber gasket with clean oil

Fig. 93 Turn the oil filler cap counterclockwise to open

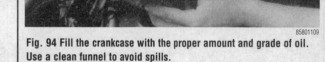

Fig. 94 Fill the crankcase with the proper amount and grade of oil. Use a clean funnel to avoid spills.

4. Place a drip pan beneath the oil pan and remove the drain plug. The oil could be very hot! Protect yourself by using rubber gloves if necessary.

5. Allow the engine to drain thoroughly.

➡**On some V8 engines a dual sump oil pan was used. When changing the oil, both drain plugs (front and side) must be removed. Failure to remove both plugs can lead to incomplete drainage and an incorrect oil level reading.**

6. When the oil has completely drained, clean the threads of the plug and coat them with non–hardening sealer or Teflon® tape and install the plug. Tighten it snugly.

➡**The threads in the oil pan are easily stripped! Do not overtighten the plug!**

7. Place the drip pan beneath the oil filter.

8. Using an oil filter wrench, turn the filter counterclockwise to remove it. The oil could be very hot! Protect yourself by using rubber gloves if necessary.

9. Wipe the contact surface of the new filter clean and coat the rubber gasket with clean engine oil.

10. Clean the mating surface of the adapter on the block.

11. Screw the new filter into position on the block using hand pressure only. Do not use a strap wrench to install the filter! Then hand–tighten the filter ½–¾ additional turn.

12. Fill the crankcase with the proper amount of oil. Check the oil level prior to starting the engine.

13. Start the engine and check for leaks.

Certain operating conditions may warrant more frequent oil changes. If the vehicle is used for short trips, where the engine does not have a chance to fully warm up before it is shut off, water condensation and low temperature deposits may make it necessary to change the oil sooner. If the vehicle is used mostly in stop–and–go traffic, corrosive acids and high temperature deposits may necessitate shorter oil changing intervals. The shorter intervals also apply to industrial or rural areas where high concentrations of dust and other airborne particulate matter contaminate the oil. Finally, if the car is used for towing trailers, a severe load is placed on the engine causing the oil to thin out sooner, necessitating shorter oil changing intervals.

Manual Transmission

FLUID RECOMMENDATIONS

- All 4–speed and 5–speed manual transmissions except for the T5OD — SAE 85W/90 gear oil
- T5OD 5–sp — Dexron®II or Mercon®ATF

SAE 85W/90 gear oil may be used in the T5OD transmission in very warm climates or if gear/bearing noise is excessive. Conversely, Dexron®II or Mercon®ATF may be used in the ET 4–speed in very cold climates, or if hard shifting is a continuing problem.

FLUID LEVEL CHECK

The fluid level should be checked every 6 months/6,000 miles, whichever comes first.

1. Park the car on a level surface, turn off the engine, apply the parking brake and block the wheels.
2. Remove the filler plug from the side of the transmission case using the proper size wrench. The fluid level should be even with the bottom of the filler hole.
3. If additional fluid is necessary, add it through the filler hole using a siphon pump or squeeze bottle.
4. Replace the filler plug; do not overtighten.

DRAIN AND REFILL

1. Place a suitable drain pan under the transmission.
2. Remove the drain plug and allow the gear lube to drain out.
3. Replace the drain plug, then remove the filler plug. Fill the transmission to the proper level with the required fluid.
4. Reinstall the filler plug.

Automatic Transmission

FLUID RECOMMENDATIONS

- 1979–80 C3 — Type F
- 1981–86 C3 — Dexron®II or Mercon®ATF
- 1979 C4 — Type F
- 1980–81 C4 — Dexron®II or Mercon®ATF
- 1982–87 C5 — Type H
- 1981–88 AOD — Dexron®II or Mercon®ATF
- 1987–88 A4LD — Dexron®II or Mercon®ATF

FLUID LEVEL CHECK

▶ **See Figures 95 and 96**

It is very important to maintain the proper fluid level in an automatic transmission. If the level is either too high or too low, poor shifting operation and

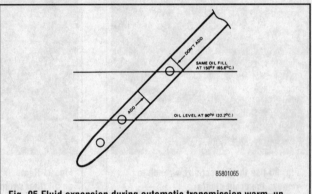

Fig. 95 Fluid expansion during automatic transmission warm–up

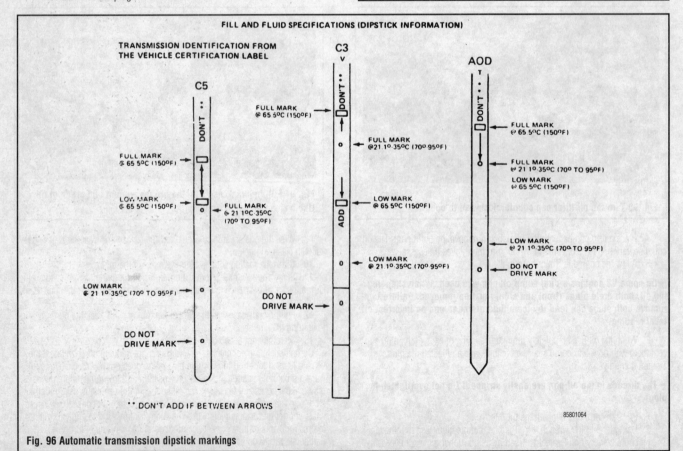

Fig. 96 Automatic transmission dipstick markings

internal damage are likely to occur. For this reason, a regular check of the fluid level is essential.

1. Drive the vehicle for 15–20 minutes to allow the transmission to reach operating temperature.

2. Park the car on a level surface, apply the parking brake and leave the engine idling. Shift the transmission to engage each gear, then place the gear selector in P (PARK).

3. Wipe away any dirt in the vicinity of the transmission dipstick to prevent it from falling into the filler tube. Withdraw the dipstick, wipe it with a clean, lint–free rag and reinsert it until it seats.

4. Withdraw the dipstick and note the fluid level. It should be between the upper (FULL) mark and the lower (ADD) mark.

5. If the level is below the lower mark, use a funnel and add fluid in small quantities through the dipstick filler neck. Keep the engine running while adding fluid and check the level after each small amount. Do not overfill.

DRAIN AND REFILL

C4 and C5 Transmissions

1. Raise the vehicle so that the transmission is readily accessible. Safely support the vehicle on jackstands.

2. Place a large drain pan under the transmission oil pan.

3. On pan fill models, disconnect the fluid filler tube from the pan and drain the fluid from the transmission. Unless further service is planned, the pan need not be removed. On case fill models, loosen the pan attaching bolts, starting at the rear of the pan, and allow the fluid to drain. Remove all attaching bolts except for two at the front, to permit further drainage. Once the fluid has drained, remove the pan and clean it thoroughly. Discard the pan gasket.

To install:

4. On pan fill models, connect the filler tube to the pan and tighten the fitting to 32–42 ft. lbs. On case fill models, place a new gasket on the pan, and install the pan on the transmission. Tighten the attaching bolts to 12–16 ft. lbs.

5. Add 3 quarts of fluid to the transmission through the filler tube.

6. Lower the vehicle. Start the engine and move the gear selector through its shift pattern. Allow the engine to reach normal operating temperature.

7. Check the transmission fluid. Add fluid, if necessary, to achieve the correct level.

C3, AOD and A4LD Transmissions

1. Raise the vehicle so that the transmission is readily accessible. Safely support the vehicle on jackstands.

2. Place a large drain pan under the transmission oil pan.

3. Loosen the pan attaching bolts and drain the fluid from the transmission.

4. When the fluid has drained to the level of the pan flange, remove the remaining pan bolts by working from the rear and both sides of the pan, allowing it to drop and drain slowly.

5. When all of the fluid has drained, remove the pan and clean it thoroughly. Discard the pan gasket.

To install:

6. Place a new gasket on the pan, and install the pan on the transmission. Tighten the attaching bolts to the following torque values:

- C3 Transmission — 12–17 ft. lbs.
- AOD Transmission — 12–16 ft. lbs. (1981–84); 6–10 ft. lbs. (1985–88)
- A4LD Transmission — 8–10 ft. lbs.

7. Add 3 quarts of fluid to the transmission through the filler tube.

8. Lower the vehicle. Start the engine and move the gear selector through its shift pattern. Allow the engine to reach normal operating temperature.

9. Check the transmission fluid. Add fluid, if necessary, to achieve the correct level.

PAN AND FILTER SERVICE

C4 and C5 Transmissions

1. Raise the vehicle so that the transmission is readily accessible. Safely support the vehicle on jackstands.

2. Place a large drain pan under the transmission oil pan.

3. On pan fill models, disconnect the fluid filler tube from the pan and drain the fluid from the transmission. On case fill models, loosen the pan attaching bolts, starting at the rear of the pan, and allow the fluid to drain. Remove all attaching bolts except for two at the front, to permit further drainage.

4. Remove the transmission oil pan attaching bolts, pan and gasket.

5. Loosen the retaining bolt(s) and remove the transmission filter screen and seal or gasket from the valve body.

6. If the filter screen is to be reused, thoroughly clean it with solvent.

7. Clean the transmission oil pan and transmission mating surfaces.

To install:

8. Install a clean filter screen and new seal or gasket.

9. Install the transmission oil pan, using a new gasket and torquing the attaching bolts to 12–16 ft. lbs.

10. Connect the filler tube to the pan and tighten the fitting to 32–42 ft. lbs. Add 3 quarts of fluid to the transmission through the filler tube.

11. Lower the vehicle. Start the engine and move the gear selector through its shift pattern. Allow the engine to reach normal operating temperature.

12. Check the transmission fluid. Add fluid, if necessary, to achieve the correct level.

C3 and A4LD Transmissions

1. Raise the vehicle so that the transmission is readily accessible. Safely support the vehicle on jackstands.

2. Place a large drain pan under the transmission oil pan.

3. Loosen the pan attaching bolts and drain the fluid from the transmission.

4. When the fluid has drained to the level of the pan flange, remove the remaining pan bolts by working from the rear and both sides of the pan, allowing it to drop and drain slowly.

5. When all of the fluid has drained, remove the pan and clean it thoroughly. Discard the pan gasket.

6. Loosen the retaining bolt(s) and remove the transmission filter screen and gasket or seals from the valve body.

7. If the filter screen is to be reused, thoroughly clean it with solvent.

8. Clean the transmission oil pan and transmission mating surfaces.

To install:

9. Install a clean filter screen and new gasket or seals.

10. Place a new gasket on the pan, and install the pan on the transmission. Tighten the attaching bolts to 12–17 ft. lbs. for the C3 transmission or 8–10 ft. lbs. for the A4LD transmission.

11. Add 3 quarts of fluid to the transmission through the filler tube.

12. Lower the vehicle. Start the engine and move the gear selector through its shift pattern. Allow the engine to reach normal operating temperature.

13. Check the transmission fluid. Add fluid, if necessary, to achieve the correct level.

AOD Transmission

1. Raise the vehicle so that the transmission is readily accessible. Safely support the vehicle on jackstands.

2. Place a large drain pan under the transmission oil pan.

3. Loosen the pan attaching bolts and drain the fluid from the transmission.

4. When the fluid has drained to the level of the pan flange, remove the remaining pan bolts by working from the rear and both sides of the pan, allowing it to drop and drain slowly.

5. When all of the fluid has drained, remove the pan and discard the pan gasket.

6. Loosen the retaining bolts and remove the oil filter, gasket and filter grommet. Retain the filter grommet for reuse, but discard the oil filter and gasket. Do not reuse or clean the filter assembly, since the filter element material will contaminate the transmission.

7. Clean the transmission oil pan and transmission mating surfaces.

To install:

8. Place the filter grommet in a new oil filter.

9. Install the new oil filter and gasket. Do not reuse the old gasket. Tighten the attaching bolts to 80–100 inch lbs.

10. Place a new gasket on the pan, and install the pan on the transmission. Tighten the attaching bolts to 12–16 ft. lbs. on 1981–84 models or 6–10 ft. lbs. on 1985–88 models.

11. Add 3 quarts of fluid to the transmission through the filler tube.

12. Lower the vehicle. Start the engine and move the gear selector through its shift pattern. Allow the engine to reach normal operating temperature.

13. Check the transmission fluid. Add fluid, if necessary, to achieve the correct level.

Rear Axle (Differential)

FLUID RECOMMENDATIONS

SAE 85W/90/95 hypoid gear oil for conventional and limited slip differentials. For limited slip differentials only, add 4 oz. of the recommended friction modifier (Ford part no. C8AZ–19B546–A).

FLUID LEVEL CHECK

▶ **See Figure 97**

Like the manual transmission, the rear axle fluid should be checked every six months/6,000 miles. A filler plug is provided near the center of the rear cover or on the upper (driveshaft) side of the gear case. Remove the plug and check to ensure that the fluid level is even with the bottom of the filler hole. Add SAE 85W/90/95 hypoid gear lube as required. If the vehicle is equipped with a limited slip rear axle, add the required special fluid. Install the filler plug but do not overtighten.

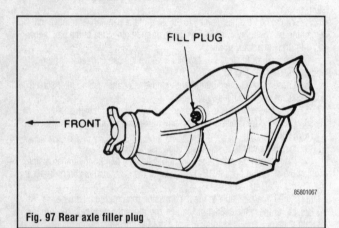

FILL PLUG

← FRONT

85801067

Fig. 97 Rear axle filler plug

DRAIN AND REFILL

Normal maintenance does not require changing the rear axle fluid. However, to do so, proceed as follows:
1. Place a large drain pan under the differential case.
2. Remove either the rear drain plug (models so equipped), the lower two cover bolts or the cover, and drain the fluid.
   To install:
3. If the rear cover was removed, clean the mounting surfaces of the cover and rear housing. Install a new gasket on early models. On late models, apply a continuous bead of Silicone Rubber Sealant (D6AZ–19562–A/B or the equivalent) around the rear housing face inside the circle of bolt holes. Install the cover and tighten the bolts. Parts must be assembled within a half hour after the sealant is applied. If the fluid was drained by removing the two lower cover bolts, apply sealant to the bolts before reinstallation.
4. Fill the rear axle through the filler hole with the proper lubricant. Add friction modifier to limited slip models as required.

Cooling System

FLUID RECOMMENDATIONS

The proper coolant for your vehicle is a 50/50 mix of an ethylene glycol–base antifreeze/coolant and water. Ethylene glycol–base antifreeze/coolant contains water pump lubricants, rust inhibitors and other corrosion inhibitors, as well as acid neutralizers. Alcohol or methanol base coolants are not recommended. Antifreeze solutions should be used, even in summer, to prevent rust and to take advantage of the solution's higher boiling point compared to plain water. This is imperative on air conditioned vehicles; the heater core can freeze if it is not protected.

FLUID LEVEL CHECK

▶ **See Figures 98, 99 and 100**

✳✳ CAUTION

Exercise extreme care when removing the cap from a hot radiator. Wait a few minutes until the engine has time to cool, then wrap a thick towel around the radiator cap and slowly turn it counterclockwise to the first stop. Step back and allow the pressure to release from the cooling system. Then, when the steam has stopped venting, press down on the cap, turn it one more stop counterclockwise and remove the cap.

The coolant level in the radiator should be checked on a monthly basis, when the engine is cold. On a cold engine, the coolant level should be maintained at one inch below the filler neck on downflow radiators, and 2½ in. below the filler neck at the "**COLD FILL**" mark on crossflow radiators. On cars equipped with the Coolant Recovery System, the radiator is normally full when the level is maintained at the "**COLD LEVEL**" mark in the translucent plastic expansion bottle. Top off as necessary with a mixture of 50% water and 50% ethylene glycol antifreeze, to ensure proper rust, freezing and boiling protection. If you have to add coolant more often than once a month or if you have to add more than one quart at a time, check the cooling system for leaks. Small amounts of coolant often escape at loose hose fittings or failing water pumps, and are evidenced by a white telltale residue.

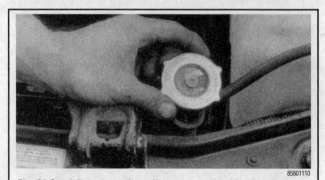

85801110

Fig. 98 Carefully remove the radiator cap, preferably when the engine is cool

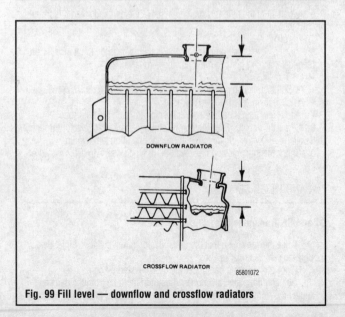

DOWNFLOW RADIATOR

CROSSFLOW RADIATOR

85801072

Fig. 99 Fill level — downflow and crossflow radiators

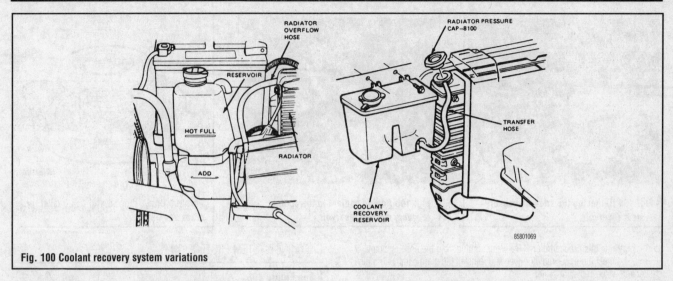

Fig. 100 Coolant recovery system variations

The presence of coolant in the crankcase oil suggests a more serious problem, such as a blown cylinder head gasket. If this situation exists, it is recommended that the engine not be operated until the problem has been identified and repaired. In so doing, engine damage should be kept to a minimum.

DRAIN AND REFILL

▶ **See Figures 101, 102, 103, 104 and 105**

❊❊ CAUTION

When draining the coolant, keep in mind that cats and dogs are attracted by the ethylene glycol antifreeze, and are quite likely to drink any that is left in an uncovered container or in puddles on the ground. This will prove fatal in sufficient quantity. Always drain the coolant into a sealable container. Coolant should be reused unless it is contaminated or several years old.

Completely draining and refilling the cooling system at least once every two years will remove accumulated rust, scale and other deposits.

1. Drain the existing coolant/water mixture. Open the radiator and engine drain petcocks (on models so equipped), or disconnect the bottom radiator hose, at the radiator outlet. Set the heater temperature controls to the full HOT position.

➡**Before opening the radiator petcock, spray it with some penetrating lubricant.**

2. Close the petcock(s) or reconnect the lower hose and fill the system with water.
3. Add a can of quality radiator flush. Be sure the flush is safe to use in engines having aluminum components.
4. Idle the engine until the upper radiator hose gets hot.
5. Drain the system again.

6. Repeat steps 2, 4 and 5 until the drained water is clear and free of scale.
7. Close all petcocks and connect all the hoses.
8. If equipped with a coolant recovery system, flush the reservoir with water and leave empty. It may be helpful to remove the reservoir before flushing, so that old coolant and water can be poured out.
9. If applicable, reinstall the coolant recovery system reservoir.
10. Determine the capacity of your cooling system. Refer to the Capacities Specifications chart in this section for details. Add a 50/50 mix of quality antifreeze/coolant and water to provide the desired protection. If equipped with a coolant recovery system, be sure to fill the reservoir to the indicated level after filling the radiator.

➡**Since a fair amount of water will remain in the system after draining, especially on engines without drain petcocks, it is a good practice to add the full allotment of undiluted antifreeze/coolant before topping off with water. This will avoid the annoying problem of insufficient room for the recommended amount of coolant. When pouring in the unmixed coolant, be sure to limit the quantity to one–half of the total cooling system capacity.**

FLUSHING AND CLEANING THE SYSTEM

In addition to the chemical flush mentioned above, a good way to eliminate or prevent the build–up of unwanted deposits is to reverse flush the entire cooling system with high pressure water. Inexpensive kits which can be permanently installed for this purpose are available at auto parts stores. If you prefer to reverse flush your vehicle's cooling system without using such a kit, proceed as follows:

1. Drain the cooling system.
2. Close the petcock or reconnect the lower radiator hose.
3. Remove the thermostat from the engine. Disconnect the upper radiator hose at the radiator neck.
4. Install a high pressure hose into the thermostat housing and allow the water pressure to reverse flush the system.

Fig. 101 Opening the radiator drain petcock

Fig. 102 Carefully lift off the cap from the coolant recovery system reservoir

Fig. 103 The coolant recovery system reservoir is retained by bolts

Fig. 104 Removing the coolant recovery system reservoir

Fig. 105 Adding coolant to the coolant recovery system reservoir

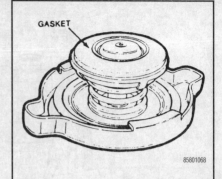
GASKET
Fig. 106 Check the radiator cap gasket for cracks or wear

5. Continue this procedure until the water coming from the hose is clean.

6. Reconnect the upper radiator hose and reinstall the thermostat with a new gasket and water–resistant sealer.

7. Refill the cooling system with a mixture of fresh coolant and water.

SYSTEM INSPECTION

Most permanent antifreeze/coolant have a colored dye added which makes the solution an excellent leak detector. When servicing the cooling system, check for leakage at:

- All hoses and hose connections
- Radiator seams, radiator core, and radiator draincock
- All engine block and cylinder head freeze (core) plugs, and drain plugs
- Edges of all cooling system gaskets (head gaskets, thermostat gasket)
- Transmission fluid cooler
- Heating system components, water pump
- Check the engine oil dipstick for signs of coolant in the engine oil
- Check the coolant in the radiator for signs of oil in the coolant

Investigate and correct any indication of coolant leakage.

Check the Radiator Cap

▶ See Figure 106

While you are checking the coolant level, check the radiator cap for a worn or cracked gasket. If the cap doesn't seal properly, fluid will be lost and the engine will overheat.

A worn cap should be replaced with a new one.

Clean Radiator of Debris

▶ See Figure 107

Periodically clean any debris such as leaves, paper, insects, etc., from the radiator fins. Pick the large pieces off by hand. The smaller pieces can be washed away with water from a hose.

Carefully straighten any bent radiator fins with a pair of needle nose pliers. Be careful, the fins are very soft. Don't wiggle the fins back and forth too much. Straighten them once and try not to move them again.

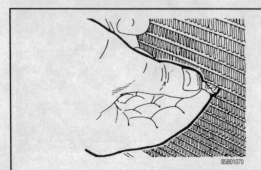
Fig. 107 Clean debris from the radiator fins

CHECKING SYSTEM PROTECTION

▶ See Figure 108

A 50/50 mix of coolant concentrate and water will usually provide protection to −35°F (−37°C). Freeze protection may be checked by using a cooling system hydrometer. Inexpensive hydrometers (floating ball types) may be obtained from a local auto supply store. Follow the directions packaged with the coolant hydrometer when checking protection.

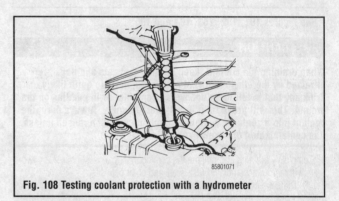
Fig. 108 Testing coolant protection with a hydrometer

Brake Master Cylinder

FLUID RECOMMENDATIONS

Use only Heavy Duty Brake Fluid meeting DOT 3 specifications. Never reuse old brake fluid.

✳✳ CAUTION

Be careful to avoid spilling any brake fluid on painted surfaces, because the paint coat will become discolored or damaged.

FLUID LEVEL CHECK

The brake fluid in the master cylinder should be checked every 6 months/6,000 miles.

➡**A slight drop in fluid level is normal as brake pads wear. However, if the level of the brake fluid is less than half the volume of the reservoir, it is advisable to check the brake system for leaks. Leaks in the hydraulic brake system most commonly occur at the wheel cylinders.**

Cast Iron Reservoir

▶ See Figures 109, 110 and 111

1. Park the vehicle on a level surface and open the hood.

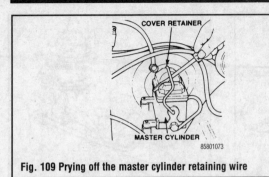

Fig. 109 Prying off the master cylinder retaining wire

2. Pry the retaining spring bar holding the cover onto the master cylinder to one side.

3. Clean any dirt from the sides and top of the cover before removal. Remove the master cylinder cover and gasket.

4. Add fluid, if necessary, to within ¼ in. of the top of the reservoir, or to the full level indicator (on models so equipped).

5. Push the gasket bellows back into the cover. Reinstall the gasket and cover and reposition the retaining spring bar.

Plastic Reservoir

Check the fluid level on the side of the reservoir. If fluid is required, remove the filler cap and gasket from the master cylinder. Fill the reservoir to the full line in the reservoir. Install the filler cap, making sure the gasket is properly seated in the cap.

Power Steering Pump

FLUID RECOMMENDATIONS

All vehicles covered by this book use Type F automatic transmission fluid in the power steering system.

FLUID LEVEL CHECK

▶ **See Figures 112, 113, 114, 115 and 116**

Check the power steering fluid level every 6 months/6,000 miles.

1. Park the vehicle on a level surface. Run the engine until normal operating temperature is reached.

2. Turn the steering all the way to the left and then all the way to the right several times. Center the steering wheel and shut off the engine.

3. Open the hood and locate the power steering pump.

4. Remove the filler cap and wipe the attached dipstick clean.

5. Re-insert the dipstick and tighten the cap. Remove the cap and note the fluid level indicated on the dipstick.

6. The level should be at any point below the Full mark, but not below the Add mark.

7. Add fluid as necessary. Do not overfill.

Chassis Greasing

➡ **Depending on the year and model, vehicles may have plugs or grease fittings in all steering/suspension linkage or pivot points. Follow the instructions under "Ball Joints" in this section, if equipped with these plugs. Newer models have sealed points and lubrication is not necessary.**

BALL JOINTS

▶ **See Figure 117**

1. Park the vehicle on a level surface, set the parking brake, block the rear wheels, raise the front end and support it with jackstands.

2. Wipe away any dirt from the ball joint lubrication plugs.

3. Pull out the plugs and install grease fittings.

4. Using a hand-operated grease gun containing multi-purpose grease, force lubricant into the joint until the joint boot swells.

5. Remove the grease fitting and push in the lubrication plug.

6. Lower the vehicle.

Fig. 110 After cleaning any dirt, remove the master cylinder cover and gasket. Note how the bellows expand to displace a low fluid level.

Fig. 111 Add new, clean brake fluid, if necessary, to fill the reservoir to the proper level

Fig. 112 A filler cap and dipstick sit atop the power steering pump's reservoir

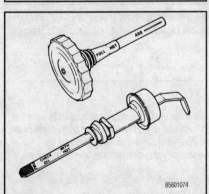

Fig. 113 Power steering pump reservoir dipsticks

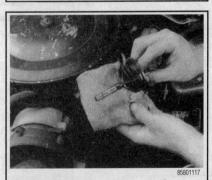

Fig. 114 Withdraw the filler cap and attached dipstick, and wipe dry with a clean, lint-free rag

Fig. 115 Re-insert the dipstick and tighten the cap. Remove the cap and note the fluid level indicated on the dipstick.

Fig. 116 Add clean Type F ATF as necessary, and recheck the fluid level

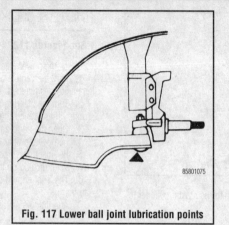

Fig. 117 Lower ball joint lubrication points

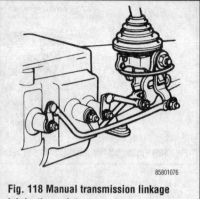

Fig. 118 Manual transmission linkage lubrication points

STEERING ARM STOPS

The steering arm stops are attached to the lower control arm. They are located between each steering arm and the upturned end of the front suspension strut.

1. Park the vehicle on a level surface, set the parking brake, block the rear wheels, raise the front end and support it with jackstands.
2. Clean the friction points and apply multi–purpose grease.
3. Lower the vehicle.

MANUAL TRANSMISSION AND CLUTCH LINKAGE

▶ **See Figure 118**

On models so equipped, apply a small amount of multi–purpose grease to the pivot points of the transmission and clutch linkage as per the chassis lubrication diagram.

AUTOMATIC TRANSMISSION LINKAGE

▶ **See Figure 119**

On models so equipped, apply a small amount of multi–purpose grease or 10W–30 engine oil to the kickdown and shift linkage at the pivot points.

PARKING BRAKE LINKAGE

▶ **See Figure 120**

At yearly intervals or whenever binding is noticeable in the parking brake linkage, lubricate the cable guides, levers and linkage with a polyethylene or lithium grease.

Body Lubrication and Maintenance

LOCK CYLINDERS

Apply graphite lubricant sparingly through the key slot. Insert the key and operate the lock several times to be sure that the lubricant is worked into the lock cylinder.

DOOR HINGES

Spray a silicone lubricant on the hinge pivot points to eliminate any binding conditions. Open and close the door several times to be sure that the lubricant is evenly and thoroughly distributed.

TRUNK LID OR HATCH

Spray a silicone lubricant on all of the pivot and friction surfaces to eliminate any squeaks or binds. Work the trunk lid or hatch to distribute the lubricant.

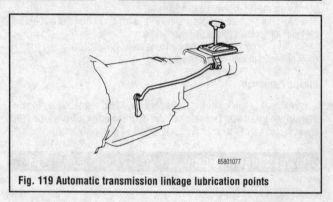

Fig. 119 Automatic transmission linkage lubrication points

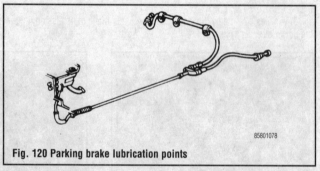

Fig. 120 Parking brake lubrication points

BODY DRAIN HOLES

Be sure that the drain holes in the doors and rocker panels are unobstructed. A small screwdriver can be used to clear them of any debris.

Front Wheel Bearings

→This section only covers service of the front wheel bearings. For information and service procedures regarding rear wheel bearings, refer to Section 8.

ADJUSTMENT

▶ **See Figure 121**

The front wheels each rotate on a set of opposed, tapered roller bearings as shown in the accompanying illustration. The grease retainer at the inside of the hub prevents lubricant from leaking onto the dust shield or rotor.

1. Raise and support the front end on jackstands.
2. Remove the wheel cover.
3. Remove the dust cap and remove excess grease from the end of the spindle.
4. Remove the cotter pin and nut retainer. Discard the cotter pin.

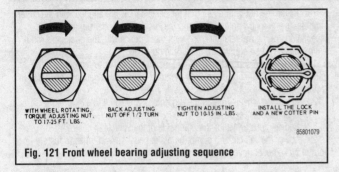

Fig. 121 Front wheel bearing adjusting sequence

5. Loosen the adjusting nut three turns. Rock the wheel, hub and rotor assembly in and out several times to push the brake pads away from the rotor.

6. While rotating the wheel, hub and rotor assembly, tighten the adjusting nut to 17–25 ft. lbs. in order to seat the bearings.

7. Back off the adjusting nut ½, then retighten the adjusting nut to 10–15 inch lbs.

8. Place the nut retainer on the adjusting nut, so that the castellations on the retainer are lined up with the cotter pin hole in the spindle.

9. Install a new cotter pin, and bend the ends around the castellated flange of the nut retainer, to prevent interference with the dust cap's radio static collector (if so equipped).

10. Check the wheel for proper rotation, then install the dust cap and wheel cover. If the wheel still does not rotate properly, clean and repack or replace the wheel bearings and cups.

11. Repeat steps 2–10 for the other side of the vehicle, if desired.

12. Lower the vehicle and pump the brake pedal several times to restore normal brake pedal travel before driving.

REMOVAL, PACKING, AND INSTALLATION

▶ **See Figures 122 and 123**

Before handling the bearings, there are a few things that you should remember to do and not to do.

Remember to DO the following:
- Remove all outside dirt from the housing before exposing the bearing.
- Treat a used bearing as gently as you would a new one.
- Work with clean tools in clean surroundings.
- Use clean, dry canvas gloves, or at least clean, dry hands.
- Clean solvents and flushing fluids are a must.
- Use clean paper when laying out the bearings to dry.
- Protect disassembled bearings from rust and dirt. Cover them up.
- Use clean rags to wipe bearings.
- Keep the bearings in oil–proof paper when they are to be stored or are not in use.
- Clean the inside of the housing before replacing the bearing.

Do NOT do the following:
- Do not work in dirty surroundings.
- Do not use dirty, chipped or damaged tools.
- Try not to work on wooden work benches or use wooden mallets.
- Do not handle bearings with dirty or moist hands.
- Do not use gasoline for cleaning; use a safe solvent.
- Do not spin–dry bearings with compressed air. They will be damaged.
- Do not spin dirty bearings.
- Avoid using cotton waste or dirty cloths to wipe bearings.
- Try not to scratch or nick bearing surfaces.
- Do not allow the bearing to come in contact with dirt or rust at any time.

1. Raise and support the front end on jackstands.
2. Remove the wheel cover. Remove the wheel.

➡**The outer bearing assembly may be removed without removing the rotor. However, in order to also remove the inner bearing assembly, you will have to first remove the caliper and hub and rotor assembly.**

3. Remove the caliper assembly from the anchor plate and wire it to the underbody to prevent damage to the brake hose. (See the brake caliper removal procedures in section 9.)

4. Remove the dust cap from the hub. Then, remove the cotter pin, nut retainer, adjusting nut and flat washer from the spindle. Remove the outer bearing assembly from the hub.

5. Pull the hub and rotor assembly off the wheel spindle.

6. Remove and discard the old grease retainer. Remove the inner bearing cone and roller assembly from the hub.

7. Clean all grease from the inner and outer bearing cups with solvent. Inspect the cups for pits, scratches, or excessive wear. If the cups are damaged, remove them with a drift.

8. Clean the inner and outer cone and roller assemblies with solvent and shake them dry. If the cone and roller assemblies show excessive wear or damage, replace them with the bearing cups as a unit.

9. Clean the spindle and the inside of the hub with solvent to thoroughly remove all old grease.

10. Covering the spindle with a clean cloth, brush all loose dirt and dust from the brake assembly. Remove the cloth carefully so as to not get dirt on the spindle.

11. If the inner and/or outer bearing cups were removed, install the replacement cups on the hub. Be sure that the cups seat properly in the hub.

✳✳ CAUTION

When installing bearing cups, support the hub and rotor assembly on a wooden block to avoid damage to the wheel studs.

12. It is imperative that all old grease be removed from the bearings and surrounding surfaces before repacking. The new lithium–based grease is not compatible with the sodium–base grease used in the past.

13. Using a bearing packer, pack the bearing cone and roller assemblies with the recommended grease. If a packer is not available, use your hands to work as much grease as possible between the rollers and cages. Grease the cup surfaces.

14. Place the inner bearing cone and roller assembly in the inner cup. Apply a light film of wheel bearing grease to the lips of a new grease retainer and install the retainer. Be sure that it is properly seated.

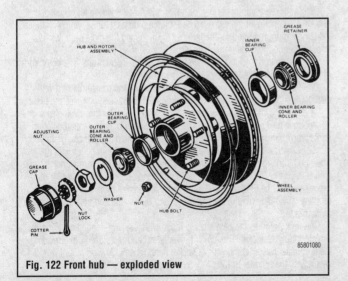

Fig. 122 Front hub — exploded view

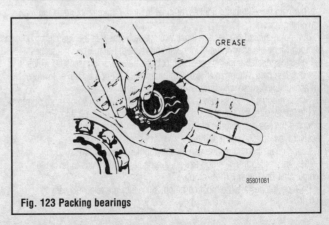

Fig. 123 Packing bearings

❋❋ CAUTION

When installing the grease retainer, support the hub and rotor assembly on a wooden block to avoid damage to the wheel studs.

15. Install the hub and rotor assembly on the spindle. To prevent damage to the grease retainer and spindle threads, keep the hub centered on the spindle.

16. Install the outer bearing cone and roller assembly and the flat washer on the spindle. Install the adjusting nut finger tight.

17. Adjust the wheel bearings by torquing the adjusting nut to 17–25 ft. lbs. with the wheel rotating to seat the bearing. Then back off the adjusting nut ½ turn. Retighten the adjusting nut to 10–15 inch lbs.

18. Install the nut retainer so that the castellations are aligned with the cotter pin hole. Install a new cotter pin. Bend the ends of the cotter pin around the castellations of the nut retainer to prevent interference with the dust cap's radio static collector (if so equipped). Install the dust cap.

19. Remove the supporting wire and install the caliper assembly over the rotor and onto the anchor plate. (See the brake caliper installation procedures in section 9.)

20. Install the wheel. Tighten the lug nuts to 80–105 ft. lbs.

21. Install the wheel cover.

22. Repeat steps 2–19 for the other side of the vehicle, if desired.

23. Lower the vehicle and pump the brake pedal several times to restore normal brake pedal travel before driving.

TRAILER TOWING

❋❋ WARNING

Ford cautions that the 4–140 turbocharged engine should not be used for trailer towing, in order to prevent engine damage. Ford also recommends a minimum 6–cylinder engine and automatic transmission as the power train for towing Class I trailers of up to 1000 lbs. An external automatic transmission oil cooler is also recommended for any trailer towing other than the temporary, cross–town variety.

General Recommendations

Your vehicle was primarily designed to carry passengers and cargo. It is important to remember that towing a trailer will place additional loads on your vehicle's engine, drive train, steering, braking and other systems. However, if you find it necessary to tow a trailer, using the proper equipment is a must.

Factory trailer towing packages are available for most vehicles. However, if you are installing a trailer hitch and wiring on your car, there are a few things that you ought to know. Local laws may require specific equipment such as trailer brakes or fender mounted mirrors. If in doubt, check with local authorities.

Trailer Weight

Trailer weight is the first, and most important, factor in determining whether or not your vehicle is suitable for towing the trailer you have in mind. The horsepower–to–weight ratio should be calculated. The basic standard is a ratio of 35:1. That is, 35 pounds of GVW for every unit of horsepower.

To calculate this ratio, multiply your engine's rated horsepower by 35, then subtract the weight of the vehicle, including passengers and luggage. The resulting figure is the ideal maximum trailer weight that you can tow. One point to consider: a numerically higher axle ratio can offset what appears to be a high trailer weight. If the weight of the trailer that you have in mind is somewhat higher than the weight you just calculated, you might consider changing your rear axle ratio to compensate.

Hitch Weight

There are three kinds of hitches: bumper mounted, frame mounted, and load equalizing.

Bumper mounted hitches are those which attach solely to the vehicle's bumper. Many states prohibit towing with this type of hitch, when it attaches to the vehicle's stock bumper, since it subjects the bumper to stresses for which it was not designed. Aftermarket rear step bumpers, designed for trailer towing, are acceptable for use with bumper mounted hitches.

Frame mounted hitches can be of the type which bolts to two or more points on the frame, plus the bumper, or just to several points on the frame. Frame mounted hitches can also be of the tongue type, for Class I towing, or, of the receiver type, for classes II and III.

Load equalizing hitches are usually used for large trailers. Most equalizing hitches are welded in place and use equalizing bars and chains to level the vehicle after the trailer is hooked up.

Bolt–on hitches are the most common, since they are relatively easy to install.

Check the gross weight rating of your trailer. Tongue weight is usually figured as 10% of gross trailer weight. Therefore, a trailer with a maximum gross weight of 2,000 lb. will have a maximum tongue weight of 200 lb. Class I trailers fall into this category. Class II trailers are those with a gross weight rating of 2,000–3,500 lb., while Class III trailers fall into the 3,500–6,000 lb. category. Class IV trailers are those over 6,000 lb. and are for use with fifth wheel trucks, only.

When you've determined the hitch that you'll need, follow the manufacturer's installation instructions, exactly, especially when it comes to fastener torques. The hitch will be subjected to a lot of stress and good hitches come with hardened bolts. Never substitute an inferior bolt for a hardened bolt.

❋❋ WARNING

The combined vehicle and trailer weight must never exceed either the gross axle weight ratings (GAWR front and rear) or the gross vehicle weight rating (GVWR). These ratings appear on the Safety Compliance Certification Label attached to the left front door lock panel or door pillar. Overloading can cause vehicle breakdown and damage, as well as possible personal injury.

Wiring

Wiring the car for towing is fairly easy. There are a number of good wiring kits available and these should be used, rather than trying to design your own. All trailers will need brake lights and turn signals as well as tail lights and side marker lights. Most states require extra marker lights for overly wide trailers. Also, most states have recently required back–up lights for trailers, and most trailer manufacturers have been building trailers with back–up lights for several years.

Additionally, some Class I, most Class II and just about all Class III trailers will have electric brakes.

All of these electric circuits require wires. When you factor in an accessories wire, to operate the trailer's internal equipment or to charge the trailer's battery, you can have as many as seven wires in the harness.

Determine the equipment on your trailer and buy the wiring kit necessary. The kit will contain all the wires needed, plus a plug adapter set which includes the female plug, mounted on the bumper or hitch, and the male plug, wired into, or plugged into the trailer harness.

When installing the kit, follow the manufacturer's instructions. The color coding of the wires is standard throughout the industry.

One point to note is that some domestic vehicles, and most imported vehicles, have separate turn signals. On most domestic vehicles, however, the brake lights and rear turn signals operate from the same bulb. For these vehicles without separate turn signals, you can purchase an isolation unit so that the brake lights won't blink whenever the turn signals are operated, or, you can go to your local electronics supply house and buy four diodes to wire in series with the brake and turn signal bulbs. Diodes will isolate the brake and turn signals. The choice is yours. The isolation units are simple and quick to install, but far more expensive than the diodes. The diodes, however, require more work to install properly, since they require the cutting of each bulb's wire and soldering in place of the diode.

One final point — the best kits are those with a spring–loaded cover on the vehicle mounted socket. This cover prevents dirt and moisture from corroding the terminals. Never let the vehicle socket hang loosely. Always mount it securely to the bumper or hitch.

Cooling

ENGINE

One of the most common, if not THE most common, problem associated with trailer towing is engine overheating.

With factory installed trailer towing packages, a heavy duty cooling system is usually included. Heavy duty cooling systems are available as optional equipment on most cars, with or without a trailer package. If you have one of these extra–capacity systems, you shouldn't have any overheating problems.

If you have a standard cooling system, without an expansion tank, you'll definitely need to get an aftermarket expansion tank kit, preferably one with at least a 2 quart capacity. These kits are easily installed on the radiator's overflow hose, and come with a pressure cap designed for expansion tanks.

Another helpful accessory is a Flex Fan. These large diameter fans are designed to provide more airflow at low speeds, with blades that have deeply cupped surfaces. The blades then flex, or flatten out, at high speeds, when less cooling air is needed. These fans are far lighter in weight than stock fans, requiring less horsepower to drive them. Also, they are far quieter than stock fans.

If you do decide to replace your stock fan with a flex fan, note that if your car has a fan clutch, a spacer between the flex fan and water pump hub will be needed.

Aftermarket engine oil coolers are helpful for prolonging engine oil life and reducing overall engine temperatures. Both of these factors increase engine life.

While not absolutely necessary in towing Class I and some Class II trailers, they are recommended for heavier Class II and all Class III towing.

Engine oil cooler systems consist of an adapter, screwed on in place of the oil filter, a remote filter mounting and a multi–tube, finned heat exchanger, which is mounted in front of the radiator or air conditioning condenser.

JACKING

▶ **See Figure 124**

Your car is equipped with either a scissors–type jack or a bumper jack. The scissors–type jack is placed under the side of the car so that it fits into the notch in the vertical rocker panel flange nearest the wheel to be changed. These jacking notches are located approximately 8 inches from the wheel opening on the rocker panel flanges. Bumper jack slots or flats are provided on the front and rear bumpers. Be sure the jack is inserted firmly and is straight before raising the vehicle.

When raising the car with a scissors–type or bumper jack follow these precautions: Park the car on a firm, level spot and put the gear selector in P (PARK) with an automatic transmission or in R (REVERSE) if your car has a manual transmission. Apply the parking brake and block the front and back of the wheel that is diagonally opposite the wheel being changed. These jacks are fine for changing a tire, but never crawl under the car when it is supported only by the jack.

❋❋ CAUTION

If you are going to work beneath the vehicle, always support it on jackstands or ramps.

TRANSMISSION

An automatic transmission is recommended for trailer towing. Modern automatics have proven reliable and, of course, easy to operate, in trailer towing.

The increased load of a trailer, however, causes an increase in the temperature of the automatic transmission fluid. Heat is the worst enemy of an automatic transmission. As the temperature of the fluid increases, the life of the fluid decreases.

It is essential, therefore, that you install an automatic transmission cooler.

The cooler, which consists of a multi–tube, finned heat exchanger, is usually installed in front of the radiator or air conditioning condenser, and hooked inline with the transmission cooler tank inlet line. Follow the cooler manufacturer's installation instructions.

Select a cooler of at least adequate capacity, based upon the combined gross weights of the car and trailer.

Cooler manufacturers recommend that you use an aftermarket cooler in addition to, and not instead of, the present cooling tank in your car radiator. If you do want to use it in place of the radiator cooling tank, get a cooler at least two sizes larger than normally necessary.

➡**A transmission cooler can sometimes cause slow or harsh shifting in the transmission during cold weather, until the fluid has a chance to warm up to normal operating temperature. Some coolers can be purchased with, or retrofitted with, a temperature bypass valve, which allows fluid to flow through the cooler only upon reaching normal operating temperature.**

❋❋ WARNING

Do not use OVERDRIVE when towing a trailer.

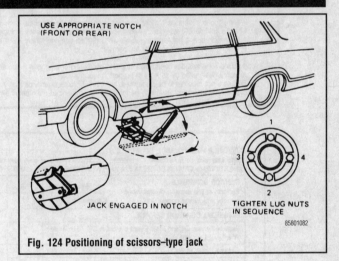

USE APPROPRIATE NOTCH (FRONT OR REAR)

JACK ENGAGED IN NOTCH

TIGHTEN LUG NUTS IN SEQUENCE

85801082

Fig. 124 Positioning of scissors–type jack

MAINTENANCE INTERVALS

CUSTOMER MAINTENANCE SCHEDULE A

Follow this Schedule if your driving habits MAINLY include one or more of the following conditions:

- Short trips of less than 16 km (10 miles) when outside temperatures remain below freezing.
- Operating during HOT WEATHER
  — Driving in stop-and-go "rush hour" traffic.
- Towing a trailer or using a car-top carrier.
- Operating in severe dust conditions.
- Extensive idling, such as police, taxi or door-to-door delivery service.

SERVICE INTERVAL Perform at the months or distances shown, whichever comes first. Miles × 1000	3	6	9	12	15	18	21	24	27	30	33	36	39	42	45	48	51	54	57	60
Kilometers × 1000	4.8	9.6	14.4	19.2	24	28.8	33.6	38.4	43.2	48	52.8	57.6	62.4	67.2	72	76.8	81.6	86.4	91.2	96
EMISSION CONTROL SERVICE																				
Replace Engine Oil and Oil Filter Every 3 Months OR	X	X	X	X	X	X	X	X	X	X	X	X	X	X	X	X	X	X	X	X
Replace Spark Plugs										X										X
Inspect Accessory Drive Belt(s)										X										X
Replace PCV Valve and Crankcase Emission Filter — 5.0L					(X)					(X)					(X)					X
Replace Air Cleaner Filter①										X										X
Replace Engine Coolant, EVERY 36 Months OR										X										X
Check Engine Coolant Protection, Hoses and Clamps	ANNUALLY																			
GENERAL MAINTENANCE																				
Inspect Exhaust Heat Shields										X										X
Change Automatic Transmission Fluid②										X										X
Lubricate Tie Rods										X										X
Inspect Disc Brake Pads and Rotors②										X										X
Inspect Brake Linings and Drums (Rear)③										X										X
Inspect and Repack Front Wheel Bearings										X										X
Rotate Tires		X					X						X				X			

① If operating in severe dust, more frequent intervals may be required. Consult your dealer.
② Change automatic transmission fluid if your driving habits frequently include one or more of the following conditions:
  • Operation during hot weather (above 32°C (90°F)) carrying heavy loads and in hilly terrain.
  • Towing a trailer or using a car top carrrier.
  • Police, taxi or door to door delivery service.
③ If your driving includes continuous stop-and-go driving or driving in mountainous areas, more frequent intervals may be required.
X All items designated by an X must be performed in all states.
(X) This item not required to be performed, however, Ford recommends that you also perform maintenance on items designated by an (X) in order to achieve best vehicle operation. Failure to perform this recommended maintenance will not invalidate the vehicle emissions warranty or manufacturer recall liability.

85801086

CUSTOMER MAINTENANCE SCHEDULE B

Follow Maintenance Schedule B if, generally, you drive your vehicle on a daily basis for more than 16 Km (10 miles) and NONE OF THE UNIQUE DRIVING CONDITIONS SHOWN IN SCHEDULE A APPLY TO YOUR DRIVING HABITS.

SERVICE INTERVALS Perform at the months or distances shown, whichever comes first. Miles x 1000	7.5	15	22.5	30	37.5	45	52.5	60
Kilometers x 1000	12	24	36	48	60	72	84	96
EMISSIONS CONTROL SERVICE								
Replace Engine Oil and Filter Every 6 Months OR 7,500 Miles Whichever Occurs First	X	X	X	X	X	X	X	X
Replace Spark Plugs				X				X
Replace Crankcase Emission Filter①				X				X
Inspect Accessory Drive Belt(s)				X				X
Replace Air Cleaner Filter①				X				X
Replace PCV Valve and Crankcase Emission Filter — 5.0L		(X)		(X)		(X)		X
Replace Engine Coolant Every 36 Months OR				X				X
Check Engine Coolant Protection, Hoses and Clamps	ANNUALLY							
GENERAL MAINTENANCE								
Check Exhaust Heat Shields				X				X
Lube Tie Rods		X③		X		X③		X
Inspect Disc Brake Pads and Rotors②				X				X
Inspect Brake Linings and Drums (Rear)②				X②				X②
Inspect and Repack Front Wheel Bearings				X				X
Rotate Tires	X		X		X		X	

① If operating in severe dust, more frequent intervals may be required. Consult your dealer.
② If your driving includes continuous stop-and-go driving or driving in mountainous areas, more frequent intervals may be required.
③ All vehicles.
X All items designated by an X must be performed in all states.
(X) This item not required to be performed, however, Ford recommends that you also perform maintenance on items designated by an (X) in order to achieve best vehicle operation. Failure to perform this recommended maintenance will not invalidate the vehicle emissions warranty or manufacturer recall liability.

85801087

CAPACITIES

Year	Engine No. Cyl. Displacement (Cu. In.)	Engine Crankcase Add 1 Qt. For New Filter	Transmission Pts. to Refill After Draining Manual	Automatic (Total Capacity)	Drive Axle (pts.)	Gasoline Tank (gals.)	Cooling System (qts.) [14] With Heater	With A/C
1979	4-140	4[3]	2.8	[2]	[1]	11.5	8.6	10.0
	4-140T	4[3]	3.5	[2]	[1]	12.5	8.6	10.2
	6-170	4.5[3]	4.5	[2]	[1]	12.5	9.2	9.4
	6-200	4	4.5	12[2]	[1]	12.5	9.0	9.0
	8-302	4	4.5	19	[1]	12.5	14.0	14.6
1980	4-140	4[3]	2.8	[2]	[1]	11.5	8.6	9.0
	4-140T	4[3]	3.5	[2]	[1]	12.5	9.2	9.2
	6-200	4	4.5	12[2]	[1]	12.5	8.1	8.1
	8-255	4	4.5	19	[1]	12.5	13.4	13.7
1981	4-140	4[3]	2.8	[4]	[1]	12.5	8.6	9.0
	4-140T	4[3]	3.5	[4]	[1]	12.5	9.2	9.2
	6-200	4	4.5	[5]	[1]	12.5	8.1	8.1
	8-255	4	4.5	19	[1]	12.5	13.4	13.7
1982	4-140	4[3]	[7]	[6]	[1]	15.4	8.6	9.4
	4-140T	4[3]	3.5	[6]	[1]	15.4	9.4	9.4
	6-200	4	4.5	[6]	[1]	15.4	8.4	8.4
	8-255	4	4.5	22	[1]	15.4	14.7	15.0
	8-302	4	4.5	22	[1]	15.4	13.1	13.4
1983	4-140	4[3]	[8]	16	[1]	15.4	8.6	9.4
	4-140T	4.5[3]	5.6	—	[9]	15.4	8.6	9.4
	6-232	4	—	22	[1]	15.4	10.7	10.8
	8-302	4	4.5	—	[1]	15.4	13.1	13.4
1984	4-140	4	2.8	16	[9]	15.4	8.6	9.4
	4-140T	4.5[3]	5.6	—	[9]	15.4	10.5	10.5
	6-232	4	—	22	[9]	15.4	10.7	10.8
	8-302	4	5.6	24.6	[9]	15.4	13.1	13.4
1985	4-140	4	2.8	16	[10]	15.4	9.2	9.9
	4-140T	4.5[3]	5.6	—	[10]	15.4	10.8	10.8
	6-232	4	—	22	[10]	15.4	11.7	11.7
	8-302	4	5.6	24.6	[10]	15.4	14.1	14.1
1986	4-140	4	2.8	16	[10]	15.4	10.0	10.0
	4-140T	4.5[3]	5.6	—	[10]	15.4	10.4	10.2
	6-232	4	—	22	[10]	15.4	11.5	11.5
	8-302	4	5.6	—	[10]	15.4	14.1	14.1
1987	4-140	4	5.6	19	[11]	15.4	10.0	10.0
	8-302	4	5.6	24.6	[11]	15.4	14.1	14.1
1988	4-140	4	5.6	19	[12]	15.4	10.0	10.0
	8-302	4	5.6	[13]	[12]	15.4	14.1	14.1

T—Turbocharged
[1] 6.75 in.—2.5 pts.
   7.50 in.—3.5 pts.
   7.50 in. limited slip—3.5 pts.
[2] C3—16 pts.; C4—14 pts.
[3] Add only 1 pt. for new filter
[4] C3—16 pts.; C4—13.5 pts.
[5] C3—16 pts.; C4—14.5 pts.
[6] C3—16 pts.; C5—22 pts.
[7] 82ET—2.8 pts.; RAD—3.5 pts.

[8] 4 spd—2.8 pts.; 5 spd—4.75 pts.
[9] 7.50 in.—3.5 pts.
   7.50 in. limited slip—3.5 pts.
   7.50 in. Ford limited slip—3.75 pts.
[10] 7.50 in.—3.5 pts.
   7.50 in. limited slip—3.75 pts.
   8.80 in.—3.75 pts.
[11] 7.50 in.—3.5 pts.
   7.50 in. limited slip—3.75 pts.
   8.80 in.—4.0 pts.
   8.80 in. limited slip—4.75 pts.

[12] 7.50 in.—3.5 pts.
   7.50 in. limited slip—3.75p ts.
   8.80 in.—4.0 pts.
   8.80 in. limited slip—4.0 pts.
[13] A4LD—19 pts.; AOD—24.6 pts.
[14] Cooling system figuers include overflow reservoir filled to FULL COLD level

858010C3A

ENGLISH TO METRIC CONVERSION: MASS (WEIGHT)

Current **mass** measurement is expressed in pounds and ounces (lbs. & ozs.). The metric unit of mass (or weight) is the kilogram (kg). Even although this table does not show conversion of masses (weights) larger than 15 lbs, it is easy to calculate larger units by following the data immediately below.

To convert ounces (oz.) to grams (g): multiply th number of ozs. by 28
To convert grams (g) to ounces (oz.): multiply the number of grams by .035

To convert pounds (lbs.) to kilograms (kg): multiply the number of lbs. by .45
To convert kilograms (kg) to pounds (lbs.): multiply the number of kilograms by 2.2

lbs	kg	lbs	kg	oz	kg	oz	kg
0.1	0.04	0.9	0.41	0.1	0.003	0.9	0.024
0.2	0.09	1	0.4	0.2	0.005	1	0.03
0.3	0.14	2	0.9	0.3	0.008	2	0.06
0.4	0.18	3	1.4	0.4	0.011	3	0.08
0.5	0.23	4	1.8	0.5	0.014	4	0.11
0.6	0.27	5	2.3	0.6	0.017	5	0.14
0.7	0.32	10	4.5	0.7	0.020	10	0.28
0.8	0.36	15	6.8	0.8	0.023	15	0.42

ENGLISH TO METRIC CONVERSION: TEMPERATURE

To convert Fahrenheit (°F) to Celsius (°C): take number of °F and subtract 32; multiply result by 5; divide result by 9

To convert Celsius (°C) to Fahrenheit (°F): take number of °C and multiply by 9; divide result by 5; add 32 to total

Fahrenheit (F)		Celsius (C)		Fahrenheit (F)		Celsius (C)		Fahrenheit (F)		Celsius (C)	
°F	°C	°C	°F	°F	°C	°C	°F	°F	°C	°C	°F
−40	−40	−38	−36.4	80	26.7	18	64.4	215	101.7	80	176
−35	−37.2	−36	−32.8	85	29.4	20	68	220	104.4	85	185
−30	−34.4	−34	−29.2	90	32.2	22	71.6	225	107.2	90	194
−25	−31.7	−32	−25.6	95	35.0	24	75.2	230	110.0	95	202
−20	−28.9	−30	−22	100	37.8	26	78.8	235	112.8	100	212
−15	−26.1	−28	−18.4	105	40.6	28	82.4	240	115.6	105	221
−10	−23.3	−26	−14.8	110	43.3	30	86	245	118.3	110	230
−5	−20.6	−24	−11.2	115	46.1	32	89.6	250	121.1	115	239
0	−17.8	−22	−7.6	120	48.9	34	93.2	255	123.9	120	248
1	−17.2	−20	−4	125	51.7	36	96.8	260	126.6	125	257
2	−16.7	−18	−0.4	130	54.4	38	100.4	265	129.4	130	266
3	−16.1	−16	3.2	135	57.2	40	104	270	132.2	135	275
4	−15.6	−14	6.8	140	60.0	42	107.6	275	135.0	140	284
5	−15.0	−12	10.4	145	62.8	44	112.2	280	137.8	145	293
10	−12.2	−10	14	150	65.6	46	114.8	285	140.6	150	302
15	−9.4	−8	17.6	155	68.3	48	118.4	290	143.3	155	311
20	−6.7	−6	21.2	160	71.1	50	122	295	146.1	160	320
25	−3.9	−4	24.8	165	73.9	52	125.6	300	148.9	165	329
30	−1.1	−2	28.4	170	76.7	54	129.2	305	151.7	170	338
35	1.7	0	32	175	79.4	56	132.8	310	154.4	175	347
40	4.4	2	35.6	180	82.2	58	136.4	315	157.2	180	356
45	7.2	4	39.2	185	85.0	60	140	320	160.0	185	365
50	10.0	6	42.8	190	87.8	62	143.6	325	162.8	190	374
55	12.8	8	46.4	195	90.6	64	147.2	330	165.6	195	383
60	15.6	10	50	200	93.3	66	150.8	335	168.3	200	392
65	18.3	12	53.6	205	96.1	68	154.4	340	171.1	205	401
70	21.1	14	57.2	210	98.9	70	158	345	173.9	210	410
75	23.9	16	60.8	212	100.0	75	167	350	176.7	215	414

2

ENGINE PERFORMANCE AND TUNE-UP

TUNE-UP PROCEDURES

In order to extract the full measure of performance and economy from your engine, it is essential that it be properly tuned at regular intervals. A regular tune-up will keep your vehicle's engine running smoothly and will help prevent the annoying minor breakdowns and poor performance associated with an untuned engine.

A complete tune-up should be performed every 12,000 miles (19,308 Km) or twelve months, whichever comes first. This interval should be halved if the vehicle is operated under severe conditions, such as trailer towing, prolonged idling, continual stop and start driving, or if starting/running problems are noticed. It is assumed that the routine maintenance described in Section 1 has been kept up, as this will have a decided effect on the results of a tune-up. All of the applicable steps of a tune-up should be followed in order, as the result is a cumulative one.

If the specifications on the tune-up sticker in the engine compartment disagree with the Tune-Up Specifications chart in this section, the figures on the sticker must be used. The sticker often reflects changes made during the production run.

Spark Plugs

▶ **See Figures 1 and 2**

A typical spark plug consists of a metal shell surrounding a ceramic insulator. A metal electrode extends downward through the center of the insulator and protrudes a small distance. Located at the end of the plug and attached to the side of the outer metal shell is the side electrode. The side electrode bends in at a 90 degree angle so that its tip is even with, and parallel to, the tip of the center electrode. The distance between these two electrodes (measured in thousandths of an inch) is called the spark plug gap. The spark plug in no way produces a spark, but merely provides a gap across which the current can arc. The ignition coil produces anywhere from 20,000–40,000 volts or more, which travels to the distributor assembly where it is distributed through the spark plug wires to the spark plugs. The current passes along the center electrode and jumps the gap to the side electrode, and, in so doing, ignites the air/fuel mixture in the combustion chamber.

SPARK PLUG HEAT RANGE

Spark plug heat range is the ability of the plug to dissipate heat. The longer the insulator (or the farther it extends into the engine), the hotter the plug will operate; the shorter the insulator, the cooler it will operate. A plug that absorbs little heat and remains too cool will quickly accumulate deposits of oil and carbon since it is not hot enough to burn them off. This leads to plug fouling and

consequently to misfiring. A plug that absorbs too much heat will have no deposits, but due to the excessive heat, the electrodes will burn away quickly. (In some instances, pre-ignition may result.) Pre-ignition takes place when plug tips get so hot that they glow sufficiently to ignite the fuel/air mixture before the actual spark occurs. This early ignition will usually cause a pinging during low speeds and heavy loads.

Original equipment plugs are compromise plugs, but most people never have occasion to change their plugs from the factory recommended heat range. As a general rule of thumb: if most of your driving is long distance, high speed travel, you may need a colder plug; if most of your driving is stop and go, you may need a hotter plug.

REMOVAL & INSTALLATION

▶ **See Figures 3 thru 8**

A set of spark plugs usually requires replacement every 20,000–30,000 miles (32,180–48,270 Km) for most cars with electronic ignition systems, or every 15,000 miles (24,135 Km) on turbocharged vehicles with electronic ignition, depending on your style of driving. In normal operation, plug gap increases about 0.001 in. (0.0254mm) for every 1,000–2,500 miles (1,609–4,023 Km). As the gap increases, the plug's voltage requirement also increases. It requires a greater voltage to jump the wider gap and about two to three times as much voltage to fire a plug at high speeds than at idle. Therefore, it is extremely important to check and/or regap each spark plug between replacements. While the need for such maintenance will be affected by your driving conditions, as well as the condition of your vehicle's ignition and fuel systems, checking the condition of your vehicle's spark plugs between tune-ups is a good practice. For vehicles regularly subjected to severe service, such as extensive idling or frequent short trips of 10 miles (16 Km) or less, it is recommended that the spark plugs be checked and regapped every 6,000 miles (9,654 Km).

When you are removing spark plugs, you should work on one at a time. Do not start by removing the plug wires (cables) all at once, because unless you number them, they may become mixed up. Take a minute before you begin and number the wires with tape. The best location for numbering is near the ends of the wires.

➡ **Apply a small amount of silicone dielectric compound (Ford part no. D7AZ-19A331-A or the equivalent) to the inside of the terminal boots whenever an ignition wire is disconnected from the plug, or coil/distributor cap connection.**

1. Twist the spark plug boot, then remove the boot and wire from the plug. Do not pull on the wire itself as this will eventually ruin the wire.

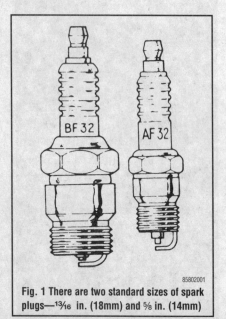

Fig. 1 There are two standard sizes of spark plugs—13/16 in. (18mm) and 5/8 in. (14mm)

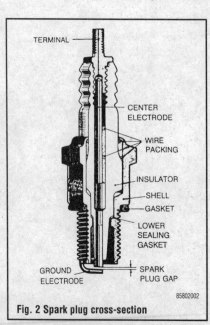

Fig. 2 Spark plug cross-section

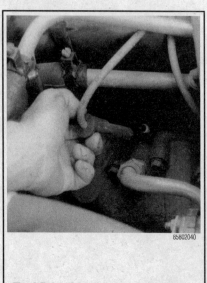

Fig. 3 Twist and pull the spark plug boot, not the wire

2. If possible, use a brush or rag to clean the area around the spark plug. Make sure that all the dirt is removed so that none will enter the cylinder after the plug is removed.

3. Remove the spark plug using either a ⅝ in. or 1³⁄₁₆ in. socket, depending on the engine. Turn the socket counterclockwise to remove the plug. Be sure to hold the socket straight on the plug to avoid breaking it, or rounding off its hexagonal wrenching surface.

4. Once the plug is out, check it against the spark plug diagnostic chart in this section to determine engine condition. This is crucial since plug readings are vital indicators of engine condition.

5. Use a round wire feeler gauge to check the plug gap. The correct size gauge should pass through the electrode gap with a slight drag. If you are in doubt, try one size smaller and one larger. The smaller gauge should go through easily while the larger one should not go through at all. If the gap is incorrect, use the electrode bending tool on the end of the gauge to adjust the gap. When adjusting, always bend the side electrode. The center electrode is non-adjustable.

6. Squirt a drop of penetrating oil on the threads of the new plug and install it. Do not oil the threads too heavily. Turn the plug in clockwise by hand until it is snug.

7. When the plug is finger-tight, tighten it with a socket. Torque to 5–10 ft. lbs. (7–14 Nm) for 4-cyl. engines or 10–15 ft. lbs. (14–20 Nm) for 6 and 8-cyl. engines. Take care not to overtighten.

8. Install the wire boot firmly over the plug. Proceed to the next plug.

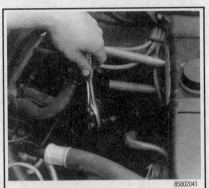

Fig. 4 Remove the spark plug using the correct size socket

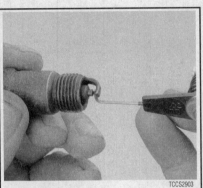

Fig. 5 Checking the spark plug gap with a feeler gauge

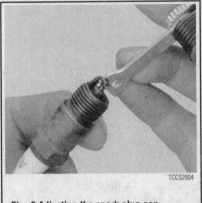

Fig. 6 Adjusting the spark plug gap

DIAGNOSIS OF SPARK PLUGS

Problem	Possible Cause	Correction
Brown to grayish-tan deposits and slight electrode wear.	• Normal wear.	• Clean, regap, reinstall.
Dry, fluffy black carbon deposits.	• Poor ignition output.	• Check distributor to coil connections.
Wet, oily deposits with very little electrode wear.	• "Break-in" of new or recently overhauled engine. • Excessive valve stem guide clearances. • Worn intake valve seals.	• Degrease, clean and reinstall the plugs. • Refer to Section 3. • Replace the seals.
Red, brown, yellow and white colored coatings on the insulator. Engine misses intermittently under severe operating conditions.	• By-products of combustion.	• Clean, regap, and reinstall. If heavily coated, replace.
Colored coatings heavily deposited on the portion of the plug projecting into the chamber and on the side facing the intake valve.	• Leaking seals if condition is found in only one or two cylinders.	• Check the seals. Replace if necessary. Clean, regap, and reinstall the plugs.
Shiny yellow glaze coating on the insulator.	• Melted by-products of combustion.	• Avoid sudden acceleration with wide-open throttle after long periods of low speed driving. Replace the plugs.
Burned or blistered insulator tips and badly eroded electrodes.	• Overheating.	• Check the cooling system. • Check for sticking heat riser valves. Refer to Section 1. • Lean air-fuel mixture. • Check the heat range of the plugs. May be too hot. • Check ignition timing. May be over-advanced. • Check the torque value of the plugs to ensure good plug-engine seat contact.
Broken or cracked insulator tips.	• Heat shock from sudden rise in tip temperature under severe operating conditions. Improper gapping of plugs.	• Replace the plugs. Gap correctly.

Fig. 7 Spark plug diagnostic chart

TUNE-UP SPECIFICATIONS

Year	Engine No. Cyl. Displacement (cu. in.)	Spark Plugs Orig. Type	Gap (in.)	Distributor	Ignition Timing (deg.)▲ Man.	Ignition Timing (deg.)▲ Auto.	Intake Valve Opens (deg.)■	Fuel Pump Pressure (psi)	Idle Speed (rpm)▲ Man.	Idle Speed (rpm)▲ Auto.
1979	4-140	AWSF-42	.034	Electronic	6B	20B	22	5.0-7.0	850	850(750)
	4-140 (Turbo)	AWSF-32	.034	Electronic	2B	—	22	6.5-7.5	900	—
	6-170	AWSF-42	.034	Electronic	—	9(6)B	28	3.5-5.8	—	650(600)②
	6-200	BSF-82	.050	Electronic	10B	10B	20	5.5-6.5	700①	550(600)②
	8-302	ASF-52	.050	Electronic	12B	6B	16	5.5-6.5	800	600
	8-302 (Calif.)	ASF-52-6	.060	Electronic	12B	6B	16	5.5-6.5	800	600
1980	4-140	AWSF-42	.035	Electronic	6B	20(12)B	22	5.0-7.0	850	750
	4-140 (Turbo)	AWSF-32	.050	Electronic	6(2)B	8(2)B	22	6.5-7.5	900	800
	6-200	BSF-82	.050	Electronic	10B	10B	20	5.5-6.5	7C0①	550(600)②
	8-255	ASF-42	.050	Electronic	8B	8B	16	4.0-6.0	500	550(500)②
1981	4-140	AWSF-42	.034	Electronic	6B	20(12)B	22	5.0-7.0	850	750
	4-140 (Turbo)	AWSF-42	.050	Electronic	6(2)B	—	22	5.5-6.5	850	750
	6-200	BSF-92	.050	Electronic	10B	10B	20	5.5-6.5	700①	550②
	8-255	ASF-52	.050	Electronic	8B	8B	16	5.0-7.0	850	550
1982	4-140	AWSF-42	.034	Electronic	6B	20(12)B	22	5.0-7.0	850	750
	4-140 (Turbo)③	AWSF-42	.034	Electronic	6B	—	20	6.5-7.5	900	700
	6-200	BSF-92	.050	Electronic	10B	10B	16	6.0-8.0	—	500
	8-255	ASF-52	.050	Electronic	—	10B	15	6.5-8.0	800	700
1983	4-140	AWSF-44	.044	Electronic	12B	—	22	5.0-7.0	850	800
	4-140 (Turbo)	AWSF-32C	.034	Electronic	④	④	22	39	850	—
	6-232	AWSF-52	.044	Electronic	④	④	13	6.0-8.0	—	700
	8-302	ASF-42	.044	Electronic	④	④	16	6.0-8.0	700	550
1984	4-140	AWSF-44	.044	Electronic	④	④	22	5.0-7.0	850	800
	6-232	AWSF-52	.044	Electronic	④	④	13	39	—	700
	8-302	ASF-42	.044	Electronic	④	④	16	6.0-8.0	700	550
1985	4-140	AWSF-44	.044	Electronic	④	④	22	6.0-8.0	850	800
	4-140 (Turbo)	AWSF-32C	.034	Electronic	④	④	22	39	850	—
	6-232	AWSF-52	.044	Electronic	④	④	13	39	—	700
	8-302	ASF-42	.044	Electronic	④	④	16	6.5-8.0	800	550
1986	4-140	AWSF-44	.044	Electronic	④	④	22	5.0-7.0	700	800
	4-140 (Turbo)	AWSF-32C	.034	Electronic	④	④	22	39	850	—
	6-232	AWSF-52	.044	Electronic	④	④	16	39	—	700
	8-302	ASF-42	.044	Electronic	④	④	22	39	700	550
1987	4-140	AWSF-44	.044	Electronic	④	④	22	39	850	800
	8-302	ASF-42	.044	Electronic	④	④	16	39	700	550
1988	4-140	AWSF-44	.044	Electronic	④	④	22	39	850	550
	8-302	ASF-42	.044	Electronic	④	④	16	39	700	550

The underhood specifications sticker often reflects tune-up specification changes in production. Sticker figures must be used if they disagree with those in this chart.
▲ Figures in parentheses are for California; automatic figures taken w/transmission in "Drive".
■ All figures are in degrees Before Top Dead Center
① 49 states: 700 w/A.C. 600 Calif. and 700 Calif. w/A/C
② Canada only
③ 900 with air conditioning
④ 700 with air conditioning

④ Refers to emission sticker
⑤ CFI—39 psi; carbureted—6.0-8.0 psi

85802OC1

A **normally worn** spark plug should have light tan or gray deposits on the firing tip.

A **carbon fouled** plug, identified by soft, sooty, black deposits, may indicate an improperly tuned vehicle. Check the air cleaner, ignition components and engine control system.

This spark plug has been left in the **engine too long**, as evidenced by the extreme gap - Plugs with such an extreme gap can cause misfiring and stumbling accompanied by a noticeable lack of power.

An **oil fouled** spark plug indicates an engine with worn poston rings and/or bad valve seals allowing excessive oil to enter the chamber.

A **bridged or almost bridged** spark plug, identified by a build-up between the electrodes caused by excessive carbon or oil build-up on the plug.

A **physically damaged** spark plug may be evidence of severe detonation in that cylinder. Watch that cylinder carefully between services, as a continued detonation will not only damage the plug, but could also damage the engine.

TCCA1P40

Fig. 8 Inspect the spark plug to determine engine running conditions

Spark Plug Wires

TESTING

▶ **See Figure 9**

Visually inspect the spark plug cables for burns, cuts, or breaks in the insulation. The cables should be supple enough to be formed into three-inch-diameter loops. Check the spark plug boots and their terminals, paying particular attention to rusted or misshapen terminals. Replace any damaged wiring. If no physical damage is obvious, the wires can be checked with an ohmmeter for excessive resistance. This is particularly important when a break occurs only in the conductive core, with no external signs of breakage. Resistance should be no more than 5,000 ohms per foot of cable length. Therefore, it is normal for resistance readings of the longer wires to be somewhat higher than those of the shorter wires.

➡On models equipped with electronic ignition, apply a small amount of silicone dielectric compound (D7AZ-19A331-A or the equivalent) to the inside of the terminal boots whenever an ignition wire is disconnected from the plug, or coil/distributor cap connection.

REMOVAL & INSTALLATION

▶ **See Figure 10**

When installing a new set of spark plug cables, replace the cables one at a time so there will be no mix-up. Start by replacing the longest cable first. Install the boot firmly over the spark plug and route the cable exactly the same as the original. (Improper arrangement of the wiring can induce voltage between the cables, resulting in misfiring and poor performance.) Insert the terminal firmly into the tower on the distributor cap. Repeat the process for each cable.

➡When removing spark plug wires, be sure to twist and pull only on the rubber boots. Never pull on the wire itself, otherwise the wire may break.

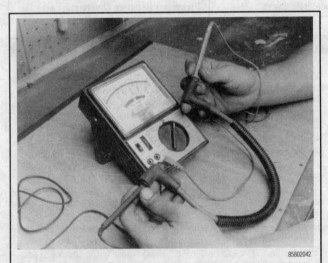

Fig. 9 Measure the resistance of disconnected spark plug wires using an ohmmeter

Fig. 10 Note the different lengths of the spark plug wires and number them before removal to avoid confusion

FIRING ORDERS

▶ **See Figures 11 thru 16**

➡To avoid confusion, remove and tag the spark plug wires one at a time, for replacement.

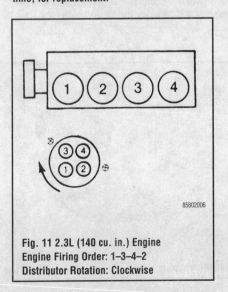

Fig. 11 2.3L (140 cu. in.) Engine
Engine Firing Order: 1-3-4-2
Distributor Rotation: Clockwise

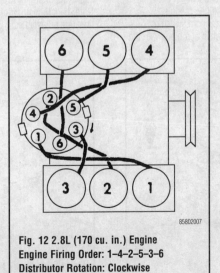

Fig. 12 2.8L (170 cu. in.) Engine
Engine Firing Order: 1-4-2-5-3-6
Distributor Rotation: Clockwise

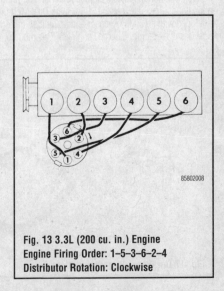

Fig. 13 3.3L (200 cu. in.) Engine
Engine Firing Order: 1-5-3-6-2-4
Distributor Rotation: Clockwise

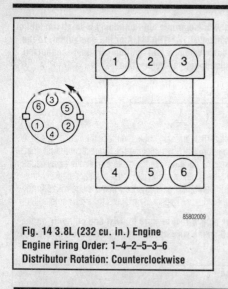

Fig. 14 3.8L (232 cu. in.) Engine
Engine Firing Order: 1–4–2–5–3–6
Distributor Rotation: Counterclockwise

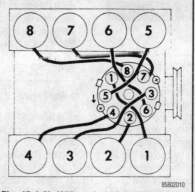

Fig. 15 4.2L (255 cu. in.), 5.0 (302 cu. in.)
except HO Engines
Engine Firing Order: 1–5–4–2–6–3–7–8
Distributor Rotation: Counterclockwise

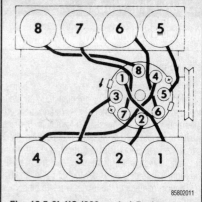

Fig. 16 5.0L HO (302 cu. in.) Engine
Engine Firing Order: 1–3–7–2–6–5–4–8
Distributor Rotation: Counterclockwise

ELECTRONIC IGNITION SYSTEMS

Description and Operation

▶ See Figures 17 and 18

Basically, four electronic ignition systems were used in Ford Motor Company vehicles from 1979–88:

- DuraSpark I—1979–1980
- DuraSpark II—1979–1988
- DuraSpark III—1980–1984
- EEC-IV Thick Film Integrated (TFI)—1984–1988

In 1977, the first DuraSpark systems were introduced. These systems, DuraSpark I and DuraSpark II, are nearly identical in operation and appearance. DuraSpark I uses a special control module which senses current flow through the ignition coil and adjusts the dwell, or coil on-time for maximum spark intensity. If the DuraSpark I module senses that the ignition is **ON**, but the distributor shaft is not turning, the current to the coil is turned OFF by the module. The DuraSpark II system does not have this feature. The coil is energized for the full amount of time that the ignition switch is **ON**. Keep this in mind when servicing the DuraSpark II system, since the ignition system could inadvertently fire while performing ignition system services (such as distributor cap removal) if the ignition is **ON**. During its limited use, DuraSpark I was initially restricted to California vehicles equipped with an 8-302 engine. The more widely used DuraSpark II systems are easily identified by their two-piece distributor cap, on which all of the terminals, including the center tower, are the same height.

On some applications over the years, the DuraSpark II system has utilized different ignition modules designed to perform additional functions. Some 1978 and later engines use a special DuraSpark Dual Mode ignition module, equipped with an altitude sensor and an ignition timing vacuum switch (or pressure switches on turbocharged engines). This module, when combined with the additional switches and sensor, varies the base engine timing according to altitude and engine load conditions. DuraSpark Dual Mode ignition modules have three wiring harnesses, rather than the standard two.

Some 1981 and later DuraSpark II systems, found in vehicles equipped with 8-255 and 8-302 cu. in. engines, utilize a Universal Ignition Module (UIM) which includes a run-retard function. By responding to a second control signal, the UIM provides additional spark timing control for certain operating conditions. The operation of this module is basically the same as that of the DuraSpark Dual Mode module.

Another variation in DuraSpark II ignition modules involves 1981 49-state and 1982 Canadian vehicles equipped with 4-140 engines and automatic transmissions. These vehicles have a Dual Mode Crank Retard ignition module, which has the same function as the DuraSpark II module, plus an ignition timing retard function that is operational during engine cranking. The spark timing retard feature eases engine starting, but allows normal timing advance as soon as the engine is running. This module can be identified by the presence of a white connector shell on the four-pin connector at the module.

In 1980, the DuraSpark III system was introduced. This version is based on the previous systems, but the input signal is controlled by the EEC (Electronic Engine Control) system, rather than as a function of engine timing and distributor armature position. The EEC system controls spark advance in response to various engine sensors. These include a crankshaft position sensor, which replaces the stator assembly and armature previously located in the distributor assembly. As a result, the DuraSpark III distributor serves only to distribute high voltage generated by the ignition coil. The relationship of the distributor rotor to cap is important for proper high voltage distribution. For this reason, the DuraSpark III distributor is secured to the engine and the distributor rotor positions are adjustable.

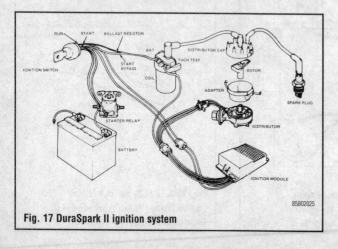

Fig. 17 DuraSpark II ignition system

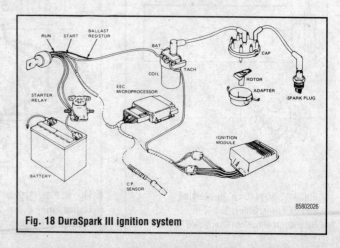

Fig. 18 DuraSpark III ignition system

➡An exception involves the 6-232 engine, in which the DuraSpark III distributor assembly is a modified DuraSpark II design. Rotor alignment is not adjustable on these applications.

The distributor, rotor, cap and control module are unique to the DuraSpark III system, while the spark plugs and plug wires are the same as those used with the DuraSpark II system. Although the DuraSpark II and III control modules are similar in appearance, they cannot be interchanged between systems.

Finally, 1984 marked the introduction of Ford's EEC-IV Thick Film Integrated (TFI) ignition system. The EEC-IV system's universal distributor has a diecast base which incorporates an externally mounted TFI-IV ignition module. It also contains a Hall effect vane switch stator assembly and provision for fixed octane adjustment. No distributor calibration is necessary and initial timing adjustment is normally not required. The primary function of the EEC-IV system's universal distributor is to direct high secondary voltage to the spark plugs. In addition, the distributor supplies crankshaft position and frequency information to a computer using a profile ignition pickup. The Hall effect switch in the distributor consists of a Hall effect device on one side and a magnet on the other side. A rotary cup which has windows and tabs rotates and passes through the space between the device and the magnet. When a window is between the sides of the switch, the magnetic path is not completed and the switch is off, sending no signal. When a tab passes between the sides of the switch, the magnetic path is completed, whereby the Hall effect device is turned on and a signal is sent. The voltage pulse (signal) is used by the EEC-IV system for sensing crankshaft position and computing the desired spark advance based on engine demand and calibration.

DURASPARK OPERATION

With the ignition switch **ON**, the primary circuit is on and the ignition coil is energized. When the armature spokes approach the magnetic pickup coil assembly, they induce the voltage which tells the amplifier module to turn the coil primary current off. A timing circuit in the amplifier module will turn the current on again after the coil field has collapsed. When the current is on, it flows from the battery through the ignition switch, the primary windings of the ignition coil, and through the amplifier module circuits to ground. When the current is off, the magnetic field in the ignition coil is allowed to collapse, inducing a high voltage into the coil's secondary windings. High voltage is produced each time the field is thus built and collapsed. When DuraSpark is used in conjunction with the EEC (DuraSpark III), the EEC computer tells the DuraSpark module when to turn the coil primary current off or on. In this case, the armature position is only a reference signal of engine timing, used by the EEC computer (in combination with other reference signals) to determine optimum ignition spark timing.

The high voltage flows through the ignition coil high tension lead to the distributor cap where the rotor distributes it to one of the cap terminals. This process is repeated for every power stroke of the engine.

Ignition system troubles are caused by a failure in the primary and/or the secondary circuit, incorrect ignition timing or incorrect distributor advance. Circuit failures may be caused by shorts, corroded or dirty terminals, loose connections, unsound wire insulation, a defective pick-up coil assembly or amplifier module, a cracked distributor cap/rotor, or fouled spark plugs.

If an engine starting or operating problem is attributed to the ignition system, start the engine and verify the complaint. On engines that will not start, be sure that there is gasoline in the fuel tank and that fuel is reaching the carburetor or injectors. Then locate the ignition system problem using the following procedures.

Diagnosis and Testing

DURASPARK I SYSTEM

The following DuraSpark II troubleshooting procedures may be used on DuraSpark I systems with a few variations. The DuraSpark I module has internal connections which shut off the primary circuit in the run mode when the engine stalls. To perform the above troubleshooting procedures, it is necessary to bypass these connections. However, with these connections bypassed, the current flow in the primary becomes so great that it will damage both the ignition coil and module unless a ballast resistor is installed in series with the primary circuit at the BATT terminal of the ignition coil. Such a resistor is available from

Ford (Motorcraft part number DY-36). A 1.3ω, 100 watt wire-wound power resistor can also be used. To install the resistor, proceed as follows:

⁎⁎ WARNING

The resistor will become very hot during testing.

1. Release the BATT terminal lead from the coil by inserting a paper clip through the hole in the rear of the horseshoe coil connector and manipulating it against the locking tab in the connector until the lead comes free.
2. Insert a paper clip in the BATT terminal of the connector on the coil. Using jumper leads, connect one end of the ballast resistor to the paper clip and the other end to the BATT terminal lead.
3. Using a straight pin, pierce both the red and white leads of the module to short these two together. This will bypass the internal connections of the module which turn off the ignition circuit when the engine is not running.

⁎⁎ CAUTION

Pierce the wires only after the ballast resistor is in place or you could damage the ignition coil and module.

4. With the ballast resistor and bypass in place, proceed with the DuraSpark II troubleshooting procedures. (After troubleshooting is completed, be sure to remove this resistor and reconnect the BATT terminal lead to the ignition coil.)

➡After performing any test which requires piercing a wire with a straight pin, remove the pin and seal the holes in the wire with a suitable RTV silicone sealer.

DURASPARK II SYSTEM

The following procedures can be used to determine whether the ignition system is working or not. If these procedures fail to correct the problem, a full troubleshooting procedure should be performed.

Preliminary Checks

◆ See Figures 19 and 20

1. Check the battery's state of charge and connections.
2. Inspect all wires and connections for breaks, cuts, abrasions, or burned spots. Repair as necessary.
3. Unplug all connectors one at a time and inspect for corroded or burned contacts. Repair and plug connectors back together. Do not remove the dielectric compound in the connectors.
4. Check for loose or damaged spark plug or coil wires. A wire resistance check is given at the end of this section. If the boots or terminals are removed on 8mm ignition wires, reline the inside of each with new silicone dielectric compound (Motorcraft part no. D7AZ-19A331-A or equivalent).

➡Besides inhibiting corrosion, silicone dielectric compound is used to reduce radio interference caused by high voltage discharges in the ignition system. Therefore, with the exception of multipoint rotors, this special grease should also be applied to the distributor rotor upon replacement.

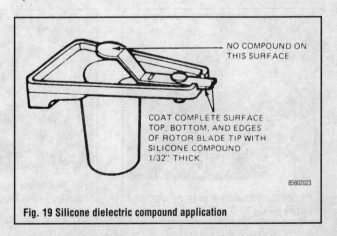

NO COMPOUND ON THIS SURFACE

COAT COMPLETE SURFACE TOP, BOTTOM, AND EDGES OF ROTOR BLADE TIP WITH SILICONE COMPOUND 1/32" THICK

85802023

Fig. 19 Silicone dielectric compound application

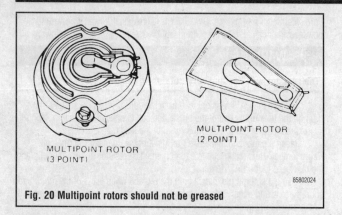

Fig. 20 Multipoint rotors should not be greased

Special Tools

▶ See Figures 21 and 22

To perform the following tests, two special tools are needed. These include an ignition test jumper wire with switch and a spark tester. Use the illustration to assemble the ignition test jumper. The spark tester is basically a spark plug with the side electrode removed. Ford offers a special tool called a Spark Tester for this purpose which, besides not having a side electrode, is equipped with a spring clip so that it can be grounded to engine metal. It is recommended that the ready-made Spark Tester be used, as there is less chance of being shocked.

Run Mode Spark Tests

▶ See Figure 23

➡ The wire colors given here are the main colors of the wires, not the dots or hashmarks.

TEST 1

▶ See Figures 24, 25 and 26

1. Remove the distributor cap and rotor from the distributor.
2. With the ignition **OFF**, turn the engine over by hand until one of the teeth on the distributor armature aligns with the magnet in the pickup coil.
3. Remove the coil wire from the distributor cap. Install the spark tester (see Special Tools) in the coil wire terminal, then, using heavy gloves and insulated pliers, hold the spark plug shell against the engine block.
4. Turn the ignition to **RUN** (not **START**) and tap the distributor body with a screwdriver handle. There should be a spark at the modified spark plug or at the coil wire terminal.
5. If a good spark is evident, the primary circuit is okay: perform the Start Mode Spark Test found later in this section. If there is no spark, proceed to TEST 2.

TEST 2

1. Unplug the module connector(s) which contain(s) the green and black module leads.

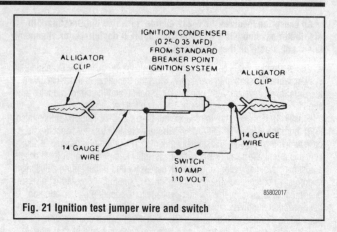

Fig. 21 Ignition test jumper wire and switch

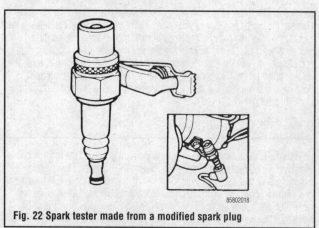

Fig. 22 Spark tester made from a modified spark plug

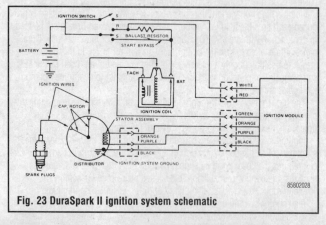

Fig. 23 DuraSpark II ignition system schematic

Fig. 24 Many distributor caps are fastened by two screws

Fig. 25 To avoid confusion, mark the distributor cap and spark plug wires before removal

Fig. 26 Lift off the distributor cap after loosening its fasteners and removing the spark plug wires

2. In the harness side of the connector(s), install the special test jumper (see Special Tools) between the leads which connect to the green and black leads of the module pig tails. Use paper clips on connector socket holes to make contact. Do not allow clips to ground.

3. Turn the ignition switch to **RUN** (not **START**) and close the test jumper switch. Leave closed for about 1 second, then open. Repeat several times. There should be a spark each time the switch is opened.

➡ **On DuraSpark I systems, it is not necessary to repeatedly open and close the test switch. Instead, leave the switch closed for at least 10 seconds, then open.**

4. If there is no spark, the problem is probably in the primary circuit through the ignition switch, the coil, the green lead or the black lead, or the ground connection in the distributor: perform TEST 3. If there is a spark, the primary circuit wiring and coil are probably okay. The problem is probably in the distributor pick-up, the module red wire, or the module: perform TEST 6. (For DuraSpark III systems, proceed to TEST 7.)

TEST 3

1. Disconnect the test jumper lead from the black lead and connect it to a good ground. Turn the test jumper switch on and off several times as in TEST 2.

2. If there is no spark, the problem is probably in the green lead, the coil, or the coil feed circuit: perform TEST 5.

3. If there is spark, the problem is probably in the black lead or the distributor ground connection: perform TEST 4.

TEST 4

1. Connect an ohmmeter between the black lead and ground. With the meter on its lowest scale, there should be no measurable resistance in the circuit. If there is resistance, check the distributor ground connection and the black lead from the module. Repair as necessary, remove the ohmmeter, plug in all connections and repeat TEST 1.

2. If there is no resistance, the primary ground wiring is okay: perform TEST 6.

TEST 5

1. Disconnect the test jumper from the green lead and ground, then connect it between the TACH TEST terminal of the coil and a good ground to the engine.

2. With the ignition switch in the **RUN** position, turn the jumper switch on. Hold it on for about 1 second then turn it off as in Test 2. Repeat several times. There should be a spark each time the switch is turned off. If there is no spark, the problem is probably in the primary circuit running through the ignition switch to the coil BATT terminal, or in the coil itself. Check coil resistance (test given later in this section), and check the coil for internal shorts or opens. Check the coil feed circuit for opens, shorts, or high resistance. Repair as necessary, re-engage all connectors and repeat TEST 1. If there is spark, the coil and its feed circuit are okay. The problem could be in the green lead between the coil and the module. Check for an open or short, then repair as necessary. Re-engage all connectors and repeat TEST 1.

TEST 6

To perform this test, a voltmeter which is not combined with a dwell meter is needed. The slight needle oscillations (½v) you will be looking for may not be detectable on the combined voltmeter/dwell meter unit.

1. Connect a voltmeter between the orange and purple leads on the harness side of the module connectors.

✳✳ CAUTION

On catalytic converter equipped cars, disconnect the air supply line between the Thermactor bypass valve and the manifold before cranking the engine without ignition. This will prevent damage to the catalytic converter. After testing, run the engine for at least 3 minutes before reconnecting the bypass valve, to clear excess fuel from the exhaust system.

2. Set the voltmeter on its lowest scale and crank the engine. The meter needle should oscillate slightly (about ½v). If the meter does not oscillate, check the circuit through the magnetic pick-up in the distributor for open, shorts, shorts to ground and resistance. Resistance between the orange and purple leads should be 400-1,000ω, and between each lead and ground should be more than 70,000ω. Repair as necessary, re-engage all connectors and repeat TEST 1.

If the meter oscillates, the problem is probably in the power feed to the module (red wire) or in the module itself: proceed to TEST 7.

TEST 7

1. Remove all meters and jumpers, then engage all connectors.

2. Turn the ignition switch to the **RUN** position and measure voltage between the battery positive terminal and engine ground. It should be 12 volts.

3. Next, measure voltage between the red lead of the module and engine ground. To make this measurement, it will be necessary to pierce the red wire with a straight pin, then connect the voltmeter to the straight pin and to ground. Do not allow the straight pin to ground itself.

4. The two readings should be within one volt of each other. If not within one volt, the problem is in the power feed to the red lead. Check for shorts, open, or high resistance and correct as necessary. After repairs, repeat TEST 1.If the readings are within one volt, the problem is probably in the module. Replace it with a good module and repeat TEST 1. If this corrects the problem, reconnect the old module and repeat TEST 1. If the problem returns, permanently install the new module.

➡ **After performing any test which requires piercing a wire with a straight pin, remove the pin and seal the holes in the wire with a suitable RTV silicone sealer.**

Start Mode Spark Test

➡ **The wire colors given here are the main colors of the wires, not the dots or hashmarks.**

1. Remove the coil wire from the distributor cap. Install the spark tester (described earlier under Special Tools) in the coil wire and ground it to engine metal, either by its spring clip or by holding the spark plug shell against the engine block with insulated pliers.

✳✳ CAUTION

On catalytic converter equipped cars, disconnect the air supply line between the Thermactor bypass valve and the manifold before cranking the engine without ignition. This will prevent damage to the catalytic converter. After testing, run the engine for at least 3 minutes before reconnecting the bypass valve, to clear excess fuel from the exhaust system.

2. Have an assistant crank the engine using the ignition switch and check for spark. If there is good spark, the problem is probably in the distributor cap, rotor, spark plug wires or spark plugs. If there is no spark, proceed to Step 3.

3. Measure the battery voltage. Next, measure the voltage at the white wire of the module while cranking the engine. To make this measurement, it will be necessary to pierce the white wire with a straight pin, then connect the voltmeter to the straight pin and to ground. Do not allow the straight pin to ground itself. The battery voltage and the voltage at the white wire should be within 1 volt of each other. If the readings are not within 1 volt of each other, check and repair the feed through the ignition switch to the white wire. Recheck for spark (TEST 1). If the readings are within 1 volt of each other, or if there is still no spark after the power feed to the white wire is repaired, proceed to Step 4.

➡ **After performing any test which requires piercing a wire with a straight pin, remove the pin and seal the holes in the wire with a suitable RTV silicone sealer.**

4. Measure the coil BATT terminal voltage while cranking the engine. The reading should be within 1 volt of battery voltage. If the readings are not within 1 volt of each other, check and repair the feed through the ignition switch to the coil. If the readings are within 1 volt of each other, the problem is probably in the ignition module. Substitute another module and repeat the test for spark (TEST 1). If this corrects the problem, reconnect the old module and repeat TEST 1. If the problem returns, permanently install the new module.

DURASPARK III SYSTEM

▶ **See Figures 27, 28, 29 and 30**

The preceding DuraSpark II troubleshooting procedures may be used on DuraSpark III systems with a few variations. In DuraSpark III systems, the inter-

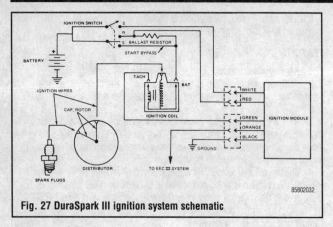

Fig. 27 DuraSpark III ignition system schematic

ruption of primary circuit current is caused by a signal from the EEC micro-processor, rather than by stator and armature juxtaposition within the distributor. Since the DuraSpark III system contains no stator or armature assembly (with the exception of its 1983–84 applications on 6-232 engines), any diagnostic procedures involving those components should be disregarded. Other than some minor wiring differences due to this design variation, the testing procedures and normal test values also apply to DuraSpark III, unless otherwise noted.

Unlike the DuraSpark II system's two different ignition modules (one identified by a yellow grommet with three connectors and eight wires, and the other identified by a blue grommet with two connectors and six wires), the Duraspark III ignition module is identifiable by its brown grommet with two connectors and only five wires. As a result, there is no purple wire coming from the DuraSpark III ignition module. Diagnostic procedures for the DuraSpark II system which refer to this wire can be disregarded.

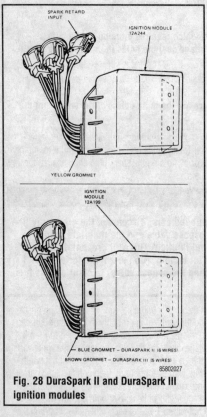

Fig. 28 DuraSpark II and DuraSpark III ignition modules

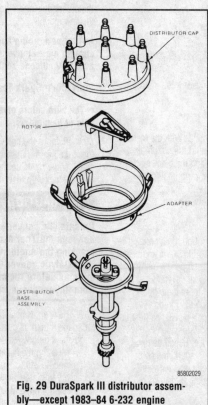

Fig. 29 DuraSpark III distributor assembly—except 1983–84 6-232 engine

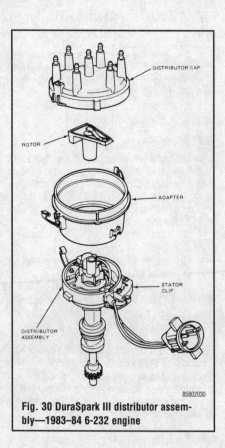

Fig. 30 DuraSpark III distributor assembly—1983–84 6-232 engine

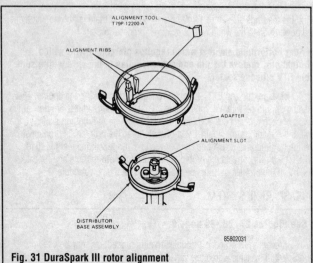

Fig. 31 DuraSpark III rotor alignment

Rotor Alignment

EXCEPT 6-232 ENGINE

▶ See Figure 31

Although initial timing is not adjustable on DuraSpark III ignition systems, rotor alignment may be adjusted. It is important to keep the rotor properly aligned, as the system is sensitive to variation. To check the rotor alignment:
1. Remove the distributor cap and rotor.
2. Rotate the engine until the No. 1 piston is on its compression stroke.

➡**In order to confirm that the No. 1 piston is on its compression stroke, rotate the crankshaft pulley (in its normal direction of rotation) until the TDC mark on the pulley and the pointer align.**

3. Slowly rotate the engine until a Rotor Alignment Tool (Ford part no. T79P-12200-A or equivalent) can be inserted into the alignment slots of the sleeve assembly and adapter.
4. Read the timing mark on the damper which is indicated by the timing pointer.
5. If the timing mark is somewhere between 4 degrees BTDC and 4 degrees ATDC, the rotor alignment is acceptable.

6. If the reading does not fall within this range, rotor alignment can be adjusted as follows:

  a. Rotate the engine until the No. 1 piston is on compression stroke.

  b. Slowly rotate the engine until the timing pointer aligns with 0 degree timing mark.

  c. Loosen the two sleeve assembly adjustment screws and insert a Rotor Alignment Tool (Ford part no. T79P-12200-A or equivalent) into the alignment slots of the sleeve assembly and adapter.

  d. Tighten the two sleeve assembly adjustment screws and remove the alignment tool.

  e. Replace the rotor and distributor cap.

6-232 ENGINE

The ignition system used by the 6-232 engine is basically a modified version of the DuraSpark II ignition. No adjustment for rotor alignment is necessary or possible.

EEC-IV THICK FILM INTEGRATED (TFI) SYSTEM

➡If the engine operates but has no power, the problem could be in the EEC system. Check the initial timing; if the engine is operating at a fixed 10 degrees BTDC, the system is in fail-safe mode. Have the EEC system checked with necessary diagnostic equipment.

Ignition Coil Secondary Voltage

1. Disconnect the secondary (high voltage) coil wire from the distributor cap and install a spark tester (see Special Tools) between the coil wire and ground.

2. Crank the engine. A good, strong spark should be noted at the spark tester. If spark is noted, but the engine will not start, check the spark plugs, spark plug wiring, and fuel system. If there is no spark at the tester:

  a. Check the ignition coil wire resistance; it should be no more than 5,000ω per foot.

  b. Inspect the ignition coil for damage and/or carbon tracking.

  c. With the distributor cap removed, verify that the distributor shaft turns with the engine. If it does not, repair the engine as required.

  d. If the fault was not found in a, b, or c, proceed to the next test.

Ignition Coil Primary Circuit Switching

1. Insert a small straight pin in the wire which runs from the coil negative (–) terminal to the TFI-IV module, about 1 in. (25.4mm) from the module.

✳✳ CAUTION

The pin must not touch ground.

2. Connect a 12V DC test lamp between the straight pin and an engine ground.

3. Crank the engine, noting the operation of the test lamp. If the test lamp flashes, proceed to the next test. If the test lamp lights but does not flash, proceed to the Wiring Harness test. If the test lamp does not light at all, or is very dim, proceed to the Primary Circuit Continuity test.

➡After performing any test which requires piercing a wire with a straight pin, remove the pin and seal the holes in the wire with suitable RTV silicone sealer.

Ignition Coil Resistance

1. Disconnect the ignition coil connector, then inspect for dirt, corrosion and damage.

2. To check the coil's primary resistance, connect an ohmmeter to the coil's positive and negative terminals. If the ohmmeter reading is 0.3-1.0ω, the primary resistance is okay.

3. To check the coil's secondary resistance, connect an ohmmeter to the coil's negative and high voltage (output) terminals. If the ohmmeter reading is 8,000-11,500ω, the secondary resistance is okay.

Replace the ignition coil if either resistance reading is out of the specified range.

Wiring Harness

▶ See Figure 32

1. Disconnect the wiring harness connector from the TFI-IV module; the connector tabs must be pushed to disengage the connector. Inspect the connector for dirt, corrosion and damage.

2. If so equipped, disconnect the wire at the S terminal of the starter relay.

3. Attach the negative lead of a voltmeter to the base of the distributor.

4. Measure the battery voltage.

5. Attach the other voltmeter lead to a small straight pin.

  a. With the ignition switch in the **RUN** position, insert the straight pin into the No. 2 terminal of the ignition module connector. Note the voltage reading and proceed to b.

  b. With the ignition switch in the **RUN** and **START** positions, move the straight pin to the No. 3 connector terminal. Again, note the voltage reading, then proceed to c.

  c. Move the straight pin to the No. 4 connector terminal, then turn the ignition switch to the **START** position. Note the voltage reading, then turn the ignition **OFF**.

6. Remove the straight pin.

7. Reconnect the wire to the S terminal of the starter relay, if applicable.

8. The voltage readings from a, b, and c should all be at least 90% of the available battery voltage. If the readings are okay, separate the wiring harness connector from the ignition module. Inspect for dirt, corrosion and/or damage, and reconnect the harness. Disconnect the pin-in-line connector and recheck for spark. If there is no spark, proceed to the Distributor/TFI-IV Module test. If any reading is less than 90% of the battery voltage, inspect the wiring, connectors, and/or ignition switch for defects. If the voltage is low only at the No. 1 terminal, proceed to the Ignition Coil Primary Voltage test.

Distributor/TFI-IV Module

▶ See Figures 33 and 34

1. Remove the distributor/module assembly from the engine, as described in Section 3.

2. Install a new TFI-IV module on the distributor and repeat the coil secondary voltage test as follows:

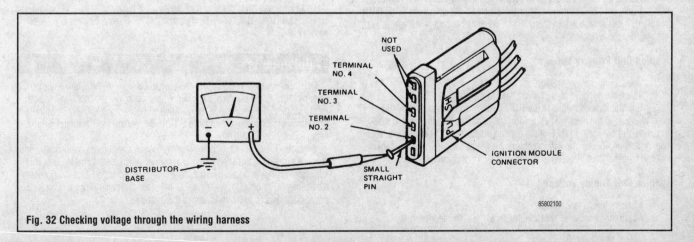

Fig. 32 Checking voltage through the wiring harness

85802100

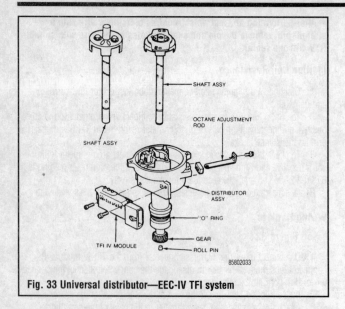

Fig. 33 Universal distributor—EEC-IV TFI system

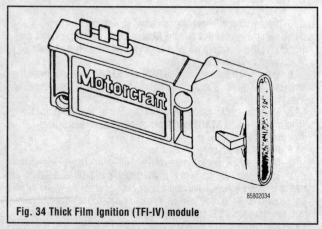

Fig. 34 Thick Film Ignition (TFI-IV) module

a. Connect the body wiring harness to the TFI-IV module.
b. Make sure that the unit is grounded with a jumper lead from the distributor to an engine ground.
c. Rotate the distributor by hand, while checking for spark at the spark tester.
3. Reinstall the distributor assembly in the engine, as described in Section 3. If the previous step produced a spark, leave the new TFI-IV module in place. If the previous step did not produce a spark, you may want to reinstall the old TFI-IV module, since the problem apparently lies elsewhere.

Primary Circuit Continuity

This test is performed in the same manner as the previous Wiring Harness test, but only the No. 2 terminal conductor is tested (ignition switch in the **RUN** position). If the voltage is less than 90% of the available battery voltage, proceed to the next test.

Ignition Coil Primary Voltage

1. Measure the battery voltage.
2. Attach the negative lead of a voltmeter to the distributor base.
3. Turn the ignition switch to the **RUN** position and connect the positive voltmeter lead to the negative (–) ignition coil terminal. Note the voltage reading, then turn the ignition **OFF**. If the reading is less than 90% of the available battery voltage, inspect the wiring between the ignition module and the negative (–) coil terminal, then proceed to the Ignition Coil Supply Voltage test.

Ignition Coil Supply Voltage

1. Measure the battery voltage.
2. Attach the negative lead of a voltmeter to the distributor base.

3. Turn the ignition switch to the **RUN** position and connect the positive voltmeter lead to the positive (+) ignition coil terminal.
Note the voltage reading, then turn the ignition **OFF**. If the reading is less than 90% of the battery voltage, check the wiring between the ignition coil and ignition switch, as well as the ignition switch itself. If the reading is at least 90% of the battery voltage, yet the engine still will not run, check the ignition coil connector and terminals for dirt, corrosion or damage.

ALL IGNITION SYSTEMS

Ignition Coil Test

The ignition coil must be diagnosed separately from the rest of the ignition system.
1. Primary resistance is measured between the two primary (low voltage) coil terminals, with the coil connector disengaged and the ignition switch **OFF**. Primary resistance must be 0.71–0.77ω for DuraSpark I, or 0.80–1.60ω for DuraSpark II and DuraSpark III. For TFI systems, the primary resistance should be 0.3-1.0ω.
2. On DuraSpark ignition systems, the secondary resistance is measured between the BATT and high voltage (secondary) terminals of the ignition coil with the ignition **OFF**, and wiring from the coil disconnected. Secondary resistance must be 7,350-8,250ω for DuraSpark I, or 7,700-10,500ω for DuraSpark II and DuraSpark III. For TFI systems, the secondary resistance should be 8,000-11,500ω.
3. If resistance tests are within specifications, but the coil is still suspected, check the coil on a coil tester by following the test equipment manufacturer's instructions for a standard coil. If the reading differs from the original test, check for a defective harness.

Ballast Resistor

➤**The ballast resistor is not used on DuraSpark I or TFI systems.**

Replace the primary circuit ballast resistor if it does not show a resistance of 0.80–1.60ω for DuraSpark II or DuraSpark III systems. This resistor, which is actually a specific length of special wire, is part of the vehicle's wiring harness inside the passenger compartment. Under no circumstances should it be cut, spliced or replaced by any other type of non-resistance wire.

Spark Plug Wire Resistance

Resistance on these wires must not exceed 5,000ω per foot. To properly measure this, remove the wires from the plugs, and remove the distributor cap. Measure the resistance through the distributor cap at that end. Do not pierce any ignition wire for any reason. Measure only from the two ends.

➤**Silicone grease (dielectric compound) must be re-applied to the spark plug wires whenever they are removed.**

When removing the wires from the spark plugs, be careful not to pull on the wires. Grasp and twist the boot to remove the wire. If you prefer, a special tool is available for this purpose.
Whenever the high tension wires are removed from the plugs, coil, or distributor, silicone grease must be applied to the boot before reconnection. Use a clean small screwdriver blade to coat the entire interior surface with Ford silicone grease D7AZ-19A331-A, Dow Corning #111, General Electric G-627, or equivalent.

Adjustments

On those systems so equipped, the air gap between the armature and magnetic pick-up coil in the distributor is not adjustable, nor are there any adjustments for the amplifier module. Inoperative components are simply replaced. Any attempt to connect components outside the vehicle may result in component failure.
On most DuraSpark III ignition systems the rotor alignment is adjustable and must be properly set as the system is sensitive to variation. In most cases this adjustment is not periodically necessary, but should checked after distributor replacement. For details, please refer to the rotor alignment procedure located under diagnosis and testing earlier in this section.

Component Replacement

DISTRIBUTOR CAP

▶ **See Figures 35, 36 and 37**

1. Loosen the distributor cap hold-down screws or, if equipped with spring clips, gently pry them away from the cap. Lift the cap straight off the distributor to prevent damage to the rotor points and spring.

2. Wipe the distributor cap with a clean, damp cloth and dry with compressed air or a lint-free cloth. Inspect the cap for cracks, broken carbon button, carbon tracks, dirt or corrosion on the terminals. Replace the cap if it is worn or damaged.

To install:

3. Position the distributor cap on the distributor base, noting the square alignment locator. Tighten the hold-down screws or reposition the spring clips.

4. Reconnect the spark plug wires, if removed. Be sure to route them in their original locations and to connect them to the proper terminals.

DISTRIBUTOR ROTOR

▶ **See Figures 38, 39, 40 and 41**

1. Remove the distributor cap, as previously described.

2. Loosen the rotor hold-down screws, if equipped, and lift the rotor straight off the distributor base assembly. If there are no hold-down screws, the rotor is a friction fit, and must be carefully pulled straight off the distributor shaft. Be sure to use steady, even effort, to avoid injury or damage to the rotor.

3. Wipe the rotor with a clean, damp cloth and dry with compressed air or a lint-free cloth. Inspect the rotor for cracks, carbon tracks, burns, damaged points or spring. Replace the rotor if it is worn or damaged.

To install:

4. Position the distributor rotor with its round and square locator pins (if equipped) matched to the distributor shaft plate and tighten the hold-down screws. For rotors without locator pins and screws, align the rotor with the bevel on the distributor shaft and push it firmly onto the shaft, with steady, even pressure.

5. Apply a coating of silicone dielectric compound to single point rotors. Be sure to only apply it to the metallic tip of the rotor which extends to the side. Do not apply any of this grease to the raised portion of the rotor contact which presses against the carbon button in the distributor cap. Also, do not apply grease to any portion of a multipoint rotor.

6. Reinstall the distributor cap, as previously described.

Fig. 35 Many distributor caps are fastened by two screws

Fig. 36 To avoid confusion, mark the distributor cap and spark plug wires before removal

Fig. 37 Lift off the distributor cap after loosening its fasteners and removing the spark plug wires

Fig. 38 If there are no hold-down screws, the rotor is retained by a friction fit

Fig. 39 Examine the rotor for cracks, burns, deposits or other damage

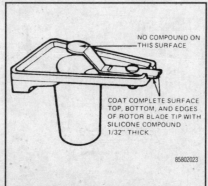

Fig. 40 Silicone dielectric compound application

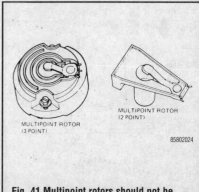

Fig. 41 Multipoint rotors should not be greased

IGNITION TIMING

General Information

▶ See Figures 42, 43, 44, 45 and 46

Ignition timing is the measurement, in degrees of crankshaft rotation, of the point at which the spark plugs fire in each of the cylinders. It is measured in degrees before or after Top Dead Center (TDC) of the compression stroke. Ignition timing is adjusted by turning the distributor body in the engine.

Ideally, the air/fuel mixture in the cylinder is ignited by the spark plug just as the piston passes TDC of the compression stroke. If this happens, the piston will begin the power stroke just as the compressed and ignited air/fuel mixture starts to expand. The expansion of the air/fuel mixture then forces the piston down on the power stroke and turns the crankshaft.

Because it takes a fraction of a second for the spark plug to ignite the mixture in the cylinder, the spark plug must fire a little before the piston reaches TDC. Otherwise, the mixture will not be completely ignited as the piston passes TDC and the full power of the explosion will not be used by the engine.

The timing measurement is given in degrees of crankshaft rotation before the piston reaches TDC (BTDC). If the setting for the ignition timing is 5 degrees BTDC, each spark plug must fire 5 degrees before each piston reaches TDC. This only holds true, however, when the engine is at idle speed.

As the engine speed increases, the pistons go faster. The spark plugs have to ignite the fuel even sooner if it is to be completely ignited when the piston reaches TDC. To do this, the distributor has a means to advance the timing of the spark as the engine speed increases. This is often accomplished by centrifugal weights within the distributor and a vacuum diaphragm assembly mounted on the side of the distributor.

➡DuraSpark III and EEC-IV Thick Film Integrated (TFI) ignition systems do not utilize centrifugal or vacuum advance, and thus, do not utilize centrifugal weights or vacuum diaphragm assemblies.

➡It is necessary to disconnect the vacuum line(s) from the diaphragm assembly (if so equipped) when the ignition timing is being set.

If the ignition is set too far advanced (BTDC), the ignition and expansion of the fuel in the cylinder will occur too soon and try to force the piston down while it is still traveling up. This causes engine ping. If the ignition spark is set too far retarded after TDC (ATDC), the piston will have already passed TDC and started on its way down when the fuel is ignited. This will cause the piston to be forced down for only a portion of its travel, resulting in poor engine performance and a lack of power.

The timing is best checked with a timing light. This device is usually connected in series with the No. 1 spark plug. The current that fires the spark plug also causes the timing light to flash.

The crankshaft pulley on 6-200 and 6-232 engines contains a notch. A scale of degrees of crankshaft rotation is attached to the engine block in such a position that the notch will pass close by the scale. On 4-140, 6-170 and V8 engines, the scale is located on the crankshaft pulley and a pointer is attached to the engine block so that the scale will pass close by. When the engine is running, the timing light is aimed at the mark on the crankshaft pulley and the scale.

ADJUSTMENT

▶ See Figures 47 and 48

➡All engines are equipped with conventional ignition timing marks and pointers. In addition, some early model engines are equipped with a monolithic timing system. The monolithic system uses a timing receptacle, which accepts an electronic probe that is connected to digital read-out equipment. When equipped, this receptacle is located at the front of most engines (except the 4-140, which has a boss for monolithic timing at the left rear of the cylinder block). Timing can also be adjusted in the conventional way. Many 1980 and later models are equipped with EEC engine controls, in which all ignition timing is controlled by the EEC module. Initial ignition timing is not adjustable and no attempt at adjustment should be made on EEC equipped vehicles. Since require-

Fig. 42 Crankshaft timing marks are used to read ignition timing

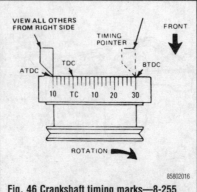

Fig. 43 Crankshaft timing marks—4-140 engine

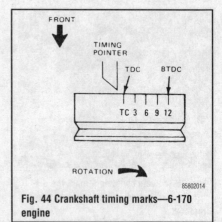

Fig. 44 Crankshaft timing marks—6-170 engine

Fig. 45 Crankshaft timing marks—6-200 and 6-232 engines

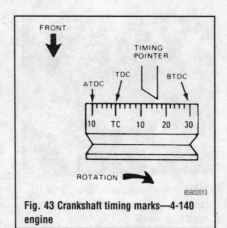

Fig. 46 Crankshaft timing marks—8-255 and 8-302 engines

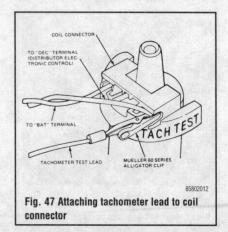

Fig. 47 Attaching tachometer lead to coil connector

Fig. 48 With the engine running at the specified rpm, aim the timing light at the timing mark and pointer

ments vary from model to model, always refer to the Vehicle Emission Control Information (VECI) label for details concerning your particular vehicle.

1. Locate the timing marks and pointer on the lower engine pulley and engine's front cover.

2. Clean the marks and apply chalk or brightly colored paint to the pointer.

3. On 1981 and later models, if the ignition module has (-12A244-) as a basic part number, disconnect the two wire connector (yellow and black wires). On engines equipped with the EEC-IV system, disconnect the single white (black on some models) wire connector near the distributor.

4. Attach a timing light and tachometer according to manufacturer's specifications.

➡The coil connector used with DuraSpark is provided with a cavity for connection of a tachometer, so that the connector does not have to be removed to check engine rpm. Install the tachometer lead with an alligator clip on its end into the cavity marked TACH TEST and connect the other lead to a good ground. If the coil connector must be removed, pull it out horizontally until it is disengaged from the coil terminal.

5. Disconnect and plug all vacuum lines leading to the distributor.

6. Start the engine, allow it to warm to normal operating temperature, then set the idle to the specifications given on the underhood sticker (for timing).

7. On 1981 and later models equipped with the module mentioned in Step 3, jumper the pins in the module connector for the yellow and black wires.

8. Aim the timing light at the timing mark and pointer on the front of the engine. If the marks align when the timing light flashes, remove the timing light, set the idle to its proper specification, and connect the vacuum lines at the distributor. If the marks do not align when the light flashes, turn the engine off and loosen the distributor hold-down clamp slightly.

9. Start the engine again, and observe the alignment of the timing marks. To advance the timing, turn the distributor opposite of its rotational direction, meaning counterclockwise on 4-140, 6-170 and 6-200 engines, and clockwise on 6-232 and V8 engines. To retard the timing, turn the distributor in its rotational direction, meaning clockwise on 4-140, 6-170 and 6-200 engines, and counterclockwise on 6-232 and V8 engines. When altering the timing, it is wise to tap the distributor lightly with a wooden hammer handle to move it in the desired direction. Grasping the distributor with your uninsulated hand may result in a painful electric shock. When the timing marks are aligned, turn the engine OFF and tighten the distributor hold-down clamp. Remove the test equipment, reconnect the vacuum hoses and white (or black) single wire connector (EEC-IV).

10. On 1981 and later models equipped with the module mentioned in Step 3, remove the jumper connected in Step 7 and reconnect the two-wire connector. Test the module operation as follows:

a. Disconnect and plug the vacuum source hose to the ignition timing vacuum switch.

b. Using an external vacuum source, apply vacuum greater than 12 in. Hg (40.52 kPa) to the switch, and compare the ignition timing with the requirements below.

- 4-cylinder: per specifications less 32–40 degrees
- 6-cylinder: per specifications less 21–27 degrees
- 8-cylinder: per specifications less 16–20 degrees

VALVE LASH

Adjustment

▸ See Figure 49

All of the Mustang and Capri engines covered by this manual utilize hydraulic valve lifters, except for the V6-170 cu in. engine. Valve systems equipped with hydraulic valve lifters operate with zero clearance in the valve train, thereby eliminating the need for adjustment. The V6-170 cu in. engine, however, is equipped with mechanical lifters that should be adjusted at the recommended intervals.

➡While all valve adjustments must be as accurate as possible, it is better to have the valve adjustment slightly loose than slightly tight, as burnt valves may result from overly tight adjustments.

1. Remove the air cleaner assembly and disconnect the negative battery cable.

2. Disconnect hoses leading to the Thermactor bypass valve.

3. Unfasten the Thermactor bypass valve mounting bracket, then remove the bracket and valve assembly.

4. Remove the two engine lifting eyes. Remove the alternator drive belt, loosen the alternator mounting bolts and pivot the alternator towards the fender.

5. Remove the spark plug wires from the spark plugs and the rocker arm covers.

6. When removing the rocker arm covers, first remove or reposition any wires and/or hoses which might block removal of the covers.

7. Torque the rocker arm support bolts to 43–49 ft. lbs. (58–66 Nm).

8. Reconnect the battery cable, place the transmission in Neutral (manual) or Park (automatic), and apply the parking brake.

9. Place a finger on the adjusting screw of the intake valve rocker arm for cylinder No. 5. You will be able to detect the slightest motion of the rocker arm in this way. (Cylinder numbering is shown under Firing Order near the beginning of the section.) Valve arrangement, from front to rear, on the left bank is I-E-E-I-E-I; on the right it is I-E-I-E-E-I.

10. Use a remote starter switch to turn the engine over until you can just feel the valve begin to open. Now the cam is in position to adjust the intake and exhaust valves on the No.1 cylinder.

Valve Clearance Adjustment V6 170 Cu. In. Engine

Adjust Both Valves For This Cylinder (Intake — 0.016 in.; Exhaust — 0.018 in.)	Intake Valve Just Opening for Cyl.:
1	5
4	3
2	6
5	1
3	4
6	2

Fig. 49 Valve clearance adjustment order

11. Adjust the No.1 intake valve so that a 0.016 in. (0.4064mm) feeler gauge has a slight drag, while a 0.017 in. (0.4318mm) feeler gauge is a tight fit. Turn the adjusting screw clockwise to decrease lash or counterclockwise to increase lash. There are no lockbolts to tighten as the adjusting screws are self-locking.

✳✳ WARNING

Do not use a step-type "go-no go" feeler gauge. When checking lash, you must insert the feeler gauge and move it parallel to the crankshaft. Do not move it in and out perpendicular to the crankshaft, as this will give an erroneous feel which will result in overtightened valves.

IDLE SPEED AND MIXTURE ADJUSTMENTS

This section contains only regular maintenance carburetor adjustments as they apply to engine tune-up. Descriptions of the carburetor and complete adjustment procedures can be found in Section 5, under Fuel System.

Carbureted Engines

➡Since the design of the 2700VV and 7200VV carburetor is different from all other Motorcraft carburetors in many respects, the adjusting procedures are necessarily different as well. Although the idle speed adjustment alone is identical, there is further information you will need to know in order to adjust the 2700VV and 7200VV properly. Refer to Section 4 for an explanation.

✳✳ WARNING

In order to limit exhaust emissions, plastic caps have been installed on the idle fuel mixture screw(s), which prevent the carburetor from being adjusted to an overly rich idle fuel mixture. Under no circumstances should these limiters be modified or removed. A satisfactory idle should be obtained within the range of the limiter(s).

ADJUSTMENT

▶ See Figures 50, 51, 52 and 53

1. Start the engine and run it at idle until it reaches normal operating temperature (about 10–15 minutes, depending on outside temperature). Stop the engine.
2. Check the ignition timing as outlined earlier in this section.
3. Remove the air cleaner, taking note of the hose locations, and check that the choke plate is fully open (in a vertical position). Check the accompanying illustrations or those in Section 5 to see where the carburetor adjustment loca-

12. Adjust the exhaust valve the same way so that a 0.018 in. (0.4572mm) feeler gauge has a slight drag, while a 0.019 in. (0.4826mm) gauge is a tight fit.
13. The rest of the valves are adjusted in the same way, in their firing order (1-4-2-5-3-6), by first positioning the cam accordingly. For details, please refer to the chart.
14. Remove all the old gasket material from the cylinder heads and rocker cover gasket surfaces, then disconnect the negative cable from the battery.
15. Remove the spark plug wires and reinstall the rocker arm covers.
16. Reinstall any hoses and wires which were removed previously.
17. Reinstall the spark plug wires, the alternator drive belt, then the Thermactor air bypass valve and its mounting bracket.
18. Reconnect the battery cable and reinstall the air cleaner assembly.
19. Start the engine, then check for oil and/or vacuum leaks.

tions are. If you cannot reach them with the air cleaner installed, leave it off temporarily. Otherwise, reinstall the air cleaner assembly including all of the hose connections.

➡Leaving the air cleaner removed will affect the idle speed. Therefore, adjust the curb idle speed to a setting 50–100 rpm higher than specified, if the air cleaner is off. When the air cleaner is reinstalled, the idle speed should return to specifications.

4. Attach a tachometer to the engine, with the positive wire connected to the distributor side of the ignition coil, and the negative wire connected to a good ground, such as an engine mount. The ignition coil connector allows a tachometer test lead with an alligator clip to be connected to the DEC (Distributor Electronic Control) terminal without removing the connector.
5. All idle speed adjustments are made with the headlights off (unless otherwise specified on the engine decal), with the air conditioning off (if so equipped), with all vacuum hoses connected, with the throttle solenoid positioner activated (connected, if so equipped), and with the air cleaner on. (See Note after Step 3.) Finally, all idle speed adjustments are made in Neutral on cars with a manual transmission, and in Drive on cars equipped with an automatic transmission.

✳✳ CAUTION

Whenever performing these adjustments, block all four wheels and set the parking brake.

6. On cars not equipped with a Throttle Solenoid Positioner (TSP), the idle speed is adjusted with the curb idle speed adjusting screw. Start the engine. Turn the curb idle speed adjusting screw inward or outward until the correct idle speed (see Tune-Up Specifications chart) is reached, remembering to make the 50–100 rpm allowance if the air cleaner is removed.
7. On cars equipped with a TSP, idle speed is adjusted by a solenoid adjusting screw (nut), in two stages. Start the engine. The higher speed is adjusted with the solenoid connected. Turn the solenoid adjusting screw (nut)

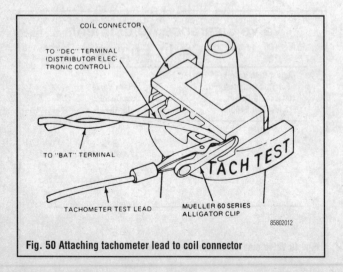

Fig. 50 Attaching tachometer lead to coil connector

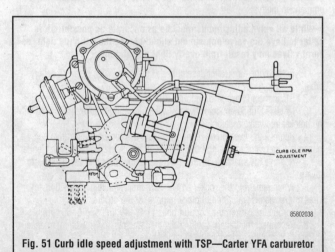

Fig. 51 Curb idle speed adjustment with TSP—Carter YFA carburetor

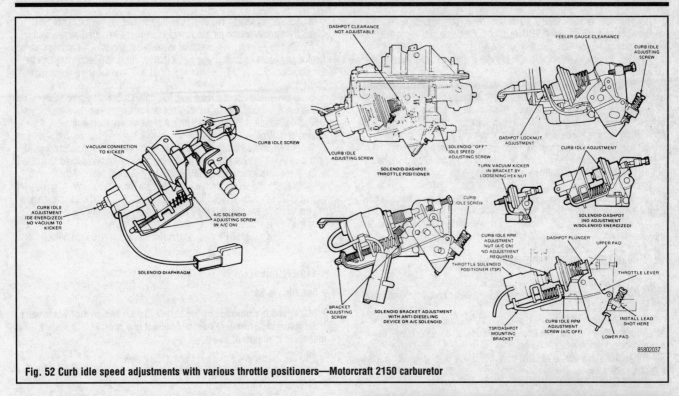

Fig. 52 Curb idle speed adjustments with various throttle positioners—Motorcraft 2150 carburetor

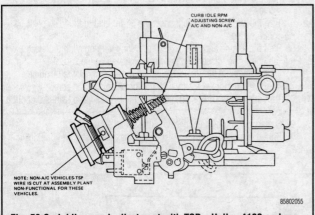

Fig. 53 Curb idle speed adjustment with TSP—Holley 4180 carburetor

Fuel Injected Engines

➡Prior to adjusting the curb idle speed, set the parking brake and block all four wheels. Make all adjustments with the engine at normal operating temperature. Be sure all accessories are turned off. If the Vehicle Emission Control Information (VECI) label gives different specs and procedures than those following, always follow the label as it will reflect production changes and calibration differences.

On vehicles equipped with EEC-IV, curb idle speed (RPM) is controlled by the EEC-IV processor and the idle speed control device. If the control system is operating properly, these speeds are self-compensating and cannot be changed by traditional adjustment techniques.

ADJUSTMENT

♦ See Figure 50

6-232 Central Fuel Injection (CFI)

➡The EEC-IV system and an idle speed motor control the curb idle speed on models equipped with the V6 engine. The idle speed is not adjustable, except for minimum and maximum throttle stop adjustment screw clearance. Too little clearance will prevent the throttle from closing as required, thus causing a faster than normal idle speed. Any other problems with the system must be checked by EEC-IV system diagnosis.

The EXACT sequence must be followed when checking the adjustment.
1. Set the parking brake and block all four wheels.
2. Connect a suitable tachometer, according to the manufacturer's instructions.
3. Adjustment is checked with the idle speed motor plunger fully retracted. Run the engine until normal operating temperature is reached. Note the idle speed, then shut the engine OFF. Remove the air cleaner assembly.
4. Locate the self-test connector and self-test input connector. Both are under the hood by the driver's side strut tower.
5. Connect a jumper wire between the single input connector and the signal return pin of the self-test connector. The signal return pin is on the upper right of the plug when the plug is held straight-on with the four prongs on the bottom facing you.

on 1 or 4-barrel carburetors, or the entire bracket on 2-barrel carburetors inward or outward until the correct higher idle speed (see Tune-Up Specifications chart) is reached, remembering to make the 50–100 rpm allowance if the air cleaner is removed. After making this adjustment on cars equipped with 2-barrel carburetors, tighten the solenoid adjusting locknut. The lower idle speed is adjusted with the solenoid lead wire disconnected near the harness (not at the carburetor). Place automatic transmission equipped cars in Neutral for this adjustment. Using the curb idle speed adjusting screw on the carburetor, turn the idle speed adjusting screw inward or outward until the correct lower idle speed (see Tune-Up Specifications chart) is reached, remembering again to make the 50–100 rpm allowance if the air cleaner is removed. Finally, reconnect the solenoid, slightly depress the throttle lever and allow the solenoid plunger to fully extend.

8. If removed, install the air cleaner. Recheck the idle speed. If it is not correct, Step 6 will have to be repeated and the appropriate corrections made.

9. To adjust the idle mixture, turn the idle mixture screw(s) inward to obtain the smoothest idle possible within the range of the limiter(s).

10. Turn the engine OFF, then disconnect the tachometer.

➡If any doubt exists as to the proper idle mixture setting for your car, have the exhaust emission level checked at a diagnostic center or garage with an exhaust (HC/CO) analyzer or an air/fuel ratio meter.

6. The motor plunger should retract when the jumper wire is connected and the ignition key turned to the **RUN** position. If not, the EEC-IV system requires testing and service.

7. Wait about ten seconds until the plunger is fully retracted. Turn the key **OFF** and remove the jumper.

8. If the idle speed was too high, remove the throttle stop adjusting screw and install a new one. With the throttle plates completely closed, turn the throttle stop adjusting screw in until a gap of 0.005 in. (0.127mm) is present between the screw tip and the throttle lever contact surface. Turn the screw in an additional 1½ turns to complete the adjustment.

9. If the idle speed was too low, remove the dust cover from the motor tip. Push the tip back toward the motor to remove any play. Measure the clearance between the motor tip and throttle lever by passing a 9/32 in. (7mm) drill bit between the tip and lever. A slight drag should be felt.

10. If adjustment is required, turn the motor bracket adjusting screw until proper clearance is obtained. Tighten the lock and install the dust cover.

11. Install the air cleaner assembly. Disconnect the tachometer and unblock the wheels.

V8 through 1985 With Central Fuel Injection (CFI)

1. Set the parking brake and block all four wheels.
2. Connect a suitable tachometer, start the engine and allow it to reach normal operating temperature.
3. Shut the engine **OFF** and restart it. Run the engine at about 2,000 rpm for a minute. Allow the engine to return to idle and stabilize for about 30 seconds. Place the gear selector in Reverse.
4. Adjust the curb idle as required using the saddle bracket adjusting screw. If the rpm figure was too low, turn the adjusting screw clockwise one full turn. If the speed was too high, turn the screw counterclockwise.
5. Repeat Steps 3 and 4 until correct idle speed is obtained. (Turn the adjusting screw in smaller increments, as you approach the correct idle speed.)
6. Shut the engine **OFF**, then disconnect the tachometer and unblock the wheels.

1986–88 V8 with Sequential Electronic Fuel Injection (SEFI)

1. Apply the parking brake, block all four wheels and place the vehicle in Neutral.
2. Connect a suitable tachometer, according to the manufacturer's instructions.
3. Start the engine and let it run until it reaches normal operating temperature, then turn the engine **OFF**.

4. Turn off all accessories and place the transmission in Park or Neutral. Check the throttle linkage for freedom of movement and correct as necessary.

5. Start the engine, then check for vacuum leaks. Place the transmission in Neutral and operate the engine at 1,800 rpm for at least 30 seconds. Place the transmission in Drive (AT) or leave in Neutral (MT) and allow the engine to stabilize.

6. Check the idle speed; if the curb idle speed falls within specifications, do not adjust. If the curb idle speed does not meet specifications, turn the engine **OFF** and disconnect the positive terminal of the battery for five minutes, then reconnect it. Repeat Steps 5 and 6.

7. If the curb idle speed is still out of specifications, the problem could be with the EEC-IV system and a diagnostic check of the system should be made.

8. If the curb idle speed is still out of specifications, back out the throttle screw until the idle speed reaches 555–595 rpm (base 8-302 with AT), 605–645 rpm (8-302 H.O. with AT), or 680–720 rpm (8-302 H.O. with MT), then back out the throttle plate stop screw ½ additional turn to bring the throttle plate linkage into the normal operating range of the ISC system.

9. Shut the engine **OFF**, then disconnect the tachometer and unblock the wheels.

4-140 EFI Turbo

▶ **See Figure 54**

➡️**Idle speed is controlled by the EEC-IV system and an air bypass valve. If the following procedure does not correct idle rpm, EEC-IV system diagnosis is required.**

1. Set the parking brake and block all four wheels.
2. Connect a suitable tachometer, according to the manufacturer's instructions.
3. Run the engine until normal operating temperature is reached. Turn off all accessories.
4. Turn the engine **OFF**. Disconnect the power lead to the idle speed bypass control valve.
5. Start the engine and run at 2,000 rpm for two minutes. If the electric cooling fan comes on, disconnect the wiring harness connector.
6. Let the engine return to normal idling rpm and check the tachometer.
7. Adjust the rpm if necessary with the throttle plate stop screw.
8. Turn the engine **OFF**, then reconnect the bypass valve lead and cooling fan harness.
9. Restart the engine and check the idle speed.
10. Shut the engine **OFF**, then disconnect the tachometer and unblock the wheels.

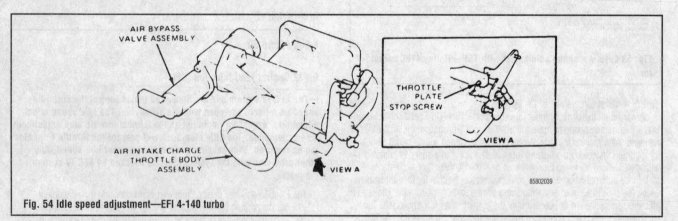

Fig. 54 Idle speed adjustment—EFI 4-140 turbo

85802039

3

ENGINE AND ENGINE REBUILDING

ENGINE ELECTRICAL

Understanding the Engine Electrical System

The engine electrical system can be broken down into three separate and distinct systems:

1. The starting system
2. The charging system
3. The ignition system

BATTERY AND STARTING SYSTEM

Basic Operating Principles

The battery is the first link in the chain of mechanisms which work together to provide cranking of the automobile engine. In most modern cars, the battery is a lead/acid electrochemical device consisting of six 2–volt subsections connected in series so the unit is capable of producing approximately 12 volts of electrical pressure. Each subsection, or cell, consists of a series of positive and negative plates held a short distance apart in a solution of sulfuric acid and water. The two types of plates are of dissimilar metals. This causes a chemical reaction to be set up, and it is this reaction which produces current flow from the battery when its positive and negative terminals are connected to an electrical appliance such as a lamp or motor. The continued transfer of electrons would eventually convert the sulfuric acid in the electrolyte to water, and make the two plates identical in chemical composition. As electrical energy is removed from the battery, its voltage output tends to drop. Thus, measuring battery voltage and battery electrolyte composition are two ways of checking the ability of the unit to supply power. During the starting of the engine, electrical energy is removed from the battery. However, if the charging circuit is in good condition and the operating conditions are normal, the power removed from the battery will be replaced by the generator (or alternator) which will force electrons back through the battery, reversing the normal flow, and restoring the battery to its original chemical state.

The battery and starting motor are linked by very heavy electrical cables designed to minimize resistance to the flow of current. Generally, the major power supply cable that leaves the battery goes directly to the starter, while other electrical system needs are supplied by a smaller cable. During starter operation, power flows from the battery to the starter and is grounded through the car's frame and the battery's negative ground strap.

The starting motor is a specially designed, direct current electric motor capable of producing a very great amount of power for its size. One thing that allows the motor to produce a great deal of power is its tremendous rotating speed. It drives the engine through a tiny pinion gear (attached to the starter's armature), which drives the very large flywheel ring gear at a greatly reduced speed. Another factor allowing it to produce so much power is that only intermittent operation is required of it. Thus, little allowance for air circulation is required, and the windings can be built into a very small space.

The starter solenoid is a magnetic device which employs the small current supplied by the starting switch circuit of the ignition switch. This magnetic action moves a plunger which mechanically engages the starter and electrically closes the heavy switch which connects it to the battery. The starting switch circuit consists of the starting switch contained within the ignition switch, a transmission neutral safety switch or clutch pedal switch, and the wiring necessary to connect these in series with the starter solenoid or relay.

A pinion, which is a small gear, is mounted to a one–way drive clutch. This clutch is splined to the starter armature shaft. When the ignition switch is moved to the **start** position, the solenoid plunger slides the pinion toward the flywheel ring gear via a collar and spring. If the teeth on the pinion and flywheel match properly, the pinion will engage the flywheel immediately. If the gear teeth butt one another, the spring will be compressed and will force the gears to mesh as soon as the starter turns far enough to allow them to do so. As the solenoid plunger reaches the end of its travel, it closes the contacts that connect the battery and starter and then the engine is cranked.

As soon as the engine starts, the flywheel ring gear begins turning fast enough to drive the pinion at an extremely high rate of speed. At this point, the one–way clutch begins allowing the pinion to spin faster than the starter shaft so that the starter will not operate at excessive speed. When the ignition switch is released from the starter position, the solenoid is de–energized, and a spring contained within the solenoid assembly pulls the gear out of mesh and interrupts the current flow to the starter.

Some starters employ a separate relay, mounted away from the starter, to switch the motor and solenoid current on and off. The relay thus replaces the solenoid electrical switch, but does not eliminate the need for a solenoid mounted on the starter used to mechanically engage the starter drive gears. The relay is used to reduce the amount of current the starting switch must carry.

THE CHARGING SYSTEM

Basic Operating Principles

The automobile charging system provides electrical power for operation of the vehicle's ignition and starting systems and all the electrical accessories. The battery serves as an electrical surge or storage tank, storing (in chemical form) the energy originally produced by the engine driven generator or alternator. The system also provides a means of regulating generator or alternator output to protect the battery from being overcharged and to avoid excessive voltage to the accessories.

The storage battery is a chemical device incorporating parallel lead plates in a tank containing a sulfuric acid/water solution. Adjacent plates are slightly dissimilar, and the chemical reaction of the two dissimilar plates produces electrical energy when the battery is connected to a load such as the starter motor. The chemical reaction is reversible, so that when the generator or alternator is producing a voltage (electrical pressure) greater than that produced by the battery, electricity is forced into the battery, and the battery is returned to its fully charged state.

The vehicle's generator or alternator is driven mechanically, through V–belts, by the engine crankshaft. It consists of two coils of fine wire, one stationary (the stator), and one movable (the rotor). The rotor may also be known as the armature, and consists of fine wire wrapped around an iron core which is mounted on a shaft. The electricity which flows through the two coils of wire (provided initially by the battery in some cases) creates an intense magnetic field around both rotor and stator, and the interaction between the two fields creates voltage, allowing the generator or alternator to power the accessories and charge the battery.

There are two types of generators: the earlier is the direct current (DC) type. The current produced by the DC generator is generated in the armature and carried off the spinning armature by stationary brushes contacting the commutator. The commutator is a series of smooth metal contact plates on the end of the armature. The commutator plates, which are separated from one another by a very short gap, are connected to the armature circuits so that current will flow in one direction only in the wires carrying the generator output. The generator stator consists of two stationary coils of wire which draw some of the output current of the generator to form a powerful magnetic field and create the interaction of fields which generates the voltage. The generator field is wired in series with the regulator.

Newer automobiles use alternating current (AC) generators or alternators, because they are more efficient, can be rotated at higher speeds, and have fewer brush problems. In an alternator, the field rotates while all of the current produced passes through only the stator winding. The brushes bear against continuous slip rings rather than a commutator. This causes the current produced to periodically reverse the direction of its flow. Diodes (electrical one–way switches) block the flow of current from traveling in the wrong direction. A series of diodes is wired together to permit the alternating flow of the stator to be converted to a pulsating, but unidirectional flow at the alternator output. The alternator's field is wired in series with the voltage regulator.

The voltage regulator, which is completely solid state, consists of transistors, diodes and resistors. Its operating functions are achieved through the arrangement of four circuit divisions: an output stage, a voltage control stage, a solid state relay, and a field circuit overcurrent protection stage. Each of these sensing and switching circuits responds directly to system voltage. When the voltage reaches the required level, the circuitry raises resistance of the generator or alternator field circuit, thereby reducing voltage output. The circuits' ability to sense and alter voltage many times each second permits precise voltage control.

While alternators are self–limiting as far as maximum current is concerned, DC generators employ a current–regulating circuit which responds directly to the total amount of current flowing through the generator circuit, rather than to the output voltage. The current regulator is similar to the voltage regulator except that all system current must flow through the regulator on its way to the various accessories.

Ignition Coil

TESTING

♦ See Figure 1

The ignition coil must be diagnosed separately from the rest of the ignition system. Resistance measurements require the use of an ohmmeter and are taken as follows:

1. Primary resistance is measured between the two primary (low voltage) coil terminals, with the coil connector disconnected and the ignition switch off. Primary resistance must be 0.71–0.7Ω for DuraSpark I, or 0.80–1.60Ω for DuraSpark II and DuraSpark III. For TFI systems, the primary resistance should be 0.3–1.0Ω.

2. On DuraSpark ignitions, the secondary resistance is measured between the BATT and high voltage (secondary) terminals of the ignition coil with the ignition off, and wiring from the coil disconnected. Secondary resistance must be 7,350–8,250Ω for DuraSpark I, or 7,700–10,500Ω for DuraSpark II and DuraSpark III. For TFI systems, the secondary resistance should be 8,000–11,500Ω.

3. If resistance tests are all right, but the coil is still suspected, test the coil on a coil tester by following the test equipment manufacturer's instructions for a standard coil. If the reading differs from the original test, check for a defective harness.

REMOVAL & INSTALLATION

♦ See Figures 2, 3 and 4

1. Disconnect the battery ground.
2. Disconnect the two small and one large wire from the coil.
3. Disconnect the condenser connector from the coil, if equipped.

85803005

Fig. 1 Ignition coil connector removal

4. Unbolt and remove the coil.
5. Installation is the reverse of removal.

Ignition Module

REMOVAL & INSTALLATION

DuraSpark Systems

Removing the module, on DuraSpark systems, is a matter of simply removing the fasteners that attach it to the fender or firewall and pulling apart the connectors. When unplugging the connectors, pull them apart with a firm, straight pull. NEVER PRY THEM APART! Prying them will cause damage. When reconnecting them, coat the mating ends with silicone dielectric grease to waterproof the connection. Press the connectors together firmly to overcome any vacuum lock caused by the grease.

➡ If the locking tabs weaken or break, don't replace the unit. Just secure the connection with electrical tape or tie straps.

Thick Film Integrated (TFI) Systems

1. Remove the distributor cap and position it aside.
2. Unplug the TFI harness connector.
3. Remove the two module attaching screws.

➡ The head of the attaching screws may differ depending on year and engine application. Some screws may be removed using a small socket while others require a Torx® bit. A tamper-resistant screw may also be used on some models. The special bit required to remove the tamper-resistant screw can usually be purchased through your local Ford dealer's parts department.

4. Carefully slide the module assembly downwards until the pins completely disengage from the distributor, then carefully pull the module from the mounting surface.

To install:

5. Coat the metal base plate of the TFI ignition module uniformly with silicone dielectric grease approximately 1/32 in. (0.79mm) thick.

6. Place the TFI module on the mounting surface, then carefully push the module upwards until the pins are completely engaged.

7. Install the mounting screws, then tighten to 20–30 inch lbs. (2.3–3.4 Nm).

8. Engage the TFI harness connector, then install the distributor cap.

Distributor

REMOVAL

♦ See Figures 5, 6, 7 and 8

1. Remove the air cleaner on V6 and V8 engines. On 4 and 6–cylinder in–line engines, removal of a Thermactor (air) pump mounting bolt and drive belt will

85803138

Fig. 2 Disconnecting the large (secondary circuit) ignition coil wire

85803139

Fig. 3 Disconnecting the small (primary circuit) ignition coil wires

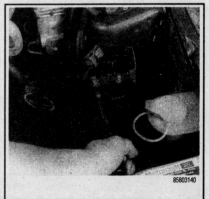

85803140

Fig. 4 Unbolting the ignition coil

allow the pump to be moved to the side and permit access to the distributor. If necessary, disconnect the Thermactor bypass valve and air supply hoses as well.

2. Remove the distributor cap and position the cap and ignition wires to the side.

3. Disconnect the wiring harness plug from the distributor connector. Disconnect and plug the vacuum hose(s) from the vacuum diaphragm assembly, if so equipped.

➡**DuraSpark III and EEC-IV Thick Film Integrated (TFI) ignition systems are not equipped with a vacuum diaphragm assembly.**

4. Rotate the engine (in normal direction of rotation) until No. 1 piston is on TDC (Top Dead Center) of the compression stroke. The TDC mark on the crankshaft pulley and the pointer should align, causing the rotor tip to point towards the No. 1 position of the distributor cap (if it was installed).

5. On DuraSpark I or II systems, turn the engine a slight bit more (if required) to align the timing marks or protrusion of the stator (pick–up coil) assembly with the nearest tooth on the armature. On DuraSpark III, the distributor sleeve groove (when looking down from the top) and the cap adapter alignment slot should align. On models equipped with EEC–IV (1984 and later), remove the rotor (2 screws) and note the position of the polarizing square and shaft plate for installation reference.

6. Scribe a mark on the distributor body and engine block to indicate the position of the rotor tip and position of the distributor in the engine. DuraSpark III and some EEC–IV system distributors are equipped with a notched base and will only locate at one position on the engine.

7. Remove the hold-down bolt and clamp located at the base of the distributor. Some DuraSpark III and EEC–IV system distributors are equipped with a special hold-down bolt that requires a Torx® Head Wrench for removal. Remove the distributor from the engine. Pay attention to the direction the rotor tip points when the drive gear disengages. For installation purposes, the rotor should be at this position to insure proper gear mesh and timing.

8. Avoid turning the engine, if possible, while the distributor is removed, since this will throw off the timing adjustment. If the engine is turned from its TDC position, TDC timing marks will have to be reset before the distributor is installed.

INSTALLATION

◆ **See Figure 9**

1. If the engine was rotated with the distributor removed, rotate the engine again until the no. 1 piston is on TDC of the compression stroke.

2. Rotate the distributor by hand to make sure it turns freely. Visually inspect for the presence of a base O–ring, if so equipped.

3. Position the distributor in the engine with the rotor aligned to the marks made on the distributor, or to the place the rotor pointed when the distributor was removed. (If a new distributor is being installed, rotate the engine until the timing marks align and the rotor is pointing towards the no. 1 cap terminal.) The stator and armature, or polarizing square and shaft plate should also be aligned. Engage the oil pump intermediate shaft and insert the distributor until fully seated on the engine.

4. If the distributor does not fully seat, turn the engine slightly to fully engage the intermediate shaft. If the armature and stator assembly poles cannot be aligned by rotating the distributor in the block, pull the distributor out of the block enough to rotate the shaft and engage a different distributor gear tooth.

5. Follow the above procedures on models equipped with an indexed distributor base. Make sure when positioning the distributor that the slot in the distributor base will engage the block tab and that the sleeve/adapter slots are aligned.

6. After the distributor has been fully seated on the block, install the hold-down clamp and bolt. On models equipped with an indexed base, tighten the mounting bolt. On other models, snug the mounting bolt so the distributor can be turned for ignition timing purposes.

7. Reconnect the wiring harness plug to the distributor connector.

8. On vehicles equipped with a DuraSpark III ignition system (except the 6–232 engine), check and adjust the rotor alignment, as necessary. For details, please refer to the ignition diagnosis and testing procedures found in 9. Install the distributor cap and ignition wires.

10. If removed, install the air cleaner or Thermactor components.

11. Check and reset the ignition timing, as necessary, on applicable models. Reconnect vacuum hose(s) to the vacuum diaphragm assembly, if so equipped.

➡**A silicone compound is used on rotor tips, distributor cap contacts and on the inside of the connectors on the spark plugs cable and module couplers. Always apply silicone dielectric compound after servicing any component of the ignition system. Various models use a multi–point rotor, which does not require the application of dielectric compound.**

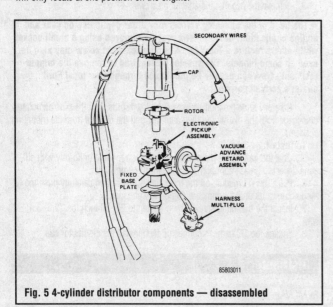

Fig. 5 4-cylinder distributor components — disassembled

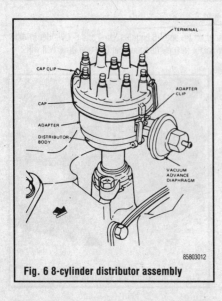

Fig. 6 8-cylinder distributor assembly

Fig. 7 Remove the hold-down bolt and clamp

Fig. 8 Lift out the distributor and its hold-down bolt and clamp

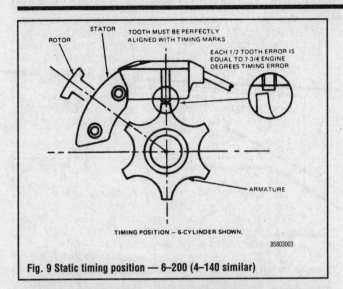

Fig. 9 Static timing position — 6–200 (4–140 similar)

Alternator

♦ **See Figures 10 and 11**

The alternator charging system consists of the alternator, voltage regulator, warning light, battery, and fusible link wire.

A failure of any component of the charging system can cause the entire system to stop functioning. Because of this, the charging system can be very difficult to troubleshoot when problems occur.

When the ignition key is turned on, current flows from the battery, through the charging system indicator light on the instrument panel, to the voltage regulator, and to the alternator. Since the alternator is not producing any current, the alternator warning light comes on. When the engine is started, the alternator begins to produce current and turns the alternator light off. As the alternator turns and produces current, the current is divided into two areas: some goes to the battery to charge the battery and power the electrical components of the vehicle, while some is returned to the alternator, enabling it to increase its output. In this situation, the alternator is receiving current from the battery and from itself. A voltage regulator is wired into the current supply to the alternator to prevent it from receiving too much current, which would cause it to put out too much current. Conversely, if the voltage regulator does not allow the alternator to receive enough current, the battery will not be fully charged and will eventually go dead.

The battery is connected to the alternator at all times, whether the ignition key is turned on or not. If the battery were shorted to ground, the alternator would also be shorted. This would damage the alternator. To prevent this, a fusible link is installed in the wiring between the battery and the alternator. If the battery is shorted, the fusible link is melted, protecting the alternator.

ALTERNATOR PRECAUTIONS

Several precautions must be observed with alternator equipped vehicles to avoid damaging the unit. They are as follows:

1. If the battery is removed for any reason, make sure that it is reconnected with the correct polarity. Reversing the battery connections may result in damage to the one-way rectifiers.

2. When utilizing a booster battery as a starting aid, always connect it as follows: positive to positive, and negative (booster battery) to a good ground on the engine of the car being started.

3. Never use a fast charger as a booster to start cars with alternating current (AC) circuits.

4. When servicing the battery with a fast charger, always disconnect the car's battery cables.

5. Never attempt to polarize an alternator.

6. Avoid long soldering times when replacing diodes or transistors. Prolonged heat is damaging to alternators.

7. Do not use test lamps of more than 12 volts (V) for checking diode continuity.

8. Do not short across or ground any of the terminals on the alternator.

9. The polarity of the battery, alternator, and regulator must be matched and considered before making any electrical connections within the system.

10. Never separate the alternator on an open circuit. Make sure that all connections within the circuit are clean and tight.

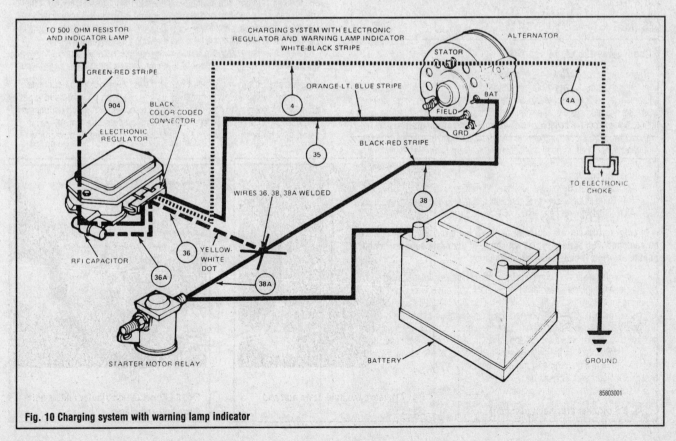

Fig. 10 Charging system with warning lamp indicator

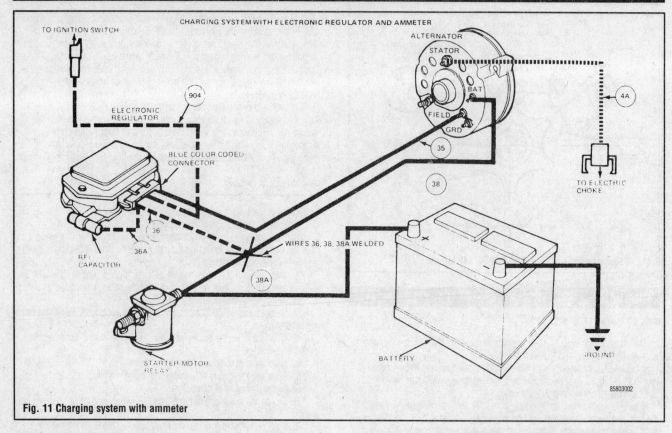

CHARGING SYSTEM WITH ELECTRONIC REGULATOR AND AMMETER

Fig. 11 Charging system with ammeter

11. Disconnect the battery terminals when performing any service on the electrical system. This will eliminate the possibility of accidental reversal of polarity.

12. Disconnect the battery ground cable if arc welding is to be done on any part of the car.

TESTING THE CHARGING SYSTEM

▶ **See Figures 12, 13, 14 and 15**

There are many possible ways in which the charging system can malfunction. Often the source of a problem is difficult to diagnose, requiring special equipment and a good deal of experience. This is usually not the case, however, where the charging system fails completely, causing the dashboard warning light to come on or the battery to "die". To troubleshoot a complete system failure, only two pieces of equipment are needed: a test light, to determine that current is reaching a certain point; and a current indicator (ammeter), to determine the direction of the current flow and its measurement in amps. This test works under three assumptions:

• The battery is known to be good and fully charged.
• The alternator belt is in good condition and adjusted to the proper tension.
• All electrical connections in the system are clean and tight.

➡ **In order for the current indicator to give a valid reading, the car must be equipped with battery cables which are of the same gauge size and quality as original equipment battery cables.**

1. Turn off all electrical components on the car. Make sure the doors of the car are closed. If the car is equipped with a clock, disconnect the clock by removing the lead wire from the rear of the clock. Disconnect the positive battery cable from the battery and connect the ground wire on a test light to the disconnected positive battery cable. Touch the probe end of the test light to the positive battery post. The test light should not light. (If the test light does light, there is a short circuit in the car's wiring. Pull the fuses one at a time, and check each circuit for a short. After locating the cause of the short, service wiring harnesses or components as required.)

2. Disconnect the voltage regulator wiring harness connector at the voltage regulator. Turn on the ignition key. Connect the wire on a test light to a good ground (engine bolt). Touch the probe end of a test light to the ignition wire con-

nector in the voltage regulator wiring harness connector. This wire corresponds to the **I** terminal on the regulator. If the test light goes on, the charging system warning light circuit is complete. If the test light does not come on and the warning light on the instrument panel is on, either the resistor wire, which is parallel with the warning light, or the wiring to the voltage regulator, is defective. If the test light does not come on and the warning light is not on, either the bulb is defective or the power supply wire form the battery through the ignition switch to the bulb has an open circuit. Reconnect the wiring harness to the regulator.

3. Examine the fusible link in the wiring harness from the starter relay to the alternator. If the insulation on this wire is cracked or split, the fusible link may be melted. Connect a test light to the fusible link by attaching the ground wire on the test light to an engine bolt and touching the probe end of the light to the bottom of the fusible link where it splices into the alternator output wire. If the bulb in the test light does not light, the fusible link is melted.

4. Start the engine and place a current indicator on the positive battery cable. Turn off all electrical accessories and make sure the doors are closed. If

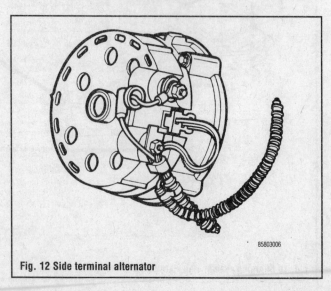

Fig. 12 Side terminal alternator

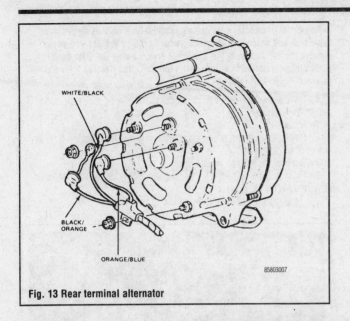

Fig. 13 Rear terminal alternator

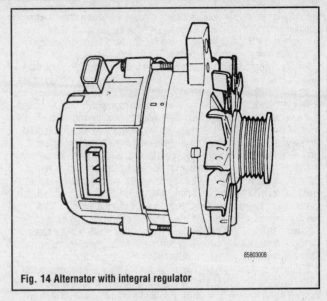

Fig. 14 Alternator with integral regulator

CHARGING SYSTEM DIAGNOSIS

CONDITION	POSSIBLE SOURCE	ACTION
• Battery Does Not Stay Charged — Engine Starts OK	• Battery.	• Test battery, replace if necessary
	• Loose or worn alternator belt.	• Adjust or replace belt
	• Wiring or cables.	• Service as required
	• Alternator.	• Test and/or replace components as required
	• Regulator.	• Test, replace if necessary
	• Other vehicle electrical systems.	• Check other systems for current draw. Service as required
• Alternator Noisy	• Loose or worn alternator belt.	• Adjust tension or replace belt
	• Bent pulley flanges.	• Replace pulley
	• Alternator.	• Service or replace alternator
• Lamps and/or Fuses Burn Out Frequently	• Wiring.	• Service as required
	• Alternator/Regulator.	• Test, service, replace if necessary
	• Battery.	• Test, replace if necessary
• Charge Indicator Lamp Flickers After Engine Starts or Comes On While Vehicle Is Being Driven	• Loose or worn alternator belt.	• Adjust tension or replace
	• Alternator.	• Service or replace
	• Field circuit ground.	• Service or replace worn or damaged wiring.
	• Regulator.	• Test, replace if necessary
	• Lamp circuit wiring and connector.	• Service as required.
	• Operation at low engine speed (idle) with heavy electrical load — IAR alternator only.	• Test, replace if neccessary.
• Charge Indicator Lamp Flickers While Vehicle Is Being Driven	• Loose or worn alternator belt.	• Adjust tension or replace belt
	• Loose or improper wiring connections.	• Service as required
	• Alternator.	• Service or replace
	• Regulator.	• Test, replace if necessary
Electronic Cluster Voltmeter • Voltmeter Bars Above Or Below Normal Area	• Loose or worn alternator belt.	• Adjust tension or replace belt
	• Damaged or worn wiring (battery to alternator for ground or open).	• Service or replace wiring.
Non-Electronic Cluster Voltmeter • Voltmeter Pointer Reads in the Read Area	• Field circuit ground.	• Service or replace wiring.
	• Alternator.	• Service or replace
	• Regulator.	• Test, replace if necessary
	• Voltmeter indicator gauge wiring and connections.	• Service as required
	• Damaged or worn gauge.	• Replace gauge
	• Other vehicle electrical system malfunction.	• Service as required.

Fig. 15 Charging system diagnosis chart

the charging system is working properly, the gauge will show a draw of less than 5 amps. If the system is not working properly, the gauge will show a draw of more than 5 amps. A charge moves the needle toward the battery, a draw moves the needle away from the battery. Turn the engine off.

5. Disconnect the wiring harness connector from the voltage regulator. If the voltage regulator is an external type (separate from the alternator), connect a male spade terminal (solderless connector) to each end of a jumper wire. Insert one end of the wire into the wiring harness connector which corresponds to the **A** terminal on the regulator. Insert the other end of the wire into the wiring harness connector which corresponds to the **F** terminal on the regulator. (If the voltage regulator is integral with the alternator housing, the three–wire connector will not have an **F** terminal. In this case, connect a male spade terminal to one end of a jumper wire, and insert it into the wiring harness connector which corresponds to the **A** terminal on the regulator. Clip or hold the other end of the jumper wire to the regulator **F** terminal screw.) Position the connector with the jumper wire installed so that it cannot contact any metal surface under the hood. Position a current indicator gauge on the positive battery cable. Have an assistant start the engine and observe the reading on the current indicator. Have your assistant slowly raise the speed of the engine to about 2,000 rpm or until the current indicator needle stops moving, whichever comes first. Do not run the engine for more than a short period of time in this condition. If the wiring harness connector or jumper wire becomes excessively hot during this test, turn off the engine and check for a grounded wire in the regulator wiring harness. If the current indicator shows a charge of about three amps less than the output of the alternator, the alternator is working properly. If the previous tests showed a draw, the voltage regulator is defective. If the gauge does not show the proper charging rate, the alternator is defective.

6. Disconnect the jumper wire and replace any faulty component.

REMOVAL & INSTALLATION

▶ See Figures 16 thru 22

1. Disconnect the negative battery cable from the battery.
2. Disconnect the wires from the alternator.
3. Loosen the alternator mounting bolts and remove the drive belt(s).

➡ Some 1981 and later cars are equipped with a ribbed, serpentine drive belt and automatic tensioner, which require the use of a prybar to remove the tension from the tensioner arm. Loosen the idler pulley pivot and adjuster bolts before using the tool. See Section 1 for further information on belt removal.

4. Remove the alternator mounting bolts and spacer (if equipped), and remove the alternator.

To install:

5. Position the alternator on its brackets and install the attaching bolts and spacer (if so equipped).
6. Connect the wires to the alternator.
7. Position the drive belt(s) on the alternator pulley, and adjust belt tension as outlined in Section 1.
8. Connect the negative battery cable.

Fig. 16 Disconnect the negative battery cable before disconnecting the alternator

Fig. 17 Disconnect the electrical leads at the alternator terminals

Fig. 18 The electrical leads are protected by rubber insulators.

Fig. 19 Some terminals simply push onto studs, while others are secured by nuts

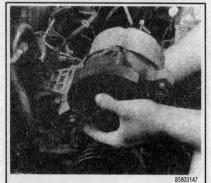

Fig. 20 Loosen the alternator mounting bolts

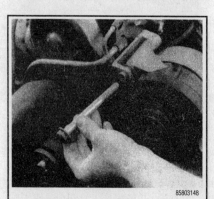

Fig. 21 After removing the drive belt(s), remove the alternator mounting bolts

Fig. 22 Lift the alternator from its mounting bracket

Voltage Regulator

Completely solid–state regulators are used. These voltage regulators are calibrated and preset by the manufacturer, so that no readjustment is required or possible. Earlier model vehicles utilized a separate or external voltage regulator, which was often mounted on the right–hand fender apron. Later model vehicles utilized an integral alternator/regulator, in which the voltage regulator was located within the alternator itself.

REMOVAL & INSTALLATION

External Voltage Regulator

▶ See Figure 23

1. Remove the battery ground cable. On models with the regulator mounted behind the battery, it is necessary to remove the battery hold-down, and to move the battery.
2. Disconnect the regulator from the wiring harness.
3. Remove the regulator mounting screws, radio suppression condenser (if so equipped) and regulator.

To install:

4. Mount the regulator to the regulator mounting plate. The radio suppression condenser mounts under one mounting screw, the ground lead under the other mounting screw. Tighten the mounting screws.
5. Connect the wiring harness to the regulator.
6. If the battery was moved to gain access to the regulator, reposition the battery and install the hold-down. Connect the battery ground cable, and test the system for proper voltage regulation.

Starter

▶ See Figures 24 and 25

All engines use a positive engagement starter.

The positive engagement starter system employs a starter relay, usually mounted inside the engine compartment on a fender wall, to transfer battery current to the starter. The relay is activated by the ignition switch and, when engaged, creates direct current from the battery to the starter windings. Simultaneously, as the armature begins to turn, the starter drive is pushed out to engage the flywheel.

REMOVAL & INSTALLATION

▶ See Figures 26, 27 and 28

1. Disconnect the negative battery cable.
2. Raise the front of the car and install jackstands beneath the frame. Firmly apply the parking brake and place blocks behind the rear wheels.
3. Tag and disconnect the wiring at the starter.
4. Turn the front wheels fully to the right. On some later models it will be necessary to remove the frame brace. On many models, it will be necessary to remove the two bolts retaining the steering idler arm to the frame to gain access to the starter.
5. Remove the starter mounting bolts and remove the starter.
6. Reverse the above procedure to install. Torque the mounting bolts to 12–15 ft. lbs. on starters with 3 mounting bolts and 15–20 ft. lbs. on starters with 2 mounting bolts. Torque the idler arm retaining bolts to 28–35 ft. lbs. (if removed). Make sure that the nut securing the heavy cable to the starter is snugged down tightly.

Sending Units and Sensors

REMOVAL & INSTALLATION

Coolant Temperature

▶ See Figures 29, 30, 31 and 32

The coolant temperature sending unit is a small, threaded device which screws into the engine block, cylinder head or intake manifold.

1. Disconnect the lead wire from the temperature sender or switch.
2. Using the proper size socket wrench, unscrew the sender or switch from its threaded engine fitting.

Fig. 23 Some vehicles contain an external voltage regulator, often mounted on the right–hand fender apron

Fig. 24 Positive engagement starters utilize a starter relay between the battery and the starter

Fig. 25 To avoid confusion, mark and tag electrical connections before disassembly

Fig. 26 Tag and disconnect the wiring at the starter

Fig. 27 Using a socket, remove the starter mounting bolts

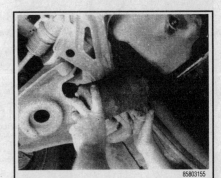

Fig. 28 Carefully lower the starter after removing the mounting bolts

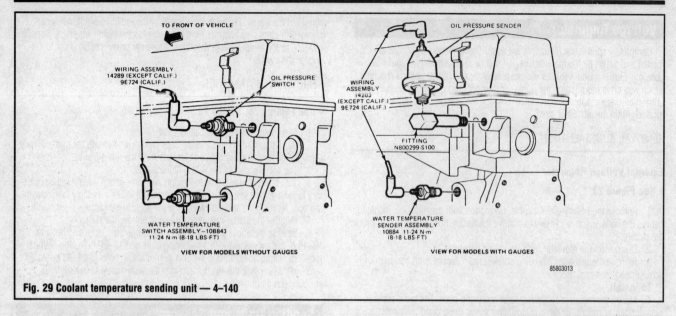

Fig. 29 Coolant temperature sending unit — 4–140

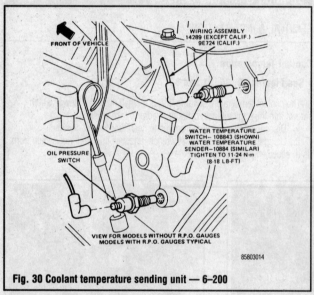

Fig. 30 Coolant temperature sending unit — 6–200

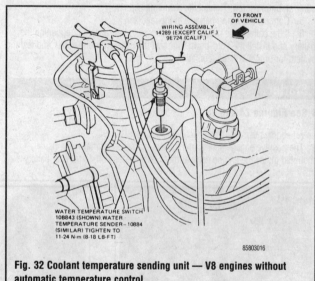

Fig. 32 Coolant temperature sending unit — V8 engines without automatic temperature control

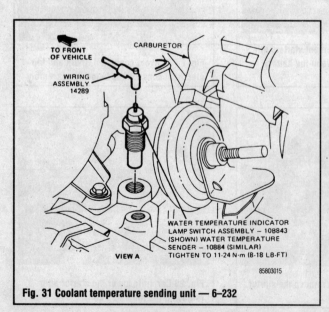

Fig. 31 Coolant temperature sending unit — 6–232

To install:

3. Prepare the new sender or switch for installation by applying a pipe sealant with Teflon® or equivalent to the threads.

➡ **Be sure to use an electrically conductive, water–resistant sealer.**

4. Remove the radiator pressure cap to relieve pressure, then install the cap.

5. Screw in the new temperature sender or switch by hand and tighten with a socket to 8–18 ft. lbs. Do not overtorque.

6. Reconnect the electrical lead wire.

7. Check the coolant level and start the engine. Check the temperature indication function.

Oil Pressure

♦ **See Figures 33, 34 and 35**

The oil pressure sending unit is a threaded device which typically screws into the engine block or cylinder head, by means of an extension fitting. The shape and location of these devices does vary. In some applications, they are similar in size and appearance to a coolant temperature sending unit. In other applications, oil pressure sending units are somewhat larger and of a different shape than coolant temperature sending units.

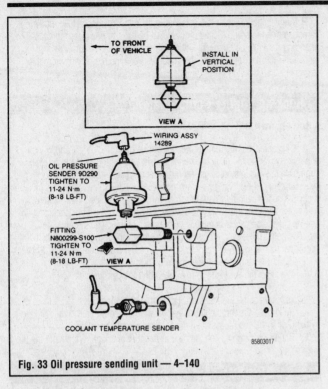

Fig. 33 Oil pressure sending unit — 4–140

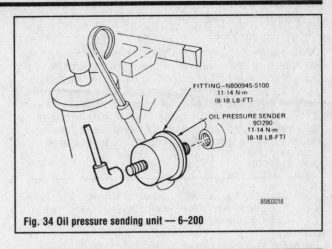

Fig. 34 Oil pressure sending unit — 6–200

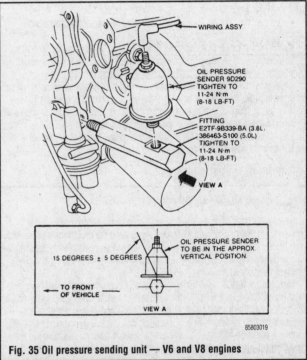

Fig. 35 Oil pressure sending unit — V6 and V8 engines

1. Disconnect the lead wire from the oil pressure sending unit.
2. Using the proper size wrench, unscrew the sending unit from its threaded fitting. If the unit screws into an extension fitting, rather than directly into the engine, do not remove the extension fitting.

To install:

3. Prepare the new sender for installation by applying a pipe sealant with Teflon® or equivalent to the threads.

➡**Be sure to use an electrically conductive, water–resistant sealer.**

4. Screw in the new oil pressure sender by hand and tighten with a wrench to 8–18 ft. lbs. Do not overtorque.
5. Reconnect the electrical lead wire.
6. Check the oil level and start the engine. Check the oil pressure indication function.

ENGINE MECHANICAL

Engine Overhaul Tips

Most engine overhaul procedures are fairly standard. In addition to specific parts replacement procedures and complete specifications for your individual engine, this section also is a guide to acceptable rebuilding procedures. Examples of standard rebuilding practice are shown and should be used along with specific details concerning your particular engine.

Competent and accurate machine shop services will ensure maximum performance, reliability and engine life.

In most instances, it is more profitable for the do–it–yourself mechanic to remove, clean and inspect the component, buy the necessary parts, and deliver these to a shop for actual machine work.

On the other hand, much of the rebuilding work (crankshaft, block, bearings, piston rods, and other components) is well within the scope of a willing, do–it–yourself mechanic.

TOOLS

The tools required for an engine overhaul or parts replacement will depend on the depth of your involvement. With a few exceptions, they will be the tools found in a mechanic's tool kit (see Section 1). More in–depth work will require any or all of the following:
- a dial indicator (reading in thousandths) mounted on a universal base
- micrometers and telescope gauges
- jaw and screw–type pullers
- scraper
- valve spring compressor
- ring groove cleaner
- piston ring expander and compressor
- ridge reamer
- cylinder hone or glaze breaker
- Plastigage®
- engine stand

The use of most of these tools is illustrated in this section. Many can be rented for a one–time use from a local parts jobber or tool supply house specializing in automotive work.

Occasionally, the use of special tools is called for. See the information on Special Tools and Safety Notice in the front of this book before substituting another tool.

INSPECTION TECHNIQUES

Procedures and specifications are given in this section for inspecting, cleaning and assessing the wear limits of most major components. Other procedures such as Magnaflux® and Zyglo® can be used to locate material flaws and stress cracks. Magnaflux® is a magnetic process applicable only to ferrous materials. The Zyglo® process coats the material with a fluorescent dye penetrant and can be used on any material. Checks for suspected surface cracks can be more readily made using spot check dye. The dye is sprayed onto the suspected area, wiped off and the area sprayed with a developer. Cracks will show up brightly.

OVERHAUL TIPS

Aluminum has become extremely popular for use in engines, due to its low weight. Observe the following precautions when handling aluminum parts:
• Never hot tank aluminum parts. (The caustic hot tank solution will eat the aluminum.)
• Remove all aluminum parts (identification tag, etc.) from engine parts prior to the tanking.
• Always coat threads lightly with engine oil or anti–seize compounds before installation, to prevent seizure.
• Never overtorque bolts or spark plugs, especially in aluminum threads.
Stripped threads in any component can be repaired using any of several commercial repair kits (Heli–Coil®, Microdot®, Keenserts®, etc.).

When assembling the engine, any parts that will have frictional contact must be prelubed to provide lubrication at initial start–up. Any product specifically formulated for this purpose can be used, but engine oil is not recommended as a prelube.

When semi–permanent (locked, but removable) installation of bolts or nuts is desired, threads should be cleaned and coated with Loctite® or another similar, commercial non–hardening sealant.

REPAIRING DAMAGED THREADS

▶ **See Figures 36, 37, 38, 39 and 40**

Several methods of repairing damaged threads are available. Heli–Coil® (shown here), Keenserts® and Microdot® are among the most widely used. All involve basically the same principle — drilling out stripped threads, tapping the hole and installing a prewound insert — making welding, plugging and oversize fasteners unnecessary.

Two types of thread repair inserts are usually supplied: a standard type for most Inch Coarse, Inch Fine, Metric Coarse and Metric Fine thread sizes, and a spark plug type to fit most spark plug port sizes. Consult the individual manufacturer's catalog to determine exact applications. Typical thread repair kits will contain a selection of prewound threaded inserts, a tap (corresponding to the outside diameter threads of the insert) and an installation tool. Spark plug inserts usually differ because they require a tap equipped with pilot threads and a combined reamer/tap section. Most manufacturers also supply blister–packed thread repair inserts separately in addition to a master kit containing a variety of taps and inserts plus installation tools.

Before effecting a repair to a threaded hole, remove any snapped, broken or damaged bolts or studs. Penetrating oil can be used to free frozen threads. The offending item can be removed with locking pliers or with a screw or stud extractor. After the hole is clear, the thread can be repaired, as shown in the series of accompanying illustrations.

Checking Engine Compression

▶ **See Figure 41**

A noticeable lack of engine power, excessive oil consumption and/or poor fuel mileage measured over an extended period are all indicators of internal engine wear. Worn piston rings, scored or worn cylinder bores, blown head gaskets, sticking or burnt valves and worn valve seats are all possible culprits here. A check of each cylinder's compression will help you locate the problem(s).

As mentioned in the Tools and Equipment portion of Section 1, a screw–in type compression gauge is more accurate than the type you simply hold against the spark plug hole, even though it takes slightly longer to use. The little bit of additional time is worth it, however, to obtain a more accurate reading. To check engine compression, follow the procedures below.
1. Warm up the engine to normal operating temperature.
2. Remove all the spark plugs.
3. Disconnect the high tension lead from the ignition coil.
4. Fully open the throttle either by operating the carburetor throttle linkage by hand or by having an assistant floor the accelerator pedal.
5. Screw the compression gauge into the no.1 spark plug hole until the fitting is snug.

✳✳ WARNING

Be careful not to crossthread the plug hole. On aluminum cylinder heads use extra care, as the threads in these heads are easily ruined.

6. Ask an assistant to depress the accelerator pedal fully (on both carbureted and fuel injected vehicles). Then, while you read the compression gauge, ask the assistant to crank the engine two or three times in short bursts using the ignition switch.
7. Read the compression gauge at the end of each series of cranks, and record the highest of these readings. Repeat this procedure for each of the engine's cylinders. Compare the highest reading for each cylinder to those of the other cylinders. Generally, a cylinder's compression pressure is acceptable if it is at least 80 percent of the highest reading of all other cylinders. For example, if the maximum reading of any cylinder in a given engine is 150 psi, then none of the highest readings of the other cylinders should fall below 120 psi.
8. If a cylinder is unusually low, pour a tablespoon of clean engine oil into the cylinder through the spark plug hole and repeat the compression test. If the compression comes up after adding the oil, it appears that the cylinder's piston rings or bore are damaged or worn. If the pressure remains low, the valves may not be seating properly (a valve job is needed), or the head gasket may be blown near that cylinder. If compression in any two adjacent cylinders is low, and if the addition of oil does not help the compression, there is leakage past

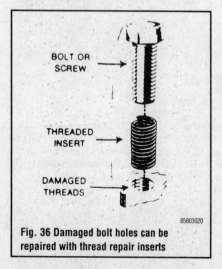

Fig. 36 Damaged bolt holes can be repaired with thread repair inserts

Fig. 37 Standard thread repair insert (left) and spark plug thread repair insert (right)

Fig. 38 Drill out the damaged threads with the specified drill bit. Drill completely through the hole or to the bottom of a blind hole.

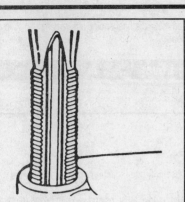

Fig. 39 Using the supplied tap, tap the hole to receive the thread insert. Keep the tap well–oiled and back it out frequently to avoid clogging the threads.

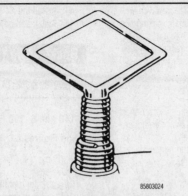

Fig. 40 Screw the insert onto the installation tool until the tang engages the slot. Screw the insert into the tapped hole until it is ¼–½ turn below the top surface. After installation, break off the tang.

Fig. 41 The screw–in type compression gauge is more accurate

the head gasket. Oil and coolant water in the combustion chamber can result from this problem. There may be evidence of water droplets on the engine dipstick when a head gasket has blown.

Engine

REMOVAL & INSTALLATION

✳✳ WARNING

Disconnect the negative battery cable before beginning any work. Always label all disconnected hoses, vacuum lines and wires, to prevent incorrect reassembly. Do not disconnect any air conditioning lines unless you are thoroughly familiar with A/C systems and the hazards involved; escaping refrigerant (Freon®) will freeze any surface it contacts, including skin and eyes. Have the system discharged professionally before required repairs are started.

1. Scribe the hood hinge outline on the underside of the hood. With the help of an assistant, unbolt the hood and remove it.
2. Drain the entire cooling system and crankcase.

✳✳ CAUTION

When draining the coolant, keep in mind that cats and dogs are attracted by the ethylene glycol antifreeze, and are quite likely to drink any that is left in an uncovered container or in puddles on the ground. This will prove fatal in sufficient quantity. Always drain the coolant into a sealable container. Coolant should be reused unless it is contaminated or several years old.

3. Remove the air cleaner and intake duct assembly. Disconnect the battery ground cable from the cylinder block. On automatic transmission equipped cars, disconnect the fluid cooler lines at the radiator. On the 4–140, remove the exhaust manifold shroud.
4. Remove the upper and lower radiator hoses and remove the radiator. If equipped with air conditioning, unbolt the compressor and position it out of the way with refrigerant lines intact. Unbolt and lay the refrigerant condenser forward without disconnecting the refrigerant lines.

➡If there is not enough slack in the refrigerant lines to position the compressor out of the way, the refrigerant in the system must be removed (using proper safety precautions) before the lines can be disconnected from the compressor. See Section 1 of this book for further information.

5. Remove the fan, fan belt and upper pulley. On models equipped with an electric cooling fan, disconnect the power lead and remove the fan and shroud as an assembly.

6. On cars with power steering, disconnect the pump and bracket assembly and secure them out of the way in a position which will prevent fluid from leaking out. Do not disconnect the hoses.
7. On the 6–232 with fuel injection, disconnect the Thermactor hose from the downstream air tube check valve.
8. Disconnect the heater hoses at their engine fittings.
9. Disconnect the alternator wires at the alternator and the positive battery cable at the starter.
10. Disconnect the accelerator cable from the carburetor or throttle body. Disconnect the speed control cable, if so equipped. Disconnect the throttle valve rod on automatic overdrive (AOD) transmissions, if so equipped.
11. Disconnect and plug the fuel line at the fuel pump or, on fuel injected models, at the fuel rail. On fuel injected vehicles, relieve pressure in the fuel lines before disconnecting.
12. Disconnect the coil primary wire at the coil. Disconnect the wires at the oil pressure and coolant temperature sending units. Disconnect the brake booster vacuum line, if so equipped.
13. Remove the starter and dust seal.
14. Remove any additional grounding straps, wiring or vacuum hoses which may interfere with removal of the engine.
15. On cars with a manual transmission, remove the clutch retracting spring. Disconnect the clutch equalizer shaft and arm bracket at the underbody rail and remove the arm bracket and equalizer shaft.
16. Raise the car and safely support on jackstands. Remove the flywheel or converter housing upper attaching bolts.
17. Disconnect the exhaust pipe or pipes at the exhaust manifold(s). Disconnect the right and left motor mount at the underbody bracket. Remove the flywheel or converter housing cover. On models so equipped, disconnect the engine roll damper on the left front of the engine from the frame.
18. On cars with a manual transmission, remove the flywheel housing lower attaching bolts. On models with an automatic transmission, disconnect the throttle valve vacuum line at the intake manifold and disconnect the converter from the flywheel. Remove the converter housing lower attaching bolts.
19. Lower the car. Support the transmission and flywheel or converter housing with a jack.
20. Attach an engine lifting hook. Lift the engine up and out of the compartment and onto a workstand.

➡On carburetor equipped models of the 6–232, it will be necessary to remove the carburetor and install an Engine Lifting Plate (Ford part no. T75T–6000–A or equivalent). Since the intake manifold is aluminum and of a lightweight design, all mounting studs must be used to secure the lifting plate. Do not remove the engine with the transmission attached when using a lifting plate.

To install:
21. Place a new gasket on the exhaust pipe flange.
22. Attach an engine sling and lifting device. Lift the engine from the workstand.
23. Lower the engine into the engine compartment. Be sure the exhaust manifold(s) is (are) in proper alignment with the muffler inlet pipe(s), and the

dowels in the block engage the holes in the flywheel housing. On cars with an automatic transmission, start the converter pilot into the crankshaft, making sure that the converter studs align with the flexplate holes. On cars with a manual transmission, start the transmission main drive gear into the clutch disc. If the engine hangs up after the shaft enters, rotate the crankshaft slowly (with transmission in gear) until the shaft and clutch disc splines mesh. Rotate 4–140 engine clockwise only, when viewed from the front.

24. Install the flywheel or converter housing upper bolts.

25. Install the engine support insulator to bracket retaining nuts. Disconnect the engine lifting sling and remove the lifting brackets. On carburetor equipped models of the 6–232, remove the Engine Lifting Plate and install the carburetor.

26. Raise the front of the car. Connect the exhaust line(s) and tighten the attachments.

27. Install the starter.

28. On cars with a manual transmission, install the remaining flywheel housing–to–engine bolts. Connect the clutch release rod. Position the clutch equalizer bar and bracket, and install the retaining bolts. Install the clutch pedal retracting spring.

29. On cars with an automatic transmission, remove the retainer holding the converter in the housing. Attach the converter to the flywheel. Install the converter housing inspection cover and the remaining converter housing retaining bolts.

30. Remove the support from the transmission and lower the car.

31. Connect the engine ground strap and coil primary wire.

32. Connect the heater hoses to the coolant outlet housing and the water pump. Connect the water temperature sending unit wire.

33. On the 6–232 with fuel injection, connect the Thermactor hose to the downstream air tube check valve.

34. Connect the accelerator cable to the carburetor or throttle body. Connect the speed control cable, if so equipped. Connect the throttle valve rod on automatic overdrive (AOD) transmissions, if so equipped.

35. On cars with an automatic transmission, connect the transmission filler tube bracket, if applicable. Connect the throttle valve vacuum line.

36. On cars with power steering, install the drive belt and power steering pump bracket. Install the bracket retaining bolts. Adjust the drive belt to proper tension.

37. Remove the plug from the fuel tank line. Connect the flexible fuel line and the oil pressure sending unit wire.

38. Install the pulley, belt, spacer, and fan. Adjust the belt tension.

39. Tighten the alternator adjusting bolts. Connect the wires and the battery ground cable. On the 4–140, install the exhaust manifold shroud.

40. Reconnect any other grounding straps, wiring or vacuum hoses which had been removed.

41. Install the radiator. Connect the radiator hoses. On air conditioned cars, install the compressor and condenser.

42. On cars with an automatic transmission, connect the fluid cooler lines. On cars with power brakes, connect the brake booster line.

43. Install an oil filter and fill the crankcase with the correct grade of oil. Run the engine at fast idle and check for leaks.

44. Install the air cleaner and make the final engine adjustments.

45. Install and adjust the hood.

Rocker Arm (Valve) Cover

REMOVAL & INSTALLATION

4–140 and 6–200 Engines

▶ See Figures 42, 43 and 44

1. Remove the air cleaner assembly and mounting brackets, if mounted on the valve cover.

2. Label for identification and remove all wires and vacuum hoses interfering with valve cover removal. Disconnect the PCV hose at the valve cover elbow (4–140) or remove the PCV valve with hose (6–200). Remove the accelerator control cable bracket if necessary.

➡4–140 Turbocharged models require removal of the air intake tube and air throttle body. Refer to the Fuel Injection portion of Section 5 for procedures.

3. Remove the valve cover retaining bolts. On 4–140 models, the front bolts equipped with rubber sealing washers must be installed in the same location to prevent oil leakage.

4. Unfasten any bolts and clamps securing hot water pipes to the valve cover. Reposition the pipes and any wiring harnesses to permit removal of the valve cover.

5. Remove the valve cover. Clean all old gasket material from the valve cover and cylinder head gasket surfaces.

6. Installation is the reverse of removal. Be sure to use a new valve cover gasket. On the 4–140 engine, coat the gasket contact surfaces of the valve cover and the Up side of the valve cover gasket with oil resistant sealing compound. When installing the valve cover gasket, make sure all the gasket locating tangs are engaged in the cover notches provided. On the 4–140 engine, tighten the bolts to 6–8 ft. lbs.; on the 6–200 engine, tighten the bolts in two steps. First, tighten the bolts to 3–5 ft. lbs. and, two minutes later, tighten them to the same specification.

V6 and V8 Engines

➡When disconnecting wires and vacuum lines, label them for installation identification.

1. Remove the air cleaner assembly. (On 1986–88 V8 engines, the air cleaner assembly does not need to be removed.)

2. On the right side:

a. Disconnect the automatic choke heat chamber hose from the inlet tube near the right valve cover, if equipped.

b. Remove the automatic choke heat tube, if equipped, and remove the PCV valve and hose from the valve cover. Disconnect the EGR valve hoses.

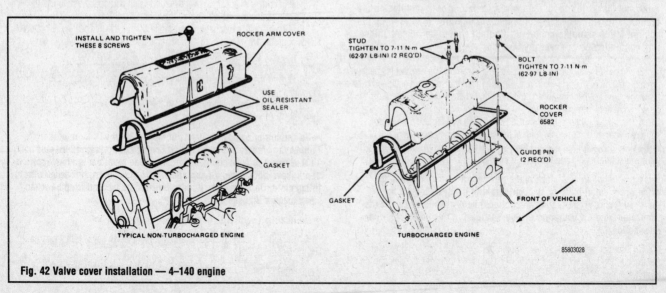

Fig. 42 Valve cover installation — 4–140 engine

Fig. 43 Remove the valve cover retaining bolts with a socket and extension, if necessary

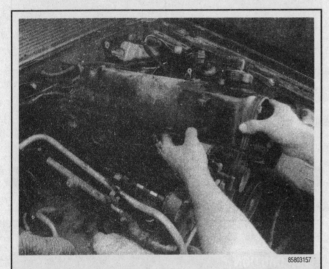

Fig. 44 Lift the valve cover from the cylinder head

c. Remove the Thermactor bypass valve and air supply hoses as necessary to gain clearance.

d. Disconnect the spark plug wires from the plugs with a twisting, pulling motion; twist and pull on the boots only, never on the wires. Position the wires and mounting bracket out of the way.

e. Remove the valve cover mounting bolts and valve cover.

3. On the left side:

a. Remove the spark plug wires and bracket.

b. Remove the wiring harness and any vacuum hose(s) from the bracket.

c. Remove the valve cover mounting bolts and valve cover.

4. Clean all old gasket material from the valve cover and cylinder head mounting surfaces.

➡ **Some 6–232 engines were not equipped with valve cover gaskets in production. Rather, RTV silicone gasket material was originally used. Scrape away the old RTV sealant and clean the cover. Spread an even bead ³/₁₆ in. (4mm) wide of RTV sealant on the valve covers and install, or install with gaskets.**

5. Installation is the reverse of removal. Be sure to use new valve cover gaskets. When installing the valve cover gaskets, make sure all the gasket tangs are engaged in the cover notches provided. On all engines other than the 6–232, tighten the bolts to 3–5 ft. lbs. (On the 6–232 engine, tighten the bolts to 80–106 inch lbs.) On the V8 engines only, retighten the bolts to the same specification two minutes later.

Rocker Arm (Cam Follower) and Hydraulic Lash Adjuster

REMOVAL & INSTALLATION

4–140 Engine

➡ **A special tool is required to compress the lash adjuster.**

1. Remove the valve cover and related parts as described above.

2. Rotate the camshaft so that the base circle of the cam is against the cam follower you intend to remove.

3. Remove the retaining spring from the cam follower, if so equipped.

4. Using special tool T74P–6565–B or a valve spring compressor tool, collapse the lash adjuster and/or depress the valve spring, as necessary, and slide the cam follower over the lash adjuster and out from under the camshaft.

5. Install the cam follower in the reverse order of removal. Make sure that the lash adjuster is collapsed and released before rotating the camshaft.

6. Clean the mounting surfaces and install the valve cover with a new gasket, as described above.

7. install the air cleaner assembly, PCV valve and any other parts which were moved.

Rocker Arm Shaft/Rocker Arms

REMOVAL & INSTALLATION

6–170 Engine

1. Remove the valve covers and related parts, as described above. If it interferes with removal, disconnect the throttle linkage to the carburetor.

2. Remove the rocker arm shaft stand attaching bolts, by loosening the bolts two turns at a time, in sequence.

3. Lift off the rocker arm shaft assembly and oil baffle.

4. Loosen the valve lash adjusting screws a few turns.

➡ **Lubricate all parts with motor oil before installation.**

5. Install the oil baffle and rocker arm shaft assembly to the cylinder head and guide the adjusting screws on to the push rods.

6. Install and tighten the rocker arm stand attaching bolts to 43–49 ft. lbs., two turns at a time, in sequence.

7. Adjust valve lash to the cold specified setting.

8. Repeat steps 2–8 for the opposite side of the engine.

9. Clean the mounting surfaces and install the valve covers with new gaskets, as described above.

10. install the air cleaner assembly, PCV valve and any other parts which were moved.

6–200 Engine

▶ See Figure 45

1. Remove the valve cover and related parts, as described above.

2. Remove the rocker arm shaft mounting bolts, two turns at a time for each bolt. Start at the end of the rocker shaft and work toward the middle.

3. Lift the rocker arm shaft assembly from the engine. Remove the pin and washer from each end of the shaft. Slide the rocker arms, spring and supports off the shaft. Keep all parts in order or label them by position.

4. Clean and inspect all parts, replace as necessary.

5. Assemble the rocker shaft parts in reverse order of removal. Be sure the oil holes in the shaft are pointed downward. install the rocker shaft assembly on the engine and tighten the mounting bolts two turns at a time, in sequence, from the front to the rear. After the supports fully contact the cylinder head, tighten the mounting bolts in the same sequence to 30–35 ft. lbs.

➡ **Lubricate all parts with motor oil before installation.**

6. Clean the mounting surfaces and install the valve cover with a new gasket, as described above.

7. install the air cleaner assembly, PCV valve and any other parts which were moved.

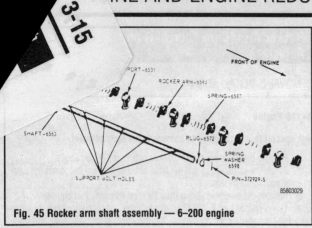

Fig. 45 Rocker arm shaft assembly — 6-200 engine

6-232 and V8 Engines

▶ **See Figures 46 and 47**

1. Remove the air cleaner assembly.
2. On the right side:
   a. Disconnect the automatic choke heat chamber air inlet hose.
   b. Remove the air cleaner and duct.
   c. Remove the automatic choke heat tube (6-232, 8-302).
   d. Remove the PCV fresh air tube from the rocker cover, and disconnect the EGR vacuum amplifier hoses.
   e. Remove the Thermactor bypass valve and air supply hoses.
   f. Disconnect the spark plug wires.
   g. Remove the valve cover mounting bolts and valve cover.
3. On the left side:
   a. Remove the wiring harness from the clips.
   b. Remove the valve cover mounting bolts and valve cover.
4. Remove the rocker arm stud nut or bolt, fulcrum seat and rocker arm.
5. Lubricate all parts with heavy SG engine oil before installation. When installing, rotate the crankshaft until the lifter is on the base of the cam circle (all the way down) and assemble the rocker arm. On V8 engines, torque the nuts or bolts to 18-25 ft. lbs. (On the 6-232 engine, tighten the bolts in two steps. First, tighten the bolts to 5-11 ft. lbs., then tighten them again to 19-25 ft. lbs. The camshaft may be in any position during the final tightening sequence.)

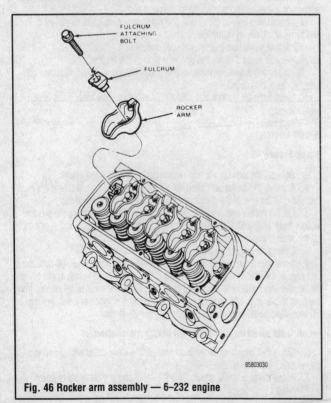

Fig. 46 Rocker arm assembly — 6-232 engine

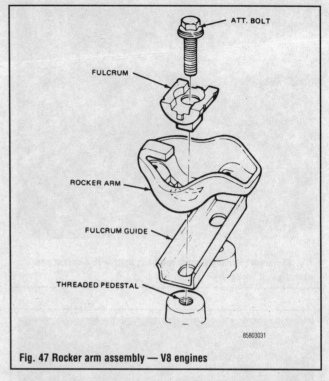

Fig. 47 Rocker arm assembly — V8 engines

➡ **Some later engines use RTV sealant instead of valve cover gaskets.**

6. Clean the mounting surfaces and install the valve covers with new gaskets or RTV sealant, as described above.
7. install the air cleaner assembly and other parts which were moved or disconnected.

Thermostat

REMOVAL & INSTALLATION

▶ **See Figures 48, 49, 50, 51 and 52**

❋❋ CAUTION

When draining the coolant, keep in mind that cats and dogs are attracted by the ethylene glycol antifreeze, and are quite likely to drink any that is left in an uncovered container or in puddles on the ground. This will prove fatal in sufficient quantity. Always drain the coolant into a sealable container. Coolant should be reused unless it is contaminated or several years old.

1. Open the drain cock and drain the radiator so the coolant level is below the coolant outlet elbow which houses the thermostat.

➡ **On some models it will be necessary to remove the distributor cap, rotor and vacuum diaphragm in order to gain access to the thermostat housing mounting bolts.**

2. Remove the outlet elbow retaining bolts and position the elbow sufficiently clear of the intake manifold or cylinder head to provide access to the thermostat.
3. Remove the thermostat and the gasket.
4. Clean the mating surfaces of the outlet elbow and the engine to remove all old gasket material and sealer. Coat the new gasket with water–resistant sealer. Position the gasket on the engine, and install the thermostat in the coolant elbow. The thermostat must be rotated clockwise to lock it into position on all 8-255 and 8-302 engines.
5. Install the outlet elbow and retaining bolts on the engine. Torque the bolts to specification.
6. Refill the radiator. Run the engine at operating temperature and check for leaks. Recheck the coolant level.

Intake Manifold

REMOVAL & INSTALLATION

1979–86 4–140 Engine w/carb

♦ See Figures 53, 54 and 55

➥ The following procedure applies only to carburetor-equipped versions of the 4–140 engine. Fuel injected models utilize a two-piece intake manifold which requires different removal and installation procedures.

1. Disconnect the negative battery cable.
2. Drain the cooling system.

✳✳ CAUTION

When draining the coolant, keep in mind that cats and dogs are attracted by the ethylene glycol antifreeze, and are quite likely to drink any that is left in an uncovered container or in puddles on the ground. This will prove fatal in sufficient quantity. Always drain the coolant into a sealable container. Coolant should be reused unless it is contaminated or several years old.

Fig. 48 Remove the outlet elbow retaining bolts and position the elbow to provide access to the thermostat

Fig. 49 Remove all old gasket material from the outlet elbow with a gasket scraper

Fig. 50 Remove the thermostat from the outlet elbow

Fig. 51 Remove and replace the gasket between the thermostat and the outlet elbow, if so equipped

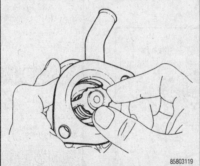

Fig. 52 On V8 engines, turn the thermostat clockwise to lock it into position on the flats in the outlet elbow

Fig. 53 The intake manifold can be removed with the carburetor attached

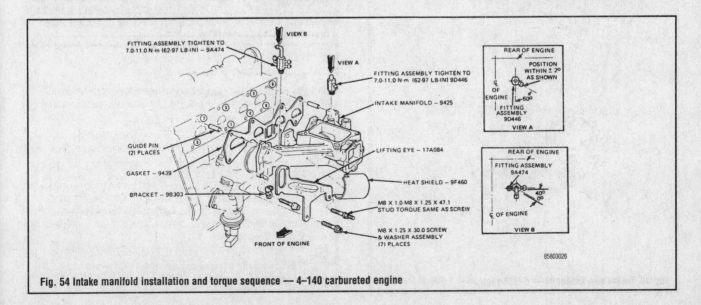

Fig. 54 Intake manifold installation and torque sequence — 4–140 carbureted engine

3. Remove the air cleaner and disconnect the throttle linkage from the carburetor.

4. Disconnect the fuel and vacuum lines from the carburetor.

5. Remove the oil dipstick and dipstick tube retaining bolt.

6. Disconnect the heat tube at the EGR valve.

7. Disconnect and remove PCV hoses at the intake manifold and the engine block.

8. Remove the distributor cap screws and distributor cap.

9. Remove the carburetor, if necessary.

10. Starting from each end and working towards the middle, remove the intake manifold attaching bolts and remove the manifold.

To install:

11. Clean all old gasket material from the manifold and cylinder head.

12. Position the intake manifold against the cylinder head and install intake manifold attaching bolts. Tighten the bolts in the proper sequence (see illustration) in two steps. First tighten them to 11–12½ ft. lbs., and then to 14–21 ft. lbs.

13. Install the carburetor with a new gasket, if it was removed.

14. Position the distributor cap and tighten its retaining screws.

15. Connect PCV hoses at the intake manifold and engine block.

16. Connect the heat tube at the EGR valve.

17. Install the oil dipstick and dipstick tube retaining bolt.

18. Connect the fuel and vacuum lines to the carburetor.

19. Connect the throttle linkage to the carburetor.

20. Install the air cleaner and fill the cooling system.

21. Connect the negative battery cable.

1984–88 4–140 Engine w/EFI

♦ See Figures 56 thru 61

1. Disconnect the negative battery cable.

2. Drain the cooling system.

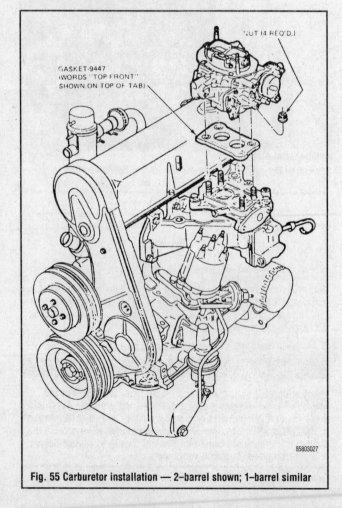

Fig. 55 Carburetor installation — 2–barrel shown; 1–barrel similar

---

⁂ CAUTION

When draining the coolant, keep in mind that cats and dogs are attracted by the ethylene glycol antifreeze, and are quite likely to drink any that is left in an uncovered container or in puddles on the ground. This will prove fatal in sufficient quantity. Always drain the coolant into a sealable container. Coolant should be reused unless it is contaminated or several years old.

3. Disconnect electrical connectors at the throttle position sensor, air bypass valve, knock sensor and EGR valve.

4. Disconnect the upper intake manifold vacuum fitting connections.

5. Disconnect the throttle linkage, speed control, if so equipped, and kickdown cable. Unbolt the accelerator cable from its bracket, and position it out of the way.

6. Disconnect the air intake hose and crankcase vent hose.

7. Disconnect the PCV system by disconnecting the hose from its fitting on the underside of the upper intake manifold.

8. Disconnect the EGR tube from the EGR valve.

9. Remove the upper intake mounting bolts and the upper intake manifold assembly.

10. Disconnect the Push Connect Fittings at the fuel supply manifold supply and return lines.

11. Disconnect the electrical connectors from all four fuel injectors and move the harness aside.

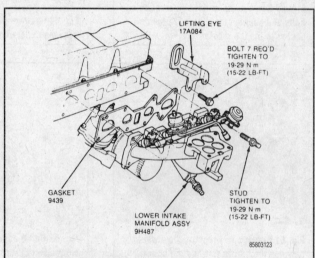

Fig. 56 Lower intake manifold installation — 1985–88 4–140 fuel injected engine; 1984 similar

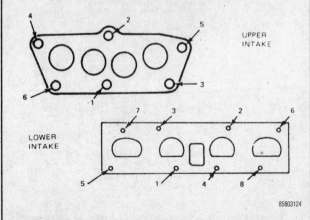

Fig. 57 Intake manifold torque sequences — 1984 4–140 fuel injected engine

12. Remove the two fuel supply manifold retaining bolts, and the fuel supply manifold/injectors assembly. If necessary, the fuel injectors can be removed from the fuel supply manifold by gently twisting and pulling.

13. Remove the four bottom retaining bolts from the lower manifold.

14. Remove the four upper retaining bolts and the lower intake manifold assembly.

To install:

15. Remove and discard the gasket between the cylinder head and lower manifold assembly. Clean and inspect the mating surfaces, and install a new gasket.

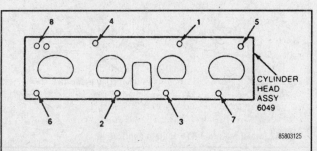

Fig. 58 Lower intake manifold torque sequence — 1985–88 4–140 fuel injected engine

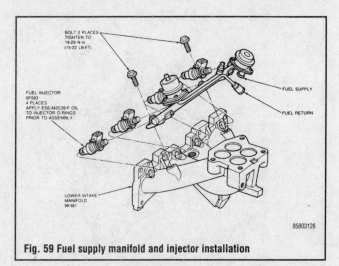

Fig. 59 Fuel supply manifold and injector installation

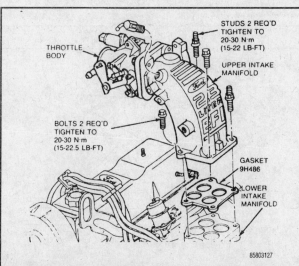

Fig. 60 Upper intake manifold installation — 1985–88 4–140 fuel injected engine; 1984 similar

16. Position the lower manifold assembly and install the four upper retaining bolts finger–tight. The front two bolts may also secure an engine lifting bracket.

17. Install the four lower bolts and, using the appropriate sequence, tighten all of the bolts to the following specifications:

- 1984–85: 12–15 ft. lbs.
- 1986: 14–21 ft. lbs.
- 1987–1988: 15–22 ft. lbs.

18. Install the fuel supply manifold and injectors with two retaining bolts, and tighten to 12–15 ft. lbs.

19. Connect the four electrical connectors to the injectors.

20. Remove and discard the gasket between the lower and upper manifold assemblies. Clean and inspect the mating surfaces. If scraping is necessary, be careful not to damage either gasket surface, or to allow material to fall into the lower manifold. Install a new gasket on the lower manifold assembly.

21. Install the upper intake manifold on the lower intake manifold. On 1984 engines, tighten the six attaching bolts, beginning with the two center ones, to 15–22 ft. lbs. On 1985–88 engines, tighten the four attaching bolts in a criss–cross pattern to 15–22 ft. lbs.

22. Connect the EGR tube to the EGR valve.

23. Connect the PCV system hose to the fitting on the underside of the upper intake manifold.

24. Connect the upper intake manifold vacuum fitting connections.

25. Install the accelerator cable and bracket assembly. Install the throttle linkage and speed control, if applicable.

26. Fasten electrical connectors at the throttle position sensor, air bypass valve, knock sensor and EGR valve.

27. Install the air intake hose and crankcase vent hose.

28. Fill the cooling system.

29. Connect the negative battery cable.

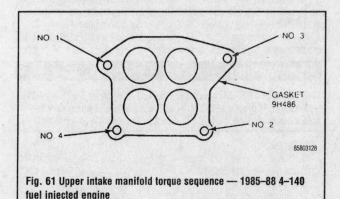

Fig. 61 Upper intake manifold torque sequence — 1985–88 4–140 fuel injected engine

6–200 Engine

On 6–cylinder inline engines, the intake manifold is integral with the cylinder head and cannot be removed.

V6 and 1979–85 V8 Engines

▶ See Figures 62, 63 and 64

➡The following procedure applies only to carburetor–equipped and CFI versions of the V6 and V8 engines. Electronically fuel injected models (EFI and SEFI) utilize a two–piece intake manifold which requires different removal and installation procedures.

1. Disconnect the negative battery cable and drain the cooling system.

❊❊❊ CAUTION

When draining the coolant, keep in mind that cats and dogs are attracted by the ethylene glycol antifreeze, and are quite likely to drink any that is left in an uncovered container or in puddles on the ground. This will prove fatal in sufficient quantity. Always drain the coolant into a sealable container. Coolant should be reused unless it is contaminated or several years old.

2. Remove the air cleaner assembly.

3. Disconnect the upper radiator hose and water pump bypass hose from the thermostat housing and/or intake manifold. Disconnect the temperature sending unit wire connector. Remove the heater hose from the choke housing bracket and disconnect the hose from the intake manifold.

4. Disconnect the automatic choke heat chamber air inlet tube and electric wiring connector from the carburetor. Remove the crankcase ventilation hose, vacuum hoses and EGR hose and coolant lines (if equipped). Label the various hoses and wiring for installation identification.

5. Disconnect the Thermactor air supply hose at the check valve. Loosen the hose clamp at the check valve bracket and remove the air bypass valve from the bracket and position to one side.

❈ CAUTION

On CFI (fuel injected) engines, system pressure must be released before disconnecting the fuel lines. See Section 5 for pressure release and fuel line procedures.

6. Remove all carburetor and automatic transmission linkage attached to the carburetor or intake manifold. Remove the speed control servo and bracket, if equipped. Disconnect the fuel line and any remaining vacuum hoses or wiring from the carburetor, CFI unit, solenoids, sensors, or intake manifold.

7. On V8 engines, disconnect the distributor vacuum hose(s) from the distributor. Remove the distributor cap and mark the relative position of the rotor on the distributor housing. Disconnect the spark plug wires at the spark plugs and the wiring connector at the distributor. Remove the distributor hold-down bolt and remove the distributor. (See Distributor Removal and Installation).

➥Distributor removal is not necessary on 6–232 engines.

8. If your car is equipped with air conditioning and the compressor or mounting brackets interfere with manifold removal, remove the brackets and compressor and position them out of the way. Do not disconnect any compressor lines.

9. Remove the intake manifold mounting bolts. Lift off the intake manifold and carburetor, or CFI unit, as an assembly.

❈ WARNING

The manifold on 6–232 engines is sealed at each end with an RTV type sealer. If prying at the front of the manifold is necessary to break the seal, take care not to damage the machined surfaces.

To install:

10. Clean all gasket mounting surfaces. 6–232 engines have an aluminum intake manifold and cylinder heads; exercise care when cleaning the old gasket material or RTV sealant from the machined surfaces.

11. End seals are not used on V6 engines. Apply a ⅛ in. (3mm) bead of RTV sealant at each end of the engine where the intake manifold seats. Install the intake gaskets and the manifold.

12. On V8 engines, make sure the intake gaskets interlock with the end seals. Use silicone rubber sealer (RTV) on the end seals.

13. After installing the intake manifold, run a finger along the manifold ends to spread the RTV sealer and to make sure the end seals have not slipped out of place.

14. Torque the manifold mounting bolts to the required specifications in the proper sequence (see illustration). Recheck the torque after the engine has reached normal operating temperature.

15. Install the air conditioning compressor and mounting brackets, if they were moved.

16. On V8 engines, connect the distributor vacuum hose(s) to the distributor.

17. Install the distributor cap and distributor. (See Distributor Removal and Installation).

18. Connect the spark plug wires at the spark plugs and the wiring connectors at the distributor.

19. Install all carburetor and automatic transmission linkage attached to the carburetor or intake manifold.

20. Install the speed control servo and bracket, if equipped.

21. Connect the fuel line and any remaining vacuum hoses or wiring at the carburetor, CFI unit, solenoids, sensors, or intake manifold.

22. Connect the Thermactor air supply hose at the check valve.

23. Install the air bypass valve on its bracket.

24. Connect the automatic choke heat chamber air inlet tube and electric wiring connector at the carburetor.

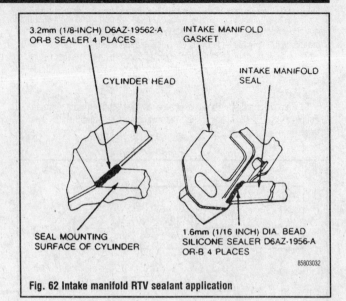

Fig. 62 Intake manifold RTV sealant application

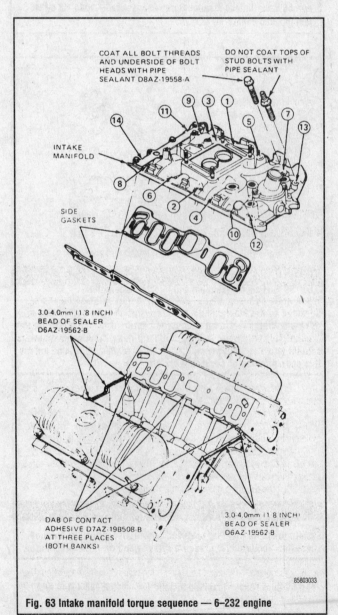

Fig. 63 Intake manifold torque sequence — 6–232 engine

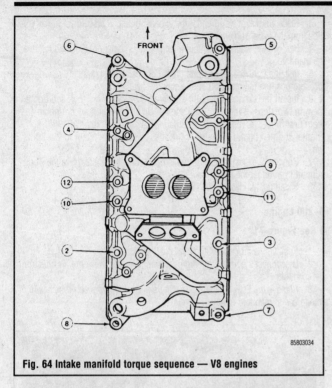

Fig. 64 Intake manifold torque sequence — V8 engines

25. Install the crankcase ventilation hose, vacuum hoses and EGR hose and coolant lines (if equipped).

26. Connect the upper radiator hose and water pump bypass hose at the thermostat housing and/or intake manifold.

27. Connect the temperature sending unit wire connector.

28. Install the heater hose on the choke housing bracket and connect the hose at the intake manifold.

29. Fill the cooling system and connect the negative battery cable.

30. Install the air cleaner assembly.

1986–88 8–302 Engine

▶ See Figures 62, 65 and 66

1. Disconnect the negative battery cable and drain the cooling system.

⁑ CAUTION

When draining the coolant, keep in mind that cats and dogs are attracted by the ethylene glycol antifreeze, and are quite likely to drink any that is left in an uncovered container or in puddles on the ground. This will prove fatal in sufficient quantity. Always drain the coolant into a sealable container. Coolant should be reused unless it is contaminated or several years old.

2. Remove the crankcase ventilation and evaporative purge hoses. Disconnect the air intake duct assembly and the automatic choke heat tube.

3. Disconnect the accelerator cable, speed control linkage and transmission TV cable, if so equipped, from the throttle body. Remove the accelerator cable bracket and disconnect the vacuum lines at the intake manifold fitting.

4. Disconnect the spark plug wires at the plugs. Remove the wires and bracket assembly from the valve cover stud, then remove the distributor cap, adapter and spark plug wire assembly.

5. Disconnect and cap the fuel supply and return lines.

⁑ CAUTION

System pressure must be released before disconnecting the fuel lines. See Section 5 for pressure release and fuel line procedures.

6. Disconnect the vacuum hoses from the distributor, if so equipped. Disconnect the distributor wiring connector. Remove the distributor hold–down bolt and remove the distributor.

7. Disconnect the upper radiator hose from the coolant outlet housing, and the water temperature sending unit wire at the sending unit. Disconnect the hose from the intake manifold. Disconnect the two throttle body cooler hoses.

8. Loosen the clamp on the water pump bypass hose at the coolant outlet housing and slide the hose off the outlet housing. Disconnect wires at the ECT, ACT, TP, ISC solenoid and EGR sensors. Disconnect the fuel injector wire connections and, on SEFI systems, the fuel charging assembly wiring.

9. Disconnect the crankcase vent hose assembly at the rear of the lower intake manifold. Disconnect the fuel evaporative purge tube, if so equipped.

10. Remove the upper intake manifold mounting bolts and the upper intake manifold. It may be necessary to pry the intake manifold away from the cylinder heads. Use caution to avoid possible damage to the gasket sealing surfaces. Remove the intake manifold gaskets and seals.

11. Remove the lower intake manifold mounting bolts and stud nuts, and remove the manifold.

To install:

12. Clean the mating surfaces of the intake manifold, cylinder heads and cylinder block. Apply RTV sealer where the intake manifold meets the cylinder heads, as in the illustration. Position new seals on the cylinder block and new gaskets on the cylinder heads. Interlock the gaskets with the seal tabs and be sure that the gasket holes are aligned with the cylinder head holes.

13. Using guide pins to ease installation, lower the intake manifold into position on the cylinder block and cylinder heads After the intake manifold is in place, run a finger around the seal area to ensure that the seals are in place. If the seals are not in place, remove the intake manifold and reposition the seals.

14. Check that the holes in the manifold gaskets and manifold are in alignment, and remove the guide pins. Install the lower intake manifold attaching bolts and nuts, and tighten them in sequence to 23–25 ft. lbs.

15. Install the water pump bypass hose and hose clamp on the coolant outlet housing. Install the hoses to the heater tubes and tighten the clamps.

16. Connect the upper radiator hose to the coolant outlet housing, and the heater hose to the intake manifold.

17. Install the distributor cap and distributor. (See Distributor Removal and Installation).

18. Position the spark plug wires in the harness brackets on the valve cover attaching stud, and connect the wires to the spark plugs.

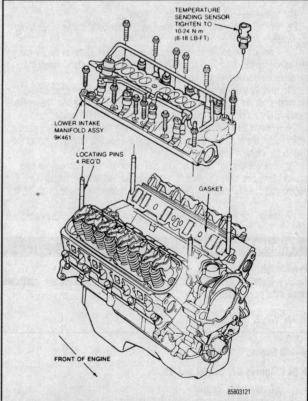

Fig. 65 Lower intake manifold assembly — V8 engine with electronic fuel injection

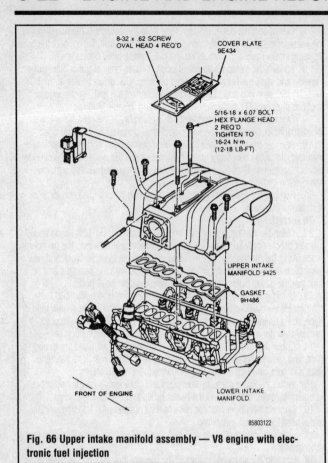

Fig. 66 Upper intake manifold assembly — V8 engine with electronic fuel injection

19. Install the upper intake manifold and tighten its attaching bolts to 12–18 ft. lbs.

20. Install the EGR spacer and throttle body.

21. Connect the crankcase vent hose and the fuel evaporative purge tube, if applicable.

22. Connect the accelerator cable and cable bracket. Connect the TV cable and speed control linkage, if so equipped, to the throttle body. Connect the transmission vacuum line, if so equipped.

23. Restore any electrical connections which were disconnected during removal. Connect any vacuum lines which were disconnected from the intake manifold during removal. Connect coolant hoses to the EGR spacer.

24. Fill and bleed the cooling system. Connect the negative battery cable.

25. Start the engine and check and adjust the ignition timing. Connect the distributor vacuum hoses, if so equipped.

26. Operate the engine at fast idle and check all hose connections and gaskets for leaks. When engine temperatures have stabilized, adjust the engine idle speed. Retighten the intake manifold attaching bolts to 23–25 ft. lbs.

27. Install the automatic choke heat tube and the air intake duct assembly.

Exhaust Manifold

➡️Although, in most cases, the engine is not equipped with factory–installed exhaust manifold gasket(s), such gaskets are available from auto parts stores.

REMOVAL & INSTALLATION

4–140 Engine

▶ See Figures 67, 68, 69 and 70

1. Remove the air cleaner.

2. Remove the heat shroud from the exhaust manifold. On turbocharged models, remove the turbocharger.

3. Place a block of wood under the exhaust pipe and disconnect the exhaust pipe from the exhaust manifold.

4. Remove the exhaust manifold attaching nuts, bolts or studs and remove the manifold.

5. Install a light coat of graphite grease on the exhaust manifold mating surface and position the manifold on the cylinder head.

6. Install the exhaust manifold attaching nuts, bolts or studs and tighten them in two steps in the sequence shown. On 1979–86 engines, tighten them first to 5–7 ft. lbs., then tighten again to 16–23 ft. lbs. On 1987–88 engines, tighten them first to 15–17 ft. lbs., then tighten again to 20–30 ft. lbs.

7. Connect the exhaust pipe to the exhaust manifold and remove the wood support from under the pipe.

8. Install the air cleaner.

6–200 Engine

▶ See Figure 71

1. Remove the air cleaner and heat duct body.

2. Disconnect the muffler inlet pipe and remove the choke hot air tube from the manifold.

3. Remove the EGR tube and any other emission components which will interfere with manifold removal.

Fig. 67 Remove the exhaust manifold attaching bolts with a socket wrench

Fig. 68 After removing the fasteners, pull the exhaust manifold from the cylinder head

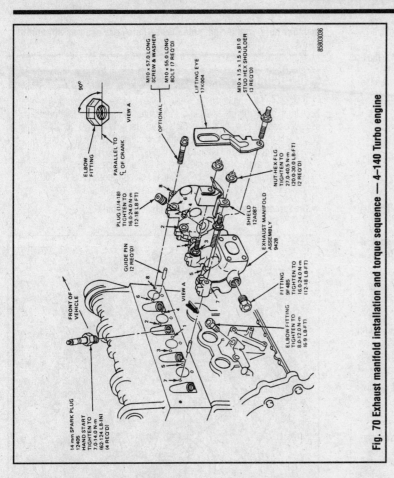

85803036

Fig. 70 Exhaust manifold installation and torque sequence — 4-140 Turbo engine

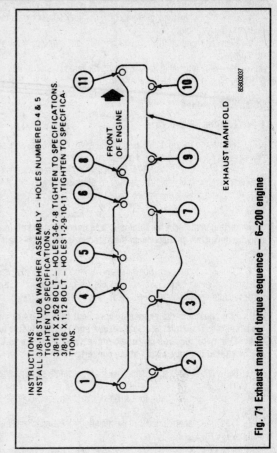

85803037

INSTRUCTIONS:
INSTALL 3/8-16 STUD & WASHER ASSEMBLY – HOLES NUMBERED 4 & 5
TIGHTEN TO SPECIFICATIONS.
3/8-16 X 2.62 BOLT – HOLES 3-6-7-8 TIGHTEN TO SPECIFICATIONS.
3/8-16 X 1.12 BOLT – HOLES 1-2-9-10-11 TIGHTEN TO SPECIFICA-
TIONS.

Fig. 71 Exhaust manifold torque sequence — 6-200 engine

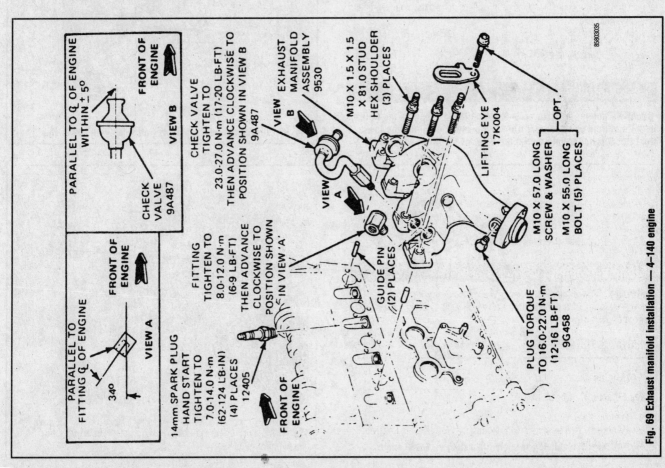

85803035

Fig. 69 Exhaust manifold installation — 4-140 engine

4. Bend the exhaust manifold attaching bolt lock tabs back, remove the bolts and the manifold.

5. Clean all manifold mating surfaces and place a new gasket on the muffler inlet pipe.

6. Re–install the manifold by reversing the removal procedure. Torque the attaching bolts in the sequence shown to 18–24 ft. lbs.

V6 and V8 Engines

▶ **See Figures 72 and 73**

1. If removing the right side exhaust manifold, remove the air cleaner and related parts and the heat stove, if so equipped.

2. On 6–232, 8–255, and 8–302, dipstick and tube removal may be required. Remove any speed control brackets that interfere.

3. Disconnect the exhaust manifold(s) from the muffler (or converter) inlet pipe(s).

➡ **On certain vehicles with automatic transmission and column shift, it may be necessary to disconnect the selector lever cross–shaft for clearance.**

4. Disconnect the spark plug wires and remove the spark plugs and heat shields. Disconnect the EGR sensor (models so equipped), and heat control valve vacuum line (models so equipped).

➡ **On some engines, the spark plug wire heat shields are removed with the manifold. Transmission dipstick tube and Thermactor air tube removal may be required on certain models. Air tube removal is possible by cutting the tube clamp at the converter.**

5. Remove the exhaust manifold attaching bolts and washers, and remove the manifold(s).

6. Inspect the manifold(s) for damaged gasket surfaces, cracks, or other defects.

7. Clean the mating surfaces of the manifold(s), cylinder head and muffler inlet pipe(s).

8. Install the manifold(s) in reverse order of removal. Starting with the centermost bolt and working outward in both directions, torque the mounting bolts to the following values:
- 6–170 — 20–30 ft. lbs.
- 6–232 — 15–22 ft. lbs.
- 8–255 — 18–24 ft. lbs.
- 8–302 — 18–24 ft. lbs.

❋❋ WARNING

Slight warpage may occur on 6–232 manifolds. Elongate the holes in the manifold as necessary. Do not, however, elongate the lower front No. 5 cylinder hole on the left side, or the lower rear No. 2 cylinder hole on the right side. These holes are used as alignment pilots.

Turbocharger

Various 4–140 engines have been modified to accept an exhaust driven turbocharger, providing increases in both horsepower and torque over normally aspirated engines. As an on–demand system, the turbocharger boosts engine output at high load/high speed conditions, while having little effect on fuel economy at moderate to light load conditions.

The turbocharger, which is mounted on the right side of the engine, consists of five major components. These include the compressor, the center housing, the outlet elbow and wastegate, the turbine and the wastegate actuator.

➡ **The turbocharger is serviced by replacement only.**

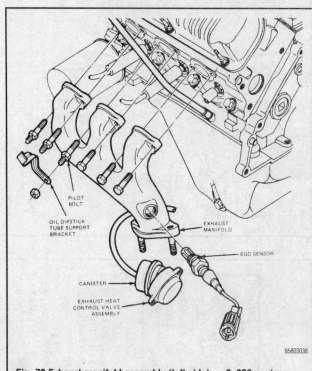

Fig. 72 Exhaust manifold assembly (left side) — 6–232 engine

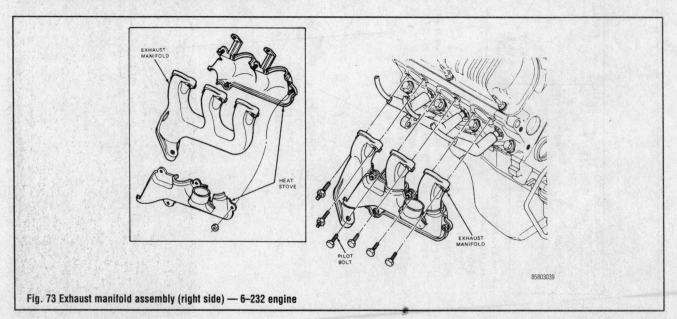

Fig. 73 Exhaust manifold assembly (right side) — 6–232 engine

REMOVAL & INSTALLATION

▶ **See Figures 74 and 75**

➡Before starting removal/service procedures, clean the area around the turbocharger with a non–caustic solution. Cover the openings of component connections to prevent the entry of dirt and foreign materials. Exercise care when handling the turbocharger so as not to nick, bend or in any way damage the compressor wheel blades.

1. Disconnect the negative battery cable.
2. Drain the cooling system.

✳✳ CAUTION

When draining the coolant, keep in mind that cats and dogs are attracted by the ethylene glycol antifreeze, and are quite likely to drink any that is left in an uncovered container or in puddles on the ground. This will prove fatal in sufficient quantity. Always drain the coolant into a sealable container. Coolant should be reused unless it is contaminated or several years old.

3. Loosen the upper clamp on the turbocharger inlet hose. Remove the two bolts mounting the throttle body discharge tube to the turbocharger.
4. Label for identification and location all vacuum hoses and tubes to the turbo and disconnect them.
5. Disconnect the PCV tube from the turbo air inlet elbow. Remove the throttle busy discharge tube and hose as an assembly.
6. Disconnect the ground wire from the air inlet elbow. Remove (disconnect) the water outlet connection (and fitting, if a new turbo unit is to be installed) from the turbo center housing.
7. Remove the turbo oil supply feed line. Disconnect the oxygen sensor connector at the turbocharger.

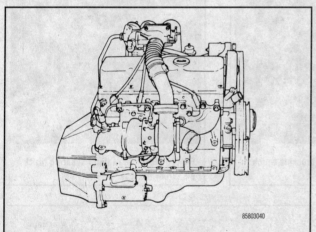

Fig. 74 Turbocharger installation — 4–140 engine

8. Raise and support the front of the vehicle on jackstands. Disconnect the exhaust pipe from the turbocharger.
9. Disconnect the oil return line from the bottom of the turbocharger. Take care not to damage or kink the line.
10. Disconnect the water inlet tube at the turbo center housing.
11. Remove the lower turbo mounting bracket–to–engine bolt. Lower the vehicle from the jackstands.
12. Remove the lower front mounting nut. Remove the three remaining mounting nuts while simultaneously sliding the turbocharger away from its mounting studs.

To install:

13. Position a new turbocharger mounting gasket in position with the bead side facing outward. Install the turbocharger in position over the four mounting studs.
14. Position the lower mounting bracket over the two bottom studs. Start the two lower, then the two upper retaining nuts. Do not tighten them completely at this time, to allow for slight turbo movement.
15. Raise and support the front of the vehicle on jackstands.
16. Connect the water inlet tube assembly.
17. Install a new oil return line gasket and connect the return line to the turbocharger. Tighten the mounting bolts to 14–21 ft. lbs.
18. Connect the exhaust pipe to the turbocharger and tighten the retaining nuts to 25–35 ft. lbs.
19. Lower the vehicle. Using four new nuts, tighten the turbocharger–to–exhaust manifold mounting nuts to 28–40 ft. lbs.
20. Connect the water outlet assembly to the turbocharger, tighten the fasteners to 11–14 ft. lbs. Hold the fitting with a wrench when tightening the line.
21. Install the air inlet tube to the turbo inlet elbow and tighten the bolts to 15–22 ft. lbs. Tighten the hose clamp to 15–22 inch lbs. .
22. Connect the PCV tube and all vacuum lines.
23. Connect the oxygen sensor and other wiring which was disconnected.
24. Install the oil supply line and the air intake tube.
25. Fill the cooling system and connect the negative battery cable.
26. Start the engine and check for coolant leaks. Check vehicle operation.

✳✳ WARNING

When installing the turbocharger, or after an oil and filter change, disconnect the distributor feed harness and crank the engine with the starter motor until the oil pressure light on the dash goes out. Oil pressure must be up before starting the engine.

Radiator

REMOVAL & INSTALLATION

▶ **See Figures 76, 77, 78 and 79**

1. Drain the cooling system.

✳✳ CAUTION

When draining the coolant, keep in mind that cats and dogs are attracted by the ethylene glycol antifreeze, and are quite likely to

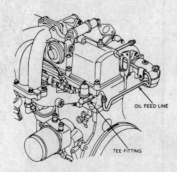

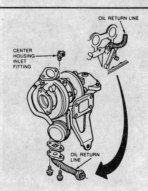

Fig. 75 Turbo oil supply and return lines — 4–140 engine

drink any that is left in an uncovered container or in puddles on the ground. This will prove fatal in sufficient quantity. Always drain the coolant into a sealable container. Coolant should be reused unless it is contaminated or several years old.

2. Disconnect the upper, lower and overflow hoses at the radiator.

3. On automatic transmission equipped cars, disconnect the transmission fluid (or "oil") cooler lines at the radiator.

4. Depending on the model, remove the two top mounting bolts and remove the radiator and shroud assembly, or remove the shroud mounting bolts and position the shroud out of the way, or remove the side mounting bolts. If the air conditioner condenser is attached to the radiator, remove the retaining bolts and position the condenser out of the way. Do not disconnect the refrigerant lines.

5. Remove the radiator attaching bolts or top brackets and lift out the radiator.

6. If a new radiator is to be installed, transfer the petcock (draincock) from the old radiator to the new one. On cars equipped with automatic transmissions, transfer the fluid cooler line fittings from the old radiator.

7. Position the radiator and install, but do not tighten, the radiator support bolts. On cars equipped with automatic transmissions, connect the fluid cooler lines. Then, tighten the radiator support bolts or shroud and mounting bolts.

8. Connect the radiator hoses. Close the radiator petcock. Fill and bleed the cooling system.

9. Start the engine and bring it to operating temperature. Check for leaks.

10. On cars equipped with automatic transmissions, check the cooler lines for leaks and interference. Check the transmission fluid level.

Engine Fan and Fan Drive Clutch

REMOVAL & INSTALLATION

♦ **See Figure 80**

1. Remove the fan shroud attaching screws.

2. Loosen the fan belt(s). Remove bolts and washers attaching the fan drive clutch to the water pump hub. Remove the fan drive clutch and fan as an assembly, along with the shroud.

3. Remove the attaching bolts and washers to separate the fan assembly from the fan drive clutch.

To install:

4. Position the fan assembly on the drive clutch. Install the bolts and washers and tighten to 12–18 ft. lbs.

5. Position the fan drive clutch, fan assembly and fan shroud, and fasten to the water pump hub. Install and tighten the clutch attaching bolts to 12–18 ft. lbs. for 1979–83 engines, or to 15–22 ft. lbs. for 1984–88 engines.

6. Install the fan belt(s) and adjust to the proper tension.

7. Install the fan shroud and adjust for equal fan–to–shroud clearance. Install and tighten the fan shroud screws.

Electro–Drive Cooling Fan

Various models, are equipped with a bracket–mounted electric cooling fan that replaces the conventional water pump mounted fan.

Operation of the fan motor is dependent on engine coolant temperature and air conditioner compressor clutch engagement. The fan will run only when the

85803164

Fig. 76 Disconnect the overflow hose leading to the coolant recovery system reservoir, if so equipped

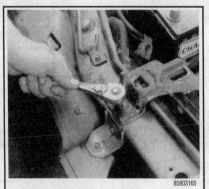

85803165

Fig. 77 Unfasten the top brackets which secure the radiator

85803166

Fig. 78 Move the radiator securing brackets out of the way

85803167

Fig. 79 Lift the radiator from the vehicle

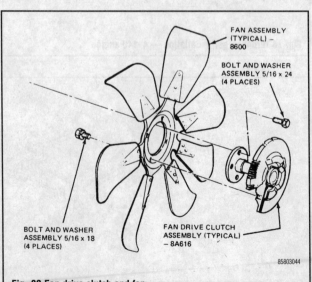

FAN ASSEMBLY (TYPICAL) – 8600

BOLT AND WASHER ASSEMBLY 5/16 x 24 (4 PLACES)

BOLT AND WASHER ASSEMBLY 5/16 x 18 (4 PLACES)

FAN DRIVE CLUTCH ASSEMBLY (TYPICAL) – 8A616

85803044

Fig. 80 Fan drive clutch and fan

coolant temperature is approximately 221°F or higher, or when the compressor clutch is engaged. The fan, motor and mount can be removed as an assembly after disconnecting the wiring harnesses and mounting bolts.

✳✳ CAUTION

The cooling fan is automatic and may come on at any time without warning even if the ignition is switched Off. To avoid possible injury, always disconnect the negative battery cable when working near the electric cooling fan.

TESTING

1. Disconnect the wiring harness at the fan motor connector.
2. Connect a jumper wire between the negative motor lead and a good ground.
3. Connect another jumper wire between the positive motor lead and the positive battery terminal.
4. If the cooling fan motor does not operate, it must be replaced.

REMOVAL & INSTALLATION

▶ **See Figures 81, 82, 83 and 84**

1. Disconnect the negative battery cable.
2. Remove the fan wiring harness from the clip.
3. Unplug the harness at the fan motor connector.

4. Remove the 4 mounting bracket attaching bolts and remove the fan and shroud assembly from the car.
5. Remove the retaining clip from the end of the motor shaft and remove the fan.
6. Remove the nuts attaching the fan motor to the mounting bracket.
7. Installation is the reverse of removal.

Water Pump

REMOVAL & INSTALLATION

▶ **See Figures 85 thru 94**

1. Drain the cooling system.

✳✳ CAUTION

When draining the coolant, keep in mind that cats and dogs are attracted by the ethylene glycol antifreeze, and are quite likely to drink any that is left in an uncovered container or in puddles on the ground. This will prove fatal in sufficient quantity. Always drain the coolant into a sealable container. Coolant should be reused unless it is contaminated or several years old.

2. Disconnect the negative battery cable.
3. On cars with power steering, remove the drive belt.

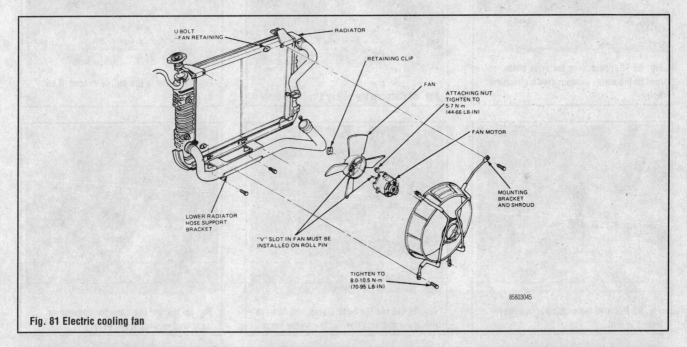

Fig. 81 Electric cooling fan

Fig. 82 Unplug the electrical connector from the fan motor

Fig. 83 Remove the 4 attaching bolts which secure the fan and shroud assembly

Fig. 84 Lift the fan and shroud assembly from the vehicle

4. If the vehicle is equipped with air conditioning, remove the idler pulley bracket and air conditioner drive belt.

5. On engines with a Thermactor air pump, remove the belt.

6. Disconnect the lower radiator hose and heater hose from the water pump.

7. On cars equipped with a belt–driven fan shroud, remove the retaining screws and position the shroud rearward.

8. Remove the fan, fan clutch and spacer from the engine. If the car is equipped with an electric motor driven fan, remove the fan as an assembly for working clearance, if necessary.

9. Remove the pulley attaching bolts, spacer (if so equipped) and pulley from the water pump hub.

10. On the 4–140 engine, remove the cam belt outer cover.

11. On cars equipped with a water pump mounted alternator, loosen the alternator mounting bolts, remove the alternator belt and remove the alternator adjusting arm bracket from the water pump. If interference is encountered, remove the air pump pulley and pivot bolts. Remove the air pump adjusting

bracket. Swing the upper bracket aside. Detach the air conditioner compressor and lay it aside. Do not disconnect any of the A/C lines. Remove any accessory mounting brackets from the water pump.

12. Loosen the bypass hose at the water pump, if so equipped.

13. Remove the water pump retaining bolts and remove the pump from the engine.

To install:

14. Clean any gasket material from the pump mounting surface. On engines equipped with a water pump backing plate, remove the plate, clean the gasket surfaces, install a new gasket and plate on the water pump.

15. Remove the heater hose fitting from the old water pump and install it on the new pump.

16. Coat both sides of the new gasket with a water–resistant sealer. Install the water pump and torque to the proper specifications.

17. Install other parts in the reverse order of removal.

18. Fill the cooling system and connect the negative battery cable.

19. Start the engine and check for leaks.

Fig. 85 After removing the drive belts, loosen the water pump pulley's attaching bolts

Fig. 86 Remove the pulley attaching bolts

Fig. 87 Remove the pulley spacer, if so equipped

Fig. 88 Remove the water pump pulley from the hub

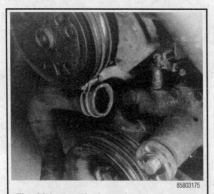

Fig. 89 Loosen the hose clamp and remove the lower radiator hose at the water pump

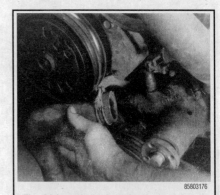

Fig. 90 Inspect the hose for damage or wear and replace if necessary

Fig. 91 Loosen and remove the water pump retaining bolts

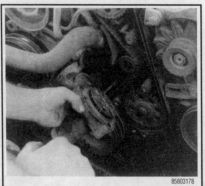

Fig. 92 Pull the water pump from the cylinder block

Fig. 93 Remove the water pump from the vehicle

Cylinder Head

REMOVAL & INSTALLATION

➡ On cars with air conditioning, remove the mounting bolts and the drive belt, and position the compressor out of the way. Remove the compressor upper mounting bracket from the cylinder head.

✳✳ CAUTION

If the compressor refrigerant lines do not have enough slack to permit repositioning of the compressor without first disconnecting the refrigerant lines, the air conditioning system will have to be discharged and evacuated. See Section 1 for details. Under no circumstances should an untrained person attempt to disconnect the air conditioning refrigerant lines.

4–140 Engine

▶ See Figures 95 thru 100

➡ Set the engine at TDC position for No. 1 piston, if possible, prior to head removal.

1. Drain the cooling system.

✳✳ CAUTION

When draining the coolant, keep in mind that cats and dogs are attracted by the ethylene glycol antifreeze, and are quite likely to drink any that is left in an uncovered container or in puddles on the ground. This will prove fatal in sufficient quantity. Always drain the coolant into a sealable container. Coolant should be reused unless it is contaminated or several years old.

2. Remove the air cleaner assembly from carburetor–equipped engines. Disconnect the negative battery cable.

3. Remove the valve cover. Note the location of the valve cover attaching screws that have rubber grommets.

4. Remove the intake and exhaust manifolds from the head. See the procedures for intake manifold, exhaust manifold and, if applicable, turbocharger removal.

5. Remove the camshaft drive belt cover. Note the location of the belt cover attaching screws that have rubber grommets.

6. Loosen the drive belt tensioner and remove the belt.

7. Remove the water outlet elbow from the cylinder head with the hose attached.

8. Remove the cylinder head attaching bolts.

9. Remove the cylinder head from the engine.

10. Clean all gasket material and carbon from the top of the cylinder block and pistons and from the bottom of the cylinder head.

11. Position a new cylinder head gasket on the engine. Rotate the camshaft so that the head locating pin is at the five o'clock position to avoid damage to the valves and pistons.

➡ If you encounter difficulty in positioning the cylinder head on the engine block, it may be necessary to install guide studs in the block to correctly align the head and the block. To fabricate guide studs, obtain two new cylinder head bolts and cut their heads off with a hacksaw. Install the bolts in the holes in the engine block which correspond with cylinder head bolt holes Nos. 3 and 4, as identified in the cylinder head bolt tightening sequence illustration. Then, install the head gasket and cylinder head over the bolts. Install the cylinder head attaching bolts, replacing the studs with the original head bolts.

12. Using a torque wrench, tighten the cylinder head bolts in two steps in the sequence shown in the illustration. First tighten them to 50–60 ft. lbs., then tighten them to 80–90 ft. lbs.

13. Install the camshaft drive belt. See Camshaft Drive Belt Installation.

14. Install the camshaft drive belt cover and its attaching bolts. Make sure the rubber grommets are installed on the bolts. Tighten the bolts to 6–13 ft. lbs.

Fig. 94 Clean any old gasket material from the water pump's mating surface. If the pump is to be reused, also clean any old gasket material from the pump.

Fig. 95 Remove the cylinder head attaching bolts

Fig. 96 Using a suitable prybar, break the seal between the cylinder head and the block. DO NOT pry on the gasket surfaces! Pry only against the casting faces

Fig. 97 Remove the cylinder head

Fig. 98 Use a gasket scraper to remove old gasket material and carbon

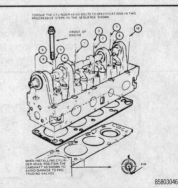

Fig. 99 Cylinder head installation and torque sequence—4–140 engine

Fig. 100 Tighten the cylinder head attaching bolts with a torque wrench

15. Install the water outlet elbow and a new gasket on the engine and tighten the attaching bolts to 12–15 ft. lbs.

16. Install the intake and exhaust manifolds. See the procedures for intake and exhaust manifold installation.

17. Install the valve cover and, if removed, the air cleaner assembly.

18. Connect the negative battery cable and fill the cooling system.

6–170 Engine

▶ See Figure 101

1. Remove the air cleaner assembly and disconnect the battery and accelerator linkage. Drain the cooling system.

✳✴ CAUTION

When draining the coolant, keep in mind that cats and dogs are attracted by the ethylene glycol antifreeze, and are quite likely to drink any that is left in an uncovered container or in puddles on the ground. This will prove fatal in sufficient quantity. Always drain the coolant into a sealable container. Coolant should be reused unless it is contaminated or several years old.

2. Remove the distributor cap with the spark plug wires attached. Remove the distributor vacuum line and distributor. Remove the hose from the water pump to the water outlet which is on the carburetor.

3. Remove the valve covers, fuel line and filter, carburetor, and the intake manifold.

4. Remove the rocker arm shaft and oil baffles. Remove the pushrods, keeping them in the proper sequence for installation.

5. Remove the exhaust manifold, referring to the appropriate procedures.

6. Remove the cylinder head retaining bolts and remove the cylinder heads and gaskets.

7. Remove all gasket material and carbon from the engine block and cylinder heads.

8. Place the head gaskets on the engine block.

➡The left and right gaskets are not interchangeable.

9. Install guide studs in the engine block. Install the cylinder head assemblies on the engine block one at a time. Tighten the cylinder head bolts in the proper sequence and in 3 steps as follows:

- Step 1 — 29–40 ft. lbs.
- Step 2 — 40–51 ft. lbs.
- Step 3 — 65–80 ft. lbs.

10. Install the intake and exhaust manifolds.

11. Install the pushrods in the proper sequence. Install the oil baffles and the rocker arm shaft assemblies. Adjust the valve clearances.

12. Install the valve covers with new gaskets.

13. Install the distributor and set the ignition timing.

14. Install the carburetor and the distributor cap with the spark plug wires.

15. Connect the accelerator linkage, fuel line and filter, and distributor vacuum line to the carburetor.

16. Install the air cleaner assembly.

17. Connect the negative battery and fill the cooling system.

6–200 Engine

▶ See Figures 102 and 103

✳✴ CAUTION

When draining the coolant, keep in mind that cats and dogs are attracted by the ethylene glycol antifreeze, and are quite likely to drink any that is left in an uncovered container or in puddles on the ground. This will prove fatal in sufficient quantity. Always drain the coolant into a sealable container. Coolant should be reused unless it is contaminated or several years old.

1. Drain the cooling system, remove the air cleaner assembly and disconnect the negative battery cable.

2. If equipped with air conditioning, remove the mounting bolts and the drive belt, and position the compressor out of the way of the cylinder head. Remove the compressor upper mounting bracket from the cylinder head.

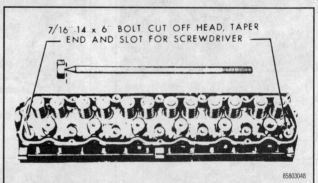

Fig. 102 Cylinder head guide stud fabrication

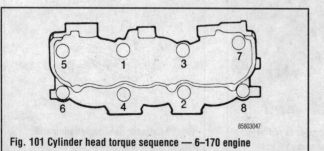

Fig. 101 Cylinder head torque sequence — 6–170 engine

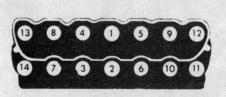

Fig. 103 Cylinder head torque sequence — 6–200 engine

➡️**If the compressor refrigerant lines do not have enough slack to permit repositioning of the compressor without first disconnecting the refrigerant lines, the air conditioning system will have to be discharged and evacuated. See Section 1 for details. Under no circumstances should an untrained person attempt to disconnect the air conditioning refrigerant lines.**

3. Disconnect the exhaust pipe at the manifold end, swing the exhaust pipe down and remove the flange gasket.

4. Disconnect the fuel and vacuum lines from the carburetor. Disconnect the intake manifold line at the intake manifold.

5. Disconnect the accelerator and retracting spring at the carburetor. Disconnect the transmission kickdown linkage, if equipped.

6. Disconnect the carburetor spacer outlet line at the spacer. Disconnect the radiator upper hose and the heater hose at the water outlet elbow. Disconnect the radiator lower hose and the heater hose at the water pump.

7. Disconnect the distributor vacuum control line at the distributor. Disconnect the gas filter line on the inlet side of the filter.

8. Disconnect and label the spark plug wires and remove the plugs. Disconnect the temperature sending unit wire.

9. Remove the rocker arm (valve) cover.

10. Remove the rocker arm shaft attaching bolts and the rocker arm and shaft assembly. Remove the valve pushrods, keeping them in order for installation in their original positions.

11. Remove the remaining cylinder head bolts and lift off the cylinder head. Do not pry under the cylinder head as damage to the mating surfaces can easily occur. To help in installation of the cylinder head, you can use a pair of 6 in. x $7/16$–14 bolts with their heads cut off and the upper portion slightly tapered and slotted (for installation and removal with a screwdriver). These will reduce the possibility of damage during head replacement.

12. Clean the cylinder head and block surfaces. Be sure of flatness and no surface damage.

13. Apply cylinder head gasket sealer to both sides of the new gasket and slide the gasket down over the two guide studs in the cylinder block.

❊❊ WARNING

Apply gasket sealer only to steel shim head gaskets. Steel/asbestos composite head gaskets are to be installed without any sealer.

14. Carefully lower the cylinder head over the guide studs. Place the exhaust pipe flange on the manifold studs, using a new gasket.

15. Coat the threads of the end bolts for the right side of the cylinder head with a small amount of water–resistant sealer. Install, but do not tighten, two head bolts at opposite ends to hold the head gasket in place. Remove the guide studs and install the remaining bolts.

16. Cylinder head torquing should proceed in three steps and in the prescribed order. Tighten them first to 50–55 ft. lbs., then give them a second tightening to 60–65 ft. lbs. The final step is to 70–75 ft. lbs., at which they should remain undisturbed.

17. Lubricate both ends of the pushrods and install them in their original locations.

18. Apply lubricant to the rocker arm pads and the valve stem tips and position the rocker arm shaft assembly on the head. Be sure the oil holes in the shaft are in a down position.

19. Tighten all the rocker shaft retaining bolts to 30–35 ft. lbs., and check that there are no tight valve adjustments.

20. Connect the exhaust pipe.

21. Reconnect the heater and radiator hoses.

22. Position the distributor vacuum line, the carburetor gas line and the intake manifold vacuum line on the engine. Fasten them to their respective connections.

23. Connect the accelerator rod and retracting spring. Connect the choke control cable and adjust the choke. Connect the transmission kickdown linkage.

24. Reconnect the vacuum line at the distributor. Connect the fuel inlet line at the fuel filter and the intake manifold vacuum line at the vacuum pump.

25. Lightly lubricate the spark plug threads and install them. Connect spark plug wires and be sure the wires are all the way down in their sockets. Connect the coolant temperature sending unit wire.

26. If equipped with air conditioning, install the compressor and mounting bracket. Install the drive belt and adjust to proper tension.

27. Connect the negative battery cable.

28. Fill the cooling system. Run the engine to stabilize all engine part temperatures.

29. Adjust engine idle speed and idle fuel air adjustment.

30. Coat one side of a new rocker arm cover gasket with oil–resistant sealer. Lay the treated side of the gasket on the cover and install the cover. Be sure the gasket seals evenly all around the cylinder head.

31. Install the air cleaner assembly.

6–232 Engine

▶ **See Figure 104**

1. Drain the cooling system.

❊❊ CAUTION

When draining the coolant, keep in mind that cats and dogs are attracted by the ethylene glycol antifreeze, and are quite likely to drink any that is left in an uncovered container or in puddles on the ground. This will prove fatal in sufficient quantity. Always drain the coolant into a sealable container. Coolant should be reused unless it is contaminated or several years old.

2. Disconnect the cable from the negative battery terminal.

3. Remove the air cleaner assembly including air intake duct and heat tube.

4. Loosen the accessory drive belt idler pulley and remove the drive belt.

5. If the left cylinder head is being removed:

a. Remove the oil filler cap.

b. If equipped with power steering, remove the pump mounting brackets' attaching bolts, leaving the hoses connected, and place the pump/bracket assembly aside in a position to prevent the fluid from leaking out.

c. If equipped with air conditioning, remove the mounting and support brackets' attaching bolts, leaving the hoses connected, and position the compressor aside.

➡️**If the compressor refrigerant lines do not have enough slack to permit repositioning of the compressor without first disconnecting the refrigerant lines, the air conditioning system will have to be discharged and evacuated. See Section 1 for details. Under no circumstances should an untrained person attempt to disconnect the air conditioning refrigerant lines.**

6. If the right cylinder head is being removed:

a. Disconnect the Thermactor diverter valve and hose assembly at the bypass valve and downstream air tube.

b. Disconnect the Thermactor tube support bracket from the rear of the cylinder head.

c. Remove the accessory drive idler.

d. Remove the alternator.

e. Remove the Thermactor pump pulley and the Thermactor pump.

f. Remove the alternator bracket.

g. Remove the PCV valve.

7. Remove the intake manifold.

8. Remove the rocker arm (valve) cover attaching screws. Loosen the silicone rubber gasket material by inserting a putty knife under the cover flange. Work the cover loosen and remove. The plastic rocker arm covers will break if they are pried excessively.

9. Remove the exhaust manifold(s).

10. Loosen the rocker arm fulcrum attaching bolts enough to allow the rocker arm to be lifted off the pushrod and rotated to one side.

11. Remove the pushrods. Label the pushrods since they should be installed in their original positions during assembly.

12. Remove the cylinder head attaching bolts. Remove the cylinder head(s).

13. Remove and discard the old cylinder head gasket(s). Discard the cylinder head bolts.

To install:

14. Lightly oil all bolt and stud bolt threads before installation, except those specifying special sealant.

15. Clean the cylinder head, intake manifold, valve cover and cylinder head gasket surfaces. If the cylinder head was removed for a cylinder head gasket replacement, check the flatness of the cylinder head and block gasket surfaces.

16. Position new head gasket(s) on the cylinder block using the dowels for alignment.

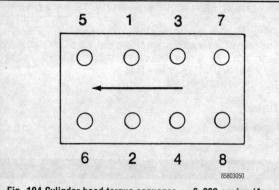

Fig. 104 Cylinder head torque sequence — 6–232 engine (Arrow points to the front)

17. Position the cylinder head(s) to the block.

18. Apply a thin coating of pipe sealant or equivalent to the threads of the short cylinder head bolts (nearest to the exhaust manifold). Do not apply sealant to the long bolts. Lightly oil the cylinder head bolt flat washers. Install the flat washers and cylinder head bolts (eight on each side).

> ✳✳ **WARNING**
>
> **Always use new cylinder head bolts to assure a leak–tight assembly. Torque retention with used bolts can vary, which may result in coolant or compression leakage at the cylinder head mating surface area.**

19. Tighten the attaching bolts in four steps in the sequence shown. Back off the attaching bolts 2–3 turns and repeat the tightening sequence. Be sure to tighten to specifications.

➡ **When the cylinder head attaching bolts have been tightened using the above sequential procedure, it is not necessary to retighten the bolts after extended engine operation. However, the bolts can be checked for tightness if desired.**

20. Dip each pushrod end in heavy engine oil. Install the push rods in their original position. For each valve, rotate the crankshaft until the tappet rests on the heel (base circle) of the camshaft lobe.

21. Position the rocker arms over the pushrods, install the fulcrums, and tighten the fulcrum attaching bolts to 61–132 inch lbs.

> ✳✳ **WARNING**
>
> **Fulcrums must be fully seated in cylinder head and pushrods must be seated in rocker arm sockets prior to final tightening.**

22. Lubricate all rocker arm assemblies with heavy engine oil. Finally tighten the fulcrum bolts to 19–25 ft. lbs. For final tightening, the camshaft may be in any position.

➡ **If the original valve train components are being installed, a valve clearance check is not required. If a component has been replaced, perform a valve clearance check.**

23. Install the exhaust manifold(s).

24. Apply a ⅛–³⁄₁₆ in. (3–4mm) bead of RTV silicone sealant to the valve cover flange, making sure the sealer fills the channel in the flange. The valve cover must be installed within 15 minutes after the silicone sealer application. After this time, the sealer may start to set–up, and its sealing effectiveness may be reduced.

25. Position the cover on the cylinder head and install the attaching bolts. Note the location of the wiring harness routing clips and spark plug wire routing clip stud bolts. Tighten the attaching bolts to 80–106 inch lbs.

26. Install the intake manifold.

27. Install the spark plugs, if necessary.

28. Connect the secondary wires to the spark plugs.

29. Install the oil filler cap. If equipped with air conditioning, install the compressor mounting and support brackets.

30. On the right cylinder head:
   a. Install the PCV valve.
   b. Install the alternator bracket. Tighten the attaching nuts to 30–40 ft. lbs.
   c. Install the Thermactor pump and pump pulley.
   d. Install the alternator.
   e. Install the accessory drive idler.
   f. Install the Thermactor diverter valve and hose assembly. Tighten the clamps securely.

31. Install the accessory drive belt and tighten to the specified tension.

32. Connect the cable to the negative battery terminal.

33. Fill the cooling system with the specified coolant.

> ✳✳ **WARNING**
>
> **This engine has an aluminum cylinder head and requires a compatible coolant formulation to avoid radiator damage.**

34. Start the engine and check for coolant, fuel, and oil leaks.

35. Check and, if necessary, adjust the curb idle speed.

36. Install the air cleaner assembly including the air intake duct and heat tube.

V8 Engines

▶ **See Figure 105**

1. Drain the cooling system.

> ✳✳ **CAUTION**
>
> **When draining the coolant, keep in mind that cats and dogs are attracted by the ethylene glycol antifreeze, and are quite likely to drink any that is left in an uncovered container or in puddles on the ground. This will prove fatal in sufficient quantity. Always drain the coolant into a sealable container. Coolant should be reused unless it is contaminated or several years old.**

2. Remove the air cleaner assembly on vehicles equipped with a carburetor or Central Fuel Injection (CFI).

3. Remove the intake manifold and the carburetor or CFI unit as an assembly. Vehicles equipped with electronic fuel injection (EFI or SEFI) have a two–piece intake manifold, requiring a different procedure. See the appropriate intake manifold removal procedure earlier in this section.

4. Disconnect the spark plug wires, marking them as to location. Position them out of the way of the cylinder head. Remove the spark plugs.

5. Disconnect the exhaust pipes at the manifolds.

6. On cars with air conditioning, remove the mounting bolts and the drive belt, and position the compressor out of the way of the left cylinder

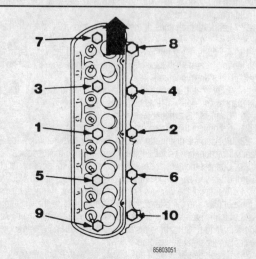

Fig. 105 Cylinder head torque sequence — V8 engines (Arrow points to the front)

head. Remove the compressor upper mounting bracket from the cylinder head.

➡️**If the compressor refrigerant lines do not have enough slack to permit repositioning of the compressor without first disconnecting the refrigerant lines, the air conditioning system will have to be discharged and evacuated. See Section 1 for details. Under no circumstances should an untrained person attempt to disconnect the air conditioning refrigerant lines.**

7. In order to remove the left cylinder head, on cars equipped with power steering, it may be necessary to remove the steering pump and bracket, remove the drive belt, and wire or tie the pump out of the way, in such a way to prevent fluid loss.

a. If the left cylinder head is to be removed on a car equipped with a Thermactor air pump system, disconnect the hose from the air manifold on the left cylinder head.

8. In order to remove the right head, it may be necessary to remove the alternator mounting bracket bolt and spacer, the ignition coil, and the air cleaner inlet duct from the right cylinder head.

a.If the right cylinder head is to be removed on a car equipped with a Thermactor system, remove the Thermactor air pump and its mounting bracket. Disconnect the hose from the air manifold on the right cylinder head.

9. Remove the valve covers.

10. Loosen the rocker arm stud nuts enough to rotate the rocker arms to the side, in order to facilitate the removal of the pushrods. Remove the pushrods in sequence, so that they may be installed in their original positions. Remove the exhaust valve stem caps, if equipped.

11. Remove the cylinder head attaching bolts, noting their positions. If required, remove the exhaust manifolds to gain access to the lower attaching bolts. Lift the cylinder head(s) off the block. Remove and discard the old cylinder head gasket(s). Clean all mounting surfaces.

To install:

12. Position the new cylinder head gasket(s) over the dowels on the block. Position new gaskets on the muffler inlet pipe(s) at the exhaust manifold flanges.

13. Position the cylinder head(s) on the block, and install the head bolts, each in its original position. On engines on which the exhaust manifolds have been removed from the heads to facilitate removal, it is necessary to properly guide the exhaust manifold studs into the muffler inlet pipe flanges when installing the head.

14. Step–torque the cylinder head retaining bolts, in the specified sequence, first to 55–65 ft. lbs., and then to 65–72 ft. lbs. If removed, tighten the exhaust manifold–to–cylinder head attaching bolts to 18–24 ft. lbs.

15. Tighten the nuts on the exhaust manifold studs at the muffler inlet flanges to 18 ft. lbs.

16. Clean and inspect the pushrods one at a time. Clean the oil passage within each pushrod with solvent and blow the passage out with compressed air. Check the ends of the pushrods for nicks, grooves, roughness, or excessive wear. Visually inspect the pushrods for straightness, and replace any bent ones. Do not attempt to straighten pushrods.

17. Install the pushrods in their original positions. Apply Lubriplate® or a similar product to the valve stem tips and to the pushrod guides in the cylinder head. Install the exhaust valve stem caps, if equipped.

18. Apply Lubriplate® or a similar product to the fulcrum seats and sockets. Turn the rocker arms to their proper position and tighten the stud nuts enough to hold the rocker arms in position. Make sure that the lower ends of the pushrods have remained properly seated in the valve lifters. Tighten the stud nuts to 17–23 ft. lbs. in the order given under preliminary valve adjustment, which follows.

19. Install the valve covers. Tighten the attaching bolts to 3–5 ft. lbs. and retorque to the same specification two minutes later.

20. Install all components which were removed in steps 6–8.

21. Install the spark plugs and spark plug wires. Be sure to route the spark plug wires in their original locations.

22. Install the intake manifold and carburetor or CFI unit, where applicable, following the appropriate procedure under Intake Manifold Installation. For vehicles equipped with EFI or SEFI, follow the procedure for replacing the two–piece intake manifold assembly.

23. Install the air cleaner assembly, if removed.

24. Fill the cooling system.

PRELIMINARY VALVE ADJUSTMENT

V6 and V8 Engines Only

▶ **See Figure 106**

This adjustment is actually part of the installation procedure for the individually mounted rocker arms found on the V–type engine, and is necessary to achieve an accurate torque value for each rocker arm nut.

By its nature, an hydraulic valve lifter will expand when it is not under load. Thus, when the rocker arms are removed and the pressure via the pushrod is taken off the lifter, the lifter expands to its maximum length. If the lifter happens to be at the top of the camshaft lobe when the rocker arm is being installed, a large amount of torque would be necessary when tightening the rocker arm nut, just to overcome the pressure of the expanded lifter. This makes it very difficult to get an accurate torque setting with individually mounted rocker arms. For this reason, the rocker arms are installed in a certain sequence which corresponds to the low points of the camshaft lobes.

1. Turn the engine until the No. 1 cylinder is at TDC of the compression stroke and the timing pointer is aligned with the mark on the crankshaft damper.

2. Scribe a mark on the damper at this point.

3. Scribe two additional marks on the damper of a V8; a single line on a V6. (see the illustration).

4. With the timing pointer aligned with Mark 1 on the damper, tighten the following valves to the specified torque:

- 6–232 Engine: No. 1 intake and exhaust; No. 3 intake and exhaust; No. 4 exhaust and No. 6 intake.
- 8–255 and 8–302 Engines (Except HO): Nos. 1, 7 and 8 Intake; Nos. 1, 5, and 4 Exhaust.
- 8–302 HO Engine: Nos. 1, 4 and 8 Intake; Nos. 1, 3 and 7 Exhaust.

5. Rotate the crankshaft 180° to point 2 and tighten the following valves:

- 6–232 Engine: No. 2 intake; No. 3 exhaust; No. 4 intake; No. 5 intake and exhaust; No. 6 exhaust.
- 8–255 and 8–302 Engines (Except HO): Nos. 5 and 4 Intake; Nos. 2 and 6 Exhaust
- 8–302 HO Engine: Nos. 3 and 7 Intake; Nos. 2 and 6 Exhaust

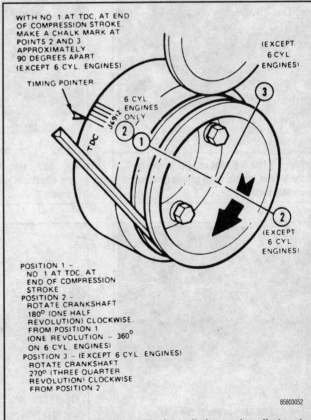

WITH NO 1 AT TDC, AT END OF COMPRESSION STROKE, MAKE A CHALK MARK AT POINTS 2 AND 3 APPROXIMATELY 90 DEGREES APART (EXCEPT 6 CYL ENGINES)

TIMING POINTER

6 CYL ENGINES ONLY

(EXCEPT 6 CYL ENGINES)

TDC

POSITION 1 – NO 1 AT TDC, AT END OF COMPRESSION STROKE
POSITION 2 – ROTATE CRANKSHAFT 180° (ONE HALF REVOLUTION) CLOCKWISE, FROM POSITION 1 (ONE REVOLUTION – 360° ON 6 CYL ENGINES)
POSITION 3 – (EXCEPT 6 CYL ENGINES) ROTATE CRANKSHAFT 270° (THREE QUARTER REVOLUTION) CLOCKWISE, FROM POSITION 2

85803052

Fig. 106 Crankshaft pulley marking for preliminary valve adjustment

6. Rotate the crankshaft 270° to point 3 and tighten the following valves:
- 8–302 Engine(Except HO): Nos. 2, 3, and 6 Intake; Nos. 7, 3 and 8 Exhaust
- 8–302 HO Engine: Nos. 2, 5 and 6 Intake; Nos. 4, 5 and 8 Exhaust

7. Rocker arm tightening specifications are:
- 6–232, 8–255, and 8–302 Engines: Tighten nut until it contacts the rocker shoulder, then torque to 18–25 ft. lbs.

CLEANING AND INSPECTION

▶ **See Figures 107 and 108**

1. Remove the cylinder head(s) from the car engine (see Cylinder Head Removal and Installation). Place the head(s) on a workbench and remove any manifolds that are still connected. Remove all rocker arm retaining parts and the rocker arms, if still installed. On the 4–140, remove the camshaft (see Camshaft Removal).

2. Turn the cylinder head over so that the mounting surface is facing up and support it evenly on wood blocks.

❉❉ WARNING

6–232 engines use aluminum cylinder heads; exercise care when cleaning.

3. Use a scraper and remove all of the gasket material stuck to the head mounting surface. Mount a wire carbon removal brush in an electric drill and clean away the carbon on the valves and head combustion chambers.

❉❉ WARNING

When scraping or decarbonizing the cylinder head, take care not to damage or nick the gasket mounting surface.

4. Number the valve heads with a permanent felt–tip marker for cylinder location.

RESURFACING

▶ **See Figures 109 and 110**

If the cylinder head is warped resurfacing by a machine shop is required. Place a straightedge across the gasket surface of the head. Using feeler gauges, determine the clearance at the center and along the length between the head and straightedge. Measure clearance at the center and along the length between the head and straightedge. Measure clearance at the center and along the lengths of both diagonals. If warpage exceeds 0.003 in. (0.08mm) in a 6 in. (152mm) span, or 0.006 in. (0.15mm) over the total length, the cylinder head must be resurfaced.

Valves

REMOVAL & INSTALLATION

▶ **See Figures 111 and 112**

1. Block the cylinder head on its side, or install a pair of head–holding brackets made especially for valve removal.

2. Using a socket slightly larger than the valve stem and keepers, place the socket over the valve stem and gently hit the socket with a plastic hammer to break loose any varnish buildup.

3. Remove the valve keepers, retainer, spring shield and valve spring using a valve spring compressor (the locking C–clamp type is the easiest kind to use).

4. Put the parts in a separate container numbered for the cylinder being worked on; do not mix them with other parts removed.

5. Remove and discard the valve stem oil seals. A new seal will be used at assembly time.

6. Remove the valves from the cylinder head and place them, in order, through numbered holes punched in a stiff piece of cardboard or wood valve holding stick.

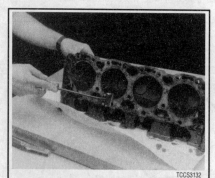

Fig. 107 Use a gasket scraper to remove the bulk of the old head gasket from the mating surface

Fig. 108 An electric drill equipped with a wire wheel will expedite complete gasket removal

Fig. 109 Check the cylinder head for warpage along the center using a straight-edge and a feeler gauge

Fig. 110 Be sure to check for warpage across the cylinder head at both diagonals

Fig. 111 Using a valve spring compressor tool to relieve spring tension from the valve caps

Fig. 112 Invert the cylinder head and with-draw the valve from the cylinder head bore

➡️The exhaust valve stems, on some engines, are equipped with small metal caps. Take care not to lose the caps. Make sure to install them at assembly time. Replace any caps that are worn.

7. Use an electric drill and rotary wire brush to clean the intake and exhaust valve ports, combustion chamber and valve seats. In some cases, the carbon will need to be chipped away. Use a blunt pointed drift for carbon chipping. Be careful around the valve seat areas.

8. Use a wire valve guide cleaning brush and safe solvent to clean the valve guides.

9. Clean the valves with a revolving wire brush. Heavy carbon deposits may be removed with the blunt drift.

➡️When using a wire brush to clean carbon on the valve ports, valves etc., be sure that the deposits are actually removed, rather than burnished.

10. Wash and clean all valve springs, keepers, retaining caps etc., in a safe solvent.

11. Clean the cylinder head with a brush and some safe solvent, and wipe dry.

12. Inspect the cylinder head, valves, valve guides, and valve seats for wear, and have them refaced or replaced as necessary.

13. Install the valves in the cylinder head, along with the metal caps, if equipped.

14. Install new valve stem oil seals.

15. Install the valve keepers, retainer, spring shield and valve spring using a valve spring compressor (the locking C–clamp type is the easiest kind to use).

16. Check the valve spring installed height, and shim or replace as necessary.

INSPECTION

▶ See Figures 113, 114 and 115

1. Check the cylinder head for cracks. Cracks in the cylinder head usually start around an exhaust valve seat because it is the hottest part of the combustion chamber. If a crack is suspected but cannot be detected visually, have the area checked with dye penetrant or other method by the machine shop.

2. After all cylinder head parts are reasonably clean, check the valve stem–to–guide clearance. If a dial indicator is not available, a visual inspection can give you a fairly good idea if the guide, valve stem or both are worn.

3. Insert the valve into the guide until slightly away from the valve seat. Wiggle the valve sideways. A small amount of wobble is normal, but excessive wobble means a worn guide or valve stem. If a dial indicator is available, mount the indicator so that the stem of the indicator is at a 90° angle to the valve stem, as close to the valve guide as possible. Move the valve off the seat, and measure the valve guide–to–stem clearance by rocking the stem back and forth to actuate the dial indicator. Measure the valve stem using a micrometer and compare to specifications to determine whether stem or guide wear is causing excessive clearance.

4. The valve guide, if worn, must be repaired before the valve seats can be resurfaced. Ford supplies valves with oversize stems to fit valve guides that are reamed to oversize for repair. The machine shop will be able to handle the guide reaming for you. In some cases, if the guide is not too badly worn, knurling may be all that is required.

5. After all valve and valve seats have been refaced, check the remaining valve train parts (springs, retainers, keepers, etc.) for wear. Check the valve springs for straightness and tension.

REFACING

1. Valves and valve seats are refaced with an electric grinding wheel. The valve seats should be a true 45° angle. Remove only enough material to clean up any pits or grooves. Be sure the valve seat is not too wide or narrow. Use a 60° grinding wheel to remove material from the bottom of the seat for raising, and a 30° grinding wheel to remove material from the top of the seat for narrowing.

2. After the valves are refaced by machine, hand lap them to the valve seat. Clean the grinding compound off and check the position of face–to–seat contact. Contact should be close to the center of the valve face. If contact is too close to the top edge of the valve, narrow the seat; if contact is too close to the bottom edge, raise the seat.

3. Valves should be refaced to a true angle of 44°. Remove only enough metal to clean up the valve face or to correct run-out. If the edge of a valve head, after machining, is 1/32 in. (0.8mm) or less, replace the valve. The tip of the valve stem should also be dressed on the valve grinding machine; however, do not remove more than 0.010 in. (0.254mm).

Valve Springs and Stem Seals

If a valve or valve seat has not been damaged, the valve spring, valve stem seal and retainer may be replaced without removing the cylinder head, by holding the affected valve against its seat using compressed air. Install a compressed air line adapter into the applicable spark plug hole. (A minimum of 140 psi line pressure is required.) If air pressure does not hold the valve shut, the valve is damaged or burnt and the cylinder head must be removed and serviced.

The 6–200 engine uses an umbrella–type oil seal, which fits on the valve stem over the top of the valve guide. The 4–140 and 6–232 engines use a positive valve stem seal with a Teflon® insert. Teflon® seals are available for other engines, but usually require valve guide machining. Consult your automotive machine shop for advice on having positive valve stem oil seals installed.

When installing valve stem oil seals, ensure that a small amount of oil is able to pass the seal to lubricate the valve stems and guide walls; otherwise, excessive wear will occur.

REPLACEMENT — HEAD INSTALLED

▶ See Figures 116, 117, 118, 119 and 120

If valve stem seal replacement is intended with the cylinder head removed from the engine, refer to the previous portion of this section on Cylinder Head Removal & Installation.

4–140 Engine

1. Remove the valve cover and associated parts as required.
2. Remove the cam follower.
3. Remove the applicable spark plug wire and spark plug, if compressed air will be used.

Fig. 113 A dial gauge may be used to check valve stem–to–guide clearance

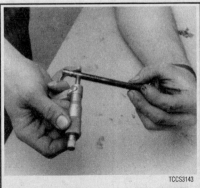
Fig. 114 Use a micrometer to measure the valve stem diameter

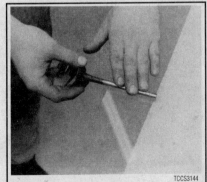
Fig. 115 Valve stems may be rolled on a flat surface to check for bends

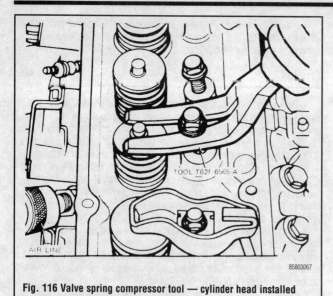

Fig. 116 Valve spring compressor tool — cylinder head installed

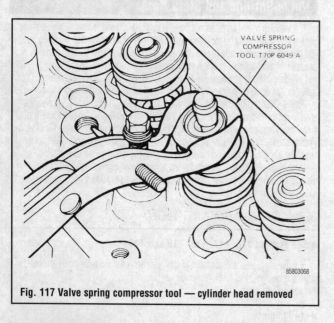

Fig. 117 Valve spring compressor tool — cylinder head removed

Fig. 118 With the valve spring out of the way, the valve stem seal may now be replaced

4. Turn on the air supply, if applicable. Using an appropriate valve spring compressor tool, compress the valve spring and remove the retainer locks, spring retainer and valve spring.

5. Remove and discard the valve stem seal.

➡ If air pressure has forced the piston to the bottom of the cylinder, any removal of air pressure will allow the valve to fall into the cylinder. A rubber band, tape or string wrapped around the end of the valve stem will prevent this situation, but will still permit enough travel to check for a binding valve.

To install:

6. Install a new valve stem seal using a plastic installation cap and Valve Seal Installer (part no. T73P–6571–A or equivalent). Remove the plastic installation cap and installation tool after the seal is in place.

7. Install the valve spring, retainer and locks.

8. Turn off the compressed air and remove the air line and adapter, if applicable. Install the spark plug and spark plug wire.

9. Apply polyethylene grease or equivalent to all contact surfaces of the cam follower and install. Check that the affected lash adjuster has been collapsed and released before rotating the camshaft.

10. Clean the valve cover mating surface and install the valve cover. Be sure to use a new gasket and oil resistant sealing compound. Tighten the attaching bolts or studs to 6–8 ft. lbs. Install any other parts which were removed in step 1.

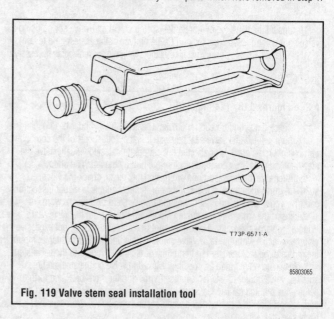

Fig. 119 Valve stem seal installation tool

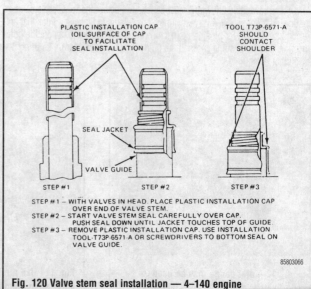

Fig. 120 Valve stem seal installation — 4–140 engine

6–170 Engine

1. Remove the air cleaner assembly.
2. Remove the valve cover.
3. Remove the applicable spark plug wire and spark plug, if compressed air will be used.
4. Remove the rocker arm shaft. Remove both valve pushrods for the cylinder being serviced.
5. Turn on the air supply, if applicable. Using an appropriate valve spring compressor tool, compress the valve spring and remove the retainer locks, spring retainer and valve spring.
6. Remove and discard the valve stem seal.

➡ If air pressure has forced the piston to the bottom of the cylinder, any removal of air pressure will allow the valve to fall into the cylinder. A rubber band, tape or string wrapped around the end of the valve stem will prevent this situation, but will still permit enough travel to check for a binding valve.

To install:

7. Install a new valve stem seal.
8. Install the valve spring, retainer and locks.
9. Apply Lubriplate®or equivalent to both ends of the push rod, the valve tips and both ends of the rocker arms. Install the pushrods, ensuring that the lower end of the rod is positioned in the tappet push rod cup.
10. Turn off the compressed air and remove the air line and adapter, if applicable. Install the spark plug and spark plug wire.
11. Install the rocker arm shaft .
12. Clean the valve cover mating surface and install the valve cover. Be sure to use a new gasket and oil resistant sealing compound. Tighten the attaching bolts to 3–5 ft. lbs.
13. Install the air cleaner assembly.

6–200 Engine

1. Remove the air cleaner assembly.
2. Remove the PCV valve and the valve cover.
3. Remove the applicable spark plug wire and spark plug, if compressed air will be used.
4. Loosen the rocker arm shaft support bolts two turns at a time, in sequence, until the valve spring pressure is relieved. Identify and remove both valve pushrods for the cylinder being serviced.
5. Tighten the attaching bolts just enough to seat the rocker arm shaft supports on the cylinder head. Push the rocker arm to one side and secure it in this position. To move the rocker arm on either end of the shaft, it will be necessary to remove the retaining pin and spring washer and slide the rocker arm off the shaft.
6. Turn on the air supply, if applicable. Using an appropriate valve spring compressor tool, compress the valve spring and remove the retainer locks, sleeve, spring retainer and valve spring.
7. Remove and discard the valve stem seal.

➡ If air pressure has forced the piston to the bottom of the cylinder, any removal of air pressure will allow the valve to fall into the cylinder. A rubber band, tape or string wrapped around the end of the valve stem will prevent this situation, but will still permit enough travel to check for a binding valve.

To install:

8. Install a new valve stem seal.
9. Position the spring over the valve. Install the spring retainer and sleeve. Compress the valve spring and install the valve spring retainer locks.
10. Apply polyethylene grease or equivalent to both ends of the push rod, the valve and push rod ends of the rocker arm, and the valve stem tip. Remove the rocker arm shaft and install the pushrods, ensuring that the lower end of each rod is positioned in the valve lifter push rod cup.
11. Slide the rocker arm back into its regular position. If a rocker arm from either end of the shaft was removed, slide it into position and install the spring washer and retainer pin.
12. Turn off the compressed air and remove the air line and adapter, if applicable. Install the spark plug and spark plug wire.
13. Install the rocker arm shaft .
14. Clean the valve cover mating surface and install the valve cover, with a new gasket. Tighten the bolts in two steps. First, tighten the bolts to 3–5 ft. lbs. and, two minutes later, tighten them to the same specification.
15. Install the PCV valve (with the vent hose and canister purge hose attached) into the valve cover mounting grommet. Install the air cleaner assembly.

6–232 and V8 Engines

1. Remove the air cleaner and intake duct assembly, on carburetor or CFI–equipped vehicles.
2. Remove the appropriate valve cover.
3. Remove the applicable spark plug wire and spark plug, if compressed air will be used.
4. Remove the rocker arm fulcrum bolts, fulcrum, rocker arm, fulcrum guide and pushrods for the cylinder being serviced. Note their positions, since they will be installed in their original locations.
5. Install the fulcrum bolt and turn on the air supply, if applicable. Using an appropriate valve spring compressor tool positioned under the head of the fulcrum bolt, compress the valve spring and remove the retainer locks, sleeve, spring retainer and valve spring.
6. Remove and discard the valve stem seal.

➡ If air pressure has forced the piston to the bottom of the cylinder, any removal of air pressure will allow the valve to fall into the cylinder. A rubber band, tape or string wrapped around the end of the valve stem will prevent this situation, but will still permit enough travel to check for a binding valve.

To install:

7. Install a new valve stem seal. Use a ⅝ in. deep well socket and a light hammer or mallet to seat the seal on the valve stem.
8. Install the valve spring, spring retainer, sleeve and retainer locks.
9. Turn off the compressed air and remove the air line and adapter, if applicable. Install the spark plug and spark plug wire.
10. Apply polyethylene grease or equivalent to both ends of the pushrods, and install the pushrods. Apply the same grease to the tip of the valve stems.
11. Apply polyethylene grease or equivalent to the pushrod sockets, underside of the fulcrum seats and the valve pad of the rocker arms. Install the rocker arms, fulcrum seats and fulcrum bolts. Tighten the bolts to 18–25 ft. lbs.
12. Clean the valve cover mating surface and install the valve cover. Be sure to use a new gasket (V8 engines) or RTV sealant (6–232 engine). When installing a valve cover gasket, make sure all the gasket tangs are engaged in the cover notches provided. On all engines other than the 6–232, tighten the bolts to 3–5 ft. lbs. (On the 6–232 engine, tighten the bolts to 80–106 inch lbs.) On the V8 engines only, retighten the bolts to the same specification two minutes later.
13. Install the air cleaner and intake duct assembly, if removed.

INSPECTION

▶ **See Figures 121 and 122**

Place the valve spring on a flat surface next to a carpenter's square. Measure the height of the spring, and rotate the spring against the edge of the square to measure distortion. If the spring height varies (by comparison) by more than ¹⁄₁₆ in. (1.6mm) or if the distortion exceeds ¹⁄₁₆ in. (1.6mm), replace the spring.

Have the valve springs tested for spring pressure at the installed and compressed (installed height minus valve lift) height using a valve spring tester. Springs should be within one pound, plus or minus each other. Replace springs as necessary.

After installing the valve spring, measure the distance between the spring mounting pad and the lower edge of the spring retainer. Compare the measurement to specifications. If the installed height is incorrect, add shim washers between the spring mounting pad and the spring. Use only washers designed for valve springs, available at most auto parts stores.

Valve Guides

REMOVAL & INSTALLATION

Worn valve guides can, in most cases, be reamed to accept a valve with an oversized stem. Valve guides that are not excessively worn or distorted may, in

Fig. 121 Use a caliper gauge to check the valve spring free length

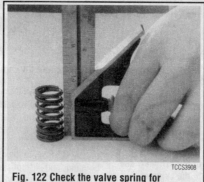

Fig. 122 Check the valve spring for squareness on a flat surface using a carpenter's square

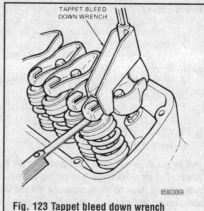

Fig. 123 Tappet bleed down wrench

some cases, be knurled rather than reamed. Knurling is a process in which metal is displaced and raised, thereby reducing clearance. Knurling also produces excellent oil control. The possibility of knurling instead of reaming the valve guides should be discussed with a machinist. However, if the valve stem is worn, reaming for an oversized valve stem is the better choice, since a new valve would be required anyway. In any event, consult with an automotive machine shop for advice.

Valve Lifters

▶ See Figure 123

All engines, other than the 6–170, utilize hydraulic valve lifters or tappets. Hydraulic valve lifters operate with zero clearance in the valve train, and because of this, the rocker arms are non-adjustable. The only means by which valve system clearances can be altered is by installing oversize or undersize pushrods; because of the hydraulic lifter's ability to compensate for slack in the valve train, all components of the valve system should be checked for wear if there is excessive play in the system.

When a valve in the engine is in the closed position, the valve lifter is resting on the base circle of the camshaft lobe and the pushrod is in its lowest position. To remove this additional clearance from the valve train, the valve lifter expands to maintain zero clearance in the valve system. When a rocker arm is loosened or removed from the engine, the lifter expands to it fullest travel. When the rocker arm is installed in the engine, the proper valve setting is obtained by tightening the rocker arm to a specified limit. However, with the lifter fully expanded, if the camshaft lobe is on a high point, it will require excessive torque to compress the lifter and obtain the proper setting. Because of this, when any component of the valve system has been removed, a preliminary valve adjustment procedure must be followed to ensure that when the rocker arm is installed on the engine and tightened, the camshaft lobe for that cylinder is in the low position.

To determine whether a shorter or longer push rod is necessary, make the following check:

Mark the crankshaft pulley as described under Preliminary Valve Adjustment procedure. Follow each step in the procedure. As each valve is positioned, mount a suitable hydraulic lifter compressor tool on the rocker arm. Slowly apply pressure to bleed down the lifter until the plunger is completely bottomed. Take care to avoid excessive pressure that might bend the pushrod. Hold the lifter in the bottom position and check available clearance between the rocker arm and the valve stem tip with a feeler gauge. If the clearance is less than specified, install an undersized pushrod. If the clearance is greater than specified, install an oversized pushrod. When compressing the valve spring to remove the pushrods, be sure the piston in the individual cylinder is below TDC to avoid contact between the valve and the piston. To replace a pushrod, it will be necessary to remove the valve rocker arm shaft assembly on 6–170 and 6–200 engines. Upon replacement of a valve pushrod, valve rocker arm shaft assembly or hydraulic valve lifter, the engine should not be cranked or rotated until the hydraulic lifters have had an opportunity to leak down to their normal operational position. The leak down rate can be accelerated by using a valve spring compressor tool on the cam follower (4–140 engine), or a tappet bleed down wrench (hydraulic lifter compressor tool) on the rocker arm (6–200, 6–232 and V8 engines), and applying pressure in a direction to collapse the lifter.

Collapsed tappet gap
4–140 and 6–200 Engines
- Allowable: 0.085–0.209 in. (2.159–5.309mm)
- Desired: 0.110–0.184 in. (2.794–4.673mm)

6–232 Engine
- Allowable: 0.088–0.189 in. (2.235–4.800mm)

8–255 Engine
- Allowable: 0.098–0.198 in. (2.489–5.029mm)
- Desired: 0.123–0.173 in. (3.124–4.394mm)

8–302 Engine
- Allowable: 0.089–0.193 in. (2.260–4.902mm)
- Desired: 0.096–0.163 in. (2.438–4.140mm)

REMOVAL & INSTALLATION

4–140 Engine

1. Remove the valve cover and associated parts as required.
2. Rotate the camshaft so that the base circle of the cam is facing the applicable cam follower.
3. Using a valve spring compressor tool, collapse the lash adjuster and/or depress the valve spring, if necessary, and slide the cam follower over the lash adjuster and out.
4. Lift out the hydraulic lash adjuster.

To install:

5. Rotate the camshaft so that the base circle of the cam is facing the applicable cam follower.
6. Place the hydraulic lash adjuster in position in the bore.
7. Using a valve spring compressor tool, collapse the lash adjuster as necessary to position the cam follower over the lash adjuster and the valve stem. If necessary, also compress the valve spring.
8. Before rotating the camshaft to the next position, be sure that the lash adjuster is fully compressed and released.
9. Clean the gasket surfaces of the valve cover and cylinder head.
10. Use a new valve cover gasket and coat the gasket contact surfaces of the valve cover and the Up side of the valve cover gasket with oil resistant sealing compound. When installing the valve cover gasket, make sure all the gasket locating tangs are engaged in the cover notches provided. Tighten the attaching bolts to 6–8 ft. lbs.
11. Install the air cleaner assembly, and any other parts, if removed.

6–170 and 6–200 Engines

1. Drain the cooling system.
2. Remove the air cleaner assembly and disconnect the battery and accelerator linkage.
3. Remove all parts necessary for cylinder head removal, including the valve cover(s). Refer to Cylinder Head Removal & Installation procedures, earlier in this section.
4. Using a magnet, remove the tappets. Place the tappets in a rack, so they can be installed in their original positions.

➡If the tappets are stuck in their bores by excessive varnish or gum, it may be necessary to use a pliers–type or claw–type tool to remove the tappets. Rotate the tappets back and forth to loosen any gum and varnish which may have formed.

To install:

5. Install new or cleaned hydraulic tappets through the pushrod openings with a magnet.

6. Install the cylinder head and all other parts which were removed or disconnected. Be sure to use new gaskets.

7. Fill the cooling system.

6–232 and V8 Engines

▶ **See Figures 124 and 125**

1. Drain the cooling system.

2. Disconnect the spark plug wires and remove the plug wire routing clips from the from the studs on the valve covers, where applicable. Lay the plug wires with the routing clips toward the front of the engine.

3. Remove the intake manifold and any associated parts.

4. Remove the valve covers and any associated parts.

5. Sufficiently loosen each rocker arm fulcrum attaching bolt to allow the rocker arm to be lifted off the pushrod and rotated to one side.

6. Remove the pushrods. Note the location of each pushrod, since when the engine is reassembled, each pushrod should be installed in its original position.

7. On those 8–302 engines with roller tappets, remove the tappet guide retainer bolts and the retainer. Remove the tappet guide plates and identify them for installation into their original positions.

8. Remove the tappets using a magnet. Note the location of each tappet, since when the engine is reassembled, each tappet should be installed in its

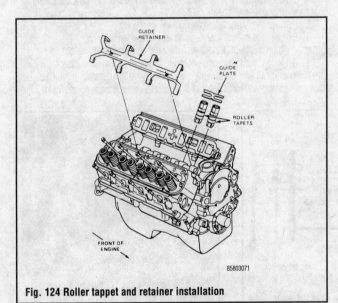

Fig. 124 Roller tappet and retainer installation

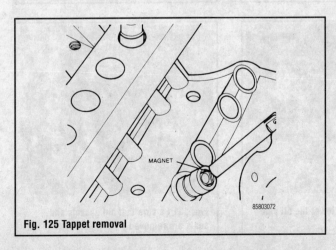

Fig. 125 Tappet removal

original position. For roller tappets, also note their original orientation, so that when installed the roller rotates in the same direction.

➡ **If the tappets are stuck in their bores by excessive varnish or gum, it may be necessary to use a pliers–type or claw–type tool to remove the tappets. Rotate the tappets back and forth to loosen any gum and varnish which may have formed.**

To install:

9. Clean the outside surface of the tappets. Lubricate each tappet and bore with heavy engine oil.

10. Install each tappet in the bore from which it was removed. If a new tappet is being installed, check the new tappet for a free fit in the particular bore for which it is intended. Be careful that roller tappets, if equipped, are installed as originally oriented.

11. If applicable, install the tappet guide plates in their original positions, followed by the tappet guide retainer and retainer bolts.

12. Dip each pushrod end in heavy engine oil and install the pushrods in their original positions. Roller tappet pushrods must be installed with the collar at the top.

13. For each valve, rotate the crankshaft until the tappet rests on the heel (base circle) of the camshaft lobe. Position the rocker arms over the pushrods. Install the fulcrums and tighten the fulcrum attaching bolts. On V8 engines, torque the bolts to 18–25 ft. lbs. On the 6–232 engine, tighten the bolts in two steps. First, tighten the bolts to 5–11 ft. lbs., then tighten them again to 19–25 ft. lbs. The camshaft may be in any position during the final tightening sequence.

14. Perform a valve clearance adjustment check, and compare the figures with the specified ranges. Longer or shorter pushrods may be substituted if some compensation is required.

15. Clean the valve cover and cylinder head mating surfaces.

➡ **Some later engines use RTV sealant instead of valve cover gaskets.**

16. Install the valve covers with new gaskets or RTV sealant, as described earlier in this section.

17. Install the intake manifold with new gaskets and seals, or sealer, where applicable.

18. Install the air cleaner assembly and other parts which were moved or disconnected.

19. Fill the cooling system.

INSPECTION

Hydraulic Valve Lash Adjusters

4–140 ENGINE

▶ **See Figure 126**

Hydraulic valve lash adjusters are used in the valve train. These units are placed at the fulcrum point of the cam followers (or rocker arms). Their action is similar to the hydraulic tappets used in push rod engines. In order to check for proper valve clearance, proceed as follows:

1. Position the camshaft so that the base circle of the lobe is facing the cam follower of the valve to be checked.

2. Using a valve spring compressor tool, slowly apply pressure to the cam follower until the lash adjuster is completely collapsed. Hold the cam follower in this position and insert a 0.045 in. (1.14mm) feeler gauge between the base circle of the cam and the follower.

➡ **The minimum gap is 0.035 in. (0.89mm) and the maximum is 0.055 in. (1.39mm). The desired gap is between 0.040 and 0.050 in. (1.02–1.27mm).**

3. If the clearance is excessive, remove the cam follower and inspect it for damage.

4. If the cam follower seems okay, measure the valve spring assembled height to be sure the valve is not sticking. See the Valve Specifications chart in this section.

5. If the valve spring assembled height is okay, check the dimensions of the camshaft.

6. If the camshaft dimensions are okay, the lash adjuster should be cleaned and tested.

7. Replace any worn parts as necessary.

➡For any repair that includes removal of the camshaft follower (rocker arm), each affected hydraulic lash adjuster must be collapsed after installation of the camshaft follower, and then released. This step must be taken prior to any rotation of the camshaft.

Hydraulic Valve Lifters

6–200, 6–232 AND V8 ENGINES

▶ **See Figure 127**

Remove the hydraulic valve lifters from their bores and remove any gum and varnish with safe solvent. Check the lifters for concave wear. If the bottom of the lifter is worn concave or flat, replace the lifter. Lifters are built with a convex bottom, so flatness indicates wear. If a worn lifter is detected, carefully check the camshaft for wear.

➡**Mark lifters for cylinder and position location. Lifters must be installed in the same bore from which they were removed.**

To test lifter leak down, submerge the lifter in a container of kerosene. Chuck a used pushrod or its equivalent into a drill press. Position the container of kerosene so the pushrod acts on the lifter plunger. Pump the lifter with the drill press until resistance increases. Pump several more times to bleed any air from the lifter. Apply very firm, constant pressure to the lifter and observe the rate which fluid bleeds out of the lifter. If the lifter bleeds down very quickly (less than 15 seconds), the lifter should be replaced. If the time exceeds 60 seconds, the lifter is sticking and should be cleaned or replaced. If the lifter is operating properly (leak down time of 15–60 seconds) and not worn, lubricate and install it in the engine.

Oil Pan

REMOVAL & INSTALLATION

➡**Always raise and safely support the vehicle on jackstands. When raising the engine, place a block of wood between the jack and jacking**

point, and either remove or open the hood. Be sure that the fan blades do not touch the radiator, and that the radiator hoses and transmission lines are not stretched.

4–140 Engine

▶ **See Figures 128, 129, 130, 131 and 132**

1. Disconnect the negative battery cable.
2. Remove the fan shroud. If equipped with an electric fan, disconnect the electrical lead and remove the fan and shroud assembly.
3. Drain the crankcase and cooling system.

✶✶ CAUTION

When draining the coolant, keep in mind that cats and dogs are attracted by the ethylene glycol antifreeze, and are quite likely to drink any that is left in an uncovered container or in puddles on the ground. This will prove fatal in sufficient quantity. Always drain the coolant into a sealable container. Coolant should be reused unless it is contaminated or several years old.

4. Disconnect the upper and lower radiator hoses at the radiator. If applicable, disconnect the automatic transmission cooler lines at the radiator.
5. Remove the right and left front engine support bolts and nuts or through–bolts. Disconnect the hydraulic damper if so equipped.
6. Using a jack, raise the engine as far as it will go. Place blocks of wood between the mounts and the chassis brackets. Remove the jack.
7. Remove the steering gear retaining nuts and bolts. Remove the bolt retaining the steering flex coupling to the steering gear. Position the steering gear forward and down.
8. Remove the shake brace and starter.
9. Remove the engine rear support–to–crossmember nuts.
10. Position a jack under the transmission and take up its weight.
11. Remove the oil pan retaining bolts. Remove the oil pan. If necessary, turn the crankshaft when removing the pan to avoid interference. It may also be necessary to remove the upper and lower rear subframe bolts on each side, and

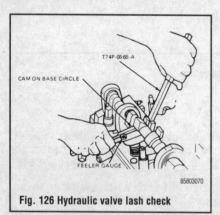

Fig. 126 Hydraulic valve lash check

Fig. 127 Check the lifter face for wear

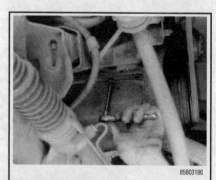

Fig. 128 Remove the oil pan retaining bolts with a socket

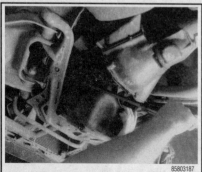

Fig. 129 If necessary, use a prybar to pivot the subframe down and provide additional clearance

Fig. 130 Withdraw and lower the oil pan from the engine

Fig. 131 Be sure that old gaskets and seals are removed

use a prybar to pivot the subframe down slightly, in order to provide sufficient clearance for pan removal.

To install:

12. Clean and inspect the oil pan and gasket surface at the cylinder block.

13. Remove and clean the oil pump pick–up tube and screen assembly, then install.

14. Position and affix the new oil pan gasket and end seals on the cylinder block with gasket cement.

15. Position the oil pan on the cylinder block and install its retaining bolts. Begin at the right rear side of the pan, and work clockwise around the pan, tightening the bolts to 6–8 ft. lbs. (7½–10 ft. lbs. for 1987–88 engines).

16. If lowered, realign the subframe and install the retaining bolts.

17. Lower the jack under the transmission and install the crossmember nuts.

18. Replace the oil filter.

19. Position the flex coupling on the steering gear and install the retaining bolt.

20. Install the steering gear.

21. Install the shake brace and starter.

22. Raise the engine enough to remove the wood blocks. Lower the engine and remove the jack. Install the engine support bolts and nuts. Connect the radiator hoses.

23. Lower the vehicle and fill the crankcase with oil and the cooling system with coolant.

24. Connect the battery.

25. Start the engine and check for leaks.

6–170 Engine

▶ **See Figure 133**

1. Disconnect the negative battery cable.

2. Remove the fan shroud attaching bolts, positioning the fan shroud back over the fan.

3. Drain the crankcase.

4. Remove the two bolts attaching the steering gear to the main crossmember and let the steering gear rest on the frame away from the oil pan.

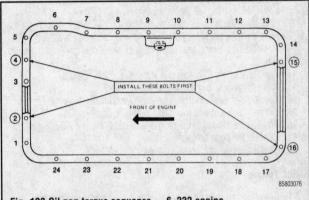

Fig. 133 Oil pan torque sequence — 6–232 engine

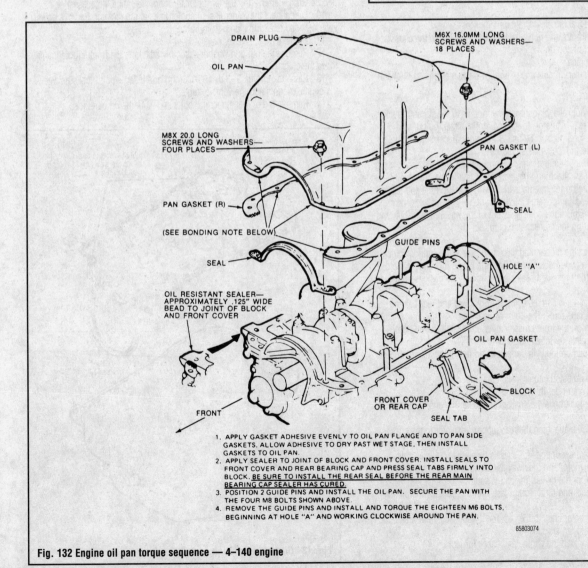

Fig. 132 Engine oil pan torque sequence — 4–140 engine

5. Remove the nuts attaching the engine mount insulators.

6. Raise the engine and place two wood blocks between the engine mounts and the vehicle frame.

7. Remove the rear K–braces.

8. Remove the oil pan attaching bolts and lower the oil pan, rotating the crankshaft as necessary to clear the counterweights.

To install:

9. Clean and inspect the oil pan and gasket surface at the cylinder block.

10. Coat the cylinder block mating surface with contact cement and position a new oil pan gasket and seals against the block.

11. Raise the oil pan into position and install the attaching bolts. Start with bolt nos. 2, 4, 15 and 16 (see the illustration).

12. After all of the bolts are in place, tighten them in sequence to 7–10 ft. lbs. Begin at the left front side of the pan, and work clockwise around the pan.

13. Position the steering gear to the main crossmember and install the two attaching bolts.

14. Position the rear K–braces and install the attaching bolts.

15. Raise the engine and remove the wood blocks.

16. Lower the engine and install the engine mount attaching nuts.

17. Fill the crankcase with the specified engine oil.

18. Position the shroud to the radiator and install the two attaching bolts.

19. Connect the negative battery cable.

20. Start the engine and check for leaks.

6–200 Engine

1. Disconnect the two oil cooler lines at the radiator, if so equipped.

2. Remove the two radiator top support bolts. Remove or position the fan shroud back over the fan.

3. Remove the oil level dipstick. Drain the crankcase.

4. Remove the four bolts and nuts attaching the sway bar to the chassis and allow the sway bar to hang down.

5. Remove the K–brace.

6. Lower the front steering rack and pinion, or the center link and linkage, if necessary for clearance.

7. Remove the starter.

8. Remove the two nuts attaching the engine mounts to the support brackets.

9. Loosen the two rear insulator–to–crossmember attaching bolts.

10. Raise the engine and place a 1¼ in. (3.175mm) spacer between the engine support insulator and the chassis brackets.

11. Position a jack under the transmission and raise it slightly.

12. Remove the oil pan attaching bolts and lower pan to the crossmember.

13. Remove the oil pump intermediate driveshaft, pick–up tube and screen assembly, and lower these components into the pan.

14. Position the transmission cooler lines out of the way, if applicable, and remove the oil pan, rotating the crankshaft if required.

To install:

15. Clean and inspect the oil pan and gasket surface at the cylinder block.

16. The oil pan has a two–piece gasket. Coat the block surface and the oil pan gasket surfaces with oil resistant sealer, and position the gaskets on the cylinder block.

17. Position the oil pan seals in the cylinder front cover and rear bearing cap.

18. Insert the gasket tabs under the front and rear seals.

19. Place the oil pan on the front crossmember and install the oil pump, intermediate driveshaft, pick–up tube and screw assembly.

20. Position the oil pan on the cylinder block and install the attaching bolts. Tighten to 7–9 ft. lbs.

21. Position the transmission cooler lines, if equipped.

22. Lower the jack from under the transmission.

23. Raise the engine to remove the spacers and lower the engine on the chassis.

24. Tighten the two nuts attaching the rear support insulator to the crossmember.

25. Install the two engine support–to–chassis through–bolts and nuts.

26. Install the starter motor and the sway bar. If moved, also install the steering rack and pinion, or the center link and linkage.

27. Install the K–brace, and fill the crankcase with oil. Replace the oil level dipstick.

28. Connect the oil cooler lines to the radiator, if applicable, and install the upper radiator support and fan shroud.

29. Lower the vehicle, start the engine and check for leaks.

6–232 Engine

▶ **See Figure 134**

1. Disconnect the negative battery cable. Remove the air cleaner assembly including the air intake duct.

2. Drain the cooling system.

❉❉ CAUTION

When draining the coolant, keep in mind that cats and dogs are attracted by the ethylene glycol antifreeze, and are quite likely to drink any that is left in an uncovered container or in puddles on the ground. This will prove fatal in sufficient quantity. Always drain the coolant into a sealable container. Coolant should be reused unless it is contaminated or several years old.

3. Remove the fan shroud attaching bolts and position the shroud back over the fan.

4. Remove the oil level dipstick.

5. If equipped, remove the screws attaching the vacuum solenoids to the dash panel. Lay the solenoids on the engine without disconnecting the vacuum hoses or electrical connectors.

6. Remove the exhaust manifold to exhaust pipe attaching nuts. Disconnect the radiator hoses from the radiator.

7. Drain the crankcase.

8. Remove the oil filter.

9. Remove the bolts attaching the shift linkage bracket to the transmission bell housing. Remove the starter motor for more clearance, if necessary.

10. Disconnect the transmission cooler lines at the radiator. Remove power steering hose retaining clamp from frame.

11. Remove the converter cover.

12. Remove the nut and washer assembly attaching the front engine insulator to the chassis.

13. Raise the engine 2–3 in. (51–76mm) and insert wood blocks between the engine mounts and the vehicle frame.

14. Remove the oil pan attaching bolts and work the oil pan loose.

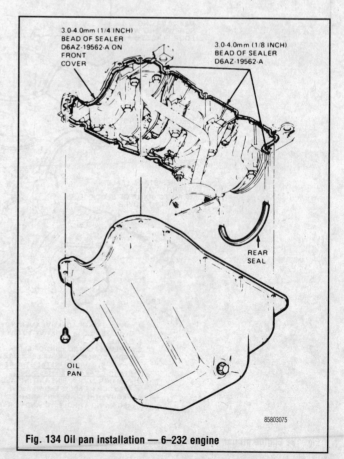

Fig. 134 Oil pan installation — 6–232 engine

15. Lower the oil pan onto the crossmember. Remove the oil pick–up tube attaching bolts and the tube support bracket attaching nut. Lower the pick–up tube/screen assembly into the pan and remove the oil pan.

16. Remove the oil pan seal from the main bearing cap.

To install:

17. Clean and inspect the gasket surfaces on the cylinder block, oil pan and oil pick–up tube.

18. Apply an 8mm bead of RTV sealer to all matching surfaces of the oil pan and the engine front cover.

19. Place the oil pick–up tube/screen assembly into the pan. Raise and support the oil pan.

20. Attach the oil pick–up tube/screen with a new gasket. Install and tighten the tube attaching bolts (15–22 ft. lbs.) and the support bracket nut (30–40 ft. lbs.).

21. Install the oil pan and pan bolts. Tighten the bolts to 80–106 inch lbs.

22. Remove the wood blocks between the engine mounts and the vehicle frame and lower the engine onto the mounts.

23. Install the nut and washer assembly attaching the front engine insulator to the chassis.

24. Install the converter cover.

25. Connect the transmission cooler lines at the radiator.

26. Install the power steering hose retaining clamp to the frame.

27. Install the starter motor, if removed .

28. Install the bolts attaching the shift linkage bracket to the transmission bell housing.

29. Install the oil filter.

30. Fill the crankcase with oil.

31. Install the exhaust manifold to exhaust pipe attaching nuts.

32. Connect the radiator hoses at the radiator.

33. Install the vacuum solenoids to the dash panel, if applicable.

34. Install the oil level dipstick and check the oil level.

35. Install the fan shroud.

36. Install the air cleaner assembly including the air intake duct.

37. Fill the cooling system.

38. Start the engine and check the fluid level in the transmission.

39. Check for engine oil or transmission fluid leaks.

V8 Engines

▶ **See Figures 135 and 136**

> ※※ **WARNING**
>
> On vehicles equipped with a dual sump oil pan, both drain plugs must be removed to thoroughly drain the crankcase. Before raising the engine for oil pan removal clearance, drain the cooling system and disconnect the hoses. Check the fan–to–radiator clearance when jacking, and remove the radiator if clearance is inadequate.

> ※※ **CAUTION**
>
> When draining the coolant, keep in mind that cats and dogs are attracted by the ethylene glycol antifreeze, and are quite likely to drink any that is left in an uncovered container or in puddles on the ground. This will prove fatal in sufficient quantity. Always drain the coolant into a sealable container. Coolant should be reused unless it is contaminated or several years old.

1. Disconnect the negative battery cable.

2. Remove the fan shroud attaching bolts, positioning the fan shroud back over the fan.

3. If equipped, also disconnect the transmission oil cooler lines at the radiator.

4. Remove the dipstick and tube assembly.

5. Drain the crankcase.

6. Disconnect the steering flex coupling. Remove the two bolts attaching the steering gear to the main crossmember and let the steering gear rest on the frame away from the oil pan. Disconnect the power steering hose retaining clamp from the frame.

7. Remove the idler arm bracket retaining bolts (models so equipped) and pull the steering linkage down and out of the way.

8. Remove the nuts and washers which attach the engine mounts to the No. 2 crossmember.

9. Raise the engine and place two wood blocks between the engine mounts and the crossmember. Remove the converter inspection cover.

10. Remove the rear K–brace (four bolts).

11. Remove the oil pan attaching bolts and lower the oil pan on the frame.

12. Remove the oil pump attaching bolts and the inlet tube attaching nut from the No. 3 main bearing cap stud, and lower the oil pump into the oil pan.

13. Remove the oil pan, rotating the crankshaft as necessary to clear the counterweights.

To install:

14. Clean and inspect the gasket mounting surfaces thoroughly. Remove the old gaskets and seals, as well as old gasket cement. Coat the surfaces on the block with contact cement and position the pan side gaskets on the engine block. Install the front cover oil seal on the cover, with the tabs over the pan side gaskets. Install the rear main cap seal with the tabs over the pan side gaskets.

15. Position the oil pump and inlet tube into the oil pan. Slide the oil pan into position under the engine. With the oil pump intermediate shaft in position in the oil pump, position the oil pump on the cylinder block, and the inlet tube on the stud of the No. 3 main bearing cap attaching bolt. Install the attaching bolts and nut and tighten to 22–32 ft. lbs. Position the oil pan on the engine and install the attaching bolts. Tighten the bolts (working from the center toward the ends) 9–11 ft. lbs. for 5/16 in. bolts and 7–9 ft. lbs. for 1/4 in. bolts.

16. Position the steering gear on the main crossmember. Install the two attaching bolts and tighten them to the specifications in Section 8. Connect the steering flex coupling.

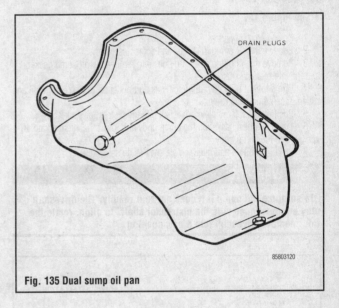

DRAIN PLUGS

85803120

Fig. 135 Dual sump oil pan

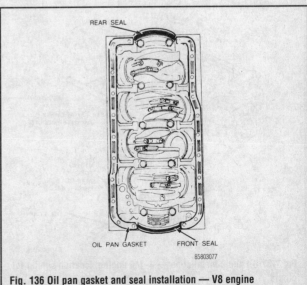

REAR SEAL

OIL PAN GASKET   FRONT SEAL

85803077

Fig. 136 Oil pan gasket and seal installation — V8 engine

17. Position the rear K–braces and install the four attaching bolts.
18. Install the converter inspection cover.
19. Raise the engine and remove the wood blocks.
20. Lower the engine and install the engine mount washers and nuts. Tighten them to the following specifications:
- 1979–81: 40–60 ft. lbs.
- 1982: 70–90 ft. lbs.
- 1983: 57–65 ft. lbs.
- 1984: 50–65 ft. lbs.
- 1985–1988: 80–106 ft. lbs.

21. Position the steering linkage and fasten the idler arm bracket retaining bolts (models so equipped).
22. Install the oil dipstick and tube assembly, and fill crankcase with the specified engine oil.
23. Connect the transmission oil cooler lines, if applicable.
24. Position the shroud on the radiator and install the two attaching bolts.
25. Connect the battery cable. Start the engine and check for leaks.

Oil Pump

REMOVAL & INSTALLATION

Except 6–232 Engine

▶ **See Figure 137**

1. Remove the oil pan.
2. Remove the oil pump inlet tube and screen assembly.
3. Remove the oil pump attaching bolts and remove the oil pump gasket and the intermediate shaft.
4. Prime the oil pump by filling the inlet and outlet ports with engine oil and rotating the pump shaft to distribute it.
5. Position the intermediate driveshaft into the distributor socket.
6. Position a new gasket on the pump body and insert the intermediate driveshaft into the pump body.
7. Install the pump and intermediate shaft as an assembly.

❊❊ WARNING

Do not force the pump if it does not seat readily. The driveshaft may be misaligned with the distributor shaft. To align, rotate the intermediate driveshaft into a new position.

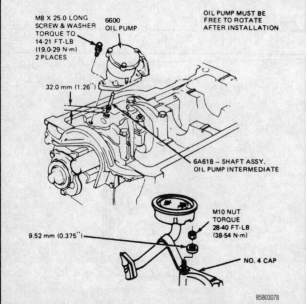

Fig. 137 Oil pump installation — 4–140 engine; location similar for others

8. Install and torque the oil pump attaching screws to:
- 4–140 and 6–200 Engines — 12–15 ft. lbs.
- 8–302 Engine — 22–32 ft. lbs.
9. Install the oil pan.

6–232 Engine

▶ **See Figure 138**

➡ **The oil pump is mounted in the front cover assembly. Oil pan removal is only necessary for pick–up tube/screen replacement or service.**

1. Raise and safely support the vehicle on jackstands.
2. Remove the oil filter.
3. Remove the cover/filter mount assembly.
4. Lift the two pump gears from their mounting pocket in the front cover.
5. Clean all gasket mounting surfaces.
6. Inspect the mounting pocket for wear. If excessive wear is present, complete timing cover assembly replacement is necessary.
7. Inspect the cover/filter mounting gasket–to–timing cover surface for flatness. Place a straightedge across the flat and check the clearance with a feeler gauge. If the measured clearance exceeds 0.004 in. (0.102mm), replace the cover/filter mount.
8. Replace the pump gears if wear is excessive.
9. Remove the plug from the end of the pressure relief valve passage using a small drill and slide hammer. Use caution when drilling.
10. Remove the spring and valve from the bore. Clean all dirt, gum and metal chips from the bore and valve. Inspect all parts for wear. Replace as necessary.
11. Install the valve and spring after lubricating them with engine oil. Install a new plug flush with the machined surface.
12. Install the pump gears and fill the pocket with petroleum jelly. Install the cover/filter mount using a new mounting gasket. Tighten the mounting bolts to 18–22 ft. lbs. Install the oil filter and add oil, as necessary, to maintain the correct level.

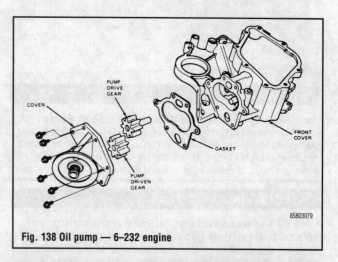

Fig. 138 Oil pump — 6–232 engine

Crankshaft Pulley (Vibration Damper)

REMOVAL & INSTALLATION

1. Remove the fan shroud, as required. If necessary, drain the cooling system and remove the radiator. Remove drive belts from the pulley.

❊❊ CAUTION

When draining the coolant, keep in mind that cats and dogs are attracted by the ethylene glycol antifreeze, and are quite likely to drink any that is left in an uncovered container or in puddles on the ground. This will prove fatal in sufficient quantity. Always drain the coolant into a sealable container. Coolant should be reused unless it is contaminated or several years old.

2. On those engines with a separate pulley, remove the retaining bolts and separate the pulley from the vibration damper.

3. Remove the vibration damper/pulley retaining bolt from the crankshaft end.

4. Using a puller, remove the damper/pulley from the crankshaft.

5. Upon installation, align the key slot of the pulley hub to the crankshaft key. Complete the assembly in the reverse order of removal. Torque the retaining bolts to specification and adjust drive belts to their proper tension.

Timing Belt Cover and Seal

➡**Replacement of the cover seal is recommended any time the front cover is removed. It is possible on the 4–140 engine to replace the front cover seal with the cover installed.**

REMOVAL & INSTALLATION

1. Remove the front seal from the cover with the cover on the engine, using a special seal removal tool (Ford part no. T74P–6700–B or equivalent).

2. Remove the timing belt outer cover, as described in the following section on Timing Belt Removal & Installation, if engine disassembly is indicated.

To install:

3. If removed, install the cover on the engine without the seal. Be sure to overlap the front and side pan gaskets. Do not tighten the attaching bolts.

4. Using a special seal installer tool (Ford part no. T74P–6150–A or equivalent), press the seal into place.

5. Properly position the cover in relation to the crankshaft, and tighten the attaching bolts to 6–9 ft. lbs.

Timing Chain Cover and Seal

➡**Replacement of the cover seal is recommended any time the front cover is removed.**

REMOVAL & INSTALLATION

1. Refer to the section on Timing Chain Removal for information on cover removal and replacement.

➡**On 6–232 engines, the seal may be removed after the crankshaft pulley is off, without removing the cover.**

2. With the cover removed from the car, drive the old seal from the rear of the cover with a pin punch. Clean out the recess in the cover.

3. Coat the new seal with grease and work it into the cover until it is fully seated. Check the seal after installation to be sure the spring is properly positioned in the seal.

Timing Gear Cover and Seal

➡**Replacement of the cover seal is recommended any time the front cover is removed.**

REMOVAL & INSTALLATION

6–170 Engine

1. Remove the oil pan, as described previously in this section.

2. Drain the coolant and remove the radiator and shroud.

❊❊ CAUTION

When draining the coolant, keep in mind that cats and dogs are attracted by the ethylene glycol antifreeze, and are quite likely to drink any that is left in an uncovered container or in puddles on the ground. This will prove fatal in sufficient quantity. Always drain the coolant into a sealable container. Coolant should be reused unless it is contaminated or several years old.

3. Remove the air conditioning compressor and bracket, if equipped.

4. Remove the alternator, Thermactor air pump and drive belts.

5. Remove the water pump and water lines, and the fan.

6. Remove the drive pulley from the crankshaft.

7. Remove the timing gear cover retaining bolts. Tap the cover lightly to break the gasket seal. Remove the timing gear cover.

8. In order to replace the cover plate gasket, remove the two cover plate retaining bolts, and remove the cover plate.

9. If necessary, remove the guide sleeves from the cylinder block.

To install:

10. Make sure that all gasket surfaces are clean. Apply sealing compound to the gasket surfaces on the cylinder block and the back side of the front cover plate. Position a new gasket and the front cover plate on the cylinder block. Temporarily install four of the timing gear cover bolts to position the gasket and cover plate in place, and install and tighten the two cover plate attaching bolts. Then, remove the four bolts which were temporarily installed.

11. If removed, fit new seal rings to the guide sleeves and, without using sealer, insert the sleeves into the cylinder block with the chamfered side of each sleeve toward the front cover.

12. Apply sealing compound to the timing gear cover gasket surface and place the gasket in position on the cover.

13. Place the timing gear cover on the engine and install the retaining bolts. Center the cover before tightening the bolts to 12–15 ft. lbs.

14. Install the drive pulley on the crankshaft and tighten the bolt to specification.

15. Install the parts removed in steps 2–5.

16. Adjust the drive belts to their proper tension and fill the cooling system.

17. Operate the engine at fast idle and check for coolant and oil leaks.

Timing Belt

The correct installation and adjustment of the camshaft drive belt is mandatory if the engine is to run properly. The camshaft controls the opening of the camshaft and the crankshaft. When any given piston is on the intake stroke, the corresponding intake valve must be open to admit air/fuel mixture into the cylinder. When the same piston is on the compression and power strokes, both valves in that cylinder must be closed. When the piston is on the exhaust stroke, the exhaust valve for that cylinder must be open. If the opening and closing of the valves is not coordinated with the movements of the pistons, the engine will run very poorly, if at all.

The camshaft drive belt also turns the engine auxiliary shaft. The distributor is driven by the engine auxiliary shaft. Since the distributor controls ignition timing, the auxiliary shaft must be coordinated with the camshaft and crankshaft, since both valves in any given cylinder must be closed and the piston in that cylinder near the top of the compression stroke when the spark plug fires.

Due to this complex interrelationship between the camshaft, the crankshaft and the auxiliary shaft, the cogged pulleys on each component must be aligned when the camshaft drive belt is installed. In order to prevent an unanticipated breakdown, and possible engine damage, it is recommended that the camshaft drive belt be replaced every 60,000 miles.

TROUBLESHOOTING

Should the camshaft drive belt jump timing by a tooth or two, the engine could still run; but very poorly. To visually check for correct timing of the crankshaft, auxiliary shaft and the camshaft, follow this procedure:

➡**There is an access plug provided in the cam drive belt cover, so that the camshaft timing can be checked without removing the cover.**

1. Remove the access plug.

2. Turn the crankshaft until the timing marks on the crankshaft indicate TDC.

3. Make sure that the timing mark on the camshaft drive sprocket is aligned with the pointer on the inner belt cover. Also, the rotor of the distributor must align with the No. 1 cylinder firing position.

❊❊ WARNING

Never turn the crankshaft of any overhead cam engine in the opposite direction of normal rotation. Backward rotation of the crankshaft may cause the timing belt to slip and alter the timing.

REMOVAL & INSTALLATION

▶ **See Figures 139 thru 149**

1. Set the engine to TDC as described in the troubleshooting section. The crankshaft and camshaft timing marks should align with their respective pointers and the distributor rotor should point to the No. 1 plug tower.

2. Loosen the adjustment bolts on the alternator and other belt–driven accessories, and remove the drive belts. To provide clearance for removing the belt outer cover and camshaft belt, remove the fan (if applicable) and pulley from the water pump hub.

3. Reposition the fuel vapor tube running to the evaporator canister, if necessary, to provide clearance for cover removal.

4. Remove the belt outer cover attaching screw and bolt.

5. Remove the belt outer cover.

6. Remove the distributor cap from the distributor and position it out of the way.

7. Loosen the belt tensioner adjustment and pivot bolts. Lever the tensioner away from the belt and retighten the adjustment bolt to hold it away.

8. Remove the crankshaft bolt and pulley. Remove the belt guide behind the pulley.

9. Remove the camshaft drive belt.

To install:

10. Install the new belt over the crankshaft sprocket first, then counterclockwise over the auxiliary shaft sprocket and the camshaft sprocket. Adjust the belt fore and aft so that it is centered on the sprockets.

11. Loosen the tensioner adjustment bolt, allowing it to spring back against the belt.

12. Rotate the crankshaft two complete turns in the normal rotational direction to remove any belt slack. Turn the crankshaft until the timing check marks

are lined up. If the timing has slipped, remove the belt and repeat the procedure.

13. Tighten the tensioner adjustment bolt to 14–21 ft. lbs., and the pivot bolt to 28–40 ft. lbs.

14. Install the distributor cap.

15. Install the belt guide, belt outer cover and crankshaft pulley. Install the water pump pulley and, if applicable, the cooling fan.

16. Install the drive belts and accessories and adjust the drive belt tension. Reposition the fuel vapor tube, if necessary.

17. Start the engine and check the ignition timing.

Timing Chain

REMOVAL & INSTALLATION

6–200 Engine

▶ **See Figure 150**

1. Drain the cooling system and crankcase.

❊❊ CAUTION

When draining the coolant, keep in mind that cats and dogs are attracted by the ethylene glycol antifreeze, and are quite likely to drink any that is left in an uncovered container or in puddles on the ground. This will prove fatal in sufficient quantity. Always drain the coolant into a sealable container. Coolant should be reused unless it is contaminated or several years old.

Fig. 139 Remove the timing belt outer cover retaining screw

Fig. 140 Remove the timing belt outer cover retaining bolt

Fig. 141 Remove the timing belt outer cover

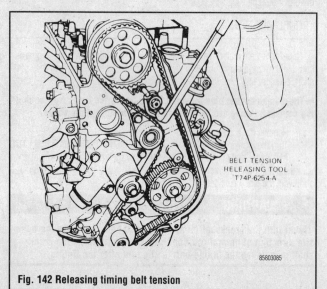

Fig. 142 Releasing timing belt tension

BELT TENSION RELEASING TOOL T74P-6254-A

2. Disconnect the upper radiator hose from the intake manifold and the lower hose from the water pump. On cars with automatic transmission, disconnect the fluid cooler lines from the radiator.

3. Remove the radiator, fan and pulley, and engine drive belts. On models with air conditioning, remove the condenser retaining bolts and position the condenser forward. Do not disconnect the refrigerant lines.

4. Remove the cylinder front cover retaining bolts and front oil pan bolts, and gently pry the cover away from the block.

5. Remove the crankshaft pulley bolt and use a puller to remove the vibration damper.

6. With a socket wrench of the proper size on the crankshaft pulley bolt, gently rotate the crankshaft in a clockwise direction until all slack is removed from the left side of the timing chain. Scribe a mark on the engine block parallel to the present position on the left side of the chain. Next, turn the crankshaft in a counterclockwise direction to remove all the slack from the right side of the chain. Force the left side of the chain outward with your fingers and measure the distance between the reference point and the present position of the chain. If the distance exceeds ½ in. (12.7mm), replace the chain and sprockets.

7. Crank the engine until the timing marks are aligned as shown in the illustration. Remove the bolt, slide the sprocket and chain forward and remove them as an assembly.

Fig. 143 Loosen the crankshaft pulley retaining bolt

Fig. 144 Remove the retaining bolt and washer

Fig. 145 Remove the crankshaft pulley

Fig. 146 Remove the belt guide to allow removal of the timing belt from the crankshaft sprocket

Fig. 147 After belt tension has been relieved, the timing belt can be removed from the camshaft sprocket

Fig. 148 After installing a timing belt, be sure that the timing marks are aligned

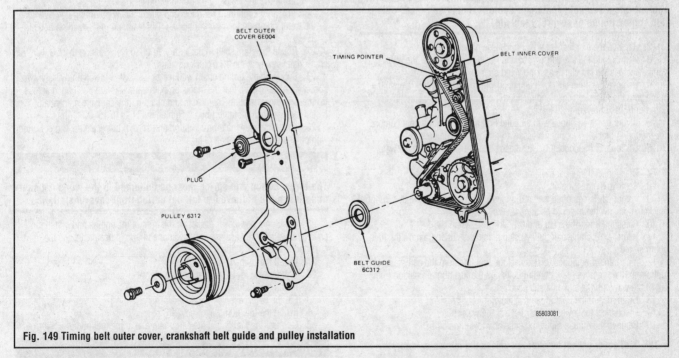

Fig. 149 Timing belt outer cover, crankshaft belt guide and pulley installation

To install:

8. Position the sprockets and chain on the engine, making sure that the timing marks are aligned, dot-to-dot.

9. Install the front cover, applying oil resistant sealer to the new gasket. Trim away the exposed portion of the old oil pan gasket flush with the front of the engine block. Cut and position the required portion of a new gasket to the oil pan, applying sealer to both sides of it.

10. Install the cylinder front cover retaining bolts and front oil pan bolts, and tighten them to 6–9 ft. lbs.

11. Install the vibration damper or pulley on the crankshaft and torque the bolt to 85–100 ft. lbs.

12. Install the fan, pulley and belts. Adjust the belt tension.

13. Install the radiator and connect the radiator hoses and transmission cooling lines, if applicable. If equipped with air conditioning, install the condenser.

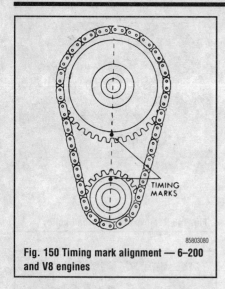

Fig. 150 Timing mark alignment — 6–200 and V8 engines

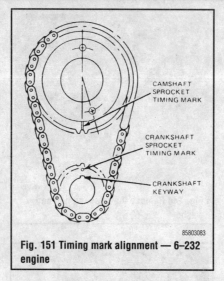

Fig. 151 Timing mark alignment — 6–232 engine

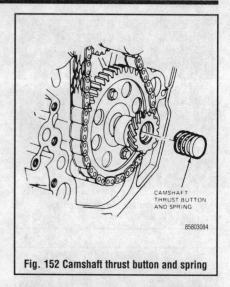

Fig. 152 Camshaft thrust button and spring

14. Fill the crankcase and cooling system. Start the engine and check for leaks.

6–232 Engine

▶ **See Figures 151 and 152**

1. Disconnect the negative battery cable from the battery. Drain the cooling system.

⁕⁕ CAUTION

When draining the coolant, keep in mind that cats and dogs are attracted by the ethylene glycol antifreeze, and are quite likely to drink any that is left in an uncovered container or in puddles on the ground. This will prove fatal in sufficient quantity. Always drain the coolant into a sealable container. Coolant should be reused unless it is contaminated or several years old.

2. Remove the air cleaner and air duct assemblies.
3. Remove the radiator fan shroud and position it back over the water pump. Remove the fan clutch assembly and shroud.
4. Remove the drive belt(s). If equipped with power steering, remove the pump with the hoses attached and position it out of the way. Be sure to keep the pump upright to prevent fluid leakage.
5. If your car is equipped with air conditioning, remove the front compressor mounting bracket. It is not necessary to remove the compressor.
6. Disconnect the coolant bypass hose and the heater hose at the water pump.
7. Disconnect the upper radiator hose at the thermostat housing.
8. Remove the distributor.
9. If your car is equipped with a trip minder, remove the flow meter support bracket and allow the meter to be supported by the hoses.
10. Raise the front of the car and support on jackstands.
11. Remove the crankshaft pulley using a suitable puller. Remove the fuel pump shield.
12. If carburetor equipped, disconnect the fuel line from the carburetor at the fuel pump, then remove the mounting bolts and the fuel pump. Position pump out of the way with the tank line still attached.
13. Drain the engine oil and remove the oil filter.
14. Disconnect the lower radiator hose at the water pump.
15. Remove the oil pan mounting bolts and lower the oil pan.

➡ **The front cover cannot be removed unless the oil pan is lowered.**

16. Lower the car from the jackstands.
17. Remove the front cover mounting bolts. It is not necessary to separate the water pump.

➡ **A front cover mounting bolt is located behind the oil filter adapter. If this bolt is not removed and the cover is pried upon, breakage will occur.**

18. Remove the timing indicator. Remove the front cover and water pump as an assembly.
19. Remove the camshaft thrust button and spring from the end of the camshaft. Remove the camshaft sprocket attaching bolts.
20. Remove the camshaft sprocket, crankshaft sprocket and timing chain by pulling forward evenly on both sprockets. If the crankshaft sprocket is difficult to remove, position two small prybars, one on each side, behind the sprocket and pry forward.

To install:

21. Clean all gasket surfaces on the front cover, cylinder block, fuel pump and oil pan.
22. Install a new front cover oil seal. If a new front cover is to be installed:
   a. Install the oil pump, oil filter adapter and intermediate shaft from the old cover.
   b. Remove the water pump from the old cover.
   c. Clean the mounting surface, and install a new mounting gasket with the water pump on the new front cover. Tighten the pump attaching bolts to 15–22 ft. lbs.
23. Rotate the crankshaft, if necessary, to bring No. 1 piston to TDC with the crankshaft keyway at the 12 o'clock position.
24. Lubricate the timing chain with motor oil. Install the chain over the two sprockets making sure that the marks on both sprockets are positioned across from each other. Install the sprockets and chain on the cam and crankshaft. Install the camshaft mounting bolts. Tighten the bolts to 15–22 ft. lbs.
25. Install the camshaft thrust button and spring. Lubricate the thrust button with polyethylene grease before installation.

⁕⁕ WARNING

The thrust button and spring must be bottomed in the camshaft seat and must not be allowed to fall out during front cover installation.

26. Position a new cover gasket on the front of the engine and install the cover and water pump assemblies. Install the timing indicator. Torque the front cover bolts to 15–22 ft. lbs.
27. Install the oil pan.
28. Connect the lower radiator hose at the water pump.
29. Install the oil filter.
30. Fill the crankcase.
31. Install the fuel pump, if removed.
32. Connect the fuel line at the carburetor and at the fuel pump, if removed.

⁕⁕ WARNING

When installing the fuel pump, turn the crankshaft 180° to position the fuel pump drive eccentric away from the fuel pump arm. Failure to turn the drive eccentric away from the pump arm can cause stress on the pump mounting threads and strip them when installing the pump.

33. Install the crankshaft pulley.

34. Install the fuel pump shield.

35. Lower the front of the car.

36. If your car is equipped with a trip minder, install the flow meter support bracket.

37. Connect the upper radiator hose at the thermostat housing.

38. Install the distributor.

39. Connect the coolant bypass hose and the heater hose at the water pump.

40. If your car is equipped with air conditioning, install the front compressor mounting bracket.

41. If equipped with power steering, install the pump. Be sure to keep the pump upright to prevent fluid leakage.

42. Install the drive belt(s) and adjust to the proper tension.

43. Install the fan clutch assembly.

44. Install the radiator fan shroud.

45. Install the air cleaner and air duct assemblies.

46. Connect the negative battery cable at the battery.

47. Fill the cooling system.

V8 Engines

▶ **See Figure 150**

1. Disconnect the negative battery cable, and drain the cooling system.

❊❊ CAUTION

When draining the coolant, keep in mind that cats and dogs are attracted by the ethylene glycol antifreeze, and are quite likely to drink any that is left in an uncovered container or in puddles on the ground. This will prove fatal in sufficient quantity. Always drain the coolant into a sealable container. Coolant should be reused unless it is contaminated or several years old.

2. Remove the air cleaner assembly, if mounted above the intake manifold.

3. Disconnect the radiator hoses and transmission cooler lines, if so equipped, and remove the radiator.

4. Disconnect the heater hose at the water pump. Slide the water pump bypass hose clamp toward the pump.

5. Loosen the alternator mounting bolts at the alternator. Remove the alternator support bolt at the water pump. Remove the Thermactor pump on all engines so equipped. If equipped with power steering or air conditioning, unbolt the component, remove the belt, and lay the pump or compressor aside with the lines attached.

6. Remove the fan, spacer, pulley, and drive belt.

7. Drain the crankcase and remove the engine oil dipstick.

8. Remove the pulley from the crankshaft pulley adapter. Remove the capscrew and washer from the front end of the crankshaft. Remove the crankshaft pulley adapter with a puller.

9. On carburetor equipped engines, disconnect the fuel outlet line at the fuel pump, then remove the fuel pump retaining bolts and lay the pump to the side.

10. Remove the front cover attaching bolts.

11. Remove the crankshaft oil slinger, if so equipped.

12. Check timing chain deflection, using the procedure outlined in Step 6 of the 6–200 engine Timing Chain Removal.

13. Rotate the engine until the sprocket timing marks are aligned as shown in the valve timing illustration.

14. Remove the camshaft sprocket bolt or capscrew, washers, and fuel pump eccentric or spacer. Slide both sprockets and chain forward and off as an assembly.

To install:

15. Position the sprockets and chain on the camshaft and crankshaft with both timing marks facing dot–to–dot on a centerline. Install the fuel pump eccentric or spacer, washers and sprocket attaching bolt or capscrew. Torque the sprocket attaching bolt or capscrew to 40–45 ft. lbs.

16. Install the crankshaft front oil slinger, if applicable.

17. Clean the front cover and mating surfaces of old gasket material. Install a new oil seal in the cover. Use a seal driver tool, if available.

18. Coat a new cover gasket with sealer and position it on the block.

➡ Trim away the exposed portion of the oil pan gasket flush with the cylinder block. Cut and position the required portion of a new gasket to the oil pan, applying sealer to both sides of it.

19. Install the front cover, using a crankshaft–to–cover alignment tool. Coat the threads of the attaching bolts with sealer. Torque the attaching bolts to 12–18 ft. lbs.

20. If removed, install the fuel pump and connect the fuel pump outlet tube.

21. Install the crankshaft pulley adapter and torque the attaching bolt. Install the crankshaft pulley.

22. Install the water pump pulley, drive belt, spacer and fan.

23. Install the alternator support bolt at the water pump. Tighten the alternator mounting bolts. Adjust the drive belt tension. Install the Thermactor pump if so equipped.

24. Install the radiator and connect all coolant and heater hoses.

25. Install the engine oil dipstick. Refill the cooling system and the crankcase.

26. Connect the negative battery cable.

27. Start the engine and operate it at fast idle. Check for leaks.

28. Install the air cleaner assembly, if removed. Adjust the ignition timing and make all final adjustments.

Timing Gears

REMOVAL & INSTALLATION

▶ **See Figure 153**

1. Drain the cooling system and crankcase. Remove the oil pan and radiator.

2. Remove the water pump and drive belt.

3. Remove the timing gear cover and camshaft timing gear.

4. Use a gear puller to remove the crankshaft gear. Remove the key from the crankshaft.

To install:

5. Align the keyway in the camshaft timing gear with the key, and slide the gear onto the shaft, making sure that it seats tightly against the spacer.

6. Check the camshaft end-play. If it is not within specifications, replace the thrust plate.

7. Position the key in the crankshaft. Align the keyway in the crankshaft gear with the key in the crankshaft, and align the timing marks. Install the gear with the use of two wrenches and a special tool designed to press the gear onto the shaft.

8. Install the timing gear cover and seal, as described previously in this section.

9. Install the water pump and drive belt. Adjust the drive belt to its proper tension.

10. Install the oil pan and radiator.

11. Fill the cooling system with coolant and the crankcase with oil.

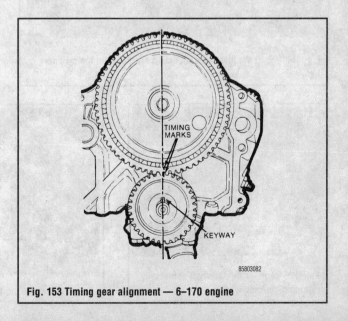

Fig. 153 Timing gear alignment — 6–170 engine

Camshaft and Bearings

REMOVAL & INSTALLATION

▶ **See Figures 154 thru 162**

4–140 Engine

➡The following procedure covers camshaft removal and installation with the cylinder head on or off the engine. If the cylinder head has been removed start at Step 9.

1. Remove the air cleaner assembly and disconnect the negative battery cable. Drain the cooling system.

✳✳ CAUTION

When draining the coolant, keep in mind that cats and dogs are attracted by the ethylene glycol antifreeze, and are quite likely to drink any that is left in an uncovered container or in puddles on the ground. This will prove fatal in sufficient quantity. Always drain the coolant into a sealable container. Coolant should be reused unless it is contaminated or several years old.

2. Remove the spark plug wires from the plugs, disconnect the retainer from the valve cover and position the wires out of the way. Disconnect the rubber vacuum lines as necessary.
3. Remove all drive belts. Remove the alternator mounting bracket–to–cylinder head mounting bolts, and position the bracket and alternator out of the way.
4. Disconnect and remove the upper radiator hose. Disconnect the radiator shroud.

5. Remove the fan blades and water pump pulley and fan shroud. Remove the valve cover and timing belt outer cover.
6. Align the engine timing marks at TDC. Remove the timing belt.
7. Jack up the front of the car and support it on jackstands. Remove the front motor mount bolts. Disconnect the lower radiator hose from the radiator. Disconnect and plug the automatic transmission cooler lines, if so equipped.
8. Position a piece of wood on a floor jack and raise the engine carefully as far as it will go. Place blocks of wood between the engine mounts and crossmember pedestals.
9. Remove the cam followers (rocker arms) as described earlier in this section.
10. Remove the camshaft sprocket and belt guide using a suitable puller. Remove the front oil seal with a sheet metal screw and slide hammer or special seal remover tool.
11. Remove the camshaft retainer located on the rear mounting stand, by unfastening the two bolts or screws.
12. Remove the camshaft by carefully withdrawing it toward the front of the engine. Caution should be used to prevent damage to the cam bearings, lobes and journals.

To install:
13. Check the camshaft journals and lobes for wear. Inspect the cam bearings. If they are worn, the cylinder head must be removed for new bearings to be installed by a machine shop.
14. Install the camshaft. Caution should be used to prevent damage to the cam bearings, lobes and journals. Coat the camshaft with heavy SG engine oil before sliding it into the cylinder head.
15. Install the camshaft retainer located on the rear mounting stand.
16. Install a new front oil seal.
17. Install the camshaft sprocket and belt guide. Apply a coat of sealer or Teflon® tape to the camshaft sprocket bolt before installation.
18. Install the cam followers as described earlier in this section.

Fig. 154 Unbolt the alternator mounting bracket from the cylinder head

Fig. 155 Loosen the camshaft sprocket retaining bolt

Fig. 156 Remove the camshaft sprocket retaining bolt and washer

Fig. 157 Remove the camshaft sprocket

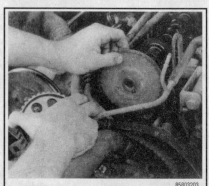

Fig. 158 Remove the camshaft belt guide

Fig. 159 Remove the front oil seal

Fig. 160 Loosen the two fasteners which secure the camshaft retainer to the rear mounting stand

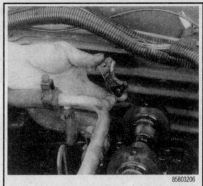

Fig. 161 Remove the camshaft retainer and its two fasteners

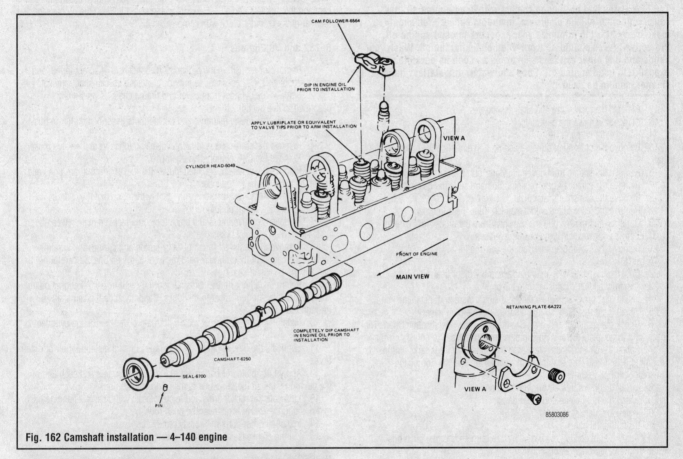

Fig. 162 Camshaft installation — 4–140 engine

✳✳ WARNING

After any procedure requiring removal of the rocker arms, each lash adjuster must be fully collapsed after assembly, then released. This must be done before the camshaft is turned. See Valve Clearance — Hydraulic Valve Lash Adjusters.

19. Remove the blocks of wood between the engine mounts and crossmember pedestals, and lower the engine onto the mounts.
20. Lower the front of the car.
21. Install the front motor mount bolts.
22. Connect the lower radiator hose at the radiator.
23. Connect the automatic transmission cooler lines, if applicable.
24. Align the engine timing marks at TDC.
25. Install the timing belt.
26. Install the timing belt outer cover and valve cover.
27. Install the fan blades and water pump pulley and fan shroud.
28. Connect and install the upper radiator hose.
29. Install the alternator and mounting bracket on the cylinder head.
30. Install all drive belts.
31. Install the spark plug wires on the plugs.
32. Connect the plug wires to the retainer on the valve cover.
33. Connect the rubber vacuum lines as necessary.
34. Fill the cooling system.
35. Install the air cleaner assembly.
36. Connect the negative battery cable.

6–170 Engine

1. Drain the coolant.

✳✳ CAUTION

When draining the coolant, keep in mind that cats and dogs are attracted by the ethylene glycol antifreeze, and are quite likely to drink any that is left in an uncovered container or in puddles on the ground. This will prove fatal in sufficient quantity. Always drain the coolant into a sealable container. Coolant should be reused unless it is contaminated or several years old.

2. Remove the radiator, fan, spacer, water pump pulley and drive belts.
3. Remove the distributor.
4. Remove the alternator.
5. Remove the Thermactor pump.
6. Remove the valve covers.
7. Remove the fuel line and filter.
8. Remove the carburetor.
9. Remove the EGR tube.
10. Remove the intake manifold.
11. Drain the crankcase.

✳✳ CAUTION

The EPA warns that prolonged contact with used engine oil may cause a number of skin disorders, including cancer! You should make every effort to minimize your exposure to used engine oil. Protective gloves should be worn when changing the oil. Wash your hands and any other exposed skin areas as soon as possible after exposure to used engine oil. Soap and water, or waterless hand cleaner, should be used.

12. Remove the rocker arm and shaft assemblies.
13. Mark and remove the pushrods.
14. Remove the oil pan.
15. Remove the crankshaft pulley attaching bolt and slide the pulley off the shaft.
16. Remove the engine front cover and water pump as an assembly.
17. Remove the camshaft gear retaining bolt and slide the gear off the shaft.
18. Remove the camshaft thrust plate.
19. Remove the valve lifters with a magnet. Keep them in order.
20. Carefully and slowly, pull the camshaft from the block. Take care to avoid hitting the lobes against the bearing surfaces.
21. Remove the key and spacer from the camshaft.

To install:
22. Coat the camshaft with an engine assembly oil or gear oil.
23. Carefully slide the camshaft into the block.
24. Install the spacer with the chamfered side inward and install the key.
25. Install the thrust plate so that it covers the main oil gallery.
26. Check the camshaft end-play. See the Camshaft Specification Chart. The spacer and thrust plate are available in different thicknesses to adjust end-play.
27. Rotate the camshaft and crankshaft to align the timing marks and install the timing gear. Make sure that the timing marks are aligned. Torque the camshaft gear bolt to 34 ft. lbs.
28. Install the lifters in their original locations.
29. Install the front cover and water pump.
30. Install the crankshaft pulley.
31. Install the oil pan.
32. Apply a light coating of chassis lube to both ends of the pushrods and install them in their original locations.
33. Install the intake manifold.
34. Install the oil baffles and rocker arm assemblies. Tighten the bolts to 45 ft. lbs. Adjust the valves.
35. Install the water pump pulley, fan spacer, fan and drive belt. Adjust the belt tension.
36. Install the:
- carburetor
- EGR tube
- fuel line
- fuel filter
- alternator
- Thermactor pump
- distributor
- radiator
37. Install and properly tension the accessory drive belt(s).
38. Fill the cooling system.
39. Adjust the timing.

40. Install the valve covers.
41. Start the engine and check the idle speed.
42. Let the engine run to normal operating temperature and check for leaks.

6–200 Engine

1. Remove the cylinder head. Refer to Cylinder Head Removal & Installation procedures, earlier in this section.
2. Remove the cylinder front cover, timing chain and sprockets as outlined previously.
3. Disconnect and remove the radiator, condenser and grille. Remove the gravel deflector.
4. Using a magnet, remove the valve lifters and keep them in order so that they can be installed in their original positions.
5. Remove the camshaft thrust plate and remove the camshaft by pulling it from the front of the engine. Use care not to damage the camshaft lobes or journals while removing the cam from the engine.
6. Before installing the camshaft, coat the lobes with engine assembly lubricant and the journals and all valve parts with heavy oil. Clean the oil passage at the rear of the cylinder block with compressed air.

6–232 and V8 Engines

1. Remove or reposition the radiator, A/C condenser, if so equipped, and grille components, as necessary, to provide clearance for camshaft removal.
2. Remove the cylinder front cover and timing chain as previously described in this section.
3. Remove the intake manifold and related parts described earlier in this section.
4. Remove the crankcase ventilation valve and tubes from the valve rocker covers. Remove the EGR cooler, if so equipped.
5. Remove the valve covers, then loosen the rocker arm fulcrum bolts and rotate the rocker arms to the side.
6. Remove the valve pushrods and identify them, so that they can be installed in their original positions.
7. Remove the valve lifters and place them in a rack, so that they can be installed in their original bores.
8. Remove the camshaft thrust plate or button and spring, and carefully remove the camshaft by pulling toward the front of the engine. Be careful not to damage the camshaft bearings.
9. Before installing, oil the camshaft journals with heavy SG engine oil and apply Lubriplate® or equivalent to the lobes. Carefully slide the camshaft through the bearings.
10. Install the camshaft thrust plate with the groove towards the cylinder block.
11. Lubricate the lifters with heavy SG engine oil and install in their original bores.
12. Apply Lubriplate® or equivalent to the valve stem tips and each end of the pushrods. Install the pushrods in their original positions.
13. Lubricate the rocker arms and fulcrum seats with heavy SG engine oil and position the rocker arms over the push rods.
14. Install all other parts previously removed.
15. Fill the crankcase and cooling system and adjust the timing.

INSPECTION

▶ **See Figure 163**

Clean the camshaft using a safe solvent, and clean all oil grooves. Visually inspect the cam lobes and bearing journals for excessive wear. If a lobe is questionable, check all lobes and journals with a micrometer.

Measure the lobes from nose to base (measurement A) and again from side to side (measurement B). The lift is determined by subtracting the second measurement from the first. If all exhaust lobes and all intake lobes are not identical, the camshaft must be reground or replaced. Measure the bearing journals and compare to specifications. If a journal is worn there is a good chance that the cam bearings are worn too, requiring replacement.

If the lobes and journals appear intact, place the front and rear cam journals in V–blocks and rest a dial indicator on the center journal. Rotate the camshaft to check for straightness; if deviation exceeds 0.001 in. (0.025mm), replace the camshaft.

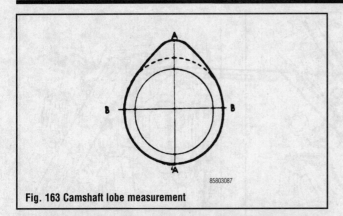

Fig. 163 Camshaft lobe measurement

Auxiliary Shaft

REMOVAL & INSTALLATION

♦ **See Figure 164**

4–140 Engine

1. Remove the camshaft drive (timing) belt outer cover.
2. Remove the timing belt. Remove the auxiliary shaft sprocket. A puller may be necessary to remove the sprocket.
3. Remove the distributor and, on carburetor–equipped engines, the fuel pump.
4. Remove the auxiliary shaft cover and thrust plate.
5. Withdraw the auxiliary shaft from the block.

✳✥ WARNING

The distributor drive gear and the fuel pump eccentric on the auxiliary shaft must not be allowed to touch the auxiliary shaft bearings during removal and installation. Completely coat the shaft with oil before sliding it into place.

6. Slide the auxiliary shaft into the housing and insert the thrust plate to hold the shaft.
7. Install a new gasket and auxiliary shaft cover.

➡ The auxiliary shaft cover and cylinder front cover share a gasket. Cut off the old gasket around the cylinder cover and use half of the new gasket on the auxiliary shaft cover.

8. If applicable, fit a new gasket onto the fuel pump and install the pump.
9. Insert the distributor and install the auxiliary shaft sprocket.
10. Align the timing marks and install the camshaft drive belt.
11. Install the drive belt outer cover.
12. Check the ignition timing.

Pistons and Connecting Rods

REMOVAL

♦ **See Figures 165, 166 and 167**

➡ Although, in most cases, the pistons and connecting rods can be removed from the engine (after the cylinder head and oil pan are removed) while the engine is still in the car, it is far easier to remove the engine from the car. If removing pistons with the engine still installed, disconnect the radiator hoses, automatic transmission cooler

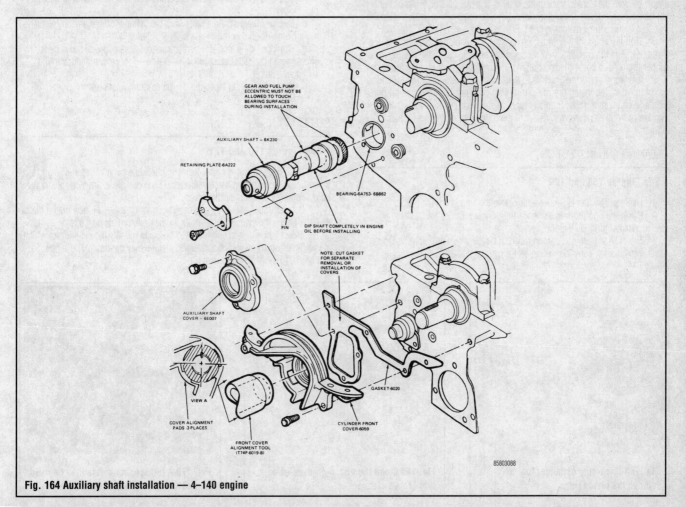

Fig. 164 Auxiliary shaft installation — 4–140 engine

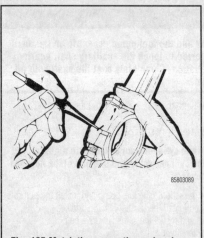

Fig. 165 Match the connecting rod and cap with scribe marks

Fig. 166 Use lengths of vacuum hose or rubber tubing to protect the crankshaft journals and cylinder walls during piston removal and installation

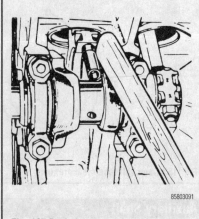

Fig. 167 Push the piston out with a hammer handle

lines, if so equipped, and radiator shroud. Unbolt front mounts before jacking up the engine. Block the engine in position with wooden blocks between the mounts.

1. Remove the engine from the car, as previously covered in this section.
2. Remove the cylinder head(s), oil pan and front cover (if necessary).
3. Using a ridge reamer, remove the ridge at the top of each cylinder bore, before removing the pistons and connecting rods. (Refer to the following section on Ridge Removal.)
4. Check the edges of the connecting rod and bearing cap for numbers or matchmarks. If none are present, mark the rod and cap numerically and in sequence from the front to back of the engine. The numbers or marks not only tell from which cylinder the piston came, but also ensures that the rod caps are installed in the correct matching position.
5. Turn the crankshaft until the connecting rod is at the bottom of its travel. Remove the two attaching nuts and the bearing cap. Take two pieces of rubber tubing and cover the rod bolts to prevent crankshaft or cylinder scoring. Use a wooden hammer handle to help push the piston and rod up and out of the cylinder. install the rod cap in its proper position. Remove all pistons and connecting rods, in this manner. Inspect the cylinder walls and deglaze or hone as necessary. (Refer to the following section on Cylinder Honing.)

CLEANING AND INSPECTION

▶ **See Figures 168 and 169**

1. Use a piston ring expander and remove the rings from the piston.
2. Clean the ring grooves using an appropriate cleaning tool, exercising care to avoid cutting too deeply.
3. Clean all varnish and carbon from the piston with a safe solvent. Do not use a wire brush or caustic solution on the pistons.

4. Inspect the pistons for scuffing, scoring, cracks, pitting or excessive ring groove wear. If wear is evident, the piston must be replaced.
5. Have the piston and connecting rod assembly checked by a machine shop for correct alignment, piston pin wear and piston diameter. If the piston has collapsed, it will have to be replaced or knurled to restore its original diameter. Connecting rod bushing replacement, piston pin fitting and piston changing can be handled by the machine shop.
6. Check used piston–to–cylinder bore clearance as follows:
   a. Measure the cylinder bore diameter with a telescope gauge.
   b. Measure the piston's outer diameter with a micrometer. When measuring the pistons for size or taper, measurements must be made with the piston pin removed.
   c. Subtract the piston diameter from the cylinder bore diameter to determine piston–to–bore clearance.
   d. Compare the piston–to–bore clearances obtained with those clearances recommended. Determine if the piston–to–bore clearance is in the acceptable range.
   e. When measuring taper, the largest reading must be at the bottom of the skirt.

SELECTING NEW PISTONS

▶ **See Figures 170 and 171**

1. If the used piston is not acceptable, check the service piston size and determine if a new piston can be selected. (Service pistons are available in standard, high limit and standard oversize.
2. If the cylinder bore must be reconditioned, measure the new piston diameter, then hone the cylinder bore to obtain the preferred clearance.
3. Select a new piston and mark the piston to identify the cylinder for which it was fitted. On some vehicles, oversize pistons may be found. These pistons will be 0.010 in. (0.254mm) oversize.

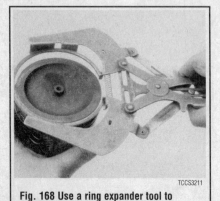

Fig. 168 Use a ring expander tool to remove the piston rings

Fig. 169 Clean the piston grooves using a ring groove cleaner

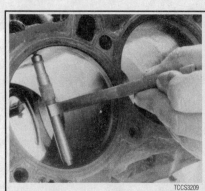

Fig. 170 A telescoping gauge may be used to measure the cylinder bore diameter

Fig. 171 Measure the piston's outer diameter using a micrometer

RIDGE REMOVAL

▶ **See Figures 172 and 173**

Because the top piston ring does not travel to the very top of the cylinder bore, a ridge is built up between the end of the travel and the top of the cylinder. Pushing the piston and connecting rod assembly past the ridge is difficult and may cause damage to the piston. If new rings are installed and the ridge has not been removed, ring breakage and piston damage can occur when the ridge is encountered at engine speed.

1. Turn the crankshaft to position the piston at the bottom of the cylinder bore. Cover the top of the piston with a rag.

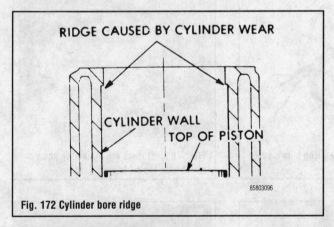

Fig. 172 Cylinder bore ridge

2. Install a ridge reamer in the bore and follow the manufacturer's instructions to remove the ridge. Use caution to avoid cutting too deeply or into the ring travel area.
3. Remove the rag and cuttings from the top of the piston.
4. Remove the ridge from each of the other cylinders, using the same procedure.

CYLINDER HONING

▶ **See Figures 174 and 175**

Check the cylinder bore for wear using a telescope gauge and a micrometer. Measure the cylinder bore diameter perpendicular to the piston pin at the point 2½ in. (63.5mm) below the top of the engine block. Measure the piston skirt perpendicular to the piston pin. The difference between the two measurement is the piston clearance. If the clearance is within specifications, finish honing or glaze breaking is all that is required. If clearance is excessive, a slightly oversized piston may be required. If greatly oversize, the engine will have to be bored and 0.010 in. (0.254mm) or larger oversized pistons installed.

1. When cylinders are being honed, follow the manufacturer's recommendations for the use of the hone.
2. Occasionally, during the honing operation, the cylinder bore should be thoroughly cleaned and the selected piston checked for correct fit.
3. When finish–honing a cylinder bore, the hone should be moved up and down at a sufficient speed to obtain a very fine uniform surface finish in a cross–hatch pattern of approximately 45–65° included angle. The finish marks should be clean, but not sharp, and free from imbedded particles and torn or folded metal.
4. Permanently mark the piston for the cylinder to which it has been fitted and proceed to hone the remaining cylinders.

✳✳ WARNING

Handle the pistons with care. Do not attempt to force the pistons through the cylinders until the cylinders have been honed to the correct size. Pistons can be distorted through careless handling.

5. Thoroughly clean the bores with hot water and detergent. Scrub well with a stiff bristle brush and rinse thoroughly with hot water. It is extremely essential that a good cleaning operation be performed. If any of the abrasive material is allowed to remain in the cylinder bores, it will rapidly wear the new rings and cylinder bores. The bores should be swabbed several times with light engine oil and a clean cloth, and then wiped with a clean dry cloth. CYLINDERS SHOULD NOT BE CLEANED WITH KEROSENE OR GASOLINE. Clean the remainder of the cylinder block to remove the excess material spread during the honing operation.

PISTON PIN REPLACEMENT

Use care at all times when handling and servicing connecting rods and pistons. To prevent possible damage to these units, do not clamp the rods or pistons in a vise, since they may become distorted. Do not allow the pistons to strike against one another, or against hard objects or bench surfaces, since distortion of the piston contour or nicks in the soft aluminum material may result.

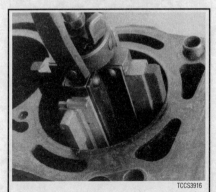

Fig. 173 Removing the ridge from the cylinder bore using a ridge reamer

Fig. 174 Using a ball–type cylinder hone is an easy way to hone the cylinder bore

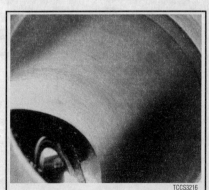

Fig. 175 A properly cross–hatched cylinder bore

1. Remove the piston rings using a suitable piston ring remover.

2. Remove the piston pin lockring, if used. Install the guide bushing of the piston pin removing and installing tool.

3. Install the piston and connecting rod assembly on a support, and place the assembly in an arbor press. Press the pin out of the connecting rod, using the appropriate piston pin tool.

4. Assembly is the reverse of disassembly. Use new lockrings where needed.

PISTON RING REPLACEMENT

▶ **See Figures 176, 177, 178, 179 and 180**

1. Take the new piston rings and compress them, one at a time into the cylinder that they will be used in. Press the ring about 1 in. (25.4mm) below the top of the cylinder block using an inverted piston.

2. Use a feeler gauge and measure the distance between the ends of the ring; this is called measuring the ring end–gap. Compare the reading to the one called for in the specification table. File the ends of the ring with a fine file to obtain the necessary clearance.

✳✳ WARNING

If inadequate ring end–gap exists, ring breakage will result.

3. Inspect the ring grooves on the piston for excessive wear or taper. If necessary, have the grooves recut for use with a standard ring and spacer. A machine shop can handle this job for you.

4. Check the ring grooves by rolling the new piston ring around the groove to check for burrs or carbon deposits. If any are found, remove them with a fine file. Hold the ring in the groove and measure side clearance with a feeler gauge. If clearance is excessive, spacer(s) will have to be added.

➡**Always add the spacer above the piston ring.**

5. Install the rings on the piston, lower oil ring first. Use a ring installing tool on the compression rings. Consult the instruction sheet that comes with the rings to be sure they are installed with the correct side up. A mark on the ring usually faces upward.

6. When installing the oil rings, first install the expanding ring in the groove. Hold the ends of the ring butted together (they must not overlap) and install the bottom rail (scraper) with the end about 1 in. (25.4mm) away from the butted end of the control ring. Install the top rail about 1 in. (25.4mm) away from the butted end of the control, but on the opposite side from the lower rail.

7. Install the two compression rings.

8. Consult the illustration for ring positioning, and arrange the rings as shown.

9. Install a ring compressor and insert the piston and rod assembly into the engine.

ROD BEARING REPLACEMENT

▶ **See Figures 181 thru 186**

Rod bearings can be installed when the pistons have been removed for servicing (rings, etc.) or, in most cases, while the engine is still in the car. Bearing replacement, however, is far easier with the engine out of the car and disassembled.

Wash the connecting rods in a cleaning solvent and dry with compressed air. Check for twisted or bent rods and inspect for nicks or cracks. Replace connecting rods that are damaged.

Inspect journals for roughness and wear. Slight roughness may be removed with a fine grit polishing cloth saturated with engine oil. Burrs may be removed with a fine oil stone by moving the stone on the journal circumference. Do not move the stone back and forth across the journal. If the journals are scored or ridged, the crankshaft must be replaced.

The connecting rod journals should be checked for out–of–roundness and correct size with a micrometer.

➡**Connecting rod journals will normally be standard size. If any undersized bearings are used, the size will be stamped on a counterweight.**

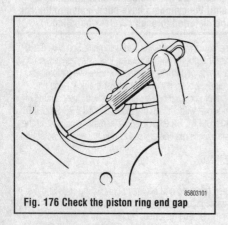

Fig. 176 Check the piston ring end gap

85803101

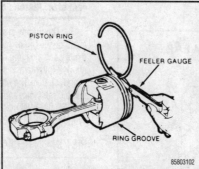

Fig. 177 Check the piston ring side clearance

85803102

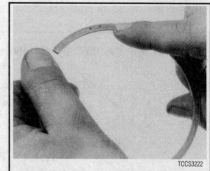

TCCS3222

Fig. 178 Most rings are marked to show which side should face upward

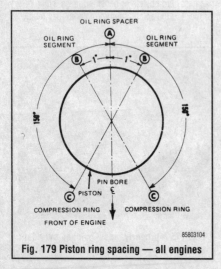

Fig. 179 Piston ring spacing — all engines

85803104

TCCS3914

Fig. 180 Using a ring compressor and hammer handle to insert the piston into the cylinder

85803207

Fig. 181 Removing the bearing cap nuts

Fig. 182 Removing the bearing cap and bearing insert

Fig. 183 The bearing insert is designed to fit securely in the bearing cap

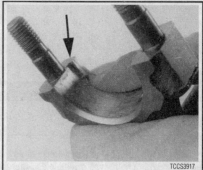

Fig. 184 The notch on the side of the bearing cap matches the groove on the bearing insert

Fig. 185 Apply a strip of gauging material to the bearing, then install and torque the cap

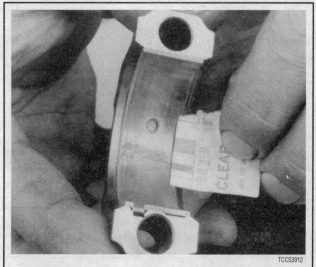

Fig. 186 After the bearing cap has been removed, use the gauge supplied with the gauging material to check bearing clearances

5. Install the new bearing inserts in the connecting rod and bearing cap, with the tangs fitting in the slots provided and lubricate them with oil.
6. Lubricate the bearing inserts with oil.
7. Position the connecting rod over the crankshaft journal and install the rod cap. Make sure the cap and rod numbers match, and torque the rod nuts to specification.

INSTALLATION

1. Lubricate the piston, bearing inserts and cylinder wall.
2. Install a ring compressor over the piston, position the piston with the mark toward the front of the engine, and carefully install.
3. Position the connecting rod with the bearing insert installed over the crankshaft journal. Install the connecting rod cap with the bearing in its proper position. Secure with rod nuts and torque to the proper specification.
4. Install the remaining rod and piston assemblies in the same manner.
5. If removed, replace the front cover and gasket or seal.
6. Install the oil pan and cylinder head(s).
7. Install the engine in the car, as previously covered in this section.

Crankshaft/Intermediate Shaft Front Oil Seal

REMOVAL & INSTALLATION

1. Remove the engine front cover.
2. Using an arbor press, press the old seal(s) out of the front cover.

If plastic gauging material is to be used:
1. Clean oil from the journal bearing cap, connecting rod and outer and inner surfaces of the bearing inserts. Position the insert so that the tang is properly aligned with the notch in the rod and cap.
2. Place a piece of plastic gauging material, such as Plastigage®, in the center of the lower bearing shell.
3. Remove the bearing cap and determine the bearing clearances by comparing the width of the flattened plastic gauging material at its widest point with the graduation on the package. The number within the graduation on the package indicates the clearance in thousandths of an inch or millimeters.
   If this clearance is excessive, replace the bearing insert and recheck the clearance with the plastic gauging material. Lubricate the bearing insert with engine oil before assembly. Repeat the procedure on the remaining connecting rod bearings. All rods must be connected to their journals when rotating the crankshaft, to prevent engine damage.
4. Clean the rod journal, the connecting rod end and the bearing cap after removing the old bearing inserts.

3. Position the new seals on the front cover and install, using the appropriate tool. Use part no. T84P–6019–B or equivalent for the crankshaft seal, and part no. T84P–6020–A or equivalent for the intermediate shaft seal.

4. Lubricate the seal lips with engine oil.

5. Install the engine front cover.

Rear Main Oil Seal

REMOVAL & INSTALLATION

➡Refer to the build dates listed below to determine if the engine is equipped with a split–type or one–piece rear main oil seal. Engines manufactured after the dates indicated have a one–piece oil seal, while those built prior to the indicated dates are equipped with a split–type seal.

- 4–140 — 9/28/81
- 6–232 — 4/1/83
- 8–302 — 12/1/82

Split–Type Seal

▶ See Figure 187

➡The rear oil seal installed in these engines is a rubber type (split–lip) seal.

1. Remove the oil pan and, if required, the oil pump.

2. Loosen all the main bearing caps, allowing the crankshaft to lower slightly.

✳✳ WARNING

The crankshaft should not be allowed to drop more than 1/32 in. (0.8mm).

3. Remove the rear main bearing cap and remove the seal from the cap and block. Be very careful not to scratch the sealing surface. Remove the old seal

retaining pin from the cap, if equipped. It is not used with the replacement seal.

4. Carefully clean the seal grooves in the cap and block with solvent.

5. Soak the new seal halves in clean engine oil.

6. Install the upper half of the seal in the block with the undercut side of the seal toward the front of the engine. Slide the seal around the crankshaft journal until 3/8 in. (9.5mm) protrudes beyond the base of the block.

7. Tighten all the main bearing caps (except the rear main bearing) to specifications.

8. Install the lower seal into the rear cap, with the undercut side facing the front of the engine. Allow 3/8 in. (9.5mm) of the seal to protrude above the surface, at the opposite end from the block seal.

9. Squeeze a 1/16 in. (1.6mm) bead of silicone sealant onto the areas shown.

10. Install the rear cap and torque to specification.

11. Install the oil pump, if applicable, and the oil pan. Fill the crankcase with oil, start the engine, and check for leaks.

One–Piece Seal

▶ See Figure 188

1. Remove the transmission, clutch, and flywheel or driveplate, after referring to the appropriate section for instructions.

2. Punch two holes in the crankshaft rear oil seal on opposite sides of the crankshaft, just above the bearing cap to the cylinder block split line. Install a sheet metal screw in each of the holes or use a small slide hammer, and pry the crankshaft rear main oil seal from the block.

✳✳ WARNING

Use extreme caution not to scratch the crankshaft oil seal surface.

3. Clean the oil seal recess in the cylinder block and main bearing cap.

4. Coat the seal and all of the seal mounting surfaces with oil and install the seal in the recess, driving it into place with an oil seal installation tool or a large socket.

5. Install the driveplate or flywheel, clutch and transmission in the reverse order of removal.

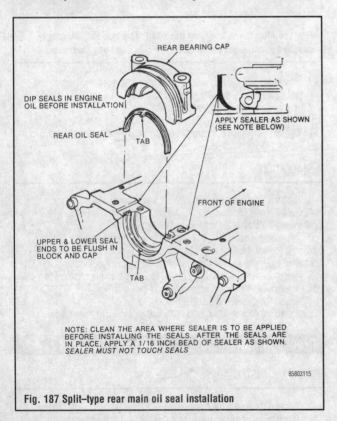

NOTE: CLEAN THE AREA WHERE SEALER IS TO BE APPLIED BEFORE INSTALLING THE SEALS. AFTER THE SEALS ARE IN PLACE, APPLY A 1/16 INCH BEAD OF SEALER AS SHOWN. *SEALER MUST NOT TOUCH SEALS*

85803115

Fig. 187 Split–type rear main oil seal installation

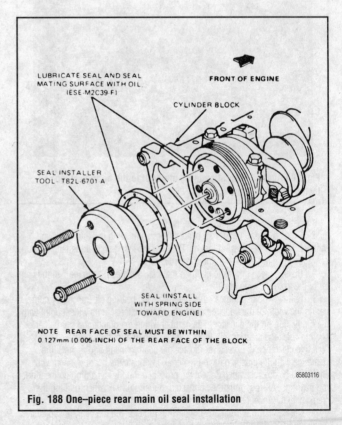

NOTE REAR FACE OF SEAL MUST BE WITHIN 0.127mm (0.005 INCH) OF THE REAR FACE OF THE BLOCK

85803116

Fig. 188 One–piece rear main oil seal installation

Crankshaft and Main Bearings

REMOVAL & INSTALLATION

In–Car Service

▶ See Figures 189 and 190

1. Main bearings may be replaced while the engine is still in the car by rolling them out and in.
2. Special roll–out pins are available from automotive parts houses, or can be fabricated from a cotter pin. The roll–out pin fits in the oil hole of the main bearing journal. When the crankshaft is rotated opposite the direction of the bearing lock tab, the pin engages the end of the bearing and rolls out the insert.

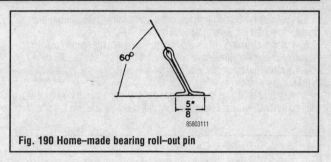

Fig. 190 Home–made bearing roll–out pin

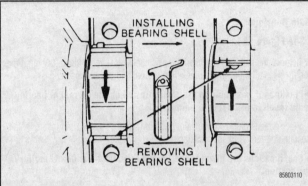

Fig. 189 Remove or install the upper bearing insert using a roll–out pin

3. Remove the main bearing cap and roll out the upper bearing insert. Remove the insert from the main bearing cap. Clean the inside of the bearing cap and crankshaft journal.
4. Lubricate and roll the upper insert into position, making sure the lock tab is anchored and the insert is not cocked. Install the lower bearing insert into the cap, lubricate it and install it on the engine. Make sure the main bearing cap is installed facing in the correct direction and torque it to specification.

Out–Of–Car Service

▶ See Figures 191, 192 and 193

1. Remove the intake manifold, cylinder heads, front cover, timing gears and/or chain, oil pan, oil pump and flywheel.
2. Remove the piston and rod assemblies. Remove the main bearing caps after marking them for position and direction.
3. Remove the crankshaft, bearing inserts and rear main oil seal. Clean the engine block and cap bearing saddles. Clean the crankshaft and inspect it for wear. Check the bearing journals with a micrometer for out–of–round condition and to determine what size main bearing inserts to install.
4. Install the main bearing upper inserts and rear main oil seal half into the engine block.

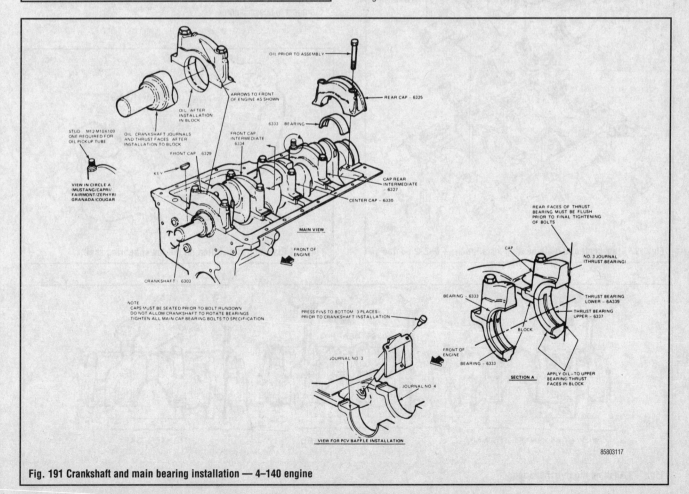

Fig. 191 Crankshaft and main bearing installation — 4–140 engine

5.   Lubricate the bearing inserts and the crankshaft journals. Slowly and carefully lower the crankshaft into position.

6.   Install the bearing inserts and rear main seal into the bearing caps. Install the caps working from the middle out. Torque the cap bolts to specification in stages, rotating the crankshaft after each torque stage. Note the illustration for thrust bearing alignment.

7.   Remove the bearing caps, one at a time, and check the oil clearance with a gauging material, such as Plastigage®. install if clearance is within specifications.

8.   Check the crankshaft end–play. (This procedure is described below.) If it is within specifications, install the connecting rod and piston assemblies with new rod bearing inserts. Check the connecting rod bearing oil clearance and side–play. (This procedure is also described below.) If they are correct, assemble the rest of the engine.

➡ **If a journal is damaged on the crankshaft, repair is possible by having the crankshaft machined to a standard undersize. In most cases, however, since the engine must be removed from the car and disassembled, some thought should be given to replacing the damaged crankshaft with a reground shaft kit. A reground crankshaft kit contains the necessary main and rod bearings for installation. The shaft has been ground and polished to undersize specifications, and will usually hold up well if installed correctly.**

CLEANING AND INSPECTION

Main Bearings

▶ **See Figure 194**

Remove the cap from the bearing to be checked. Using a clean, dry rag, thoroughly clean all oil from the crankshaft journal and bearing insert.

➡**Plastigage® is soluble in oil, therefore, oil on the journal or bearing could result in erroneous readings.**

Place a piece of Plastigage® along the full width of the bearing insert, install the cap, and torque to specification.

➡**Specifications are given in the Engine Specifications Chart, earlier in this section.**

Remove the bearing cap, and determine the bearing clearance by comparing the width of the Plastigage® to the scale on the Plastigage® envelope. Journal taper is determined by comparing the width of the bearing insert. Install the cap, and torque it to specification.

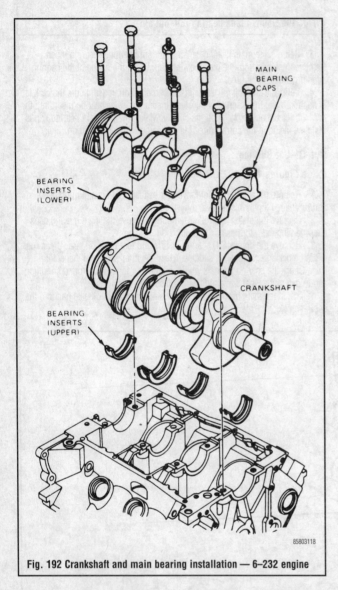

Fig. 192 Crankshaft and main bearing installation — 6–232 engine

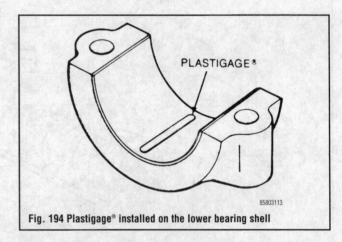

Fig. 194 Plastigage® installed on the lower bearing shell

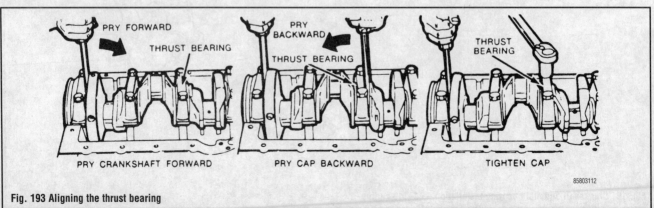

Fig. 193 Aligning the thrust bearing

➡Do not rotate the crankshaft with the Plastigage® installed. If the bearing insert and journal appear intact, and are within tolerances, no further main bearing service is required. If the bearing or journal appear defective, the cause of failure should be determined before replacement.

Crankshaft End–Play/Connecting Rod Side–Play

♦ See Figure 195

Place a pry bar between a main bearing cap and crankshaft casting, taking care not to damage any journals. Pry backward and forward, measuring the distance between the thrust bearing and crankshaft with a feeler gauge. Compare the reading with specifications. If too great a clearance is determined, a main bearing with a larger thrust surface or crankshaft machining may be required. Check with an automotive machine shop for their advice.

Connecting rod clearance between the rod and crankthrow casting can be checked with a feeler gauge. Pry the rod carefully to one side as far as possible and measure the distance on the other side of the rod.

COMPLETING THE REBUILDING PROCESS

Fill the oil pump with oil, to prevent cavitating (sucking air) on initial engine start up. Install the oil pump and the pickup tube on the engine. Coat the oil pan gasket as necessary, and install the gasket and the oil pan. Mount the flywheel and the crankshaft vibration damper or pulley on the crankshaft.

➡Always use new bolts when installing the flywheel. Inspect the clutch shaft pilot bushing in the crankshaft. If the bushing is excessively worn, remove it with an expanding puller and a slide hammer, and tap a new bushing into place.

Position the engine, cylinder head side up. Lubricate the lifters, and install them into their bores. Install the cylinder head, and torque it as specified. Insert the pushrods (where applicable), and install the rocker shaft(s) or rocker arms.

Install the intake and exhaust manifolds, the carburetor, if applicable, and the distributor and spark plugs. Mount all accessories and install the engine in the car. Fill the radiator with coolant, and the crankcase with high quality engine oil.

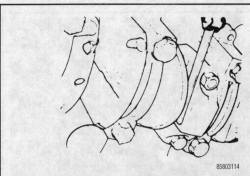

Fig. 195 Check the connecting rod side clearance with a feeler gauge

BREAK–IN PROCEDURE

Start the engine, and allow it to run at low speed for a few minutes, while checking for leaks. Stop the engine, check the oil level, and fill as necessary. Restart the engine, and fill the cooling system to capacity. Check and adjust the ignition timing. Run the engine at low to medium speed (800–2,500 rpm) for approximately ½ hour, and retorque the cylinder head bolts. Road test the car, and check again for leaks.

➡Some gasket manufacturers recommend not retorquing the cylinder head(s) due to the composition of the head gasket. Follow the directions in the gasket set.

Flywheel/Flex Plate and Ring Gear

➡Flex plate is the term for a flywheel mated with an automatic transmission.

REMOVAL & INSTALLATION

All Engines

♦ See Figures 196 thru 201

➡The ring gear is replaceable only on engines mated with a manual transmission. Engines with automatic transmissions have ring gears which are welded to the flex plate.

1. Remove the transmission and transfer case.
2. Remove the clutch, if equipped, or torque converter from the flywheel.
3. Loosen the flywheel bolts a little at a time in a criss–cross pattern to avoid warping the flywheel and remove the flywheel.
4. On cars with manual transmissions, replace the pilot bearing in the end of the crankshaft after removing the flywheel.
5. The flywheel should be checked for cracks and glazing. It can be resurfaced by a machine shop.
6. If the ring gear is to be replaced, drill a hole in the gear between two teeth, being careful not to contact the flywheel surface. Using a cold chisel at this point, crack the ring gear and remove it.
7. Polish the inner surface of the new ring gear and heat it in an oven to about 600°F (316°C). Quickly place the ring gear on the flywheel and tap it into place, making sure that it is fully seated.

✷✷ WARNING

Never heat the ring gear past 800°F (426°C), or the tempering will be destroyed.

8. Position the flywheel on the end of the crankshaft. Torque the bolts a little at a time, in a criss–cross pattern, to the torque figure shown in the Torque Specifications Chart.
9. Install the clutch or torque converter.
10. Install the transmission and transfer case.

Fig. 196 The flywheel is accessible after removing the clutch or torque converter

Fig. 197 Use a spray solvent to clean away dirt

Fig. 198 Matchmark the flywheel and pilot hole before removing the flywheel

Fig. 199 Using a torque wrench or breaker bar, loosen the flywheel bolts a little at a time in a criss–cross pattern

Fig. 200 Remove the flywheel bolts and the flywheel

Fig. 201 Replace the pilot bearing on vehicles equipped with a manual transmission, before replacing the flywheel

EXHAUST SYSTEM

✳ CAUTION

For a number of reasons, exhaust system work can be dangerous. Always observe the following safety precautions.

Safety Precautions

1. Support the vehicle securely by using jackstands or equivalent under the frame of the vehicle.
2. Wear safety goggles to protect your eyes from metal chips that may become airborne while working on the exhaust system.
3. Avoid working on a hot exhaust system. Be especially careful when working around the catalytic converter. The converter rises to a high temperature after only a few minutes of engine operation.
4. If you use a torch, be careful not to get close to any fuel lines or components that may burn or explode.
5. Always use the proper tool for the job.
6. Once the exhaust system has been repaired, make sure that all connections are tight and do not leak exhaust fumes. If allowed to enter the vehicle's passenger compartment, exhaust gases can cause serious personal injury or death.

Special Tools

A number of special exhaust system tools can be rented or purchased from a local auto parts store. It may also be quite helpful to use solvents designed to loosen rusted nuts and bolts. Remember that these products are often flammable; apply only to parts when they are cool.

Muffler

▸ See Figure 202

REMOVAL & INSTALLATION

➡ The following applies to exhaust systems using clamped joints. Some models use welded joints at the muffler. These joints will, of course, have to be cut.

1. Disconnect the negative battery cable.
2. Raise and safely support the vehicle using jackstands placed under the frame.
3. On 1983–88 vehicles, disconnect the lower shock absorber mountings.

This will allow the rear axle to lower providing additional clearance. Be careful not to stretch the brake hose.

4. Disconnect the muffler and tailpipe support brackets from the exhaust system, as equipped.
5. Separate the inlet of the muffler from the exhaust system. This can be done by removing the muffler clamp or flange mounting bolts, as equipped.
6. Remove the clamp from the muffler outlet to allow removal of the tailpipe. Separate the tailpipe and remove the muffler. If equipped with a one piece tailpipe and muffler, remove the muffler and tailpipe assembly as a unit.
7. Installation is the reverse of removal. Always use new clamps when replacing exhaust system components. Install exhaust system components loosely, then align system checking that all clearances are satisfactory. Torque support bracket bolts to 14 ft. lbs., flange nuts to 30 ft. lbs. and clamp nuts to 35 ft. lbs.

Fig. 202 The muffler is located between an inlet pipe and the tailpipe

Front Exhaust Pipe (Y–Pipe or Inlet Pipe)

➡Some vehicles were factory–equipped with a one–piece inlet pipe/catalytic converter assembly. Replacement components may vary in design and number of parts.

REMOVAL & INSTALLATION

1. Disconnect the negative battery cable.
2. Raise and safely support the vehicle using jackstands placed under the frame.
3. On cars equipped with an exhaust shield, remove the shield(s).
4. Support the exhaust system to prevent component damage during removal.
5. Disconnect the downstream injection air hose at the check valve, or the air injection tube at the catalytic converter, if so equipped.
6. Separate the Y–pipe or inlet pipe from its adjacent components. This can be done by removing flange mounting bolts or pipe clamps, as equipped.
7. Disconnect the muffler and/or tailpipe support brackets, if necessary, to provide sufficient clearance, and remove the Y–pipe or inlet pipe.
8. Installation is the reverse of removal. Always use new clamps and replace pipe end–to–manifold packing(s). Always install all parts loosely and align the system so that clearances between the system components and surrounding parts are adequate. Torque support bracket bolts to 14 ft. lbs., flange nuts to 30 ft. lbs. and manifold nuts to 35 ft. lbs.

Underbody Catalytic Converter

◆ See Figures 203, 204 and 205

Underbody catalytic converters were designed in a variety of shapes and sizes. Although their placement and positioning does vary, they are all designed to convert noxious emissions of hydrocarbons and carbon monoxide into harmless carbon dioxide and water. For further information on emission controls, see Section 4.

➡Although most vehicles utilize a single underbody converter, some vehicles are also equipped with one or two light–off converters. These auxiliary converters are typically part of the inlet pipe or Y–pipe assembly, but on some vehicles, they are separate components. Removal and installation of these separate converters is covered below.

REMOVAL & INSTALLATION

1. Disconnect the negative battery cable.
2. Raise and safely support the vehicle using jackstands placed under the frame.
3. Remove the exhaust shield(s), if so equipped.
4. Support the exhaust system to prevent component damage during removal.
5. Disconnect the downstream injection air hose at the check valve, if so equipped.
6. Separate the underbody converter from its adjacent components. This can be done by removing flange mounting bolts or pipe clamps, as equipped.
7. Slide the muffler inlet pipe rearward, if necessary, and remove the converter.
8. Installation is the reverse of removal. Always use new clamps and replace old gaskets. Always install all parts loosely and align the system, making sure that all clearances between the system parts and surrounding components are adequate. Torque support bracket bolts to 14 ft. lbs., flange nuts to 30 ft. lbs. and manifold nuts to 35 ft. lbs.

Light–Off Converter

REMOVAL & INSTALLATION

1. Disconnect the negative battery cable.
2. Raise and safely support the front end on jackstands.
3. Remove the bolts connecting the light–off converter outlet pipe to the underbody converter inlet pipe.
4. Loosen the U–clamp which attaches the air injection tube to the light–off converter outlet pipe.
5. Remove the air injection tube from the light–off converter pipe muzzle connection.
6. Remove the four nuts securing the light–off converter to the exhaust manifold.
7. Remove the light–off converter assembly from the vehicle.
8. Remove the upper and lower heat shields from the converter.
9. Installation is the reverse of removal. Always use new clamps and replace old gaskets. Always install all parts loosely and align the system, making sure that all clearances between the system parts and surrounding components are adequate. Torque the flange nuts to 30 ft. lbs., the manifold nuts to 35 ft. lbs. and the clamp nuts to 13 ft. lbs.

Fig. 203 The underbody catalytic converter is typically located between the front exhaust pipe and the muffler inlet pipe

Fig. 204 The front exhaust pipe is sometimes integral with the catalytic converter

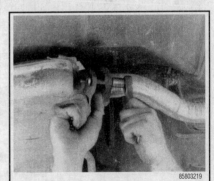

Fig. 205 Replace old gaskets, where applicable, and torque fasteners to the recommended specifications

GENERAL ENGINE SPECIFICATIONS

Year	Code	Engine Displacement Cu. In.	Carburetor Type	Net Horsepower (@ rpm)	Net Torque @ rpm (ft. lbs.)	Bore × Stroke (in.)	Compression Ratio	Oil Pressure @ rpm (psi)
1987	A	4-140	EFI	90 @ 3800	130 @ 2800	3.781 × 3.126	9.5:1	50 @ 2000
	E	8-302 HO	SEFI	①	300 @ 3200	4.00 × 3.00	9.2:1	40-60 @ 2000
1988	A	4-140	EFI	90 @ 3800	130 @ 2800	3.781 × 3.126	9.5:1	50 @ 2000
	E	8-302 HO	SEFI	②	300 @ 3200	4.00 × 3.00	9.2:1	40-60 @ 2000

NOTE: Horsepower and torque are SAE net figures. They are measured at the rear of the transmission with all accessories installed and operating. Since the figures vary when a given engine is installed in different models, some are representative rather than exact.

① CFI—50 states; 2 bbl—Canada
② Equipped with intercooler and boost control (SVO Mustang only)
③ CFI with MT (Canada only)
④ 175 @ 4400, increased to 200 @ 5000 in mid-year
⑤ 210 @ 3000, increased to 240 @ 3200 in mid-year
⑥ MT—225 @ 4200, AT—225 @ 4000

85803C1A

GENERAL ENGINE SPECIFICATIONS

Year	Code	Engine Displacement Cu. In.	Carburetor Type	Net Horsepower (@ rpm)	Net Torque @ rpm (ft. lbs.)	Bore × Stroke (in.)	Compression Ratio	Oil Pressure @ rpm (psi)
1979	Y	4-140	2 bbl	88 @ 4800	118 @ 2800	3.781 × 3.126	9.0:1	50 @ 2000
	W	4-140 (Turbo)	2 bbl	—	—	3.781 × 3.126	9.0:1	55 @ 2000
	Z	6-170	2 bbl	109 @ 4800	142 @ 2800	3.66 × 2.70	8.7:1	40-55 @ 1500
	T	6-200	1 bbl	85 @ 3600	154 @ 1600	3.68 × 3.126	8.6:1	30-50 @ 2000
	F	8-302	2 bbl	140 @ 3600	250 @ 1800	4.00 × 3.00	8.4:1	40-60 @ 2000
	F	8-302 (Calif.)	2 bbl	143 @ 3600	243 @ 2200	4.00 × 3.00	8.1:1	40-60 @ 2000
1980	A	4-140	2 bbl	88 @ 4600	119 @ 2600	3.781 × 3.126	9.0:1	50 @ 2000
	A	4-140 (Calif.)	2 bbl	89 @ 4800	122 @ 2600	3.781 × 3.126	9.0:1	50 @ 2000
	T	4-140 (Turbo)	2 bbl	—	—	3.781 × 3.126	9.0:1	55 @ 2000
	B	6-200	1 bbl	90 @ 3800	160 @ 1600	3.68 × 3.126	8.6:1	30-50 @ 2000
	D	8-255	2 bbl/VV	118 @ 3800	193 @ 2200	3.68 × 3.00	8.8:1	40-60 @ 2000
1981	A	4-140	2 bbl	88 @ 4600	119 @ 2600	3.781 × 3.126	9.0:1	50 @ 2000
	A	4-140 (Calif.)	2 bbl	89 @ 4800	122 @ 2600	3.781 × 3.126	9.0:1	50 @ 2000
	T	4-140 (Turbo)	2 bbl	—	—	3.781 × 3.126	9.0:1	55 @ 2000
	B	6-200	1 bbl	90 @ 3800	160 @ 1600	3.68 × 3.126	8.6:1	30-50 @ 2000
	D	8-255	2 bbl/VV	118 @ 3800	193 @ 2200	3.68 × 3.00	8.8:1	40-60 @ 2000
1982	A	4-140	2 bbl	88 @ 4600	118 @ 2600	3.781 × 3.126	9.0:1	50 @ 2000
	T	4-140 (Turbo)	2 bbl	—	—	3.781 × 3.126	9.0:1	55 @ 2000
	B	6-200	1 bbl	88 @ 3800	158 @ 1400	3.68 × 3.126	8.6:1	30-50 @ 2000
	D	8-255	2 bbl	111 @ 3400	205 @ 2690	3.68 × 3.00	8.2:1	40-60 @ 2000
	F	8-302	2 bbl	155 @ 4200	235 @ 2490	4.00 × 3.00	8.4:1	40-60 @ 2000
1983	A	4-140	1 bbl	88 @ 4600	118 @ 2800	3.781 × 3.126	9.0:1	50 @ 2000
	W	4-140 (Turbo)	EFI	145 @ 4600	180 @ 3600	3.781 × 3.126	8.0:1	50 @ 2000
	3	6-232	CFI	112 @ 4000	175 @ 2600	3.810 × 3.390	8.7:1	40-60 @ 2000
	F	8-302 HO	4 bbl	140 @ 3400	265 @ 2000	4.00 × 3.00	8.4:1	40-60 @ 2000
1984	A	4-140	1 bbl	88 @ 4000	122 @ 2400	3.781 × 3.126	9.0:1	50 @ 2000
	W	4-140 (Turbo)	EFI	145 @ 4600	180 @ 3600	3.781 × 3.126	8.0:1	50 @ 2000
	T	4-140 (Turbo)②	EFI	175 @ 4400	155 @ 3000	3.810 × 3.390	8.0:1	40-60 @ 2000
	3	6-232	①	—	—	3.810 × 3.390	8.6:1	40-60 @ 2000
	F	8-302	CFI	165 @ 3800	245 @ 2000	4.00 × 3.00	8.3:1	40-60 @ 2000
	M	8-302 HO	4 bbl	175 @ 4000	245 @ 2200	4.00 × 3.00	8.3:1	40-60 @ 2000
1985	A	4-140	1 bbl	88 @ 4200	122 @ 2600	3.781 × 3.126	9.5:1	50 @ 2000
	W	4-140 (Turbo)	EFI	145 @ 4600	180 @ 3600	3.781 × 3.126	8.0:1	50 @ 2000
	T	4-140 (Turbo)②	EFI	⑥	⑥	3.781 × 3.126	8.0:1	40-60 @ 2000
	3	6-232	①	120 @ 5600	205 @ 1600	3.810 × 3.390	8.7:1	40-60 @ 2000
	F	8-302	①	180 @ 4200	260 @ 2600	4.00 × 3.00	8.3:1	40-60 @ 2000
	M	8-302 HO	4 bbl	210 @ 4400	270 @ 3200	4.00 × 3.00	8.3:1	40-60 @ 2000
1986	A	4-140	1 bbl	88 @ 4200	122 @ 2600	3.781 × 3.126	9.5:1	50 @ 2000
	T	4-140 (Turbo)②	EFI	200 @ 5000	240 @ 3200	3.781 × 3.126	8.0:1	40-60 @ 2000
	3	6-232	①	120 @ 3600	205 @ 1600	3.810 × 3.390	8.7:1	40-60 @ 2000
	M	8-302 HO	SEFI	200 @ 4000	285 @ 3000	4.000 × 3.000	9.2:1	40-60 @ 2000

85803C1

VALVE SPECIFICATIONS

Year	Engine Displacement cu. in.	Seat Angle (deg.)	Face Angle (deg.)	Spring Test Pressure (lbs. @ in.)①	Spring Installed Height (in.)	Stem-to-Guide Clearance (in.) Intake	Stem-to-Guide Clearance (in.) Exhaust	Stem Diameter (in.) Intake	Stem Diameter (in.) Exhaust
1979	4-140	45	44	③	1¹¹/₁₆	0.0010-0.0027	0.0015-0.0032	0.3420	0.3415
	6-170	45	44	⑩	1¹⁹/₃₂	0.0008-0.0025	0.0018-0.0035	0.3163	0.3153
	6-200	45	44	⑪	1¹⁹/₃₂	0.0008-0.0025	0.0010-0.0027	0.3104	0.3104
	8-302	45	44	④	②	0.0010-0.0027	0.0015-0.0032	0.3420	0.3429
1980	4-140	45	44	③	1¹¹/₁₆	0.0010-0.0027	0.0015-0.0032	0.3420	0.3415
	6-200	45	44	④	1¹⁹/₃₂	0.0008-0.0025	0.0010-0.0027	0.3104	0.3104
	8-255	45	44	⑤	②	0.0010-0.0027	0.0015-0.0032	0.3400	0.3415
1981	4-140	45	44	③	1¹¹/₁₆	0.0010-0.0027	0.0015-0.0032	0.3420	0.3415
	6-200	45	44	④	1¹⁹/₃₂	0.0008-0.0025	0.0010-0.0027	0.3104	0.3104
	8-255	45	44	⑤	②	0.0010-0.0027	0.0015-0.0032	0.3400	0.3415
1982	4-140	45	44	③	1¹¹/₁₆	0.0010-0.0027	0.0015-0.0032	0.3420	0.3415
	6-200	45	44	④	1¹⁹/₃₂	0.0008-0.0025	0.0010-0.0027	0.3104	0.3104
	8-255	45	44	⑤	②	0.0010-0.0027	0.0015-0.0032	0.3400	0.3415
1983	4-140	45	44	③	1¹¹/₁₆	0.0010-0.0027	0.0015-0.0032	0.3420	0.3415
	6-232	45	44	⑨	1³/₄	0.0010-0.0027	0.0015-0.0032	0.3420	0.3415
	8-302	45	44	⑥	②	0.0010-0.0027	0.0015-0.0032	0.3420	0.3415
1984	4-140	45	44	③	1¹¹/₁₆	0.0010-0.0027	0.0015-0.0032	0.3420	0.3415
	6-232	45	44	⑨	1³/₄	0.0010-0.0027	0.0015-0.0032	0.3420	0.3415
	8-302	45	44	⑥	②	0.0010-0.0027	0.0015-0.0032	0.3420	0.3415
1985	4-140	45	44	③	1¹¹/₁₆	0.0010-0.0027	0.0015-0.0032	0.3420	0.3415
	6-232	45	44	⑨	1³/₄	0.0010-0.0027	0.0015-0.0032	0.3420	0.3415
	8-302	45	44	⑥	②	0.0010-0.0027	0.0015-0.0032	0.3420	0.3415
1986	4-140	45	44	③	1¹¹/₁₆	0.0010-0.0027	0.0015-0.0032	0.3420	0.3415
	6-232	45	44	⑨	1³/₄	0.0010-0.0027	0.0015-0.0032	0.3420	0.3415
	8-302	45	44	⑥	②	0.0010-0.0027	0.0015-0.0032	0.3420	0.3415
1987	4-140	45	44	③	1¹¹/₁₆	0.0010-0.0027	0.0015-0.0032	0.3420	0.3415
	8-302	45	44	⑥	②	0.0010-0.0027	0.0015-0.0032	0.3420	0.3415
1988	4-140	45	44	③	1¹¹/₁₆	0.0010-0.0027	0.0015-0.0032	0.3420	0.3415
	8-302	45	44	⑥	②	0.0010-0.0027	0.0015-0.0032	0.3420	0.3415

① Simulating springs installed and valves closed
② Intake: 1¹¹/₁₆
   Exhaust: 1¹⁹/₃₂
③ Intake and Exhaust: 71-79 @ 1.56
④ Intake: 74-82 @ 1.78
   Exhaust: 76-84 @ 1.60
⑤ Intake: 74-82 @ 1.78
   Exhaust: 71-79 @ 1.60
⑥ Intake and Exhaust: 71-79 @ 1.52
⑦ Intake: 74-82 @ 1.78
   Exhaust: 77-85 @ 1.60
⑧ Intake and Exhaust: 51-57 @ 1.59
⑨ Intake and Exhaust: 75 @ 1.70
⑩ Intake and Exhaust: 60-68 @ 1.59
⑪ Intake and Exhaust: 67-74 @ 1.52

85803C2

CAMSHAFT SPECIFICATIONS
(All measurements given in inches)

Engine cu. in. (liter)	Journal Diameter 1	2	3	4	5	Bearing Clearance	Lobe Lift Intake	Lobe Lift Exhaust	Endplay
4-140 (2.3L)	1.7713-1.7720	1.7713-1.7720	1.7713-1.7720	1.7713-1.7720	—	0.001-0.003	0.2437①	0.2437①	0.001-0.007
6-170 (2.8L)	1.6497-1.6505	1.6347-1.6355	1.6197-1.6205	1.6047-1.6055	—	0.001-0.0026	0.2555	0.2555	0.008-0.004
6-200 (3.3L)	1.8095-1.8105	1.8095-1.8105	1.8095-1.8105	1.8095-1.8105	—	0.001-0.003	0.245	0.245	0.001-0.007
6-232 (3.8L)	2.0505-2.0515	2.0505-2.0515	2.0505-2.0515	2.0505-2.0515	—	0.001-0.003	0.240	0.241	②
8-255 (4.2L)	2.0805-2.0815	2.0655-2.0665	2.0505-2.0515	2.0355-2.0365	2.0205-2.0215	0.001-0.003	0.2375	0.2375	0.001-0.007
8-302 (5.0L)	2.0805-2.0815	2.0655-2.0665	2.0505-2.0515	2.0355-2.0365	2.0205-2.0215	0.001-0.003	0.2375③	0.2374③	0.001-0.003

① 84 and later: 0.2381
② Endplay controlled by button and spring on camshaft end
③ HO engine: Intake—0.2600; Exhaust—0.2780

85803C3

CRANKSHAFT AND CONNECTING ROD SPECIFICATIONS (Cont.)

All measurements are given in inches.

Year	Engine ID/VIN	Engine Displacement (cu. in.)	Main Brg. Journal Dia.	Crankshaft Main Brg. Oil Clearance	Shaft End-play	Thrust on No.	Journal Diameter	Connecting Rod Oil Clearance	Side Clearance
1984	A	140	2.3982-2.3990	0.0008-0.0026	0.0040-0.0080	3	2.0465-2.0472	0.0008-0.0026	0.0035-0.0105
	W	140	2.3982-2.3990	0.0008-0.0026	0.0040-0.0080	3	2.0465-2.0472	0.0008-0.0026	0.0035-0.0105
	T	140	2.3982-2.3990	0.0008-0.0026	0.0040-0.0080	3	2.0465-2.0472	0.0008-0.0026	0.0035-0.0105
	3	232	2.5190-2.5198	0.0005-0.0023	0.0040-0.0080	3	2.3103-2.3111	0.00086-0.0027	0.0047-0.0114
	F	302	2.2482-2.2490	0.0004-0.0021①	0.0040-0.0080	3	2.1228-2.1236	0.0008-0.0024	0.0100-0.0200
	M	302	2.2482-2.2490	0.0004-0.0021①	0.0040-0.0080	3	2.1228-2.1236	0.0008-0.0024	0.0100-0.0200
1985	A	140	2.3982-2.3990	0.0008-0.0026	0.0040-0.0080	3	2.0465-2.0472	0.0008-0.0026	0.0035-0.0105
	W	140	2.3982-2.3990	0.0008-0.0026	0.0040-0.0080	3	2.0465-2.0472	0.0008-0.0026	0.0035-0.0105
	T	140	2.3982-2.3990	0.0008-0.0026	0.0040-0.0080	3	2.0465-2.0472	0.0008-0.0026	0.0035-0.0105
	3	232	2.5190-2.5198	0.0005-0.0023	0.0040-0.0080	3	2.3103-2.3111	0.00086-0.0027	0.0047-0.0114
	F	302	2.2482-2.2490	0.0004-0.0021	0.0040-0.0080	3	2.1228-2.1236	0.0008-0.0024	0.0100-0.0200
	M	302	2.2482-2.2490	0.0004-0.0021	0.0040-0.0080	3	2.1228-2.1236	0.0008-0.0024	0.0100-0.0200
1986	A	140	2.3982-2.3990	0.0008-0.0026	0.0040-0.0080	3	2.0465-2.0472	0.0008-0.0026	0.0035-0.0105
	T	140	2.3982-2.3990	0.0008-0.0026	0.0040-0.0080	3	2.0465-2.0472	0.0008-0.0026	0.0035-0.0105
	3	232	2.5190-2.5198	0.0005-0.0023	0.0040-0.0080	3	2.3103-2.3111	0.00086-0.0027	0.0047-0.0114
	M	302	2.2482-2.2490	0.0004-0.0021	0.0040-0.0080	3	2.1228-2.1236	0.0008-0.0024	0.0100-0.0200
1987	A	140	2.3982-2.3990	0.0008-0.0026	0.0040-0.0080	3	2.0465-2.0472	0.0008-0.0026	0.0035-0.0105
	E	302	2.2482-2.2490	0.0004-0.0021	0.0040-0.0080	3	2.1228-2.1236	0.0008-0.0024	0.0100-0.0200
1988	A	140	2.3982-2.3990	0.0008-0.0026	0.0040-0.0080	3	2.0465-2.0472	0.0008-0.0026	0.0035-0.0105
	E	302	2.2482-2.2490	0.0004-0.0021	0.0040-0.0080	3	2.1228-2.1236	0.0008-0.0024	0.0100-0.0200

① 0.0001-0.0017 No. 1 bearing only
② 0.0001-0.0030 No. 1 bearing only

85803C5

CRANKSHAFT AND CONNECTING ROD SPECIFICATIONS

All measurements are given in inches.

Year	Engine ID/VIN	Engine Displacement (cu. in.)	Main Brg. Journal Dia.	Crankshaft Main Brg. Oil Clearance	Shaft End-play	Thrust on No.	Journal Diameter	Connecting Rod Oil Clearance	Side Clearance
1979	Y	140	2.3982-2.3990	0.0008-0.0026	0.0040-0.0080	3	2.0464-2.0472	0.0008-0.0026	0.0035-0.0105
	W	140	2.3982-2.3990	0.0008-0.0026	0.0040-0.0080	3	2.0464-2.0472	0.0008-0.0026	0.0035-0.0105
	Z	170	2.2433-2.2441	0.0005-0.0019	0.0040-0.0080	3	2.1252-2.1260	0.0005-0.0022	0.0040-0.0110
	T	200	2.2482-2.2490	0.0008-0.0024	0.0040-0.0080	5	2.1232-2.1240	0.0008-0.0026	0.0035-0.0105
	F	302	2.2482-2.2490	0.0004-0.0021①	0.0040-0.0080	3	2.1228-2.1236	0.0007-0.0024	0.0100-0.0200
1980	A	140	2.3982-2.3990	0.0008-0.0026	0.0040-0.0080	3	2.0464-2.0472	0.0008-0.0026	0.0035-0.0105
	T	140	2.3982-2.3990	0.0008-0.0026	0.0040-0.0080	3	2.0464-2.0472	0.0008-0.0026	0.0035-0.0105
	B	200	2.2482-2.2490	0.0008-0.0026	0.0040-0.0080	5	2.1232-2.1240	0.0008-0.0024	0.0035-0.0105
	D	255	2.2482-2.2490	0.0008-0.0026	0.0040-0.0080	3	2.1228-2.1236	0.0008-0.0024	0.0100-0.0200
1981	A	140	2.3982-2.3990	0.0008-0.0026	0.0040-0.0080	3	2.0462-2.0472	0.0008-0.0026	0.0035-0.0105
	T	140	2.3982-2.3990	0.0008-0.0026	0.0040-0.0080	3	2.0462-2.0472	0.0008-0.0026	0.0035-0.0105
	B	200	2.2482-2.2490	0.0008-0.0026	0.0040-0.0080	5	2.1232-2.1240	0.0008-0.0024	0.0035-0.0105
	D	255	2.2482-2.2490	0.0008-0.0021①	0.0040-0.0080	3	2.1228-2.1236	0.0008-0.0024	0.0100-0.0200
1982	A	140	2.3982-2.3990	0.0008-0.0026	0.0040-0.0080	3	2.0465-2.0472	0.0008-0.0026	0.0035-0.0105
	T	140	2.3982-2.3990	0.0008-0.0026	0.0040-0.0080	3	2.0465-2.0472	0.0008-0.0026	0.0035-0.0105
	B	200	2.2482-2.2490	0.0008-0.0026	0.0040-0.0080	5	2.1232-2.1240	0.0008-0.0024	0.0035-0.0105
	D	255	2.2482-2.2490	0.0004-0.0021①	0.0040-0.0080	3	2.1228-2.1236	0.0008-0.0024	0.0100-0.0200
1983	A	140	2.3982-2.3990	0.0008-0.0026	0.0040-0.0080	3	2.0465-2.0472	0.0008-0.0026	0.0035-0.0105
	W	140	2.3982-2.3990	0.0008-0.0026	0.0040-0.0080	3	2.0465-2.0472	0.0008-0.0026	0.0035-0.0105
	3	232	2.5190-2.5198	0.0005-0.0023	0.0040-0.0080	3	2.3103-2.3111	0.00086-0.0027	0.0047-0.0114
	F	302	2.2482-2.2490	0.0004-0.0021①	0.0040-0.0080	3	2.1228-2.1236	0.0008-0.0024	0.0100-0.0200

85803C4

PISTON AND RING SPECIFICATIONS
(All measurements are given in inches)

Engine Displacement (cu. in.)	Piston Clearance	Ring Gap			Ring Side Clearance			Water Limit
		Top Compression	Bottom Compression	Oil① Control	Top Compression	Bottom Compression	Oil Control	
4-140 (2.3L)	0.0014–0.0022	0.010–0.020	0.010–0.020	0.015–0.055	0.002–0.004	0.002–0.004	Snug	0.006
4-140 (2.3L) ('79–'82 Turbo)	0.0034–0.0042	0.010–0.020	0.010–0.020	0.015–0.055	0.002–0.004	0.002–0.004	Snug	0.006
4-140 (2.3L) ('83–'86 Turbo)	0.0030–0.0038	0.010–0.020	0.010–0.020	0.015–0.055	0.002–0.004	0.002–0.004	Snug	0.006
6-170 (2.8L)	0.0011–0.0019	0.015–0.023	0.015–0.023	0.015–0.055	0.002–0.0033	0.002–0.0033	Snug	0.006
6-200 (3.3L)	0.0013–0.0021	0.008–0.016	0.008–0.016	0.015–0.055	0.002–0.004	0.002–0.004	Snug	0.006
6-232 (3.8L)	0.0014–0.0028	0.010–0.020	0.010–0.020	0.015–0.055	0.002–0.004	0.002–0.004	Snug	0.006
8-255 (4.2L)	0.0018–0.0026	0.010–0.020	0.010–0.020	0.015–0.055	0.002–0.004	0.002–0.004	Snug	0.006
8-302 (5.0L)	0.0018–0.0026	0.010–0.020	0.010–0.020	0.015–0.055	0.002–0.004	0.002–0.004	Snug	0.006

① Steel rails

85803007

TORQUE SPECIFICATIONS

Component	U.S.	Metric
Starter		
4-140 cid engine		
3 mounting bolts	12–15 ft. lbs.	16–20 Nm
2 mounting bolts	15–20 ft. lbs.	20–27 Nm
6-170 cid engine		
3 mounting bolts	12–15 ft. lbs.	16–20 Nm
2 mounting bolts	15–20 ft. lbs.	20–27 Nm
6-200 cid engine		
3 mounting bolts	12–15 ft. lbs.	16–20 Nm
2 mounting bolts	15–20 ft. lbs.	20–27 Nm
6-232 cid engine		
3 mounting bolts	12–15 ft. lbs.	16–20 Nm
2 mounting bolts	15–20 ft. lbs.	20–27 Nm
8-255 cid engine		
3 mounting bolts	12–15 ft. lbs.	16–20 Nm
2 mounting bolts	15–20 ft. lbs.	20–27 Nm
8-302 cid engine		
3 mounting bolts	12–15 ft. lbs.	16–20 Nm
2 mounting bolts	15–20 ft. lbs.	20–27 Nm
Coolant temperature sending unit		
4-140 cid engine	8–18 ft. lbs.	11–24 Nm
6-170 cid engine	8–18 ft. lbs.	11–24 Nm
6-200 cid engine	8–18 ft. lbs.	11–24 Nm
6-232 cid engine	8–18 ft. lbs.	11–24 Nm
8-255 cid engine	8–18 ft. lbs.	11–24 Nm
8-302 cid engine	8–18 ft. lbs.	11–24 Nm
Oil pressure sending unit		
4-140 cid engine	8–18 ft. lbs.	11–24 Nm
6-170 cid engine	8–18 ft. lbs.	11–24 Nm
6-200 cid engine	8–18 ft. lbs.	11–24 Nm
6-232 cid engine	8–18 ft. lbs.	11–24 Nm
8-255 cid engine	8–18 ft. lbs.	11–24 Nm
8-302 cid engine	8–18 ft. lbs.	11–24 Nm
Rocker arm (valve) cover bolts		
4-140 cid engine	6–8 ft. lbs.	8–11 Nm
6-170 cid engine	3–5 ft. lbs.	4–7 Nm
6-200 cid engine	3–5 ft. lbs.	4–7 Nm
6-232 cid engine	80–106 inch lbs.	9–12 Nm
8-255 cid engine	3–5 ft. lbs.	4–7 Nm
8-302 cid engine	3–5 ft. lbs.	4–7 Nm
Rocker arm bolts or rocker arm shaft bolts		
6-170 cid engine	43–49 ft. lbs.	58–67 Nm
6-200 cid engine	30–35 ft. lbs.	41–48 Nm
6-232 cid engine		
First step	5–11 ft. lbs.	7–15 Nm
Second step	19–25 ft. lbs.	26–34 Nm
8-255 cid engine	18–25 ft. lbs.	24–34 Nm
8-302 cid engine	18–25 ft. lbs.	24–34 Nm
Thermostat housing bolts		
4-140 cid engine	14–21 ft. lbs.	19–29 Nm
6-170 cid engine	12–15 ft. lbs.	16–20 Nm
6-200 cid engine	12–15 ft. lbs.	16–20 Nm
6-232 cid engine	15–22 ft. lbs.	20–30 Nm
8-255 cid engine	9–12 ft. lbs.	12–16 Nm
8-302 cid engine	9–12 ft. lbs.	12–16 Nm

85803009

TORQUE SPECIFICATIONS

Component	U.S.	Metric
Intake manifold to cylinder block		
4-140 cid engine		
Carburetor-equipped		
First step	11-12½ ft. lbs.	15-17 Nm
Second step	14-21 ft. lbs.	19-29 Nm
EFI-equipped		
Lower manifold		
1983-85	12-15 ft. lbs.	16-20 Nm
1986	14-21 ft. lbs.	19-29 Nm
1987-88	15-22 ft. lbs.	20-30 Nm
Upper manifold-to-lower manifold		
1984-88	15-22 ft. lbs.	20-30 Nm
Intake manifold to cylinder block		
6-170 cid engine		
Bolt/nut		
First step	3-6 ft. lbs.	4-8 Nm
Second step	6-11 ft. lbs.	8-15 Nm
Third step	11-15 ft. lbs.	15-20 Nm
Fourth step	15-18 ft. lbs.	20-24 Nm
Stud	10-12 ft. lbs.	14-16 Nm
6-232 cid engine		
First step	7 ft. lbs.	10 Nm
Second step	15 ft. lbs.	20 Nm
Third step	24 ft. lbs.	33 Nm
8-255 cid engine	18-20 ft. lbs.	24-27 Nm
8-302 cid engine		
1979-85 one-piece manifold	23-25 ft. lbs.	31-34 Nm
1986-88 lower manifold	23-25 ft. lbs.	31-34 Nm
1986-88 upper manifold-to-lower manifold	12-18 ft. lbs.	16-24 Nm
Exhaust manifold to cylinder block		
4-140 cid engine		
1979-86	5-7 ft. lbs.	7-10 Nm
First step	16-23 ft. lbs.	22-31 Nm
1987-88		
First step	15-17 ft. lbs.	20-23 Nm
Second step	20-30 ft. lbs.	27-41 Nm
6-170 cid engine	20-30 ft. lbs.	27-41 Nm
6-200 cid engine	18-24 ft. lbs.	24-33 Nm
6-232 cid engine	15-22 ft. lbs.	20-30 Nm
8-255 cid engine	18-24 ft. lbs.	24-33 Nm
8-302 cid engine	18-24 ft. lbs.	24-33 Nm
Turbocharger		
To intake manifold (1979-82)		
Vertical nuts	13-19 ft. lbs.	18-26 Nm
Horizontal nuts	9-13 ft. lbs.	12-18 Nm
To exhaust manifold (1984-86)		
Nuts	28-40 ft. lbs.	38-54 Nm
	12-18 ft. lbs.	16-24 Nm
Engine cooling fan-to-drive clutch bolts	12-18 ft. lbs.	16-24 Nm
Engine cooling fan drive clutch-to-water pump bolts		
1979-83 engines	12-18 ft. lbs.	16-24 Nm
1984-88 engines	15-22 ft. lbs.	20-30 Nm

85803C10

TORQUE SPECIFICATIONS

Component	U.S.	Metric
Water pump-to-cylinder block bolts		
4-140 cid engine	14-21 ft. lbs.	19-29 Nm
6-170 cid engine	7-9 ft. lbs.	10-12 Nm
6-200 cid engine	15-20 ft. lbs.	20-27 Nm
6-232 cid engine	15-22 ft. lbs.	20-30 Nm
8-255 cid engine	12-18 ft. lbs.	16-24 Nm
8-302 cid engine	12-18 ft. lbs.	16-24 Nm
Cylinder head bolts		
4-140 cid engine		
First step	50-60 ft. lbs.	68-82 Nm
Second step	80-90 ft. lbs.	109-122 Nm
6-170 cid engine		
First step	29-40 ft. lbs.	39-54 Nm
Second step	40-51 ft. lbs.	54-69 Nm
Third step	65-80 ft. lbs.	88-109 Nm
6-200 cid engine		
First step	50-55 ft. lbs.	68-75 Nm
Second step	60-65 ft. lbs.	82-88 Nm
Third step	70-75 ft. lbs.	95-102 Nm
Cylinder head bolts		
6-232 cid engine		
First step		
1983	47 ft. lbs.	64 Nm
1984-86	37 ft. lbs.	50 Nm
Second step		
1983	55 ft. lbs.	75 Nm
1984-86	45 ft. lbs.	61 Nm
Third step		
1983	63 ft. lbs.	86 Nm
1984-86	52 ft. lbs.	71 Nm
Fourth step ①		
1983	74 ft. lbs.	101 Nm
1984-86	59 ft. lbs.	80 Nm
8-255 cid engine		
First step	55-65 ft. lbs.	75-88 Nm
Second step	65-72 ft. lbs.	88-98 Nm
8-302 cid engine		
First step	55-65 ft. lbs.	75-88 Nm
Second step	65-72 ft. lbs.	88-98 Nm
Oil pan bolts		
4-140 cid engine		
1979-86	6-8 ft. lbs.	8-11 Nm
1987-88	7½-10 ft. lbs.	10-13½ Nm
6-170 cid engine	7-9 ft. lbs.	10-14 Nm
6-200 cid engine	7-9 ft. lbs.	10-12 Nm
6-232 cid engine	80-106 inch lbs.	9-12 Nm
8-255 cid engine		
5/16 in. bolts	9-11 ft. lbs.	12-15 Nm
1/4 in. bolts	7-9 ft. lbs.	10-12 Nm
8-302 cid engine		
5/16 in. bolts	9-11 ft. lbs.	12-15 Nm
1/4 in. bolts	7-9 ft. lbs.	10-12 Nm

85803C11

TORQUE SPECIFICATIONS

Component	U.S.	Metric
Crankshaft pulley-to-damper bolts		
6-170 cid engine	18-25 ft. lbs.	24-34 Nm
6-200 cid engine	35-50 ft. lbs.	48-68 Nm
6-232 cid engine	20-28 ft. lbs.	27-38 Nm
8-255 cid engine	35-50 ft. lbs.	48-68 Nm
8-302 cid engine	35-50 ft. lbs.	48-68 Nm
Damper or pulley-to-crankshaft bolt		
4-140 cid engine		
1979-1986	100-120 ft. lbs.	136-163 Nm
1987-1988	103-133 ft. lbs.	140-181 Nm
6-170 cid engine	92-103 ft. lbs.	125-140 Nm
6-200 cid engine	85-100 ft. lbs.	116-136 Nm
6-232 cid engine	93-121 ft. lbs.	126-165 Nm
8-255 cid engine	70-90 ft. lbs.	95-122 Nm
8-302 cid engine	70-90 ft. lbs.	95-122 Nm
Camshaft sprocket (or gear) bolt or capscrew		
4-140 cid engine	50-71 ft. lbs.	68-97 Nm
6-170 cid engine	30-36 ft. lbs.	41-49 Nm
6-200 cid engine	35-45 ft. lbs.	48-61 Nm
6-232 cid engine	15-22 ft. lbs.	20-30 Nm
8-255 cid engine	40-45 ft. lbs.	54-61 Nm
8-302 cid engine	40-45 ft. lbs.	54-61 Nm
Connecting rod nuts		
4-140 cid engine		
First step	25-30 ft. lbs.	34-41 Nm
Second step	30-36 ft. lbs.	41-49 Nm
6-170 cid engine	21-25 ft. lbs.	29-34 Nm
6-200 cid engine	21-26 ft. lbs.	29-35 Nm
6-232 cid engine	31-36 ft. lbs.	42-49 Nm
8-255 cid engine	19-24 ft. lbs.	26-33 Nm
8-302 cid engine	19-24 ft. lbs.	26-33 Nm
Flywheel-to-crankshaft bolts		
4-140 cid engine	54-64 ft. lbs.	73-87 Nm
6-170 cid engine	64-69 ft. lbs.	87-94 Nm
6-200 cid engine	75-85 ft. lbs.	102-116 Nm
6-232 cid engine	54-64 ft. lbs.	73-87 Nm
8-255 cid engine	75-85 ft. lbs.	102-116 Nm
8-302 cid engine	75-85 ft. lbs.	102-116 Nm
Main bearing cap bolts		
4-140 cid engine		
First step	50-60 ft. lbs.	68-82 Nm
Second step	80-90 ft. lbs.	109-122 Nm
6-170 cid engine	65-75 ft. lbs.	88-102 Nm
6-200 cid engine	60-70 ft. lbs.	82-95 Nm
6-232 cid engine	65-81 ft. lbs.	88-110 Nm
8-255 cid engine	60-70 ft. lbs.	82-95 Nm
8-302 cid engine	60-70 ft. lbs.	82-95 Nm

85803C12

TORQUE SPECIFICATIONS

Component	U.S.	Metric
Front cover-to-cylinder block bolts		
4-140 cid engine	6-9 ft. lbs.	8-12 Nm
6-170 cid engine	12-15 ft. lbs.	16-20 Nm
6-200 cid engine	6-9 ft. lbs.	8-12 Nm
6-232 cid engine	15-22 ft. lbs.	20-30 Nm
8-255 cid engine	12-18 ft. lbs.	16-24 Nm
8-302 cid engine	12-18 ft. lbs.	16-24 Nm
Spark plugs		
4-140 cid engine	5-10 ft. lbs.	7-14 Nm
6-170 cid engine	10-15 ft. lbs.	14-20 Nm
6-200 cid engine	10-15 ft. lbs.	14-20 Nm
6-232 cid engine	5-11 ft. lbs.	7-15 Nm
8-255 cid engine	10-15 ft. lbs.	14-20 Nm
8-302 cid engine		
1979-87	10-15 ft. lbs.	14-20 Nm
1988	5-10 ft. lbs.	7-14 Nm
EGR valve mounting bolts or nuts		
4-140 cid engine	14-21 ft. lbs.	19-29 Nm
6-170 cid engine	12-15 ft. lbs.	16-20 Nm
6-200 cid engine	12-18 ft. lbs.	16-24 Nm
6-232 cid engine	15-22 ft. lbs.	20-30 Nm
8-255 cid engine	12-18 ft. lbs.	16-24 Nm
8-302 cid engine	12-18 ft. lbs.	16-24 Nm

① After completing the fourth step, back off the cylinder head bolts 2-3 revolutions and repeat all four steps.

85803C13

USING A VACUUM GAUGE

White needle = steady needle   *Dark needle = drifting needle*

The vacuum gauge is one of the most useful and easy-to-use diagnostic tools. It is inexpensive, easy to hook up, and provides valuable information about the condition of your engine.

Indication: Normal engine in good condition

Gauge reading: Steady, from 17–22 in./Hg.

Indication: Sticking valve or ignition miss

Gauge reading: Needle fluctuates from 15–20 in./Hg. at idle

Indication: Late ignition or valve timing, low compression, stuck throttle valve, leaking carburetor or manifold gasket.

Gauge reading: Low (15–20 in./Hg.) but steady

Indication: Improper carburetor adjustment, or minor intake leak at carburetor or manifold

NOTE: Bad fuel injector O-rings may also cause this reading.

Gauge reading: Drifting needle

Indication: Weak valve springs, worn valve stem guides, or leaky cylinder head gasket (vibrating excessively at all speeds).

NOTE: A plugged catalytic converter may also cause this reading.

Gauge reading: Needle fluctuates as engine speed increases

Indication: Burnt valve or improper valve clearance. The needle will drop when the defective valve operates.

Gauge reading: Steady needle, but drops regularly

Indication: Choked muffler or obstruction in system. Speed up the engine. Choked muffler will exhibit a slow drop of vacuum to zero.

Gauge reading: Gradual drop in reading at idle

Indication: Worn valve guides

Gauge reading: Needle vibrates excessively at idle, but steadies as engine speed increases

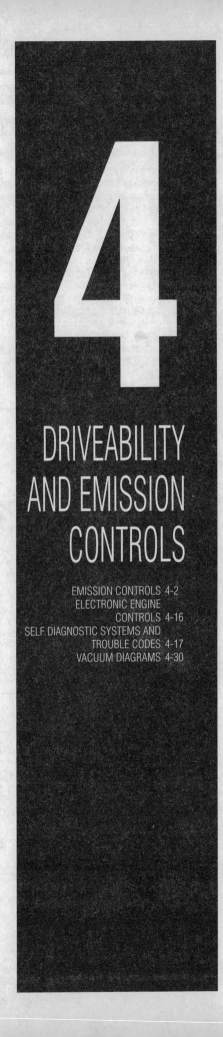

4

DRIVEABILITY
AND EMISSION
CONTROLS

EMISSION CONTROLS

Positive Crankcase Ventilation System

▶ **See Figure 1**

All models covered in this book are equipped with a Positive Crankcase Ventilation (PCV) system to control crankcase blow-by vapors. The system consists of a PCV valve, a non-ventilated oil filler cap, an oil separator and a pair of hoses that supply filtered intake air to the rocker arm cover, while delivering crankcase vapors from the rocker arm cover to the intake manifold, carburetor or throttle body. The PCV valve is often mounted in a grommet on top of the rocker arm cover. On engines equipped with an externally mounted oil separator, the PCV valve may instead be located between a vent hose and a manifold vacuum source. The system functions as follows:

When the engine is running, a small portion of the gases which are formed in the combustion chamber leak by the piston rings and enter the crankcase. Since these gases are under pressure, they tend to escape from the crankcase and enter the atmosphere. If these gases are allowed to remain in the crankcase for any period of time, they contaminate the engine oil and cause sludge to build up. If the gases are allowed to escape into the atmosphere, they pollute the air with unburned hydrocarbons. The job of the crankcase emission control equipment is to recycle the gases back into the engine combustion chamber where they are burned.

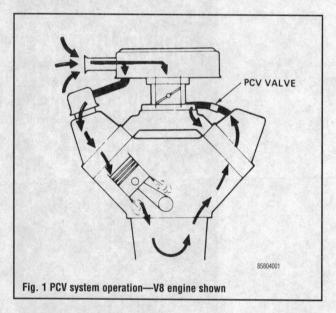

Fig. 1 PCV system operation—V8 engine shown

TESTING

1. Remove the PCV valve from the rocker arm cover grommet or other underhood location.
2. Shake the PCV valve. If the valve rattles when shaken, reinstall and proceed to Step 3. If the valve does not rattle, it is sticking and must be replaced.
3. With the engine at idle, disconnect the hose from the air cleaner and feel for vacuum at the hose. Some vacuum indicates that the system is okay. If there is no vacuum, proceed to Step 4.
4. No vacuum indicates that either the system is plugged or the evaporative valve is leaking. Proceed as follows:
   a. Disconnect the evaporative hose, cap the tee and retest. Some vacuum indicates that the PCV system is okay. Check the evaporative system.
   b. If there is still no vacuum, check for vacuum back through the system (oil filler cap, PCV valve, hoses and oil separator). Also check the rocker arm cover(s) for correct bolt torque and/or a gasket leak. Service as necessary.

REMOVAL & INSTALLATION

Since the PCV valve works under severe load, it is very important that it be replaced at the interval specified in the maintenance chart (see Section 1).

On many engines, the PCV valve is mounted in a grommet in the rocker arm cover. On 4-140 engines equipped with an externally mounted oil separator, the PCV valve is positioned between two or more hoses near the intake manifold.
1. Remove the PCV valve from the grommet in the rocker arm cover, if applicable.
2. Disconnect the hose(s) from the valve.

➡ **Do not attempt to clean a used valve.**

To install:
3. Connect the hose(s) to the new PCV valve.
4. Insert valve into the rocker arm grommet, if applicable.

Fuel Evaporative Control System

▶ **See Figures 2 and 3**

This system is designed to prevent the evaporation of unburned gasoline. The system consists of a vacuum/pressure relief fuel filler cap, an expansion area at the top of the fuel tank, a foam-filled vapor separator mounted on top of the fuel tank, a carbon canister which stores fuel vapors and a number of hoses which connect the various components. The system functions as follows:

Changes in ambient temperature cause the gasoline in fuel tanks to expand or contract. If this expansion and consequent vaporization takes place in a conventional fuel tank, the vapors escape through the filler cap or vent hose and pollute the atmosphere. The fuel evaporation emission control system prevents this by routing the gasoline vapors to the engine where they are burned.

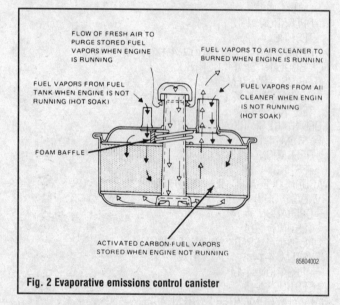

Fig. 2 Evaporative emissions control canister

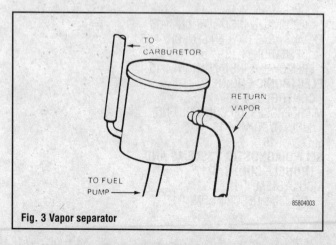

Fig. 3 Vapor separator

As the gasoline in the fuel tank of a parked car begins to expand due to heat, the vapor that forms moves to the top of the fuel tank. The tanks are enlarged so that there is an area representing 10–20% of the total fuel tank volume above the level of the fuel tank filler tube where these gases may collect. The vapors travel upward into the vapor separator, which prevents liquid gasoline from escaping the fuel tank. The vapor then travels through the separator outlet hose to the charcoal canister in the engine compartment. The vapor enters the canister, passes through a charcoal filter, and then exits through the canister's atmospheric outlet. As the vapor passes through the charcoal, hydrocarbons are removed, so pollutants passing through to the atmosphere are reduced.

When the engine is started, intake vacuum draws fresh air into the canister. As the entering air passes through the charcoal in the canister, it picks up the hydrocarbons that were deposited by the fuel vapors. This mixture of hydrocarbons and fresh air is then carried through a hose to the carburetor or air cleaner assembly. It combines with the incoming air/fuel mixture in the carburetor or throttle body, and enters the combustion chambers of the engine where it is burned.

SERVICE

The only required service for the evaporative emissions control system is inspection of the various components at the interval specified in the maintenance chart (see Section 1). If the charcoal element in the canister becomes gummed up, the entire canister should be replaced. Disconnect the canister purge hose from the air cleaner fitting, loosen the canister retaining bracket and lift out the canister. Installation is the reverse of removal.

Thermactor System

▶ **See Figures 4 thru 9**

One form or other of this system is found in most models sold in the 50 states. The managed air Thermactor emission control system makes use of a belt-driven air pump to inject fresh air into the hot exhaust stream through the engine exhaust ports. The result is the extended burning of those fumes which were not completely ignited in the combustion chamber, and the subsequent reduction of some hydrocarbon and carbon monoxide content of the exhaust emissions, by turning them into harmless carbon dioxide and water.

The managed air Thermactor system is composed of the following components:

1. Air supply pump (belt-driven)
2. Air bypass valve
3. Check valves
4. Air manifolds (internal or external)
5. Air supply tubes (on external manifolds only)

Air for the Thermactor system is cleaned by means of a centrifugal filter fan mounted on the air pump driveshaft. The air filter does not require a replaceable element.

To prevent excessive pressure, the air pump is equipped with a pressure relief valve which uses a replaceable plastic plug to control the pressure setting.

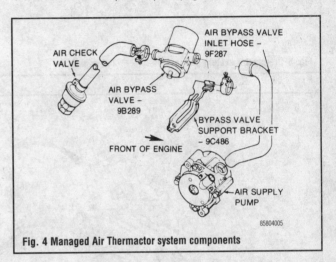

Fig. 4 Managed Air Thermactor system components

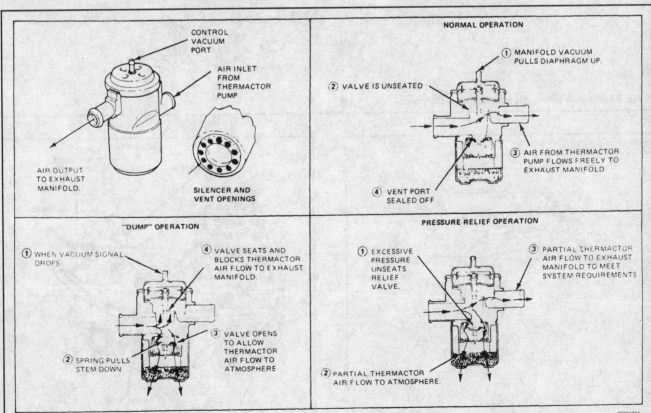

Fig. 5 Air bypass valve—normally closed

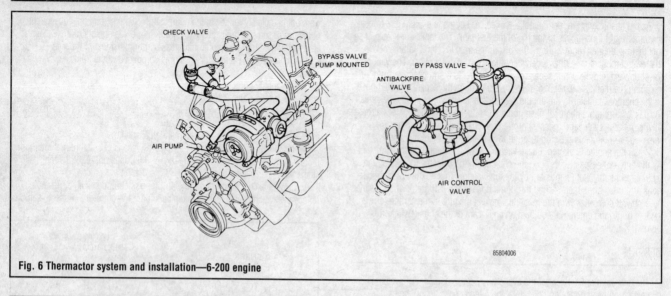

85804006

Fig. 6 Thermactor system and installation—6-200 engine

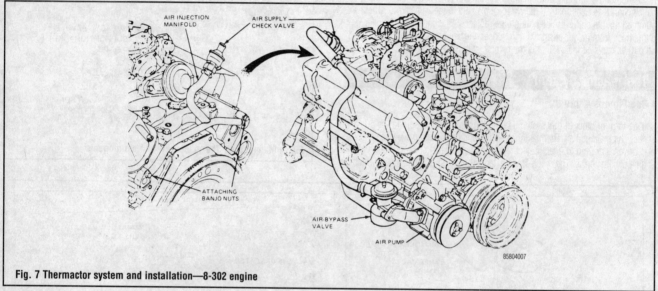

85804007

Fig. 7 Thermactor system and installation—8-302 engine

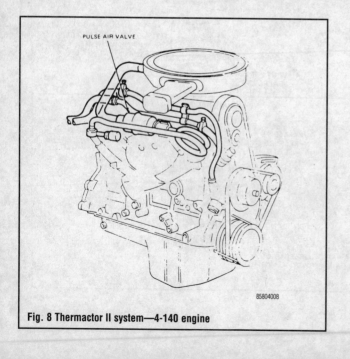

85804008

Fig. 8 Thermactor II system—4-140 engine

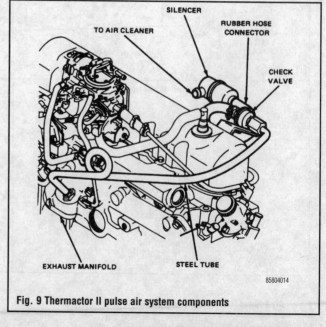

85804014

Fig. 9 Thermactor II pulse air system components

The Thermactor air pump has sealed bearings which are lubricated for the life of the unit. The pump also utilizes a preset rotor vane and bearing clearances, which do not require any periodic adjustments.

The air supply from the pump is controlled by the air bypass valve, sometimes called a dump valve. During deceleration, the air bypass valve opens, momentarily diverting the air supply through a silencer and into the atmosphere, thus preventing backfires within the exhaust system.

A check valve is incorporated in the air inlet side of the air manifolds. Its purpose is to prevent exhaust gases from backing up into the Thermactor system. This valve is especially important in the event of drive belt failure, and during deceleration, when the air bypass valve is dumping the air supply.

The air manifolds and air supply tubes channel air from the Thermactor air pump into the exhaust ports of each cylinder, thus completing the cycle of the Thermactor system.

Another version of the Thermactor system is the called the Thermactor II or pulse air system. Instead of an air pump, this system uses natural pulses present in the exhaust system to pull air into the exhaust manifold through pulse air valves. The pulse air valve is connected to the manifold with a long tube and to the air cleaner or silencer with a hose.

SERVICE

The entire Thermactor system should be checked periodically according to the maintenance chart in Section 1. Use the following procedure to determine if the system is functioning properly.

➡️See Section 1 for belt adjustment and replacement procedures.

1. Remove the air cleaner assembly, if necessary.
2. Inspect all components of the Thermactor system for any loose connections or other abnormal conditions. Repair or replace them as necessary.
3. If so equipped, inspect the air pump drive belt for wear and tension. Adjust or replace it as necessary.
4. With the transmission in neutral or park and the parking brake on, start the engine and bring it to normal operating temperature.
5. Stop the engine and connect a tachometer. Remove the air supply hose at the check valve. If the engine has two check valves, remove both air supply hoses at the check valves and plug off one hose. Position the open hose so that the air blast emitted is harmlessly dissipated.
6. Start the engine and accelerate to 1,500 rpm. Place a hand over the open hose. Air flow should be heard and felt. If no air flow is noted, the air bypass valve is defective and should be replaced. The procedure is outlined later in this section.
7. Let the engine speed return to normal idle. Pinch off and remove the vacuum hose from the bypass valve. Accelerate the engine to 1,500 rpm. With a hand held over the open end of the check valve hose (same as in Step 6), virtually no air flow should be felt or heard. If air flow is noted, the bypass valve is defective and should be replaced.
8. Let the engine speed return to normal idle and reinstall the vacuum hose on the bypass valve vacuum hose nipple. Check hose routing to be sure it is not pinched or restricting normal vacuum signal flow.
9. With a hand held over the open end of the check valve hose (same as in Step 6), rapidly increase the engine speed to approximately 2,500 rpm. Immediately release the throttle so the engine returns to normal idle. Air flow should be

felt and/or heard momentarily diminishing or cutting off completely during deceleration. If the air flow does not momentarily diminish or cut off, repeat this procedure using an engine speed of 3,000–3,200 rpm. If air flow does not respond correctly during the deceleration from 3,000–3,200 rpm, the vacuum differential control valve should be replaced. Of course, this step should be omitted if the system is not equipped with a differential vacuum valve.

❄❄ CAUTION

The check valve may be hot and capable of causing a burn if the hands are not protected.

10. Accelerate the engine to 1,500 rpm and check for any exhaust gas leakage at the check valve. There should be virtually no pressure felt or heard when a hand is held over the open end of the check valve for approximately 15 seconds. If excessive leakage is noted, replace the check valve(s).
11. If the engine is equipped with two check valves, repeat Step 10 for the second valve.
12. Stop the engine and remove all test equipment. Reconnect all related components and reinstall the air cleaner, if removed.

REMOVAL & INSTALLATION

Thermactor Air Pump

▸ See Figures 10, 11, 12 and 13

1. Disconnect the air outlet hose at the air pump.
2. Loosen the pump belt tension adjuster.
3. Disengage the drive belt.

Fig. 10 Remove the air pump drive belt

Fig. 11 On some vehicles, the air pump mounting bracket is fastened to the cylinder head

Fig. 12 Remove the air pump mounting bolts

Fig. 13 Remove the air pump from the vehicle

4. Remove the mounting bolts and air pump (or air pump and bracket assembly).

To install:

5. Position the air pump (or air pump and bracket assembly) and install the mounting bolts.

6. Place the drive belt in the pulley and attach the adjusting arm to the air pump.

7. Adjust the drive belt tension to specification and tighten the adjusting arm and mounting bolts.

8. Connect the air outlet hose to the air pump.

Air Pump Filter Fan

▶ **See Figure 14**

1. Loosen the air pump adjusting arm bolt and mounting bracket bolt to relieve drive belt tension.

2. Remove the drive pulley attaching bolts and pull the drive pulley off the air pump shaft.

3. Pry the outer disc loose, then pull off the centrifugal filter fan with slip-joint pliers.

❄❄ CAUTION

Do not attempt to remove the metal drive hub.

4. Install a new filter fan by drawing it into position, using the pulley and bolts as an installer. Draw the fan evenly by alternately tightening the bolts, making certain that the outer edge of the fan slips into the housing.

➡**A slight interference with the housing bore is normal. After a new fan is installed, it may squeal upon initial operation, until its outer diameter sealing lip has worn in, which may require 20–30 miles of operation.**

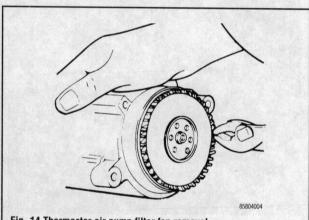

Fig. 14 Thermactor air pump filter fan removal

Thermactor Check Valve

1. Disconnect the air supply hose at the valve. (Use a 1¼ in. crowfoot wrench; the valve has a standard, right-hand pipe thread.)

2. Clean the threads on the air manifold adapter (air supply tube on the 8-302 engine) with a wire brush. Do not blow compressed air through the check valve in either direction.

3. Install the check valve and tighten.

4. Connect the air supply hose.

Thermactor Air Bypass Valve

1. Disconnect the air and vacuum hoses at the air bypass valve body.

2. Position the air bypass valve, and connect the respective hoses.

Vacuum Differential Control Valve

1. Remove the hose connections.

2. Unbolt the valve at its mounting bracket.

3. Install in reverse order.

Improved Combustion (IMCO) System

SYSTEM DESCRIPTION

All models are equipped with the Improved Combustion (IMCO) System. The IMCO system controls emissions arising from the incomplete combustion of the air/fuel mixture in the cylinders. The IMCO system incorporates a number of modifications to the distributor spark control system, the fuel system, and the internal design of the engine.

Internal engine modifications include: elimination of surface irregularities and crevices as well as a low surface area-to-volume ratio in the combustion chambers, a high velocity intake manifold combined with short exhaust ports, selective valve timing, along with a higher temperature and capacity cooling system.

Modifications to the fuel system include: recalibrated carburetors or fuel injection to achieve a leaner air/fuel mixture, more precise calibration of the choke mechanism, the installation of idle mixture limiter caps and a heated air intake system.

Modifications to the distributor spark control system include: a modified centrifugal advance curve, the use of dual diaphragm distributors on most applications, a ported vacuum switch, a deceleration valve and a spark delay valve.

OPERATION

Heated Air Intake System

▶ **See Figures 15, 16 and 17**

The heated air intake portion of the air cleaner consists of a thermostat, or a bimetal switch with a vacuum motor, and a spring-loaded temperature control

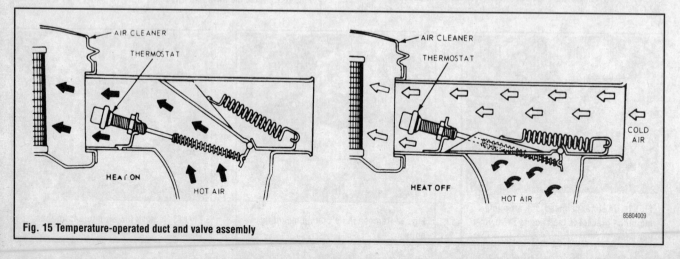

Fig. 15 Temperature-operated duct and valve assembly

door in the snorkel of the air cleaner. The temperature control door is located between the end of the air cleaner snorkel and the duct that carries heated air up from the exhaust manifold. When the underhood temperature is below 90°F (32°C), the temperature control door blocks off underhood or ducted air from entering the air cleaner, allowing only heated air from the exhaust manifold to be drawn into the air cleaner. When the underhood temperature rises above 130°F (54°C), the temperature control door blocks off heated air from the exhaust manifold, allowing only underhood or ducted air to be drawn into the air cleaner.

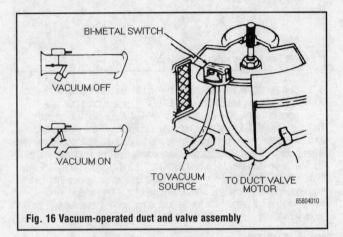

Fig. 16 Vacuum-operated duct and valve assembly

In addition to a bimetal switch, some vacuum-operated duct and valve assemblies also utilize a cold weather modulator, located in the air cleaner assembly. During engine operation in cold ambient temperatures, the cold weather modulator prevents the control door from opening to non-heated intake air. Once the air flowing through the snorkel reaches 55°F (13°C), the cold weather modulator stops operating and the bimetal switch takes control.

By controlling the temperature of the engine intake air this way, exhaust emissions are lowered and fuel economy is improved. In addition, throttle plate icing is reduced, while cold weather driveability is improved.

Dual Diaphragm Distributors

Dual diaphragm distributors are installed in most models and appear in many different engine/transmission/equipment combinations. The best way to tell if you have one is to take a look at your distributor. One vacuum hose running from the vacuum capsule indicates a single diaphragm distributor. Two vacuum hoses means that you have a dual diaphragm unit.

The dual diaphragm is a two-chambered housing which is mounted on the side of the distributor. The outer side of the housing is a distributor vacuum advance mechanism, connected to the carburetor or throttle body by a vacuum hose. The purpose of the vacuum advance (as the name might imply) is to advance ignition timing according to the conditions under which the engine is operating. This device has been used on automobiles for many years, and its chief advantage is economical engine operation. The second side of the dual diaphragm has been added to help control engine exhaust emissions at idle and during deceleration.

The inner side of the dual diaphragm is connected by a vacuum hose to the intake manifold. When the engine is idling or decelerating, intake manifold vac-

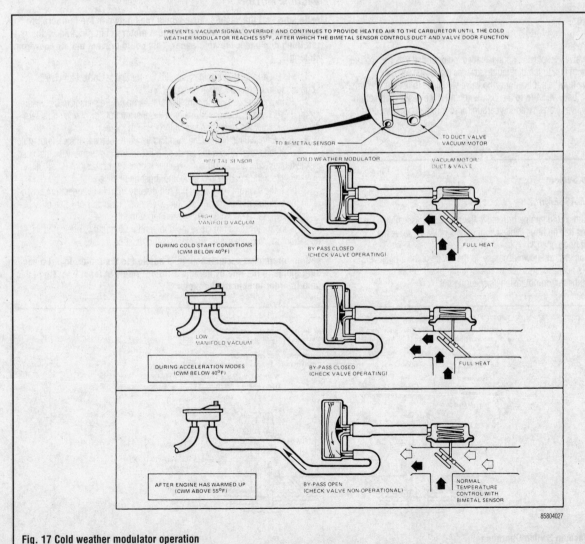

Fig. 17 Cold weather modulator operation

uum is high and carburetor/throttle body vacuum is low. Under these conditions, intake manifold vacuum, applied to the inner side of the dual diaphragm, retards ignition timing to promote more complete combustion of the air/fuel mixture in the engine combustion chambers.

Ported Vacuum Switch (Distributor Vacuum Control Valve)

▶ **See Figure 18**

The distributor vacuum control valve is a temperature sensitive valve which screws into the water jacket of the engine. Three vacuum lines are attached to the vacuum control valve: one which runs from the carburetor or throttle body to the control valve, one which runs from the control valve to the distributor vacuum advance (outer) chamber, and one which runs from the intake manifold to the control valve.

During normal engine operation, vacuum from the carburetor or throttle body passes through the top port of the control valve, through the valve to the middle port, and out the middle port on the valve to the distributor vacuum advance chamber. When the engine is idling however, carburetor or throttle body vacuum is very low, so there is little, if any, vacuum in the passageways described above.

If the engine should begin to overheat while idling, a check ball inside the distributor vacuum control valve which normally blocks off the lower port of the valve (intake manifold vacuum), moves upward to block off the top port (carburetor or throttle body vacuum). This applies intake manifold vacuum to the distributor vacuum advance chamber. Since intake manifold vacuum is very high while the engine is idling, ignition timing is advanced by the application of intake manifold vacuum. This raises the engine idle speed and helps to cool the engine.

Spark Delay Valve

▶ **See Figure 19**

The spark delay valve is a plastic, spring-loaded, color-coded valve which is installed in the vacuum line to the distributor advance diaphragm on many models. Under heavy throttle applications, the valve will close, blocking normal carburetor or throttle body vacuum to the distributor. After the designated period of closed time, the valve opens, restoring carburetor or throttle body vacuum to the distributor.

TESTING

Heated Air Intake System

DUCT AND VALVE ASSEMBLY

1. Either start with a cold engine or remove the air cleaner assembly from the engine for at least half an hour. While cooling the air cleaner, leave the engine compartment hood open.

2. Tape a thermometer, of known accuracy, to the inside of the air cleaner assembly so that it is near the temperature sensor unit. Install the air cleaner assembly on the engine but do not fasten its securing nut.

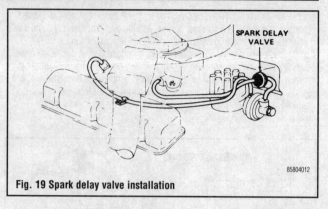

Fig. 19 Spark delay valve installation

3. Start the engine. With the engine cold and the outside temperature less than 90°F (32°C), the door should be in the HEAT ON position (closed to outside air).

4. Operate the throttle lever rapidly to ½-¾ of its opening and release it. The air door should open to allow outside air to enter and then close again.

5. Allow the engine to warm up to normal temperature. Watch the door. When it opens to the outside air, remove the cover from the air cleaner assembly. The temperature should be over 90°F (32°C) and no more than 130°F (54°C); 105°F (41°C) is about normal. If the door does not work within these temperature ranges, or fails to work at all, check for linkage or door binding.

If binding is not present and the air door is not working, proceed with the following vacuum motor tests, if so equipped.

VACUUM MOTOR

➡ **Be sure that the vacuum hose which runs between the temperature sensor (bimetal switch) and the vacuum motor is not pinched by the retaining clip under the air cleaner. This could prevent the air door from closing.**

1. Check all the vacuum lines and fittings for leaks. Correct any leaks. If none are found, proceed with the test.

2. Remove the hose which runs from the temperature sensor to the vacuum motor. (This hose may connect to a cold weather modulator or vacuum retard delay valve, which in turn connects to the vacuum motor.)

3. Run a hose directly from the manifold vacuum source to the vacuum motor.

   a. If the motor closes the air door, it is functioning properly. In that case, the temperature sensor (or cold weather modulator or vacuum retard delay valve, if so equipped) is defective and must be replaced.

   b. If the vacuum hose does not run directly from the temperature sensor to the vacuum motor, identify the faulty sensor, modulator or valve by separately bypassing each component and repeating the test.

4. If the motor does not close the door, and no binding is present in its operation, the vacuum motor is defective and must be replaced.

➡ **If an alternative vacuum source is applied to the motor, insert a vacuum gauge in the line by using a T-fitting. Apply at least 9 in. Hg of vacuum in order to operate the motor.**

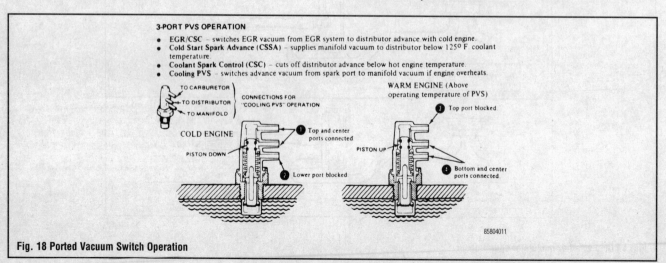

3-PORT PVS OPERATION

- **EGR/CSC** – switches EGR vacuum from EGR system to distributor advance with cold engine.
- **Cold Start Spark Advance (CSSA)** – supplies manifold vacuum to distributor below 125° F. coolant temperature.
- **Coolant Spark Control (CSC)** – cuts off distributor advance below hot engine temperature.
- **Cooling PVS** – switches advance vacuum from spark port to manifold vacuum if engine overheats.

TO CARBURETOR
TO DISTRIBUTOR
TO MANIFOLD

CONNECTIONS FOR "COOLING PVS" OPERATION

COLD ENGINE

PISTON DOWN

1 Top and center ports connected

2 Lower port blocked.

WARM ENGINE (Above operating temperature of PVS)

PISTON UP

3 Top port blocked.

4 Bottom and center ports connected.

Fig. 18 Ported Vacuum Switch Operation

Dual Diaphragm Distributor Advance/Retard Mechanisms

1. Connect a timing light to the engine. Check the ignition timing.

❊❊ WARNING

Before proceeding with the tests, disconnect any spark control devices, distributor vacuum valves, etc. If these are left connected, inaccurate results may be obtained.

2. Remove the retard hose from the distributor and plug it. Increase the engine speed. The timing should advance. If it fails to do so, then the vacuum unit is faulty and must be replaced.

3. Check the timing with the engine at normal idle speed. Unplug the retard hose and connect it to the vacuum unit. The timing should instantly be retarded 4–10 degrees. If this does not occur, the retard diaphragm has a leak and the vacuum unit must be replaced.

Ported Vacuum Switch (Distributor Vacuum Control Valve)

1. Check to make sure that the all-season cooling mixture meets specifications, and that the correct radiator cap is in place and functioning.
2. Check the routing and connection of all vacuum hoses.
3. Attach a tachometer to the engine.
4. Start the engine and bring it up to normal operating temperature. The engine must not be overheated.
5. Note the engine rpm, with the transmission in Neutral, and the throttle in the curb idle position.
6. Disconnect the vacuum hose from the intake manifold at the temperature sensing valve. Plug or clamp the hose.
7. Note the idle rpm with the hose disconnected. If there is no change in rpm, the valve is good. If there is a drop of 100 or more rpm, the valve should be replaced. Connect the vacuum line.
8. Safely block the radiator air flow or disable the cooling fan to induce a higher-than-normal temperature. Be careful not to contact an operating fan.
9. Continue to operate until the engine temperature or heat indicator reading is above normal. If the engine speed by this time has increased 100 or more rpm, the temperature sensing valve is satisfactory. If not, it should be replaced.
10. Unblock the radiator air flow or restore the cooling fan to its normal operation.

Spark Delay Valve

▶ See Figure 20

➡ **If the distributor vacuum line contains a cut-off solenoid, it must be open during this test.**

1. Detach the vacuum line from the distributor at the spark delay valve end. Connect a vacuum gauge to the valve, in its place.
2. Connect a tachometer to the engine. Start the engine and rapidly increase its speed to 2,000 rpm with the transmission in Neutral.

Valve Color	ID #	Time Delay (seconds)	
		Min.	Max.
Black/Gray	1	1	4
Black/Brown	2	2	5
Black/White	5	4	12
Black/Yellow	10	5.8	14
Black/Blue	15	7	16
Black/Green	20	9	20
Black/Orange	30	13	24
Black/Red	40	15	28
White/Brown*	2	2	5
White/Green*	20	9	20

*Dual delay, all others are single delay

85804013

Fig. 20 Spark delay valve color coding

3. As soon as the engine speed is increased, the vacuum gauge reading should drop to zero.
4. Hold the engine speed at a steady 2,000 rpm. It should take longer than two seconds for the gauge to register 6 in. Hg. (20 kpa). If it takes less than two seconds, the valve is defective and must be replaced.
5. If it takes longer than the number of seconds specified in the application chart for the gauge to reach 6 in. Hg (20 kpa), disconnect the vacuum gauge from the spark delay valve. Disconnect the hose which runs from the spark delay valve to the carburetor or throttle body at the valve end. Connect the vacuum gauge to this hose.
6. Start the engine and increase its speed to 2,000 rpm. The gauge should indicate 10–16 in. Hg (34–54 kpa). If it does not, there is a blockage in the carburetor or throttle body vacuum port, or else the hose itself is plugged or broken. If the gauge reading is within specifications, the valve is defective.
7. Reconnect all vacuum lines and remove the tachometer, once testing is completed.

REMOVAL & INSTALLATION

Heated Air Intake System

TEMPERATURE OPERATED DUCT AND VALVE ASSEMBLY

1. Remove the hex-head cap screws which secure the air intake duct and valve assembly to the air cleaner housing. (If secured by rivets, remove the entire air cleaner assembly and drive out the rivets with appropriate tools.)
2. Remove the duct and valve assembly from the air cleaner housing.
3. If inspection reveals that the valve plate is sticking or the thermostat is malfunctioning, remove the thermostat and valve plate as follows:
   a. Detach the valve plate tension spring from the valve plate using long-nose pliers.
   b. Loosen the thermostat locknut and unscrew the thermostat from the mounting bracket.
   c. Grasp the valve plate and withdraw it from the opening.
   To install:
4. If it was necessary to disassemble the thermostat and valve plate, assemble the unit as follows: Install the locknut on the thermostat, and screw the thermostat into the mounting bracket. Install the valve plate tension spring on the valve plate and duct.
5. Position the duct and valve assembly to the air cleaner housing and heat riser tube. Install the attaching cap screws or new pop rivets.

VACUUM OPERATED DUCT AND VALVE ASSEMBLY

1. Disconnect the vacuum hose at the vacuum motor.
2. Remove the hex-head cap screws which secure the air intake duct and valve assembly to the air cleaner housing. (If secured by rivets, remove the entire air cleaner assembly and drive out the rivets with appropriate tools.)
3. Remove the duct and valve assembly from the air cleaner housing.
   To install:
4. Position the duct and valve assembly to the air cleaner housing and heat riser tube. Install the attaching cap screws or new pop rivets.
5. Connect the vacuum line at the vacuum motor.

Ported Vacuum Switch (Distributor Vacuum Control Valve)

1. Drain about one gallon of coolant out of the radiator.

❊❊ CAUTION

When draining the coolant, keep in mind that cats and dogs are attracted by the ethylene glycol antifreeze, and are quite likely to drink any that is left in an uncovered container or in puddles on the ground. This will prove fatal in sufficient quantity. Always drain the coolant into a sealable container. Coolant should be reused unless it is contaminated or several years old.

2. Tag the vacuum hoses that run to the control valve and disconnect them.
3. With a proper size wrench, unscrew and remove the control valve. Be careful to only place the wrench on the hexagonal base of the valve.
   To install:
4. Screw in the control valve and tighten with a proper size wrench. Be careful not to overtighten.

5. Connect the vacuum hoses.
6. Fill the cooling system.

Spark Delay Valve

1. Locate the spark delay valve in the distributor vacuum line.
2. Disconnect the attached vacuum hoses and remove the valve.

To install:

3. Install a new spark delay valve in-line, making sure that the black end of the valve is connected to the vacuum hose from the carburetor or throttle body, and the color-coded end is connected to the line from the distributor.

Exhaust Gas Recirculation System

OPERATION

▶ **See Figures 21 and 22**

All models are equipped with an Exhaust Gas Recirculation (EGR) system to control oxides of nitrogen.

For V8 engines, exhaust gases travel through the exhaust gas crossover passage in the intake manifold. On 6-200 engines, an external tube carries exhaust manifold gases to a carburetor spacer. On such spacer-equipped engines, a por-

tion of the gases is diverted into a spacer mounted under the carburetor or adjacent to the throttle body. For floor entry models, a regulated portion of exhaust gases enters the intake manifold through a pair of small holes drilled in the floor of the intake manifold riser. The EGR control valve, which is attached to the rear of the spacer or intake manifold, consists of a vacuum diaphragm with an attached plunger that normally blocks exhaust gases from entering the intake manifold.

On all models, the EGR valve is controlled by a vacuum line from the carburetor or throttle body which passes through a ported vacuum switch. The EGR ported vacuum switch provides vacuum to the EGR valve at coolant temperatures above 125°F (52°C). The vacuum diaphragm then opens the EGR valve, permitting exhaust gases to flow through the spacer and enter the combustion chambers. The exhaust gases are relatively oxygen-free, and tend to dilute the combustion charge. This lowers peak combustion temperature, thereby reducing oxides of nitrogen.

TESTING

1. Allow the engine to warm up, so that the coolant temperature reaches at least 125°F (52°C).
2. Disconnect the vacuum hose which runs from the temperature cut-in valve to the EGR valve at the EGR valve end. Connect a vacuum gauge to this hose with a T-fitting.
3. Increase the engine speed. The gauge should indicate a vacuum. If no vacuum is present, check the following:
   a. The carburetor or throttle body— look for a clogged vacuum port.
   b. The vacuum hoses — including the vacuum hoses to the transmission modulator.
   c. The temperature cut-in valve — if no vacuum is present at its outlet with the engine temperature above 125°F (52°C) and vacuum is available from the carburetor or throttle body, the valve is defective.
4. If the vehicle passes all of the above tests, check the EGR valve itself.
5. Connect an outside vacuum source and a vacuum gauge to the valve.
6. Apply vacuum to the EGR valve. The valve should open at 3–10 in. Hg (10–34 kpa), the engine idle speed should slow down and the idle should become more rough.
7. If this does not happen (that is, the EGR valve remains closed), the EGR valve is defective and must be replaced.
8. If the valve stem moves but the idle remains the same, the valve orifice is clogged and must be cleaned.

➡**If an outside vacuum source is not available, disconnect the hose which runs between the EGR valve and the temperature cut-in valve and plug the hose connections on the cut-in valve. Connect the EGR valve hose to a source of intake manifold vacuum and watch the idle. The results should be the same as in Steps 6–7.**

SERVICE

Since the EGR system channels exhaust gases through quite narrow passages, deposits are likely to build up and eventually block the flow of gases. This necessitates servicing of the system at the interval specified in the maintenance chart (see Section 1). EGR system service consists of cleaning or replacing the EGR valve and cleaning all the exhaust gas channels.

Cleaning

EGR VALVE

▶ **See Figures 23 and 24**

Remove the EGR valve for cleaning, as described later in this section. Do not strike or pry on the valve diaphragm housing or supports, as this may damage the valve operating mechanism and/or change the valve calibration. Check the orifice in the EGR valve body for deposits. A small hand drill with a diameter of 0.060 in. (1.5mm) or less may be used to clean the hole if plugged. Extreme care must be taken to avoid enlarging the hole or damaging the surface of the orifice plate.

➡**The remainder of this procedure refers only to EGR valves which can be disassembled. Valves which are riveted or otherwise permanently assembled cannot be cleaned and should be replaced if clogged.**

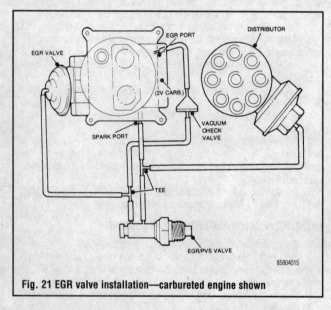

Fig. 21 EGR valve installation—carbureted engine shown

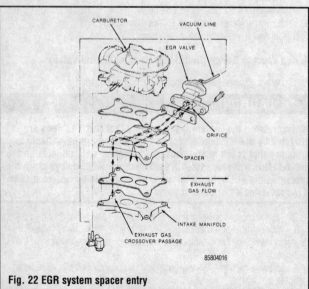

Fig. 22 EGR system spacer entry

Separate the diaphragm section from the main mounting body. Clean the valve plates, stem, and the mounting plate, using a small power-driven rotary type wire brush. Take care not to damage the parts. Remove deposits between the stem and valve disc by using a steel blade or shim approximately 0.028 in. (0.7mm) thick in a sawing motion around the stem shoulder at both sides of the disc. The poppet must wobble and move axially before assembly.

Clean the cavity and passages in the main body of the valve with a power-driven rotary wire brush. If the orifice plate has a hole with a diameter of less than 0.050 in. (1.27mm), it must be removed for cleaning. Remove all loosened debris using compressed air. Reassemble the diaphragm section on the main body using a new gasket between them. Clean the orifice plate and the counter-bore in the valve body. Reinstall the orifice plate using a small amount of contact cement to retain the plate during assembly of the valve and spacer. Apply cement only to the outer edges of the orifice plate to avoid restriction of the orifice.

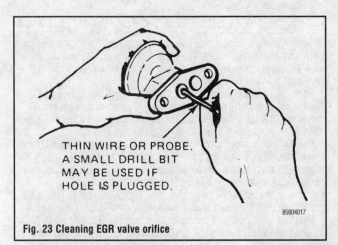

Fig. 23 Cleaning EGR valve orifice

EGR SUPPLY PASSAGES AND CARBURETOR SPACER

▶ See Figure 25

Remove the carburetor and carburetor spacer on engines so equipped. On fuel injected engines, remove the throttle body assembly and EGR spacer. Clean the supply tube with a small power-driven rotary type wire brush or blast cleaning equipment. Clean the exhaust gas passages in the spacer using a suitable wire brush and/or scraper. The machined holes in the spacer can be cleaned by using a suitable round wire brush. Hard, encrusted material should be probed loose first, then brushed out.

EGR EXHAUST GAS CHANNEL

Clean the intake manifold exhaust gas channel, where applicable, using a suitable carbon scraper. Clean the exhaust gas entry port in the intake manifold by hand passing a suitable drill bit through the holes to auger out the deposits. Do not use a wire brush. The manifold riser bore(s) should be suitably plugged during the above action to prevent any of the residue from entering the induction system.

REMOVAL & INSTALLATION

EGR Valve

▶ See Figures 26, 27, 28 and 29

1. Disconnect the negative battery cable.
2. Disconnect the vacuum line from the EGR valve. Also, disconnect the wire at the EGR Valve Position (EVP) sensor, if so equipped.
3. Disconnect the exhaust gas inlet line at the EGR valve.
4. Remove the mounting bolts or stud nuts and remove the EGR valve.
5. Remove the stud nuts, then remove the EVP sensor from the EGR valve, if so equipped.
   To install:
6. Installation is the reverse of removal. Be sure to remove all old gasket material from both the EGR valve and its mating surface before installation. Also, be sure to use a new gasket.

Fig. 24 Carefully open any ports which are blocked by deposits

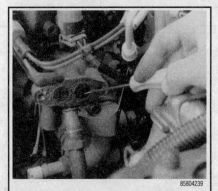

Fig. 25 Check the supply passages for obstructions and clear as necessary

Fig. 26 Disconnect the vacuum line from the EGR valve

Fig. 27 Using a wrench, disconnect the exhaust gas inlet fitting at the EGR valve

Fig. 28 Remove the mounting bolts or nuts and the EGR valve

Fig. 29 Remove the old gasket and replace with a new one

Venturi Vacuum Amplifier System

OPERATION

▶ **See Figures 30 and 31**

Many models use a venturi vacuum amplifier in conjunction with the EGR system. The amplifier is used to boost a relatively weak venturi vacuum signal (in the throat of the carburetor or throttle body) into a strong intake manifold vacuum signal in order to operate the EGR valve. This device improves drive-ability by more closely matching venturi airflow and EGR flow.

The amplifier features a vacuum reservoir and check valve to maintain an adequate vacuum supply regardless of variations in engine manifold vacuum. Also used in conjunction with the amplifier is a relief valve, which will cancel the output EGR vacuum signal whenever the venturi vacuum signal is equal to, or greater than, the intake manifold vacuum. Thus, the EGR valve may close at or near wide-open throttle acceleration, when maximum power is needed.

TESTING

1. Connect a vacuum gauge to port O of the amplifier. Do not remove the connection at port R. The gauge may read as much as 2 in. Hg (6.75 kpa) at idle.
2. Disconnect the venturi vacuum hose at the carburetor or throttle body, and increase engine speed to 2000 rpm (3000 for the 4-140 engine). Vacuum should not change.
3. Maintain a high engine speed and connect the venturi vacuum hose. The gauge should read at least 4 in. Hg (13.5 kpa).
4. Return to idle. The gauge should return to its initial reading.
5. If the above conditions are not met, replace the venturi vacuum amplifier.

REMOVAL & INSTALLATION

1. Tag and disconnect the vacuum hoses at the venturi vacuum amplifier.
2. Remove the fasteners which secure the venturi vacuum amplifier and remove the unit.

To install:

3. Installation is the reverse of removal. Be sure to connect the vacuum hoses to their proper ports. Replace any vacuum hoses which are cracked or brittle.

EGR/Coolant Spark Control (EGR/CSC) System

OPERATION

▶ **See Figure 32**

The EGR/CSC system is used on most vehicles. It regulates both distributor spark advance and the EGR valve operation according to coolant temperature by sequentially switching vacuum signals. The major EGR/CSC system components are:

1. A 95°F (35°C) EGR Ported Vacuum Switch (EGR-PVS)
2. Spark Delay Valve (SDV)
3. Vacuum Check Valve (VCV)

When the engine coolant temperature is below 82°F (28°C), the EGR-PVS admits carburetor or throttle body EGR port vacuum (occurring at about 2,500 rpm) directly to the distributor advance diaphragm, through the one-way check valve. At the same time, the EGR-PVS shuts off EGR port vacuum to the EGR valve and transmission diaphragm.

When engine coolant temperature is 95°F (35°C) and above, the EGR-PVS is actuated and directs EGR port vacuum to the EGR valve and transmission, instead of to the distributor. At temperatures between 82–95°F (28–35°C), the EGR-PVS may be opened, closed or in mid-position.

The SDV delays carburetor or throttle body spark vacuum to the distributor advance diaphragm by restricting the vacuum signal through the SDV for a pre-determined time. During normal acceleration, little or no vacuum is admitted to the distributor advance diaphragm until acceleration is completed. This is accomplished because of the time delay of the SDV and the rerouting of the EGR port vacuum when the engine coolant temperature is 95°F (35°C) or higher.

The check valve blocks off vacuum signal from the SDV to the EGR-PVS, so that spark port vacuum will not be dissipated when the EGR-PVS is actuated above 95°F (35°C).

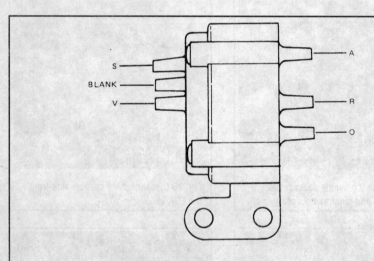

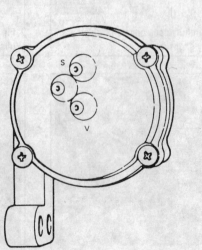

CODE FOR PORT CONNECTIONS:

O — OUTPUT TO EGR
R — FROM RESERVOIR
S — VACUUM SOURCE (SPARK OR EGR PORT)
V — VENTURI VACUUM
A — ATMOSPHERE (VENT)

85804023

Fig. 30 EGR venturi vacuum amplifier

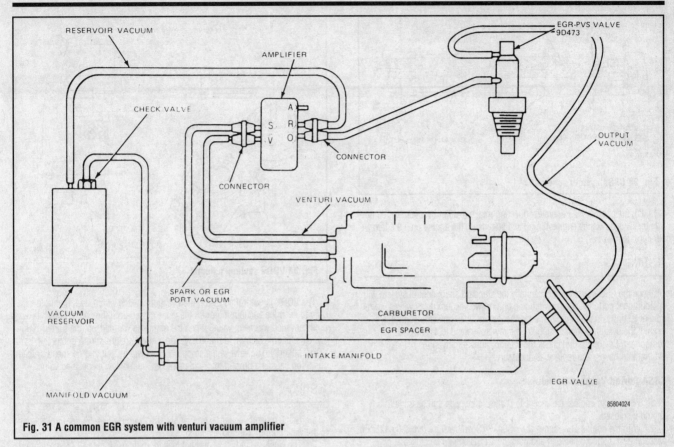

Fig. 31 A common EGR system with venturi vacuum amplifier

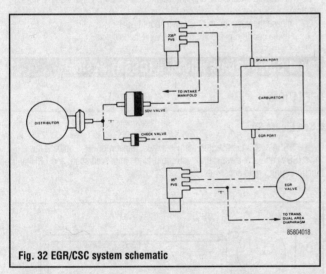

Fig. 32 EGR/CSC system schematic

The 235°F (113°C) PVS is not part of the EGR/CSC system, but is connected to the distributor vacuum advance to prevent engine overheating while idling. At idle speed, no vacuum is generated at either the carburetor/throttle body spark port or at the EGR port, and engine timing is fully retarded. When engine coolant temperatures reaches 235°F (113°C), however, the valve is actuated to admit intake manifold vacuum to the distributor advance diaphragm. This advances the engine timing and speeds up the engine. The increase in coolant flow and fan speed lowers engine temperature.

TESTING

EGR-PVS

1. With a cold engine, the passage between the upper and middle ports should be open, and the passage between the lower and middle ports should be closed.

2. With the engine at or above the EGR-PVS temperature (typically 95°F), the passage between the lower and middle ports should be open, and the passage between the upper and middle ports should be closed.

Spark Delay Valve

1. Disconnect the vacuum lines which run to the spark delay valve and connect a hand vacuum pump.
2. Operate the pump and note if vacuum can be achieved.
   a. A valve with one black or white side and one colored side is good if vacuum can be built up in one direction, but not in the other direction, and if the vacuum slowly decreases.
   b. A valve with both sides the same color is good if vacuum can be built up in both directions before visibly decreasing.

Vacuum Check Valve

1. Connect a hand vacuum pump to the vacuum (black) side of the valve.
2. Apply 16 in. Hg (54 kpa) of vacuum.
3. If vacuum remains above 15 in. Hg (50.7 kpa) for 10 seconds, the valve is acceptable.

Cold Start Spark Advance (CSSA) System

OPERATION

▶ See Figure 33

Some vehicles are equipped with the CSSA System. It is a modification of the existing spark control system to aid in cold start driveability. The system uses a coolant temperature sensing ported vacuum switch located on the thermostat housing. When the engine is cold (below 125°F/113°C), it momentarily traps spark port vacuum on the distributor advance diaphragm. After the engine warms up, normal spark control resumes. The 235°F (113°C) PVS is not part of the CSSA system, but is connected to the distributor vacuum advance to prevent engine overheating at idle. Should the coolant temperature exceed 235°F

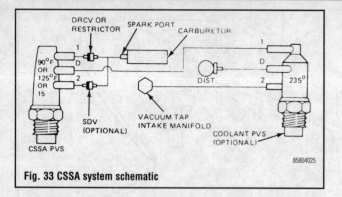

Fig. 33 CSSA system schematic

(113°C), the coolant PVS operates, directing intake manifold vacuum to the distributor. This advances engine timing and speeds up the engine until the temperature decreases.

TESTING

Since the CSSA System is essentially the standard spark control system with an additional ported vacuum switch and one or two vacuum delay valves, component testing is done in the same manner as on other emission control systems. If the system is malfunctioning, simply isolate and test each specific component. Be sure to first check the vacuum lines for any signs of leaking or deteriorated hoses, and replace as necessary.

CSSA Ported Vacuum Switch

1. With a cold engine, passage 1 to D should be open and passage 2 to D should be closed.
2. With the engine at or above the CSSA-PVS temperature (typically 125°F), passage 2 to D should be open and passage 1 to D should be closed.

Distributor Retard Control Valve (DRCV)

1. Disconnect the vacuum lines which run to the distributor retard control valve and connect a hand vacuum pump to the DRCV.
2. Operate the pump and note if vacuum can be achieved.
   a. A valve with one black or white side and one colored side is good if vacuum can be built up in one direction, but not in the other direction, and if the vacuum slowly decreases.
   b. A valve with both sides the same color is good if vacuum can be built up in both directions before visibly decreasing.

Spark Delay Valve

1. Disconnect the vacuum lines which run to the spark delay valve and connect a hand vacuum pump.
2. Operate the pump and note if vacuum can be achieved.
   a. A valve with one black or white side and one colored side is good if vacuum can be built up in one direction, but not in the other direction, and if the vacuum slowly decreases.
   b. A valve with both sides the same color is good if vacuum can be built up in both directions before visibly decreasing.

Vacuum Operated Heat Control Valve (VOHV)

OPERATION

▶ See Figure 34

To further aid cold start driveability during engine warm-up, many V6 and V8 engines use a VOHV located between the exhaust manifold and the exhaust inlet (header) pipe.

When the engine is first started, the valve is closed, blocking exhaust gases from exiting one bank of cylinders. These gases are then diverted back through the intake manifold crossover passage under the carburetor or fuel injection throttle body. The result is quick heat to the carburetor and choke assembly or to the CFI throttle body.

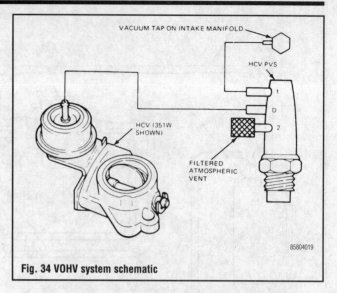

Fig. 34 VOHV system schematic

The VOHV is controlled by a ported vacuum switch which uses manifold vacuum to keep the vacuum motor on the valve closed until the coolant reaches a predetermined warm-up value. When the engine is warmed-up, the ported switch shuts off vacuum to the VOHV, and a strong return spring opens the VOHV butterfly. The valve will also open before warm-up if engine speed or load condition causes a drop in intake manifold vacuum below a specified value.

TESTING

1. Using a hand vacuum pump, apply 10–15 in. Hg (34–51 kpa) of vacuum to the vacuum motor for 60 seconds.
2. The valve should close and not leak more than 2 in. Hg (6.75 kpa) during this time.
3. Release the vacuum and the valve should open.
4. If these conditions are not met, the valve is defective.

Dual Signal Spark Advance (DSSA) System

OPERATION

▶ See Figure 35

The DSSA system is used on many engines. It incorporates a spark delay valve (SDV) and a one-way check valve to provide improved spark and EGR function during mild acceleration.

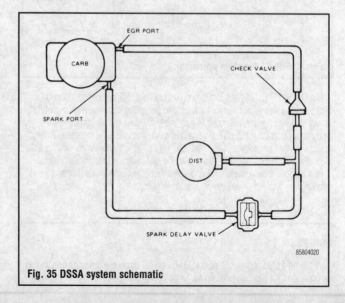

Fig. 35 DSSA system schematic

The check valve prevents spark port vacuum from reaching the EGR valve and causing excessive EGR valve flow. It also prevents EGR port vacuum, which could result in improper spark advance due to a weakened signal. The SDV permits application of full EGR port vacuum to the distributor advance diaphragm during mild acceleration. During steady speed or cruise conditions, EGR port vacuum is applied to the EGR valve, while spark port vacuum is applied to the distributor advance diaphragm.

TESTING

Since the DSSA System is essentially the standard spark control system with an added spark delay valve and a vacuum check valve, component testing is done in the same manner as on other emission control systems. If the system is malfunctioning, simply isolate and test each specific component. Be sure to first check the vacuum lines for any signs of leaking or deteriorated hoses, and replace as necessary.

Spark Delay Valve

1. Disconnect the vacuum lines which run to the spark delay valve and connect a hand vacuum pump.
2. Operate the pump and note if vacuum can be achieved.
   a. A valve with one black or white side and one colored side is good if vacuum can be built up in one direction, but not in the other direction, and if the vacuum slowly decreases.
   b. A valve with both sides the same color is good if vacuum can be built up in both directions before visibly decreasing.

Vacuum Check Valve

1. Connect a hand vacuum pump to the vacuum (black) side of the valve.
2. Apply 16 in. Hg (54 kpa) of vacuum.
3. If vacuum remains above 15 in. Hg (50.7 kpa) for 10 seconds, the valve is acceptable.

Catalytic Converter System

OPERATION

▶ **See Figure 36**

All models, including Canadian, are equipped with a catalytic converter system to meet 1975 Federal and California emission control standards. California models are equipped with two or more converters, while models sold in the other 49 states and Canada have at least one unit. The catalytic converter works as a gas reactor, which speeds up the heat producing chemical reaction between various exhaust gas components. In so doing, the catalytic converter reduces air pollutants in the engine exhaust. The catalyst material, contained inside the converter, is made of a ceramic substrate that is coated with a high surface area alumina, and is impregnated with catalytically active, precious metals. The conventional oxidation catalyst, containing Platinum and Palladium, is effective at converting noxious emissions of hydrocarbons (HC) and carbon monoxide (CO) into harmless carbon dioxide and water. A three-way catalyst, containing Platinum and Rhodium, is also effective against hydrocarbons and carbon monoxide, as well as nitrogen oxides (NOx). If a vehicle's engine is properly tuned, a catalytic converter is designed to last at least 50,000–100,000 miles before replacement, although it may last indefinitely if not subjected to prolonged overheating and overly rich fuel mixtures.

Besides the variety of underbody catalytic converters, many vehicles utilize one or more light-off converters. These auxiliary catalytic converters are mounted forward of the underbody converter(s), and are often an integral part of the front pipe assembly. They are designed to operate effectively at engine warm-up, before the main converter reaches the temperature required for maximum efficiency.

In order to maintain the converter's oxygen supply at a high enough level to promote oxidation, the oxidation catalyst requires the use of a secondary air source. This is provided by the Thermactor air injection system.

➡**Lead-free gasoline must be used on all converter-equipped vehicles.**

REMOVAL & INSTALLATION

For removal and installation of catalytic converters, refer to Section 3 of this manual.

Exhaust Gas Oxygen Sensor

OPERATION

▶ **See Figure 37**

The exhaust gas oxygen sensor supplies a signal to the Electronic Control Assembly (ECA) indicating either a rich or lean condition during engine operation. The oxygen sensor is located in the exhaust manifold.

REMOVAL & INSTALLATION

▶ **See Figures 38 and 39**

1. Unplug the electrical connector.
2. Using a proper size wrench, unscrew the sensor.
To install:
3. Coat the sensor's threads with anti-seize compound.
4. Screw in the sensor and torque it to 12 ft. lbs. (16 Nm).
5. Engage the electrical connector.

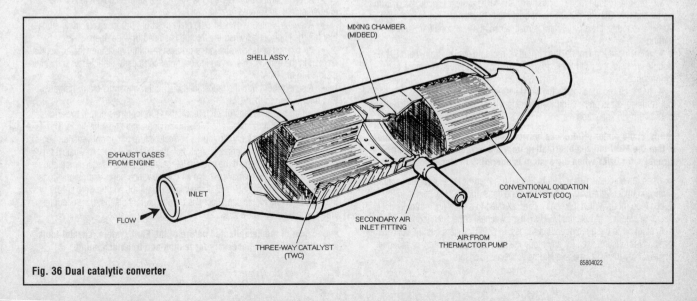

Fig. 36 Dual catalytic converter

85804022

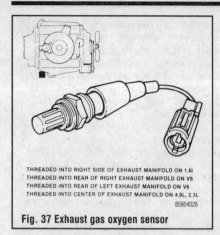

THREADED INTO RIGHT SIDE OF EXHAUST MANIFOLD ON 1.6I
THREADED INTO REAR OF RIGHT EXHAUST MANIFOLD ON V8
THREADED INTO REAR OF LEFT EXHAUST MANIFOLD ON V6
THREADED INTO CENTER OF EXHAUST MANIFOLD ON 4.9L, 2.3L

85804026

Fig. 37 Exhaust gas oxygen sensor

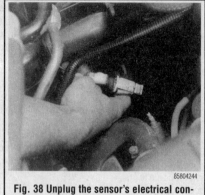

85804244

Fig. 38 Unplug the sensor's electrical connector

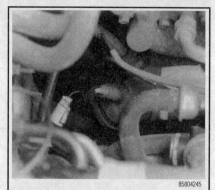

85804245

Fig. 39 The oxygen sensor threads into the exhaust manifold

ELECTRONIC ENGINE CONTROLS

➡Since late 1979, emission controls and air/fuel mixtures have been controlled by various electronic methods. On selected applications, an electronically controlled feedback carburetor was used, in conjunction with various vacuum check valves, solenoids and regulators, to precisely calibrate fuel metering. On other applications, these electronic systems monitor and control fuel injection. The electronic control boxes (or microprocessors) can be calibrated and programmed in order to be used by different engines and under different conditions.

Microprocessor Control Unit (MCU) System

The Microprocessor Control Unit (MCU) system was used on some of the 4 and 8-cylinder vehicles covered by this manual from 1980–83. Although the MCU system is basically the same for all engines, it was confined to applications using a feedback carburetor. The heart of the MCU system's operation is the fuel control system. Strict fuel control is necessary to keep the air/fuel ratio at a proper chemical balance of 14.7:1, so that maximum catalytic efficiency is maintained.

The fuel control loop is comprised of the Microprocessor Control Unit (MCU) module, an Exhaust Gas Oxygen (EGO) sensor, and a Feedback Carburetor (FBC). 4-cylinder engines also incorporate a fuel control solenoid. In order to maintain the critical air/fuel ratio, the EGO sensor monitors the exhaust emissions by measuring the amount of oxygen in the exhaust gases. It then provides a voltage signal to the MCU module to indicate lean or rich engine operation. The feedback carburetor varies the air/fuel ratio based on oxygen measurements taken by the EGO sensor. Since good emissions and fuel economy do not always correlate with driveability, the MCU system is designed to operate in three fuel control modes: initialization, open loop and closed loop.

• The initialization mode occurs when the MCU system is activated by turning the ignition **ON** and persists for a brief moment after the engine is started. During this mode, the air/fuel ratio is maintained at a rich condition for easy starting.

• In the open loop mode, the air/fuel ratio output signals from the MCU module are held at a fixed level, adjusting fuel to assure good response and performance.

• In the closed loop mode, the MCU system leans out the air/fuel ratio so that sufficient air is present in the mixture for nearly complete combustion of the fuel's hydrogen and carbon.

➡One of the major differences between open and closed loop operation is that the MCU utilizes information from the oxygen sensor to control air/fuel ratio ONLY when the system is operating in closed loop.

When the engine is running at its normal (warmed-up) operating temperature range and under light-load, part-throttle conditions, the MCU system is in the closed loop mode. When the engine is accelerated to a wide-open throttle, decelerated, or standing at idle, the MCU system switches to the open loop mode.

In addition to the three operating modes, the MCU system has the built-in capability for testing itself for any mode malfunction. This self-test is intended to check only the MCU module and its associated sensors.

➡Because of the complicated nature of the Ford system, special tools and procedures are necessary for testing and troubleshooting.

EEC-IV

Most 1984–88 vehicles covered by this manual use the EEC-IV system. As is the case with its EEC-I, II and III predecessors, the heart of the EEC-IV system is a microprocessor. Unlike its predecessors, however, the EEC-IV microprocessor is not properly called an Electronic Control Assembly (ECA). Instead, the EEC-IV microprocessor is called a Powertrain Control Module (PCM), by virtue of its added transmission control function.

EEC-IV marked the disappearance of separate ECA and calibration assemblies, which was the norm for its predecessors. Instead, the calibration assembly became a program stored on a Read Only Memory (ROM) chip, within the PCM.

The PCM is given responsibility for the operation of the emission control devices, cooling fan(s), ignition/timing advance and, in some cases, automatic transmission functions. Because the EEC-IV system oversees both the ignition timing and the fuel injector (or feedback carburetor) operation, a precise air/fuel ratio will be maintained under all operating conditions. The PCM receives electrical input from several sensors, switches and relays located on and around the engine:

• A potentiometer senses the position of the vane airflow meter in the engine's air induction system and generates a voltage signal that varies with the amount of air drawn into the engine.

• A sensor in the area of the vane airflow meter measures the temperature of the incoming air and transmits a corresponding electrical signal.

• Another temperature sensor inserted in the engine coolant tells if the engine is cold or warmed up.

• A switch, which senses throttle plate position, produces electrical signals that tell the control unit when the throttle is closed or wide open.

• An oxygen sensor probe in the exhaust manifold measures the amount of oxygen in the exhaust gas, as an indication of combustion efficiency, and sends a signal to the PCM.

• A sensor built into the redesigned distributor transmits crankshaft position information to the PCM.

Based on combinations of such input, the PCM controls output to various devices and actuators concerned with engine operation and emissions. The PCM relies on these signals to form a correct picture of current vehicle operation. If any of the input signals is incorrect, the PCM will react to whatever data is received. For example, if the coolant temperature sensor is inaccurate and reads too low, the PCM may perceive an engine which never warms up. Consequently, the engine settings will be maintained as if the engine were cold. Because so many inputs can affect one output, correct diagnostic procedures are essential on these systems.

➡Because of the complicated nature of the Ford system, special tools and procedures are necessary for testing and troubleshooting.

SELF DIAGNOSTIC SYSTEMS AND TROUBLE CODES

MCU System

GENERAL DESCRIPTION

The MCU system was the first to incorporate both a special test connector and the Self-Test Automatic Readout (STAR) hand-held scan tool for diagnostics. The MCU module is devoted to monitoring both input and output functions within the system. This ability forms the core of the self-diagnostic system. If a problem is detected within a circuit, the controller will recognize the fault, assign it an identification code, and store the code in a memory section. Fault codes are represented by two-digit numbers, which may be retrieved during diagnosis.

While the MCU system is capable of recognizing many internal problems, certain faults will not be recognized. Because the computer system reads only electrical signals, it cannot sense or react to mechanical or vacuum faults affecting engine operation. Some of these faults may affect another component which will set a code. For example, the MCU monitors the output signal to the fuel control solenoid or feedback carburetor, but cannot detect a defective choke diaphragm. As long as the output driver responds correctly, the computer will read the system as functioning correctly. However, the improper choke pull-off may result in a rich mixture. This would, in turn, be detected by the oxygen sensor and noticed as a constantly rich signal by the MCU. Once the signal falls outside the pre-programmed limits, the engine control assembly would notice the fault and set an identification code.

TOOLS AND EQUIPMENT

Hand-Held Scan Tools

Although stored codes may be read through an analog voltmeter, the use of a hand-held scan tool such as Ford's Self-Test Automatic Readout (STAR) tester, or equivalent, is highly recommended. There are many manufacturers of such tools, but you must be certain that the tool is appropriate for the intended use.

The STAR tester is designed to communicate directly with the MCU system and interpret electrical signals. The scan tool allows any stored faults to be read from the engine controller memory. Use of the scan tool provides additional data during troubleshooting, but does not eliminate the need for diagnostic work. The scan tool makes information collection easier, but the data must still be correctly interpreted by an operator familiar with the system.

Other Diagnostic Tools

An analog (needle type) voltmeter with a voltage scale of 0–20 volts DC may be used to read stored fault codes if the STAR tester is not available. The codes are transmitted as visible needle sweeps on the face of the instrument.

Other necessary tools for testing/troubleshooting include a timing light, a vacuum gauge (for some applications), and a jumper wire. A quality tachometer, preferably with an inductive (clip-on) pickup and a range of 0–3000 rpm, will also be required to verify test rpm on 4-140 engines during Self-Test procedures.

DIAGNOSIS AND TESTING

Diagnosis of a driveability problem requires attention to detail and following the diagnostic procedures in the correct order. Resist the temptation to begin extensive testing before completing the preliminary diagnostic steps. The preliminary or visual inspection must be completed in detail before diagnosis begins. In many cases, this will shorten diagnostic time and often cure the problem without electronic testing.

Visual Inspection

This is possibly the most critical step of diagnosis. A detailed examination of all connectors, wiring and vacuum hoses can often lead to a repair without further diagnosis. Performance of this step relies on the skill of the person performing it; a careful inspector will check the undersides of hoses as well as the integrity of hard-to-reach hoses blocked by the air cleaner or other components.

Wiring should be checked carefully for any sign of strain, burning, crimping or terminal pull-out from a connector.

You should always check connectors at components or in harnesses as required. Pushing them together will usually reveal a loose fit. Pay particular attention to ground circuits, making sure they are not loose or corroded. Remember to inspect connectors and hose fittings at components not mounted on the engine, such as the evaporative canister or relays mounted on the fender aprons. Any component or wiring in the vicinity of a fluid leak or spillage should be given extra attention during inspection.

Additionally, inspect maintenance items such as belt condition and tension, battery charge and condition, and the radiator cap carefully. Any of these simple items may affect the system enough to set a fault.

Reading Codes With a Hand-Held Scan Tool

▶ **See Figures 40 and 44**

A hand-held scan tool, such as the STAR tester, may be used to retrieve stored fault codes. Simply engage the tester's service connectors to the vehicle's Self-Test connectors.

Follow the directions given later in this section under Quick Test Procedures for performing the Key On Engine Off (KOEO) and Key On Engine Running (KOER) tests. Be sure to release the tester's push button, if applicable, before beginning the Self-Test.

Digital codes, such as "23", will be output and displayed as numbers on the hand-held scan tool. (The codes may also be read using an analog voltmeter. For further details on this alternative method, please refer to the following portion of this section.)

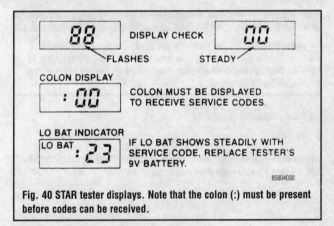

Fig. 40 STAR tester displays. Note that the colon (:) must be present before codes can be received.

Reading Codes With an Analog Voltmeter

▶ **See Figures 41 and 45**

In the absence of a scan tool, an analog voltmeter may be used to retrieve stored fault codes. Set the meter range to read 0–15 volts DC. Connect the positive (+) lead of the meter to the positive battery terminal and connect the negative (–) lead of the meter to the self-test output pin of the diagnostic connector.

Follow the directions for performing the KOEO and KOER tests. To activate the tests, use a jumper wire to connect the signal return pin on the diagnostic connector to the self-test input connector. The self-test input line is the separate wire and connector that is located with or near the diagnostic connector.

The codes will be transmitted as groups of needle sweeps, whose cadence corresponds to the codes' numerical representation. Please refer to the accompanying illustration for details on counting the needle sweeps in order to determine the transmitted code.

SELF-TESTING (GENERATING STORED CODES)

Quick Test Procedures

The MCU system may be interrogated for stored codes using the Quick Test Procedures. These Quick Test procedures include: Key On Engine Off (KOEO)

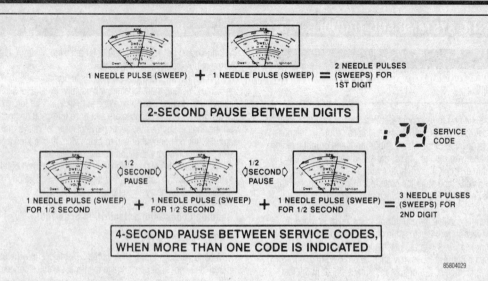

1 NEEDLE PULSE (SWEEP) + 1 NEEDLE PULSE (SWEEP) = 2 NEEDLE PULSES (SWEEPS) FOR 1ST DIGIT

2-SECOND PAUSE BETWEEN DIGITS

:23 SERVICE CODE

1 NEEDLE PULSE (SWEEP) FOR 1/2 SECOND + 1 NEEDLE PULSE (SWEEP) FOR 1/2 SECOND + 1 NEEDLE PULSE (SWEEP) FOR 1/2 SECOND = 3 NEEDLE PULSES (SWEEPS) FOR 2ND DIGIT

1/2 SECOND PAUSE   1/2 SECOND PAUSE

4-SECOND PAUSE BETWEEN SERVICE CODES, WHEN MORE THAN ONE CODE IS INDICATED

85804029

Fig. 41 Code display patterns on an analog voltmeter

and Key On Engine Running (KOER). These diagnostic procedures must be performed correctly if the system is to run the internal Self-Test checks and provide accurate fault codes.

If the vehicle passes both sections of the Quick Test, the MCU system is all right and the vehicle's problem exists elsewhere. Once the Quick Test has been performed and all fault codes recorded, refer to the code charts found later in this section.

✳✳ CAUTION

To prevent injury and/or property damage, always block the drive wheels, firmly apply the parking brake, place the transmission in Park or Neutral and turn all electrical loads off before performing the Quick Test procedures.

KEY ON ENGINE OFF (KOEO)

▶ See Figures 42 thru 47

➡**Unless instructed otherwise, do not disconnect any sensor with the key ON or a service code may be stored.**

1. Verify that the vacuum hoses are connected to the air cleaner. The air cleaner must be installed during these tests.
2. Start the engine and use an analog voltmeter to verify that there is power to the choke. Let the engine idle until it reaches normal operating temperature and the throttle is off fast idle. Turn the engine **OFF**.
3. Connect the scan tool or analog voltmeter to the self-test connectors, as shown. When using a voltmeter, connect a jumper wire from the Self-Test Trigger to the ground terminal of the Self-Test connector. When using a STAR tester, make certain the test button is unlatched or up.
4. Perform all of the following set-up procedures which apply:
   a. On 4-140 engines with a vacuum purge valve, disconnect (but do not plug) the hose from the canister control valve that runs to the carbon canister. (This will disable the canister purge system during the test.)
   b. On 8-255 engines with a vacuum delay valve, uncap the restrictor near the tee in the Thermactor diverter vacuum control line.
   c. On 8-cylinder engines, remove the PCV valve from the breather cap on the valve cover.
   d. On 8-cylinder engines, use a tee to connect a vacuum gauge to the canister purge solenoid valve hose on the carbon canister side of the hose.
5. Make sure that the carburetor throttle linkage is off the high step of its cam.
6. Activate the test button on the STAR tester, if applicable. This will ready the Self-Test mode.
7. Turn the ignition switch **ON**, but do not start the engine.

➡**Do not depress the throttle on gasoline engines during the test.**

8. The KOEO codes will be transmitted.
9. Record all service codes displayed, and proceed with the Key On Engine Running (KOER) test.

➡**For a translation of potential MCU service codes, please refer to the charts later in this section.**

KEY ON ENGINE RUNNING (KOER)

➡**Unless instructed otherwise, do not disconnect any sensor with the key ON or a service code may be stored.**

1. On vehicles equipped with a 4-140 engine and a 5-speed transmission, locate and tape the hole on top of the wide-open-throttle vacuum valve. (Be sure to remove the tape after this test is completed.)
2. Verify that the engine is still at normal operating temperature.
3. Activate or latch the self-test button on the scan tool, if applicable.
4. For all vehicles **except** those equipped with an 8-cylinder engine, perform the following procedures. (For those vehicles equipped with an 8-cylinder engine, proceed to step 5.)
   a. Start the engine and, within 20 seconds, increase the engine speed to 3,000 rpm.
   b. Hold the rpm steady until a service code is received on the voltmeter or STAR tester. (The Self-Test sequence may run 10–40 seconds.) Return the engine to idle as soon as service code output begins.

➡**If, within the first seven seconds of starting the engine, the voltmeter does not pulse (sweep), or pulses more than two times, check the engine's TACH lead for continuity. Likewise, if the STAR tester's code does not change, or displays a code other than "20" or "30", check the TACH lead.**

   c. Observe and record the voltmeter's pulses or the STAR tester's service code.

➡**If Code 33 appears (or any code not listed on the appropriate MCU code translation chart), the KOER test was not properly initiated.**

5. For all vehicles equipped with an 8-cylinder engine, perform the following procedures:
   a. Start the engine and run it at 2,000 rpm for two minutes. (This action warms up the oxygen sensor.)
   b. Turn the engine **OFF**, then immediately restart and idle the engine.
   c. Observe the voltmeter and vacuum gauge for initialization pulses after restarting the engine. (The throttle kicker will also extend at this time, increasing rpm, and remain on throughout the test. If not, the engine rpm is out of specification.)

➡**If there are no initialization pulses on the voltmeter or vacuum gauge, or an erroneous service code appears on the STAR tester, there is no Self-Test output.**

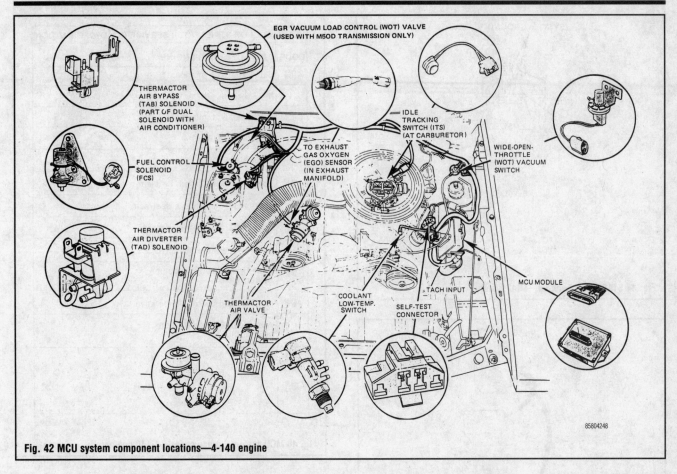

Fig. 42 MCU system component locations—4-140 engine

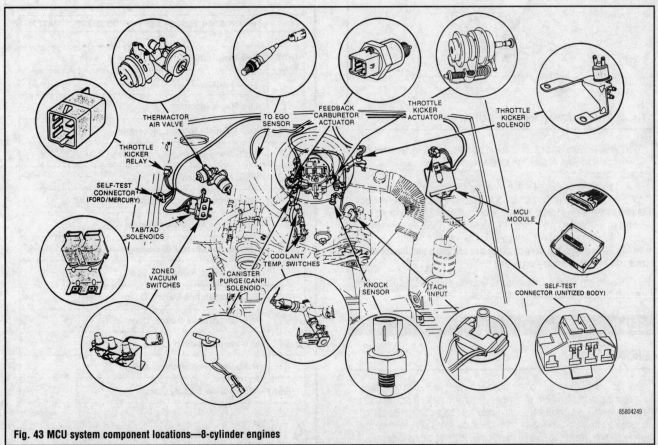

Fig. 43 MCU system component locations—8-cylinder engines

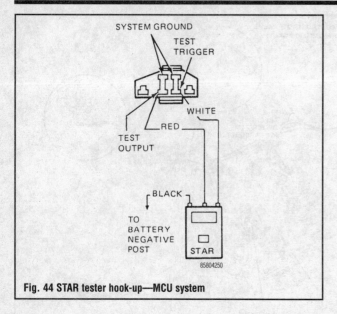

Fig. 44 STAR tester hook-up—MCU system

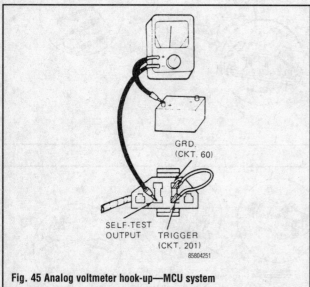

Fig. 45 Analog voltmeter hook-up—MCU system

d. After four one-second initialization pulses appear, observe and record the voltmeter's pulses or the STAR tester's service code for vehicles without a knock sensor.

e. For vehicles equipped with a knock sensor, immediately after four initial pulses occur, simulate spark knock by placing a ⅜ in. socket extension on the intake manifold, near the base of the knock sensor, and tapping lightly with a small hammer for approximately 15 seconds. Then, observe and record the voltmeter's pulses or the STAR tester's service code.

➡ **Within 90 seconds, the service codes are complete and the throttle kicker will retract, thereby decreasing rpm.**

6. Turn the engine **OFF**. Disconnect all test equipment and restore all components to their pre-test configuration/condition.

EEC-IV System

GENERAL DESCRIPTION

One part of the Powertrain Control Module (PCM) is devoted to monitoring both input and output functions within the system. This ability forms the core of the self-diagnostic system. If a problem is detected within a circuit, the controller will recognize the fault, assign it an identification code, and store the code in a memory section. The stored code(s) may then be retrieved during diagnosis.

VOLTMETER OR STAR TESTER SERVICE CODE INFORMATION	
CODE	**2.3L, 4-CYLINDER ENGINE**
:00	Self-Test, Not Functional
:11	MCU System, OK
:33	RUN Test, Not Initiated
:41	EGO, Always Lean
:42	EGO, Always Rich
:44	Thermactor Air System Problem
:45	Thermactor Air, Always Upstream
:46	Thermactor Air, Not Bypassing
:51	LOW-Temperature Switch, Open
:53	Wide-Open-Throttle Vacuum Switch, Open
:62	Idle Tracking Switch, Inoperative
:63	Wide-Open-Throttle Vacuum Switch, Closed

Fig. 46 MCU system service codes—4-140 engine

VOLTMETER OR STAR TESTER SERVICE CODE INFORMATION	
CODE	
:00	Self-Test, Not Functional
:11	MCU System, OK
:12	Idle Speed, Incorrect
:25	Knock Sensor System, Inoperative
:41	EGO, Always Lean
:42	EGO, Always Rich
:44	Thermactor Air System Problem
:45	Thermactor Air, Always Upstream
:46	Thermactor Air, Not Bypassing
:51	Hi/Lo Vacuum Switch(es), Open
:53	Dual Temperature Switch, Open
:54	MID-Temperature Switch, Open
:55	MID-Vacuum Switch, Open
:61	Hi/Lo Vacuum Switch(es), Closed
:65	MID-Vacuum Switch, Closed

Fig. 47 MCU system service codes—8-cylinder engines

The EEC-IV system is capable of storing both ongoing ("hard") and intermittent ("soft") faults. As a result, it is possible to monitor irregularities which may not be immediately present.

While the EEC-IV system is capable of recognizing many internal faults, certain faults will not be recognized. Because the computer system reads only electrical signals, it cannot sense or react to mechanical or vacuum faults affecting engine operation. Some of these faults may affect another component which will set a code. For example, the PCM monitors the output signal to the fuel injectors, but cannot detect a partially clogged injector. As long as the output driver responds correctly, the computer will read the system as functioning correctly. However, the improper flow of fuel may result in a lean mixture. This would, in turn, be detected by the oxygen sensor and noticed as a constantly lean signal by the PCM. Once the signal falls outside the pre-programmed limits, the engine control assembly would notice the fault and set an identification code.

Additionally, the EEC-IV system employs adaptive fuel logic. This process is used to compensate for normal wear and variability within the fuel system. Once the engine enters steady-state operation, the engine control assembly watches the oxygen sensor signal for a bias or tendency to run slightly rich or lean. If such a bias is detected, the adaptive logic corrects the fuel delivery to bring the air/fuel mixture towards a 14.7:1 or "centered" ratio. This compensating shift is stored in a non-volatile memory which is retained by battery power even with the ignition switched **OFF**. The correction factor is then available the next time the vehicle is operated.

➡**If the negative battery cable is disconnected for longer than 5 minutes, the adaptive fuel factor will be lost. After repair, it will be necessary to drive the car at least 10 miles to allow the processor to relearn the correct factors. If possible, the driving period should include steady-throttle open road driving. During the drive, the vehicle may exhibit driveability symptoms not noticed before. These symptoms should clear as the PCM computes the correction factor. The PCM will also store Code "19" indicating loss of power to the controller.**

Failure Mode Effects Management (FMEM)

The engine controller assembly contains back-up programs which allow the engine to operate if a sensor signal is lost. If a sensor's input is seen to be out of range—either high or low—the FMEM program is used. The processor substitutes a fixed value for the missing sensor signal. The engine will continue to operate, although performance and driveability may be noticeably reduced. This function of the controller is sometimes referred to as the limp-in or fail-safe mode. If the missing sensor signal is restored, the FMEM system immediately returns the system to normal operation.

Hardware Limited Operation Strategy (HLOS)

This mode is only used if the microprocessor fails to operate, or if the fault is too extreme for the FMEM circuit to handle. In this mode, the processor has ceased all computation and control, and the entire system is run on fixed values. The vehicle may be operated, but performance and driveability will be greatly reduced. The fixed or default settings provide minimal calibration, allowing the vehicle to be carefully driven in for service.

TOOLS AND EQUIPMENT

Hand-Held Scan Tools

Although stored codes may be read using a suitable analog voltmeter, the use of a hand-held scan tool, such as Ford's Self-Test Automatic Readout (STAR) tester or the second generation SUPER STAR tester, or equivalent, is highly recommended. There are many manufacturers of such tools, but the purchaser must be certain that the tool is appropriate for the intended use.

Both the STAR and SUPER STAR testers are designed to communicate directly with the EEC-IV system and interpret the electrical signals. The scan tool allows any stored faults to be read from the engine controller memory. Use of the scan tool provides additional data during troubleshooting, but does not eliminate the use of the charts. The scan tool makes information collection easier, but the data must still be correctly interpreted by an operator familiar with the system.

Other Diagnostic Tools

▶ **See Figure 48**

The most commonly required electrical diagnostic tool is the digital multimeter, allowing voltage, ohms (resistance) and amperage to be read by one instrument. Many of the diagnostic charts require the use of a voltmeter or ohmmeter during diagnosis.

The multimeter must be a high impedance unit, with 10 megohms of impedance in the voltmeter. This type of meter will not place an additional load on the circuit it is testing; this is extremely important in low voltage circuits. The multimeter must be of high quality in all respects. It should be handled carefully and protected from impact or damage. Replace the batteries frequently in the unit.

Additionally, an analog (needle type) voltmeter may be used to read stored fault codes if the STAR tester is not available. The codes are transmitted as visible needle sweeps on the face of the instrument.

Although code retrieval does not require additional equipment, diagnostic procedures such as pinpoint testing will be easier with a "breakout box", a device which connects into the EEC-IV harness and provides testing ports for the dozens of wires in the harness. Direct testing of the harness connectors at the terminals or by backprobing is not recommended; damage to the wiring and terminals is almost certain to occur.

Other necessary tools for testing/troubleshooting include a quality tachometer with inductive (clip-on) pickup, a fuel pressure gauge with system adapters and a vacuum gauge with an auxiliary source of vacuum.

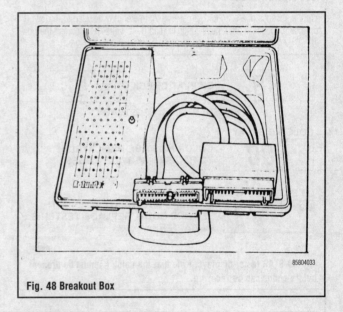

85804033

Fig. 48 Breakout Box

DIAGNOSIS AND TESTING

Diagnosis of a driveability problem requires attention to detail and following the diagnostic procedures in the correct order. Resist the temptation to begin extensive testing before completing the preliminary diagnostic steps. The preliminary or visual inspection must be completed in detail before diagnosis begins. In many cases, this will shorten diagnostic time and often cure the problem without electronic testing.

Visual Inspection

This is possibly the most critical step of diagnosis. A detailed examination of all connectors, wiring and vacuum hoses can often lead to a repair without further diagnosis. Performance of this step relies on the skill of the person performing it; a careful inspector will check the undersides of hoses as well as the integrity of hard-to-reach hoses blocked by the air cleaner or other components. Wiring should be checked carefully for any sign of strain, burning, crimping or terminal pull-out from a connector.

You should always check connectors at components or in harnesses as required. Pushing them together will usually reveal a loose fit. Pay particular attention to ground circuits, making sure they are not loose or corroded.

Remember to inspect connectors and hose fittings at components not mounted on the engine, such as the evaporative canister or relays mounted on the fender aprons. Any component or wiring in the vicinity of a fluid leak or spillage should be given extra attention during inspection.

Additionally, inspect maintenance items such as belt condition and tension, battery charge and condition, and the radiator cap carefully. Any of these simple items may affect the system enough to set a fault.

Reading Codes With a Hand-Held Scan Tool

▶ See Figures 49 and 51

A hand-held scan tool, such as the STAR or SUPER STAR tester, may be used to retrieve stored fault codes. Simply connect the tester's service connectors to the vehicle's Self-Test connectors.

Follow the directions given later in this section under Quick Test Procedures for performing the KOEO and KOER tests. Be sure to release the tester's push button, if applicable, before beginning the Self-Test.

Digital codes, such as "23", will be output and displayed as numbers on the hand-held scan tool. (The codes may also be read using an analog voltmeter. For further details on this alternative method, please refer to the following portion of this section.)

Reading Codes With an Analog Voltmeter

▶ See Figures 50 and 51

In the absence of a scan tool, an analog voltmeter may be used to retrieve stored fault codes. Set the meter range to read 0–15 volts DC. Connect the pos-

itive (+) lead of the meter to the positive battery terminal and connect the negative (−) lead of the meter to the self-test output pin of the diagnostic connector.

Follow the directions for performing the KOEO and KOER tests. To activate the tests, use a jumper wire to connect the signal return pin on the diagnostic connector to the self-test input connector. The self-test input line is the separate wire and connector with or near the diagnostic connector.

The codes will be transmitted as groups of needle sweeps, whose cadence corresponds to the codes' numerical representation. Please refer to the accompanying illustration for details on counting the needle sweeps in order to determine the transmitted code. Continuous Memory (intermittent fault) codes, if present, are separated from the KOEO codes by a 6-second delay, a single sweep and another 6-second delay.

SELF-TESTING (GENERATING STORED CODES)

Quick Test Procedures

The EEC-IV system may be interrogated for stored codes using the Quick Test Procedures. These tests will reveal "on-demand" faults immediately present during the test, as well as any intermittent or "continuous" codes set within the previous 20 warm-up cycles. If a code was set before a problem self-corrected (such as a momentarily loose connector), the code will be erased if the problem does not reoccur within 20 subsequent warm-up cycles.

The Quick Test procedure is divided into multiple sections, the most common of which are: Key On Engine Off (KOEO), Key On Engine Running (KOER), and Continuous Testing. Other tests may be performed, including Output State checking and, on SEFI engines, cylinder balance testing. These series of diagnostic procedures must be performed correctly if the system is to run the internal Self-Test checks and provide accurate fault codes.

If the vehicle passes all three sections of the Quick Test, the EEC-IV system is all right and the vehicle's problem exists elsewhere. Once the Quick Test has been performed and all fault codes recorded, refer to the code charts found later in this section.

➡ **In all cases, code 11 is used to indicate PASS during testing. Note that the PASS code may appear, followed by other stored codes. These are codes from the Continuous Memory and may indicate intermittent faults, even though the system does not presently contain the fault. The PASS designation only indicates that the system passes all internal tests at the moment.**

✳✳ CAUTION

To prevent injury and/or property damage, always block the drive wheels, firmly apply the parking brake, place the transmission in Park or Neutral and turn all electrical loads off before performing the Quick Test procedures.

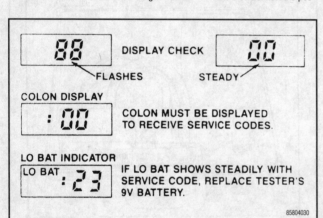

DISPLAY CHECK
FLASHES   STEADY

COLON DISPLAY
COLON MUST BE DISPLAYED TO RECEIVE SERVICE CODES.

LO BAT INDICATOR
IF LO BAT SHOWS STEADILY WITH SERVICE CODE, REPLACE TESTER'S 9V BATTERY.

85804030

Fig. 49 STAR tester displays. Note that the colon (:) must be present before codes can be received.

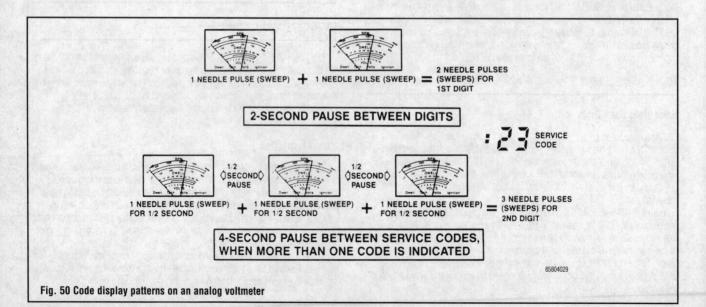

1 NEEDLE PULSE (SWEEP) + 1 NEEDLE PULSE (SWEEP) = 2 NEEDLE PULSES (SWEEPS) FOR 1ST DIGIT

2-SECOND PAUSE BETWEEN DIGITS

:23 SERVICE CODE

1 NEEDLE PULSE (SWEEP) FOR 1/2 SECOND + 1/2 SECOND PAUSE + 1 NEEDLE PULSE (SWEEP) FOR 1/2 SECOND + 1/2 SECOND PAUSE + 1 NEEDLE PULSE (SWEEP) FOR 1/2 SECOND = 3 NEEDLE PULSES (SWEEPS) FOR 2ND DIGIT

4-SECOND PAUSE BETWEEN SERVICE CODES, WHEN MORE THAN ONE CODE IS INDICATED

85804029

Fig. 50 Code display patterns on an analog voltmeter

KEY ON ENGINE OFF (KOEO)

▶ See Figures 51 and 52

➡Unless instructed otherwise, do not disconnect any sensor with the key ON or a service code may be stored.

1. Connect the scan tool or voltmeter to the self-test connectors. When using a STAR tester, make certain the test button is unlatched or up.
2. Start the engine and run it until normal operating temperature is reached.
3. Turn the engine **OFF** for 10 seconds.
4. Activate the test button on the STAR tester, if applicable. This will ready the Self-Test mode.
5. Turn the ignition switch **ON**, but do not start the engine.

➡Do not depress the throttle on gasoline engines during the test.

6. The KOEO codes will be transmitted. Six to nine seconds after the last KOEO code, a single separator pulse will be transmitted. Six to nine seconds after this pulse, the codes from the Continuous Memory will be transmitted.
7. Record all service codes displayed.

KEY ON ENGINE RUNNING (KOER)

▶ See Figure 53

➡Unless instructed otherwise, do not disconnect any sensor with the key ON or a service code may be stored.

1. Make certain the self-test button is released or de-activated on the STAR tester, if applicable.
2. Start the engine and run it at 2000 rpm for two minutes. This action warms up the oxygen sensor.
3. Turn the ignition switch **OFF** for 10 seconds.
4. Activate or latch the self-test button on the scan tool, if applicable.
5. Start the engine. The engine identification code will be transmitted. This is a single digit number representing half the number of cylinders in a gasoline engine. On the STAR tester, this number may appear with a zero (for example, 20 = 2). The code is used to confirm that the correct processor is installed and that the Self-Test has begun.
6. If the vehicle is equipped with a Brake On/Off (BOO) switch, the brake pedal must be depressed and released after the ID code is transmitted.

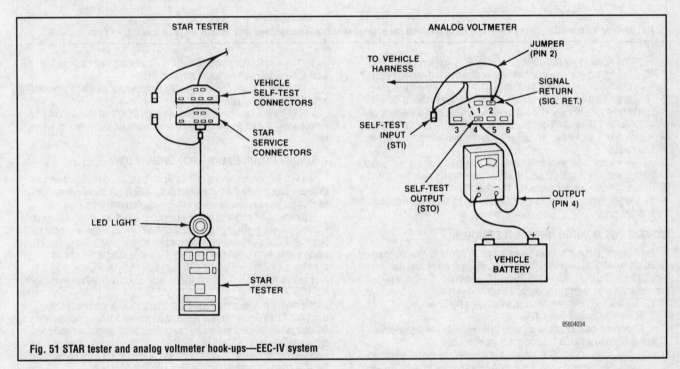

Fig. 51 STAR tester and analog voltmeter hook-ups—EEC-IV system

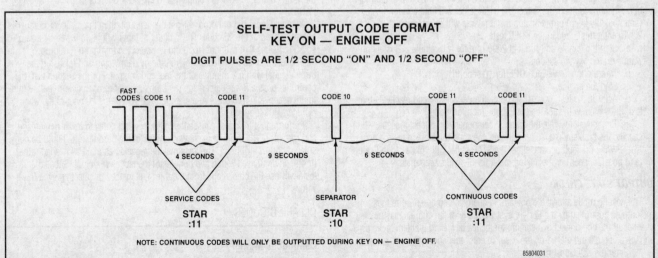

Fig. 52 Code transmission during KOEO test. Note that the Continuous Memory codes are transmitted after a pause, a separator code, and another pause.

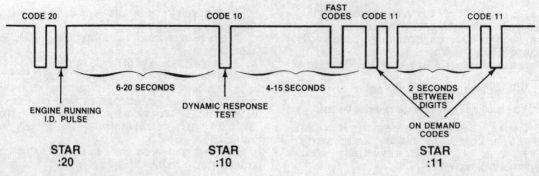

SELF-TEST OUTPUT CODE FORMAT
KEY ON — ENGINE RUNNING

DIGIT PULSES ARE 1/2 SECOND "ON" AND 1/2 SECOND "OFF"

Fig. 53 Code transmission during KOER testing begins with the engine identification code, and may include a dynamic response code

7. If the vehicle is equipped with a Power Steering Pressure Switch (PSPS), the steering wheel must be turned at least ½ turn and released within 2 seconds after the engine ID code is transmitted.

8. Certain Ford vehicles will display a dynamic response code 6–20 seconds after the engine ID code. This will appear as one pulse on a voltmeter or as a "10" on the STAR tester. When this code appears, briefly take the engine to wide open throttle. This allows the system to test the throttle position and vane air flow sensors.

9. All relevant codes will be displayed and should be recorded. Remember that codes refer only to faults present during this test cycle. Codes stored in Continuous Memory are **not** displayed in this test mode.

10. Do not depress the throttle during testing unless a dynamic response code is displayed.

CONTINUOUS MONITOR (WIGGLE TEST MODE)

Once entered, this mode allows the technician to attempt to recreate intermittent faults by wiggling or tapping components, wiring or connectors. The test may be performed during either KOEO or KOER procedures. The test requires the use of either an analog voltmeter or a hand-held scan tool.

1. To enter the Continuous Monitor mode during KOEO testing:
   a. Turn the ignition switch **ON**.
   b. Activate the test, wait 10 seconds, then deactivate and reactivate the test; the system will enter the continuous monitor mode.
   c. Tap, move or wiggle the harness, component or connector suspected of causing the problem; if a fault is detected, the code will store in the memory. When the fault occurs, either the STAR tester will light a red indicator (and possibly beep) or the analog meter needle will sweep once.

2. To enter this mode in the KOER test:
   a. Start the engine and run it at 2000 rpm for two minutes. This action warms up the oxygen sensor.
   b. Turn the ignition switch **OFF** for 10 seconds.
   c. Start the engine.
   d. Activate the test, wait 10 seconds, then deactivate and reactivate the test; the system will enter the continuous monitor mode.
   e. Tap, move or wiggle the harness, component or connector suspected of causing the problem; if a fault is detected, the code will store in the memory.
   f. When the fault occurs, either the STAR tester will light a red indicator (and possibly beep) or the analog meter needle will sweep once.

OUTPUT STATE CHECK

This testing mode allows the operator to energize and de-energize most of the outputs controlled by the EEC-IV system. Many of the outputs may be checked at the component by listening for a click or feeling the item move or engage using a hand placed on the case. To enter this check:

1. Enter the KOEO test mode.
2. When all codes have been transmitted, depress the accelerator all the way to the floor and release it.

3. The output actuators are now all ON. Depressing the throttle pedal to the floor again switches all the actuator outputs OFF.

4. This test may be performed as often as necessary, switching between ON and OFF by depressing the throttle.

5. Exit the test by turning the ignition switch **OFF**, then disconnecting the jumper wire at the diagnostic connector or releasing the test button on the scan tool.

CYLINDER BALANCE TEST—SEFI ENGINES ONLY

The EEC-IV system allows a cylinder balance test to be performed on engines equipped with the Sequential Electronic Fuel Injection system. Cylinder balance testing identifies a weak or non-contributing cylinder.

Enter the cylinder balance test by depressing and releasing the throttle pedal within 2 minutes of the last code output in the KOER test. The idle speed will become fixed and engine rpm is recorded for later reference. The engine control assembly will shut off the fuel to the highest-numbered cylinder (4 or 8), allow the engine to stabilize and then record the rpm. The injector is turned back on and the next one shut off and the process continues through cylinder No. 1.

The controller selects the highest rpm drop from all the cylinders tested, multiplies it by a percentage and arrives at an rpm drop value for all cylinders. For example, if the greatest drop for any cylinder was 150 rpm, the processor applies a multiple of 65% and arrives at 98 rpm. The processor then checks the recorded rpm drops, checking that each was at least 98 rpm. If all cylinders meet the criteria, the test is complete and the PCM outputs Code 90, indicating PASS.

If one cylinder did not drop at least this amount, then that cylinder number is output instead of the 90 code. The cylinder number will be followed by a zero, so 30 indicates that cylinder No. 3 did not meet the minimum rpm drop.

The test may be repeated a second time by depressing and releasing the throttle pedal within 2 minutes of the last code output. For the second test, the controller uses a lower percentage (and thus a lower rpm) to determine the minimum acceptable rpm drop. Again, either Code 90 or the number of the weak cylinder will be output.

Performing a third test causes the PCM to select an even lower percentage and rpm drop. If a cylinder is shown as weak in the third test, it should be considered non-contributing. The tests may be repeated as often as needed if the throttle is depressed within two minutes of the last code output. Subsequent tests will use the percentage from the third test instead of selecting even lower values.

CLEARING CODES

Continuous Memory Codes

These codes are retained in memory for 20 warm-up cycles. To clear the codes for the purposes of testing or confirming repair, perform the KOEO test.

When the fault codes begin to display, de-activate the test by either disconnecting the jumper wire (if using a voltmeter) or releasing the test button on the hand-held scanner. Stopping the test during code transmission will erase the Continuous Memory. Do not disconnect the negative battery cable to clear these codes; the Keep Alive memory will be cleared and a new code (19) will be stored for loss of PCM power.

Keep Alive Memory

The Keep Alive Memory (KAM) contains the adaptive factors used by the processor to compensate for component tolerances and wear. It should not be routinely cleared during diagnosis. If an emissions related part is replaced during repair, the KAM must be cleared. Failure to clear the KAM may cause severe driveability problems since the correction factor for the old component will be applied to the new component.

To clear the Keep Alive Memory, disconnect the negative battery cable for at least 5 minutes. After the memory is cleared and the battery reconnected, the vehicle must be driven at least 10 miles so that the processor may relearn the needed correction factors. The distance to be driven depends on the engine and vehicle, but all drives should include steady-throttle cruising on open roads. Certain driveability problems may be noted during the drive because the adaptive factors are not yet functioning.

ON-DEMAND SERVICE CODES

SERVICE CODE	EXPLANATION OF SERVICE CODE	POSSIBLE CAUSES OF CONCERN		POSSIBLE SYMPTOMS
12 KOER	Indicates the system is not capable of raising engine speed above curb idle.	Non-EEC:	— Engine running rough/missing. — Throttle linkage binding. — Improper vehicle prep. (e.g., warm-up).	— Rough idle or stalls due to lack of rpm increase with added loads (e.g., Power Steering lock or A/C "on").
		EEC:	— ISC motor/TKS system/ISC solenoid problems. — Wire harness problems. — ECA problems.	
13 KOER	Indicates that the engine did not return to a specified lower rpm prior to entering the "goose" test portion of Quick Test.	Non-EEC:	— Improper curb idle set. — Throttle/TVS linkage binding. — Improper throttle stop set. — Improper cruise control set.	— Idle speed concerns (may be accompanied by code 58).
		EEC:	— ISC motor/ISC solenoid problems. — Idle tracking switch problems. — Wire harness problems. — ECA problems.	
15 KOEO	Indicates an ECA failure.	EEC:	— ECA problems.	— Erratic operation or no start.
16 KOER	Indicates that the fuel system has been driven "lean" until the rpm drops, but the EGO sensor continues to indicate "rich."	EEC:	— Contaminated EGO sensor. — Wire harness problems. — ECA problems.	— System may correct "lean" inducing stumbles or hesitation.
17 KOER	Indicates that with thermactor air upstream the fuel system has been driven "lean" until the rpm drops, but the EGO sensor continues to indicate "rich" (5.0L CFI only).	EEC:	— Contaminated or disconnected EGO sensor. — Wire harness problems. — ECA problems.	— System may correct "rich" causing reduced MPG or black smoke.

21 KOEO	Indicates that the engine coolant temperature is out of range.	Non-EEC:	— Engine not up to operating temperature or, in the case of a no-start, test performed in cool ambient conditions.
			— Engine over operating temperature.
			  • Low coolant.
			  • Stuck thermostat.
			  • Cooling fan problems.
				— Reduced MPG.
				— Rough idle.
				— Improper idle speed.
				— Detonation.

		EEC:	— ECT sensor problems. — Wire harness problems. — ECA problems.	
21 KOER	Indicates that the engine coolant is not at normal operating temperature.	Non-EEC:	— Engine not warmed up. — Thermostat stuck open. — Low coolant level. — Coolant fan not operating. — Thermostat stuck closed. — Radiator blockage (internal or external). — Improper spark timing. — Fuel problems.	— Reduced MPG. — Rough idle. — Improper idle speed. — Detonation.
		EEC:	— ECT sensor problems. — Wire harness problems. — ECA problems.	

85804035

Fig. 54 1984–88 Ford EEC-IV Vehicles 2-Digit On-Demand Service Codes

ON-DEMAND SERVICE CODES (Fig. 56)

SERVICE CODE	EXPLANATION OF SERVICE CODE		POSSIBLE CAUSES OF CONCERN	POSSIBLE SYMPTOMS
26 KOEO	Indicates that the VAF meter is not in its closed position.	Non-EEC:	– Obstruction in VAF meter.	– No-start. – Stalls. – Runs rough. – Hesitates.
		EEC:	– VAF Meter problems. – Wire harness problems. – ECA problems.	
26 KOER	Indicates that the VAF meter is not at the normal position for Quick Test conditions.	Non-EEC:	– Unmetered air leaks. – Improper idle speeds. – Engine not at normal operating temperature.	– Stalls. – Runs rough. – Hesitates.
		EEC:	– VAF meter problems. – Wire harness problems. – ECA problems.	
31 KOEO/ KOER	Indicates that the EGR valve is not in its normal closed position.	Non-EEC:	– Sticking damaged EGR valve. – Vacuum trapped at EGR valve.	– Stalls. – Runs rough. – Dies at idle. – Detonation.
		EEC:	– EGR solenoid problems. – EVP sensor problems. – Wire harness problems. – ECA problems.	
32 KOER	Indicates that the system is not able to open and maintain a specified EGR valve position.	Non-EEC:	– Stuck or damaged EGR valve. – Vacuum leaks.	– Detonation. – Poor performance.
		EEC:	– EGR solenoid problems. – EVP sensor problems. – Wire harness problems. – ECA problems.	
33 KOER	Indicates that the EGR valve has not returned to its normal closed position after the EGR test.	Non-EEC:	– Stuck or damaged EGR valve.	– Decel stall. – Runs rough.
		EEC:	– EGR solenoid problems. – EVP sensor problems.	
34 KOER	Indicates that, with engine rpm elevated and stabilized, a specified rpm drop did not occur when EGR was turned "on."	Non-EEC:	– Stuck or damaged EGR valve. – BVT:EGR problems. – Vacuum leaks. – Improper exhaust back-pressure.	– Detonation.
		EEC:	– EGR solenoid problems. – Wire harness problems. – ECA problems.	
35 KOER	Indicates that the engine rpm is too low for the EGR test.	Non-EEC:	– Base engine problems.	– May run rough. – Lacks power.
		EEC:	– ISC problems.	
41* KOER	Indicates that the EGO sensor output voltage is always less than 0.5 volts ("lean") during the fuel test.	Non-EEC:	– Improper fuel delivery. – Carburetor/Throttle-Body injector problem. – Vacuum leaks. – Unmetered air. – Thermactor air is always upstream.	– Runs rough. – Stalls. – Hesitates. – Runs "lean." – May correct "rich" if sensor or harness related. ● Spark plugs fouled. ● Reduced MPG.
		EEC:	– EGO sensor problems. – Wire harness problems. – ECA problems.	

85804037

Fig. 56 1984-88 Ford EEC-IV Vehicles 2-Digit On-Demand Service Codes (Continued)

ON-DEMAND SERVICE CODES (Fig. 55)

SERVICE CODE	EXPLANATION OF SERVICE CODE		POSSIBLE CAUSES OF CONCERN	POSSIBLE SYMPTOMS
22 KOEO	Indicates that the MAP:BP sensor is out of range. The sensor(s) should read atmospheric pressure.	Non-EEC:	– Unusually high atmospheric pressure. – Vacuum trapped at MAP sensor.	– No-start. – Stalls. – Detonation. – Reduced MPG. – Loss of power.
		EEC:	– MAP:BP sensor problems. – Wire harness problems. – ECA problems.	
22 KOER	Indicates that the MAP:BP sensor is not at normal vacuum levels for Quick Test. The MAP sensor should indicate engine manifold vacuum. The BP sensor should indicate atmospheric pressure.	Non-EEC:	– Base engine problems (MAP). ● Compression problems. ● Improper timing. ● Vacuum leaks. ● Excess EGR. – Vacuum line connected to BP sensor (BP).	– Stalls. – Detonation. – Reduced MPG. – Loss of power.
		EEC:	– MAP:BP sensor problems. – Wire harness problems. – ECA problems.	
23 KOEO	Indicates that the TP sensor is not at the proper closed throttle position. Failure may occur either above or below the proper closed throttle position.	Non-EEC:	– Improper base adjustment of curb set. ISC motor, TSP, TKS, or cruise control linkage.	– No-start (EFI/CFI). – Hesitation. – Stalls. – Low/high idle. – Poor performance. – Reduced MPG.
		EEC:	– TKS:ISC motor problems. – Wire harness problems. – TP sensor problems. – ECA problems.	
23 KOER	Indicates that the TP sensor is not at the normal throttle position for Quick Test conditions.	Non-EEC:	– Improper base adjustment of curb set. ISC motor, TSP, TKS, or cruise control linkage.	– Hesitation. – Stalls. – Low/high idle. – Poor performance. – Reduced MPG.
		EEC:	– TKS:ISC motor problems. – Wire harness problems. – TP sensor problems. – ECA problems.	
24 KOEO	Indicates that the Air Charge Vane Air temperature is out of range.	Non-EEC:	– Vehicle testing performed in ambient temperature less than +50 deg. F. – Improper air cleaner duct/door operation.	– Poor idle. – Reduced MPG.
		EEC:	– ACT sensor problems. – Wire harness problems. – ECA problems.	
24 KOER	Indicates that the ACT:VAT sensor is not at normal engine operating temperature.	Non-EEC:	– Improper operation of the air cleaner duct door. – Cooling system problems. – Base timing problems.	– Poor idle. – Reduced MPG.
		EEC:	– ACT:VAT sensor problems. – Wire harness problems. – ECA problems.	
25 KOER	Indicates that knock was not sensed during the "goose" test.	Non-EEC:	– Base timing problems.	– Detonation. – Poor performance.
		EEC:	– Knock sensor problems. – Wire harness problems. – ECA problems.	

85804036

Fig. 55 1984-88 Ford EEC-IV Vehicles 2-Digit On-Demand Service Codes (Continued)

ON-DEMAND SERVICE CODES

SERVICE CODE	EXPLANATION OF SERVICE CODE	POSSIBLE CAUSES OF CONCERN	POSSIBLE SYMPTOMS
48 KOER	Indicates that the system does not have proper side-to-side fuel control (3.8L only.)	Non-EEC: — Catalyst blockage. — Stuck injector. — Plugged injector. EEC: — Wire harness problems. — Injector connections reversed. — EGO connections reversed. — One injector disconnected. — One EGO disconnected. — EGO sensor problems. — ECA problems.	— Stumbles. — Stalls. — Reduce MPG. — Black smoke.
51 KOEO	Indicates that the ECT signal failed at the high end (approximately 5.0 volts). Failure mode indicates – 40 deg. F.	EEC: — ECT sensor problems. — Wire harness problems. — ECA problems.	— Hard to start Hot. — Black smoke. — Reduced MPG.
53 KOEO	Indicates that the TP signal has failed at the high end (approximately 5.0 volts). Failure mode indicates WOT.	EEC: — Wire harness problems. • Open signal return circuit. • TP signal shorted to VREF. — TP sensor problems. — ECA problems.	— No start (EFI/CFI). — Poor part throttle performance.
54 KOER	Indicates that the ACT signal has failed at the high end (approximately 5.0 volts). Failure mode indicates – 40 deg. F.	EEC: — Wire harness problems. • ACT signal shorted to signal return. • ACT signal open. — ACT sensor problems. — ECA problems.	— Reduced MPG. — Black smoke.
56 KOEO	Indicates that the VAF signal has failed at the high end (approximately 5.0 volts). Failure mode indicates wide open throttle.	EEC: — Wire harness problems. — VAF sensor problems. — ECA problems.	— Black smoke.
58 KOER	Indicates that the ITS is not in contact with the throttle lever with the ISC motor extended.	Non-EEC: — Improper throttle plate stop adjustment. — Throttle linkage binding. — Cruise control misadjusted. — Improper ISC adjustment. EEC: — ITS problems. — Wire harness problems. — ECA problems.	— Improper idle speeds. — Stalls.
61 KOEO	Indicates that the ECT signal has failed at the low end (approximately 0.0 volts). Failure mode indicates + 240 deg. F.	EEC: — ECT sensor problems. — Wire harness problems. — ECA problems.	— Hard start/no start (cold).
63 KOEO	Indicates that the TP signal has failed at the low end (approximately 0.0 volts). Failure mode indicates closed throttle.	EEC: — Wire harness problems. • Vref open. • TP signal shorted to signal return. • TP signal open. — TP sensor problems. — ECA problems.	— Runs rough. — Stumbles. — Stalls.

Fig. 58 1984–88 Ford EEC-IV Vehicles 2-Digit On-Demand Service Codes (Continued)

ON-DEMAND SERVICE CODES

SERVICE CODE	EXPLANATION OF SERVICE CODE	POSSIBLE CAUSES OF CONCERN	POSSIBLE SYMPTOMS
42* KOER	Indicates that the EGO sensor output voltage is always greater than 0.5 volts ("rich") during the fuel test.	Non-EEC: — Improper fuel delivery. — Carburetor/Throttle-Body injector problems. — Obstructed air intake. — Ignition system problems. — Cannister purge problems. EEC: — EGO sensor problems. — Wire harness problems. — ECA problems.	— Runs rough. — Runs "rich". — Reduced MPG. — Spark plugs fouled. — May correct "lean" if sensor or harness related. • Hesitations • Stalls.
43* KOER	Indicates that the EGO sensor has cooled down and may not have given the proper responses during Quick Test.	Non-EEC: — Vehicle not properly prepared for test (Run at 2000 rpm for 2 minutes prior to test). — Engine below operating temperature.	— Usually no drive complaint.
44* KOER	Indicates that there is a thermactor problem.	Non-EEC: — Air pump problems. — Thermactor valve problems. EEC: — Thermactor solenoid problems. — Wire harness problems. — ECA problems.	— Usually no drive complaint.
45* KOER	Indicates that thermactor air is always upstream during Quick Test.	Non-EEC: — Air pump problems. — Thermactor valve problems. EEC: — Thermactor solenoid problems. — Wire harness problems. — ECA problems.	— Catalyst over temperature.
46* KOER	Indicates that the system is unable to bypass (vent to atmosphere) thermactor air.	Non-EEC: — Air pump problems. — Thermactor valve problems. EEC: — Thermactor solenoid problems. — Wire harness problems. — ECA problems.	— Catalyst over temperature.
47* KOER	Indicates that, even though thermactor air is upstream and fuel control is max., the EGO sensor indicates "rich".	Non-EEC: — Improper fuel delivery. — Carburetor/Throttle-Body injector problems. — Obstructed air intake. — Ignition system problems. EEC: — EGO sensor problems. — Wire harness problems. — ECA problems.	— Runs "rich". — Runs rough. — Reduced MPG. — Spark plugs fouled. — May correct "lean" if sensor or harness related. • Hesitations • Stalls.

Fig. 57 1984–88 Ford EEC-IV Vehicles 2-Digit On-Demand Service Codes (Continued)

ON-DEMAND SERVICE CODES

SERVICE CODE	EXPLANATION OF SERVICE CODE	POSSIBLE CAUSES OF CONCERN	POSSIBLE SYMPTOMS
64 KOEO	Indicates that the ACT/VAT signal has failed at the low end (approximately 0.0 volts). Failure mode indicates +240 deg	EEC: — ACT/VAT sensor problems. — Wire harness problems. — ECA problems.	— Runs rough. — Stumbles. — Stalls.
66 KOEO	Indicates that the VAF signal has failed at the low end (approximately 0.0 volts). Failure mode indicates closed throttle.	EEC: — Wire harness problems. — VAF sensor problems. — ECA problems.	— Stumbles. — Stalls.
67 KOEO	Indicates that the system is receiving an improper neutral/drive or A/C clutch status input.	Non-EEC: — Vehicle in gear or A/C "on." EEC: — Neutral drive switch problems. — Wire harness problems. — ECA problems.	— Improper ISC. — Stalls.
68 KOEO	Indicates that the ITS is in contact with the throttle lever with the ISC motor retracted.	Non-EEC: — Improper ISC motor adjustment. EEC: — ITS problems. — Wire harness problems. — ECA problems.	— Improper idle speed control. — Stalls.
72 KOER	Indicates that the MAP sensor has not detected a sufficient manifold vacuum change during the "goose" test	Non-EEC: — Vacuum leaks. — Base engine problems. EEC: — Map sensor problems. — ECA problems.	— Stumbles. — Hesitations. — Stalls.
73 KOER	Indicates that the system has not detected a sufficient TP change during the "goose" test.	EEC: — TP sensor stuck at WOT — TP sensor not tracking throttle shaft. — ECA problems.	— Stumbles. — Hesitations.
76 KOER	Indicates that the system has not detected a sufficient VAF change during the "goose" test	Non-EEC: — Unmetered air entering engine. EEC: — VAF meter sticking. — ECA problems.	— Stumbles. — Hesitations.
77 KOER	Indicates that the operator did not do a brief WOT.	Non-EEC: — Operator did not do a brief WOT. EEC: — ECA problems.	—
81 KOEO	Indicates a TAD circuit fault. (For 2.8L only, code indicates a TAB circuit fault.)	EEC: — Open shorted TAD solenoid. — Wire harness problems. — ECA problems.	— Thermactor service code KOER.
82 KOEO	Indicates a TAB circuit fault. (For 2.8L only, code indicates a TAD circuit fault.)	EEC: — Open shorted TAB solenoid. — Wire harness problems. — ECA problems.	— Thermactor service code KOER.
83 KOEO	Indicates an EGRC circuit fault.	EEC: — Open shorted EGRC solenoid. — Wire harness problems. — ECA problems.	— No EGR control. — Detonation.
84 KOEO	Indicates an EGRV circuit fault.	EEC: — Open shorted EGRV solenoid. — Wire harness problems. — ECA problems.	— Improper EGR control. — Stalls. — Runs rough.
85 KOEO	Indicates a CANP circuit fault.	EEC: — Open shorted CANP valve. — Wire harness problems. — ECA problems.	— Customer complaints of gasoline odor.
86 KOEO	Indicates a WAC circuit fault.	EEC: — Open shorted WAC controller. — Wire harness problems. — ECA problems.	— No A/C operation. — No WOT-A/C cutoff.

Fig. 59 1984–88 Ford EEC-IV Vehicles 2-Digit On-Demand Service Codes (Continued)

ON-DEMAND SERVICE CODES

SERVICE CODE	EXPLANATION OF SERVICE CODE	POSSIBLE CAUSES OF CONCERN	POSSIBLE SYMPTOMS
87 KOEO	Indicates a fuel pump relay circuit fault	EEC: — Inertia switch problems. — Open short fuel pump relay. — Wire harness problems. — ECA problems.	— No start. — Pump runs with key in "off" position.
	or a TCP circuit fault (2.8L only).	EEC: — TCP solenoid problems. — Wiring harness problems. — ECA problems.	— Poor cold start driveaway.
88 KOEO	Indicates a TKS circuit fault (5.0L CFI only)	EEC: — Open shorted TKS solenoid. — Wire harness problems. — ECA problems.	— High idle speeds. — Stalls (low idle speeds).
	or a VVC circuit fault (2.8L only).	EEC: — VVC relay problems. — Wiring harness problems. — ECA problems.	— Poor cold start driveaway. — Spark plug loading. — Reduced MPG. — Black smoke.
89 KOEO	Indicates an exhaust heat control circuit fault.	EEC: — Open shorted EHC solenoid. — Wire harness problems. — ECA problems.	— Stumbles. — Hesitations cold.
91 KOER	Indicates that the right EGO sensor output voltage is always less than 0.5 volts ("lean") during the fuel test (3.8L only).	Non-EEC: — Improper fuel delivery. — Carburetor/Throttle-Body injector problems. — Vacuum leaks. — Unmetered air. — Thermactor air is always upstream. EEC: — EGO sensor problems. — Wire harness problems. — ECA problems.	— Runs rough. — Stalls. — Hesitates. — Runs "lean". — May correct "rich" if sensor or harness related. ● Spark plugs fouled. ● Reduced MPG.
92 KOER	Indicates that the right EGO sensor output voltage is always greater than 0.5 volts ("rich") during the fuel test (3.8L only).	Non-EEC: — Improper fuel delivery. — Carburetor/Throttle-Body injector problems. — Obstructed air intake. — Ignition system problems. EEC: — EGO sensor problems. — Wire harness problems. — ECA problems.	— Runs rough. — Runs "rich". — Reduced MPG. — Spark plugs fouled. — May correct "lean" if sensor or harness related. ● Hesitations. ● Stalls.
93 KOER	Indicates that the right EGO sensor has cooled down and may not have given the proper responses during Quick Test (3.8L only).	Non-EEC: — Vehicle not properly prepared for test (Run at 2000 rpm for 2 minutes prior to test). — Engine below operating temperature.	— Usually no drive complaint.
94 KOER	Indicates that there is a thermactor problem on the right bank (3.8L only).	Non-EEC: — Air pump problems. EEC: — Thermactor solenoid problems. — Wire harness problems. — ECA problems.	— Usually no drive complaint.
95 KOER	Indicates that the right bank thermactor air is always upstream during Quick Test (3.8L only).	Non-EEC: — Air pump problems. — Thermactor valve problems. EEC: — Thermactor solenoid problems. — Wire harness problems. — ECA problems.	— Catalyst over temperature.

Fig. 60 1984–88 Ford EEC-IV Vehicles 2-Digit On-Demand Service Codes (Continued)

CONTINUOUS CODES

SERVICE CODE	EXPLANATION OF SERVICE CODE	POSSIBLE CAUSES OF CONCERN	POSSIBLE SYMPTOMS
31 Cont.	Indicates that the EVP sensor signal has been off scale at the high or low end during recent operation.	Non-EEC: — EGR valve sticks at wide open. EEC: — EGR over travel (normal condition on some applications, refer to diagnostics manual). — EVP sensor problems. — Wire harness problems. — ECA problems.	— Detonation. — Hard to start. — No start. — Runs rough. — Stalls. — Dies at idle.
53 Cont.	Indicates that the TP sensor signal has been off scale at the high end during recent operation.	EEC: — Wire harness problems. • Open signal return. • Signal short circuit to Vref. — TP sensor problems. — ECA problems.	— No start (CFI/EFI). — Detonation. — Stumbles. — Poor performance.
54 Cont.	Indicates that the ACT/VAT sensor signal has been off scale at the high end during recent operation.	EEC: — ACT/VAT sensor problems — Wire harness open circuit — ECA problems.	— Runs rough. — Black smoke. — Reduced MPG.
56 Cont.	Indicates that the VAF meter signal has been off scale at the high end during recent operation.	EEC: — VAF sensor problems. — Wire harness problems. — ECA problems.	— No start. — Stumbles. — Stalls. — Runs only at WOT.
61 Cont.	Indicates that the ECT sensor signal has been off scale at the low end during recent operation.	EEC: — ECT sensor problems. — Wire harness shorted to ground. — ECA problems.	— Runs rough. — Stalls. — Erratic idle
63 Cont.	Indicates that the TP sensor signal has been off scale at the low end during recent operation.	EEC: — Wire harness problems. • Vref open. • Signal line open. • Signal shorted to sensor return. — TP sensor problems. — ECA problems.	— Poor performance. — Stumbles. — Detonation.
64 Cont.	Indicates that the ACT/VAT sensor signal has been off scale at the low end during recent operation.	EEC: — ACT/VAT sensor problems. — Wire harness shorted to ground. — ECA problems.	— Runs rough. — Stalls. — Erratic idle.
65 Cont.	Indicates that during recent operation a charging system over-voltage condition (greater than 17.5 v) has occurred.	Non-EEC: — Voltage regulator problems. — Alternator problems. EEC: — Wire harness problems. — ECA problems.	— Lamp burnout. — Electronic-component burnout (e.g. TFI, ECA, Radio, etc.)
66 Cont.	Indicates that the VAF meter signal has been off scale at the low end during recent operation.	EEC: — Wire harness problems. • Vref circuit open. • Signal circuit open. • Signal circuit shorted to signal return. — VAF meter problems. — ECA problems.	— No start. — Stalls. — Lacks power. — Runs only at WOT.

Fig. 63 1984–88 Ford EEC-IV Vehicles 2-Digit Continuous Codes (Continued)

85804044

ON-DEMAND SERVICE CODES

SERVICE CODE	EXPLANATION OF SERVICE CODE	POSSIBLE CAUSES OF CONCERN	POSSIBLE SYMPTOMS
96 KOER	Indicates that the system is unable to bypass (vent to atmosphere) thermactor air on the right bank (3.8L only).	Non-EEC: — Air pump problems. — Thermactor valve problems. EEC: — Thermactor solenoid problems. — Wire harness problems. — ECA problems.	— Catalyst over temperature.
97 KOER	Indicates that, even though thermactor air is upstream and fuel control is max. "lean," the right EGO sensor indicates "rich" (3.8L only).	Non-EEC: — Improper fuel delivery. — Carburetor/Throttle-Body Injector problems. — Obstructed air intake. — Ignition system problems. EEC: — EGO sensor problems. — Wire harness problems. — ECA problems.	— Runs "rich." — Runs rough. — Reduced MPG. — Spark plugs fouled. — May correct "lean" if sensor or harness related. • Hesitations. • Stalls.

Fig. 61 1984–88 Ford EEC-IV Vehicles 2-Digit On-Demand Service Codes (Continued)

85804042

CONTINUOUS CODES

SERVICE CODE	EXPLANATION OF SERVICE CODE	POSSIBLE CAUSES OF CONCERN	POSSIBLE SYMPTOMS
13 Cont.	Indicates that during recent operation, while in the normal operating mode an ISC command to extend the ISC motor shaft occurred without a corresponding TP sensor change.	Non-EEC: — Throttle shaft binding. — Improper ISC adjustment. EEC: — ISC motor problems. — TP sensor problems. — Wire harness problems. — ECA problems.	— Improper idle speed — Possible stalls.
14 Cont.	Indicates that erratic operation or intermittent loss of PIP information to the ECA has occurred during recent operation.	Non-EEC: — Distributor pickup problems. — TFI module problems. EEC: — Wire harness problems. — ECA problems.	— Engine miss. — Surge. — Rough idle. — Stall.
15 Cont.	Indicates loss of Keep-Alive-Memory during recent operation.	EEC: — Loss of Keep-Alive-Memory battery power. — Wire harness problems. — ECA problems.	— No codes in memory.
18 Cont.	Indicates that during recent operation the ECA received a PIP signal input without receiving a corresponding tach signal input.	Non-EEC: — Ignition coil problems. — TFI module problems. — Vehicle wire harness. EEC: — Wire harness problems. — ECA problems.	— No start. — Stalls. — Idles/runs rough.
21 Cont.	Indicates that during a single drive cycle the engine has reached normal operating temperature and then has cooled down.	Non-EEC: — Thermostat failure. — Coolant loss. EEC: — ECT sensor problems. — Wire harness problems. — ECA problems.	— Reduced MPG. — Heater output loss.
22 Cont.	Indicates that a gross MAP/BP sensor signal error has occurred during recent operation.	Non-EEC: — Basic engine problems. • Compression problems. • Improper timing. • Vacuum leaks. EEC: — MAP/BP sensor problems. — Wire harness problems. — ECA problems.	— Detonation. — Poor performance. — Reduced MPG. — Surge. — Stumbles.

Fig. 62 1984–88 Ford EEC-IV Vehicles 2-Digit Continuous Codes

85804043

VACUUM DIAGRAMS

Each vehicle is equipped with a decal containing emission control data specific to that vehicle and engine. The decal is typically located on the underside of the hood, but might instead be found on the fan shroud, the coil appearance cover or elsewhere. These specifications are critical to the effective servicing of the applicable system. In addition to the tune-up specifications and procedures, the emission control data decal includes a color-coded schematic of the engine vacuum system. The color coding on the schematic represents the actual color coding on the vacuum hoses, although there may be some exceptions.

Since this book covers approximately two hundred calibrations, all of which correspond to a specific vacuum diagram, it is not feasible to include

a schematic of every vacuum system. In addition, mid-year production changes often result in different vacuum schematics from those which are published. For this reason, the best source for vacuum diagrams is the vehicle's emission control data decal. The following vacuum diagrams cover most, but not all, calibrations pertaining to the 1979-88 Mustang and Capri. For ease of use, these diagrams are arranged by engine size within each model year.

If your exact calibration is not covered here, use a similar configuration as a guide or see your local dealer about purchasing a replacement sticker.

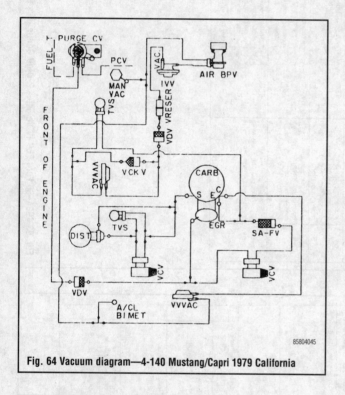

Fig. 64 Vacuum diagram—4-140 Mustang/Capri 1979 California

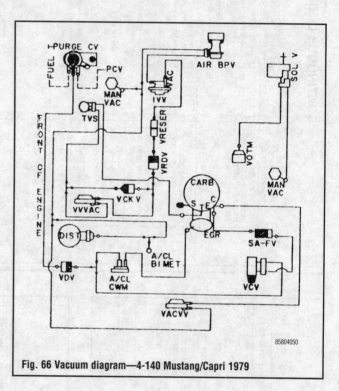

Fig. 66 Vacuum diagram—4-140 Mustang/Capri 1979

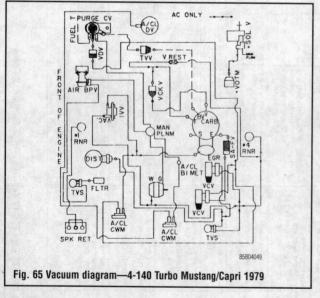

Fig. 65 Vacuum diagram—4-140 Turbo Mustang/Capri 1979

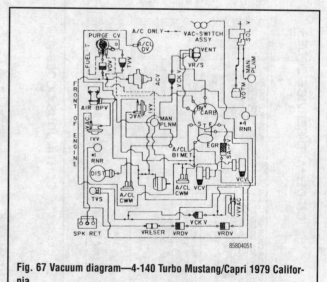

Fig. 67 Vacuum diagram—4-140 Turbo Mustang/Capri 1979 California

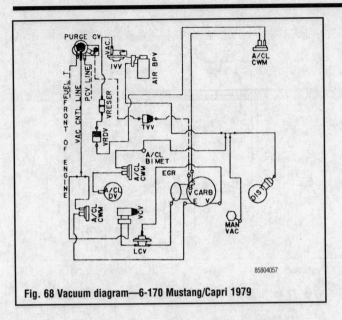

Fig. 68 Vacuum diagram—6-170 Mustang/Capri 1979

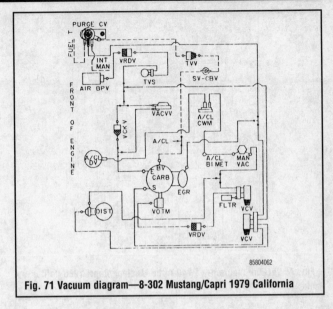

Fig. 71 Vacuum diagram—8-302 Mustang/Capri 1979 California

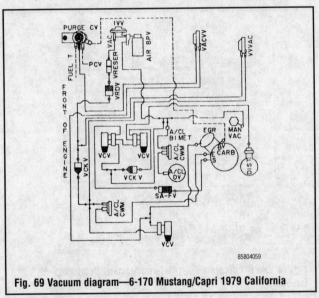

Fig. 69 Vacuum diagram—6-170 Mustang/Capri 1979 California

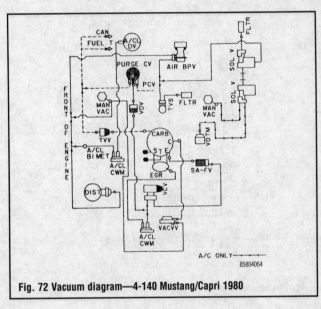

Fig. 72 Vacuum diagram—4-140 Mustang/Capri 1980

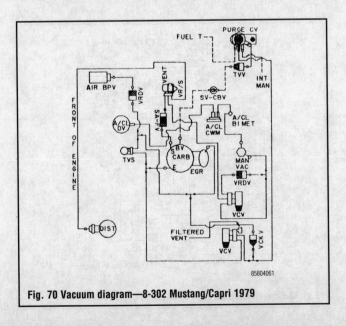

Fig. 70 Vacuum diagram—8-302 Mustang/Capri 1979

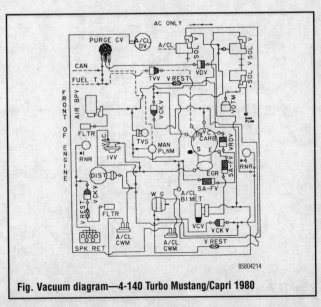

Fig. Vacuum diagram—4-140 Turbo Mustang/Capri 1980

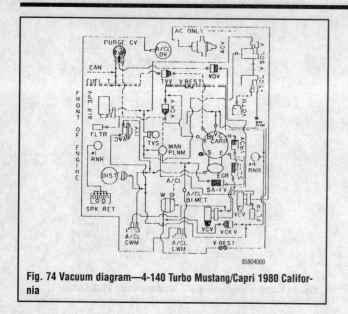

Fig. 74 Vacuum diagram—4-140 Turbo Mustang/Capri 1980 California

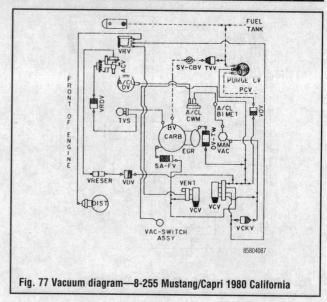

Fig. 77 Vacuum diagram—8-255 Mustang/Capri 1980 California

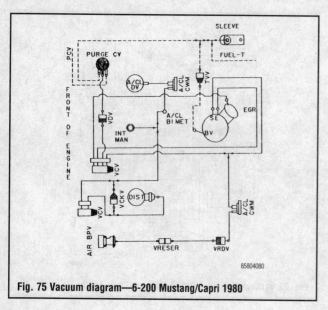

Fig. 75 Vacuum diagram—6-200 Mustang/Capri 1980

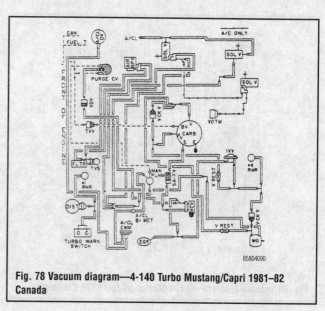

Fig. 78 Vacuum diagram—4-140 Turbo Mustang/Capri 1981–82 Canada

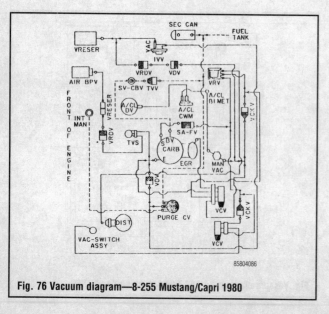

Fig. 76 Vacuum diagram—8-255 Mustang/Capri 1980

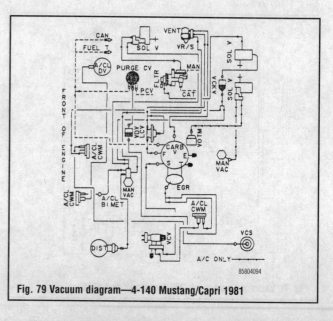

Fig. 79 Vacuum diagram—4-140 Mustang/Capri 1981

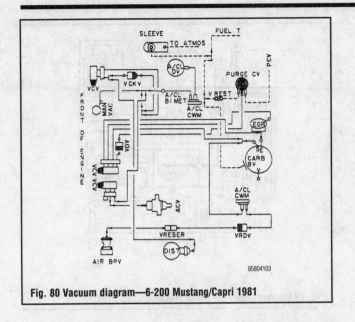

Fig. 80 Vacuum diagram—6-200 Mustang/Capri 1981

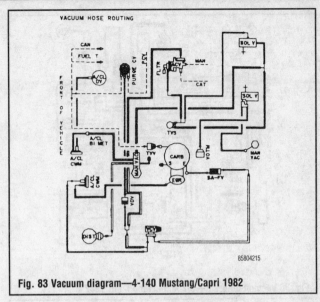

Fig. 83 Vacuum diagram—4-140 Mustang/Capri 1982

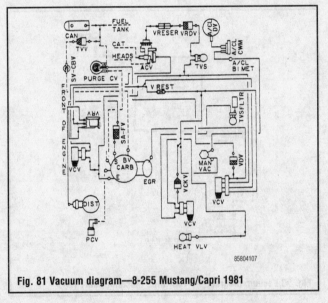

Fig. 81 Vacuum diagram—8-255 Mustang/Capri 1981

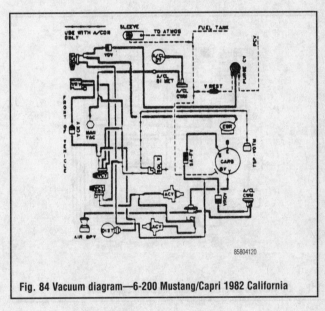

Fig. 84 Vacuum diagram—6-200 Mustang/Capri 1982 California

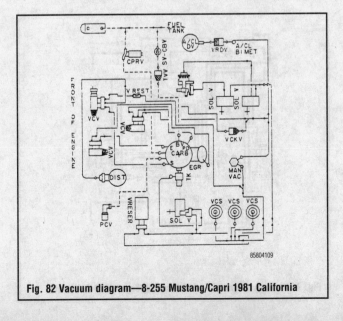

Fig. 82 Vacuum diagram—8-255 Mustang/Capri 1981 California

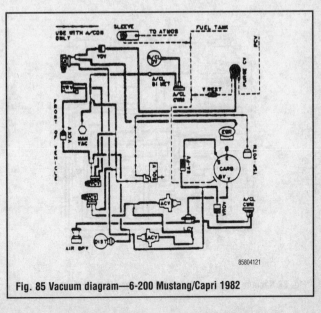

Fig. 85 Vacuum diagram—6-200 Mustang/Capri 1982

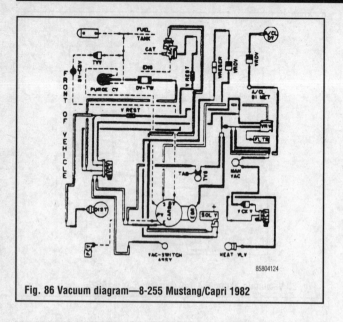

Fig. 86 Vacuum diagram—8-255 Mustang/Capri 1982

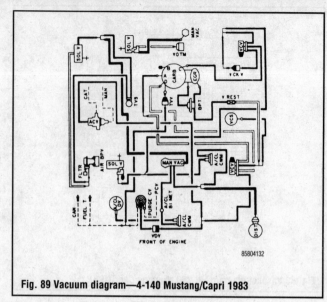

Fig. 89 Vacuum diagram—4-140 Mustang/Capri 1983

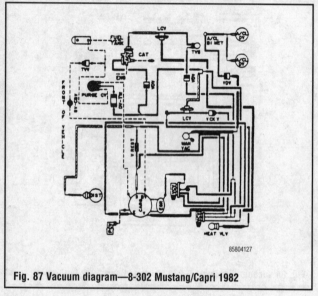

Fig. 87 Vacuum diagram—8-302 Mustang/Capri 1982

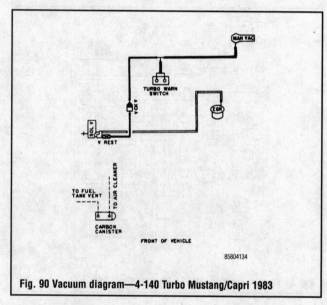

Fig. 90 Vacuum diagram—4-140 Turbo Mustang/Capri 1983

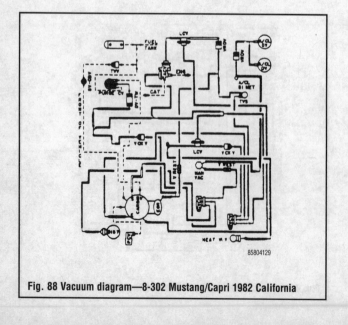

Fig. 88 Vacuum diagram—8-302 Mustang/Capri 1982 California

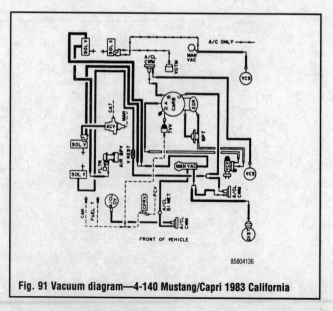

Fig. 91 Vacuum diagram—4-140 Mustang/Capri 1983 California

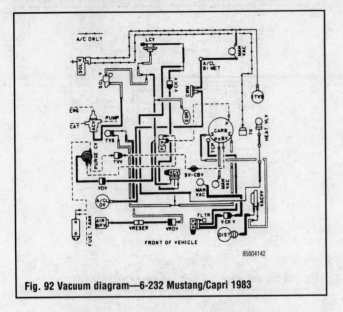

Fig. 92 Vacuum diagram—6-232 Mustang/Capri 1983

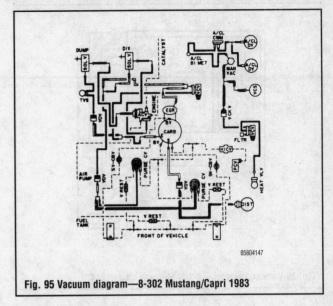

Fig. 95 Vacuum diagram—8-302 Mustang/Capri 1983

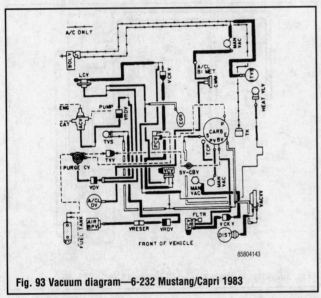

Fig. 93 Vacuum diagram—6-232 Mustang/Capri 1983

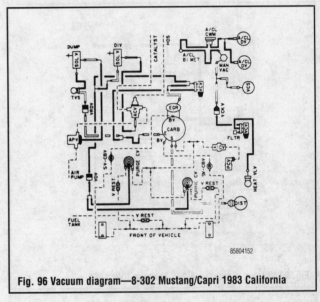

Fig. 96 Vacuum diagram—8-302 Mustang/Capri 1983 California

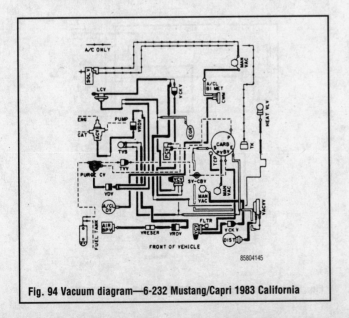

Fig. 94 Vacuum diagram—6-232 Mustang/Capri 1983 California

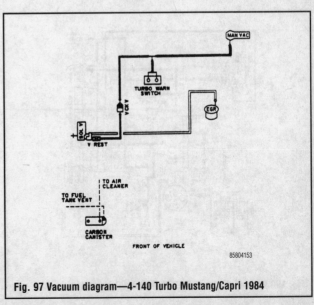

Fig. 97 Vacuum diagram—4-140 Turbo Mustang/Capri 1984

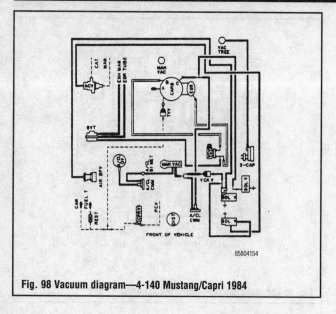

Fig. 98 Vacuum diagram—4-140 Mustang/Capri 1984

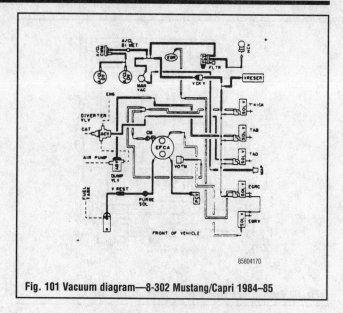

Fig. 101 Vacuum diagram—8-302 Mustang/Capri 1984–85

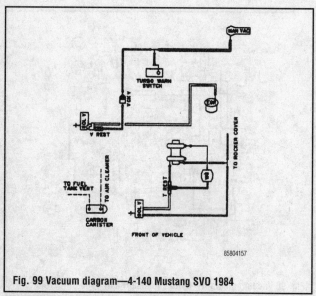

Fig. 99 Vacuum diagram—4-140 Mustang SVO 1984

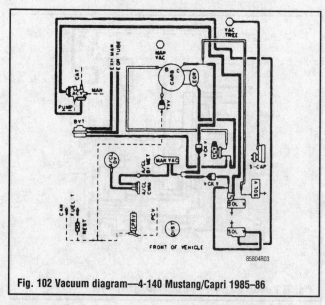

Fig. 102 Vacuum diagram—4-140 Mustang/Capri 1985–86

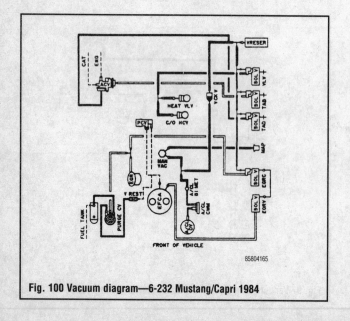

Fig. 100 Vacuum diagram—6-232 Mustang/Capri 1984

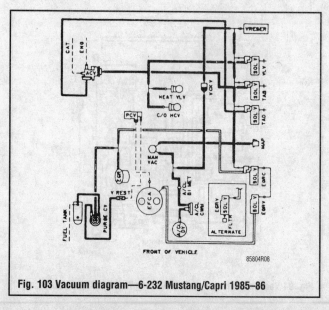

Fig. 103 Vacuum diagram—6-232 Mustang/Capri 1985–86

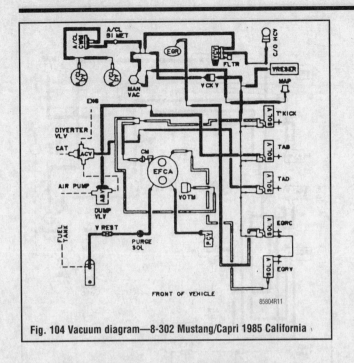

Fig. 104 Vacuum diagram—8-302 Mustang/Capri 1985 California

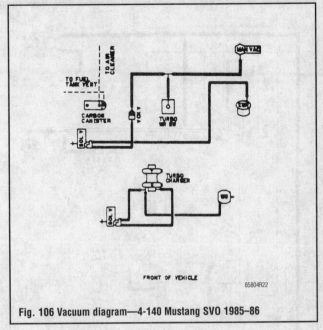

Fig. 106 Vacuum diagram—4-140 Mustang SVO 1985–86

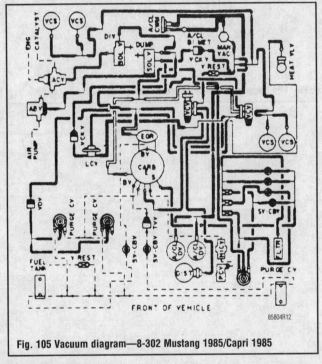

Fig. 105 Vacuum diagram—8-302 Mustang 1985/Capri 1985

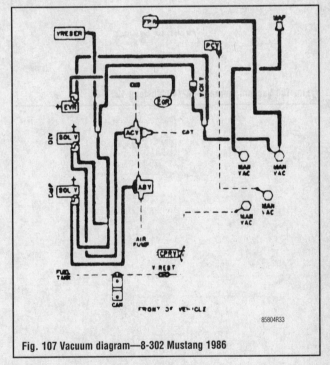

Fig. 107 Vacuum diagram—8-302 Mustang 1986

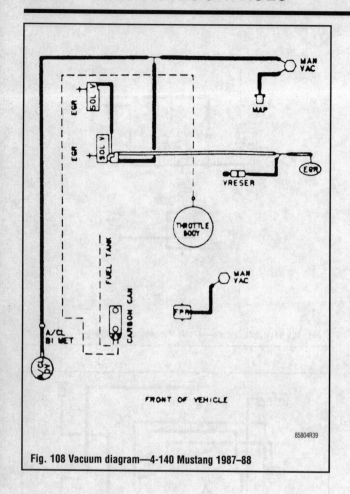

Fig. 108 Vacuum diagram—4-140 Mustang 1987–88

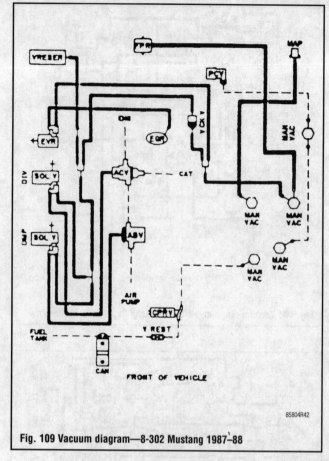

Fig. 109 Vacuum diagram—8-302 Mustang 1987–88

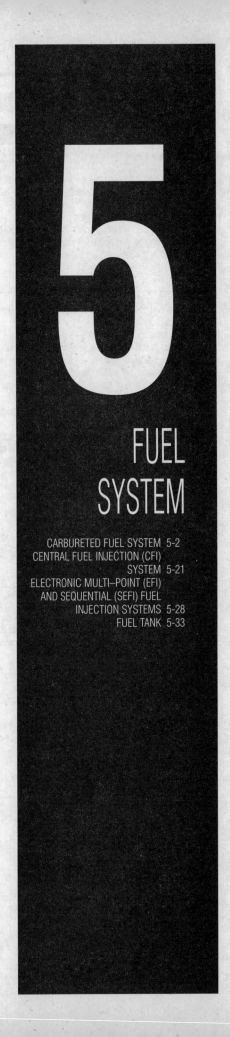

5

FUEL
SYSTEM

CARBURETED FUEL SYSTEM

Mechanical Fuel Pump

♦ **See Figures 1 and 2**

A single–action, diaphragm–type mechanical fuel pump is found on all carbureted models, with the possible exception of 1980–82 4–140 turbo models equipped with an automatic transmission.

The mechanical fuel pump, which is driven by the camshaft, is located at the lower left side of the cylinder block on the 6–170 engine, at the right front cover on the 6–232 engine, and at the left side of the cylinder block or front cover on 4–140, 6–200 and V8 models.

TESTING

No adjustments may be made to the fuel pump. Before removing and replacing the old fuel pump, the following test may be made while the pump is still installed on the engine.

1. If a fuel pressure gauge is available, connect the gauge to the engine and operate the engine until the pressure stops rising. Stop the engine and take the reading. If the reading is within the specifications given in the Tune–Up Specifications chart in Section 2, the malfunction is not in the fuel pump. Also check the pressure drop after the engine is stopped. A large pressure drop below the minimum specification indicates leaky valves. If the pump proves to be satisfactory, check the fuel tank and inlet line.

2. If a fuel pressure gauge is not available, disconnect the fuel line at the pump outlet, place a vessel beneath the pump outlet, and crank the engine. A good pump will force the fuel out of the outlet in steady spurts. One pint in 25–30 seconds is a good flow. A worn diaphragm spring may not provide proper pumping action.

3. As a further test, disconnect and plug the fuel line from the tank at the pump, and hold your thumb over the pump inlet. If the pump is functioning properly, no suction indicates that the pump diaphragm is leaking, or that the diaphragm linkage is worn.

4. Check the crankcase for gasoline. A ruptured diaphragm may leak fuel into the engine.

REMOVAL & INSTALLATION

➡**Before removing the pump, rotate the engine so that the low point of the cam lobe is against the pump arm. This can be determined by rotating the engine with the fuel pump mounting bolts loosened slightly. When tension (resistance) is removed from the arm, proceed.**

1. Disconnect and plug the inlet and outlet lines at the fuel pump.
2. Remove the fuel pump retaining bolts and carefully pull the pump and old gasket away from the cylinder block or cover.
3. Discard the old gasket. Clean the mating surfaces on the block or cover and position a new gasket, using oil–resistant sealer.
4. Mount the fuel pump and gasket to the engine block or cover, being careful to insert the pump lever (rocker arm) in the engine block, aligning it correctly above the camshaft lobe.

➡**If resistance is felt while positioning the fuel pump on the block, the camshaft lobe is probably on the high position. To ease installation, connect a remote engine starter switch to the engine and tap the switch until resistance fades.**

5. While holding the pump securely against the block, install the retaining bolts. On 4 and 6–cylinder engines, torque the bolts to 12–15 ft. lbs.; on V8 engines, torque the bolts to 20–24 ft. lbs.
6. Unplug and reconnect the fuel lines at the pump.
7. Start the engine and check for fuel leaks. Also check for oil leaks where the fuel pump attaches to the block.

Quick–Connect Fuel Line Fittings

REMOVAL & INSTALLATION

➡**Quick–Connect (push) type fuel fittings are used on most models equipped with a pressurized fuel system. The fittings must be disconnected using proper procedures or the fitting may be damaged. Two types of retainers are used on the push connect fittings. Line sizes of ⅜ in. and ⁵⁄₁₆ in. use a hairpin clip retainer, and ¼ in. line connectors use a duck bill clip retainer.**

Hairpin Clip

♦ **See Figure 3**

1. Clean all dirt and/or grease from the fitting. Using finger pressure only, spread the two clip legs about ⅛ in. (3mm) each to disengage from the fitting, and pull the clip outward from the fitting. In order to avoid damage or breakage, do not use any tools.
2. Grasp the fitting and hose assembly and pull away from the steel line. Twist the fitting and hose assembly slightly while pulling, if necessary, when a sticking condition exists.
3. It is recommended that the original clip not be reused in the fitting. Insert a new clip into any two adjacent openings with the triangular portion pointing away from the fitting opening. Push on the clip to fully engage the body, so that the legs of the clip lock onto the outside of the body.
4. Inspect the fitting and inside of the connector to insure freedom of dirt or obstruction. Install the fitting into the connector and push together. A click will be heard when the hairpin clip makes a proper connection. Pull on the line to insure full engagement.

Duck Bill Clip

♦ **See Figures 4 and 5**

1. The preferred method of clip removal requires a special tool, Ford Tool No. T82L–9500–AH or equivalent. (If the tool is not available, proceed to Step 2). Align the slot on the push connect disconnection tool with either tab on the retaining clip. Insert the tool to disengage the clip and pull the line from the connector.

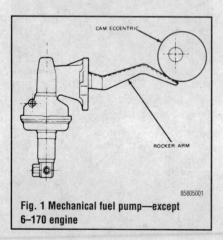

Fig. 1 Mechanical fuel pump—except 6–170 engine

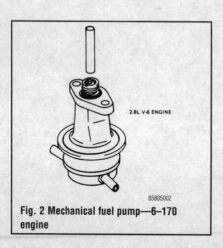

Fig. 2 Mechanical fuel pump—6–170 engine

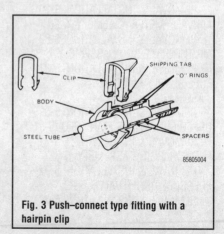

Fig. 3 Push–connect type fitting with a hairpin clip

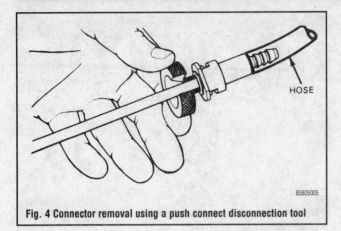

Fig. 4 Connector removal using a push connect disconnection tool

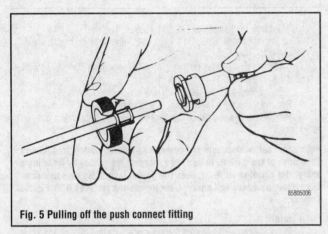

Fig. 5 Pulling off the push connect fitting

2. If the special clip tool is not available, use a pair of narrow 6 in. (152mm) locking pliers with a jaw width of 0.2 in. (5mm) or less. Align the jaws of the pliers with the openings of the fitting case and compress the part of the retaining clip that engages the case. Compressing the retaining clip will release the fitting, which may be pulled from the connector. Both sides of the clip must be compressed at the same time to disengage.

3. It is recommended that the retaining clip not be reused. Insert one of a new retaining clip's serrated edges on the duck bill portion into one of the window openings of the body. Push on the other side until the clip snaps into place.

4. Push the line into the steel connector until a click is heard, indicating that the clip is in place. Pull on the line to insure full engagement.

Carburetors—Except Motorcraft 2700VV and

➡ **Servicing of the 2700VV and 7200VV models immediately follows the other carburetors.**

OPERATIONAL TESTS

Electric Choke

▶ **See Figure 6**

Most carbureted models use a temperature–sensitive, electrically assisted choke to reduce exhaust emissions of carbon monoxide during warm–up. The system consists of a choke cap, a thermostatic spring, a bimetal sensing disc (switch) and a ceramic positive temperature coefficient (PTC) heater. Even though current is constantly supplied to it with the engine running, the temperature sensing disc limits the duration of choke assist. At temperatures below approximately 60°F (16°C), the switch is open and no current is supplied to the ceramic heater, thereby resulting in normal, unassisted thermostatic spring choke action. When the temperature rises above 60°F (16°C), the temperature sensing disc closes and current is supplied to the heater which, in turn, acts on

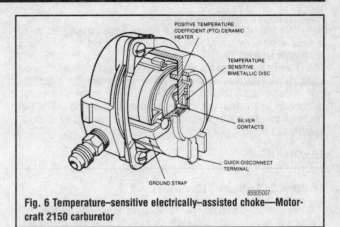

Fig. 6 Temperature–sensitive electrically–assisted choke—Motorcraft 2150 carburetor

the thermostatic spring. Once the heater starts, it causes the thermostatic spring to pull the choke plate(s) open within 1½ minutes, which is sooner than it would open if non–assisted.

Over the years, various Ford and Mercury vehicles have also employed a constantly operating, full electric choke. This system, which lacks a temperature–sensing switch, heats whenever the engine is running.

1. Detach the electrical lead from the choke cap.

2. Use a jumper lead to connect the terminal on the choke cap and the wire terminal, so that the electrical circuit is still completed.

3. Start the engine.

4. Hook up a test light between the connector on the choke lead and ground.

5. The test light should glow. If it does not, current is not being supplied to the electrically assisted choke.

6. Connect the test light between the power supply terminal on the alternator (or other source, if applicable) and the terminal on the choke cap. If the light now glows, replace the lead, since it is not passing current to the choke assist.

❋❋ CAUTION

Do not ground the terminal on the alternator while performing Step 6.

7. If the light still does not glow, the fault lies somewhere in the electrical system. Check the system out. If the electrically assisted choke receives power but still does not appear to be functioning properly, reconnect the choke lead and proceed with the rest of the test.

8. Tape the bulb end of a thermometer to the metallic portion of the choke housing.

9. If the electrically assisted choke operates below 55°F (13°C), it is defective and must be replaced.

10. Allow the engine to warm up to 80–100°F (27–38°C); at these temperatures the choke should operate for about 1½ minutes.

11. If it does not operate for this length of time, check the bimetallic spring to see if it is connected to the tang on the choke lever.

12. If the spring is connected and the choke is not operating properly, replace the cap assembly.

Throttle Solenoid (Anti–Dieseling Solenoid)

1. Turn the ignition key on and open the throttle. The solenoid plunger should extend (solenoid energized).

2. Turn the ignition off. The plunger should retract, allowing the throttle to close.

➡ **With the anti–dieseling solenoid de–energized, the carburetor idle speed adjusting screw must make contact with the throttle shaft to prevent the throttle plates from jamming in the throttle bore when the engine is turned off.**

3. If the solenoid is functioning properly and the engine is still dieseling, check for one of the following:

   a. High idle or engine shut off speed

   b. Engine timing not set to specification

   c. Binding throttle linkage

   d. Too low an octane fuel being used

Correct any of these problems as necessary.

4. If the solenoid fails to function as outlined in Steps 1 and 2, disconnect the solenoid leads; the solenoid should de–energize. If it does not, it is jammed and must be replaced.

5. Connect the solenoid to a 12–volt power source and to ground. Open the throttle so that the plunger can extend. If it does not, the solenoid is defective.

6. If the solenoid is functioning correctly and no other source of trouble can be found, the fault probably lies in the wiring between the solenoid and the ignition switch or in the ignition switch itself. Remember to reconnect the solenoid when finished testing.

ADJUSTMENTS

Automatic Choke Housing (Choke Cap)

Original equipment carburetors on 1979 vehicles, as well as some later applications, have adjustable choke caps. On a vehicle of this type, the reaction of the choke to engine temperature can be controlled by positioning and rotating the cap in relation to an index mark or reference point. In spite of their adjustability, these carburetors each have a preferred setting, as determined by the manufacturer. Most original equipment carburetors on 1980 and later vehicles utilize adjustment–limiting or non–adjustable choke caps. The inclusion of a locking/indexing plate or spacer with locating tabs eliminates the need for choke cap adjustment. Nevertheless, the removal and installation procedures for these non–adjustable choke caps are essentially the same as those for their adjustable counterparts. One significant difference is in the type of fastener used to retain the caps. Generally, regular slotted screws are used to retain adjustable choke caps, thereby permitting easy removal. Non–adjustable choke caps, on the other hand, are retained by a combination of screws and either rivets or break-away screws. Such unslotted–head fasteners require different removal tools and techniques, as described below.

1979 CARBURETORS

▶ See Figure 7

1. Remove the air cleaner assembly.
2. Loosen the thermostatic spring housing retaining screws.
3. Set the spring housing to the specified index mark, by rotating the housing. (Refer to the appropriate Carburetor Specifications chart, later in this section.)

➡If the choke cap was removed, be sure that the choke cap gasket or spacer is in place and that the choke cap engages the bimetal loop on the choke thermostatic lever.

4. Line up the holes in the choke cap retainer, if removed, and fasten the retaining screws.
5. Install the air cleaner assembly, if no further adjustments are required at this time.

1980–86 CARBURETORS

➡The carburetors used on most 1980 and later vehicles have adjustment–limiting or non–adjustable choke caps which must line up with a locking/indexing plate or spacer. Although non–adjustable, these choke caps may have to be removed if defective, or when performing other carburetor procedures.

1. Remove the air cleaner assembly from the carburetor.
2. If the choke cap retainer is fastened with unslotted–head fasteners, determine whether those fasteners are rivets or break-away screws.

➡Break-away screws are threaded like regular screws, but once they are sufficiently tightened, the slotted upper portion breaks off. Unlike rivets, they can be unscrewed if a new slot if created.

3. To remove break-away screws, use a hacksaw to carefully cut a slot in the head of each break-away screw, so that they can be removed with a straight–blade screwdriver. Proceed to step 5.
4. To remove rivets, proceed as follows:

➡This procedure must be followed to retain the hole size.

a. Check the choke cap retainer rivets to determine if the mandrel is well below the rivet head. If the mandrel appears to be at or within the rivet head thickness, drive it down or out with a ¼ in. (1.6mm) diameter punch.

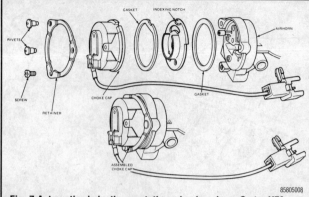

Fig. 7 Automatic choke thermostatic spring housing—Carter YFA carburetor

85805008

b. Use a ⅛ in. diameter or No. 30 (.1285 in. diameter) drill bit for drilling the rivet heads. Drill into the rivet head until the rivet head comes loose from the rivet body.

c. After the rivet head is removed, drive the remaining portion of the rivet out of the hole with an ⅛ in. diameter punch.

d. Repeat Step 4 for the remaining rivet.
5. Remove the screw(s) with a proper size screwdriver.
6. Remove the retainer, choke cap, locking/indexing plate and/or gasket(s), as equipped.

➡On some carburetors, epoxy cement was applied during production to both sides of the gasket. In this case, remove the gasket by inserting a sharp, flat chisel or knife between the gasket layers. Be sure to clean any remaining epoxy and gasket from the mating surfaces with a gasket scraper.

To install:

7. Install the choke cap gasket(s) and locking/indexing plate or spacer, as equipped. (Replace any damaged gasket(s) and be sure to apply epoxy cement or equivalent to any gasket which was originally cemented.)
8. Install the choke cap, making certain that the bimetal loop is positioned around the choke lever tang.
9. While holding the cap in place, actuate the choke plate to make certain the bimetal loop is properly engaged with the lever tang. Set the retainer over the choke cap and orient the retainer to match the holes in the casting. (The holes are not equally spaced on some models.) Make sure the retainer is not upside down.

➡1983–84 Holley 4180 carburetors have an adjustable choke cap, which must be aligned with the proper index mark. (Refer to the Carburetor Specifications Chart, found later in this section.) To properly position the cap, loosely install the choke cap retainer screws before aligning the cap. Once the cap is properly positioned, tighten the retainer screws.

10. To replace break-away screws, install new break-away screws and tighten until their heads break off. (If you prefer, these fasteners may be replaced by conventional screws of the same installed size.)
11. To replace rivets, proceed as follows:

a. Place a rivet in the rivet gun and trigger it lightly to retain the rivet (⅛ in. diameter x ½ in. long x ¼ in. diameter head).

b. Press the rivet fully into the casting after passing through the retainer and "pop" the rivet, so that the mandrel breaks off. Be careful that the rivet mandrel does not lodge in the carburetor mechanism when it separates from the rivet.

c. Repeat this step for the remaining rivet.
12. Install and tighten the remaining conventional screw(s).
13. Install the air cleaner assembly, if no further adjustments are required at this time.

Fast Idle Speed

▶ See Figures 8 and 9

➡Be sure that the curb idle speed and idle mixture are set to specification before adjusting the fast idle speed.

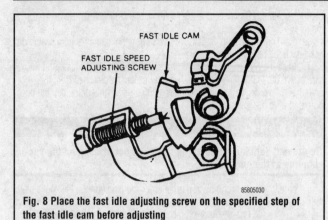

Fig. 8 Place the fast idle adjusting screw on the specified step of the fast idle cam before adjusting

Fig. 9 Turn the fast idle adjusting screw to obtain the specified setting—Carter YFA feedback carburetor shown

1. Remove the air cleaner assembly, if necessary.
2. Place the transmission in Neutral or Park and bring the engine to normal operating temperature.
3. Turn off the ignition. If so equipped, set the A/C selector to the Off position.
4. Disconnect the vacuum hose at the EGR valve and plug the hose.
5. If so equipped, disconnect the wire to the electric PVS.
6. Place the fast idle adjusting screw on the specified step of the fast idle cam.
7. Connect a suitable tachometer.
8. Start the engine without touching the accelerator pedal.
9. Adjust the fast idle speed to specification by turning the adjusting screw.
10. Rev the engine momentarily to allow the engine to return to idle and turn off the ignition.
11. Disconnect and remove the tachometer.
12. Remove the plug from the EGR vacuum hose and reconnect the hose.
13. If so equipped, reconnect the wire to the electric PVS.
14. Install the air cleaner assembly, if no further adjustments are required at this time.

Fast Idle Cam Setting

MOTORCRAFT 2150

▶ See Figure 10

1. Remove the air cleaner assembly.
2. Loosen the choke cap. (If the cap has an adjustment–limiting design, remove the fasteners as described above, temporarily remove the locking/indexing plate and install the cap with conventional screws.) Do not tighten the screws.
3. Rotate the choke thermostatic housing counterclockwise to lightly close the choke plate, and then an additional 90° in the same direction. Tighten the screws to hold this setting.
4. Cycle the throttle to set the fast idle cam.
5. Activate the pulldown motor by applying an external vacuum source to

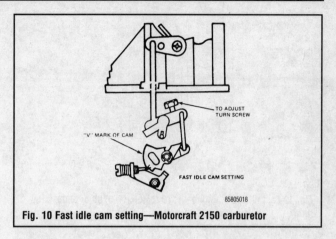

Fig. 10 Fast idle cam setting—Motorcraft 2150 carburetor

it, or by pushing the choke pulldown diaphragm's connecting link into the retracted position.
6. Cycle the throttle and observe the fast idle cam. It should drop to the kickdown step, and the fast idle screw should be opposite the V–notch on the cam.
7. To align the fast idle speed screw with the notch on the cam, turn the hex head screw in the plastic fast idle cam lever.
8. Reset the choke housing cap to its proper position. (Be sure to replace the locking/indexing plate, if so equipped, and install new fasteners where necessary.)
9. If disconnected, reconnect the vacuum hose to the pulldown motor.
10. Install the air cleaner assembly, if no further adjustments are required at this time.

CARTER YFA

▶ See Figure 11

1. Position the fast idle screw on the second (kickdown) step of the fast idle cam, against the shoulder of the high step.
2. Apply light closing pressure on the choke plate.
3. Check the clearance between the lower edge of the choke plate and the air horn wall.
4. Adjust, if necessary, by bending the choke plate connecting rod.

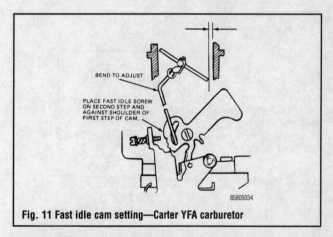

Fig. 11 Fast idle cam setting—Carter YFA carburetor

MOTORCRAFT 5200 OR 6500—1979

▶ See Figure 12

1. Place the fast idle screw on the second (kickdown) step of the fast idle cam, against the shoulder of the top step.
2. Place a 5/16 in. drill bit between the lower edge of the choke plate and the air horn wall. Apply light closing pressure on the choke plate to hold the drill bit in place.
3. Measure the clearance between the tang on the choke lever and the arm on the fast idle cam. This measurement should be 0.010 in. maximum.

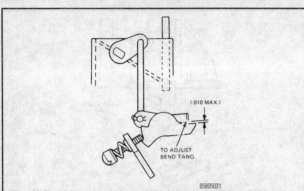

Fig. 12 Fast idle cam setting—1979 Motorcraft 5200 or 6500 carburetor

4. If the clearance is out of specification, bend the choke lever tang to adjust.

MOTORCRAFT 5200 OR 6500—1980–82

1. Place the fast idle screw on the second (kickdown) step of the fast idle cam, against the shoulder of the top step.

2. Apply light downward pressure on the choke lever tang and, using the proper size drill bit (as indicated in the Carburetor Specifications chart, later in this section), check the clearance between the lower edge of the choke plate and the air horn wall.

3. If the clearance is out of specification, replace the choke lever. Do not attempt to bend the choke lever tang, since it is hardened.

HOLLEY 1946

▸ **See Figure 13**

1. Position the fast idle adjusting screw on the second (kickdown) step of the fast idle cam, against the shoulder of the top step.

2. Apply light closing pressure on the choke plate.

3. Check the fast idle cam setting by placing a drill bit of the specified size (as indicated in the Carburetor Specifications chart, later in this section), between the upper edge of the choke plate and the air horn wall.

4. If necessary, bend the fast idle cam link to adjust.

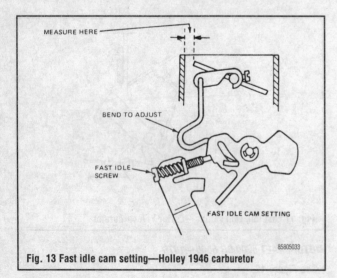

Fig. 13 Fast idle cam setting—Holley 1946 carburetor

HOLLEY 4180

1. Remove the spark delay valve, if so equipped, from the Distributor vacuum advance line, and route the vacuum line directly to the advance side of the distributor.

2. Trace the EGR signal vacuum line from the EGR valve to the carburetor and if there is EGR/PVS valve or temperature vacuum switch located in the vac-

uum line routing, disconnect the EGR vacuum line at the EGR valve and plug the line.

3. If not equipped with an EGR/PVS valve or temperature vacuum switch do not detach the EGR vacuum line.

4. Trace the purge valve vacuum line from the purge valve located on the canister, to the first point where the vacuum line can be detached from the underhood hose routing. Disconnect the vacuum line at that point, cap the open port, and plug the vacuum line.

✳✳ WARNING

To prevent damage to the purge valve, do not disconnect the vacuum line at the purge valve.

5. With the engine running at normal operating temperature, the choke plate fully opened and the manual transmission in Neutral (or automatic transmission in Park), place the fast idle lever on the second or kickdown step of the fast idle cam.

6. Adjust the fast idle screw to within 100 rpm of the speed specified on the Vehicle Emission Control Decal.

7. Reconnect all vacuum lines.

Choke Plate Pulldown Clearance

MOTORCRAFT 2150

▸ **See Figures 14 and 15**

1. Remove the air cleaner assembly.

2. Loosen the choke cap. (If the cap has an adjustment–limiting design, remove the fasteners as described above, temporarily remove the locking/indexing plate and install the cap with conventional screws.) Do not tighten the screws.

3. Rotate the choke thermostatic housing counterclockwise to lightly close the choke plate, and then an additional 90° in the same direction. Tighten the screws to hold this setting.

4. Activate the pulldown motor by applying an external vacuum source to it, or by pushing the choke pulldown diaphragm's connecting link into the retracted position.

5. Using a drill bit of the specified diameter (as indicated in the Carburetor Specifications chart, later in this section), measure the clearance between the lower edge of the choke plate and the air horn wall.

6. Turn the adjusting screw on the pulldown motor clockwise to decrease the pulldown, or counterclockwise to increase it.

➡**After each pulldown adjustment, it is necessary to check the fast idle cam setting. That procedure is covered later in this section.**

7. After the final adjustment, reset the choke housing cap to its proper position. (Be sure to replace the locking/indexing plate, if so equipped, and install new fasteners where necessary.)

8. If disconnected, reconnect the vacuum hose to the pulldown motor.

9. Install the air cleaner assembly, if no further adjustments are required at this time.

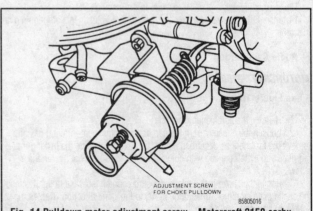

Fig. 14 Pulldown motor adjustment screw—Motorcraft 2150 carburetor

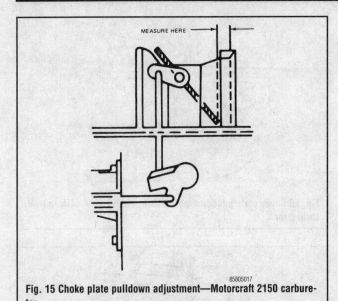

Fig. 15 Choke plate pulldown adjustment—Motorcraft 2150 carburetor

CARTER YFA—PISTON–TYPE CHOKE

♦ See Figure 16

1. Remove the air cleaner assembly.
2. Remove the retainer, choke cap and gasket, as described previously in this section.
3. Bend a 0.026 in. (0.66mm) diameter wire gauge at a 90° angle, approximately 1/8 in. (3mm) from one end. Insert the bent end of the gauge between the choke piston slot and the right hand slot in the choke housing. Rotate the choke piston lever counterclockwise until the gauge is shut in the piston slot.
4. Apply light pressure on the choke piston lever to hold the gauge in place. Then, measure the clearance between the lower edge of the choke plate and the carburetor bore using a drill bit with a diameter equal to the specified pulldown clearance. (Refer to the Carburetor Specifications chart, later in this section.)
5. Bend the choke piston lever to obtain the proper clearance. Be careful not to distort the piston link.
6. Install the gasket, choke cap and retainer.
7. Fasten the retainer screw(s) and apply new rivets, where necessary.
8. Install the air cleaner assembly, if no further adjustments are required at this time.

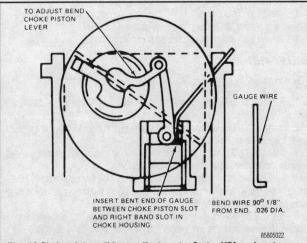

Fig. 16 Choke plate pulldown adjustment—Carter YFA carburetor with piston–type choke

CARTER YFA—DIAPHRAGM–TYPE CHOKE

♦ See Figure 17

1. Activate the pulldown motor by applying an external vacuum source.
2. Close the choke plate as far as possible without forcing it.
3. Using a drill bit of the specified size (as indicated in the Carburetor Specifications chart, later in this section), measure the clearance between the lower edge of the choke plate and the air horn wall.
4. If adjustment is necessary, bend the choke diaphragm link as required.
5. Reconnect the pulldown motor vacuum line.

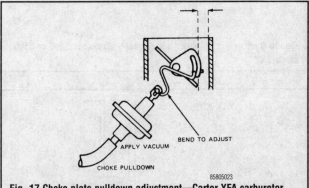

Fig. 17 Choke plate pulldown adjustment—Carter YFA carburetor with diaphragm–type choke

MOTORCRAFT 5200 OR 6500—1979

1. Remove the retaining screws and ring retaining the choke thermostatic spring housing.
2. Remove the thermostatic spring housing and the electric choke heater.
3. Set the fast idle cam on the second step.
4. Attach a rubber band to the choke operating lever to take up any slack in the linkage.
5. Push the diaphragm stem against its stop with a screwdriver, and insert a drill bit of the specified diameter (as indicated in the Carburetor Specifications chart, later in this section), between the lower edge of the choke plate and the air horn wall.
6. Turn the diaphragm adjusting screw in or out to get the proper clearance.
7. Install the electric choke heater, thermostatic spring housing, retaining ring and attaching screws. (Be sure that the choke plate is in the fully closed position before installing the electric choke heater.)
8. Rotate the housing to the specified index mark and tighten the screws.

MOTORCRAFT 5200 OR 6500—1980–82

♦ See Figures 18 and 19

1. Remove the retainer, choke cap and locking/indexing plate as described earlier in this section.
2. Remove the plastic dust cover, if so equipped.
3. Set the fast idle adjusting screw on the high step of the fast idle cam.
4. Attach a rubber band, as illustrated, to remove slack from the choke linkage. Push the diaphragm stem against its stop with a screwdriver, and insert a drill bit of the specified diameter (as indicated in the Carburetor Specifications chart, later in this section), between the lower edge of the choke plate and the air horn wall.
5. If the original choke pulldown diaphragm cover is still in place, and an adjustment is necessary, a service replacement kit will be required. This kit contains a new choke pulldown diaphragm cover, adjusting screw and a cup plug. Proceed as follows:
   a. Remove the three choke pulldown diaphragm cover retaining screws and the cover.
   b. Install a new cover and adjusting screw.
6. Turn the diaphragm adjusting screw clockwise to decrease, or counterclockwise to increase the clearance.
7. When the adjustment is complete, install a new cup plug in the choke pulldown adjustment access opening.

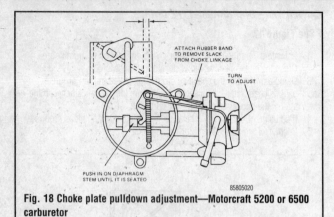

Fig. 18 Choke plate pulldown adjustment—Motorcraft 5200 or 6500 carburetor

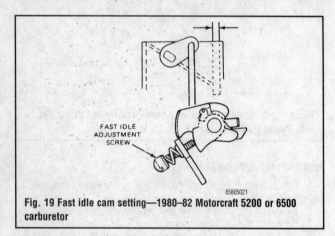

Fig. 19 Fast idle cam setting—1980–82 Motorcraft 5200 or 6500 carburetor

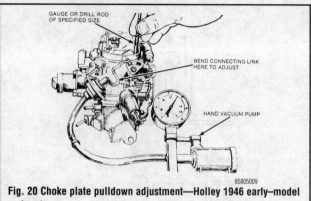

Fig. 20 Choke plate pulldown adjustment—Holley 1946 early–model carburetor

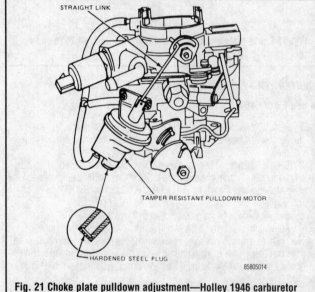

Fig. 21 Choke plate pulldown adjustment—Holley 1946 carburetor

8. Remove the rubber band and install the plastic dust cover, if so equipped.

9. Install the locking and indexing plate, the choke cap and retainer. Be sure that the bimetal loop is properly engaged.

10. Fasten the retainer screw(s) and apply new rivets, where necessary.

HOLLEY 1946

▶ See Figures 20 and 21

➡Early models of this carburetor can be adjusted, if necessary, without drilling or removing the carburetor. If the choke pulldown diaphragm's connecting link has a U–shaped bend, adjustments are simply made by bending the link.

1. Remove the retainer and choke cap, as described above. (If the pulldown diaphragm's connecting link has a U–shaped bend, simply loosen the choke cap's retainer screws, and proceed to step 4.)

2. Temporarily remove the choke locking and indexing plate.

3. Loosely reassemble the choke cap and retainer with the two screws.

4. Rotate the cap counterclockwise to lightly close the choke plate, and then an additional 90° in the same direction. Tighten the screws to hold this setting.

5. Activate the pulldown motor by applying an external vacuum source.

6. Using a drill bit of the specified diameter (as indicated in the Carburetor Specifications chart, later in this section), measure the clearance between the upper edge of the choke plate and the air horn wall.

➡The remaining steps only apply to those carburetors in which the pull-down diaphragm has a straight connecting link. For early models with a U–shaped link, bend the link until the specified clearance is achieved, then set the choke cap to the original setting and tighten the screws.

7. If an adjustment is necessary, drill a 3/32 in. diameter hole through the hardened steel plug at the base of the pulldown motor, and remove the plug with a tap. (It may be necessary to first remove the carburetor, in order to allow sufficient access. If so, follow the instructions later in this section.)

8. Repeat steps 6 and 7, and turn the adjusting screw in or out as required until the adjustment is within specifications.

9. Install a new steel plug in the adjusting screw access hole.

10. Remove the screws, retainer and choke cap.

11. Install the choke locking and indexing plate, along with the choke cap, retainer and screws. Install new rivets, as described above.

12. Install the carburetor and related parts, if removed.

HOLLEY 4180

▶ See Figure 22

1. Remove the choke thermostat housing, gasket and retainer, as described above.

2. Insert a thin piece of wire into the choke piston bore to move the piston down against the stop screw.

3. Maintain light closing pressure on the choke plate, and measure the gap between the lower edge of the choke plate and the air horn wall.

4. Turn the adjustment screw clockwise to decrease or counterclockwise to increase the gap setting. Be sure to close the choke plate during adjustment, to avoid turning the screw into the side of the piston.

5. Remove the wire and install the choke thermostat housing, gasket and retainer. Use new fasteners when replacing rivets or break-away screws.

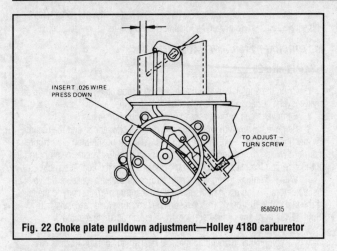

Fig. 22 Choke plate pulldown adjustment—Holley 4180 carburetor

Dechoke Clearance

MOTORCRAFT 2150

♦ See Figure 23

1. Hold the throttle in the wide open position.
2. Using the proper size drill bit (as indicated in the Carburetor Specifications chart, later in this section), measure the clearance between the lower edge of the choke plate and the air horn wall.
3. If adjustment is necessary, carefully bend the metal tang on the fast idle speed lever attached to the throttle shaft. To avoid a wide open throttle sticking condition, be sure that the tang does not touch the radius of the cam.
4. Rotate the throttle lever to assure minimal throttle effort during dechoke tang engagement.

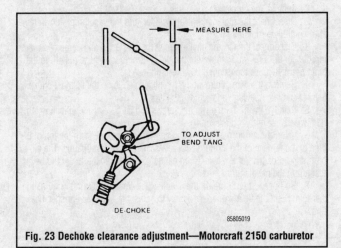

Fig. 23 Dechoke clearance adjustment—Motorcraft 2150 carburetor

CARTER YFA

♦ See Figure 24

1. Remove the air cleaner assembly.
2. Hold the throttle plate fully open and close the choke plate as far as possible without forcing it. Use a drill bit of the proper diameter to check the clearance between the choke plate and air horn.
3. If the clearance is not within specification, adjust by bending the arm on the choke lever of the throttle lever. Bending the arm downward will decrease the clearance, and bending it upward will increase the clearance. Always recheck the clearance after making any adjustment.

MOTORCRAFT 5200 OR 6500

Dechoke clearance cannot be adjusted. It is controlled by the fast idle cam settings.

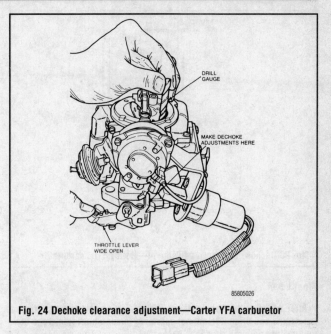

Fig. 24 Dechoke clearance adjustment—Carter YFA carburetor

HOLLEY 1946

♦ See Figure 25

1. Remove the air cleaner assembly.
2. With the engine off, hold the throttle in the wide open position.
3. Insert a drill bit of the specified diameter (as indicated in the Carburetor Specifications chart, later in this section), between the upper edge of the choke plate and the air horn wall.
4. With a slight pressure against the choke shaft, a slight drag should be felt when the gauge is withdrawn.
5. To adjust, bend the unloader tab on the throttle lever.
6. Install the air cleaner assembly, if no further adjustments are required at this time.

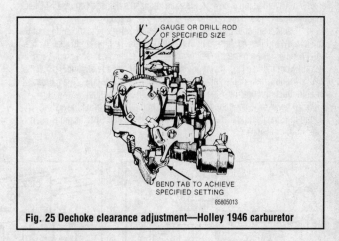

Fig. 25 Dechoke clearance adjustment—Holley 1946 carburetor

HOLLEY 4180

♦ See Figure 26

1. Verify that the choke cap is set to the proper index mark, and adjust if necessary.
2. Hold the throttle in the wide open position.
3. Apply light closing pressure on the choke plate and measure the gap between the lower edge of the choke plate and the air horn wall.
4. If adjustment is necessary, bend the pawl on the fast idle lever.

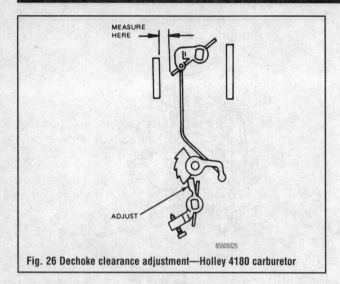

Fig. 26 Dechoke clearance adjustment—Holley 4180 carburetor

Float Level

➡After adjusting the float level and assembling all components, start the engine and bring it to normal operating temperature. Adjust the idle fuel mixture and idle speed, as necessary.

MOTORCRAFT 2150—DRY ADJUSTMENT

▶ See Figure 27

➡The dry float adjustment, performed with the carburetor removed from the engine, is a preliminary fuel level adjustment only. The final, wet float adjustment must be made after the carburetor is mounted on the engine.

1. Remove the air horn attaching screws and lockwashers, and the carburetor identification tag.
2. Remove the air horn and gasket. Remove any fuel in the air horn.
3. Raise the float to seat the inlet needle, if necessary, by depressing the float tab. (Avoid using excessive pressure, as needle damage can result.) Check that the float is raised and the fuel inlet needle is seated.
4. Using a suitable gauge, check the distance between the top surface of the main body and the top surface of the float. Depress the float tab to seat the fuel inlet needle. Take a measurement near the center of the float, at a point ⅛ in. (3mm) from the free end. If you are using a prefabricated float gauge, place the gauge in the corner of the enlarged end section of the fuel bowl. The gauge should touch the float near the end, but not on the end radius.
5. If necessary, bend the tab on the end of the float to bring the setting within the specified limits (as indicated in the Carburetor Specifications chart, later in this section).

6. Install the air horn with a new gasket, and fasten with the lockwashers and screws. Be sure to install the identification tag in its proper location.

MOTORCRAFT 2150—WET ADJUSTMENT

▶ See Figure 28

1. Bring the engine to its normal operating temperature, park the car on as nearly level a surface as possible, and stop the engine.
2. Remove the air cleaner assembly from the carburetor.
3. Remove the air horn attaching screws and lockwashers, and the carburetor identification tag. Leave the air horn and gasket in position on the carburetor main body. Start the engine, let it idle for several minutes, rotate the air horn out of the way, and remove the gasket to provide access to the float assembly.
4. With the engine idling, use a standard depth scale to measure the vertical distance from the top machined surface of the carburetor main body to the level of the fuel in the fuel bowl. This measurement must be made at least ¼ in. (6mm) away from any vertical surface, to insure an accurate reading.
5. Stop the engine before making any adjustment to the float level. Adjustment is accomplished by bending the float tab (which contacts the fuel inlet valve) up or down as required to raise or lower the fuel level. After making an adjustment, start the engine, and allow it to idle for several minutes before repeating the fuel level check. Repeat as necessary until the proper fuel level is attained.
6. Install the air horn with a new gasket, and fasten with the lockwashers and screws. Be sure to install the identification tag in its proper location.
7. Check the idle speed, fuel mixture, and throttle positioner adjustments. Install the air cleaner assembly.

CARTER YFA

▶ See Figure 29

➡The dry float fuel level adjustment is a final float or fuel level adjustment.

1. Remove the air cleaner assembly.
2. Disconnect the fuel inlet line at the filter, and the vacuum pulldown hose at the pulldown motor.
3. Disconnect the electric choke wire at the connector and at the clip on the throttle control bracket. Remove the throttle control bracket assembly from the main body. Remove the external bowl vent line.
4. Remove the wire clip retaining the link which joins the fast idle choke lever to the fast idle cam, and remove the link.
5. Remove the air horn attaching screws and carburetor identification tag. Remove the air horn and gasket.
6. Invert the air horn assembly and check the clearance from the top of the float to the surface of the air horn with a T–scale or float level gauge. The air horn should be held at eye level when gauging, and the float arm should be resting on the needle pin.
7. Do not exert pressure on the needle valve when measuring or adjusting the float. Bend the float arm as necessary to adjust the float level to specifications.

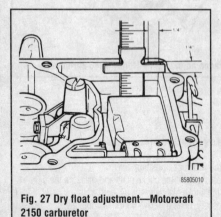

Fig. 27 Dry float adjustment—Motorcraft 2150 carburetor

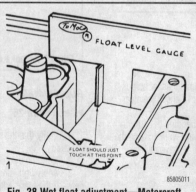

Fig. 28 Wet float adjustment—Motorcraft 2150 carburetor

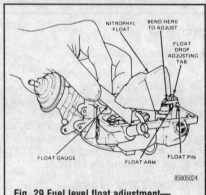

Fig. 29 Fuel level float adjustment—Carter YFA carburetor

Do not bend the tab at the end of the float arm, as it prevents the float from striking the bottom of the fuel bowl when empty and keeps the needle in place.

8. Install the air horn with a new gasket. Be sure to install the identification tag in its proper location and tighten the attaching screws to 27–37 inch lbs.
9. Connect the external bowl vent line.
10. Install the throttle control bracket assembly on the main body.
11. Position the link and plastic bushing which join the fast idle cam to the fast idle choke lever, and retain them in place on the fast idle cam with the plastic bushing and wire clip. Make sure that the mechanical fuel bowl vent rod is engaged with the forked actuating lever, if so equipped.
12. Connect the fuel inlet line to the fuel filter, and the vacuum line to the pulldown motor.
13. Connect the electric choke wire, and clip the wire to the throttle control bracket.
14. Install the air cleaner assembly.

MOTORCRAFT 5200 OR 6500

1. Remove the bowl cover (air horn) attaching screws and lockwashers.
2. Remove the plastic retainer bushings from the choke rod and remove the air horn. Be sure that the gasket is not attached.
3. Turn the air horn upside down. With the float tang resting lightly on the spring loaded fuel inlet needle, measure the clearance between the edge of the float and the air horn.
4. To adjust the float level, bend the float tang. Make sure that both floats are adjusted equally.
5. Hold the air horn in its normal position to check and adjust the float drop, if necessary.
6. Position the air horn and gasket on the main body, and install the attaching screws and lockwashers. Tighten the attaching screws to 20 inch lbs.
7. Install the plastic retainer bushings on the choke rod.

HOLLEY 1946

▸ See Figure 30

➡This setting of the float level adjustment must be done with the carburetor removed from the engine.

1. Remove the air horn attaching screws and carburetor identification tag. Remove the air horn and gasket.
2. Place a finger over the hinge pin retainer and invert the main body. Catch the accelerator pump check ball and weight when they fall out.
3. Lay a ruler across the housing under the floats. The lowest point of the floats should be just touching the ruler for all except California models. For California models, the ruler should just contact the heel (raised step) of the floats.
4. Bend the float tangs to adjust. Once this adjustment is correct, turn the main body right side up and check the float alignment. The floats should move freely without touching the fuel bowl walls. If the floats are misaligned, straighten them by bending the float arms. Recheck the float level adjustment, and adjust if necessary.

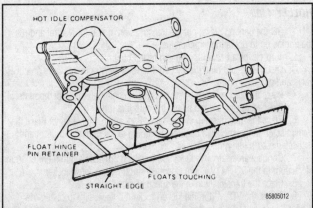

Fig. 30 Float level adjustment—Holley 1946 carburetor

5. Insert the accelerator pump check ball and weight.
6. Install the air horn with a new gasket, and fasten with the screws. Be sure to install the identification tag in its proper location.

HOLLEY 4180

To perform a preliminary dry float adjustment on both the primary and secondary fuel bowl float assemblies, remove each fuel bowl and invert it, allowing the float to rest on the fuel inlet valve and seat assembly. The fuel inlet valve and seat can be rotated until the float is parallel with the fuel bowl floor (actually, the top of the fuel bowl chamber when inverted). Note that this is an initial dry float setting which must be rechecked with the carburetor assembled and on the engine to obtain the proper wet fuel level.

➡This carburetor has an externally adjustable needle and seat assembly which allows the fuel level to be checked and adjusted without removing the carburetor from the engine.

1. Run the engine with the vehicle resting on a level surface until the engine reaches normal operating temperature.
2. Remove the air cleaner assembly.
3. Place a suitable container or an absorbent cloth below the fuel level sight plug in the fuel bowl.
4. Run the engine at 1000 rpm for about 30 seconds to stabilize the fuel level.
5. Stop the engine and remove the sight plug and gasket on the primary float bowl. The fuel level in the bowl should be at the lower edge of the sight plug hole, plus or minus 1/16 in. If the level is too high, loosen one of the lower fuel bowl retaining screws and drain the fuel from the bowl.

Never loosen the lockscrew or nut, or attempt to adjust the fuel level with the sight plug removed or the engine running, since fuel will spray out, creating a fire hazard!

6. To adjust the fuel level, loosen the lockscrew on top of the fuel bowl just enough to allow the adjusting nut to be turned. Turn the adjusting nut about 1/2 turn clockwise to lower the fuel level, or about 1/2 turn counterclockwise to raise the fuel level. (By turning the adjusting nut 5/16 of a turn, the fuel level will change 1/16 in. at the sight plug.) Tighten the lock screw and install the sight plug, using the old gasket.
7. Start the engine and allow the fuel level to stabilize again, by running the engine at 1000 rpm for about 30 seconds. Stop the engine and re–check the fuel level as outlined in Step 5.
8. Repeat the procedure in Step 6 until the fuel level is at the bottom of the sight plug hole. Install the sight plug using a new gasket.
9. Repeat Steps 5–8 for the secondary fuel bowl adjustment.

➡The secondary throttle must be used to stabilize the fuel level in the secondary fuel bowl.

10. Install the air cleaner assembly if no further adjustments are necessary.

Accelerator Pump Stroke

MOTORCRAFT 2150—WITHOUT ADJUSTMENT–LIMITING FEATURE

▸ See Figure 31

In order to keep the exhaust emission level of the engine within the specified limits, the accelerator pump stroke has been preset at the factory. The additional holes are provided for differing engine–transmission–body applications only. The primary throttle shaft lever (over-travel lever) has four holes to control the pump stroke. The accelerating pump operating rod should be in the over-travel lever hole number listed in the Carburetor Specifications chart, and in the inboard hole (hole closest to the pump plunger) in the accelerating pump link. If the pump stroke has been changed from the specified settings, use the following procedure to correct the stroke.

1. Remove the air cleaner assembly.
2. Use a small screwdriver to pry up on the tab portion of the retainer clip, which snaps over the accelerator pump rod. Disengage the rod.
3. Position the clip over the specified hole in the over-travel lever. (See the Carburetor Specifications chart, later in this section.) Insert the rod through the hole in the clip and the over-travel lever.
4. Snap the end of the clip over the rod.

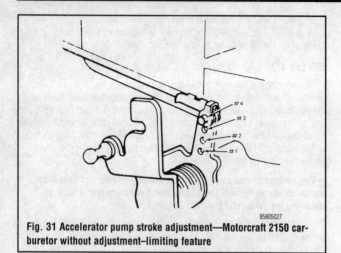

Fig. 31 Accelerator pump stroke adjustment—Motorcraft 2150 carburetor without adjustment–limiting feature

5. Install the air cleaner assembly, if no further adjustments are required at this time.

MOTORCRAFT 2150—WITH ADJUSTMENT–LIMITING FEATURE

▶ See Figure 32

1. Remove the air cleaner assembly.
2. Support the area below the roll pin to prevent damage to the accelerator pump housing.
3. Use a blunt–tipped punch and a small hammer to drive out the roll pin attaching the accelerator pump link to the accelerator pump housing.
4. Lift the pump link and rod up and over the carburetor until the keyed end of the rod is aligned with the keyed hole in the pump over-travel lever.
5. Reposition the rod in the specified hole, and reassemble the pump link and rod assembly. If replacement is necessary, an accelerator rod and swivel (Ford part no. 9F687 or equivalent) should be used.
6. Install the roll pin.
7. Install the air cleaner assembly, if no further adjustments are required at this time.

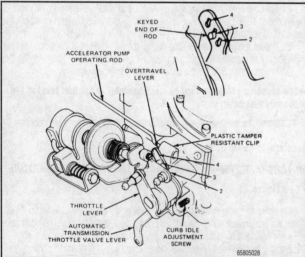

Fig. 32 Accelerator pump stroke adjustment—Motorcraft 2150 carburetor with adjustment–limiting feature

HOLLEY 1946

▶ See Figure 33

➥The accelerator pump stroke is pre-set at the factory and should not be adjusted in an effort to improve driveability. After disassembling the carburetor, be sure to return the accelerator pump operating link to its proper slot in the throttle return spring arm.

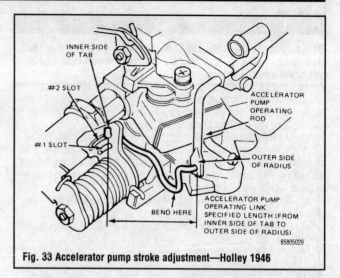

Fig. 33 Accelerator pump stroke adjustment—Holley 1946

1. Check the length of the accelerator pump operating link from its outside edge at the accelerator pump rod to its inside edge at the applicable slot. The measurement should be 2.140–2.160 in. (1979–81) or 2.385–2.405 in. (1982).
2. Adjust to the proper length, if necessary, by bending the loop in the operating link.

Accelerating Pump Lever

HOLLEY 4180

1. Hold the primary throttle plates in the wide open position.
2. Using a feeler gauge, check the clearance between the accelerating pump operating lever adjustment screw head and the pump arm while depressing the pump arm with your finger.
3. To make an adjustment, loosen and hold the adjusting screw locknut and turn the adjusting screw inward to increase, or outward to decrease the adjustment. ½ turn will change the clearance by approximately 0.015 in. (0.381 mm). When the adjustment is complete, hold the adjusting screw stationary and tighten the locknut.

Throttle Positioner Clearance

ALL CARBURETORS

1. Check that the engine idle speed and mixture settings are correct and that the engine is at normal operating temperature.
2. Loosen the dashpot or solenoid locking nut.
3. With the throttle held closed, depress the plunger with a screwdriver blade and measure the clearance between the throttle lever and the plunger tip. If the clearance is not within specifications, turn the dashpot or solenoid until the proper clearance is obtained between the throttle lever and the plunger tip.
4. Tighten the locking nut and recheck the adjustment. Readjust if necessary.

Vacuum Operated Throttle Modulator

HOLLEY 4180

1. Set the parking brake, put the transmission in Park or Neutral and run the engine up to operating temperature.
2. Turn off the air conditioning and heater controls.
3. Disconnect and plug the vacuum hoses at the air control valve and EGR valve and purge control valve.
4. Place the transmission in the position specified on the underhood decal.
5. If necessary, check and adjust the curb idle rpm.
6. Place the transmission in Neutral or Park and rev the engine. Place the transmission in the specified position according to the underhood decal and recheck the curb idle rpm. Readjust if necessary.
7. Connect an external vacuum source which provides a minimum of 10 in. of vacuum to the VOTM (Vacuum Operated Throttle Modulator) kicker.
8. Place the transmission in the specified position.
9. Adjust the VOTM (throttle kicker) locknut if necessary to obtain the proper idle rpm.
10. Reconnect all vacuum hoses.

Throttle and Downshift Linkage

WITH MANUAL TRANSMISSION

Throttle linkage adjustments are not normally required, unless the carburetor or linkage has been removed from the car or otherwise disturbed. In all cases, the car is first brought to operating temperature, with the choke open and the fast idle adjusting screw off the fast idle cam. The idle speed is then set to specifications (see Section 2).

Secondary Throttle Plate

HOLLEY 4180

1. Remove the carburetor from the engine.
2. Hold the secondary throttle plates closed.
3. Turn the secondary throttle shaft lever stop screw out until the secondary throttle plates seat in the throttle bores.
4. Turn the screw back in until the screw just touches the secondary lever, and then ¼ additional turn.

REMOVAL & INSTALLATION

Motorcraft 2150

➡**On vehicles with an automatic transmission, the transmission kickdown lever or the throttle valve lever must be adjusted whenever the carburetor assembly is removed for service or replacement.**

1. Remove the air cleaner assembly.
2. Disconnect the throttle cable from the throttle lever.
3. Disconnect all vacuum lines, emission hoses, the fuel line, electrical connection and choke heat tube at the carburetor.
4. Remove the carburetor retaining nuts. Lift off the carburetor carefully, taking care not to spill any fuel. Remove the carburetor mounting gasket and discard it. Remove the carburetor mounting spacer, if so equipped, from the intake manifold.
   To install:
5. Prior to installation, clean the gasket mounting surfaces of the intake manifold, spacer (if so equipped), and carburetor. When using a spacer, use two new gaskets, sandwiching the spacer between the gaskets. If a spacer is not used, only one new carburetor mounting gasket is required.
6. Position and connect the choke heat tube.
7. Install the spark and EGR port vacuum lines, if so equipped, before bolting the carburetor in place.
8. Place the new gasket(s) and spacer (if so equipped) on the carburetor mounting studs. Position the carburetor on top of the gasket and hand–tighten the retaining nuts. Then tighten the nuts in a crisscross pattern to 14–16 ft. lbs.
9. Connect the fuel line, throttle cable, transmission linkage, emission hoses and vacuum lines.
10. Install the air cleaner assembly.
11. Adjust the engine idle speed and mixture settings, if necessary, as outlined in Section 2. Be sure that the accelerator pump rod is set in the specified hole. (Refer to the Carburetor Specifications chart, later in this section.)

Carter YFA

▶ **See Figures 34, 35, 36 and 37**

1. Remove the air cleaner assembly.
2. Disconnect the throttle cable or rod at the throttle lever.
3. Disconnect the appropriate vacuum lines.
4. Disconnect the fuel bowl vent hose at the air horn.
5. Disconnect the fuel line at the fuel filter.
6. Disconnect the electrically assisted choke wire at its connector.
7. Disconnect the electrical connections for the throttle control, idle tracking switch and WOT air conditioning cut–off switch, if so equipped.
8. On feedback model carburetors, disconnect the feedback solenoid, DC idle speed control motor and throttle position sensor wires.
9. Remove the carburetor retaining nuts. Lift off the carburetor carefully, taking care not to spill any fuel. Remove the carburetor mounting gasket and discard it. Remove the carburetor mounting spacer, if so equipped, from the intake manifold.
   To install:
10. Prior to installation, clean the gasket mounting surfaces of the intake manifold, spacer (if so equipped), and carburetor. When using a spacer, use two new gaskets, sandwiching the spacer between the gaskets. If a spacer is not used, only one new carburetor mounting gasket is required.
11. Place the new gasket(s) and spacer (if so equipped) on the carburetor mounting studs. Position the carburetor on top of the gasket and hand tighten the retaining nuts. Then tighten the nuts in a crisscross pattern to 12–15 ft. lbs.
12. Connect the fuel line, throttle cable or rod, and the appropriate vacuum lines.
13. Connect the fuel bowl vent hose to the air horn.
14. Connect the electrical connections for the throttle control, idle tracking switch and WOT air conditioning cut–off switch, if so equipped.
15. Connect the electrically assisted choke wire. On feedback model carburetors, connect the feedback solenoid, DC idle speed control motor and throttle position sensor wires.

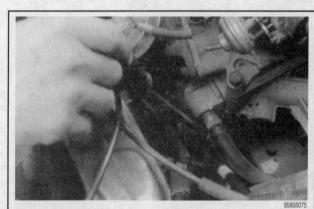

Fig. 34 Disconnect and tag all hoses and vacuum lines before removing the carburetor

Fig. 35 On feedback model carburetors, unplug the feedback solenoid's electrical connector

Fig. 36 Remove the carburetor retaining nuts

Fig. 37 Carefully lift the carburetor from the intake manifold or carburetor spacer

16. Install the air cleaner assembly.
17. Check and adjust the engine idle speed settings, as outlined in Section 2.

Holley 5200 or 6500

1. Remove the air cleaner assembly.
2. Disconnect the throttle cable from the throttle lever.
3. Disconnect the canister bowl vent tube, bowl vent tube, vacuum throttle kicker tube (if so equipped), and feedback tube (model 6500 only).
4. Disconnect the distributor vacuum tube, Thermactor dump valve vacuum tube, EGR vacuum tube and external choke pulldown vacuum tube (if so equipped).
5. Disconnect the fuel inlet line.
6. Disconnect the electric choke cap, bowl vent switch connector, throttle solenoid connector (if so equipped) and idle tracking switch connector.
7. Remove the carburetor retaining nuts. Lift off the carburetor carefully, taking care not to spill any fuel. Remove the carburetor mounting gasket and discard it. Remove the carburetor mounting spacer, if so equipped, from the intake manifold.
To install:
8. Prior to installation, clean the gasket mounting surfaces of the intake manifold, spacer (if so equipped), and carburetor. When using a spacer, use two new gaskets, sandwiching the spacer between the gaskets. If a spacer is not used, only one new carburetor mounting gasket is required.
9. Place the new gasket(s) and spacer (if so equipped) on the carburetor mounting studs. Position the carburetor on top of the gasket and hand tighten the retaining nuts. Then tighten the nuts in a crisscross pattern to 10–14 ft. lbs.
10. Connect the electric choke, bowl vent switch, throttle solenoid (if so equipped) and idle tracking switch.
11. Connect the canister bowl vent tube, bowl vent tube, vacuum throttle kicker tube (if so equipped), and feedback tube (model 6500 only).
12. Connect the distributor vacuum tube, Thermactor dump valve vacuum tube, EGR vacuum tube and external choke pulldown vacuum tube (if so equipped).
13. Connect the fuel inlet line.
14. Connect the throttle cable at the throttle lever.
15. Install the air cleaner assembly.
16. Adjust the curb idle and fast idle speed settings, if necessary, as outlined in Section 2.

Holley 1946

1. Remove the air cleaner assembly.
2. Disconnect the throttle cable from the throttle lever.
3. Disconnect the distributor vacuum line, EGR vacuum line, venturi vacuum line and fuel line.
4. Disconnect the choke heat tube, if so equipped.
5. Disconnect the throttle solenoid positioner and choke cap at their electrical connections.
6. Disconnect the canister bowl vent electrical connector and the canister vent hose.
7. Remove the carburetor retaining nuts. Lift off the carburetor carefully, taking care not to spill any fuel. Remove the carburetor mounting gasket and discard it. Remove the carburetor mounting spacer, if so equipped, from the intake manifold.
To install:
8. Prior to installation, clean the gasket mounting surfaces of the intake manifold, spacer (if so equipped), and carburetor. When using a spacer, use two new gaskets, sandwiching the spacer between the gaskets. If a spacer is not used, only one new carburetor mounting gasket is required.
9. Place the new gasket(s) and spacer (if so equipped) on the carburetor mounting studs. Position the carburetor on top of the gasket and hand tighten the retaining nuts. Then tighten the nuts in a crisscross pattern to 12–15 ft. lbs.
10. Connect the fuel line, throttle cable, distributor vacuum line, EGR vacuum line, and venturi vacuum line.
11. Connect the canister vent hose and the canister bowl vent electrical connector.
12. Connect the choke heat tube, if so equipped.
13. Connect the throttle solenoid positioner and choke cap at their electrical connections.
14. Install the air cleaner assembly.
15. Adjust the curb idle and fast idle speed settings, if necessary, as out-

lined in Section 2. (On 1979 models, also adjust the slow idle speed with the throttle solenoid positioner OFF.)

Holley 4180

1. Remove the air cleaner assembly.
2. Disconnect the throttle rod from the throttle lever.
3. Disconnect the distributor vacuum lines, PCV hose, fuel line and any electrical connections.
4. Disconnect the choke heat tube, if so equipped.
5. Remove the carburetor retaining nuts. Lift off the carburetor carefully, taking care not to spill any fuel. Remove the carburetor mounting gasket and discard it. Remove the carburetor mounting spacer from the intake manifold.
To install:
6. Prior to installation, clean the gasket mounting surfaces of the intake manifold, spacer and carburetor. When using a spacer, use two new gaskets, sandwiching the spacer between the gaskets.
7. Place the new gaskets and spacer on the carburetor mounting studs. Position the carburetor on top of the gasket and hand tighten the retaining nuts. Then tighten the nuts in a crisscross pattern to 14–20 ft. lbs.
8. Connect the throttle rod, vacuum lines, PCV hose, fuel line and electrical connections.
9. Connect the choke heat tube, if so equipped.
10. Install the air cleaner assembly.
11. Check and adjust the idle speed settings, if necessary, as outlined in Section 2.

Carburetors—Motorcraft 2700VV and 7200VV

ADJUSTMENTS

Since the design of the 2700VV (variable venturi) carburetor differs considerably from the other carburetors in the Ford lineup, an explanation of the theory and operation is presented here.

In exterior appearance, the variable venturi carburetor is similar to a conventional carburetor and, like a conventional carburetor, it uses a normal float and fuel bowl system. However, the similarity ends there. In place of the normal choke plate and fixed area venturis, the 2700VV carburetor has a pair of small oblong castings in the top of the upper carburetor body where you would normally expect to see the choke plate. These castings slide back and forth across the top of the carburetor in response to fuel–air demands. Their movement is controlled by a spring–loaded diaphragm valve regulated by a vacuum signal taken below the venturis in the throttle bores. As the throttle is opened, the strength of the vacuum signal increases, opening the venturis and allowing more air to enter the carburetor.

Fuel is admitted into the venturi area by means of tapered metering rods that fit into the main jets. These rods are attached to the venturis, and, as the venturis open or close in response to air demand, the fuel needed to maintain the proper mixture increases or decreases as the metering rods slide in the jets. In comparison to a conventional carburetor with fixed venturis and a variable air supply, this system provides much more precise control of the fuel–air supply during all modes of operation. Because of the variable venturi principle, there are fewer fuel metering systems and fuel passages. The only auxiliary fuel metering systems required are an idle trim, accelerator pump (similar to a conventional carburetor), starting enrichment, and cold running enrichment.

➡**Adjustment, assembly and disassembly of this carburetor require special tools for some of the operations. These tools are available (see the Tools and Equipment Section). Do not attempt any operations on this carburetor without first checking to see if you need the special tools for that particular operation. The adjustment and repair procedures given here mention when and if you will need the special tools.**

The Motorcraft model 7200 variable venturi (VV) carburetor shares most of its design features with the model 2700VV. The major difference between the two is that the 7200VV is designed to work with Ford's EEC (electronic engine control) feedback system. The feedback system precisely controls the air/fuel ratio by varying signals to the feedback control monitor located on the carburetor, which opens or closes the metering valve in response. This expands or reduces the amount of control vacuum above the fuel bowl, leaning or enriching the mixture accordingly.

Fast Idle Speed

▶ **See Figure 38**

1. Remove the air cleaner assembly, if necessary.
2. Place the transmission in Neutral or Park and connect a suitable tachometer.
3. Start the engine and bring it to normal operating temperature.
4. Disconnect and plug the EGR vacuum line.
5. Place the fast idle lever on the specified step of the fast idle cam. (Refer to the engine compartment sticker or the Carburetor Specifications chart for the proper setting.) If so equipped, make sure that the high speed cam positioner lever is disengaged.
6. Turn the fast idle speed screw clockwise to increase or counterclockwise to decrease the fast idle speed.
7. Rev the engine momentarily, place the fast idle lever on the specified step and recheck the fast idle rpm.
8. Shut off the ignition. Disconnect and remove the tachometer.
9. Remove the plug from the EGR vacuum line and connect the line.
10. Install the air cleaner assembly, if no further adjustments are required at this time.

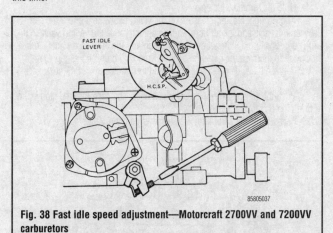

Fig. 38 Fast idle speed adjustment—Motorcraft 2700VV and 7200VV carburetors

Fast Idle Cam Setting

▶ **See Figure 39**

You will need a special choke adjustment tool for this job: Ford calls it a stator cap (#T77L–9848–A or equivalent). It fits over the choke thermostatic lever when the choke cap is removed.

1. Remove the choke coil cap. On 1980 and later California models, the choke cap is riveted in place. The top rivets will have to be drilled out. The bottom rivet will have to be driven out from the rear. New rivets must be used upon installation.
2. Place the fast idle lever in the corner of the specified step of the fast idle cam, counting the highest step as first. (Refer to the engine compartment sticker

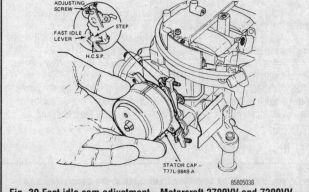

Fig. 39 Fast idle cam adjustment—Motorcraft 2700VV and 7200VV carburetors

or the Carburetor Specifications chart for the proper setting.) Be sure that the high speed cam positioner, if so equipped, is retracted.

3. If the adjustment is being made with the carburetor removed, hold the throttle lightly closed with a rubber band to maintain cam position.
4. Turn the stator cap clockwise until the lever contacts the fast idle cam adjusting screw.
5. Turn the fast idle cam adjusting screw until the index mark on the cap lines up with the specified mark on the choke casting.
6. Remove the stator cap and install the choke coil cap. Set it to the specified casting mark.

High Cam Speed Positioner

1979

▶ **See Figure 40**

1. Place the high cam speed positioner in the corner of the specified cam step, counting the highest step as the first.
2. Place the fast idle lever in the corner of the positioner.
3. Hold the throttle firmly closed.
4. Remove the diaphragm cover. Adjust the diaphragm assembly clockwise until it lightly bottoms. Turn it counterclockwise ½–1½ turns until the vacuum port and diaphragm hole line up.
5. Replace the diaphragm cover.

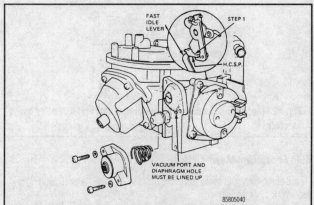

Fig. 40 High cam speed positioner adjustment—Motorcraft 2700VV carburetor

Float Level

▶ **See Figure 41**

1. Remove the carburetor from the engine.
2. Remove the upper body assembly and the upper body gasket.
3. Invert the upper body and measure the vertical distance between the cast surface of the upper body and the bottom of the float. (The normal range is 1.015–1.065 inches.)

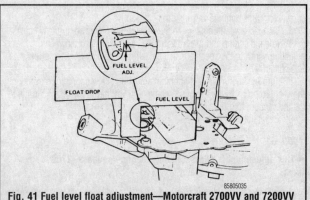

Fig. 41 Fuel level float adjustment—Motorcraft 2700VV and 7200VV carburetors

4. To adjust, bend the float operating lever away from the fuel inlet needle valve to decrease the setting, or toward the needle valve to increase the setting. Make sure that the float remains parallel to the gasket surface.

5. Check the float drop and adjust, if necessary, as described below.

6. Install a new upper body gasket and reinstall the upper body assembly.

Float Drop

▶ **See Figure 42**

1. Remove the carburetor upper body assembly and upper body gasket.

2. Hold the upper body assembly upright and measure the vertical distance between the cast surface of the upper body and the bottom of the float. (The normal range is 1.435–1.485 inches.)

3. To adjust, bend the stop tab on the float lever away from the hinge pin to increase the setting, or toward the hinge pin to decrease the setting.

4. Install a new upper body gasket and reinstall the upper body assembly.

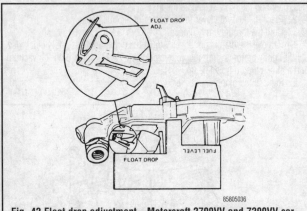

Fig. 42 Float drop adjustment—Motorcraft 2700VV and 7200VV carburetors

Cold Enrichment Metering Rod

A dial indicator and stator cap (Ford part #T77L–9848–A or equivalent) are required for this adjustment.

1. Remove the choke coil cap. See Step 1 of the Fast idle Cam Adjustment.

2. Attach a weight to the choke coil mechanism to seat the cold enrichment rod.

3. Install and zero–set a dial indicator with the tip of the top of the enrichment rod. Raise and release the weight to verify zero on the dial indicator.

4. With the stator cap at the index position, the dial indicator should read the specified dimension. Turn the adjusting nut to correct it.

5. Install the choke cap at the correct setting.

Control Vacuum

1979

1. Make sure the idle speed is correct.

2. Using a 5/16 in. Allen wrench, turn the venturi valve diaphragm adjusting screw clockwise until the valve is firmly closed.

3. Connect a vacuum gauge to the vacuum tap on the venturi valve cover.

4. Idle the engine and use a 1/8 in. Allen wrench to turn the venturi bypass adjusting screw to the specified vacuum setting. You may have to correct the idle speed.

5. Turn the venturi valve diaphragm adjusting screw counterclockwise until the vacuum drops to the specified setting. You will have to work the throttle to get the vacuum to drop.

6. Reset the idle speed.

1980–82

➡**This adjustment is necessary only on non–feedback (2700VV) systems.**

1. Remove the carburetor. Remove the venturi valve diaphragm plug with a center–punch.

2. If the carburetor has a venturi valve bypass, remove it by removing the

two cover retaining screws; invert and remove the bypass screw plug from the cover with a drift. Install the cover.

3. Install the carburetor. Start the engine and allow it to reach normal operating temperature. Connect a vacuum gauge to the venturi valve cover. Set the idle speed to 500 rpm with the transmission in Drive.

4. Push and hold the venturi valve closed. Adjust the bypass screw to obtain a reading of 8 in. Hg on the vacuum gauge. Make sure the idle speed remains constant. Open and close the throttle and check the idle speed.

5. With the engine idling, adjust the venturi valve diaphragm screw to obtain a reading of 6 in. Hg. Set the curb idle to specification. Install new venturi valve bypass and diaphragm plugs.

Venturi Valve Limiter

▶ **See Figure 43**

1. Remove the carburetor. Take off the venturi valve cover and the two rollers.

2. Use a center punch to loosen the expansion plug at the rear of the carburetor main body on the throttle side. Remove it.

3. Use an Allen wrench to remove the venturi valve wide open stop screw.

4. Hold the throttle wide open.

5. Apply a light closing pressure on the venturi valve and check the gap between the valve and the air horn wall. To adjust, move the venturi valve to the wide open position and insert an Allen wrench into the stop screw hole. Turn clockwise to increase the gap. Remove the wrench and check the gap again.

6. Replace the wide open stop screw and turn it clockwise until it contact the valve.

7. Push the venturi valve wide open and check the gap. Turn the stop screw to bring the gap to specifications.

8. Reassemble the carburetor with a new expansion plug.

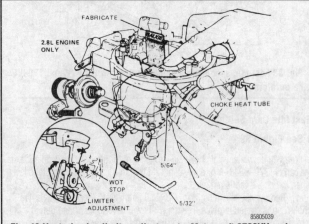

Fig. 43 Venturi valve limiter adjustment—Motorcraft 2700VV and 7200VV carburetors

Control Vacuum Regulator

The cold enrichment metering rod adjustment must be checked and set before making this adjustment.

1. After adjusting the cold enrichment metering rod, leave the dial indicator in place but remove the stator cap. Do not re–zero the dial indicator.

2. Press down on the C.V.R. rod until it bottoms on its seat. Measure this amount of travel with the dial indicator.

3. If the adjustment is incorrect, hold the 3/8 in. C.V.R. adjusting nut with a box wrench to prevent it from turning. Use a 3/16 in. Allen wrench to turn the C.V.R. rod; turning counterclockwise will increase the travel, and vice–versa.

REMOVAL & INSTALLATION

➡**On vehicles with an automatic transmission, the transmission kickdown lever or the throttle valve lever must be adjusted whenever the carburetor assembly is removed for service or replacement.**

1. Remove the air cleaner assembly.
2. Disconnect the throttle cable from the throttle lever.
3. Disconnect the vacuum lines, emission hoses, fuel line and electrical connection.
4. On EEC–equipped vehicles, disconnect the throttle position sensor connector at the loom.
5. Remove the carburetor retaining nuts. Lift off the carburetor carefully, taking care not to spill any fuel. Remove the carburetor mounting gasket and discard it. Remove the carburetor mounting spacer, if so equipped, from the intake manifold.

To install:

6. Prior to installation, clean the gasket mounting surfaces of the intake manifold, spacer (if so equipped), and carburetor. When using a spacer, use two new gaskets, sandwiching the spacer between the gaskets. If a spacer is not used, only one new carburetor mounting gasket is required.

7. Install the spark and EGR port vacuum lines, if so equipped, before bolting the carburetor in place.
8. On EEC–equipped vehicles, connect the throttle position sensor plug, and secure the wire loom.
9. Place the new gasket(s) and spacer (if so equipped) on the carburetor mounting studs. Position the carburetor on top of the gasket and hand tighten the retaining nuts. Then tighten the nuts in a crisscross pattern to 12–15 ft. lbs.
10. Connect the fuel line, throttle cable, and all vacuum lines and emission hoses which were removed.
11. Install the air cleaner assembly.
12. Check and adjust the engine idle speed settings, as outlined in Section 2.

Motorcraft 2150 Specifications

Year	(9510)* Carburetor Identification	Dry Float Level (in.)	Wet Float Level (in.)	Pump Setting Hole # ①	Choke Plate Pulldown (in.)	Fast Idle Cam Linkage Clearance (in.)	Fast Idle (rpm)	Dechoke (in.)	Choke Setting
1979	D9AE-AHA	7/16	13/16	3	0.147	①	②	0.250	3 Rich
	D9AE-AJA	7/16	13/16	3	0.147	①	②	0.250	3 Rich
	D9AE-ANB	7/16	13/16	3	0.129	①	②	—	1 Rich
	D9AE-APB	7/16	13/16	3	0.129	①	②	—	1 Rich
	D9AE-AVB	7/16	13/16	3	0.129	①	②	—	1 Rich
	D9AE-AYA	7/16	13/16	3	0.129	①	②	—	1 Rich
	D9AE-AYB	7/16	13/16	3	0.129	①	②	—	1 Rich
	D9AE-TB	7/16	13/16	3	0.129	①	②	—	2 Rich
	D9AE-UB	7/16	13/16	3	0.129	①	②	—	2 Rich
	D9BE-VB	7/16	13/16	3	0.153	①	②	0.250	2 Rich
	D9BE-YB	7/16	13/16	3	0.153	①	②	—	2 Rich
	D9DE-NB	7/16	13/16	3	0.153	①	②	0.250	2 Rich
	D9DE-RA	7/16	13/16	2	0.125	①	②	0.115	3 Rich
	D9DE-RB	7/16	13/16	2	0.125	①	②	0.115	3 Rich
	D9DE-RD	7/16	13/16	2	0.125	①	②	—	3 Rich
	D9DE-SA	7/16	13/16	2	0.125	①	②	0.250	3 Rich
	D9DE-SC	7/16	13/16	2	0.125	①	②	—	3 Rich
	D9ME-BA	7/16	13/16	2	0.136	①	②	0.115	Index
	D9ME-CA	7/16	13/16	2	0.136	①	②	0.115	Index
	D9OE-CB	7/16	13/16	3	0.132	①	②	0.115	3 Rich
	D9OE-DB	7/16	13/16	3	0.132	①	②	—	3 Rich
	D9OE-EA	7/16	13/16	3	0.132	①	②	0.115	2 Rich
	D9OE-FA	7/16	13/16	3	0.132	①	②	0.115	2 Rich
	D9SE-GA	7/16	13/16	3	0.150	①	②	0.250	2 Rich
	D9VE-LC	7/16	13/16	3	0.145	①	②	0.250	3 Rich
	D9VE-SA	7/16	13/16	3	0.147	①	②	—	3 Rich
	D9VE-UB	7/16	13/16	3	0.155	①	②	0.250	3 Rich
	D9VE-VA	3/8	3/4	3	0.145	①	②	—	3 Rich
	D9VE-YB	3/8	3/4	2	0.145	①	②	0.250	3 Rich
	D9WE-CB	7/16	13/16	3	0.132	①	②	—	3 Rich
	D9WE-DB	7/16	13/16	3	0.132	①	②	—	3 Rich
	D9WE-EB	7/16	13/16	3	0.132	①	②	—	2 Rich
	D9WE-FB	7/16	13/16	3	0.132	①	②	—	2 Rich
	D9WE-JA	7/16	13/16	3	0.150	①	②	0.250	2 Rich
	D9WE-MB	7/16	13/16	3	0.132	①	②	—	1 Rich
	D9WE-NB	7/16	13/16	3	0.132	①	②	—	1 Rich
	D9YE-EA	7/16	13/16	3	0.118	①	②	0.115	1 Rich
	D9YE-FA	7/16	13/16	3	0.118	①	②	0.115	1 Rich
	D9YE-AB	7/16	13/16	3	0.118	①	②	0.115	Index
	D9YE-BB	7/16	13/16	3	0.118	①	②	0.115	Index

858050C1

Motorcraft 2150 Specifications (cont.)

Year	(9510)* Carburetor Identification	Dry Float Level (in.)	Wet Float Level (in.)	Pump Setting Hole #⊙	Choke Plate Pulldown (in.)	Fast Idle Cam Linkage Clearance (in.)	Fast Idle (rpm)	Dechoke (in.)	Choke Setting
1981	E1AE-ZA	7/16	0.810	3	0.124	⊖	⊕	0.250	⊕
	E1AE-ADA	7/16	0.810	3	0.124	⊖	⊕	0.250	⊕
	E1AE-AEA	7/16	0.810	3	0.124	⊖	⊕	0.250	⊕
	E1AE-TA	—	0.810	2	0.104	⊖	⊕	0.250	⊕
	E1AE-UA	—	0.810	2	0.104	⊖	⊕	0.250	⊕
1982	E22E-BAA	13/32	0.780	2	0.172	⊖	1400	0.250	⊕
	E22E-BBA	13/32	0.780	2	0.172	⊖	1400	0.250	⊕
1983	E3CE-LA	7/16	0.810	3	0.103	⊖	2200	0.250	⊕
	E3CE-MA	7/16	0.810	3	0.103	⊖	2200	0.250	⊕
	E3CE-JA	7/16	0.810	3	0.103	⊖	2200	0.250	⊕
	E3CE-KA	7/16	0.810	3	0.103	⊖	2200	0.250	⊕
	E3CE-NA	7/16	0.810	3	0.120	⊖	2100	0.250	⊕
	E3CE-PA	7/16	0.810	3	0.120	⊖	2100	0.250	⊕

⊙ With link in inbound hole of pump lever
⊕ See underhood sticker
⊖ Opposite V notch

85805C2A

Motorcraft 2150 Specifications (cont.)

Year	(9510)* Carburetor Identification	Dry Float Level (in.)	Wet Float Level (in.)	Pump Setting Hole #⊙	Choke Plate Pulldown (in.)	Fast Idle Cam Linkage Clearance (in.)	Fast Idle (rpm)	Dechoke (in.)	Choke Setting
1979	D9YE-CA	7/16	13/16	2	0.118	⊖	⊕	0.115	Index
	D9YE-DA	7/16	13/16	2	0.118	⊖	⊕	0.115	Index
	D9ZE-AYA	7/16	13/16	3	0.138	⊖	⊕	0.115	Index
	D9ZE-BFB	7/16	13/16	2	0.125	⊖	⊕	—	3 Rich
	D9ZE-BGB	7/16	13/16	2	0.125	⊖	⊕	—	3 Rich
	D9ZE-BHB	7/16	13/16	2	0.125	⊖	⊕	0.250	3 Rich
	D9ZE-BJB	7/16	13/16	2	0.125	⊖	⊕	—	3 Rich
1980	E04E-PA, RA	—	13/16	2	0.104	⊖	⊕	1/4	⊕
	E0BE-AUA	—	13/16	3	0.116	⊖	⊕	1/4	⊕
	E0DE-SA, TA	—	13/16	2	0.104	⊖	⊕	1/4	⊕
	E0KE-CA, DA	—	13/16	3	0.116	⊖	⊕	1/4	⊕
	E0KE-GA, HA	—	13/16	3	0.116	⊖	⊕	1/4	⊕
	E0KE-JA, KA	—	13/16	3	0.116	⊖	⊕	1/4	⊕
	D84E-TA, UA	—	13/16	2	0.125	⊖	⊕	1/4	⊕
	E04E-ADA, AEA	—	13/16	2	0.104	⊖	⊕	1/4	⊕
	E04E-CA	—	13/16	2	0.104	⊖	⊕	1/4	⊕
	E04E-EA, FA	—	13/16	2	0.104	⊖	⊕	1/4	⊕
	E04E-JA, KA	—	13/16	2	0.137	⊖	⊕	1/4	⊕
	E04E-SA, TA	—	13/16	3	0.104	⊖	⊕	1/4	⊕
	E04E-VA, YA	—	13/16	2	0.104	⊖	⊕	1/4	⊕
	E0DE-TA, VA	—	13/16	2	0.104	⊖	⊕	1/4	⊕
	E0SE-GA, HA	—	13/16	2	0.104	⊖	⊕	1/4	⊕
	E0SE-LA, MA	—	13/16	2	0.104	⊖	⊕	1/4	⊕
	E0SE-NA	—	13/16	2	0.104	⊖	⊕	1/4	⊕
	E0SE-PA	—	13/16	2	0.104	⊖	⊕	1/4	⊕
	E0VE-FA	—	13/16	2	0.104	⊖	⊕	1/4	⊕
	E0WF-BA, CA	—	13/16	2	0.137	⊖	⊕	1/4	⊕
	D9AE-ANA, APA	—	13/16	3	0.129	⊖	⊕	1/4	⊕
	D9AE-AVA, AYA	—	13/16	3	0.129	⊖	⊕	1/4	⊕
	D0AE-AGA	—	13/16	3	0.159	⊖	⊕	1/4	⊕
1981	E1KE-CA	7/16	0.810	3	0.124	⊖	⊕	0.250	⊕
	E1KE-EA	7/16	0.810	3	0.124	⊖	⊕	0.250	⊕
	E1KE-DA	7/16	0.810	3	0.124	⊖	⊕	0.250	⊕
	E1KE-FA	7/16	0.810	3	0.124	⊖	⊕	0.250	⊕
	E1WE-FA	7/16	0.810	3	0.120	⊖	⊕	0.250	⊕
	E1WE-EA	7/16	0.810	2	0.120	⊖	⊕	0.250	⊕
	E1WE-CA	7/16	0.810	2	0.120	⊖	⊕	0.250	⊕
	E1WE-DA	7/16	0.810	2	0.120	⊖	⊕	0.250	⊕
	E1AE-YA	7/16	0.810	3	0.124	⊖	⊕	0.250	⊕

85805C2

Carter YFA Specifications

Year	Model ①	Float Level (in.)	Fast Idle Cam (in.)	Choke Plate Pulldown (in.)	Unloader (in.)	Dechoke (in.)	Choke
1983	E32E-LA	0.650	0.140	0.260	—	0.220	—
	E32E-MA	0.650	0.140	0.260	—	0.220	—
	E32E-TB	0.650	0.140	0.240	—	0.220	—
	E32E-UA	0.650	0.140	0.240	—	0.220	—
	E32E-VA	0.650	0.140	0.260	—	0.220	—
	E32E-YA	0.650	0.140	0.260	—	0.220	—
	E32E-NB	0.650	0.160	0.260	—	0.220	—
	E32E-PB	0.650	0.160	0.260	—	0.220	—
	E32E-ASA	0.650	0.160	0.260	—	0.220	—
	E32E-APA	0.650	0.140	0.240	—	0.220	—
	E32E-ARA	0.650	0.140	0.240	—	0.220	—
	E32E-ADA	0.650	0.140	0.260	—	0.220	—
	E32E-AEA	0.650	0.140	0.260	—	0.220	—
	E32E-ACA	0.650	0.140	0.260	—	0.220	—
	E32E-ATA	0.650	0.160	0.260	—	0.220	—
	E32E-ABA	0.650	0.140	0.260	—	0.220	—
	E32E-UB	0.650	0.140	0.240	—	0.220	—
	E32E-TC	0.650	0.140	0.240	—	0.220	—
1984-86	E42E-HC, DB	0.650	0.140	0.260	—	0.270	—
	E42E-MA, NA	0.650	0.140	0.240	—	0.270	—
	E42E-PA, RA	0.650	0.140	0.260	—	0.270	—
	E52E-CA	0.650	0.140	0.260	—	0.270	—
	E42E-PB, RB	0.650	0.140	0.240	—	0.270	—

① Model number located on the tag or casting

Holley 5200 (Non-Feedback) and 6500 (Feedback) Specifications

Year	Carburetor Identification	Dry Float Level (in.)	Pump Hole Setting	Choke Plate Pulldown (in.)	Fast Idle Cam Linkage (in.)	Dechoke (in.)	Choke Setting
1979	D9BE-AAA/ADA	0.460	2	0.236	0.118	0.236	2 Rich
	D9BE-ABA/ACA	0.460	2	0.236	0.118	0.236	1 Rich
	D9EE-ANA/APA	0.460	2	0.236	0.118	0.236	2 Rich
	D9ZE-MD/ND	0.460	3	0.236	0.118	0.236	2 Rich
1980	E0EE-GA/RA	0.460	2	0.197	0.079	0.197	—
	E0EE-JA/TA	0.460	2	0.197	0.079	0.197	—
	E0EE-NA/VA	0.460	2	0.236	0.118	0.394	—
	E0EE-NC/NV	0.460	2	0.236	0.118	0.157	—
	E0EE-ND/VD	0.460	2	0.236	0.118	0.393	—
	E0ZE-AAA	0.460	3	0.276	0.157	0.236	—
	E0ZE-ACA	0.460	2	0.276	0.157	0.236	—
	E0ZE-AFC/SC	0.460	—	0.236	0.118	0.393	—
1981	E1DE-DA	0.460	3	0.240	0.120	0.400	—
	E1DE-EA	0.460	3	0.240	0.120	0.400	—
	E1ZE-RA	0.460	3	0.240	0.120	0.400	—
	E1ZE-SA	0.460	3	0.240	0.120	0.400	—
	E1ZE-VA	0.460	2	0.200	0.080	0.200	—
	E1ZE-YA	0.460	2	0.200	0.080	0.200	—
1982	E2ZE-ADA	0.460	2	0.275	0.118	0.393	—
	E2ZE-APA	0.460	2	0.275	0.118	0.393	—
	E2ZE-ARA	0.460	2	0.275	0.118	0.393	—
	E2ZE-UA	0.460	3	0.275	0.118	0.393	—
	E2ZE-VA	0.460	3	0.275	0.118	0.393	—

85805C3

85805C4

Holley 1946 Specifications

Year	Part Number	Float Level (in.)	Choke Pulldown (in.)	Dechoke (in.)	Fast Idle Cam (in.)	Accelerator Pump Stroke Slot
1979	D9BE-AEA	0.69	0.080	0.150	0.055	#2
	D9BE-AHA	0.69	0.150	0.150	0.130	#2
	D9BE-AJA	0.69	0.150	0.150	0.130	#2
	D9BE-AMA	0.69	0.095	0.150	0.070	#2
	D9BE-BKA	0.69	0.080	0.150	0.055	#2
	D9BE-LA	0.69	0.080	0.150	0.055	#2
1980	E0ZE-GA	0.69	0.110	0.150	0.05-0.09	#2
	E0ZE-BBA	0.69	0.120	0.150	0.086	#2
	E0BE-CA	0.69	0.100	0.150	0.070	#2
	E0BE-AA	0.69	0.100	0.150	0.070	#2
	E0BE-AAA	0.69	0.115	0.150	0.090	#1
	E0BE-ZA	0.69	0.115	0.150	0.090	#1
	E0ZE-EA	0.69	0.110	0.150	0.070	#2
	E0ZE-DA	0.69	0.110	0.150	0.070	#2
1981	E1BE-AFA	0.69	0.113	0.150	0.082	#2
	E1BE-AKA	0.69	0.113	0.150	0.082	#2
	E0BE-CA	0.69	0.100	0.150	0.070	#2
	E0BE-AA	0.69	0.100	0.150	0.070	#2
1982	E1BE-AGA	0.69	0.120	0.150	0.086	#2
	E2BE-CA	0.69	0.110	0.150	0.078	#2
	E2BE-BA	0.69	0.110	0.150	0.078	#2
	E2BE-JA	0.69	0.110	0.150	0.078	#2
	E2BE-HA	0.69	0.110	0.150	0.078	#2
	E2BE-TA	0.69	0.110	0.150	0.078	#2
	E2BE-SA	0.69	0.110	0.150	0.078	#2

85805C5

Motorcraft Model 7200 VV Specifications

Year	Model	Float Level (in.)	Float Drop (in.)	Fast Idle Cam Setting (notches)	Cold Enrichment Metering Rod (in.)	Control Vacuum (in. H_2O)	Venturi Valve Limiter (in.)	Choke Cap Setting (notches)
1979	D9AE-ACA	1.015-1.065	1 15/32	1 Rich/3rd step	0.125	7.5	0.73-0.7 ①	Index
	D9ME-AA	1.015-1.065	1 15/32	1 Rich/3rd step	0.125	7.5	0.73-0.7 ①	Index
1980	All	1.015-1.065	1 15/32	1 Rich/3rd step	0.125	⊚	⊚	Index
1981	D9AE-AZA	1.015-1.065	1.435-1.485	1 Rich/3rd step	0.125	⊚	⊚	Index
	E1AE-LA	1.015-1.065	1.435-1.485	0.360/2nd step	⊚	⊚	⊚	1 Rich
	E1AE-SA	1.015-1.065	1.435-1.485	0.360/2nd step	⊚	⊚	⊚	1 Rich
	E1AE-KA	1.010-1.070	1.430-1.490	0.360/2nd step	⊚	⊚	⊚	Index
	E1DE-AA	1.010-1.070	1.430-1.490	0.360/2nd step	⊚	⊚	⊚	Index
	E1VE-AA	1.015-1.065	1.435-1.485	0.360/2nd step	⊚	⊚	⊚	Index
1982	E2AE-LB	1.010-1.070	1.430-1.490	0.360/2nd step	⊚	⊚	⊚	Index
	E2DE-NA	1.010-1.070	1.430-1.490	0.360/2nd step	⊚	⊚	⊚	Index
	E2AE-LC	1.010-1.070	1.430-1.490	0.360/2nd step	⊚	⊚	⊚	Index
	E2SE-FA	1.010-1.070	1.430-1.490	0.360/2nd step	⊚	⊚	⊚	Index
	E2SE-GB	1.010-1.070	1.430-1.490	0.360/2nd step	⊚	⊚	⊚	Index
	E2SE-GA	1.010-1.070	1.430-1.490	0.360/2nd step	⊚	⊚	⊚	Index
	E2AE-RA	1.010-1.070	1.430-1.490	0.360/2nd step	⊚	⊚	⊚	Index
	E1AE-ACA	1.010-1.070	1.430-1.490	0.360/2nd step	⊚	⊚	⊚	Index
	E2SE-DB	1.010-1.070	1.430-1.490	0.360/2nd step	⊚	⊚	⊚	Index
	E2SE-DA	1.010-1.070	1.430-1.490	0.360/2nd step	⊚	⊚	⊚	Index
	E1AE-SA	1.010-1.070	1.430-1.490	0.360/2nd step	⊚	⊚	⊚	1 Rich
	E2AE-MA	1.010-1.070	1.430-1.490	0.360/2nd step	⊚	⊚	⊚	1 Rich
	E2AE-MB	1.010-1.070	1.430-1.490	0.360/2nd step	⊚	⊚	⊚	1 Rich
	E2AE-TA	1.010-1.070	1.430-1.490	0.360/2nd step	⊚	⊚	⊚	Index
	E2AE-TB	1.010-1.070	1.430-1.490	0.360/2nd step	⊚	⊚	⊚	Index
	E25E-AC	1.010-1.070	1.430-1.490	0.360/2nd step	⊚	⊚	⊚	Index
	E1AE-AGA	1.010-1.070	1.430-1.490	0.360/2nd step	⊚	⊚	⊚	Index
	E2AE-NA	1.010-1.070	1.430-1.490	0.360/2nd step	⊚	⊚	⊚	Index

① Limiter Stop Setting: 0.99-1.01
② See text
③ Opening gap: 0.99-1.01
④ Closing gap: 0.39-0.41
⑤ See underhood decal
⑥ Maximum opening: 99/1.01
⑦ Wide open on throttle: 94/.98
⑧ Maximum opening: 99/1.01
⑨ Wide open on throttle: 74/.76
⑩ 0°F: 0.490 @ starting position
⑪ 75°F: 0.475 @ starting position
⑫ 0°F: 0.525 @ starting position
⑬ 75°F: 0.445 @ starting position
⑭ Maximum opening: 99/1.01
⑮ Wide open on throttle: 39/.41

⑯ 0°F: 0.490 @ starting position
⑰ 75°F: 0.445 @ starting position
⑱ 0°F: 0.525 @ starting position
⑲ 75°F: 0.475 @ starting position
⑳ 0°F: 0.490 @ starting position
㉑ 75°F: 0.460 @ starting position
㉒ Maximum opening: 99/1.01
㉓ Wide open on throttle: 74/.76
㉔ Maximum opening: 99/1.01
㉕ Wide open on throttle: 48/.52

85805C8

Holley 4180 Specifications

Year	(9510)* Carburetor Identification	Dry Float Level (in.)	Wet Float Level (in.)	Pump Setting Hole	Choke Plate Pulldown	Fast Idle Cam Linkage Clearance	Fast Idle (rpm)	Dechoke (in.)	Choke Setting
1983-85	E32E-AUA	⊙	⊙	#1	0.195-0.215	NA	⊙	0.300	3 Rich
	E32E-BGA	⊙	⊙	#1	0.195-0.215	NA	⊙	0.300	3 Rich
	E32E-AUB	⊙	⊙	#1	0.205	NA	⊙	0.300	3 Rich
	E32E-BGB	⊙	⊙	#1	0.205	NA	⊙	0.300	3 Rich
	E4ZE-SA	⊙	⊙	#1	0.195-0.215	NA	⊙	0.300	1 Lean

NA—Not available
⊙ Bottom of sight plug
⊙ See text
⊙ See underhood sticker

85805C6

Motorcraft Model 2700 VV Specifications

Year	Model	Float Level (in.)	Float Drop (in.)	Fast Idle Cam Setting (notches)	Cold Enrichment Metering Rod (in.)	Control Vacuum (in. H$_2$O)	Venturi Valve Limiter (in.)	Choke Cap Setting (notches)	Control Vacuum Regulator Setting (in.)
1979	D9ZE-LB	1³/₆₄	1¹⁵/₃₂	1 Rich/2nd step	0.125	①	②	Index	0.230
	D84E-KA	1³/₆₄	1¹⁵/₃₂	1 Rich/3rd step	0.125	5.5	6¹/₆₄	Index	—
1980	All	1³/₆₄	1¹⁵/₃₂	1 Rich/4th step	0.125	③	④	⑤	0.075
1981	E1AE-AAA	1.010–1.070	1.430–1.490	1 Rich/4th step	⑥	③	④	Index	—
	D9AE-AZA	1.015–1.065	1.435–1.485	1 Rich/4th step	0.125	③	④	Index	—

① Venturi Air Bypass: 6.8–7.3
  Venturi Valve Diaphragm: 4.6–5.1
② Limter Setting: .38–.42
  Limiter Stop Setting: .73–.77
③ See text
④ Opening gap: 0.99–1.01
  Closing gap: 0.94–0.98
⑤ See underhood decal
⑥ 0°F: 0.490 @ starting position
  75°F: 0.475 @ starting position

858050C7

CENTRAL FUEL INJECTION (CFI) SYSTEM

Description

Central Fuel Injection (CFI) is a throttle body injection system in which two fuel injectors are mounted in a common throttle body, spraying fuel down through the throttle valves at the bottom of the body and into the intake manifold.

All 1984–86 models with CFI are equipped with two electric pumps. A low pressure pump is mounted in the tank and a high pressure pump is externally mounted.

Electric fuel pump circuits are equipped with an interlock system which provides power to the pump during start–up, through the starter relay, and provides operating voltage during engine operation. Should the engine lose oil pressure, the pump is automatically disconnected, stopping the engine.

Fuel is supplied from the fuel tank by the combination of a low pressure, in–tank fuel pump and a high pressure, in–line fuel pump. The fuel passes through a filter and is sent to the throttle body where a regulator keeps the fuel delivery pressure at a constant 39 psi. The two fuel injectors are mounted vertically above the throttle plates and are connected in line with the fuel pressure regulator. Excess fuel supplied by the pump, but not needed by the engine, is returned to the fuel tank by a steel fuel return line.

The fuel injection system is linked with and controlled by the Electronic Engine Control (EEC) system.

Relieving Fuel System Pressure

➡On vehicles with fuel injected engines, fuel lines remain pressurized even after the ignition is switched off. Therefore, it is critical to relieve pressure from the fuel system before disconnecting any fuel line or component.

On 6–232 and 8–302 engines with CFI, relieve the system pressure at the pressure relief valve mounted on the throttle body. (This valve can be located after removing the air cleaner assembly.) Use Pressure Gauge Tool no. T80L–9974–A, or equivalent, and drain the system through the drain tube.

Electric Fuel Pump

Although Mustang and Capri employed carbureted fuel systems prior to 1984, some 1980 vehicles with the 4–140 turbo engine and automatic transmission were equipped with an early version of CFI (known then as Electronic Fuel Injection). As a result, these models also utilized an electric fuel pump, instead of the traditional low pressure, mechanical pump. Unlike the typical high pressure fuel pumps found on fuel injected systems of the mid–to–late 1980's, the electric pump used in 1980 was a low pressure in–tank version, which did not feed an external, high pressure pump. (This configuration represents an exception, however, as most fuel injected systems in subsequent years utilized either a single, in–tank high pressure pump or a combination of an in–tank low pressure pump and an external high pressure fuel pump.)

REMOVAL & INSTALLATION

✳✳ CAUTION

Before servicing any part of the fuel injection, it is necessary to depressurize the system. A special tool is available for testing and bleeding the system.

Low Pressure In–Tank Fuel Pump—1980 and 1984–86

▶ See Figures 44 and 45

1. Disconnect the negative battery cable.
2. Depressurize the system and drain as much gas from the tank as possible by pumping it out through the filler neck.
3. Raise and support the rear end on jackstands.
4. Disconnect the fuel supply, return and vent lines at the right and left side of the frame.
5. Disconnect the wiring to the fuel pump.
6. Support the gas tank, loosen and remove the mounting straps. Remove the gas tank.
7. Disconnect the lines and harness at the pump flange.
8. Clean the outside of the mounting flange and retaining ring. Turn the fuel pump lock ring counterclockwise and remove.
9. Remove the fuel pump.
10. Clean the mounting surfaces. Put a light coat of grease on the mounting surfaces and on the new sealing ring. Install the new fuel pump.
11. Installation is in the reverse order of removal. Fill the tank with at least 10 gallons of gas. Turn the ignition key **ON** for three seconds. Repeat 6 or 7

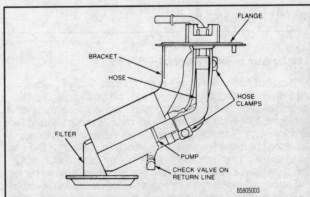

FLANGE
BRACKET
HOSE
HOSE CLAMPS
FILTER
PUMP
CHECK VALVE ON RETURN LINE

85805003

Fig. 44 Low pressure in–tank electric fuel pump used with the 4–140 turbo engine equipped with an automatic transmission

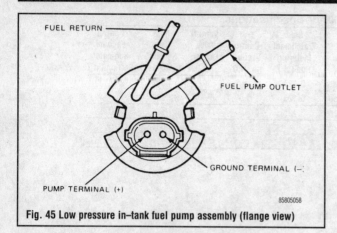

Fig. 45 Low pressure in–tank fuel pump assembly (flange view)

times until the fuel system is pressurized. Check for any fitting leaks. Start the engine and check for leaks.

High Pressure In–Line Fuel Pump—1984–86

♦ **See Figure 46**

1. Disconnect the negative battery cable.
2. Depressurize the fuel system.
3. Raise and support the rear of the vehicle on jackstands.
4. Disconnect the inlet and outlet fuel lines.
5. Disconnect the electrical harness connection.
6. Bend down the retaining tab and remove the pump from the mounting bracket ring.
7. Install in the reverse order, making sure the pump is indexed correctly in the mounting bracket insulator.

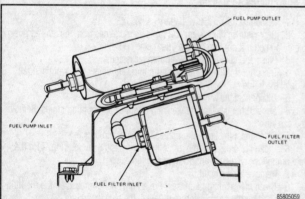

Fig. 46 High pressure in–line electric fuel pump and fuel filter assembly

TESTING AND ADJUSTMENT

Low Pressure In-Tank Fuel Pump—1984–86

Disconnect the electrical connector at the fuel pump. Connect a voltmeter to the body wiring harness connector. Turn the key **ON** while watching the voltmeter. The voltage should rise to battery voltage, then return to zero after about one second. If the voltage is not as specified, check the inertia switch and the electrical system. Connect an ohmmeter to the in–line pump wiring harness connector. If no continuity is present, check the continuity directly at the in–line pump terminals. If there is no continuity at the in–line pump terminals, replace the in-line pump. If continuity is present, service or replace the wiring harness.

Connect an ohmmeter across the body wiring harness connector. If continuity is present (about 5 ohms), the low pressure pump circuit is OK. If no conti-

nuity is present, remove the fuel tank and check for continuity at the in–tank pump flange terminals on top of the tank. If continuity is absent at the in–tank pump flange terminals, replace the assembly. If continuity is present at the in–tank pump, but not in the harness connector, service or replace the wiring harness at the in–tank pump.

High Pressure In–Line Fuel Pump—1984–86

Disconnect the electrical connector at the fuel pump. Connect a voltmeter to the body wiring harness connector. Turn the key **ON** while watching the voltmeter. The voltage should rise to battery voltage, then return to zero after about one second. If the voltage is not as specified, check the inertia switch and the electrical system. Connect an ohmmeter to the in–line pump wiring harness connector. If no continuity is present, check the continuity directly at the in–line pump terminals. If there is no continuity at the in–line pump terminals, replace the in–line pump. If continuity is present, service or replace the wiring harness.

Connect an ohmmeter across the body wiring harness connector. If continuity is present (about 5 ohms), the low pressure pump circuit is OK. If no continuity is present, remove the fuel tank and check for continuity at the in–tank pump flange terminals on top of the tank. If continuity is absent at the in–tank pump flange terminals, replace the assembly. If continuity is present at the in–tank pump, but not in the harness connector, service or replace the wiring harness at the in–tank pump.

Fuel Charging Assembly

♦ **See Figures 47 and 48**

The fuel charging throttle body mounts to the conventional carburetor pad of the intake manifold. Mounted above the throttle body is the fuel charging main body. This fuel charging assembly is comprised of six types of components which precisely allocate fuel and air to the engine. The result is an ideal ratio for providing performance and economy, while controlling exhaust emissions. The six types of components are:
- butterfly valves
- fuel injector nozzles
- fuel pressure regulator
- fuel pressure diagnostic valve
- cold engine speed control (or idle speed controller DC motor actuator)
- throttle position sensor

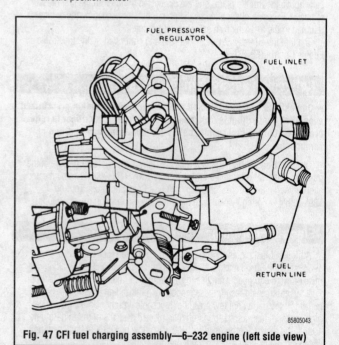

Fig. 47 CFI fuel charging assembly—6–232 engine (left side view)

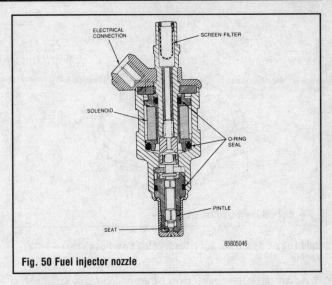

Fig. 48 CFI fuel charging assembly—6–232 engine (front view)

DESCRIPTION

Butterfly Valves (Air Flow Control)

▶ See Figure 49

The two butterfly valves, which are mounted in a two–piece, die–cast aluminum housing called the throttle body, control air flow to the engine. The butterfly valves, or throttle valves, are identical in design to the throttle plates of a conventional carburetor and are actuated by a similar linkage and pedal cable arrangement.

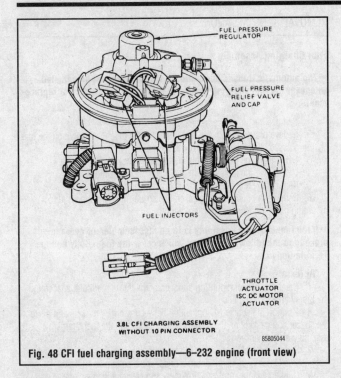

Fig. 49 Air flow control

Fuel Injector Nozzles

▶ See Figure 50

The two fuel injector nozzles, which are mounted in the throttle body, are electro–mechanical devices that meter and atomize the fuel delivered to the engine. The injector valve bodies consist of a solenoid actuated pintle and needle valve assembly. An electrical control signal from the EEC electronic processor activates the solenoid, causing the pintle to move inward off its seat, allowing fuel to flow. The fuel flow through the injector is controlled by the amount of time the injector solenoid holds the pintle off its seat.

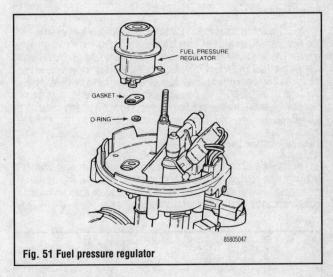

Fig. 50 Fuel injector nozzle

Fuel Pressure Regulator

▶ See Figure 51

The fuel pressure regulator is mounted on the throttle body. The regulator smooths out fuel pressure drops from the fuel pump. It is not sensitive to back pressure in the return line to the tank.

A second function of the pressure regulator is to maintain fuel supply pressure upon engine and fuel pump shut down. The regulator acts as a check valve and traps fuel between itself and the fuel pump. This promotes rapid start ups and helps prevent fuel vapor formation in the lines, or vapor lock. The regulator makes sure that the pressure of the fuel at the injector nozzles stays at a constant 39 psi.

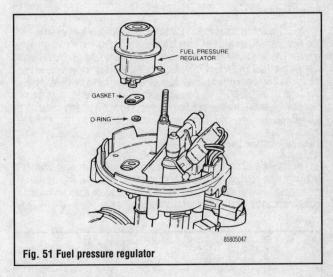

Fig. 51 Fuel pressure regulator

Fuel Pressure Diagnostic Valve

▶ See Figure 52

A Schrader–type diagnostic pressure valve is located at the top of the throttle body. This valve can be used by service personnel to monitor fuel pressure, bleed down the system pressure prior to maintenance and to bleed out air which may have been introduced during assembly or filter servicing. A special Ford Tool (T80L–9974–A) is used to accomplish these procedures.

✳✳ CAUTION

Under no circumstances should compressed air be forced into the fuel system using the diagnostic valve.

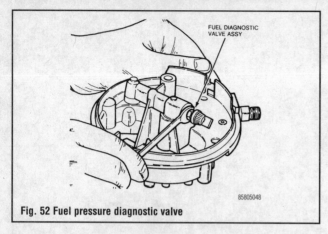

Fig. 52 Fuel pressure diagnostic valve

Cold Engine Speed Control (Throttle Stop Cam Positioner)—8–302 engine

The cold engine speed control serves the same purpose as the fast idle speed device on a carbureted engine, which is to raise engine speed during cold engine idle. A throttle stop cam positioner is used on the 8–302 engine. The cam is positioned by a bimetal spring and an electric heating element. The cold engine speed control is attached to the throttle body. As the engine heats up, the fast idle cam on the cold engine speed control is gradually repositioned by the bimetal spring, heating element and EEC computer until normal idle speed is reached. The EEC computer automatically kicks down the fast idle cam to a lower step (lower engine speed) by supplying vacuum to the automatic kickdown motor which physically moves the high speed cam a predetermined time after the engine starts.

Idle Speed Controller (ISC) DC Motor Actuator—6–232 engine

▶ See Figure 53

The DC motor actuator controls idle speed by modulating the throttle lever. The resulting airflow regulation permits the desired engine rpm for warm engine operation, as well as the additional engine speed required during cold engine idle. An Idle Tracking Switch (ITS), integral to the DC motor, determines when the throttle lever has contacted the actuator, thereby signaling the need to control engine rpm. The DC motor extends or retracts a linear shaft through a gear reduction system. The motor direction is determined by the polarity of the applied voltage.

Throttle Position Sensor

This sensor is attached to the throttle body and is used to monitor changes in throttle plate position. The throttle position sensor sends this information to the computer, which uses it to select proper air/fuel mixture, spark timing and EGR control under different engine operating conditions.

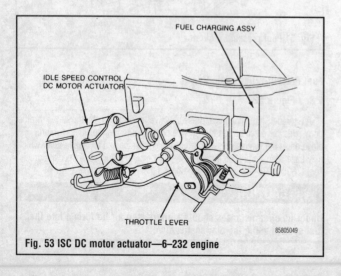

Fig. 53 ISC DC motor actuator—6–232 engine

Fuel Charging Assembly

➡**The automatic transmission throttle valve lever must be adjusted whenever the fuel charging assembly is removed for service or replacement.**

1. Remove the air cleaner assembly.
2. Relieve pressure from the fuel system at the diagnostic valve on the fuel charging assembly, as described above.
3. Disconnect the throttle cable and transmission throttle valve lever.
4. Disconnect the fuel, vacuum and electrical connections.
5. Remove the fuel charging assembly retaining nuts.
6. Remove the fuel charging assembly, spacer (if so equipped), and mounting gasket(s) from the intake manifold.

➡**If the fuel charging assembly is to be disassembled or overhauled, proceed to the following sections which cover the Main Body and the Throttle Body.**

To install:

7. Clean the gasket mounting surfaces of the intake manifold, spacer and the fuel charging assembly.
8. Position the spacer (if applicable) between two new gaskets and place the spacer and gaskets on the intake manifold. Position the fuel charging assembly on the gasket.
9. Secure the fuel charging assembly with the attaching nuts. Snug the nuts, then alternately tighten them in a criss–cross pattern to 10 ft. lbs.
10. Connect the fuel and vacuum lines, and electrical connectors.
11. Connect the throttle cable and transmission throttle valve lever.
12. Start the engine and check for leaks. Adjust engine idle speed, if necessary.
13. Install the air cleaner assembly.

Main Body

▶ See Figures 54 thru 59

1. Remove the air cleaner mounting stud, in order to separate the main (upper) body from the throttle body.
2. Turn the fuel charging assembly over and remove the four screws from the bottom of the throttle body.
3. Separate the throttle body (lower section) from the main body.
4. Remove the old gasket. If it is stuck and scraping is necessary, use only a plastic or wood scraper. Take care not to damage the gasket surfaces.
5. Remove the three pressure regulator mounting screws. Remove the pressure regulator, gasket and O–ring.
6. Disconnect the electrical connectors at each injector by pulling outward on the connector, and not on the wire. Loosen, but do not remove, the wiring harness retaining screw(s). Push in on the harness tabs to remove it from the upper body.
7. Remove the fuel injector retaining fastener. Remove the injector retainer.
8. Pull the injectors, one at a time, from the upper body. Mark the injectors for identification, since they must be reinstalled in the same position (choke or

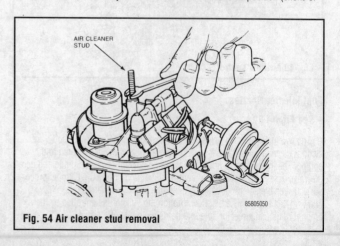

Fig. 54 Air cleaner stud removal

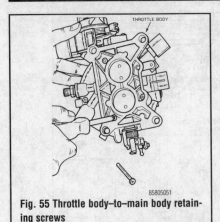

Fig. 55 Throttle body–to–main body retaining screws

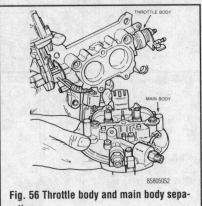

Fig. 56 Throttle body and main body separation

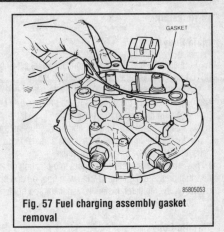

Fig. 57 Fuel charging assembly gasket removal

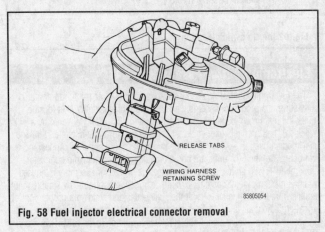

Fig. 58 Fuel injector electrical connector removal

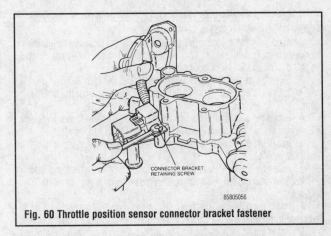

Fig. 60 Throttle position sensor connector bracket fastener

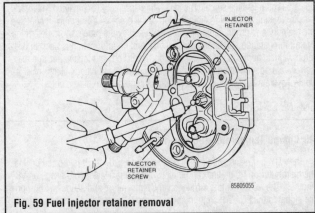

Fig. 59 Fuel injector retainer removal

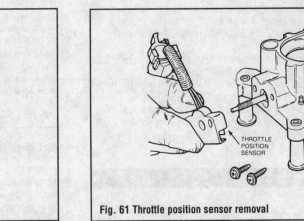

Fig. 61 Throttle position sensor removal

throttle side). Each injector is equipped with a small O–ring. If the O–ring does not come out with the injector, carefully pick it out of the cavity in the throttle body.

9. Using a wrench, unscrew the fuel pressure diagnostic valve assembly.

Throttle Body

▸ **See Figures 60 and 61**

1. Note the position of the index mark on the choke cap housing. Remove the choke cap retainer screws or rivets.

2. Remove the choke cap retaining ring, choke cap and gasket, if so equipped.

3. Remove the thermostat lever screw and lever, if so equipped.

4. Remove the fast idle cam assembly and control rod positioner, if so equipped.

➡The Idle Speed Controller (ISC) system is used on the 6–232 engine, in place of the choke pulldown system.

5. Hold the control diaphragm cover in position, if so equipped, and remove the two mounting screws. Carefully remove the cover, spring and pull down diaphragm.

6. Remove the fast idle retaining nut, fast idle cam adjuster lever, fast idle lever, spring and E–clip.

7. Remove the throttle position sensor connector bracket fastener. Mark the throttle body and throttle position sensor for correct installation position. Remove the throttle position sensor retaining screws and slide the sensor off of the throttle shaft.

8. Remove the throttle positioner mounting bolt and remove the throttle positioner, if so equipped. (If equipped instead with an ISC DC motor actuator, remove the mounting bolts and the motor.)

9. Perform any necessary cleaning or repair.

To install:

Main Body

1. Install the fuel pressure diagnostic valve assembly. Tighten the valve to 48–84 inch lbs. and the cap to 5–10 inch lbs.

2. Lubricate new injector O–rings with a light grade oil and install one on each injector. Install the injectors in their appropriate choke or throttle side position. Use a light, twisting, pushing motion to seat the injectors.

3. Install the injector retainer and tighten the fastener to 30–60 inch lbs.

4. Install the injector wiring harness and snap into position. Tighten the harness retaining screw(s) to 8–10 inch lbs.

5. Snap the electrical connectors into position on the injectors. Lubricate a new fuel pressure regulator O–ring with light oil and install the O–ring and new gasket on the regulator. Install the regulator and tighten the retaining screws to 27–40 inch lbs.

Throttle Body

1. Install the throttle positioner or ISC DC motor onto the throttle body. Tighten the mounting bolt(s) to 32–44 inch lbs.

2. Hold the throttle sensor (potentiometer) with the location identification mark (see step 7, above) in the 12 o'clock position. The two rotary tangs should be at 3 o'clock and 9 o'clock positions.

3. Slide the sensor onto the throttle shaft with the identification mark still in the 12 o'clock position. Hold the sensor firmly against the throttle body.

4. Rotate the sensor until the identification marks on the sensor and body are aligned. Install the retaining screws and tighten to 11–16 inch lbs.

5. Install the throttle position sensor connector bracket fastener and tighten to 18–22 inch lbs.

6. Install the E–clip, fast idle lever and spring, fast idle adjustment lever and fast idle retaining nut, if so equipped. Tighten the retaining nut to 16–20 inch lbs.

7. Install the pull down diaphragm, spring and cover, if so equipped. Hold the cover in position and tighten the retaining screws to 13–19 inch lbs.

8. Install the fast idle control rod positioner, fast idle cam and thermostat lever, if so equipped. Tighten the retaining screw to 13–19 inch lbs.

9. Install the choke cap gasket, if so equipped, and the choke cap and retaining ring. Be sure that the choke cap bimetal spring is properly inserted between the fingers of the thermostat lever.

10. Install the choke cap retaining screws loosely and rotate the cap so that the index mark is properly aligned. Tighten the screws 13–18 inch lbs. If equipped with rivets, install new rivets and snug them with the rivet gun. Do not break off the rivets until the choke cap's index mark is properly aligned.

11. Install a new gasket between the main body and the throttle body. Place the throttle body on the main body and install the four retaining screws loosely. Install the air cleaner stud and tighten to 70–95 inch lbs. Tighten the four retaining screws to 27–40 inch lbs.

Fuel System Inertia Switch

▶ **See Figure 62**

In the event of a collision, the electrical contacts in the inertia switch open and the fuel pump automatically shuts off. The fuel pump will shut off even if the engine does not stop running. The engine, however, will stop a few seconds after the fuel pump stops. It is not possible to restart the engine until the inertia switch is manually reset. The switch is located in the luggage compartment on the left hinge support of 2–door sedans or in the spare tire well of 3–door sedans. To reset, depress the button on top of the switch.

➡**In the reset position, the button can be depressed an additional 1.5mm (¹⁄₁₆ inch) against a spring. This is a normal condition.**

✷✷ CAUTION

Do not reset the inertia switch until the complete fuel system has been inspected for leaks.

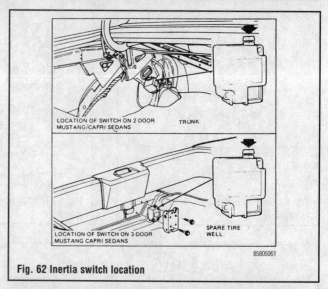

Fig. 62 Inertia switch location

Electronic Control Assembly (ECA)

The Electronic Control Assembly (ECA) is a solid–state micro–computer consisting of a processor assembly and a calibration assembly. It is located under the instrument panel or passenger's seat and is usually covered by a kick panel. 1981–82 models use an EEC–III engine control system, while 1983 and later models use EEC–IV. Although the two systems are similar in appearance and operation, the ECA units are not interchangeable. A multi-pin connector links the ECA with all system components. The processor assembly is housed in an aluminum case. It contains circuits designed to continuously sample input signals from the engine sensors. It then calculates and sends out proper control signals to adjust air/fuel ratio, spark timing and emission system operation. The processor also provides a continuous reference voltage to the B/MAP, EVP and TPS sensors. EEC–III reference voltage is 8–10 volts, while EEC–IV systems use a 5–volt reference signal. The calibration assembly is contained in a black plastic housing which plugs into the top of the processor assembly. It contains the memory and programming information used by the processor to determine optimum operating conditions. Different calibration information is used in different vehicle applications, such as California or Federal models. For this reason, careful identification of the engine, year, model and type of electronic control system is essential to insure correct component replacement.

ENGINE SENSORS

Air Charge Temperature Sensor (ACT)

The ACT is threaded into the intake manifold air runner. It is located behind the distributor on V6 engines and directly below the accelerator linkage on V8 engines. The ACT monitors air/fuel charge temperature and sends an appropriate signal to the ECA. This information is used to correct fuel enrichment for variations in intake air density due to temperature changes.

Barometric & Manifold Absolute Pressure Sensors (B/MAP)

The B/MAP sensor on V8 engines is located on the right fender panel in the engine compartment. The MAP sensor used on V6 engines is separate from the barometric sensor and is located on the left fender panel in the engine compartment. The barometric sensor signals the ECA of changes in atmospheric pressure and density to regulate calculated air flow into the engine. The MAP sensor monitors and signals the ECA of changes in intake manifold pressure which result from engine load, speed and atmospheric pressure changes.

Crankshaft Position (CP) Sensor

The purpose of the CP sensor is to provide the ECA with an accurate ignition timing reference (when the piston reaches 10°BTDC) and injector operation information (twice each crankshaft revolution). The crankshaft vibration damper is fitted with a 4–lobe pulse ring. As the crankshaft rotates, the pulse ring lobes interrupt the magnetic field at the tip of the CP sensor.

EGR Valve Position Sensor (EVP)

This sensor, mounted on EGR valve, signals the computer of EGR opening so that it may subtract EGR flow from total air flow into the manifold. In this way, EGR flow is excluded from air flow information used to determine mixture requirements.

Engine Coolant Temperature Sensor (ECT)

The ECT is threaded into the intake manifold water jacket directly above the water pump bypass hose. The ECT monitors coolant temperature and signals the ECA, which then uses these signals for mixture enrichment (during cool operation), ignition timing and EGR operation. The resistance value of the ECT increases with temperature, causing a voltage signal drop as the engine warms up.

Exhaust Gas Oxygen Sensor (EGO)

The EGO is mounted in the right side exhaust manifold on V8 engines, in the left and right side exhaust manifolds on V6 models. The EGO monitors oxygen content of exhaust gases and sends a constantly changing voltage signal to the ECA. The ECA analyzes this signal and adjusts the air/fuel mixture to obtain the optimum (stoichiometric) ratio.

Knock Sensor (KS)

This sensor is used on various models equipped with the 6–232 engine. It is attached to the intake manifold in front of the ACT sensor. The KS detects engine vibrations caused by preignition or detonation and provides information to the ECA, which then retards the timing to eliminate detonation.

Thick Film Integrated Module Sensor (TFI)

The TFI module sensor plugs into the distributor just below the distributor cap and replaces the CP sensor on some engines. Its function is to provide the ECA with ignition timing information, similar to what the CP sensor provides.

Throttle Position Sensor (TPS)

The TPS is mounted on the right side of the throttle body, directly connected to the throttle shaft. The TPS senses the throttle movement and position, and transmits an appropriate electrical signal to the ECA. These signals are used by the ECA to adjust the air/fuel mixture, spark timing and EGR operation according to engine load at idle, part throttle, or full throttle. The TPS is nonadjustable.

CFI COMPONENT TESTING

➡Diagnostic and test procedures on the EEC–III and EEC–IV electronic control systems require the use of special test equipment. Have these systems tested professionally.

Before beginning any component testing, always check the following:
• Check the fuel and ignition systems to ensure that there is fuel and spark.
• Remove the air cleaner assembly and inspect all vacuum and pressure hoses for proper connection to fittings. Check for damaged or pinched hoses.
• Inspect all sub–system wiring harnesses for proper connections to the EGR solenoid valves, injectors, sensors, etc.
• Check for loose or detached connectors and broken or detached wires. Check that all terminals are seated firmly and are not corroded. Look for partially broken or frayed wires or any shorting between the wires.
• Inspect the sensors for physical damage. Inspect the vehicle electrical system. Check the battery for full charge and cable connections for tightness.
• Inspect the relay connector and make sure the ECA power relay is securely attached and making a good ground connection.

Solenoid and Sensor Resistance Tests

All CFI components must be disconnected from the circuit before testing the resistance with a suitable ohmmeter. Replace any component whose measured resistance does not agree with the specifications chart. Shorting the wiring harness across a solenoid valve can burn out the circuitry in the ECA that controls

the solenoid valve actuator. Exercise caution when testing the solenoid valves to avoid accidental damage to the ECA.

Fuel Pressure Tests

The diagnostic pressure valve (Schrader type) is located at the top of the fuel charging main body. This valve provides a convenient point for service personnel to monitor fuel pressure, bleed down the system pressure prior to maintenance, and to bleed out air which may become trapped in the system during filter replacement. A pressure gauge with an adapter is required to perform pressure tests.

✳✳ CAUTION

Under no circumstances should compressed air be forced into the fuel system using the diagnostic valve. Depressing the pin in the diagnostic valve will relieve system pressure by expelling fuel into the throttle body.

System Pressure Test

Testing fuel pressure requires the use of a special pressure gauge (T80L–9974–A or equivalent) that attaches to the diagnostic pressure tap on the fuel charging assembly. Depressurize the fuel system before disconnecting any lines.
1. Disconnect the fuel return line at the throttle body (in–tank high pressure pump) and connect the hose to a 1–quart calibrated container. Connect a pressure gauge.
2. Disconnect the electrical connector at the fuel pump. The connector is located ahead of the fuel tank (in–tank high pressure pump) or just forward of the pump outlet (in–line high pressure pump). Connect an auxiliary wiring harness to the connector of the fuel pump. Energize the pump for 10 seconds by applying 12 volts to the auxiliary harness connector, allowing the fuel to drain into the calibrated container. Note the fuel volume and pressure gauge reading.
3. Correct fuel pressure should be 35–45 psi (241–310 kPa). Fuel volume should be 10 oz. in 10 seconds (minimum) and fuel pressure should maintain a minimum of 30 psi (206 kPa) immediately after pump cut–off.

If the pressure condition is met, but the fuel flow is not, check for blocked filter(s) and fuel supply lines. After correcting the problem, repeat the test procedure. If the fuel flow is still inadequate, replace the high pressure pump. If the flow specification is met but the pressure is not, check for a worn or damaged pressure regulator valve on the throttle body. If both the pressure and fuel flow specifications are met, but the pressure drops excessively after de–energizing, check for a leaking injector valve(s) and/or pressure regulator valve. If the injector valves and pressure regulator valve are okay, replace the high pressure pump. If no pressure or flow is seen in the fuel system, check for blocked filters and fuel lines. If no trouble is found, replace the in–line fuel pump, in–tank fuel pump and the fuel filter inside the tank.

Fuel Injector Pressure Test

1. Connect pressure gauge T80L–9974–A, or equivalent, to the fuel pressure test fitting. Disconnect the coil connector from the coil. Disconnect the electrical lead from one injector and pressurize the fuel system. Disable the fuel pump by disconnecting the inertia switch or the fuel pump relay and observe the pressure gauge reading.
2. Crank the engine for 2 seconds. Turn the ignition OFF and wait 5 seconds, then observe the pressure drop. If the pressure drop is 2–16 psi (14–110 kPa), the injector is operating properly. Reconnect the injector, activate the fuel pump, then repeat the procedure for the other injector.
3. If the pressure drop is less than 2 psi (14 kPa) or more than 16 psi (110 kPa), switch the electrical connectors on the injectors and repeat the test. If the pressure drop is still incorrect, replace the disconnected injector with one of the same color code, then reconnect both injectors properly and repeat the test.
4. Disconnect and plug the vacuum hose at the EGR valve. It may be necessary to disconnect the idle speed control (6–232) or the throttle kicker solenoid (8–302) and use the throttle body stop screw to set the engine speed. Start and run the engine at 1,800 rpm (2,000 rpm on 1984 and later models). Disconnect the left injector electrical connector. Note the rpm after the engine stabilizes around 1,200 rpm. Reconnect the injector and allow the engine to return to high idle.
5. Perform the same procedure for the right injector. Note the difference between the rpm readings of the left and right injectors. If the difference is 100 rpm or less, check the oxygen sensor. If the difference is more than 100 rpm, replace both injectors.

ELECTRONIC MULTI–POINT (EFI) AND SEQUENTIAL (SEFI) FUEL INJECTION SYSTEMS

Description

The Electronic Fuel Injection (EFI) system is classified as a multi–point, pulse time, mass air flow (or speed density control) fuel injection system. Fuel is metered into the intake air stream in accordance with engine demand through four injectors mounted on a tuned intake manifold. In addition, a blow–through turbocharger system is utilized on 1984—86 4–140 engines to reduce fuel delivery time and increase power.

The Sequential Electronic Fuel Injection (SEFI) system is classified as a multi–point, pulse time, speed density control, fuel injection system. Fuel is metered into each intake port in sequence with the engine firing order, in accordance with engine demand through eight injectors mounted on a tuned intake manifold.

An on–board vehicle electronic engine control (EEC) computer accepts input from various engine sensors to compute the required fuel flow rate necessary to maintain a prescribed air/fuel ratio throughout the entire engine operational range. The computer then outputs a command to the fuel injectors to meter the approximate quantity of fuel.

The EFI fuel delivery sub–system consists of a high pressure, chassis–mounted, electric fuel pump delivering fuel from the fuel tank through a 20 micron fuel filter to a fuel charging manifold assembly. The SEFI fuel delivery sub–system consists of a low pressure in–tank mounted fuel pump, a fuel filter/reservoir and a high pressure electric fuel pump delivering fuel from the fuel tank through a 20 micron fuel filter to a fuel charging manifold assembly.

The fuel charging manifold assembly incorporates electrically actuated fuel injectors directly above each of the engine's intake ports. The injectors, when energized, spray a metered quantity of fuel into the intake air stream.

A constant fuel pressure drop is maintained across the injector nozzles by a pressure regulator. The regulator is connected in series with the fuel injectors and positioned downstream from them. Excess fuel supplied by the pump, but not required by the engine, passes through the regulator and returns to the fuel tank through a fuel return line.

All EFI injectors are energized simultaneously, once every crankshaft revolution. SEFI injectors, on the other hand, are energized in sequence with the engine firing order, either once every crankshaft revolution (1986–87) or every other revolution (1988 models). The period of time that the injectors are energized (injector on–time or the pulse width) is controlled by the vehicle's Engine Electronic Control (EEC) computer, which responds to input from various engine sensors. In this manner, the EEC computer determines the required fuel flow rate, in order to maintain a prescribed air/fuel ratio throughout the entire engine operational range. In addition, on turbocharged models, air entering the engine is measured by a vane air flow meter, located between the air cleaner and the fuel charging manifold assembly. This air flow information is used in conjunction with input from the other engine sensors to compute the required fuel flow rate. The computer determines the needed injector pulse width and outputs a command to the injector to meter the exact quantity of fuel.

Relieving Fuel System Pressure

➡On vehicles with fuel injected engines, fuel lines remain pressurized even after the ignition is switched off. Therefore, it is critical to relieve pressure from the fuel system before disconnecting any fuel line or component.

As a safety feature, electronic fuel injected engines are equipped with a pressure relief valve. On the 4–140 engine with EFI, this valve is located in the flexible fuel supply tube approximately 12 in. (305mm) back from where it connects to the engine fuel rail, on the driver's side of the engine compartment. On the 8–302 engine with SEFI, the valve is located in the metal fuel line at the left front corner of the engine. Before opening the fuel system on EFI or SEFI engines, relieve fuel pressure as follows:

1. Remove the fuel tank cap.
2. Disconnect the vacuum hose from the fuel pressure regulator located on the engine fuel rail.
3. Using a hand vacuum pump, apply about 25 in. Hg pressure to the pressure regulator. Fuel pressure will be released into the fuel tank through the fuel return hose.

Electric Fuel Pump

All 1984–86 EFI and 1986–88 SEFI models are equipped with two electric pumps. A low pressure pump is mounted in the tank and a high pressure pump is externally mounted.

All 1987–88 EFI models are equipped with a single, in–tank, high pressure fuel pump.

Regardless of the design, all of these electric fuel pump circuits are equipped with an interlock system which provides power to the pump during start–up, through the starter relay, and provides operating voltage during engine operation. Should the engine lose oil pressure, the pump is automatically disconnected, stopping the engine.

REMOVAL & INSTALLATION

✳✳ CAUTION

Before servicing any part of the fuel injection, it is necessary to depressurize the system. A special tool is available for testing and bleeding the system.

Low Pressure In–Tank Fuel Pump—1984–88

▶ See Figure 63

1. Disconnect the negative battery cable.
2. Depressurize the system and drain as much gas from the tank as possible by pumping it out through the filler neck.
3. Raise and support the rear end on jackstands.
4. Disconnect the fuel supply, return and vent lines at the right and left side of the frame.
5. Disconnect the wiring to the fuel pump.
6. Support the gas tank, loosen and remove the mounting straps. Remove the gas tank.
7. Disconnect the lines and harness at the pump flange.
8. Clean the outside of the mounting flange and retaining ring. Turn the fuel pump lock ring counterclockwise and remove.
9. Remove the fuel pump.
10. Clean the mounting surfaces. Put a light coat of grease on the mounting surfaces and on the new sealing ring. Install the new fuel pump.
11. Installation is in the reverse order of removal. If you have a single high pressure pump system, fill the tank with at least 10 gallons of gas. Turn the ignition key ON for three seconds. Repeat 6 or 7 times until the fuel system is pressurized. Check for any fitting leaks. Start the engine and check for leaks.

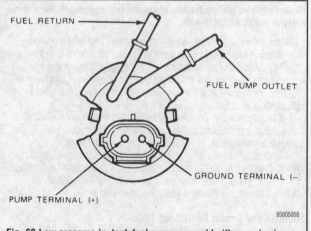

FUEL RETURN

FUEL PUMP OUTLET

GROUND TERMINAL (–)

PUMP TERMINAL (+)

85805058

Fig. 63 Low pressure in–tank fuel pump assembly (flange view)

High Pressure External Fuel Pump—1984–88

▶ **See Figure 64**

1. Disconnect the negative battery cable.
2. Depressurize the fuel system.
3. Raise and support the rear of the vehicle on jackstands.
4. Disconnect the inlet and outlet fuel lines.
5. Disconnect the electrical harness connection.
6. Bend down the retaining tab and remove the pump from the mounting bracket ring.
7. Install in reverse order, making sure the pump is indexed correctly in the mounting bracket insulator.

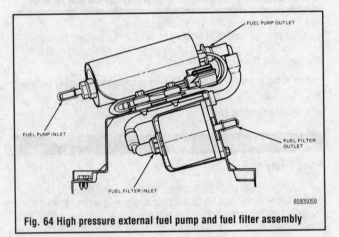

Fig. 64 High pressure external fuel pump and fuel filter assembly

High Pressure In–Tank Fuel Pump—1987–88

▶ **See Figure 65**

1. Depressurize the system.
2. Disconnect the negative battery cable.
3. Drain as much gas from the tank as possible by pumping it out through the filler neck.
4. Raise and support the rear end on jackstands.
5. Disconnect the filler hose, fuel supply, return and vent lines at the right and left side of the frame.
6. Disconnect the wiring to the fuel pump.
7. Support the gas tank, and loosen and remove the mounting straps. Remove the gas tank.
8. Disconnect the lines and harness at the pump flange.

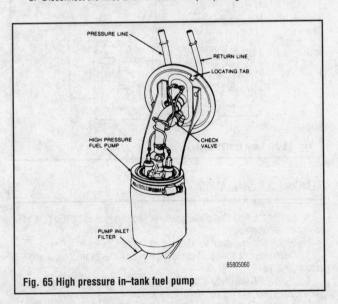

Fig. 65 High pressure in–tank fuel pump

9. Clean the outside of the mounting flange and retaining ring. Turn the fuel pump lock ring counterclockwise and remove.
10. Remove the fuel pump.
11. Clean the mounting surfaces. Put a light coat of grease on the mounting surfaces and on the new sealing ring. Install the new fuel pump.
12. Installation is in the reverse order of removal. If you have a single high pressure pump system, fill the tank with at least 10 gallons of gas. Turn the ignition key ON for three seconds. Repeat 6 or 7 times until the fuel system is pressurized. Check for any fitting leaks. Start the engine and check for leaks.

TESTING AND ADJUSTMENT

Low Pressure In–Tank Fuel Pump—1984–88

Disconnect the electrical connector at the fuel pump. Connect a voltmeter to the body wiring harness connector. Turn the key **ON** while watching the voltmeter. The voltage should rise to battery voltage, then return to zero after about 1 second. If the voltage is not as specified, check the inertia switch and the electrical system. Connect an ohmmeter to the in–line pump wiring connector. If no continuity is present, check the continuity directly at the in–line pump terminals. If there is no continuity at the in–line pump terminals, replace the in–line pump. If continuity is present, service or replace the wiring harness.

Connect an ohmmeter across the body wiring harness connector. If continuity is present (about 5 ohms), the low pressure pump circuit is OK. If no continuity is present, remove the fuel tank and check for continuity at the in–tank pump flange terminals on top of the tank. If continuity is absent at the in–tank pump flange terminals, replace the assembly. If continuity is present at the in–tank pump, but not in the harness connector, service or replace the wiring harness at the in–tank pump.

High Pressure External Fuel Pump—1984–88

Disconnect the electrical connector at the fuel pump. Connect a voltmeter to the body wiring harness connector. Turn the key **ON** while watching the voltmeter. The voltage should rise to battery voltage, then return to zero after about 1 second. If the voltage is not as specified, check the inertia switch and the electrical system. Connect an ohmmeter to the in–line pump wiring connector. If no continuity is present, check the continuity directly at the in–line pump terminals. If there is no continuity at the in–line pump terminals, replace the in–line pump. If continuity is present, service or replace the wiring harness.

Connect an ohmmeter across the body wiring harness connector. If continuity is present (about 5 ohms), the low pressure pump circuit is OK. If no continuity is present, remove the fuel tank and check for continuity at the in–tank pump flange terminals on top of the tank. If continuity is absent at the in–tank pump flange terminals, replace the assembly. If continuity is present at the in–tank pump, but not in the harness connector, service or replace the wiring harness at the in–tank pump.

High Pressure In–Tank Fuel Pump—1987–88

Disconnect the electrical connector just forward of the fuel tank. Connect a voltmeter to the body wiring harness connector. Turn the key ON while watching the voltmeter. Voltage should rise to battery voltage, then return to zero after about 1 second. Momentarily turn the key to the **START** position. Voltage should rise to about 8 volts while cranking. If the voltage is not as specified, check the electrical system.

Fuel Injectors

The fuel injector nozzles are electro–mechanical devices which both meter and atomize fuel delivered to the engine. The injectors are mounted in the lower intake manifold and are positioned so that their tips are directing fuel just ahead of the engine intake valves. The injector bodies consist of a solenoid–actuated pintle and needle valve assembly. An electrical control signal from the Electronic Engine Control unit activates the injector solenoid causing the pintle to move inward off its seat, allowing fuel to flow. Since the injector flow orifice is fixed and the fuel pressure drop across the injector tip is constant, fuel flow to the engine is regulated by how long the solenoid is energized. Atomization is obtained by contouring the pintle at the point where the fuel separates.

REMOVAL & INSTALLATION

♦ See Figures 66 and 67

1. Disconnect the fuel supply and return lines.
2. Remove the vacuum line from the fuel pressure regulator.
3. Disconnect the wiring harness.
4. Remove the fuel injector manifold assembly.
5. Carefully remove the connector(s) from the individual injector(s).
6. Grasping the injector body, pull up while gently rocking the injector from side to side.
7. Inspect the screen filter at the top of each injector. If clogged, replace the complete injector assembly.
8. Inspect the injector O–rings (two per injector) for signs of deterioration. Replace as needed.
9. Inspect the injector plastic hat (covering the injector pintle) and washer for signs of deterioration. Replace as needed. If a hat is missing, look for it in the intake manifold.
10. Installation is the reverse of removal. Lubricate all O–rings with a light oil. Carefully seat the fuel injector manifold assembly on the four injectors and secure the manifold with the attaching bolts. Torque the bolts 15–22 ft. lbs.

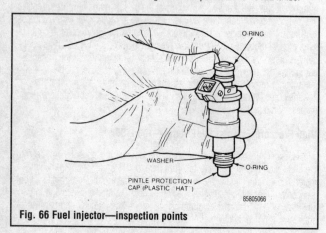

Fig. 66 Fuel injector—inspection points

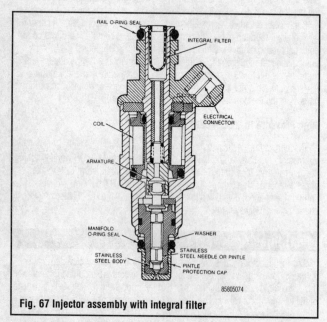

Fig. 67 Injector assembly with integral filter

Fuel Pressure Regulator

The fuel pressure regulator is attached to the fuel supply manifold assembly downstream of the fuel injectors. It regulates the fuel pressure supplied to the injectors. The regulator is a diaphragm operated relief valve in which one side of the diaphragm senses fuel pressure and the other side is subjected to intake manifold pressure. The nominal fuel pressure is established by a spring preload applied to the diaphragm. Balancing one side of the diaphragm with manifold pressure maintains a constant fuel pressure drop across the injectors. Fuel, in excess of that used by the engine, is bypassed through the regulator and returns to the fuel tank.

REMOVAL & INSTALLATION

✳ WARNING

Before attempting this procedure, depressurize the fuel system.

1. Remove the vacuum line at the pressure regulator.
2. Remove the three Allen retaining screws from the regulator housing.
3. Remove the pressure regulator, gasket and O–ring. Discard the gasket and inspect the O–ring for deterioration.

➡ **If scraping is necessary be careful not to damage the gasket surface.**

4. Installation is the reverse of removal. Lubricate the O–ring with light oil prior to installation. Tighten the three screws 27–40 inch lbs.

Air Vane Meter Assembly

♦ See Figure 68

The air vane meter assembly, found on the 4–140 turbo engine, is located between the air cleaner and the throttle body and is mounted on a bracket near the left or right hand corner of the engine compartment. The air vane meter contains two sensors which furnish input to the Electronic Control Assembly: a vane airflow sensor and a vane air temperature sensor. The air vane meter measures the mass of air flow to the engine. Air flow through the body moves a vane mounted on a pivot pin. This vane is connected to a variable resistor (potentiometer) which, in turn, is connected to a 5–volt reference voltage. The output of this potentiometer varies depending on the volume of air flowing through the sensor. The temperature sensor in the air vane meter measures the incoming air temperature. These two inputs, air volume and temperature, are used by the Electronic Control Assembly to compute the mass air flow. This valve is then used to compute the fuel flow necessary for the optimum air/fuel ratio which is fed to the injectors.

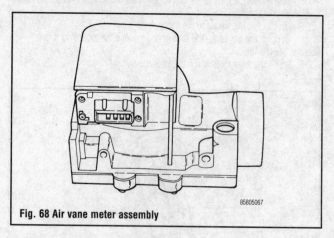

Fig. 68 Air vane meter assembly

REMOVAL & INSTALLATION

1. Loosen the hose clamp which secures engine air cleaner outlet hose to the vane meter assembly.
2. Remove air intake and outlet tube from the air cleaner.
3. Disengage four spring clamps and remove air cleaner front cover and air cleaner filter panel.
4. Remove the two screw and washer assemblies which secure the air meter to its bracket. Remove the air vane meter assembly.
5. Installation is the reverse of removal.

Air Throttle Body Assembly

The throttle body assembly controls air flow to the engine through a single butterfly–type valve. The throttle position is controlled by conventional cable/cam throttle linkage. The body is a single–piece die casting made of aluminum. It has a single bore with an air bypass channel around the throttle plate. This bypass channel controls both cold and warm engine idle air flow control as regulated by an air bypass valve assembly mounted directly to the throttle body. The valve assembly is an electromechanical device controlled by the EEC computer. It incorporates a linear actuator which positions a variable area metering valve.

Other features of the air throttle body assembly include:
- An adjustment screw to set the throttle plate at a minimum idle airflow position.
- A preset stop to locate the WOT position.
- A throttle body mounted throttle position sensor.
- A PCV fresh air source located upstream of the throttle plate.
- Individual ported vacuum taps (as required) for PCV and EVAP control signals.

REMOVAL & INSTALLATION

▶ See Figure 69

1. Remove the four throttle body nuts. Make sure that the throttle position sensor connector and the air bypass valve connector have been disconnected from the harness. Disconnect the air cleaner outlet tube.
2. Identify and disconnect the vacuum hoses.
3. Remove the throttle bracket.
4. Carefully separate the throttle body from the upper intake manifold.
5. Remove and discard the gasket between the throttle body and the upper intake manifold.

✳✳ WARNING

If scraping is necessary, be careful not to damage the gasket surfaces, or allow any material to drop into the manifold.

6. Installation is the reverse of removal. Tighten the throttle body–to–upper intake manifold nuts 12–15 ft. lbs.

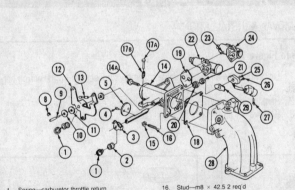

1. Spring—carburetor throttle return
2. Bushing—accelerator pump overtravel spring (2)
3. Lever—engine throttle
4. Screw—m4 × .7 × 8
5. Plate—air intake charge throttle
6. Shaft—air intake charge throttle
7. Spring—secondary throttle return
8. E-ring
9. Hub—throttle control
10. Spacer
11. Washer—nylon (2)
12. Lever—throttle control
13. Rod—engine secondary throttle control
14. Body—air intake charge throttle
14A. Bolt m8 × 1.25 × 30 hex flange head 2 req'd
15. Nut—m8 2 req'd
16. Stud—m8 × 42.5 2 req'd
17A. Screw throttle stop
17B. Spring—throttle return control
18. Gasket—air charge control to intake manifold
19. Gasket—air bypass valve
20. Seal—throttle control shaft
21. Bushing—carburetor throttle shaft
22. Valve assy—throttle air bypass
23. Bolt—m6 × 1.0 × 20 hex head flange
24. Valve assy—throttle air bypass (alt.)
25. Potentiometer throttle position
26. Screw and washer assy m4 × 22
27. Screw—m4 × 0.7 × 14.0 hex. washer tap
28. Manifold—intake upper
29. Gasket tps

85805064

Fig. 69 Air throttle body and upper intake manifold assemblies— 4–140 engine

Fuel Supply Manifold Assembly

The fuel supply manifold assembly is the component that delivers high pressure fuel from the vehicle's fuel supply line to the fuel injectors. The assembly consists of a single preformed tube or stamping with four (or eight) injector connectors, a mounting flange for the fuel pressure regulator, a pressure relief valve for diagnostic testing or field service fuel system pressure bleed down and mounting attachments which locate the fuel manifold assembly and provide fuel injector retention. On 1987–88 4–140 engines, the fuel supply manifold assembly is also equipped with a fuel pressure pulse damper, at the fuel supply fitting. This damper is designed to reduce pressure pulsation in the fuel lines, which may cause a ticking or hydraulic hammering noise.

REMOVAL & INSTALLATION

▶ See Figure 70

1. Remove the fuel tank cap. Release the pressure from the fuel system.
2. Disconnect the fuel supply and return lines.
3. Disconnect the wiring harness from the injectors.
4. Disconnect the vacuum line from the fuel pressure regulator valve.
5. Remove the two fuel injector manifold retaining bolts.
6. Carefully disengage the manifold from the fuel injectors. Remove the manifold.
7. Installation is the reverse of removal. Torque the fuel manifold bolts 15–22 ft. lbs.

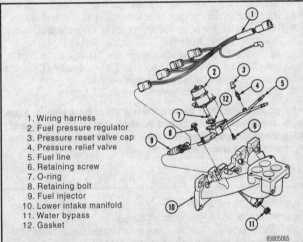

1. Wiring harness
2. Fuel pressure regulator
3. Pressure reset valve cap
4. Pressure relief valve
5. Fuel line
6. Retaining screw
7. O-ring
8. Retaining bolt
9. Fuel injector
10. Lower intake manifold
11. Water bypass
12. Gasket

85805065

Fig. 70 Fuel supply and lower intake manifold assemblies—4–140 engine

Upper (Air) Intake Manifold

The air intake manifold is a two piece (upper and lower intake manifold) aluminum casting. Runner lengths are tuned to optimize engine torque and power output. The manifold provides mounting flanges for the air throttle body assembly, fuel supply manifold and accelerator control bracket and the EGR valve and supply tube. Vacuum taps are provided to support various engine accessories. Pockets for the fuel injectors are machined to prevent both air and fuel leakage. The pockets, in which the injectors are mounted, are placed to direct the injector fuel spray immediately in front of each engine intake valve.

REMOVAL & INSTALLATION

1. Disconnect the air cleaner outlet tube from the air intake throttle body.
2. Unplug the throttle position sensor from the wiring harness.
3. Unplug the air by–pass valve connector.
4. Remove the three upper manifold retaining bolts.
5. Remove the upper manifold assembly.
6. Remove and discard the gasket from the lower manifold assembly.

✳✳ WARNING

If scraping is necessary, be careful not to damage gasket surfaces, or allow any material to drop into the lower manifold.

7. Installation is the reverse of removal. Tighten the upper intake manifold bolts 15–22 ft. lbs. Use a new gasket between the manifolds.

Fuel Charging Assembly

➡If any of the sub–assemblies are to be serviced and/or removed, with the fuel charging assembly mounted to the engine, the following steps must be taken.

1. Make sure the ignition key is in the off position.
2. Drain the coolant from the radiator.

✳✳ CAUTION

When draining the coolant, keep in mind that cats and dogs are attracted by the ethylene glycol antifreeze, and are quite likely to drink any that is left in an uncovered container or in puddles on the ground. This will prove fatal in sufficient quantity. Always drain the coolant into a sealable container. Coolant should be reused unless it is contaminated or several years old.

3. Disconnect the negative battery cable.
4. Remove the fuel cap to relieve fuel tank pressure.
5. Relieve the pressure from the fuel system at the pressure relief valve. Special tool T80L–9974–A or equivalent is needed for this procedure.
6. Disconnect the fuel supply line.
7. Identify and disconnect the fuel return lines and vacuum connections.
8. Disconnect the injector wiring harness by disconnecting the ECT sensor in the heater supply tube, under the lower intake manifold.
9. Disconnect the air bypass connector from the EEC harness.

➡Not all assemblies may be serviceable while on the engine. In some cases, removal of the fuel charging assembly may facilitate service of the various sub–assemblies. To remove the entire fuel charging assembly, the following should be observed.

REMOVAL & INSTALLATION

1. Remove the engine air cleaner outlet tube between the vane air meter and air throttle body by loosening the two clamps.
2. Disconnect and remove the accelerator and speed control cables (if so equipped) from the accelerator mounting bracket and throttle lever.
3. Disconnect the top manifold vacuum fitting connections by disconnecting:
   a. Rear vacuum line at the dash panel vacuum tree.
   b. Front vacuum line at the air cleaner and fuel pressure regulator.
4. Disconnect the PCV system by removing the following:
   a. Two large forward facing connectors on the throttle body and intake manifold.

   b. Throttle body port hose at the straight plastic connector.
   c. Canister purge line at the straight plastic connector.
   d. PCV hose at the valve cover.
   e. Unbolt the PCV separator support bracket from the cylinder head and remove the PCV system.
5. Disconnect the EGR tube from the upper intake manifold by removing the two flange nuts.
6. Remove the dipstick and its tube.
7. Remove the fuel return line.
8. Remove the six manifold retaining bolts.
9. Remove the manifold with the wiring harness and gasket.
10. Installation is the reverse of removal. Tighten the manifold bolts 12–15 ft. lbs.

Pressure Relief Valve

REMOVAL & INSTALLATION

▶ **See Figure 71**

1. If the fuel charging assembly is mounted on the engine, the fuel system must be depressurized.
2. Using an open end wrench or suitable deep well socket, remove the pressure relief valve from the injection manifold.
3. Installation is the reverse of removal. Torque the valve 48–84 inch lbs.

Throttle Position Sensor

REMOVAL & INSTALLATION

▶ **See Figure 72**

1. Disconnect the throttle position sensor from the wiring harness.
2. Remove the two retaining screws.
3. Remove the throttle position sensor.
4. Installation is the reverse of removal. Torque the sensor screws 11–16 inch lbs.

➡This throttle position sensor is not adjustable.

Air Bypass Valve Assembly

REMOVAL & INSTALLATION

▶ **See Figure 73**

1. Disconnect the air bypass valve assembly connector from the wiring harness.
2. Remove the two air bypass valve retaining screws.
3. Remove the air bypass valve and gasket.

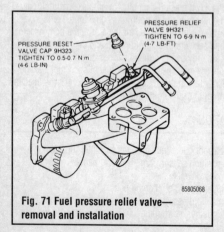

Fig. 71 Fuel pressure relief valve— removal and installation

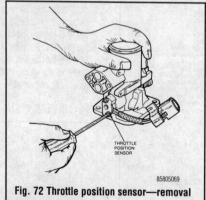

Fig. 72 Throttle position sensor—removal and installation

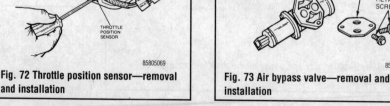

Fig. 73 Air bypass valve—removal and installation

If necessary to remove the gasket by scraping, be careful not to damage the gasket surface.

4. Installation is the reverse of removal. Torque the air bypass valve assembly 71–102 inch lbs.

Fuel System Inertia Switch

▶ **See Figure 74**

In the event of a collision, the electrical contacts in the inertia switch open and the fuel pump automatically shuts off. The fuel pump will shut off even if the engine does not stop running. The engine, however, will stop a few seconds after the fuel pump stops. It is not possible to restart the engine until the inertia switch is manually reset. The switch is located in the luggage compartment on the left hinge support of 2–door sedans or in the spare tire well of 3–door sedans. To reset, depress the button on top of the switch.

➥**In the reset position, the button can be depressed an additional 1.5mm (¹⁄₁₆ inch) against a spring. This is a normal condition.**

✳✳ **CAUTION**

Do not reset the inertia switch until the complete fuel system has been inspected for leaks.

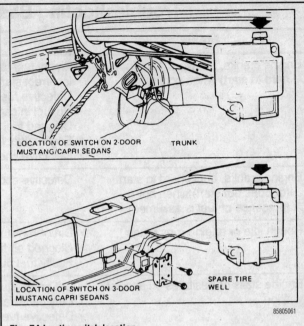

LOCATION OF SWITCH ON 2-DOOR MUSTANG/CAPRI SEDANS   TRUNK

LOCATION OF SWITCH ON 3-DOOR MUSTANG CAPRI SEDANS   SPARE TIRE WELL

85805061

Fig. 74 Inertia switch location

FUEL TANK

✳✳ **CAUTION**

NEVER SMOKE AROUND OR NEAR GASOLINE! GASOLINE VAPORS ARE EXTREMELY FLAMMABLE! EVEN THE PROXIMITY OF LIGHTED SMOKING MATERIAL CAN CAUSE AN EXPLOSION AND FIRE!

Tank Assembly

➥**On engines with fuel injection, relieve the pressure from the fuel system before disconnecting any fuel line. On 6–232 and 8–302 engines with CFI, relieve the system pressure at the pressure relief valve mounted on the throttle body and drain the system through the drain tube. (Special tool T80L–9974–A, or its equivalent, is needed for this procedure.) On the 4–140 engine with EFI, this valve is located in the flexible fuel supply tube, approximately 12 in. (305mm) back from where it connects to the engine fuel rail on the driver's side of the engine compartment. On the 8–302 engine with SEFI, the valve is located in the metal engine fuel line at the left front corner of the engine. Before opening the fuel system on an EFI or SEFI engine, relieve fuel system pressure as described earlier in this section.**

REMOVAL & INSTALLATION

1. Raise and support the rear end on jackstands.
2. Disconnect the battery ground cable.
3. Siphon off as much gasoline as possible into an approved container.

➥**On fuel injected vehicles, the fuel tank has small reservoirs inside to maintain the fuel level at or near the fuel pick–up. These reservoirs are difficult to drain since they may block the siphoning hose. You will have to try different angles and repeated attempts with the siphoning hose. Be patient.**

4. Place a pan under the fuel fill hose and disconnect the fuel filler hose at the tank. Pour any drained fuel into an approved container.
5. Place a floor jack, cushioned with a length of wood, under the fuel tank.
6. Remove the fuel tank strap nuts and lower the fuel tank just enough to disconnect the fuel liquid and vapor lines, and the fuel sending unit wire. Remove the air deflector from the tank retaining straps. The deflector is retained with pop rivets. On cars equipped with a metal retainer which fastens the filler pipe to the tank, remove the screw attaching the retainer to the fuel tank flange.
7. Continue lowering the tank once all lines are disconnected, and remove it from the car.
8. Installation is the reverse of removal. The fuel vapor line should be taped in position in the ribbed channel atop the tank.

Troubleshooting Basic Fuel System Problems

Problem	Cause	Solution
Engine cranks, but won't start (or is hard to start) when cold	• Empty fuel tank • Incorrect starting procedure • Defective fuel pump • No fuel in carburetor • Clogged fuel filter • Engine flooded • Defective choke	• Check for fuel in tank • Follow correct procedure • Check pump output • Check for fuel in the carburetor • Replace fuel filter • Wait 15 minutes; try again • Check choke plate
Engine cranks, but is hard to start (or does not start) when hot— (presence of fuel is assumed)	• Defective choke	• Check choke plate
Rough idle or engine runs rough	• Dirt or moisture in fuel • Clogged air filter • Faulty fuel pump	• Replace fuel filter • Replace air filter • Check fuel pump output
Engine stalls or hesitates on acceleration	• Dirt or moisture in the fuel • Dirty carburetor • Defective fuel pump • Incorrect float level, defective accelerator pump	• Replace fuel filter • Clean the carburetor • Check fuel pump output • Check carburetor
Poor gas mileage	• Clogged air filter • Dirty carburetor • Defective choke, faulty carburetor adjustment	• Replace air filter • Clean carburetor • Check carburetor
Engine is flooded (won't start accompanied by smell of raw fuel)	• Improperly adjusted choke or carburetor	• Wait 15 minutes and try again, without pumping gas pedal • If it won't start, check carburetor

TCCA5C01

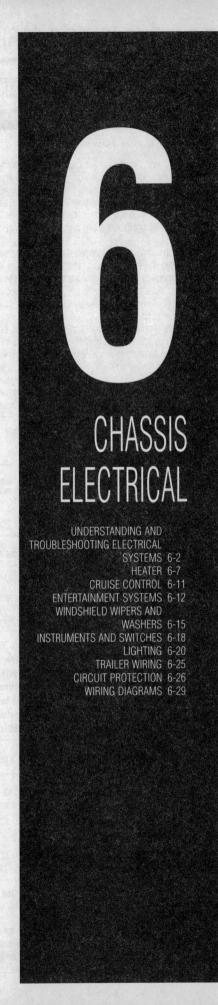

6

CHASSIS ELECTRICAL

UNDERSTANDING AND TROUBLESHOOTING ELECTRICAL SYSTEMS

Basic Electrical Theory

▶ **See Figure 1**

For any 12 volt, negative ground, electrical system to operate, the electricity must travel in a complete circuit. This simply means that current (power) from the positive (+) terminal of the battery must eventually return to the negative (-) terminal of the battery. Along the way, this current will travel through wires, fuses, switches and components. If, for any reason, the flow of current through the circuit is interrupted, the component fed by that circuit will cease to function properly.

Perhaps the easiest way to visualize a circuit is to think of connecting a light bulb (with two wires attached to it) to the battery—one wire attached to the negative (-) terminal of the battery and the other wire to the positive (+) terminal. With the two wires touching the battery terminals, the circuit would be complete and the light bulb would illuminate. Electricity would follow a path from the battery to the bulb and back to the battery. It's easy to see that with longer wires on our light bulb, it could be mounted anywhere. Further, one wire could be fitted with a switch so that the light could be turned on and off.

The normal automotive circuit differs from this simple example in two ways. First, instead of having a return wire from the bulb to the battery, the current travels through the frame of the vehicle. Since the negative (-) battery cable is attached to the frame (made of electrically conductive metal), the frame of the vehicle can serve as a ground wire to complete the circuit. Secondly, most automotive circuits contain multiple components which receive power from a single circuit. This lessens the amount of wire needed to power components on the vehicle.

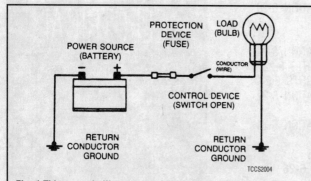

Fig. 1 This example illustrates a simple circuit. When the switch is closed, power from the positive (+) battery terminal flows through the fuse and the switch, and then to the light bulb. The light illuminates and the circuit is completed through the ground wire back to the negative (-) battery terminal. In reality, the two ground points shown in the illustration are attached to the metal frame of the vehicle, which completes the circuit back to the battery

HOW DOES ELECTRICITY WORK: THE WATER ANALOGY

Electricity is the flow of electrons—the subatomic particles that constitute the outer shell of an atom. Electrons spin in an orbit around the center core of an atom. The center core is comprised of protons (positive charge) and neutrons (neutral charge). Electrons have a negative charge and balance out the positive charge of the protons. When an outside force causes the number of electrons to unbalance the charge of the protons, the electrons will split off the atom and look for another atom to balance out. If this imbalance is kept up, electrons will continue to move and an electrical flow will exist.

Many people have been taught electrical theory using an analogy with water. In a comparison with water flowing through a pipe, the electrons would be the water and the wire is the pipe.

The flow of electricity can be measured much like the flow of water through a pipe. The unit of measurement used is amperes, frequently abbreviated as amps (a). You can compare amperage to the volume of water flowing through a pipe. When connected to a circuit, an ammeter will measure the actual amount of current flowing through the circuit. When relatively few electrons flow through a circuit, the amperage is low. When many electrons flow, the amperage is high.

Water pressure is measured in units such as pounds per square inch (psi); The electrical pressure is measured in units called volts (v). When a voltmeter is connected to a circuit, it is measuring the electrical pressure.

The actual flow of electricity depends not only on voltage and amperage, but also on the resistance of the circuit. The higher the resistance, the higher the force necessary to push the current through the circuit. The standard unit for measuring resistance is an ohm. Resistance in a circuit varies depending on the amount and type of components used in the circuit. The main factors which determine resistance are:

• Material—some materials have more resistance than others. Those with high resistance are said to be insulators. Rubber materials (or rubber-like plastics) are some of the most common insulators used in vehicles as they have a very high resistance to electricity. Very low resistance materials are said to be conductors. Copper wire is among the best conductors. Silver is actually a superior conductor to copper and is used in some relay contacts, but its high cost prohibits its use as common wiring. Most automotive wiring is made of copper.

• Size—the larger the wire size being used, the less resistance the wire will have. This is why components which use large amounts of electricity usually have large wires supplying current to them.

• Length—for a given thickness of wire, the longer the wire, the greater the resistance. The shorter the wire, the less the resistance. When determining the proper wire for a circuit, both size and length must be considered to design a circuit that can handle the current needs of the component.

• Temperature—with many materials, the higher the temperature, the greater the resistance (positive temperature coefficient). Some materials exhibit the opposite trait of lower resistance with higher temperatures (negative temperature coefficient). These principles are used in many of the sensors on the engine.

OHM'S LAW

There is a direct relationship between current, voltage and resistance. The relationship between current, voltage and resistance can be summed up by a statement known as Ohm's law.

Voltage (E) is equal to amperage (I) times resistance (R): $E = I \times R$
Other forms of the formula are $R = E/I$ and $I = E/R$

In each of these formulas, E is the voltage in volts, I is the current in amps and R is the resistance in ohms. The basic point to remember is that as the resistance of a circuit goes up, the amount of current that flows in the circuit will go down, if voltage remains the same.

The amount of work that the electricity can perform is expressed as power. The unit of power is the watt (w). The relationship between power, voltage and current is expressed as:

Power (w) is equal to amperage (I) times voltage (E): $W = I \times E$

This is only true for direct current (DC) circuits; The alternating current formula is a tad different, but since the electrical circuits in most vehicles are DC type, we need not get into AC circuit theory.

Electrical Components

POWER SOURCE

Power is supplied to the vehicle by two devices: The battery and the alternator. The battery supplies electrical power during starting or during periods when the current demand of the vehicle's electrical system exceeds the output capacity of the alternator. The alternator supplies electrical current when the engine is running. Just not does the alternator supply the current needs of the vehicle, but it recharges the battery.

The Battery

In most modern vehicles, the battery is a lead/acid electrochemical device consisting of six 2 volt subsections (cells) connected in series, so that the unit is capable of producing approximately 12 volts of electrical pressure. Each subsection consists of a series of positive and negative plates held a short distance apart in a solution of sulfuric acid and water.

The two types of plates are of dissimilar metals. This sets up a chemical reaction, and it is this reaction which produces current flow from the battery when its positive and negative terminals are connected to an electrical load . The power removed from the battery is replaced by the alternator, restoring the battery to its original chemical state.

The Alternator

On some vehicles there isn't an alternator, but a generator. The difference is that an alternator supplies alternating current which is then changed to direct current for use on the vehicle, while a generator produces direct current. Alternators tend to be more efficient and that is why they are used.

Alternators and generators are devices that consist of coils of wires wound together making big electromagnets. One group of coils spins within another set and the interaction of the magnetic fields causes a current to flow. This current is then drawn off the coils and fed into the vehicles electrical system.

GROUND

Two types of grounds are used in automotive electric circuits. Direct ground components are grounded to the frame through their mounting points. All other components use some sort of ground wire which is attached to the frame or chassis of the vehicle. The electrical current runs through the chassis of the vehicle and returns to the battery through the ground (-) cable; if you look, you'll see that the battery ground cable connects between the battery and the frame or chassis of the vehicle.

➡ **It should be noted that a good percentage of electrical problems can be traced to bad grounds.**

PROTECTIVE DEVICES

▶ **See Figure 2**

It is possible for large surges of current to pass through the electrical system of your vehicle. If this surge of current were to reach the load in the circuit, the surge could burn it out or severely damage it. It can also overload the wiring, causing the harness to get hot and melt the insulation. To prevent this, fuses, circuit breakers and/or fusible links are connected into the supply wires of the electrical system. These items are nothing more than a built-in weak spot in the system. When an abnormal amount of current flows through the system, these protective devices work as follows to protect the circuit:

• Fuse—when an excessive electrical current passes through a fuse, the fuse "blows" (the conductor melts) and opens the circuit, preventing the passage of current.

• Circuit Breaker—a circuit breaker is basically a self-repairing fuse. It will open the circuit in the same fashion as a fuse, but when the surge subsides, the circuit breaker can be reset and does not need replacement.

• Fusible Link—a fusible link (fuse link or main link) is a short length of special, high temperature insulated wire that acts as a fuse. When an excessive electrical current passes through a fusible link, the thin gauge wire inside the link melts, creating an intentional open to protect the circuit. To repair the circuit, the link must be replaced. Some newer type fusible links are housed in plug-in modules, which are simply replaced like a fuse, while older type fusible links must be cut and spliced if they melt. Since this link is very early in the electrical path, it's the first place to look if nothing on the vehicle works, yet the battery seems to be charged and is properly connected.

✳✳ CAUTION

Always replace fuses, circuit breakers and fusible links with identically rated components. Under no circumstances should a component of higher or lower amperage rating be substituted.

SWITCHES & RELAYS

▶ **See Figures 3 and 4**

Switches are used in electrical circuits to control the passage of current. The most common use is to open and close circuits between the battery and the various electric devices in the system. Switches are rated according to the amount of amperage they can handle. If a sufficient amperage rated switch is not used in a circuit, the switch could overload and cause damage.

Some electrical components which require a large amount of current to operate use a special switch called a relay. Since these circuits carry a large amount of current, the thickness of the wire in the circuit is also greater. If this large wire were connected from the load to the control switch, the switch would have to carry the high amperage load and the fairing or dash would be twice as large to accommodate the increased size of the wiring harness. To prevent these problems, a relay is used.

Relays are composed of a coil and a set of contacts. When the coil has a current passed though it, a magnetic field is formed and this field causes the contacts to move together, completing the circuit. Most relays are normally open, preventing current from passing through the circuit, but they can take any electrical form depending on the job they are intended to do. Relays can be considered "remote control switches." They allow a smaller current to operate devices that require higher amperages. When a small current operates the coil, a larger current is allowed to pass by the contacts. Some common circuits which may use relays are the horn, headlights, starter, electric fuel pump and other high draw circuits.

LOAD

Every electrical circuit must include a "load" (something to use the electricity coming from the source). Without this load, the battery would attempt to deliver its entire power supply from one pole to another. This is called a "short circuit." All this

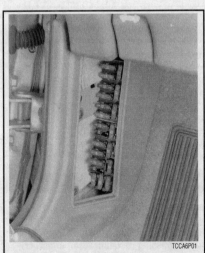

TCCA6P01

Fig. 2 Most vehicles use one or more fuse panels. This one is located on the driver's side kick panel

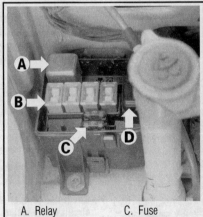

A. Relay
B. Fusible link
C. Fuse
D. Flasher

TCCA6P02

Fig. 3 The underhood fuse and relay panel usually contains fuses, relays, flashers and fusible links

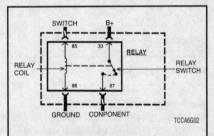

TCCA6G02

Fig. 4 Relays are composed of a coil and a switch. These two components are linked together so that when one operates, the other operates at the same time. The large wires in the circuit are connected from the battery to one side of the relay switch (B+) and from the opposite side of the relay switch to the load (component). Smaller wires are connected from the relay coil to the control switch for the circuit and from the opposite side of the relay coil to ground

electricity would take a short cut to ground and cause a great amount of damage to other components in the circuit by developing a tremendous amount of heat. This condition could develop sufficient heat to melt the insulation on all the surrounding wires and reduce a multiple wire cable to a lump of plastic and copper.

WIRING & HARNESSES

The average vehicle contains meters and meters of wiring, with hundreds of individual connections. To protect the many wires from damage and to keep them from becoming a confusing tangle, they are organized into bundles, enclosed in plastic or taped together and called wiring harnesses. Different harnesses serve different parts of the vehicle. Individual wires are color coded to help trace them through a harness where sections are hidden from view.

Automotive wiring or circuit conductors can be either single strand wire, multi-strand wire or printed circuitry. Single strand wire has a solid metal core and is usually used inside such components as alternators, motors, relays and other devices. Multi-strand wire has a core made of many small strands of wire twisted together into a single conductor. Most of the wiring in an automotive electrical system is made up of multi-strand wire, either as a single conductor or grouped together in a harness. All wiring is color coded on the insulator, either as a solid color or as a colored wire with an identification stripe. A printed circuit is a thin film of copper or other conductor that is printed on an insulator backing. Occasionally, a printed circuit is sandwiched between two sheets of plastic for more protection and flexibility. A complete printed circuit, consisting of conductors, insulating material and connectors for lamps or other components is called a printed circuit board. Printed circuitry is used in place of individual wires or harnesses in places where space is limited, such as behind instrument panels.

Since automotive electrical systems are very sensitive to changes in resistance, the selection of properly sized wires is critical when systems are repaired. A loose or corroded connection or a replacement wire that is too small for the circuit will add extra resistance and an additional voltage drop to the circuit.

The wire gauge number is an expression of the cross-section area of the conductor. Vehicles from countries that use the metric system will typically describe the wire size as its cross-sectional area in square millimeters. In this method, the larger the wire, the greater the number. Another common system for expressing wire size is the American Wire Gauge (AWG) system. As gauge number increases, area decreases and the wire becomes smaller. An 18 gauge wire is smaller than a 4 gauge wire. A wire with a higher gauge number will carry less current than a wire with a lower gauge number. Gauge wire size refers to the size of the strands of the conductor, not the size of the complete wire with insulator. It is possible, therefore, to have two wires of the same gauge with different diameters because one may have thicker insulation than the other.

It is essential to understand how a circuit works before trying to figure out why it doesn't. An electrical schematic shows the electrical current paths when a circuit is operating properly. Schematics break the entire electrical system down into individual circuits. In a schematic, usually no attempt is made to represent wiring and components as they physically appear on the vehicle; switches and other components are shown as simply as possible. Face views of harness connectors show the cavity or terminal locations in all multi-pin connectors to help locate test points.

CONNECTORS

▶ See Figures 5 and 6

Three types of connectors are commonly used in automotive applications—weatherproof, molded and hard shell.

• Weatherproof—these connectors are most commonly used where the connector is exposed to the elements. Terminals are protected against moisture and dirt by sealing rings which provide a weathertight seal. All repairs require the use of a special terminal and the tool required to service it. Unlike standard blade type terminals, these weatherproof terminals cannot be straightened once they are bent. Make certain that the connectors are properly seated and all of the sealing rings are in place when connecting leads.

• Molded—these connectors require complete replacement of the connector if found to be defective. This means splicing a new connector assembly into the harness. All splices should be soldered to insure proper contact. Use care when probing the connections or replacing terminals in them, as it is possible to create a short circuit between opposite terminals. If this happens to the wrong terminal pair, it is possible to damage certain components. Always use jumper wires between connectors for circuit checking and NEVER probe through weatherproof seals.

• Hard Shell—unlike molded connectors, the terminal contacts in hard-shell connectors can be replaced. Replacement usually involves the use of a special terminal removal tool that depresses the locking tangs (barbs) on the connector terminal and allows the connector to be removed from the rear of the shell. The connector shell should be replaced if it shows any evidence of burning, melting, cracks, or breaks. Replace individual terminals that are burnt, corroded, distorted or loose.

Fig. 5 Hard shell (left) and weatherproof (right) connectors have replaceable terminals

Fig. 6 Weatherproof connectors are most commonly used in the engine compartment or where the connector is exposed to the elements

Test Equipment

Pinpointing the exact cause of trouble in an electrical circuit is most times accomplished by the use of special test equipment. The following describes different types of commonly used test equipment and briefly explains how to use them in diagnosis. In addition to the information covered below, the tool manufacturer's instructions booklet (provided with the tester) should be read and clearly understood before attempting any test procedures.

JUMPER WIRES

✳✳ CAUTION

Never use jumper wires made from a thinner gauge wire than the circuit being tested. If the jumper wire is of too small a gauge, it may overheat and possibly melt. Never use jumpers to bypass high resistance loads in a circuit. Bypassing resistances, in effect, creates a short circuit. This may, in turn, cause damage and fire. Jumper wires should only be used to bypass lengths of wire or to simulate switches.

Jumper wires are simple, yet extremely valuable, pieces of test equipment. They are basically test wires which are used to bypass sections of a circuit. Although jumper wires can be purchased, they are usually fabricated from lengths of standard automotive wire and whatever type of connector (alligator clip, spade connector or pin connector) that is required for the particular application being tested. In cramped, hard-to-reach areas, it is advisable to have insulated boots over the jumper wire terminals in order to prevent accidental grounding. It is also advisable to include a standard automotive fuse in any jumper wire. This is commonly referred to as a "fused jumper". By inserting an in-line fuse holder between a set of test leads, a fused jumper wire can be used for bypassing open circuits. Use a 5 amp fuse to provide protection against voltage spikes.

Jumper wires are used primarily to locate open electrical circuits, on either the ground (-) side of the circuit or on the power (+) side. If an electrical component fails to operate, connect the jumper wire between the component and a good ground. If the component operates only with the jumper installed, the ground circuit is open. If the ground circuit is good, but the component does not operate, the circuit between the power feed and component may be open. By moving the jumper wire successively back from the component toward the power source, you can isolate the area of the circuit where the open is located. When the component stops functioning, or the power is cut off, the open is in the segment of wire between the jumper and the point previously tested.

You can sometimes connect the jumper wire directly from the battery to the "hot" terminal of the component, but first make sure the component uses 12 volts in operation. Some electrical components, such as fuel injectors or sensors, are designed to operate on about 4 to 5 volts, and running 12 volts directly to these components will cause damage.

TEST LIGHTS

▶ **See Figure 7**

The test light is used to check circuits and components while electrical current is flowing through them. It is used for voltage and ground tests. To use a 12 volt test light, connect the ground clip to a good ground and probe wherever necessary with the pick. The test light will illuminate when voltage is detected. This does not necessarily mean that 12 volts (or any particular amount of voltage) is present; it only means that some voltage is present. It is advisable before using the test light to touch its ground clip and probe across the battery posts or terminals to make sure the light is operating properly.

✳✳ WARNING

Do not use a test light to probe electronic ignition, spark plug or coil wires. Never use a pick-type test light to probe wiring on computer controlled systems unless specifically instructed to do so. Any wire insulation that is pierced by the test light probe should be taped and sealed with silicone after testing.

Like the jumper wire, the 12 volt test light is used to isolate opens in circuits. But, whereas the jumper wire is used to bypass the open to operate the load, the 12 volt test light is used to locate the presence of voltage in a circuit. If the test light illuminates, there is power up to that point in the circuit; if the test light does not illuminate, there is an open circuit (no power). Move the test light in successive steps back toward the power source until the light in the handle illuminates. The open is between the probe and a point which was previously probed.

The self-powered test light is similar in design to the 12 volt test light, but contains a 1.5 volt penlight battery in the handle. It is most often used in place of a multimeter to check for open or short circuits when power is isolated from the circuit (continuity test).

The battery in a self-powered test light does not provide much current. A weak battery may not provide enough power to illuminate the test light even when a complete circuit is made (especially if there is high resistance in the circuit). Always make sure that the test battery is strong. To check the battery, briefly touch the ground clip to the probe; if the light glows brightly, the battery is strong enough for testing.

➡**A self-powered test light should not be used on any computer controlled system or component. The small amount of electricity transmitted by the test light is enough to damage many electronic automotive components.**

MULTIMETERS

Multimeters are an extremely useful tool for troubleshooting electrical problems. They can be purchased in either analog or digital form and have a price range to suit any budget. A multimeter is a voltmeter, ammeter and ohmmeter (along with other features) combined into one instrument. It is often used when testing solid state circuits because of its high input impedance (usually 10 megaohms or more). A brief description of the multimeter main test functions follows:

• Voltmeter—the voltmeter is used to measure voltage at any point in a circuit, or to measure the voltage drop across any part of a circuit. Voltmeters usually have various scales and a selector switch to allow the reading of different voltage ranges. The voltmeter has a positive and a negative lead. To avoid damage to the meter, always connect the negative lead to the negative (-) side of the circuit (to ground or nearest the ground side of the circuit) and connect the positive lead to the positive (+) side of the circuit (to the power source or the nearest power source). Note that the negative voltmeter lead will always be black and that the positive voltmeter will always be some color other than black (usually red).

• Ohmmeter—the ohmmeter is designed to read resistance (measured in ohms) in a circuit or component. Most ohmmeters will have a selector switch which permits the measurement of different ranges of resistance (usually the selector switch allows the multiplication of the meter reading by 10, 100, 1,000 and 10,000). Some ohmmeters are "auto-ranging" which means the meter itself will determine which scale to use. Since the meters are powered by an internal battery, the ohmmeter can be used like a self-powered test light. When the ohmmeter is connected, current from the ohmmeter flows through the circuit or component being tested. Since the ohmmeter's internal resistance and voltage are known values, the amount of current flow through the meter depends on the resistance of the circuit or component being tested. The ohmmeter can also be used to perform a continuity test for suspected open circuits. In using the meter for making continuity checks, do not be concerned with the actual resistance readings. Zero resistance, or any ohm reading, indicates continuity in the circuit. Infinite resistance indicates an opening in the circuit. A high resistance reading where there should be none indicates a problem in the circuit. Checks for short circuits are made in the same manner as checks for open circuits, except that the circuit must be isolated from both power and normal ground. Infinite resistance indicates no continuity, while zero resistance indicates a dead short.

✳✳ WARNING

Never use an ohmmeter to check the resistance of a component or wire while there is voltage applied to the circuit.

• Ammeter—an ammeter measures the amount of current flowing through a circuit in units called amperes or amps. At normal operating voltage, most circuits have a characteristic amount of amperes, called "current draw" which can be measured using an ammeter. By referring to a specified current draw rating, then measuring the amperes and comparing the two values, one can determine what is happening within the circuit to aid in diagnosis. An open circuit, for example, will not allow any current to flow, so the ammeter reading will be zero. A damaged component or circuit will have an increased current draw, so the reading will be high. The ammeter is always connected in series with the circuit being tested. All of the current that normally flows through the circuit must also flow through the ammeter; if there is any other path for the current to follow, the ammeter reading

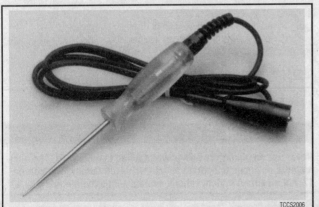

TCCS2006

Fig. 7 A 12 volt test light is used to detect the presence of voltage in a circuit

will not be accurate. The ammeter itself has very little resistance to current flow and, therefore, will not affect the circuit, but it will measure current draw only when the circuit is closed and electricity is flowing. Excessive current draw can blow fuses and drain the battery, while a reduced current draw can cause motors to run slowly, lights to dim and other components to not operate properly.

Troubleshooting Electrical Systems

When diagnosing a specific problem, organized troubleshooting is a must. The complexity of a modern automotive vehicle demands that you approach any problem in a logical, organized manner. There are certain troubleshooting techniques, however, which are standard:

• Establish when the problem occurs. Does the problem appear only under certain conditions? Were there any noises, odors or other unusual symptoms? Isolate the problem area. To do this, make some simple tests and observations, then eliminate the systems that are working properly. Check for obvious problems, such as broken wires and loose or dirty connections. Always check the obvious before assuming something complicated is the cause.

• Test for problems systematically to determine the cause once the problem area is isolated. Are all the components functioning properly? Is there power going to electrical switches and motors. Performing careful, systematic checks will often turn up most causes on the first inspection, without wasting time checking components that have little or no relationship to the problem.

• Test all repairs after the work is done to make sure that the problem is fixed. Some causes can be traced to more than one component, so a careful verification of repair work is important in order to pick up additional malfunctions that may cause a problem to reappear or a different problem to arise. A blown fuse, for example, is a simple problem that may require more than another fuse to repair. If you don't look for a problem that caused a fuse to blow, a shorted wire (for example) may go undetected.

Experience has shown that most problems tend to be the result of a fairly simple and obvious cause, such as loose or corroded connectors, bad grounds or damaged wire insulation which causes a short. This makes careful visual inspection of components during testing essential to quick and accurate troubleshooting.

Testing

OPEN CIRCUITS

▶ See Figure 8

This test already assumes the existence of an open in the circuit and it is used to help locate the open portion.

1. Isolate the circuit from power and ground.
2. Connect the self-powered test light or ohmmeter ground clip to the ground side of the circuit and probe sections of the circuit sequentially.
3. If the light is out or there is infinite resistance, the open is between the probe and the circuit ground.

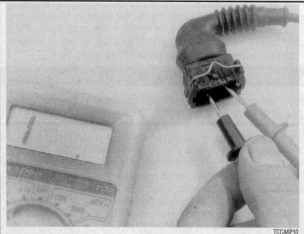

TCCA6P10

Fig. 8 The infinite reading on this multimeter indicates that the circuit is open

4. If the light is on or the meter shows continuity, the open is between the probe and the end of the circuit toward the power source.

SHORT CIRCUITS

➡**Never use a self-powered test light to perform checks for opens or shorts when power is applied to the circuit under test. The test light can be damaged by outside power.**

1. Isolate the circuit from power and ground.
2. Connect the self-powered test light or ohmmeter ground clip to a good ground and probe any easy-to-reach point in the circuit.
3. If the light comes on or there is continuity, there is a short somewhere in the circuit.
4. To isolate the short, probe a test point at either end of the isolated circuit (the light should be on or the meter should indicate continuity).
5. Leave the test light probe engaged and sequentially open connectors or switches, remove parts, etc. until the light goes out or continuity is broken.
6. When the light goes out, the short is between the last two circuit components which were opened.

VOLTAGE

This test determines voltage available from the battery and should be the first step in any electrical troubleshooting procedure after visual inspection. Many electrical problems, especially on computer controlled systems, can be caused by a low state of charge in the battery. Excessive corrosion at the battery cable terminals can cause poor contact that will prevent proper charging and full battery current flow.

1. Set the voltmeter selector switch to the 20V position.
2. Connect the multimeter negative lead to the battery's negative (-) post or terminal and the positive lead to the battery's positive (+) post or terminal.
3. Turn the ignition switch **ON** to provide a load.
4. A well charged battery should register over 12 volts. If the meter reads below 11.5 volts, the battery power may be insufficient to operate the electrical system properly.

VOLTAGE DROP

▶ See Figure 9

When current flows through a load, the voltage beyond the load drops. This voltage drop is due to the resistance created by the load and also by small resistances created by corrosion at the connectors and damaged insulation on the wires. The maximum allowable voltage drop under load is critical, especially if there is more than one load in the circuit, since all voltage drops are cumulative.

1. Set the voltmeter selector switch to the 20 volt position.
2. Connect the multimeter negative lead to a good ground.
3. Operate the circuit and check the voltage prior to the first component (load).
4. There should be little or no voltage drop in the circuit prior to the first component. If a voltage drop exists, the wire or connectors in the circuit are suspect.
5. While operating the first component in the circuit, probe the ground side of the component with the positive meter lead and observe the voltage readings. A small voltage drop should be noticed. This voltage drop is caused by the resistance of the component.
6. Repeat the test for each component (load) down the circuit.
7. If a large voltage drop is noticed, the preceding component, wire or connector is suspect.

RESISTANCE

▶ See Figures 10 and 11

✳✳ WARNING

Never use an ohmmeter with power applied to the circuit. The ohmmeter is designed to operate on its own power supply. The normal 12 volt electrical system voltage could damage the meter!

1. Isolate the circuit from the vehicle's power source.
2. Ensure that the ignition key is **OFF** when disconnecting any components or the battery.

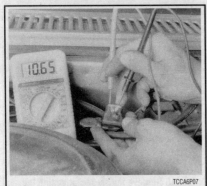

Fig. 9 This voltage drop test revealed high resistance (low voltage) in the circuit

Fig. 10 Checking the resistance of a coolant temperature sensor with an ohmmeter. Reading is 1.04 kilohms

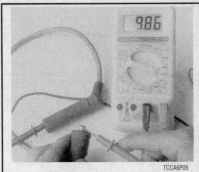

Fig. 11 Spark plug wires can be checked for excessive resistance using an ohmmeter

3. Where necessary, also isolate at least one side of the circuit to be checked, in order to avoid reading parallel resistances. Parallel circuit resistances will always give a lower reading than the actual resistance of either of the branches.

4. Connect the meter leads to both sides of the circuit (wire or component) and read the actual measured ohms on the meter scale. Make sure the selector switch is set to the proper ohm scale for the circuit being tested, to avoid misreading the ohmmeter test value.

Wire and Connector Repair

Almost anyone can replace damaged wires, as long as the proper tools and parts are available. Wire and terminals are available to fit almost any need. Even the specialized weatherproof, molded and hard shell connectors are now available from aftermarket suppliers.

Be sure the ends of all the wires are fitted with the proper terminal hardware and connectors. Wrapping a wire around a stud is never a permanent solution and will only cause trouble later. Replace wires one at a time to avoid confusion. Always route wires exactly the same as the factory.

➡ If connector repair is necessary, only attempt it if you have the proper tools. Weatherproof and hard shell connectors require special tools to release the pins inside the connector. Attempting to repair these connectors with conventional hand tools will damage them.

HEATER

Blower Motor

REMOVAL & INSTALLATION

Except Air Conditioned Vehicles

◗ See Figures 12, 13 and 14

➡ The right side ventilator assembly must be removed for access to the blower motor and wheel.

1. Remove the retaining screw from the right register duct mounting bracket.

2. Remove the screws holding the control cable lever assembly to the instrument panel.

3. Remove the glove box liner and door assembly.

4. Remove the plastic rivets securing the grille to the floor outlet, and remove the grille.

5. Remove the right register duct and register assembly:

a. Remove the register duct bracket retaining screw on the lower edge of the instrument panel, and disengage the duct from the opening and then remove them through the glove box opening.

b. Insert a thin blade under the retaining tab and pry the tab toward the louvers until retaining tab pivot clears the hole in the register opening. Pull the register assembly end out from the housing only enough to prevent the pivot from going back into the pivot hole. Pry the other retaining tab loose and remove the register assembly from the opening.

6. Remove the retaining screws securing the ventilator assembly to the blower housing. The upper right screw can be reached with a long extension through the register opening; the upper left screw can be reached through the glove box opening. The other two screws are on the bottom of the assembly.

7. Slide the assembly to the right, then down and out from under the instrument panel.

8. Remove the motor lead wire connector from the register and push it back through the hole in the case. Remove the right side cowl trim panel for access, and remove the ground terminal lug retaining screw.

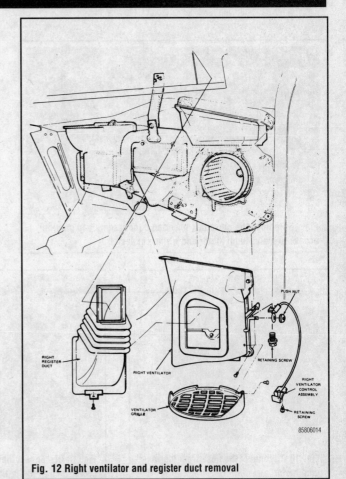

Fig. 12 Right ventilator and register duct removal

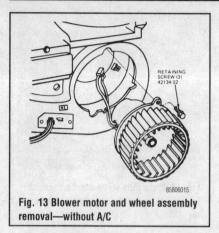

Fig. 13 Blower motor and wheel assembly removal—without A/C

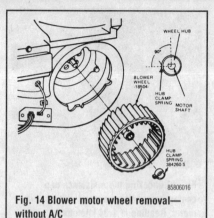

Fig. 14 Blower motor wheel removal—without A/C

Fig. 15 Remove the screws attaching the glove box liner and door assembly to the hinge

9. Remove the hub clamp spring from the motor shaft and remove the blower wheel.

10. Remove the blower motor bolts from the housing and remove the motor.

11. Service as required and reinstall in the reverse order of removal.

Air Conditioned Vehicles

▶ See Figures 15 thru 25

➡The air inlet duct and blower housing assembly must be removed for access to the blower motor.

1. Remove the glove box liner and door assembly.
2. Disconnect the hose from the vacuum motor.
3. Remove the instrument panel lower right side to cowl attaching bolt.
4. Remove the screw attaching the brace to the top of the air inlet duct.
5. Disconnect the blower motor wire at the electrical connector.
6. Remove the housing lower support bracket to case nut.

7. Remove the side cowl trim panel and remove the ground wire screw.

8. Remove the screw attaching the top of the air inlet duct to the evaporator case.

9. Move the air inlet duct and housing assembly down and away from the evaporator case.

10. Remove the four blower motor mounting plate screws then remove the blower motor and wheel as an assembly from the housing. Do not remove the mounting plate from the motor.

11. Service as required and reinstall in the reverse order of removal. Tape the blower motor power lead to the air inlet duct to keep the wire away from the blower outlet during installation.

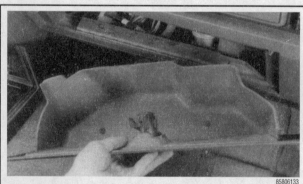

Fig. 16 Remove the glove box liner and door assembly to provide access to the vacuum motor and wiring connector

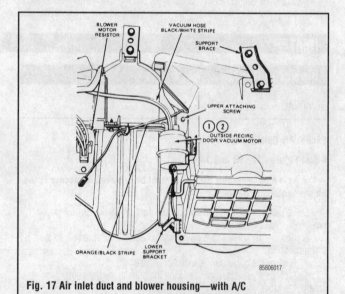

Fig. 17 Air inlet duct and blower housing—with A/C

Fig. 18 Disconnect the hose from the vacuum motor

Fig. 19 Disconnect the blower motor power lead at the in-line wire connector

Fig. 20 Remove the housing lower support bracket to case nut

Fig. 21 Remove the screw attaching the top of the air inlet duct to the evaporator case

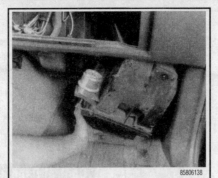

Fig. 22 Move the air inlet duct and housing assembly down and away from the evaporator case

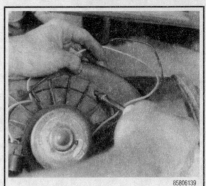

Fig. 23 Remove the four blower motor mounting plate screws

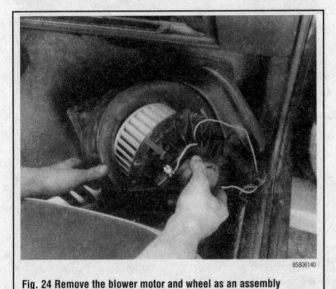

Fig. 24 Remove the blower motor and wheel as an assembly

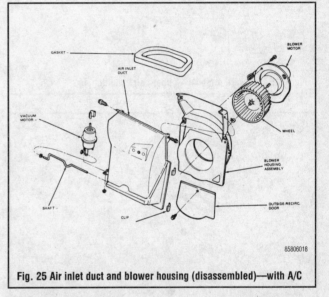

Fig. 25 Air inlet duct and blower housing (disassembled)—with A/C

Heater Core

REMOVAL & INSTALLATION

Except Air Conditioned Vehicles

♦ See Figure 26

➡It is not necessary to remove the heater case for access to the heater core.

1. Drain enough coolant from the radiator to drain the heater core.
2. Loosen the heater hose clamps on the engine side of the firewall and disconnect the heater hoses. Cap the heater core tubes.
3. Remove the glove box liner and door assembly.
4. Remove the instrument panel-to-cowl brace retaining screws and remove the brace.
5. Move the temperature lever to WARM.
6. Remove the heater core cover screws. Remove the cover through the glove box.
7. Loosen the heater case mounting nuts on the engine side of the firewall.
8. Push the heater core tubes and seals toward the interior of the car to loosen the core.
9. Remove the heater core through the glove box opening.
10. Service as required and reinstall in the reverse order of removal.

Air Conditioned Vehicles

♦ See Figure 27

✳✳ WARNING

Removal of the heater/air conditioner (evaporator) housing requires evacuation and recovery of the air conditioner refrigerant. This operation requires special tools and a thorough familiarity with automotive refrigerant systems. Failure to follow proper safety precautions may cause personal injury. If you are not familiar with these systems, it is recommended that discharging and charging of the A/C system be performed by an experienced professional mechanic. For discharging, recovery, evacuating and charging procedures, see Section 1.

➡The instrument panel must be removed for access to the heater core.

1. Using an approved refrigerant recovery/recycling station which meets SAE standards, discharge the system at the service access port on the underside of the combination valve. See Section 1.
2. Disconnect the negative battery cable.
3. Remove the instrument panel pad:
   a. Remove the screws attaching the instrument cluster trim panel to the pad.
   b. Remove the screw attaching the pad to the panel at each defroster opening.

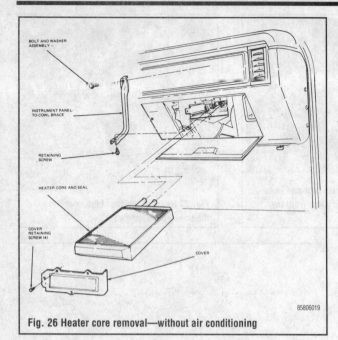

Fig. 26 Heater core removal—without air conditioning

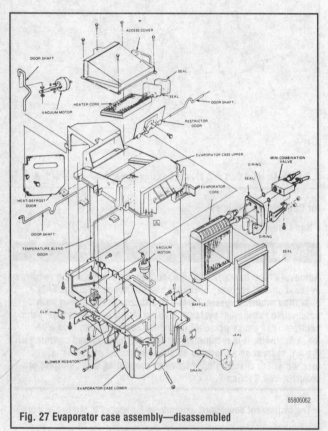

Fig. 27 Evaporator case assembly—disassembled

c. Remove the screws attaching the edge of the pad to the panel.

4. Remove the instrument panel (as described in Section 10) and lay it on the front seat.

5. Drain the cooling system and disconnect the heater hoses at the core tubes.

6. Disconnect the refrigerant lines at the combination valve. Use a back-up wrench on the suction throttling valve manifold. Cap all openings immediately!

7. Disconnect the wiring at the blower resistor. Remove the screw attaching the air inlet duct and blower housing assembly support brace to the cowl top panel.

8. Disconnect the black vacuum supply hose at the check valve, in the engine compartment.

9. Also in the engine compartment, remove the 2 nuts retaining the evaporator case to the firewall.

10. In the passenger compartment, remove the screw attaching the evaporator case support bracket to the cowl top panel.

11. Remove the nut retaining the left end of the evaporator case to the firewall and the nut retaining the bracket below the evaporator case, to the dash panel.

12. Carefully pull the case away from the firewall and remove the case from the car.

13. Remove the heater core access cover retaining screws and the cover.

14. Lift the heater core and seals from the evaporator case.

15. Service as required and reinstall in the reverse order of removal.

Control Panel

REMOVAL & INSTALLATION

Except 1987–88 Mustang

▶ **See Figure 28**

1. Remove the three retaining screws securing the top edge of the instrument cluster bezel and remove the instrument cluster bezel for access to the control panel assembly.

2. Remove the four retaining screws securing the control panel assembly to the instrument panel and pull the assembly rearward from the instrument panel for access to the electrical wire harness connectors and the control housing attachments.

3. Disengage the function and temperature control cable assemblies from the heater case assembly.

4. Disconnect the blower speed switch and the control illumination wire harness connectors.

5. Remove the control panel assembly with the control cables.

6. Remove the push nut retaining the function cable end loop or the function control lever.

7. Depress the white locking tang on the end of the function control cable housing then disengage the function control cable with housing assembly from the function lever tang and the frame of the control assembly.

8. Remove the push nut retaining the temperature cable end loop or the temperature control lever.

9. Depress the black locking tang on the end of the temperature control cable housing assembly, then disengage the function control cable with housing assembly from the temperature lever tang and frame of the control panel assembly.

To install:

10. Slip the end wire loop of the temperature control cable and housing assembly over the tang on the rear of the temperature control lever. (The wire loop coil should face outward, away from the base of the tang on the temperature control lever.) Slide the cable housing end into the bracket of the control assembly frame until the locking tang snaps into position then install the push nut to retain the cable end loop on the lever.

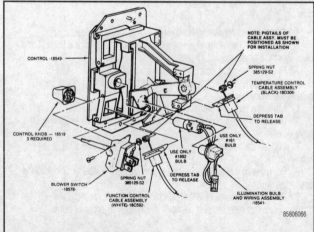

Fig. 28 Control panel disassembled—except 1987–88 Mustang

11. Repeat step 10 for connection of the function control cable and housing assembly.

12. Feed the control cables through the panel opening and position the control panel assembly near the instrument panel opening.

13. Connect the wire harness connectors for the control illumination and the blower speed switch.

14. Align the upper and lower alignment tabs on the back of the control panel assembly with the upper hole and lower slot of the instrument panel, then position the control assembly onto the instrument panel.

15. Install and tighten the four control panel assembly retaining screws.

16. Install the four lower locking tabs of the instrument cluster bezel into the tab slots at the lower edge of the instrument panel cluster area, and press the instrument cluster bezel into position.

17. Install and tighten the three instrument cluster bezel retaining screws in the holes at the top edge of the instrument cluster bezel.

18. Install the function and temperature control cable assemblies on the heater case assembly.

19. Test the system for proper operation.

1987–88 Mustang

▶ **See Figure 29**

1. Disconnect the negative battery cable.
2. Snap the control opening finish panel away from the instrument panel.
3. Remove the 4 control panel assembly-to-instrument panel screws.
4. Pull the control panel assembly towards you.
5. Disconnect the wiring from the panel connectors.
6. Disconnect the vacuum harness and the temperature control cable from the control panel.
7. If necessary, pull the control knobs off their shafts.

To install:

8. Push the control knobs onto their shafts, if removed.
9. Connect the temperature control cable to the control panel assembly.
10. Connect the wire connector and vacuum harness to the control panel assembly.

➡**If so equipped, push on the vacuum harness retaining nuts; do not try to screw them on!**

11. Position the control panel assembly in the instrument panel opening and install the 4 screws.

12. Install the control opening finish panel by snapping it into place.

13. Connect the negative battery cable.

14. Check the system for proper operation.

CRUISE CONTROL

General Information

The speed control system is electronically controlled and vacuum operated. The controls are located on the steering wheel.

The system is designed to operate at speeds above 35 mph (50 km/h). The use of the speed control is not recommended when driving conditions do not permit maintaining a constant speed, such as in heavy traffic or on roads that are winding, icy, snow covered or slippery.

Diagnostic Procedures

Whenever a speed control malfunction occurs, first verify that the speed control wire harness is properly connected to all connectors before starting repairs. A poor connection can cause a complete or intermittent malfunction and is also the only connection in the circuit that cannot be tested. For this reason, a loose connection may be misdiagnosed as a component malfunction.

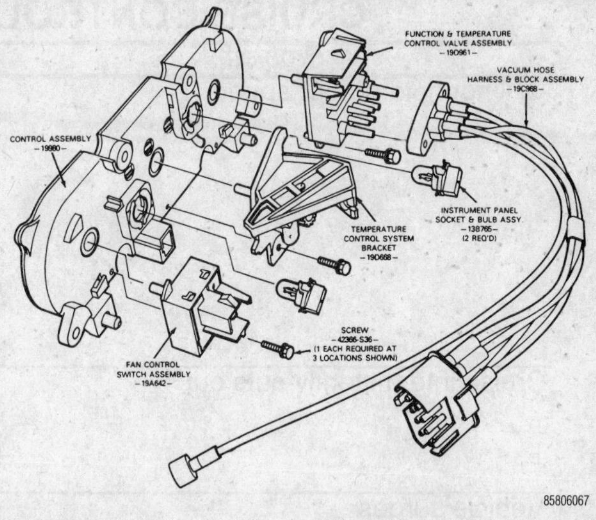

Fig. 29 Control panel disassembled—1987–88 Mustang

Air Conditioning Components

REMOVAL & INSTALLATION

Repair or service of air conditioning components is not covered by this manual, because of the risk of personal injury or death, and because of the legal ramifications of servicing these components without the proper EPA certification and experience. Cost, personal injury or death, environmental damage, and legal considerations (such as the fact that it is a federal crime to vent refrigerant into the atmosphere), dictate that the A/C components on your vehicle should be serviced only by a Motor Vehicle Air Conditioning (MVAC) trained, and EPA certified automotive technician.

➡**If your vehicle's A/C system uses R-12 refrigerant and is in need of recharging, the A/C system can be converted over to R-134a refrigerant (less environmentally harmful and expensive). Refer to Section 1 for additional information on R-12 to R-134a conversions, and for additional considerations dealing with your vehicle's A/C system.**

Also, check all vacuum connections for tightness and cracked hoses. Road test the vehicle to verify speed control problems. The road test should include attention to the speedometer. Speedometer operation should be smooth and without flutter at all speeds. A flutter in the speedometer indicates a problem which might cause surging in the speed control system. The cause of any speedometer problems should be corrected before any more diagnosis is done.

If the road test verifies an inoperative system with correct speedometer operation, follow these steps:

1. Inspect the cruise control fuse, and replace if it has blown.
2. Check for a loose electrical or vacuum connection at the servo unit.
3. Check for vacuum supply and correct position of the vacuum check valve in the hose from the servo unit to the vacuum source.
4. Remove corrosion from all electrical terminals in the speed control system.
5. Verify that both ends of the speed control cable are securely attached. If either end is loose, the speed control system will be inoperative.

CRUISE CONTROL TROUBLESHOOTING

Problem	Possible Cause
Will not hold proper speed	Incorrect cable adjustment
	Binding throttle linkage
	Leaking vacuum servo diaphragm
	Leaking vacuum tank
	Faulty vacuum or vent valve
	Faulty stepper motor
	Faulty transducer
	Faulty speed sensor
	Faulty cruise control module
Cruise intermittently cuts out	Clutch or brake switch adjustment too tight
	Short or open in the cruise control circuit
	Faulty transducer
	Faulty cruise control module
Vehicle surges	Kinked speedometer cable or casing
	Binding throttle linkage
	Faulty speed sensor
	Faulty cruise control module
Cruise control inoperative	Blown fuse
	Short or open in the cruise control circuit
	Faulty brake or clutch switch
	Leaking vacuum circuit
	Faulty cruise control switch
	Faulty stepper motor
	Faulty transducer
	Faulty speed sensor
	Faulty cruise control module

Note: Use this chart as a guide. Not all systems will use the components listed.

TCCA6C01

ENTERTAINMENT SYSTEMS

Radio/Tape Player

REMOVAL & INSTALLATION

▶ See Figures 30, 31, 32, 33 and 34

Conventional and Premium Sound Systems—Monaural and Stereo

As originally offered on the 1979–88 Mustang/Capri, the premium sound system had either four or six speakers and was available with both conventional stereo and electronically tuned radios. The premium sound system's unique wiring provides separate return lines to the speakers, which are driven at all times by a premium sound amplifier.

➡**For vehicles equipped with a floor console, refer to**

1. Disconnect the negative battery cable.
2. Disconnect the electrical, speaker, and antenna leads from the radio.
3. Remove the two upper mounting screws, if so equipped. Otherwise, remove the knobs, discs, control shaft nuts and washers from the radio shafts.
4. Remove the ash receptacle and bracket, or floor console, if applicable, to provide sufficient clearance for removal of the radio.

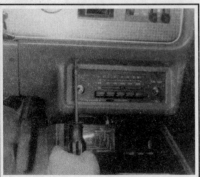
85806142
Fig. 30 Some radios are retained from the front by a pair of upper mounting screws

85806143
Fig. 31 Remove the volume and tuning knobs if the radio must be separated from its trim panel

85806144
Fig. 32 After removing the knobs, remove any selector discs or washers from the radio shafts

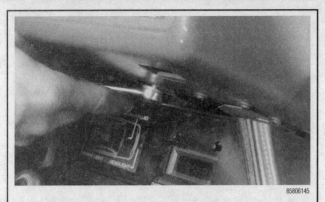
Fig. 33 Remove the rear support mounting screw

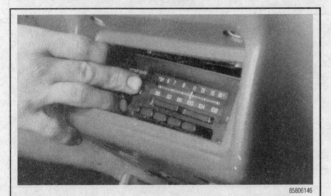
Fig. 34 Push the radio rearward and lower it for removal

5. Remove the rear support attaching screw from the radio.
6. Remove the instrument panel lower reinforcement, if necessary.
7. On vehicles equipped with premium sound, remove the radio support attaching nut, ground cable and bracket from the radio.
8. Remove the heater or air conditioning floor ducts.
9. Remove the radio from the rear support, then drop the radio down and out from behind the instrument panel.
10. To install, reverse the removal procedure. After connecting the battery cable, check the radio for proper operation and reset the memory buttons, if applicable.

Electronic Stereo Systems

EXCEPT 1987–88 MUSTANG

1. Disconnect the negative battery cable.
2. Remove the center instrument trim panel.
3. Remove the four screws retaining the radio and mounting bracket to the instrument panel.
4. Push the radio to the front and raise the rear of the radio slightly so that the rear support bracket clears the clip in the instrument panel. Slowly pull the radio out of the instrument panel.
5. Disconnect the wiring connectors and antenna cable.
6. If installing a new radio, remove the rear support bracket from the radio by removing the rear nut.
7. To install, reverse the removal procedure. After connecting the battery cable, check the radio for proper operation and reset the memory buttons, if applicable.

1987–88 MUSTANG

▶ **See Figure 35**

1. Disconnect the negative battery cable.
2. Install radio removal tools T85M-19061-A or equivalent into the radio face plate.
3. Apply a light spreading force on the tools and pull radio from the console.
4. Disconnect the wiring connectors and antenna cable.

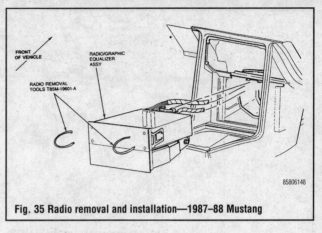
Fig. 35 Radio removal and installation—1987–88 Mustang

To install:
5. Connect the wiring connectors and antenna cable to the radio.
6. Slide the radio into the console, ensuring that the rear bracket is engaged on the upper support rail.
7. Connect the negative battery cable. Check the radio for proper operation and reset the memory buttons.

Amplifier

REMOVAL & INSTALLATION

▶ **See Figure 36**

1. Remove the instrument panel pad.
2. Remove the two screws attaching the amplifier to the instrument panel.
3. Disconnect the ground wire from the stud on the rear of the radio.
4. Disengage the electrical connectors and remove the amplifier.
5. To install, reverse the removal procedure.

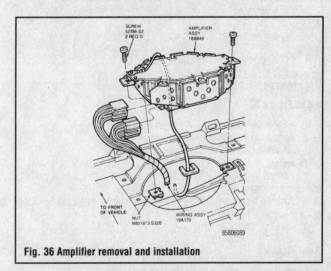
Fig. 36 Amplifier removal and installation

Speakers

REMOVAL & INSTALLATION

Instrument Panel Mounted

▶ **See Figure 37**

EXCEPT 1988 MUSTANG

1. Remove the instrument panel pad.
2. Remove the speaker retaining screws.

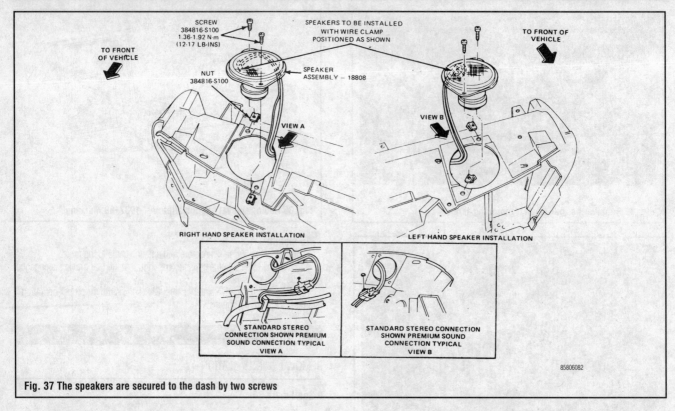

Fig. 37 The speakers are secured to the dash by two screws

3. Lift the speaker and disconnect the lead at the connector.
4. To install, reverse the removal procedure.

1988 MUSTANG

1. Remove the retaining screw at the side of the instrument panel.
2. Use a fabricated hook to disengage the clips and remove the speaker grills.
3. Remove the speaker retaining screws. Lift the speaker and disconnect the wiring.
4. To install, reverse the removal procedure.

Door Mounted

▶ See Figure 38

1. Remove the door trim panel.
2. Remove the three speaker retaining screws.
3. Lift the speaker and disconnect the speaker wires.
   To install:
4. Connect the speaker wires, position the speaker to the door side panel and install the retaining screws.
5. Push the locator clip into the hole in the door inner panel, and check the speaker operation before tightening.
6. Install the door trim panel.

Rear Mounted

2-DOOR

1. From within the luggage compartment, disconnect the speaker wiring.
2. Remove the speaker cover, speaker retaining nuts and speaker from the underside of the package shelf.
3. To install, reverse the removal procedure.

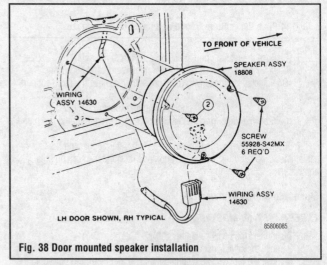

Fig. 38 Door mounted speaker installation

3-DOOR

1. Remove the speaker and grille assembly retaining screws from the quarter trim panel.
2. Lift the speaker and the grille assembly from the trim panel. Disconnect the speaker wires.
3. Remove the nuts retaining the speaker to the grille assembly and remove the speaker.
4. To install, reverse the removal procedures.

WINDSHIELD WIPERS AND WASHERS

Wiper Arm

REMOVAL & INSTALLATION

▶ **See Figures 39, 40, 41 and 42**

➡To prevent glass and/or paint damage, do not pry the wiper arm from the pivot shaft with a metallic or sharp tool.

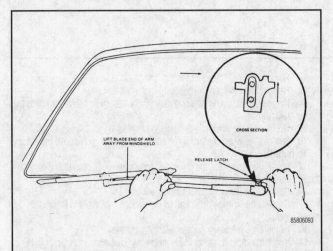

Fig. 39 Installation of the wiper arm and blade assembly to the pivot shaft

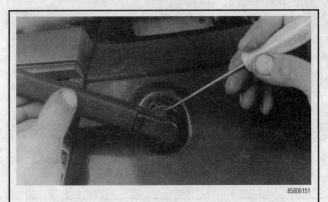

Fig. 40 A slide latch secures the wiper arm to the pivot shaft

1. Raise the blade end of the arm off of the windshield and move the slide latch away from the pivot shaft. This will unlock the wiper arm from the pivot shaft and hold the blade end of the arm off of the glass at the same time.
2. Pull the wiper arm off of the pivot shaft.
To install:
3. Push the main arm head over the pivot shaft. Be sure that the pivot shaft is in the PARK position, and that the blade assembly is correctly positioned. (Dimension X in the illustration represents the distance between the blade saddle centerline and the lower weatherstrip or moulding.) Dimension X should be 1.8–3.0 in. (45.7–76.2mm) on the driver's side and 2.3–3.5 in. (58.4–88.9mm) on the passenger's side.
4. While applying downward pressure on the arm head to ensure full seating, raise the other end of the arm far enough to allow the latch to slide under the pivot shaft and into the latched position. Use finger pressure only to slide the latch.
5. Lower the blade to the windshield. (If the blade does not touch the windshield, the slide latch is not completely in place. If this occurs, repeat the previous step.)

Rear Window Wiper Blade and Arm

REMOVAL & INSTALLATION

▶ **See Figure 43**

1. Raise the blade end of the arm off the rear window. Move the slide latch away from the pivot shaft, and hold the blade end of the arm off the glass at the same time.
2. Pull the wiper arm off of the pivot shaft.
To install:
3. Be sure that the pivot shaft is in the PARK position and that the blade assembly is positioned properly. The distance between the blade saddle centerline and the lower weatherstrip or moulding should be 1–2.5 inches.

Fig. 41 With the slide latch in the unlocked position, the wiper arm can be pulled off the pivot shaft

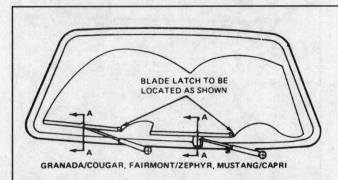

Fig. 42 Wiper arm and blade adjustment to Dimension "X"

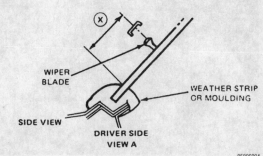

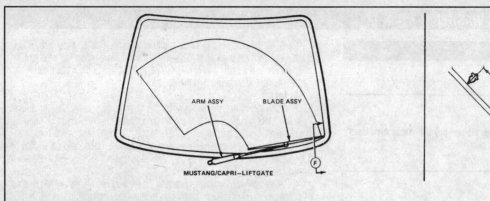
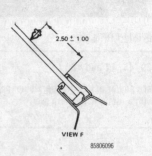

Fig. 43 Rear wiper arm and blade adjustment

4. Push the arm over the pivot shaft and hold it while raising the blade end of the wiper arm. Push the latch into the lock under the pivot shaft.

5. Lower the blade to the rear window. (If the blade does not touch the window, the slide latch is not completely in place. If this occurs, repeat the previous step.)

Wiper Motor

REMOVAL & INSTALLATION

▶ See Figures 44, 45, 46, 47 and 48

➡Use care when handling the motor to avoid damaging the ceramic magnets. Do not strike or tap the motor with a hammer or other object.

1. Disconnect the negative battery cable.

2. Remove the right hand wiper arm and blade assembly.

3. Remove the cowl top grille attaching screws and grille.

4. Remove the retaining clip and disconnect the linkage drive arm from the motor crank pin.

5. Disconnect the wiper motor's wiring connector.

6. Remove the wiper motor's three attaching screws and remove the motor.

To install:

7. Install the motor and the three attaching screws. Tighten to 60–85 inch lbs (6.78–9.60 Nm).

8. Connect the wiper motor's wiring connector.

9. Connect the linkage drive arm to the motor crank pin and install the retaining clip.

10. Install the cowl top grille and attaching screws.

11. Install the wiper arm and blade assembly. Ensure that the motor is in PARK and that the distance between the blade saddle centerline and the weath-

Fig. 44 The cowl top grille is retained by screws

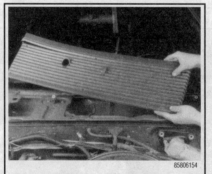

Fig. 45 Removal of the cowl top grille provides access to the wiper linkage and motor connection

Fig. 46 Remove the retaining clip and disconnect the linkage drive arm from the motor crank pin before removing the motor

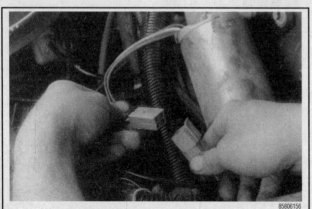

Fig. 47 Disconnect the wiper motor's wiring connector before removing the motor

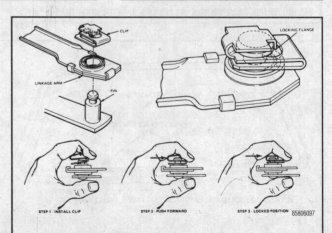

Fig. 48 Installation of the wiper linkage retainer clip

erstrip or moulding (Dimension X in the illustration) is 2.3–3.5 inches (58.4–88.9mm).

12. Connect the negative battery cable.

Rear Wiper Motor and Linkage

REMOVAL & INSTALLATION

▶ **See Figure 49**

1. Turn the ignition switch **OFF.**
2. Remove the wiper arm and blade assembly from the pivot shaft, as described earlier in this section.
3. Remove the pivot shaft nut and spacers.
4. Open the hatch and remove the inner trim panel.
5. Disconnect the wiper motor wiring.
6. Remove the motor and bracket attaching screws and remove the motor, bracket and linkage assembly.
7. Installation is the reverse of removal.

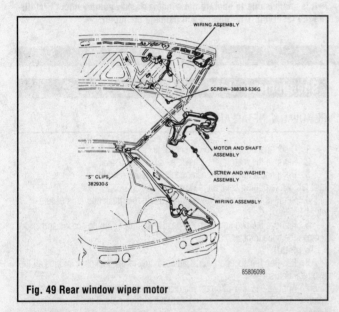

Fig. 49 Rear window wiper motor

Wiper Linkage

REMOVAL & INSTALLATION

▶ **See Figures 44, 45, 48 and 50**

➡**The pivot shaft and linkage assemblies are connected together with non-removable plastic ball joints. The left-hand shaft, right-hand pivot shafts and linkage are serviced as one unit.**

1. Disconnect the negative battery cable.
2. Remove both wiper arm assemblies.
3. Remove the cowl top grille attaching screws and grille.
4. Remove the wiper linkage retainer clip, and disconnect the linkage drive arm from the motor crankpin.
5. Remove the two screws retaining the right-hand pivot shaft to the cowl.
6. Remove the large nut, washer and spacer from the left-hand pivot shaft.
7. Remove the linkage and pivot shaft assembly from the cowl.

To install:

8. Position and attach the linkage along with the pivot shaft assembly to the cowl using the proper fasteners. Tighten the screws to 60–85 inch lbs. (6.78–9.60 Nm) and the nut to 70–110 inch lbs. (7.91–12.43 Nm). Be sure to include the washer and spacer on the left-hand pivot shaft.
9. Connect the linkage drive arm to the motor crankpin and secure with the retainer clip.
10. Attach the cowl top grille with its retaining screws.

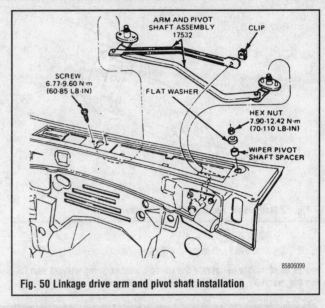

Fig. 50 Linkage drive arm and pivot shaft installation

11. Replace both wiper arm assemblies. Be sure that the motor is in the PARK position. Install both wiper arm assemblies to provide the proper distance between the blade saddle centerline and the weatherstrip or moulding (Dimension X in the accompanying illustration).
12. Connect the negative battery cable.

Windshield Washer Motor

REMOVAL & INSTALLATION

▶ **See Figures 51 and 52**

1. Remove the reservoir, as described above.
2. Using a small screwdriver, pry out the motor retaining ring.
3. Using pliers, grip one edge of the electrical connector ring, then pull the motor, seal and impeller from the reservoir.

➡**If the seal and impeller come apart from the motor, it can all be re-assembled.**

To install:

4. Take the time to clean out the reservoir before installing the motor.
5. Coat the seal with a dry lubricant, such as powdered graphite or spray Teflon®. This will aid assembly.
6. Align the small projection on the motor end cap with the slot in the reservoir and install the motor so that the seal seats against the bottom of the motor cavity.
7. Press the retaining ring into position. A 1-inch, 12-point socket or a smooth 1-inch piece of plastic tubing will do nicely as an installation tool.
8. Install the reservoir and connect the wiring.

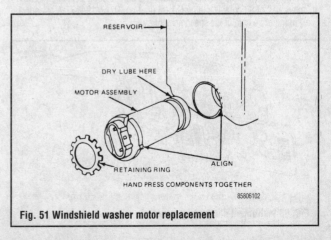

Fig. 51 Windshield washer motor replacement

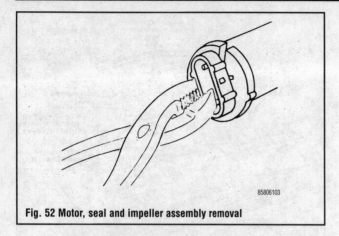

Fig. 52 Motor, seal and impeller assembly removal

9. Fill the reservoir and operate the washer system.

➡️**It is unadvisable to operate the window washer pump without first filling the reservoir. Dry-running will damage the motor.**

INSTRUMENTS AND SWITCHES

Instrument Cluster

REMOVAL & INSTALLATION

▶ **See Figure 53**

❄ WARNING

Extreme care must be exercised during this procedure to avoid damage to the cluster dash components. Wooden paddles should be used to separate components, as required. Tape or cover dash areas that may be damaged by the removal and installation of dash components.

➡️**During the procedures, slight variations may be required from the general outline, due to minor production changes.**

1. Disconnect the negative battery cable.
2. Remove the 3 upper retaining screws from the cluster trim cover and remove the cover.
3. Remove the 2 upper and 2 lower screws retaining the cluster to the instrument panel. On Mustang SVO, disconnect the turbo boost pressure hose at the shake brace.
4. Pull the cluster away from the panel, then disconnect the speedometer cable and printed circuit connectors.
5. Remove the cluster.
6. Installation is the reverse of removal. Be sure to apply a 3/16 in. (4.76mm) diameter ball of Silicone Damping Grease (part no. D7AZ-19A331-A or equivalent) in the drive hole of the speedometer head.

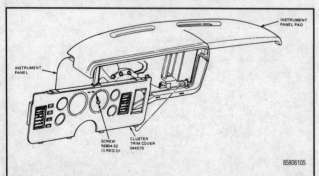

Fig. 53 Instrument cluster trim panel

Rear Window Washer Motor

REMOVAL & INSTALLATION

1. Remove the rear window washer reservoir, as described above.
2. Using a small, flat-bladed screwdriver, pry out the motor assembly. Remove the screen and the seal.
3. Flush the reservoir and clean any foreign material from the motor cavity or the reservoir.
   To install:
4. Lubricate the outside of the seal with a dry lubricant (such as powdered graphite) to prevent the seal from sticking during reassembly.
5. Insert the screen in the seal, and insert the seal all the way down in the cavity.
6. Align the motor in the cavity on the reservoir, and insert the motor in the seal using hand pressure only.
7. Install the rear window washer reservoir, as described above.
8. Fill the reservoir and operate the washer system.

➡️**It is unadvisable to operate the window washer pump without first filling the reservoir. Dry-running will damage the motor.**

Speedometer Head

REMOVAL & INSTALLATION

1. Disconnect the negative battery cable.
2. Remove the instrument cluster, as described above.
3. Disconnect the speedometer cable by depressing the flat, quick-disconnect tab, while pulling back on the cable.
4. Remove the seven screws which retain the mask and lens assembly.
5. Remove the two speedometer head assembly retaining screws and remove the speedometer.
   To install:
6. Position the speedometer head assembly to the backplate and install the two retaining screws.
7. Apply a 3/16 in. (4.76mm) diameter ball of Silicone Damping Grease (part no. D7AZ-19A331-A or equivalent) in the drive hole of the speedometer head.
8. Position the mask and lens assembly to the backplate, then install the seven attaching screws.
9. Connect the speedometer cable and install the instrument cluster.
10. Connect the negative battery cable.

Tachometer

REMOVAL & INSTALLATION

1. Disconnect the negative battery cable.
2. Remove the instrument cluster, as described above.
3. Remove the screws which attach the mask and lens to the cluster backplate, then remove the mask and lens.
4. Remove the three nuts which attach the tachometer to the cluster backplate and remove the tachometer.
   To install:
5. Position the tachometer to the cluster backplate and install the attaching nuts.
6. If another tachometer is being installed, be sure that the mode selector switch is set to correspond to the correct number of engine cylinders.
7. Position the lens and mask to the cluster backplate, then install the attaching screws.
8. Install the instrument cluster.
9. Connect the negative battery cable and check the tachometer operation.

Speedometer Cable

REMOVAL & INSTALLATION

Core and Casing

▶ See Figure 54

➡ **Depending on year and model, some dash panels or the instrument cluster may require removal to gain access to the rear of the speedometer.**

1. Disconnect the negative battery cable.
2. Reach up behind the speedometer and depress the flat, quick-disconnect tab, while pulling back on the cable.
3. Push the cable and grommet through the opening in the floorpan or dash panel.
4. Raise and safely support the car on jackstands and disengage the cable from all retaining clips.
5. Remove the speedometer cable mounting bolt and clip at the transmission, then pull the cable from the transmission.

➡ **On vehicles equipped with cruise control, remove the speedometer cable by pulling it out of the speed sensor. Do not attempt to remove the spring retainer clip with the cable attached to the sensor.**

6. Remove the speedometer cable from the vehicle.
To install:
7. Insert the new speedometer cable through the O-ring and into the speedometer driven gear. On vehicles equipped with cruise control, insert the cable into the speed sensor.
8. Attach the speedometer cable mounting bolt and clip at the transmission.
9. Engage the cable in the retaining clips and route it through the opening in the floorpan or dash panel. Be careful to observe the proper routing, particularly in relation to other cables. Push the grommet in place.
10. Lower the vehicle and remove the jackstands.
11. Apply a 3/16 in. (4.76mm) diameter ball of Silicone Damping Grease (part no. D7AZ-19A331-A or equivalent) in the drive hole of the speedometer head.
12. Push connect the speedometer cable to the speedometer head. Install the instrument cluster or any dash panels which were removed.
13. Connect the negative battery cable.

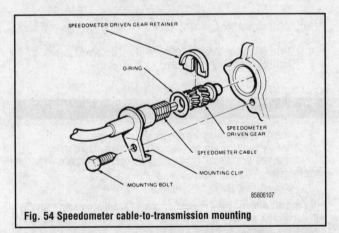

Fig. 54 Speedometer cable-to-transmission mounting

Oil Pressure Gauge

REMOVAL & INSTALLATION

1. Disconnect the negative battery cable.
2. Remove the instrument cluster, as earlier in this section.
3. Remove the screws which attach the lens and mask assembly to the cluster backplate. Remove the mask and lens assembly.
4. Remove the two retaining nuts and the oil pressure gauge.

To install:
5. Position the oil pressure gauge to the cluster backplate and install the two retaining nuts.
6. Position the lens and mask assembly to the cluster backplate, then install the retaining screws.
7. Install the instrument cluster, as described above.
8. Connect the negative battery cable and check the oil pressure gauge operation.

Fuel Gauge

REMOVAL & INSTALLATION

1. Disconnect the negative battery cable.
2. Remove the instrument cluster, as described earlier in this section.
3. From the front side of the cluster, remove the retaining screws, then separate the cluster mask and lens assembly from the backplate. (These screws also retain the cluster lens to the mask.)
4. Remove the two fuel gauge retaining nuts from the rear side of the cluster. Withdraw the gauge from the front side of the backplate.
To install:
5. Position the gauge to the cluster backplate and install the two retaining nuts from the rear side.
6. Position the mask and lens assembly to the cluster backplate and install the retaining screws.
7. Install the cluster assembly.
8. Connect the negative battery cable and check the gauge operation.

Temperature Gauge

REMOVAL & INSTALLATION

1. Disconnect the negative battery cable.
2. Remove the instrument cluster, as described earlier in this section.
3. Remove the screws that retain the mask and lens to the cluster backplate, then remove the mask and lens.
4. Remove the two temperature gauge retaining nuts and remove the gauge.
To install:
5. Position the gauge to the cluster backplate and install the two retaining nuts.
6. Position the mask and lens assembly to the cluster backplate, then install the retaining screws.
7. Install the cluster assembly.
8. Connect the negative battery cable and check gauge operation.

Windshield Wiper Switch

REMOVAL & INSTALLATION

▶ See Figures 55 and 56

1. Disengage the negative battery cable.
2. Remove the split steering column cover retaining screws.
3. Separate the two halves and remove the wiper switch retaining screws.
4. Disconnect the wire connector and remove the wiper switch.
5. Installation is the reverse of the removal procedure.

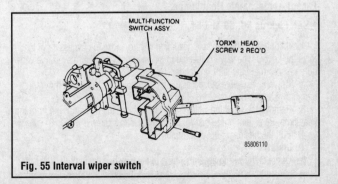

Fig. 55 Interval wiper switch

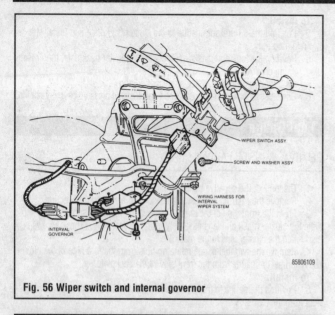

Fig. 56 Wiper switch and internal governor

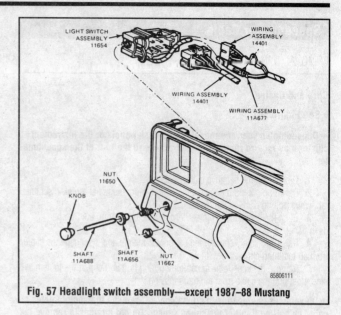

Fig. 57 Headlight switch assembly—except 1987–88 Mustang

Headlight Switch

REMOVAL & INSTALLATION

Except 1987–88 Mustang

▶ See Figure 57

1. Disconnect the negative battery cable.
2. Pull the control knob to the full ON position. Reach up from underneath the instrument panel and press the release button on the switch housing. With the release button pressed in, pull the knob out of the switch.
3. Unscrew the bezel nut using Tool T65L-700-A or equivalent to detach the switch assembly from the instrument panel, and lower the switch assembly.
4. Disconnect the wiring assembly and remove the switch.
5. Installation is the reverse of removal.

1987–88 Mustang

▶ See Figure 58

1. Disconnect the negative battery cable.
2. Disengage the 2 locking tabs on the left side of the switch (behind the switch's paddles) by pushing the tabs in with a small screwdriver and pulling on the paddles.

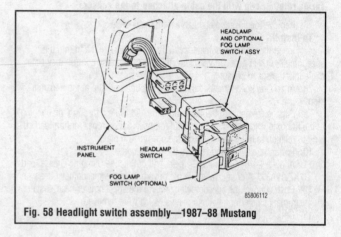

Fig. 58 Headlight switch assembly—1987–88 Mustang

3. Using a screwdriver, pry the right side of the switch out of the instrument panel.
4. Pull the switch completely out of the panel and disconnect the wiring.
5. Installation is the reverse of removal.

LIGHTING

Headlights

REMOVAL & INSTALLATION

Except Aerodynamic Headlamps

▶ See Figures 59, 60 and 61

1. If equipped with movable headlamp covers, close the bypass valve to raise the covers. The valve is located in the vacuum lines near the reserve vacuum reservoir and the left front fender.
2. On vehicles with exposed headlamps, remove the headlamp trim mounting screws and remove the trim, if so equipped.
3. Remove the retaining ring screws and remove the retaining ring from the headlamp. Be careful not to disturb the aim adjusting screws.
4. Pull the headlamp out and unplug it.
To install:
5. Connect the wiring assembly plug to the new headlamp bulb. Place the bulb in position by aligning the glass tabs with the positioning slots.

6. Attach the bulb retaining ring with the retaining ring screws.
7. Attach the headlamp trim with its mounting screws, if applicable.
8. If equipped with movable headlamp covers, open the bypass valve to lower the covers.
9. Check the headlamp bulb aim and adjust as necessary.

➡If correctly aimed before removal, a sealed beam headlamp normally will not require aiming upon installation. Aiming may be required, however, if any adjusting screws are turned.

Aerodynamic Headlamps

BULB ASSEMBLY

✳✳ CAUTION

The halogen bulb contains pressurized gas. If the bulb is dropped or scratched it will shatter. Also, avoid touching the bulb glass with your bare fingers. Grasp the bulb only by its plastic base. Oil from bare skin will cause hot spots on the glass surface and lead to pre-

Fig. 59 Remove the upper and lower retaining ring screws

Fig. 60 Remove the retaining ring to access the sealed beam headlamp

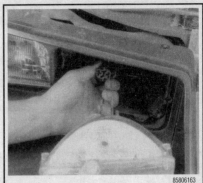

Fig. 61 Remove the headlamp and unplug the electrical connector

mature burnout. If you do touch the glass, clean it prior to installation.

1. Make sure that the headlamp switch is OFF.
2. Raise the hood. The bulb protrudes from the rear of the headlamp assembly.
3. Unplug the electrical connector from the bulb.
4. Rotate the bulb retaining ring approximately ⅛ turn counterclockwise and remove it.
5. Pull the bulb straight back out of its socket. Do not rotate it.
6. When installing the bulb, push it into position, turning it slightly right or left to align the grooves in the forward part of the base with the tabs in the socket. When they are aligned, push the bulb firmly into position until the mounting flange on the base contacts the rear face of the socket.
7. Install the locking ring, turning it until a stop is felt.
8. Push the electrical connector onto the bulb until it snaps into position.
9. Check the headlamp operation.

➡️If correctly aimed before removal, an aerodynamic headlamp normally will not require aiming after bulb installation.

HEADLAMP ASSEMBLY—EXCEPT MUSTANG SVO

▶ See Figure 62

1. Make sure that the headlamp switch is OFF.
2. Raise the hood. The bulb protrudes from the rear of the headlamp assembly.
3. Unplug the electrical connector from the bulb.
4. Remove the 3 nuts and washers from the rear of the headlamp.
5. Push forward on the headlamp at the bulb socket. It may be necessary to loosen the parking lamp and cornering lamp fasteners.
6. Remove the 3 clips which attach the headlamp to the black ring by prying them out from the base with a flat-bladed screwdriver.
7. Installation is the reverse of removal. Make sure that the black rubber shield is securely crimped on the headlamp.
8. Check the headlamp operation.

➡️If correctly aimed before removal, an aerodynamic headlamp normally will not require aiming after installation.

HEADLAMP ASSEMBLY—MUSTANG SVO

▶ See Figure 63

1. Make sure that the headlamp switch is OFF.
2. Raise the hood. The bulb protrudes from the rear of the headlamp assembly.
3. Unplug the electrical connector from the bulb.
4. Push down on the rubber tipped retainer clip to disengage the lower clip.

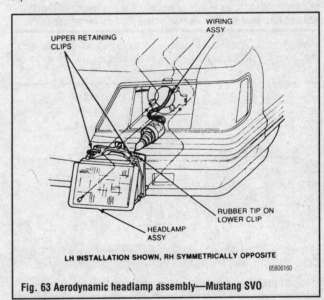

Fig. 63 Aerodynamic headlamp assembly—Mustang SVO

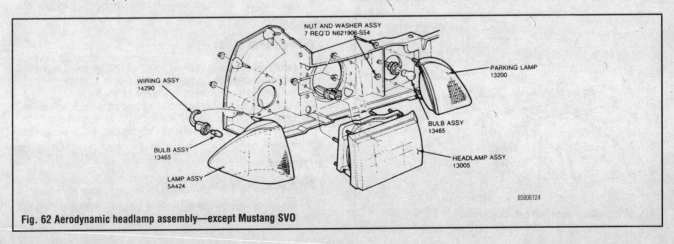

Fig. 62 Aerodynamic headlamp assembly—except Mustang SVO

5. Squeeze the upper retainer to disengage, but do not remove the clips.

6. Pull the headlamp assembly forward to remove.

To install:

7. Align two upper bosses on the headlamp with the end of the upper screw heads in the lamp opening. Depress the shield along both sides to insert it in lamp opening, and push the upper bosses to snap engage the screw heads.

8. Tuck the remaining shield in with fingertips. Push the lower outboard corner to snap engage the remaining clip.

9. Pull up on the rubber tipped clip to ensure engagement.

10. Push the electrical connector onto the bulb until it snaps into position.

11. Check the headlamp operation.

➡️**If correctly aimed before removal, an aerodynamic headlamp normally will not require aiming after installation.**

AIMING THE HEADLIGHTS

▶ **See Figures 64 and 65**

The headlights must be properly aimed to provide the best, safest road illumination. The lights should be checked for proper aim and adjusted as necessary. Certain state and local authorities have requirements for headlight aiming; these should be checked before adjustment is made.

❋❋ CAUTION

About once a year, when the headlights are replaced or when any time front end work is performed on your vehicle, the headlights should be accurately aimed by a reputable repair shop using the proper equipment. Headlights not properly aimed can make it virtually impossible to see and may blind other drivers on the road, possibly causing an accident. Note that the following procedure is a temporary fix, until you can take your vehicle to a repair shop for a proper adjustment.

Headlight adjustment may be temporarily made using a wall or on the rear of another vehicle. When adjusted, the lights should not glare in oncoming car or truck windshields, nor should they illuminate the passenger compartment of vehicles in front of you. These adjustments should always be fine-tuned by a repair shop equipped with aiming tools. Improper adjustments may be both dangerous and illegal.

For most of the vehicles covered by this manual, horizontal and vertical aiming of each headlamp assembly is provided by two adjusting screws which move the housing against the tension of a coil spring. There is no adjustment for focus; this is done during headlight manufacturing.

➡️**Because the composite headlight assembly is bolted into position, no adjustment should be necessary or possible. Some applications, however, may be bolted to an adjuster plate or may be retained by adjusting screws. If so, follow this procedure when adjusting the lights, BUT always have the adjustment checked by a reputable shop.**

Before removing the headlight bulb or disturbing the headlamp in any way, note the current settings in order to ease headlight adjustment upon reassembly. If the high or low beam setting of the old lamp still works, this can be done using the wall of a garage or a building:

1. Park the vehicle on a level surface, with the fuel tank about ½ full and with the vehicle empty of all extra cargo (unless normally carried). The vehicle should be facing a wall which is no less than 6 feet (1.8m) high and 12 feet (3.7m) wide. The front of the vehicle should be about 25 feet from the wall.

2. If aiming is to be performed outdoors, it is advisable to wait until dusk in order to properly see the headlight beams on the wall. If done in a garage, darken the area around the wall as much as possible by closing shades or hanging cloth over the windows.

3. Turn the headlights **ON** and mark the wall at the center of each light's low beam, then switch on the brights and mark the center of each light's high beam. A short length of masking tape which is visible from the front of the vehicle may be used. Although marking all four positions is advisable, marking one position from each light should be sufficient.

4. If neither beam on one side is working, and if another like-sized vehicle is available, park the second one in the exact spot where the vehicle was and mark the beams using the same-side light. Then switch the vehicles so the one to be aimed is back in the original spot. It must be parked no closer to or farther away from the wall than the second vehicle.

5. Perform any necessary repairs, but make sure the vehicle is not moved, or is returned to the exact spot from which the lights were marked. Turn the headlights **ON** and adjust the beams to match the marks on the wall.

6. Have the headlight adjustment checked as soon as possible by a reputable repair shop.

Signal and Marker Lights

REMOVAL & INSTALLATION

Parking/Turn Signal/Front Side Marker Lights

On some models, light bulb removal is simply a matter of reaching behind the fender or bumper and removing the bulb and socket assembly. Generally, if there are no screws retaining a lamp assembly from the exterior, bulb removal can be performed using Method "A". On other models, the lamp assembly must be unfastened to expose the bulb and socket. For these, please follow Method "B".

METHOD "A"

▶ **See Figures 66 and 67**

1. Reach behind the lamp assembly. Rotate the bulb and socket approximately ⅛ turn counterclockwise, then remove them as an assembly.

2. Remove the bulb from the socket and insert a new one.

3. Position the bulb and socket behind the lamp assembly. Be sure to line up the locking tabs on the socket with the opening in the lamp assembly.

4. Rotate the bulb and socket assembly approximately ⅛ turn clockwise to lock it in place.

METHOD "B"

▶ **See Figures 68, 69 and 70**

1. Remove the exposed screw(s) retaining the lamp assembly to the fascia.

2. Remove the lamp assembly with the attached bulb and socket assembly.

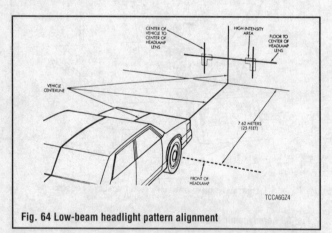

Fig. 64 Low-beam headlight pattern alignment

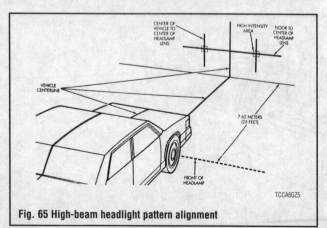

Fig. 65 High-beam headlight pattern alignment

Fig. 66 A parking lamp bulb can be removed with its socket from the rear

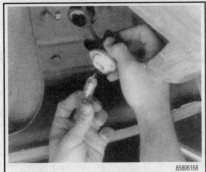

Fig. 67 A small amount of lithium grease on the base of a bulb helps resist corrosion

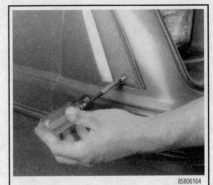

Fig. 68 The lamp assembly is secured to the fascia by a screw

3. Rotate the bulb and socket approximately ⅛ turn counterclockwise, then remove them as an assembly.

4. Remove the bulb from the socket and insert a new one.

5. Position the bulb and socket behind the lamp assembly. Be sure to line up the locking tabs on the socket with the opening in the lamp assembly.

6. Rotate the bulb and socket assembly approximately ⅛ turn clockwise to lock it in place.

7. Position the lamp assembly with the attached bulb and socket assembly.

8. Install the exposed screw(s) retaining the lamp assembly to the fascia.

Rear Lamp/Rear Side Marker Lights

⏵ See Figures 71 and 72

1. From inside the trunk or hatch, turn the bulb socket counterclockwise to the stop, then remove the socket and bulb from the lamp body.

2. Remove the bulb from the socket and insert a new one.

3. Position the socket behind the lamp body. Index the smallest tab to locate the locking tabs and press the socket into the lamp body. Turn the socket clockwise to the stop in order to lock it in place.

High-Mount Brake Lamp

2-DOOR COUPE

⏵ See Figure 73

1. From inside the luggage compartment, locate the high-mount brake lamp wiring under the package tray. Disengage the wiring from the plastic clip.

2. Remove the 2 protective caps from the lamp cover.

3. Remove the 2 screws from the sides of the lamp.

4. Pull the lamp assembly toward the front of the vehicle. The bulb socket(s) can be removed by turning counterclockwise.

5. Pull the bulb from the socket and insert a new one.

6. Installation is the reverse of removal.

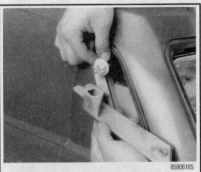

Fig. 69 Remove the lamp assembly from the exterior to access the bulb and socket assembly

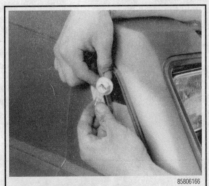

Fig. 70 This type of bulb simply pulls straight out

Fig. 71 Rear lamp light bulbs are easily accessible from inside the luggage compartment

Fig. 72 This type of bulb must be lightly depressed and rotated counterclockwise before removing it from its socket

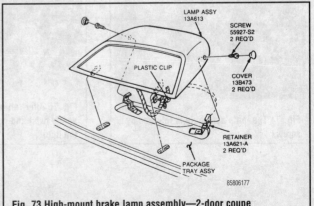

Fig. 73 High-mount brake lamp assembly—2-door coupe

HATCHBACK

▶ **See Figures 74, 75 and 76**

1. Remove the 2 screws from the lamp assembly.
2. Pull the lamp assembly outward and disengage the strain relief clip.
3. Twist and pull the bulb socket(s) to remove.
4. Pull the bulb from the socket and insert a new one.
5. Installation is the reverse of removal.

CONVERTIBLE

1. Remove the luggage crossbar.
2. Remove the 2 lamp assembly screws.
3. Lift up the lamp and pull off the strain relief clip.
4. Twist and pull the bulb socket(s) to remove.
5. Pull the bulb from the socket and insert a new one.
6. Installation is the reverse of removal.

Fog Lights

REMOVAL & INSTALLATION

Fog Lamp Bulb

1. Remove the two screws that retain the lens assembly to the lamp housing.
2. Remove the lens and body assembly from the lamp housing, then turn it access the rear of the lamp body.
3. Release the bulb socket retainer from its locking tabs.
4. Remove the bulb and socket assembly from the lamp body, then pull the bulb directly out of the socket.

❊ WARNING

Do not touch the new halogen bulb with bare hands. This will cause contamination of the quartz, which may result in early failure of the lamp. Do not remove the protective plastic sleeve until the lamp is inserted into the socket. If you inadvertently touch the quartz, clean it prior to installation.

To install:

5. Insert the new bulb into the socket, and the socket into the lamp body. Attach the bulb socket retainer.
6. Position the lens and body assembly right side up (as indicated on the lens) into the lamp housing.
7. Secure the lens assembly to the lamp housing with the two screws and test the lamp for proper operation.

AIMING

▶ **See Figure 77**

If necessary, turn the adjusting nut on each fog lamp until the beams fall within the range indicated by the accompanying illustration.

Light Bulb Specifications

Function	Trade Number
Exterior illumination	
Headlamps	H4656
	Low Beam
	H4651
	High Beam
Front park/Turn lamps	1157
Front side marker lamps	194
Rear tail/Stop lamps & turn	1157
License plate lamp	168
Back-up lamp	156
Interior illumination	
Turn signal indicator	194
Electric de-ice nomenclature (opt.)	**
Heater control nomenclature	161
A/C control nomenclature (opt.)	161
Glove compartment lamp (opt.)	1816
Courtesy lamp—under instrument panel (opt.)	N.A.
Ash tray lamp (opt.)	1892
Digital clock lamp (Opt.)	194
High beam indicator	194
Warning lamps	194
Gauge illumination—all	
Dome lamp (standard)	906
Dome/Map lamp (opt.): dome	906
map	1816
Trunk compartment lamp (opt.)	89
Engine compartment lamp (opt.)	89
Automatic transmission "PRND21" indicator (floor)	1893
Radio lamps	
Dial illumination	1893
AM, AM/FM	
AM/FM/MPX/Tape	
Premium sound indicator	
Stereo indicator lamp	

858060C1

85806171
Fig. 74 The lamp assembly is retained by screws

85806172
Fig. 75 After removing the lamp assembly, gently twist and pull the socket to expose the bulb

85806173
Fig. 76 This type of bulb simply pulls straight out

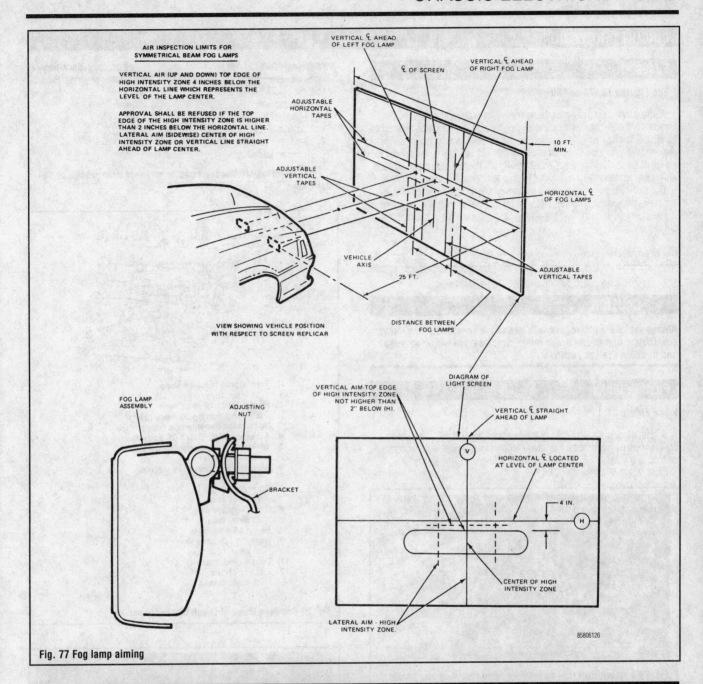

Fig. 77 Fog lamp aiming

TRAILER WIRING

Wiring the car for towing is fairly easy. There are a number of good wiring kits available and these should be used, rather than trying to design your own. All trailers will need brake lights and turn signals as well as tail lights and side marker lights. Most states require extra marker lights for overwide trailers. Also, most states have recently required back-up lights for trailers, and most trailer manufacturers have been building trailers with back-up lights for several years. Additionally, some Class I, most Class II and just about all Class III trailers will have electric brakes.

Add to this number an accessories wire, to operate trailer internal equipment or to charge the trailer's battery, and you can have as many as seven wires in the harness.

Determine the equipment on your trailer and buy the wiring kit necessary. The kit will contain all the wires needed, plus a plug adapter set which includes the female plug, mounted on the bumper or hitch, and the male plug, wired into, or plugged into the trailer harness.

When installing the kit, follow the manufacturer's instructions. The color coding of the wires is, normally standard throughout the industry.

One point to note, most domestic vehicles, and most imported vehicles, have separate turn signals. On some domestic vehicles, the brake lights and rear turn signals operate with the same bulb. For those vehicles with separate turn signals, you can purchase an isolation unit so that the brake lights will not blink whenever the turn signals are operated, or you can go to your local electronics supply house and buy four diodes to wire in series with the brake and turn signal bulbs. Diodes will isolate the brake and turn signals. The choice is yours. The isolation units are simple and quick to install, but far more expensive than the diodes. The diodes, however, require more work to install properly, since they require the cutting of each bulb's wire and soldering in place of the diode.

One final point, the best kits are those with a spring loaded cover on the vehicle mounted socket. This cover prevents dirt and moisture from corroding the terminals. Never let the vehicle socket hang loosely. Always mount it securely to the bumper or hitch.

CIRCUIT PROTECTION

Fuses

▶ See Figures 78, 79 and 80

A fuse panel is used to house the numerous fuses protecting the various branches of the electrical system and is often the most accessible component of the circuit. The fuse panel is usually mounted on the left side of the passenger compartment, under the dash, either on the side kick panel or on the firewall to the left of the steering column. Certain models will have the fuse panel exposed while other models will have it covered with a removable trim cover.

Due to differing equipment levels and design changes, the specific circuits and their corresponding fuse locations vary from vehicle to vehicle. Therefore, it is advisable to refer to the fuse panel schematic in the vehicle or to the applicable owner's manual.

REPLACEMENT

Fuses are simply pulled out and pushed in for replacement.

❊❊ CAUTION

Always replace a blown fuse with one of the specified rating. Never substitute a higher amperage rating, since severe wiring damage and possible fire can result.

Fusible Links

▶ See Figure 81

A fusible link is a short length of insulated wire, integral with the engine compartment wiring harness. It is several wire gauges smaller than the circuit it protects and is located in-line with the positive terminal of the battery.

Fig. 78 A screwdriver may be required when removing trim panels in order to access the fuse panel

Fig. 79 The fuse panel is sometimes concealed behind a removable cover

When heavy current flows or when a short to ground occurs in the wiring harness, the fusible link burns out and protects the alternator or wiring. Production fusible links are color coded:

- 12 gauge: Grey
- 14 gauge: Dark Green
- 16 gauge: Black
- 18 gauge: Brown
- 20 gauge: Dark Blue

➡**Replacement fusible link color coding may vary from production link color coding.**

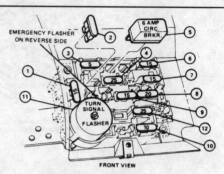

1. Turn signal back-up lamps 15 amp. fuse
2. Heater (std.) 15 amp. fuse air conditioning 30 amp. fuse
3. Instrument panel lamps 5 amp. fuse
4. Accessory-A/C clutch 25 amp. fuse
5. Windshield wiper/washer 6 amp. circuit breaker
6. Stop lamps-emergency warning amp. fuse
7. Courtesy lamps 15 amp. fuse
8. Cigar lighter-horn 20 amp. fuse
9. Radio 15 amp. fuse
10. Warning lamps 10 amp. fuse
11. Turn signal flasher
12. Electric choke 25 amp. fuse

Fig. 80 Common fuse and circuit breaker panel

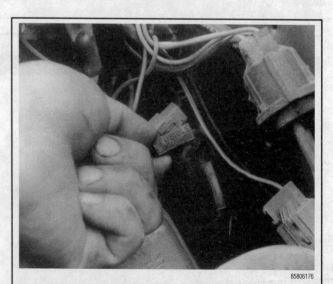
Fig. 81 Fusible links may be marked for identification

REPLACEMENT

▶ **See Figure 82**

1. Determine which circuit is damaged, its location and the cause of the open fusible link. If the damaged fusible link is one of three fed by a common No. 10 or 12 gauge feed wire, determine the specific affected circuit.

2. Disconnect the negative battery cable.

3. Cut the damaged fusible link from the wiring harness and discard it. If the fusible link is one of three circuits fed by a single feed wire, cut it out of the harness at each splice end and discard it.

4. Identify and procure the proper fusible link and butt connectors for attaching the fusible link to the harness.

5. To repair any fusible link in a 3-link group with one feed:

   a. After cutting the open link out of the harness, cut each of the remaining undamaged fusible links close to the feed wire weld.

   b. Strip approximately ½ in. (13mm) of insulation from the detached ends of the two good fusible links. Then insert two wire ends into one end of a butt connector and carefully push one stripped end of the replacement fusible link into the same end of the butt connector, then crimp all three firmly together.

➡ **Care must be taken when fitting the three fusible links into the butt connector, as the internal diameter is a snug fit for three wires. Make sure to use a proper crimping tool. Pliers, side cutters, etc. will not apply the proper crimp to retain the wires and withstand a pull test.**

   c. After crimping the butt connector to the three fusible links, 1mm) of insulation from the wire end of the circuit from which the blown fusible link was removed, and firmly crimp a butt connector or equivalent to the stripped wire. Then, insert the end of the replacement link into the other end of the butt connector and crimp firmly.

   e. Using rosin core solder with a consistency of 60 percent tin and 40 percent lead, solder the connectors and the wires at the repairs and insulate with electrical tape.

6. To replace any fusible link on a single circuit in a harness, cut out the damaged portion, strip approximately ½ in. (13mm) of insulation from the two wire ends and attach the appropriate replacement fusible link to the stripped wire ends with two proper size butt connectors. Solder the connectors and wires, then insulate with tape.

7. To repair any fusible link which has an eyelet terminal on one end such as the charging circuit, cut off the open fusible link behind the weld, strip approximately ½ in. (13mm) of insulation from the cut end and attach the

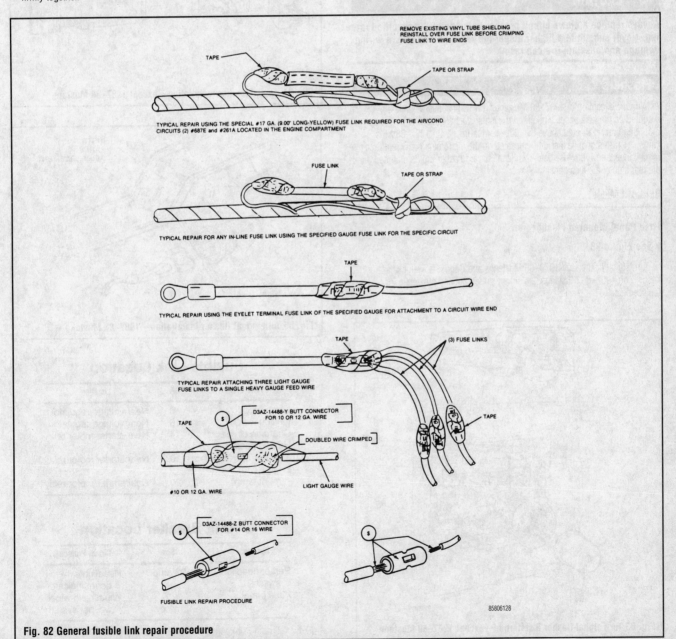

Fig. 82 General fusible link repair procedure

appropriate new eyelet fusible link to the cut stripped wire with an appropriate size butt connector. Solder the connectors and wires at the repair and insulate with tape.

8. Connect the negative battery cable to the battery and test the system for proper operation.

➡**Do not mistake a resistor wire for a fusible link. The resistor wire is generally longer and has print stating, "Resistor: don't cut or splice."**

Circuit Breakers

Circuit breakers are used on certain electrical components requiring high amperage, such as the headlamp circuit, electrical seats and/or windows to name a few. The advantage of the circuit breaker is its ability to open and close the electrical circuit as the load demands, rather than the necessity of a part replacement, should the circuit be opened with another protective device in line.

REPLACEMENT

Circuit breakers are simply pulled out and pushed in for replacement.

✳✳ CAUTION

Always replace a blown circuit breaker with one of the specified rating. Never substitute a higher amperage rating, since severe wiring damage and possible fire can result.

Flashers

With the exception of 1987–88 Mustangs, turn signal flasher units are mounted on the fuse panel, while hazard flasher units are attached to a relay mounting bracket located above the glove compartment. On 1987–88 Mustangs, the turn signal flasher unit is located on the instrument panel reinforcement flange, above the fuse panel, while the hazard flasher unit is mounted on the rear side of the fuse panel.

REPLACEMENT

Fuse Panel Mounted Flasher

▸ **See Figure 83**

Turn signal flashers on 1979–86 Mustangs and Capris, as well as hazard flashers on 1987–88 Mustangs, are simply pulled out and pushed in for replacement.

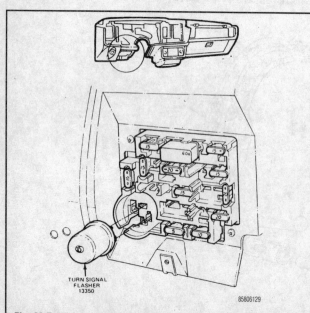

Fig. 83 Turn signal flasher installation—except 1987–88 Mustang

Slot Mounted Flasher

▸ **See Figures 84 and 85**

1. Rotate the flasher 90 degrees counterclockwise to disengage it from the mounting slot.
2. Disconnect the wiring plug.
To install:
3. Lock the flasher in place by inserting the tab in the slot and rotating 90 degrees clockwise.
4. Reconnect the wiring plug.

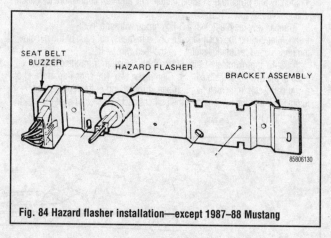

Fig. 84 Hazard flasher installation—except 1987–88 Mustang

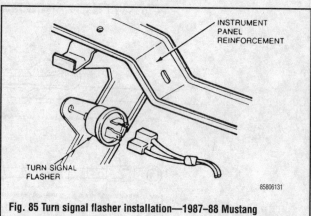

Fig. 85 Turn signal flasher installation—1987–88 Mustang

Fusible Link Location

Fuse Link	GA	Location
Lamp feed	16	Near voltage regulator
Ignition feed	16	Near voltage regulator
Charging circuit	14	Near starter motor relay
Heated backlite and power door locks	16	Near starter motor relay
Engine compartment lamp	20	Near starter motor relay

Circuit Breaker Location

Location	Size	Circuit Protected
Part of headlight switch	22 amp.	Headlights, high-beam indicator
Fuse panel	6 amp.	Windshield wiper-washer system

858060C2

WIRING DIAGRAMS

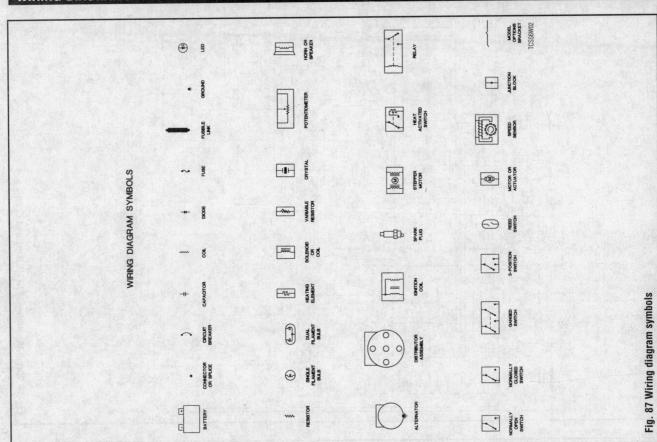

Fig. 87 Wiring diagram symbols

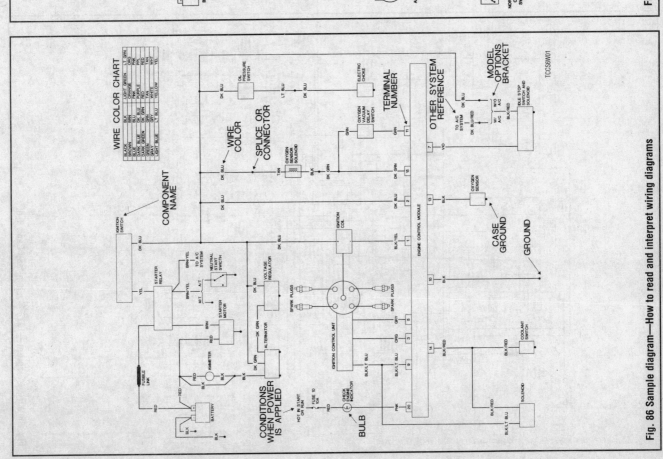

Fig. 86 Sample diagram—How to read and interpret wiring diagrams

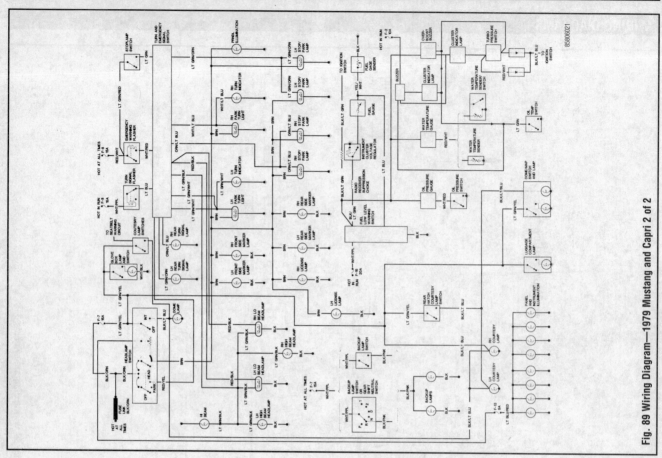

Fig. 89 Wiring Diagram—1979 Mustang and Capri 2 of 2

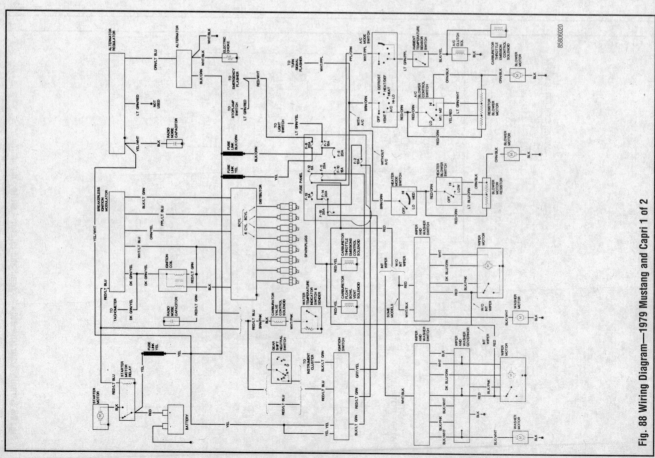

Fig. 88 Wiring Diagram—1979 Mustang and Capri 1 of 2

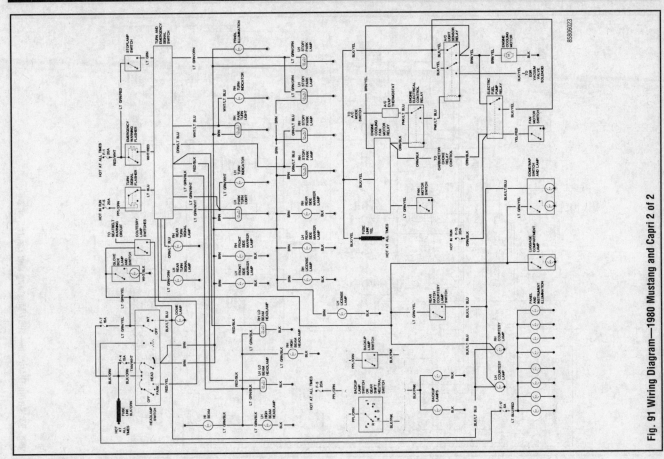

Fig. 91 Wiring Diagram—1980 Mustang and Capri 2 of 2

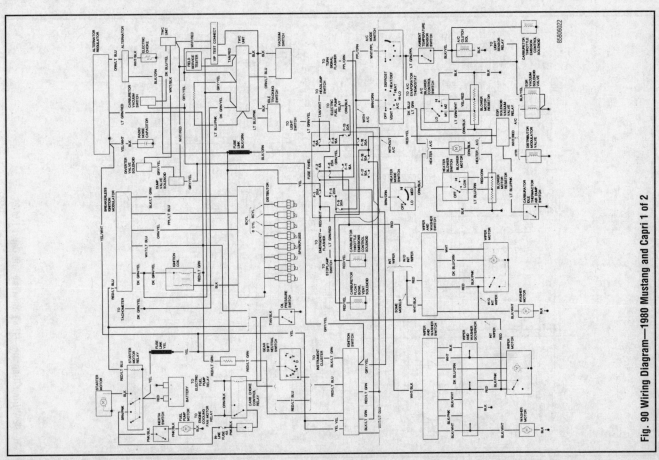

Fig. 90 Wiring Diagram—1980 Mustang and Capri 1 of 2

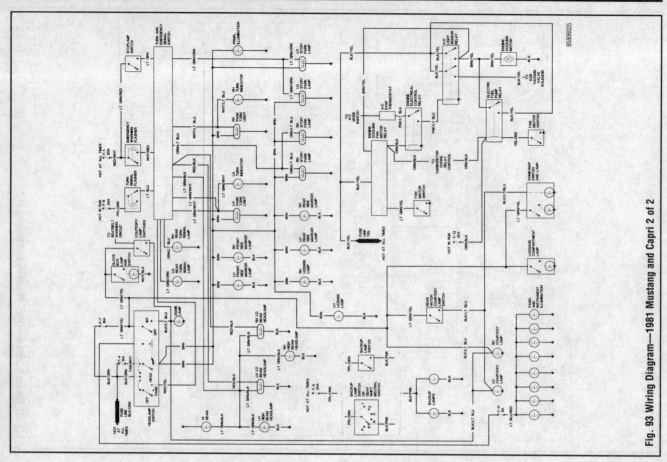

Fig. 93 Wiring Diagram—1981 Mustang and Capri 2 of 2

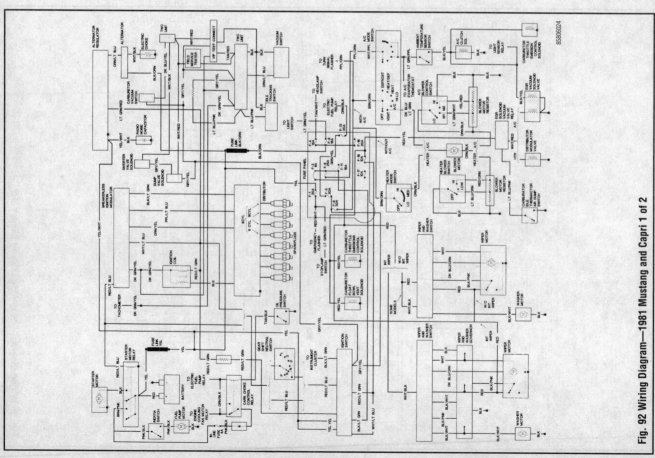

Fig. 92 Wiring Diagram—1981 Mustang and Capri 1 of 2

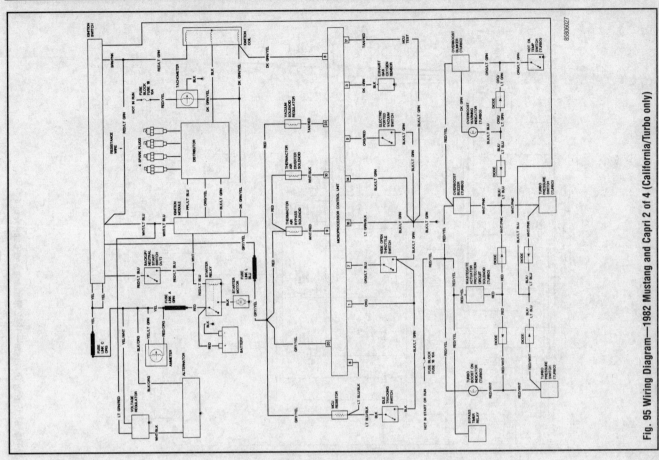

Fig. 95 Wiring Diagram—1982 Mustang and Capri 2 of 4 (California/Turbo only)

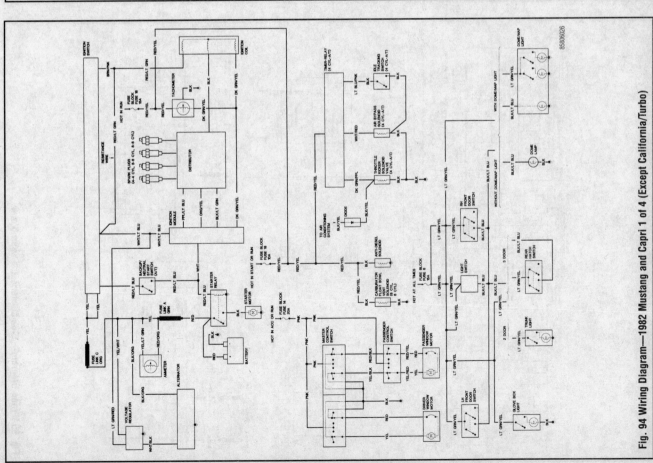

Fig. 94 Wiring Diagram—1982 Mustang and Capri 1 of 4 (Except California/Turbo)

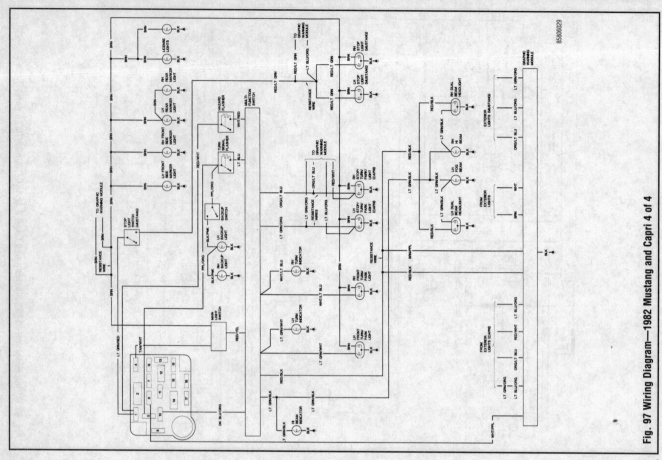

Fig. 97 Wiring Diagram—1982 Mustang and Capri 4 of 4

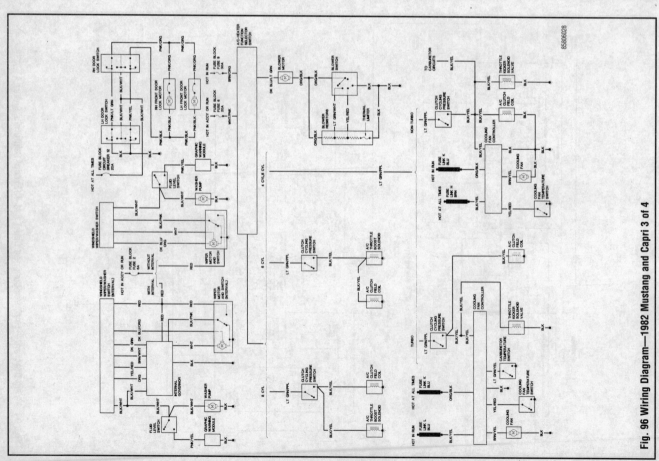

Fig. 96 Wiring Diagram—1982 Mustang and Capri 3 of 4

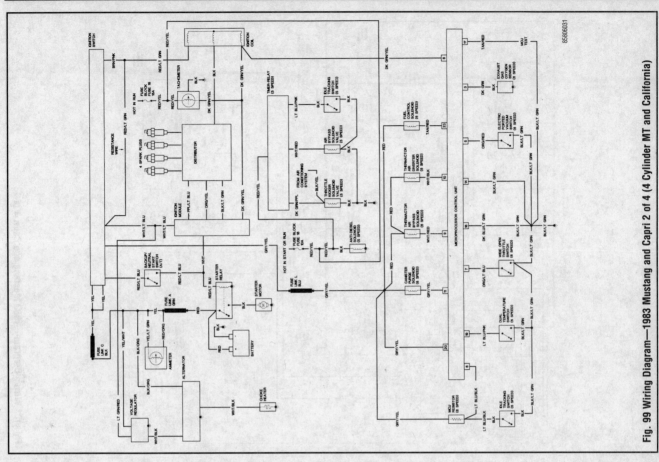

Fig. 99 Wiring Diagram—1983 Mustang and Capri 2 of 4 (4 Cylinder MT and California)

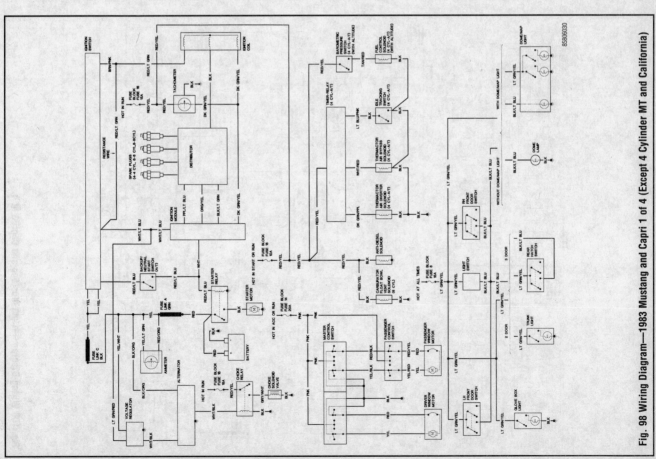

Fig. 98 Wiring Diagram—1983 Mustang and Capri 1 of 4 (Except 4 Cylinder MT and California)

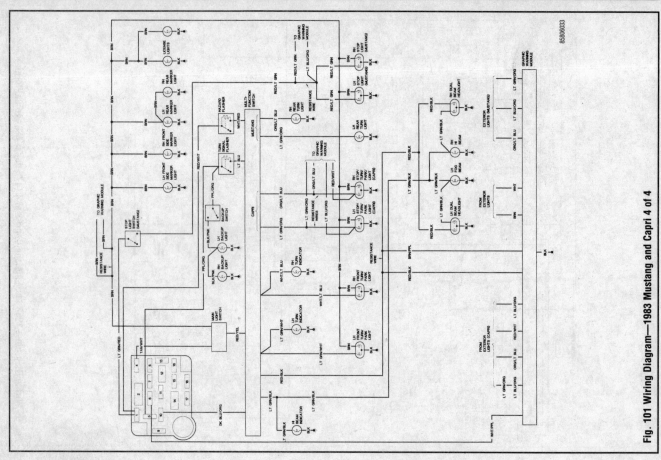

Fig. 101 Wiring Diagram—1983 Mustang and Capri 4 of 4

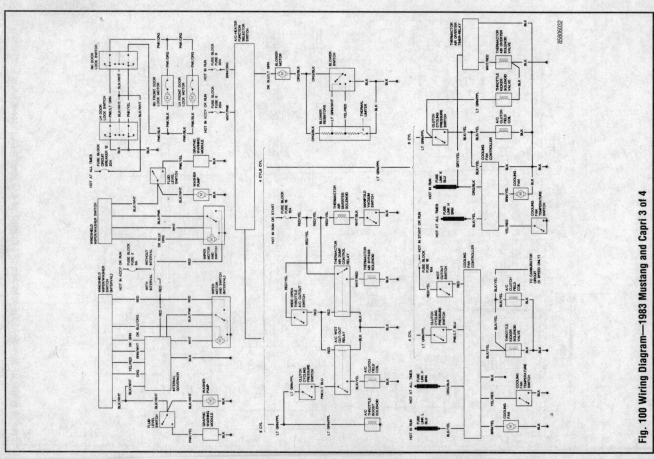

Fig. 100 Wiring Diagram—1983 Mustang and Capri 3 of 4

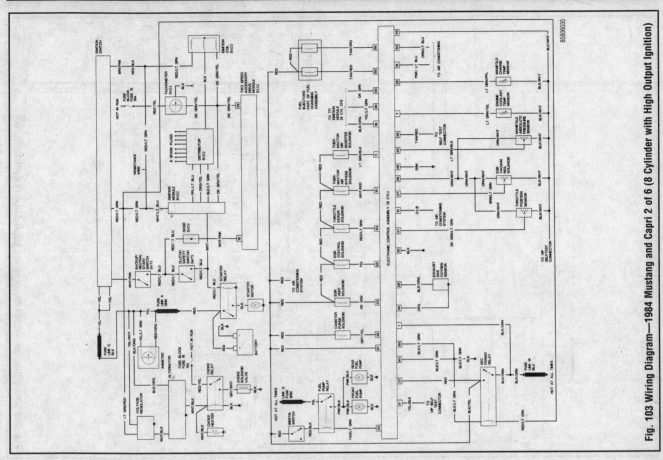

Fig. 103 Wiring Diagram—1984 Mustang and Capri 2 of 6 (8 Cylinder with High Output Ignition)

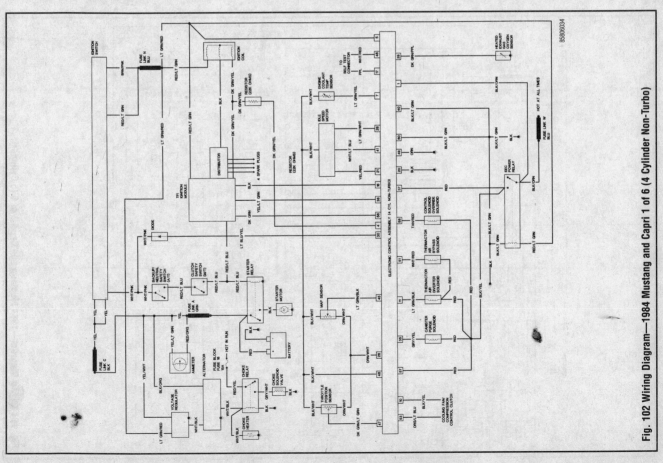

Fig. 102 Wiring Diagram—1984 Mustang and Capri 1 of 6 (4 Cylinder Non-Turbo)

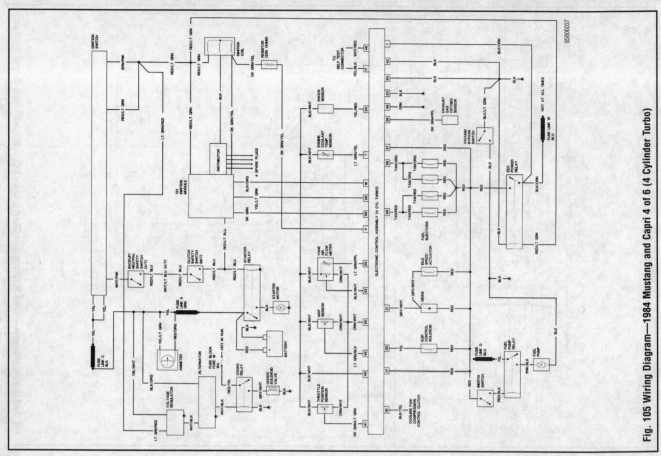

Fig. 105 Wiring Diagram—1984 Mustang and Capri 4 of 6 (4 Cylinder Turbo)

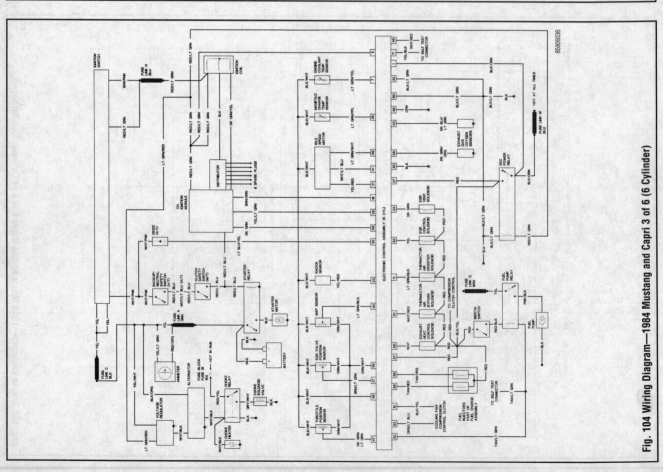

Fig. 104 Wiring Diagram—1984 Mustang and Capri 3 of 6 (6 Cylinder)

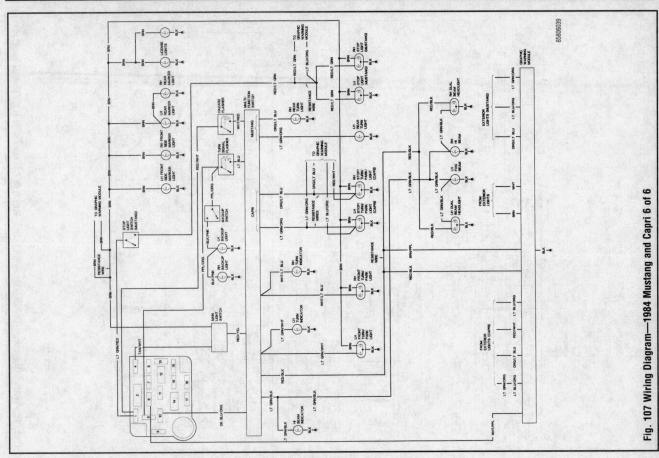

Fig. 107 Wiring Diagram—1984 Mustang and Capri 6 of 6

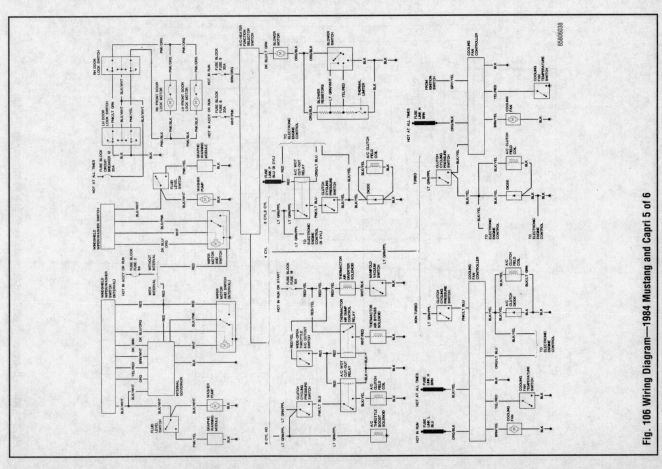

Fig. 106 Wiring Diagram—1984 Mustang and Capri 5 of 6

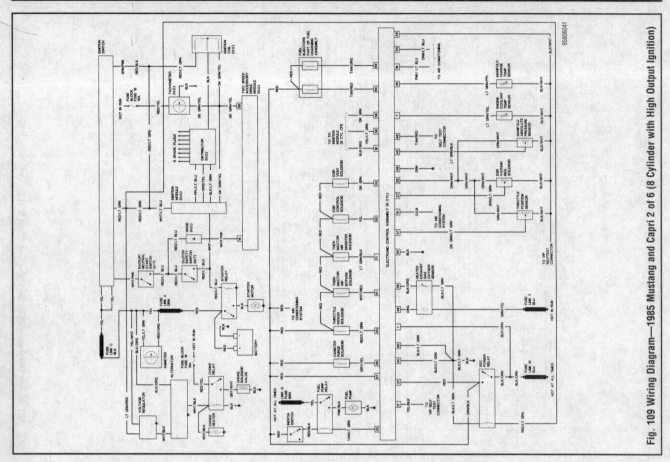

Fig. 109 Wiring Diagram—1985 Mustang and Capri 2 of 6 (8 Cylinder with High Output Ignition)

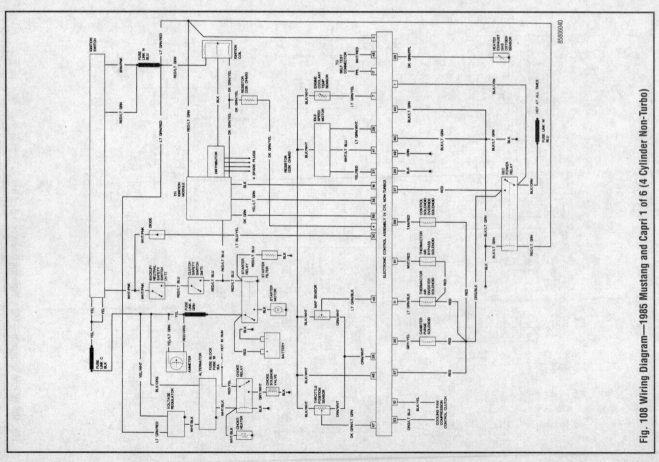

Fig. 108 Wiring Diagram—1985 Mustang and Capri 1 of 6 (4 Cylinder Non-Turbo)

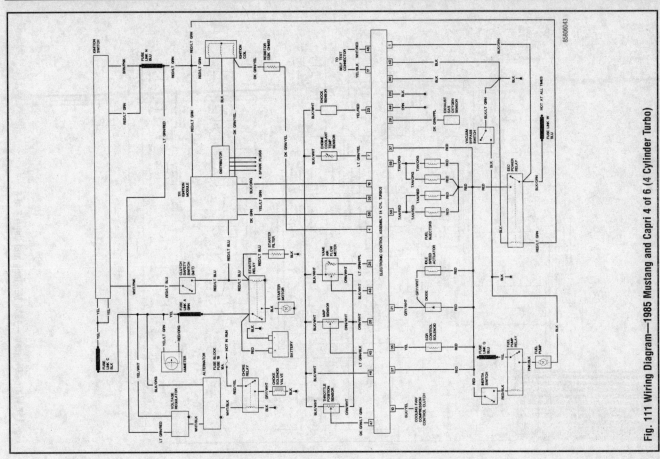

Fig. 111 Wiring Diagram—1985 Mustang and Capri 4 of 6 (4 Cylinder Turbo)

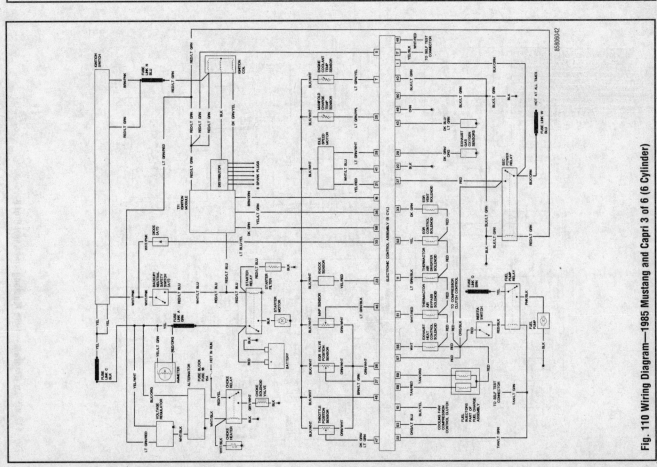

Fig. 110 Wiring Diagram—1985 Mustang and Capri 3 of 6 (6 Cylinder)

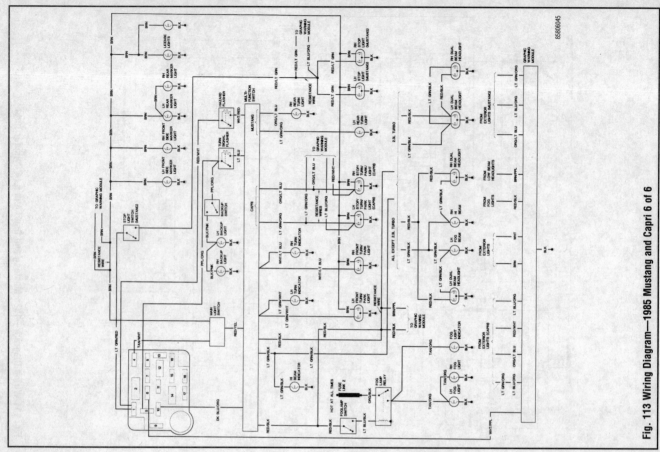

Fig. 113 Wiring Diagram—1985 Mustang and Capri 6 of 6

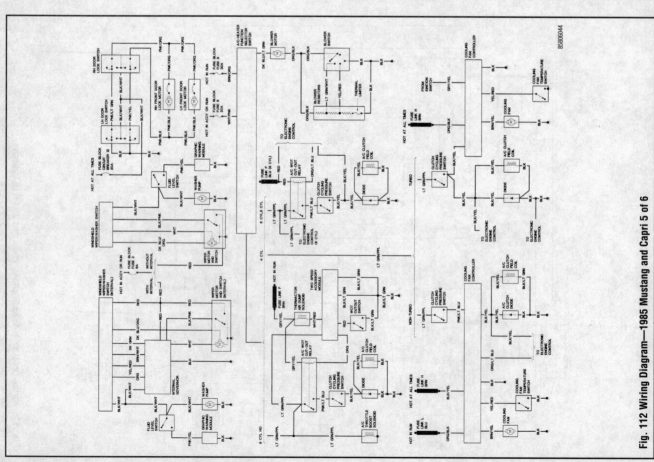

Fig. 112 Wiring Diagram—1985 Mustang and Capri 5 of 6

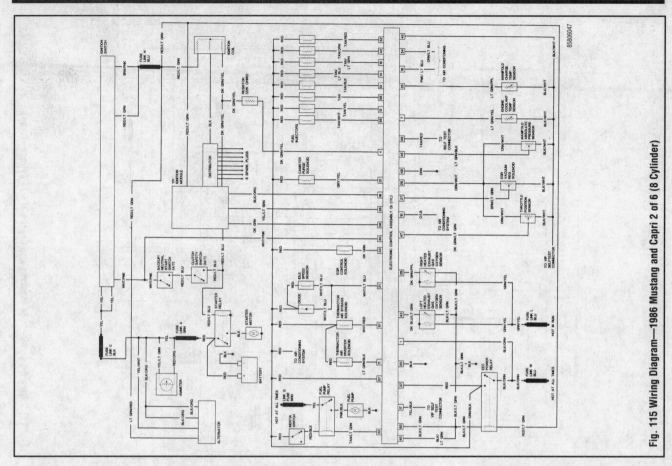

Fig. 115 Wiring Diagram—1986 Mustang and Capri 2 of 6 (8 Cylinder)

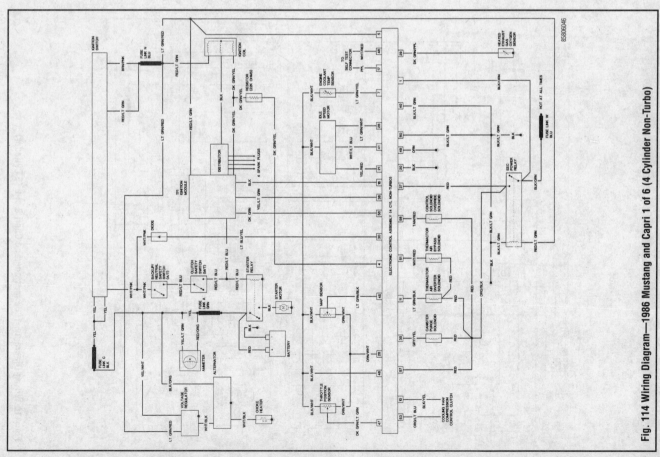

Fig. 114 Wiring Diagram—1986 Mustang and Capri 1 of 6 (4 Cylinder Non-Turbo)

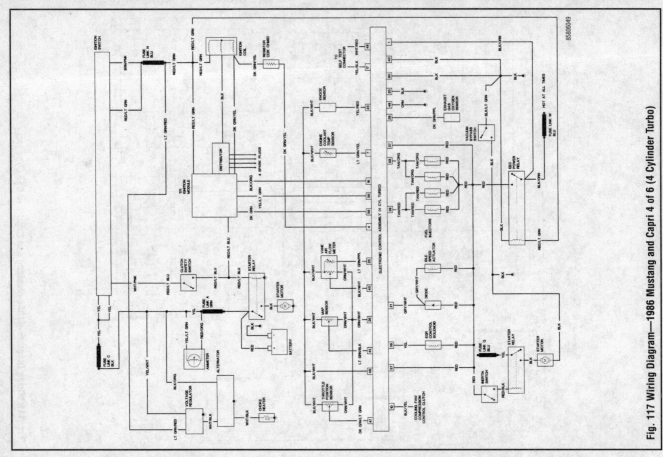

Fig. 117 Wiring Diagram—1986 Mustang and Capri 4 of 6 (4 Cylinder Turbo)

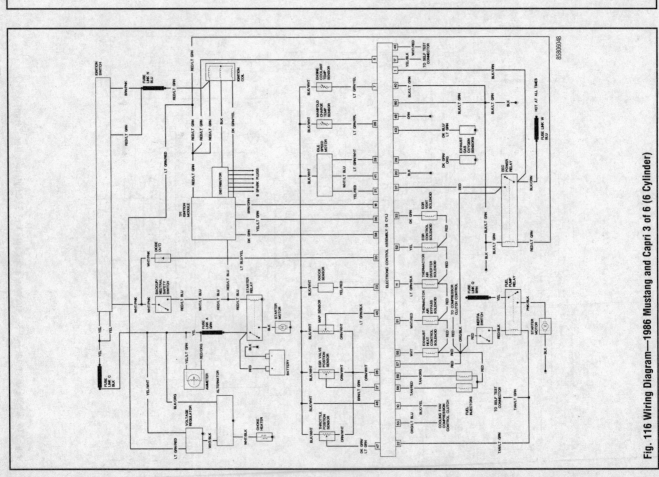

Fig. 116 Wiring Diagram—1986 Mustang and Capri 3 of 6 (6 Cylinder)

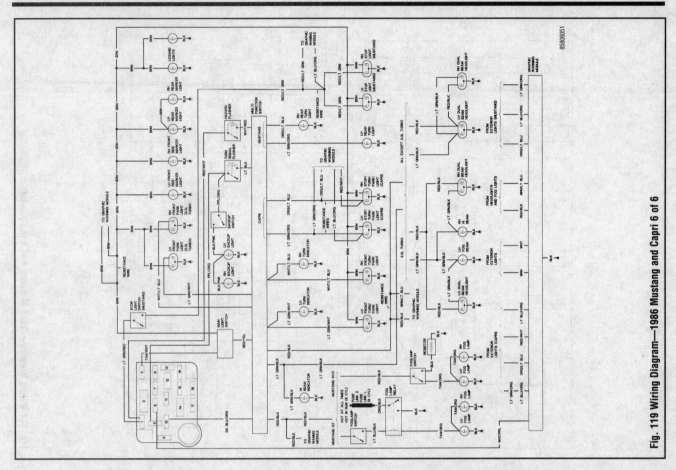

Fig. 119 Wiring Diagram—1986 Mustang and Capri 6 of 6

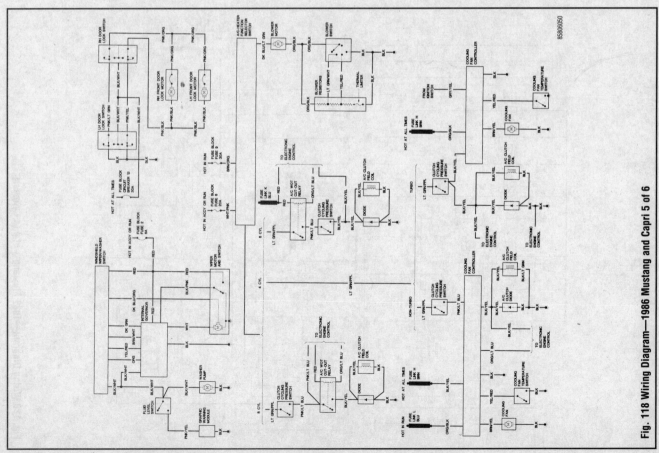

Fig. 118 Wiring Diagram—1986 Mustang and Capri 5 of 6

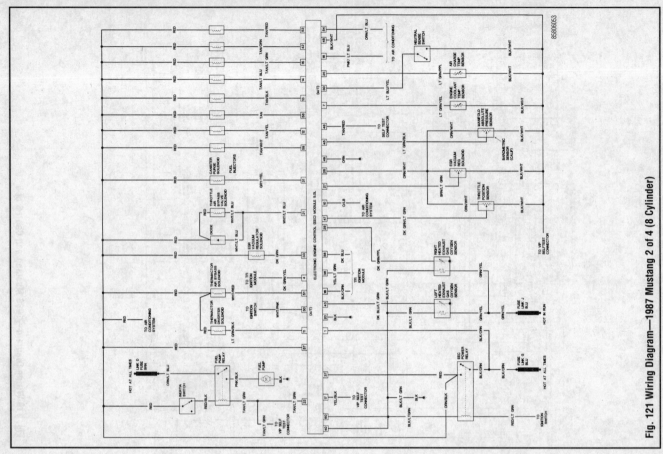

Fig. 121 Wiring Diagram—1987 Mustang 2 of 4 (8 Cylinder)

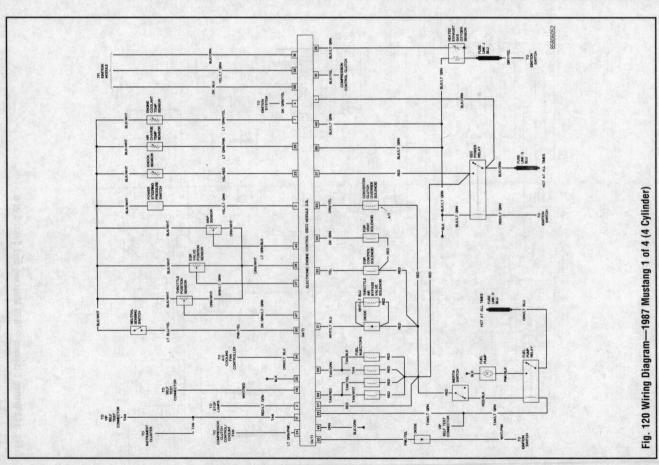

Fig. 120 Wiring Diagram—1987 Mustang 1 of 4 (4 Cylinder)

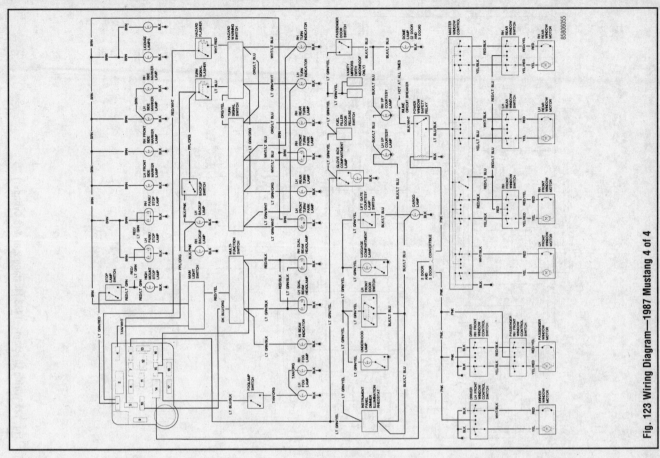

Fig. 123 Wiring Diagram—1987 Mustang 4 of 4

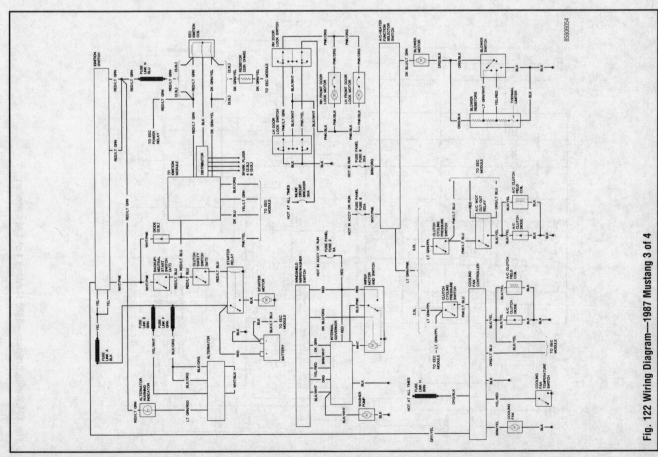

Fig. 122 Wiring Diagram—1987 Mustang 3 of 4

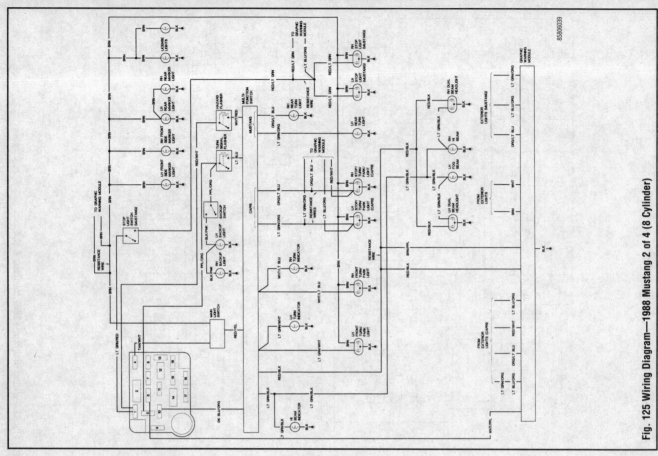

Fig. 125 Wiring Diagram—1988 Mustang 2 of 4 (8 Cylinder)

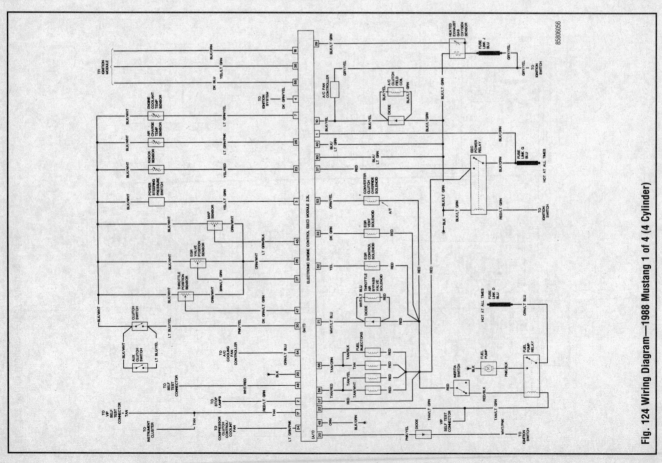

Fig. 124 Wiring Diagram—1988 Mustang 1 of 4 (4 Cylinder)

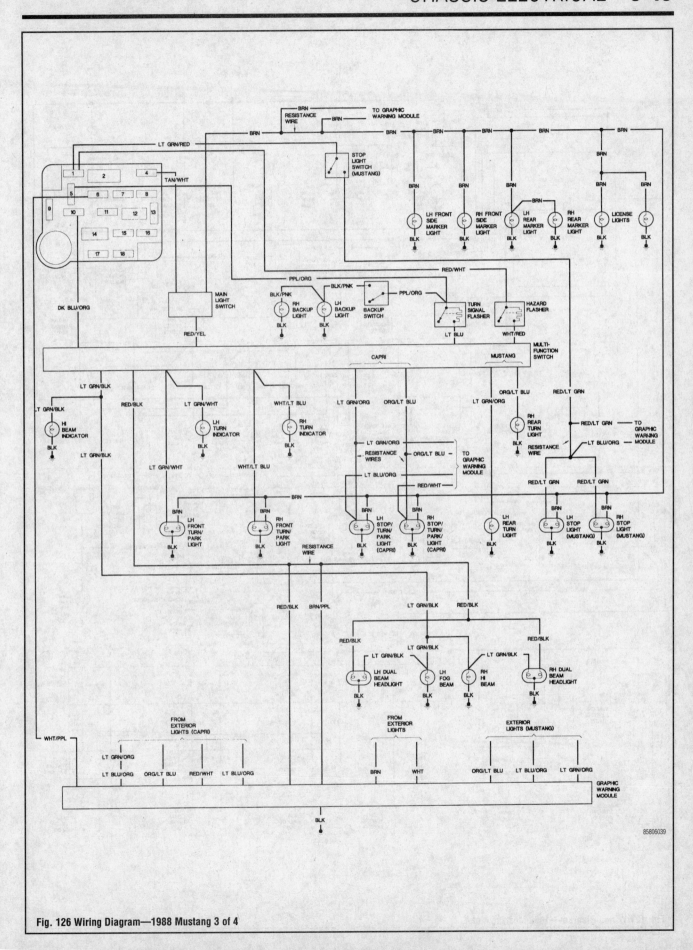

Fig. 126 Wiring Diagram—1988 Mustang 3 of 4

85806039

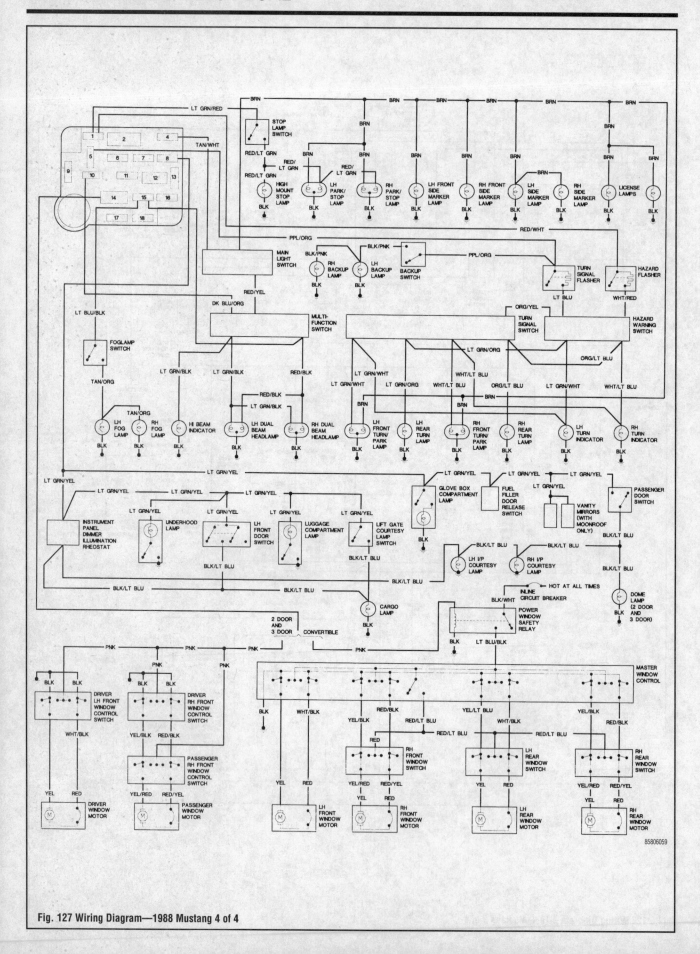

Fig. 127 Wiring Diagram—1988 Mustang 4 of 4

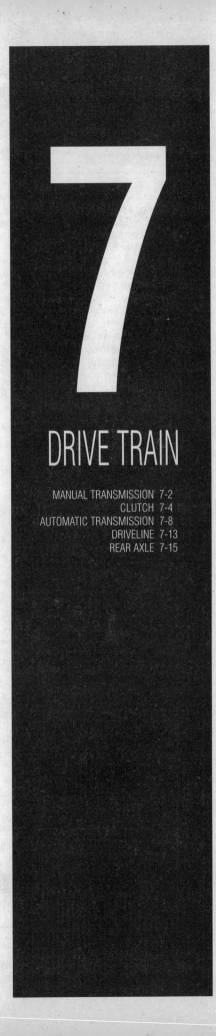

7

DRIVE TRAIN

MANUAL TRANSMISSION

Shift Lever

REMOVAL & INSTALLATION

▶ **See Figures 1, 2, 3, 4 and 5**

1. Place the gear shift lever in the Neutral position.
2. If applicable, remove the attaching screws at the rear of the coin tray and lift to release from the front hold down notch on the boot retainer. Lift the tray over the gear shift lever boot.
3. If equipped with a console tray assembly, use a putty knife to pry up the rear of the cover plate behind the gear shift selector, and remove the screw securing the tray assembly to the rear bracket. Push the tray assembly forward to disengage from the front bracket, and remove the tray assembly.
4. If equipped with a floor console (rather than a console tray assembly), pry up the front of the cover plate, then slide the plate forward and lift over the gear shift lever boot. Remove the screws securing the finish panel to the console and remove the finish panel.
5. Remove the capscrews attaching the boot to the floor pan and move the boot upward, out of the way.

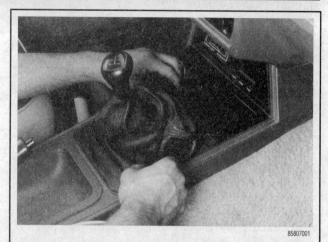

Fig. 1 Remove the cover plate after disengaging its locating pins and tabs

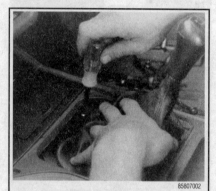

Fig. 2 Unfasten the screws which attach the gear shift lever boot to the floor pan

Fig. 3 With the boot positioned out of the way, remove the gear shift lever attaching bolts

Fig. 4 After removing the gear shift lever attaching bolts, the lever and boot can be withdrawn from the extension housing

6. Remove the lever attaching bolts.
7. Remove the lever and boot assembly from the extension housing.
8. Remove the gearshift knob and locknut and slide the boot off the lever.
9. Installation is the reverse of removal.

Back–Up Light Switch

REMOVAL & INSTALLATION

▶ **See Figure 6**

1. Place the shift lever in neutral.
2. Raise and support the car on jackstands.
3. Unplug the electrical connector at the switch.
4. Unscrew the switch from the transmission extension housing.
5. Screw the new switch into place and tighten it to 60 inch lbs. (7 Nm).
6. Connect the wiring.

Transmission

REMOVAL & INSTALLATION

▶ **See Figures 7 thru 14**

➡ The following procedure may be performed without removing the fly-wheel housing, if the transmission case mounting bolts are accessible.

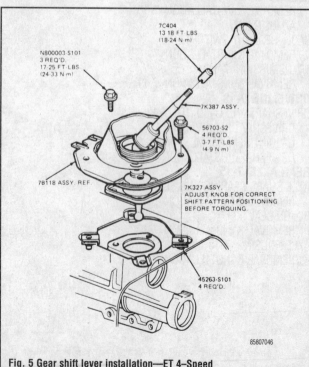

Fig. 5 Gear shift lever installation—ET 4–Speed

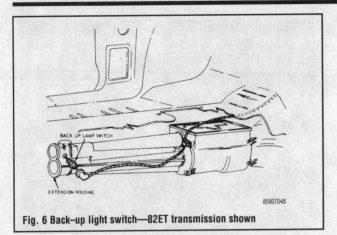

Fig. 6 Back-up light switch—82ET transmission shown

If any of these bolts are fastened from inside the bellhousing, or if the clutch assembly requires servicing, remove the transmission with the flywheel housing.

✳✳ CAUTION

The clutch driven disc may contain asbestos, which has been determined to be a cancer causing agent. NEVER clean clutch surfaces with compressed air! Avoid inhaling any dust from any clutch surface! When cleaning clutch surfaces, use a commercially available brake cleaning fluid.

1. Remove the boot retainer and gear shift lever from the extension housing. If the car is equipped with a 4-speed transmission, remove the bolts that secure the shift control bracket to the extension housing.

2. Working from above, remove the upper clutch housing-to-engine bolts on vehicles with the ET 4-speed transmission.

3. Raise and safely support the car.

4. Matchmark the driveshaft and axle flange for reassembly. Disconnect the driveshaft at the rear universal joint and remove the driveshaft. Plug the extension housing.

5. Disconnect the starter electrical cable and remove the starter motor, if the clutch assembly is to be removed.

6. Remove the clutch housing dust cover and disconnect the clutch release cable from the release lever, if the clutch assembly is to be removed.

7. Disconnect the speedometer cable at the transmission extension. Disconnect the seat belt sensor wires and the back-up lamp switch wires.

8. Remove the two rear support bracket insulator nuts from the underside of the crossmember.

9. Remove the two crossmember-to-body attaching bolts, and remove the crossmember.

10. If necessary, remove the bolts holding the extension housing to the rear support, and slide the catalytic converter heat shield mounting bracket forward.

11. Place a jack (equipped with a protective piece of wood) under the rear of the engine oil pan. Raise or lower the engine slightly as necessary to provide access to the bolts.

12. Remove the transmission-to-flywheel housing bolts, or the flywheel housing-to-engine bolts, if the clutch assembly is to also be removed. If applicable, remove the bolts that secure the engine rear plate to the front lower part of the bellhousing.

13. Slide the transmission or transmission/flywheel housing assembly back and out of the car. It may be necessary to remove the catalytic converter or to slide the catalytic converter bracket forward, in order to provide clearance on some models.

14. If the transmission and flywheel housing assembly were removed as a unit, they can be separated after removing the clutch release lever. Remove the clutch release lever by pulling it through the window in the housing until the retainer spring disengages from the pivot, and unbolt the flywheel housing from the transmission.

To install:

15. If applicable, install a new shift rod seal in the flywheel housing, if the old seal is damaged.

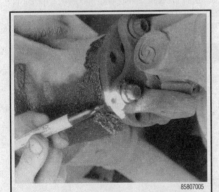

Fig. 7 Matchmark the driveshaft and axle flange for reassembly

Fig. 8 Disconnect the driveshaft at the rear universal joint and remove the driveshaft

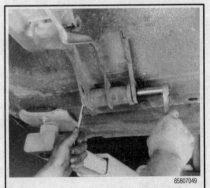

Fig. 9 Two wrenches may be needed to loosen the crossmember mounting bolts

Fig. 10 Remove the crossmember-to-body mounting bolts

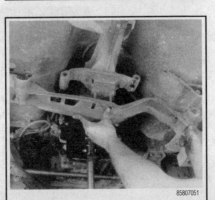

Fig. 11 Lower the crossmember from the rear mount and underbody

Fig. 12 A jack with a protective block of wood can be used to help support the transmission

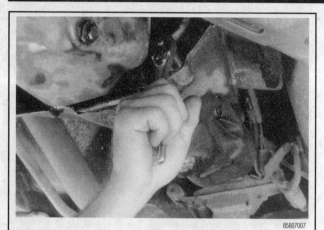

Fig. 13 Remove the bolts that secure the engine rear cover plate to the front lower part of the bellhousing

Fig. 14 The rear cover plate aligns with the bellhousing

16. If the flywheel housing was removed, position it against the transmission case, then install and tighten the attaching bolts to 35–45 ft. lbs. (47–61 Nm). Lubricate and install the clutch release lever and bearing, if applicable.

17. If the flywheel housing was removed, make sure that its mating surface and that of the engine block are clean. Any missing or damaged mounting dowels must be replaced. Apply a film of Standard Transmission Lubricant (Part no. D8DZ–19C547–A) or equivalent to the input shaft bearing retainer.

18. If the transmission and flywheel housing were removed, position them as an assembly against the engine block. It may be necessary to put the transmission in gear and rotate the output shaft to align the input shaft and clutch splines. Install and tighten the attaching bolts to 38–61 ft. lbs. (51–82 Nm) on V8 engines, 38–55 ft. lbs. (51–74 Nm) on the 6–200 engine, and 28–38 ft. lbs. (38–51 Nm) on 4–140 and 6–232 engines.

19. If only the transmission was removed, move it back just far enough for the pilot shaft to clear the clutch housing, then upward and into position against the flywheel housing. Install and tighten the transmission attaching bolts to 35–55 ft. lbs. (47–74 Nm).

20. If applicable, reposition the catalytic converter heat shield mounting bracket.

21. Install the crossmember and torque the mounting bolts to 20–30 ft. lbs. (27–40 Nm). Slowly lower the engine onto the crossmember.

22. Torque the rear mount attaching nuts to 30–50 ft. lbs. (40–67 Nm).

23. Install the starter motor and connect the starter electrical cable, if applicable.

24. If applicable, apply Multi–Purpose Long–Life Lubricant (C1AZ–19590–B or equivalent) to the ball end of the clutch release cable, and connect the cable to the release lever. Install the clutch housing dust cover.

25. Connect the speedometer cable. Connect the seat belt sensor wires and the back–up lamp switch wires.

26. Remove the plug from the extension housing and install the driveshaft, aligning the marks made previously.

27. Refill the transmission to its proper level and lower the vehicle.

28. On floorshift models, install the boot retainer and shift lever. If the car is equipped with a 4–speed transmission, fasten the bolts that secure the shift control bracket to the extension housing.

CLUTCH

➡ **All Mustang and Capri models covered by this book employ a mechanically actuated clutch system, in which clutch release is accomplished through a cable linkage system.**

Adjustments

1979–80 models require a clutch pedal height adjustment. 1981 and later models are equipped with a self–adjusting clutch.

PEDAL HEIGHT

Except 6–200 Engine

1. Raise and support the front end on jackstands.
2. Remove the dust shield.
3. Loosen the clutch cable locknut.
4. To raise the clutch pedal, turn the adjusting nut clockwise; to lower the clutch pedal, turn the adjusting nut counterclockwise. The pedal height should be:
   - 4–cylinder: 5.3 in.
   - 8–cylinder: 6.5 in.
5. Tighten the locknut. When the pedal is properly adjusted, the pedal can be raised about 2¾ in. on vehicles with a 4–140 engine, and about 1½ in. on vehicles with a V8 engine, before reaching the pedal stop.
6. Install the dust shield.

6–200 Engine

1. Raise and support the front end on jackstands.
2. Pull the clutch cable toward the front of the car until the adjusting nut can be rotated. In order to free the nut from the rubber insulator, it may be

necessary to block the clutch release forward so the clutch is partially disengaged.

3. Rotate the adjusting nut to obtain a pedal height of 5.3 in.
4. Depress the pedal a few times and recheck the adjustment. When the pedal is properly adjusted, it can be raised about 2¾ in. to reach the pedal stop.

FREE PLAY

The free play in the clutch is adjusted by a built–in mechanism that allows the clutch controls to be self–adjusted during normal operation.

Self–Adjusting Clutch

The self–adjusting clutch control mechanism is automatically adjusted during normal operation by a device on the clutch pedal. The system consists of a spring–loaded gear quadrant, a spring–loaded pawl, and a clutch cable which is spring–loaded to preload the clutch release lever bearing to compensate for movement of the release lever, as the clutch disc wears. The spring–loaded pawl, located at the top of the clutch pedal, engages the gear quadrant when the clutch pedal is depressed, and pulls the cable through its continuously adjusted stroke. Clutch cable adjustments are not required because of this feature.

INSPECTION

The self–adjusting feature should be checked every 5,000 miles. This is accomplished by insuring that the clutch pedal travels to the top of its upward position. Grasp the clutch pedal with your hand or put your foot under the clutch pedal, pull up on the pedal until it stops. Very little effort is required (about 10 lbs.) During the application of upward pressure, a click may be heard, which means an adjustment was necessary and has been accomplished.

STARTER/CLUTCH INTERLOCK SWITCH

The starter/clutch switch is designed to prevent starting the engine unless the clutch pedal is fully depressed. The switch is connected between the ignition switch and the starter motor relay coil and maintains an open circuit with the clutch pedal up (clutch engaged).

The switch is designed to self–adjust automatically the first time the clutch pedal is pressed to the floor. The self–adjuster consists of a two–piece clip snapped together over a serrated rod. When the plunger or rod is extended, the clip bottoms out on the switch body and allows the rod to ratchet over the serrations to a position determined by the clutch pedal travel limit. In this way, the switch is set to close the starter circuit when the clutch is pressed all the way to the floor (clutch disengaged).

Testing Continuity

▶ See Figure 15

1. Disconnect in–line wiring connector at jumper harness.
2. Using a test lamp or continuity tester, check that switch is open with clutch pedal up (clutch engaged), and closed at approximately 1 in. (25.4mm) from the clutch pedal full down position (clutch disengaged).
3. If switch does not operate, check to see if the self–adjusting clip is out of position on the rod. It should be near the end of the rod.
4. If the self–adjusting clip is out of position, remove and reposition the clip to about 1 in. (25.4mm) from the end of the rod.
5. Reset the switch by pressing the clutch pedal to the floor.
6. Repeat Step 2. If the switch is damaged, replace it.

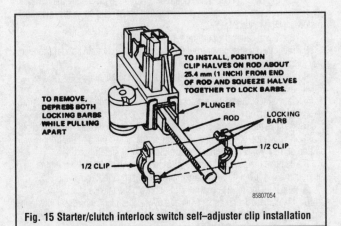

Fig. 15 Starter/clutch interlock switch self–adjuster clip installation

Starter/Clutch Interlock Switch

REMOVAL & INSTALLATION

1. Disconnect the wiring connector.
2. Remove the retaining pin from the clutch pedal.
3. Remove the switch bracket attaching screw.
4. Lift the switch and bracket assembly upward to disengage tab from the pedal support.
5. Move the switch outward to disengage actuating rod eyelet from the clutch pedal pin, and remove switch from the vehicle.

To install:

✳✳ WARNING

Always install the switch with the self–adjusting clip about 1 in. (25.4mm) from the end of the rod. The clutch pedal must be fully up (clutch engaged). Otherwise, the switch may be misadjusted.

6. Place the eyelet end of the rod onto the pivot pin.
7. Swing the switch assembly around to line up hole in the mounting boss with the hole in the bracket.
8. Install the attaching screw.
9. Replace the retaining pin in the pivot pin.
10. Connect the wiring connector.

Clutch Interlock Switch

REMOVAL & INSTALLATION

1. Remove the switch mounting bracket nuts.
2. Disconnect the wiring.
3. Remove the switch and bracket.
4. Installation is the reverse of removal.

Self–Adjusting Assembly

REMOVAL & INSTALLATION

▶ See Figure 16

1. Disconnect the battery cable from the negative terminal of the battery.
2. Remove the steering wheel using a steering wheel puller, Tool T67L–3600–A or equivalent.
3. Remove the lower dash panel section to the left of the steering column.

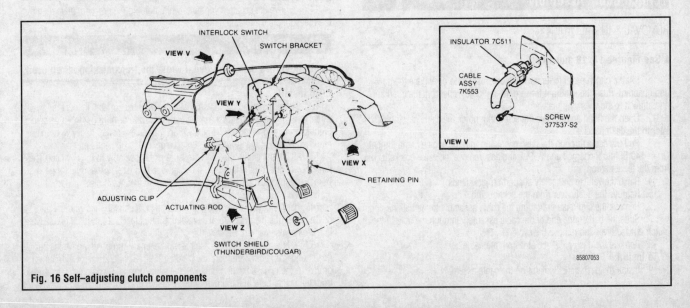

Fig. 16 Self–adjusting clutch components

4. Remove the shrouds from the steering column.

5. Disconnect the brake lamp switch and the master cylinder pushrod from the brake pedal.

6. Rotate the clutch quadrant forward and unhook the clutch cable from the quadrant. Allow the quadrant to slowly swing rearward.

7. Remove the bolt holding the brake pedal support bracket lateral brace to the left side of the vehicle.

8. Disconnect all electrical connectors from the steering column.

9. Remove the 4 nuts that hold the steering column to the brake pedal support bracket and lower the steering column to the floor.

10. Remove the 4 booster nuts that hold the brake pedal support bracket to the dash panel.

11. Remove the bolt that holds the brake pedal support bracket to the underside of the instrument panel, and remove the brake pedal support bracket assembly from the vehicle.

12. Remove the clutch pedal shaft nut and the clutch pedal, as outlined above.

13. Slide the self–adjusting mechanism out of the brake pedal support bracket.

14. Examine the self–adjusting mechanism shaft bushings on either side of the brake pedal support bracket, and replace if worn.

To install:

15. Lubricate the self–adjusting mechanism shaft with motor oil and install the mechanism into the brake pedal support bracket.

16. Position the quadrant towards the top of the vehicle. Align the flats on the shaft with the flats in the clutch pedal assembly, and install the retaining nuts. Tighten to 32–50 ft. lbs. (43–67 Nm).

17. Position the brake pedal support bracket assembly beneath the instrument panel, aligning the four holes with the studs in the dash panel. Install the four nuts loosely.

18. Install the bolt through the support bracket and into the instrument panel. Tighten to 13–25 ft. lbs. (18–34 Nm).

19. Tighten the four booster nuts that hold the brake pedal support bracket to the dash panel to 13–25 ft. lbs. (18–34 Nm).

20. Connect the brake lamp switch and the master cylinder pushrod to the brake pedal.

21. Attach the clutch cable to the quadrant.

22. Position the steering column onto the four studs in the support bracket and start the four nuts.

23. Connect the steering column electrical connectors.

24. Install the steering column shrouds.

25. Install the brake pedal support lateral brace.

26. Tighten the steering column attaching nuts to 20–37 ft. lbs. (27–50 Nm).

27. Install the lower dash panel section.

28. Install the steering wheel.

29. Connect the battery cable to the negative terminal on the battery.

30. Check the steering column for proper operation.

31. Depress the clutch pedal several times to adjust the cable.

Clutch Cable Assembly

REMOVAL & INSTALLATION

▶ **See Figures 17, 18 and 19**

1. Lift the clutch pedal to its upwardmost position to disengage the pawl and quadrant. Push the quadrant forward, unhook the cable from the quadrant and allow it to slowly swing rearward.

2. Open the hood and remove the screw that holds the cable assembly isolator to the dash panel.

3. Pull the cable through the dash panel and into the engine compartment. On 4–140 EFI turbocharged and 8–302 engines, remove the cable bracket screw from the fender apron.

4. Raise the vehicle and safely support on jackstands.

5. Remove the dust cover from the bellhousing.

6. Remove the clip retainer holding the cable assembly to the bellhousing.

7. Slide the ball on the end of the cable assembly through the hole in the clutch release lever and remove the cable.

8. Remove the dash panel isolator from the cable.

To install:

9. Install the dash panel isolator on the cable assembly.

10. Insert the cable through the hole in the bellhousing and through the hole in the clutch release lever. Slide the ball on the end of the cable assembly away from the hole in the clutch release lever.

11. Install the clip retainer that holds the cable assembly to the bellhousing.

12. Install the dust cover on the bellhousing.

13. Push the cable assembly into the engine compartment and lower the vehicle. On 4–140 EFI turbocharged and 8–302 engines, install the cable bracket screw in the fender apron.

14. Push the cable assembly into the hole in the dash panel and secure the isolator with a screw.

15. Install the cable assembly by lifting the clutch pedal to disengage the pawl and quadrant, then, pushing the quadrant forward, hook the end of the cable over the rear of the quadrant.

16. Depress the clutch pedal several times to adjust the cable.

Driven Disc and Pressure Plate

REMOVAL & INSTALLATION

▶ **See Figures 20 thru 29**

✳✳ CAUTION

The clutch driven disc may contain asbestos, which has been determined to be a cancer causing agent. Never clean clutch surfaces with compressed air! Avoid inhaling any dust from any clutch surface! When cleaning clutch surfaces, use a commercially available brake cleaning fluid.

1. Lift the clutch pedal to its uppermost position to disengage the pawl and quadrant. Push the quadrant forward, unhook the cable and allow the quadrant to slowly swing rearward.

2. Raise and safely support the vehicle.

3. Remove the dust cover from the flywheel/clutch housing and disconnect the clutch cable from the release lever.

4. Unfasten the retaining clip and remove the clutch cable from the flywheel housing.

5. Disconnect the starter electrical cable and remove the starter motor from the flywheel housing.

6. Remove the transmission and driveshaft, as described earlier in this section.

7. Remove the bolts securing the engine rear cover plate to the front lower portion of the flywheel housing. Remove the flywheel/clutch housing.

8. Remove the clutch release lever from the housing by pulling it through the housing window until the retainer spring is disengaged from the pivot.

9. Separate the release bearing and hub from the release lever.

10. Matchmark the pressure plate and flywheel to facilitate reassembly in the same position. Loosen the six pressure plate attaching bolts evenly to release the spring pressure.

11. Remove the six attaching bolts while holding the pressure plate. Remove the pressure plate and clutch disc.

✳✳ WARNING

Do not depress the clutch pedal while the transmission is removed.

To install:

12. Before installing the clutch, clean the flywheel surface. Inspect the flywheel and pressure plate for wear, warpage, scoring, or burn marks (blue color). Light scoring and wear may be cleaned up with emery paper; heavy wear may require refacing of the flywheel or replacement of the damaged parts.

13. Attach the clutch disc and pressure plate assembly to the flywheel. The three dowel pins on the flywheel, if so equipped, must be properly aligned. Damaged pins must be replaced. Avoid touching the clutch plate surface. Tighten the bolts finger tight.

14. Insert a clutch alignment arbor and align the clutch disc with the pilot bushing. Torque the pressure plate retaining bolts to 12–24 ft. lbs. (17–32 Nm) in a cross–wise pattern. Remove the clutch alignment arbor.

15. Lightly lubricate the release bearing retainer journal, using Multi–Purpose Long–Life Lubricant (part no. C1AZ–19590–B) or equivalent. Fill the groove in the release bearing hub with the same grease. Clean all excess grease from the inside bore of the hub to prevent clutch disc contamination.

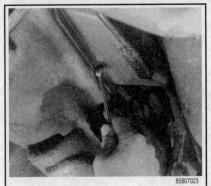

Fig. 17 Remove the bolt(s) retaining the dust cover to the bellhousing

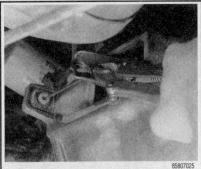

Fig. 18 Slide the ball on the end of the cable assembly through the hole in the clutch release lever

Fig. 19 Install the clip retainer

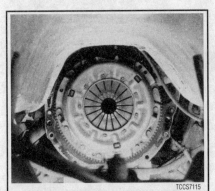

Fig. 20 View of the clutch and pressure plate assembly

Fig. 21 Removing the pressure plate attaching bolts

Fig. 22 Removing the pressure plate and driven disc

Fig. 23 The clutch driven disc may contain asbestos; handle it carefully

Fig. 24 The flywheel surface should be flat

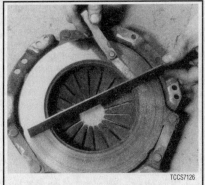

Fig. 25 Inspect the pressure plate for excessive wear

16. Attach the release bearing and hub to the release lever.

17. Lightly lubricate the release lever ball and pocket with the aforementioned lubricant.

18. Lightly lubricate the outside diameter of the transmission front bearing retainer with the same lubricant.

19. Install the release lever and bearing assembly in the flywheel housing.

20. Inspect the flywheel housing dowel holes for misalignment and wear. Also check that the dowels are in good condition; missing or damaged dowels must be replaced.

21. Install the flywheel housing and the bolts which secure the engine rear cover plate to the front lower portion of the flywheel housing.

22. Install the transmission and driveshaft, as described earlier in this section.

23. Connect the clutch cable to the flywheel housing and fasten the retaining clip.

24. Connect the clutch cable to the release lever and install the dust cover.

25. Install the starter motor and connect the starter electrical cable.

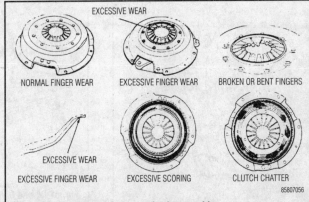

Fig. 26 Telltale signs of a worn clutch assembly

Fig. 27 Use a torque wrench to tighten the bolts in a cross–wise pattern

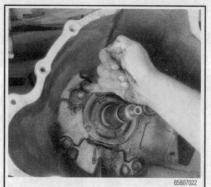

Fig. 28 Lightly grease the ball on which the release lever assembly pivots

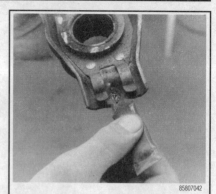

Fig. 29 Lightly grease the release lever pocket which pivots on the ball

26. Install the clutch cable assembly by lifting the clutch pedal to disengage the pawl and quadrant, pushing the quadrant forward and hooking the end of the cable over the rear of the quadrant. Cycle the clutch pedal several times to adjust the cable.

AUTOMATIC TRANSMISSION

Adjustments

BANDS

➡No external adjustments are possible on AOD transmissions.

C3 Front Band

♦ See Figure 30

1. Wipe clean the area around the adjusting screw on the side of the transmission, near the left front corner of the transmission.
2. Remove the adjusting screw locknut and discard it.
3. Install a new locknut on the adjusting screw but do not tighten it.
4. Tighten the adjusting screw to exactly 10 ft. lbs. (14 Nm).
5. Back off the adjusting screw exactly 2 turns.
6. Hold the adjusting screw so that it does not turn and tighten the adjusting screw locknut to 35–45 ft. lbs. (47–61 Nm).

C4 and C5 Intermediate Band

♦ See Figure 31

1. Clean all the dirt from the adjusting screw and remove and discard the locknut.
2. Install a new locknut on the adjusting screw using a torque wrench, tighten the adjusting screw to 10 ft. lbs. (14 Nm).
3. Back off the adjusting screw exactly 1¾ turns for the C4 and 4¼ turns for the C5.

4. Hold the adjusting screw steady and tighten the locknut to 35 ft. lbs. (47 Nm).

C4 and C5 Low–Reverse Band

♦ See Figure 32

1. Clean all dirt from around the band adjusting screw, and remove and discard the locknut.
2. Install a new locknut of the adjusting screw. Using a torque wrench, tighten the adjusting screw to 10 ft. lbs. (14 Nm).
3. Back off the adjusting screw exactly three full turns.
4. Hold the adjusting screw steady and tighten the locknut to 35 ft. lbs. (47 Nm).

SHIFT LINKAGE

Floor or Console Shift

SOLID LINK TYPE

♦ See Figure 33

1. Place the transmission shift lever in the DRIVE position (OVERDRIVE for the A4LD transmission), against the rearward DRIVE (or OVERDRIVE) stop.

➡The shift lever should be held against the rearward DRIVE (OVERDRIVE) stop when the linkage is adjusted.

2. Raise the vehicle and loosen the manual lever shift rod retaining nut. Move the transmission manual lever to the DRIVE (OVERDRIVE) position.

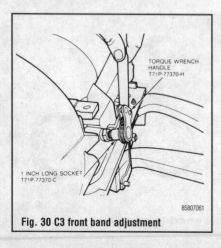

Fig. 30 C3 front band adjustment

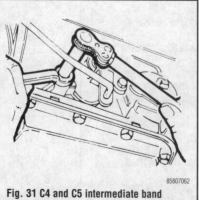

Fig. 31 C4 and C5 intermediate band adjustment

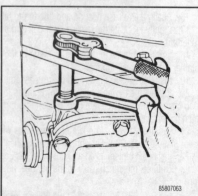

Fig. 32 C4 and C5 low–reverse band adjustment

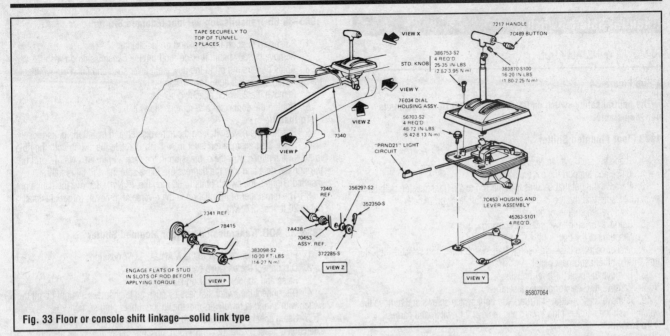

Fig. 33 Floor or console shift linkage—solid link type

➤**DRIVE is the second detent from the rear of the transmission; OVER-DRIVE is the third detent from the full counterclockwise position.**

3. With the transmission shift lever and manual lever in position, tighten the attaching nut to 10–15 ft. lbs. (14–20 Nm); on the A4LD transmission, tighten the nut to 10–20 ft. lbs. (14–27 Nm).

4. Lower the vehicle and check the transmission operation for all selector lever detent positions.

CABLE TYPE

1. Place the transmission shift lever in the DRIVE position, against the rearward DRIVE stop.

➤**The shift lever should be held against the rearward DRIVE stop when the linkage is adjusted.**

2. Raise the vehicle and loosen the manual lever shift rod retaining nut. Move the transmission manual lever to the DRIVE position. DRIVE is the third detent from the rear of the transmission (or second detent from the full counterclockwise position).

3. With the transmission shift lever and manual lever in position, tighten the attaching nut to 10–20 ft. lbs. (14–19 Nm).

4. Lower the vehicle and check the transmission operation for all selector lever detent positions.

Column Shift

1. With the engine off, place the gear selector in the D (Drive) position, or D (Overdrive) position (AOD). Either hang a weight on the shifter or have an assistant sit in the car and hold the selector against the stop.

2. Loosen the adjusting nut or clamp at the shift lever so that the shift rod if free to slide. On models with a shift cable, remove the nut from the transmission lever and disconnect the cable from the transmission.

3. Place the manual shift lever on the transmission in the D (Drive) or D (Overdrive) position. This is the second detent position from the full counterclockwise position.

4. Tighten the adjusting bolt. On cars with a cable, position the cable end on the transmission lever stud, aligning the flats. Tighten the adjusting nut.

5. Check the pointer alignment and transmission operation for all selector positions. If not correct, adjust linkage.

DOWNSHIFT (THROTTLE) LINKAGE

All Models Except AOD Transmission

1. With the engine off, disconnect the throttle and downshift return springs, if equipped.

2. Hold the carburetor throttle lever in the wide open position against the stop.

3. Hold the transmission downshift linkage in the full downshift position against the internal stop.

4. Turn the adjustment screw on the carburetor downshift lever to obtain 0.010–0.080 in. (0.254–2.032mm) clearance between the screw tip and the throttle shaft lever tab.

5. Release the transmission and carburetor to their normal free positions. Install the throttle and downshift return springs, if removed.

AOD Transmission

1. With the engine off, remove the air cleaner and make sure the fast idle cam is released; the throttle lever must be at the idle stop.

2. Turn the linkage lever adjusting screw counterclockwise until the end of the screw is flush with the face of the lever.

3. Turn the linkage adjustment screw in until there is a maximum clearance of 0.005 in. (0.127mm) between the throttle lever and the end of the adjustment screw.

4. Turn the linkage lever adjusting screw clockwise three full turns. A minimum of one turn is permissible if the screw travel is limited.

5. If it is not possible to turn the adjusting screw at least one full turn or if the initial gap of 0.005 in. (0.127mm) could not be obtained, perform the linkage adjustment at the transmission.

AOD Transmission—Alternate Method

If you are unable to adjust the throttle valve control linkage at the carburetor, as described above, proceed as follows.

1. At the transmission, loosen the 8 mm bolt on the throttle (TV) control rod sliding trunnion block. Make sure the trunnion block slides freely on the control rod.

2. Push up on the lower end of the TV control rod to insure that the carburetor linkage lever is held against the throttle lever. When the pressure is released, the control rod must stay in position.

3. Force the TV control lever on the transmission against its internal stop. While maintaining pressure tighten the trunnion block bolt. Make sure the throttle lever is at the idle stop.

AOD IDLE SPEED

Whenever it is necessary to adjust the idle speed by more than 50 rpm either above or below the factory specifications, the adjustment screw on the linkage lever at the carburetor should used. 1½ turns either way will change the idle speed by 50–100 rpm; 2½ turns either way will change the idle speed by 100–150 rpm.

After making any idle speed adjustments, make sure the linkage lever and throttle lever are in contact with the throttle lever at its idle stop and verify that the shift lever is in N (neutral).

Neutral Safety Switch

REMOVAL & INSTALLATION

▶ **See Figure 34**

➡ The neutral safety switch on C3, AOD and A4LD transmissions is non–adjustable.

1979 Floor Mounted Shifter

1. Place the shift lever in NEUTRAL.
2. Raise and support the car on jackstands.
3. Remove the nut that secures the shift rod to the transmission manual lever. Make sure that the rod is free on the selector lever grommet.
4. Remove the shift lever handle.
5. Remove the shift lever selector housing.
6. Disconnect the dial light.
7. Disconnect the back–up/neutral start switch wires and selector indicator light wires at the instrument panel.
8. Remove the selector lever housing.
9. Remove the selector pointer shield.
10. Remove the 2 neutral start/back–up light switch screws and remove the switch. Push the harness plug inward and remove the switch and harness.

To install:

11. Before installing the new switch, be sure that the selector lever is against the neutral detent stop and the actuator lever is properly aligned in the neutral position.
12. Position the harness and switch in the housing. Install the two screws loosely.
13. Put the selector lever in PARK and hold it against the forward stop.
14. Move the switch to the end of its rearward travel.
15. Hold the switch in this position and tighten the two attaching screws.
16. The remainder of installation is the reverse of removal. Check the operation of the switch.

1981–84 Transmissions w/Floor Mounted Shifter

1. Raise and support the front end on jackstands.
2. Remove the downshift linkage rod from the transmission downshift lever.
3. Apply penetrating oil to the downshift lever shaft and nut. Remove the transmission downshift outer lever retaining nut and lever.
4. Remove the 2 switch attaching screws.
5. Unplug the connector and remove the switch.

To install:

6. Position the new switch on the transmission and install the bolts loosely.
7. Place the transmission lever in NEUTRAL, rotate the switch until the hole in the switch aligns with the depression in the case and insert a No. 43 drill bit through the hole and into the depression. Make sure the drill bit is fully inserted. Tighten the switch bolts to 60 inch lbs. (7 Nm). Remove the gauge pin.
8. The remainder of installation is the reverse of removal. Torque the shaft nut to 20 ft. lbs. (27 Nm).

1985–88 C5 Transmission w/Floor Mounted Shifter

1. Raise and support the front end on jackstands.
2. Remove the downshift linkage rod from the transmission downshift lever.
3. Apply penetrating oil to the downshift lever shaft and nut. Remove the transmission downshift outer lever retaining nut and lever.
4. Remove the 2 switch attaching screws.
5. Unplug the connector and remove the switch.

To install:

6. Position the new switch on the transmission and install the bolts loosely.
7. Place the transmission lever in NEUTRAL, rotate the switch until the hole in the switch aligns with the depression in the case and insert a No. 43 drill bit through the hole and into the depression. Make sure the drill bit is fully inserted. Tighten the switch bolts to 60 inch lbs. (7 Nm). Remove the gauge pin.
8. The remainder of installation is the reverse of removal. Torque the shaft nut to 20 ft. lbs. (27 Nm).

1984–88 AOD Transmission w/Floor Mounted Shifter

1. Place the selector lever in the MANUAL LOW position.
2. Disconnect the negative battery cable.
3. Raise and support the car on jackstands.
4. Disconnect the switch harness by pushing the harness straight up off the switch with a long screwdriver underneath the rubber plug section.
5. Using special tool socket T74P–77247–A, or equivalent, on a ratchet extension at least 9½ in. (241mm) long, unscrew the switch. Once the tool is on the switch, reach around the rear of the transmission over the extension housing.
6. Installation is the reverse of removal. Use a new O–ring, and torque the switch to 8–11 ft. lbs. (11–15 Nm).

ADJUSTMENT

▶ **See Figures 35 and 36**

1. Loosen the neutral start switch attaching bolts.
2. Position the manual lever in the park position.
3. Insert a ³⁄₃₂ in. drill through the switch, and move the switch as necessary to allow the drill to rest against the case.
4. Tighten the switch attaching bolts to 55–75 inch lbs. (6–8 Nm) and remove the drill.

Back–up Light Switch

➡ Vehicles with a floor mounted shifter incorporate the back–up light switch into the neutral safety switch. For those vehicles, see the Neutral Safety Switch section, above.

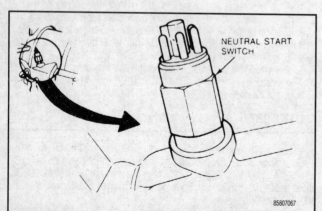

Fig. 34 Neutral safety switch used on C3, AOD and A4LD transmissions

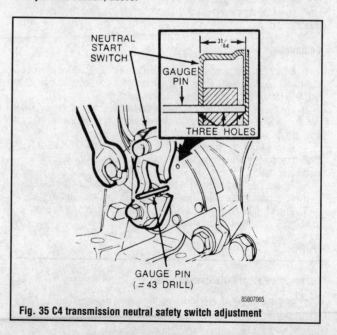

Fig. 35 C4 transmission neutral safety switch adjustment

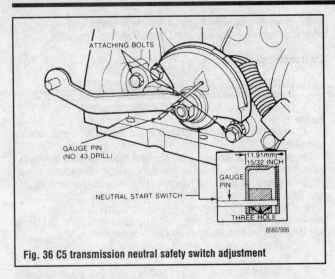

Fig. 36 C5 transmission neutral safety switch adjustment

REMOVAL & INSTALLATION

Column Mounted Shifter

1. Working under the instrument panel, disconnect the wiring at the switch.
2. Remove the 2 screws securing the switch to the steering column and remove the switch.

To install:

3. Check the column to make sure that the metal switch actuator is secured to the shift tube and that it is seated as far as possible forward against the shift tube bearing. Also check for a broken or damaged actuator.
4. When installing the new switch, align the hole in the switch with the hole in the bracket and insert a No. 43 drill through the holes.
5. Place the shift lever in the DRIVE position and hold it against the detent. Install and tighten the switch mounting screws.
6. Remove the drill bit and connect the wires.

Transmission

REMOVAL & INSTALLATION

C3 Transmission

1. Raise and safely support the vehicle.
2. Place a drain pan under the transmission fluid pan. Starting at the rear of the pan and working toward the front, loosen the attaching bolts and allow the fluid to drain. Then remove all of the pan attaching bolts except two at the front, to allow the fluid to further drain. After all the fluid has drained, install two bolts on the rear side of the pan to temporarily hold it in place.
3. Remove the converter drain plug access cover and adapter plate bolts from the lower end of the converter housing.
4. Remove the four flywheel to converter attaching nuts. Crank the engine to turn the converter to gain access to the nuts, using a wrench on the crankshaft pulley attaching bolt. On belt driven overheat camshaft engines, never turn the engine backwards.
5. Crank the engine until the converter drain plug is accessible and remove the plug. Place a drain pan under the converter to catch the fluid. After all the fluid has been drained from the converter, reinstall the plug and tighten to specification.
6. Remove the driveshaft and install the extension housing seal replacer tool in the extension housing.
7. Remove the speedometer cable from the extension housing.
8. Disconnect the shift rod at the transmission manual lever. Disconnect the downshift rod at the transmission downshift lever.
9. Remove the starter–to–converter housing attaching bolts and position the starter out of the way.
10. Disconnect the neutral start switch wires from the switch.
11. Remove the vacuum line from the transmission vacuum unit.
12. Position a transmission jack under the transmission and raise it slightly.
13. Remove the engine rear support–to–crossmember nut.

14. Remove the crossmember–to–frame side support attaching bolts and remove the crossmember.
15. Remove the inlet pipe steady rest from the inlet pipe and rear engine support; then disconnect the muffler inlet pipe at the exhaust manifold and secure it.
16. Lower the jack under the transmission and allow the transmission to hang.
17. Position a jack to the front of the engine and raise the engine to gain access to the two upper converter housing–to–engine attaching bolts.
18. Disconnect the oil cooler lines at the transmission. Plug all openings to keep out dirt.
19. Remove the lower converter housing–to–engine attaching bolts.
20. Remove the transmission filter tube.
21. Secure the transmission to the jack with a safety chain.
22. Remove the two upper converter housing–to–engine attaching bolts. Move the transmission to the rear and down to remove it from under the vehicle.

To install:

23. Tighten the converter drain plug to 20–30 ft. lbs. (27–40 Nm) if not previously done.
24. Position the converter to the transmission making sure the converter hub is fully engaged in the pump gear. The dimension given in the illustration is for guidance only. It does not indicate engagement.
25. With the converter properly installed, place the transmission on the jack and secure with safety chain.
26. Rotate the converter so the drive studs and drain plug are in alignment with their holes in the flywheel.
27. With the transmission mounted on a transmission jack, move the converter and transmission assembly forward into position being careful not to damage the flywheel and the converter pilot. During this move, to avoid damage, do not allow the transmission to get into a nosed down position as this will cause the converter to move forward and disengage from the pump gear. The converter must rest squarely against the flywheel. This indicates that the converter pilot is not binding in the engine crankshaft.
28. Install the two upper converter housing–to–engine attaching bolts and tighten to 28–38 ft. lbs. (38–51 Nm).
29. Remove the safety chain from the transmission.
30. Insert the filler tube in the stub tube and secure it to the cylinder block with the attaching bolt. Tighten the bolt to 28–38 ft. lbs. (38–51 Nm). If the stub tube is loosened or dislodged, it should be replaced.
31. Install the oil cooler lines in the retaining clip at the cylinder block. Connect the lines to the transmission case.
32. Remove the jack supporting the front of the engine.
33. Position the muffler inlet pipe support bracket to the converter housing and install the four lower converter housing–to–engine attaching bolts. Tighten the bolts to 28–38 ft. lbs. (38–51 Nm).
34. Raise the transmission. Position the crossmember to the frame side supports and install the attaching bolts. Tighten the bolts to 30–40 ft. lbs.
35. Lower the transmission and install the rear engine support–to–crossmember nut. Tighten the nut to 30–40 ft. lbs. (41–54 Nm).
36. Remove the transmission jack.
37. Install the vacuum hose on the transmission vacuum unit. Install the vacuum line into the retaining clip.
38. Connect the neutral start switch plug to the switch.
39. Install the starter and tighten the attaching bolts.
40. Install the four flywheel–to–converter attaching nuts.
41. Install the converter drain plug access cover and adapter plate bolts. Tighten the bolts to 15–20 ft. lbs. (20–27 Nm).
42. Connect the muffler inlet pipe to the exhaust manifold.
43. Connect the transmission shift rod to the manual lever.
44. Connect the downshift rod to the downshift lever.
45. Connect the speedometer cable to the extension housing.
46. Install the driveshaft. Tighten the companion flange U–bolt attaching nuts to 30 ft. lbs. (40 Nm).
47. Adjust the manual and downshift linkage as required.
48. Lower the vehicle. Fill the transmission to the proper level with the recommended fluid. Pour in 5 quarts of fluid, then run the engine and add fluid as required.
49. Check the transmission, converter assembly and oil cooler lines for leaks.

C4 Transmission

1. Raise and safely support the vehicle.
2. place the drain pan under the transmission fluid pan. Remove the fluid filler tube from the pan and drain the transmission fluid. On some models it

may be necessary to loosen the pan attaching bolts and allow the fluid to drain. Start loosening the bolts at the rear of the pan and work toward the front. Finally remove all of the pan attaching bolts except two at the front, to allow the fluid to further drain. After the fluid has drained, install two bolts on the rear side of the pan to temporarily hold it in place.

3. Remove the converter drain plug access cover from the lower end of the converter housing.

4. Remove the converter–to–flywheel attaching nuts. Place a wrench on the crankshaft pulley attaching bolt to turn the converter to gain access to the nuts.

5. With the wrench on the crankshaft pulley attaching bolt, turn the converter to gain access to the converter drain plug. Then, remove the plug. Place a drain pan under the converter to catch the fluid. After the fluid has been drained from the converter, reinstall the plug.

6. Remove the driveshaft and install the extension housing seal replacer tool in the extension housing.

7. Remove the vacuum line hose from the transmission vacuum unit. Disconnect the vacuum line from the retaining clip. Disconnect the transmission regulated spark (T.R.S.) switch wire at the transmission, if so equipped.

8. Remove the engine support to crossmember bolts or nuts.

9. Remove the speedometer cable from the extension housing.

10. Disconnect the oil cooler lines from the transmission case.

11. Disconnect the selector rod or cable at the transmission manual lever. Disconnect the downshift rod at the transmission downshift lever.

12. On console and floor shift vehicles, disconnect the column lock rod at the transmission, if so equipped.

13. Disconnect the starter cable. Remove the starter attaching bolts and remove the starter from the converter housing.

14. Remove the bolt that secures the transmission fluid filler tube to the cylinder head and lift the fluid fitter tube from the case.

15. Position the transmission jack to support the transmission and secure the transmission to the jack with a safety chain.

16. Remove the crossmember attaching bolts and lower the crossmember.

17. Remove the five converter housing–to–engine attaching bolts. Lower the transmission and remove it from under the vehicle.

To install:

18. Torque the converter drain plug to 20–30 ft. lbs. (27–40 Nm).

19. Position the converter to the transmission making sure the converter drive flats are fully engaged in the pump gear.

20. With the converter properly installed, place the transmission on the jack. Secure the transmission to the jack with a safety chain.

21. Rotate the converter so that the studs and drain plug are in alignment with their holes in the flywheel.

22. With the transmission mounted on a transmission jack, move the converter and transmission assembly forward into position, using care not to damage the flywheel and the converter pilot. The converter must rest squarely against the flywheel. This indicates that the converter pilot is not binding in the engine crankshaft.

23. Install the five converter housing–to–engine attaching bolts. Torque the bolts to 23–28 ft. lbs. (31–38 Nm). Remove the safety chain from the transmission.

24. Position the crossmember and install the attaching bolts. Torque the bolts to 40–50 ft. lbs. (54–67 Nm).

25. Lower the transmission and install the engine support to crossmember bolts or nuts. Torque the bolts or nuts to 30–40 ft. lbs. (41–54 Nm).

26. Install the flywheel to the converter attaching nuts. Torque the nuts to 23–28 ft. lbs. (31–38 Nm).

27. Remove the transmission jack. Install the fluid filler tube in the transmission case or pan. Secure the tube to the cylinder head with the attaching bolt. Install the vacuum hose on the transmission vacuum unit. Install the vacuum line retaining clip. Connect the transmission regulated spark (T.R.S.) switch wires to the switch, if so equipped.

28. Connect the fluid cooling lines to the transmission case.

29. Connect the downshift rod to the downshift lever.

30. Connect the selector rod or cable to the transmission manual lever. Connect the column lock rod on console and floor shift vehicles, if so equipped.

31. Connect the speedometer cable to the extension housing.

32. Install the converter housing cover and torque the attaching bolts to 12–16 ft. lbs. (16–21 Nm).

33. Install the starter and torque the attaching bolts to 25–30 ft. lbs. (34–40 Nm). Connect the starter cable.

34. Install the driveshaft. Torque the companion flange U–bolts attaching nuts to 25–30 ft. lbs. (34–40 Nm).

35. Lower the vehicle. Fill the transmission to the proper level with the recommended fluid. Adjust the manual and downshift linkage as required.

C5 Transmission

1. Open the hood and install protective covers on the fenders.

2. Disconnect the battery negative cable.

3. On models equipped with a 6–232 engine, remove the air cleaner assembly.

4. Remove the fan shroud attaching bolts and position the shroud back over the fan.

5. On models equipped with a 6–232 engine, loosen the clamp and disconnect the Thermactor® air injection hose at the catalytic converter check valve. The check valve is located on the right side of the engine compartment near the dash panel.

6. On models equipped with a 6–232 engine, remove the two transmission–to–engine attaching bolts located at the top of the transmission bell housing. These bolts are accessible from the engine compartment.

7. Raise and safely support the vehicle.

8. Remove the driveshaft.

9. Disconnect the muffler inlet pipe from the catalytic converter outlet pipe. Support the muffler/pipe assembly by wiring it to a convenient underbody bracket.

10. Remove the nuts attaching the exhaust pipe(s) to the exhaust manifold(s).

11. Pull back on the catalytic coverts to release the converter hangers from the mounting bracket.

12. Remove the speedometer clamps bolt and pull the speedometer out of the extension housing.

13. Separate the neutral start switch harness connector.

14. Disconnect the kickdown rod at the transmission lever.

15. Disconnect the shift linkage at the linkage bellcrank. On vehicles equipped with floor mounted shift, remove the shift cable routing bracket attaching bolts and disconnect the cable at the transmission lever.

16. Remove the converter dust shield.

17. Remove the torque converter to drive plate attaching nuts. To gain access to the converter nuts, turn the crankshaft and drive plate using a ratchet handle and socket on the crankshaft pulley attaching bolt.

18. Remove the starter attaching bolts.

19. Loosen the nuts attaching the rear support to the No. 3 crossmember.

20. Position a transmission jack under the transmission oil pan. Secure the transmission to the jack with a safety chain.

21. Remove the through bolts attaching the No. 3 crossmember to the body brackets.

22. Lower the transmission enough to allow access to the cooler line fittings. Disconnect the cooler lines.

23. On models with the 6–232, remove the (4) remaining transmission–to–engine attaching bolts (2 on each side). On all models, remove the (6) transmission–to–engine attaching bolts.

24. Pull the transmission back to disengage the converter studs from the drive plate. Lower the transmission out of the vehicle.

To install:

25. Raise the transmission into the vehicle. As the transmission is being slowly raised into position, rotate the torque converter until the studs and drain plug are aligned with the holes in the drive plate.

26. Move the converter/transmission assembly forward against the back of the engine. Make sure the converter studs engage the drive plate and that the transmission dowels on the back of the engine engage the bolts holes in the bellhousing.

27. On models equipped with a 6–232 engine, install four transmission–to–engine attaching bolts (2 on each side). On all other models, install the (6) transmission–to–engine attaching bolts. Tighten the attaching bolts to 40–50 ft. lbs. (54–67 Nm).

28. Connect the cooler lines.

29. Raise the transmission and install the No. 3 crossmember through bolts. Tighten the attaching nuts to 20–30 ft. lbs. (27–40 Nm).

30. Remove the safety chain and transmission jack.

31. Tighten the rear support attaching nuts to 30–50 ft. lbs. (41–67 Nm).

32. Position the starter and install the attaching bolts.

33. Install the torque converter to drive plate attaching nuts. Tighten the attaching nuts to 20–30 ft. lbs. (27–40 Nm).

34. Position the dust shield and on vehicles with a column mounted shift, position the linkage bellcrank bracket. Install the attaching bolts and tighten to 12–16 ft. lbs. (16–21 Nm).

35. Connect the shift linkage to the linkage bellcrank. On vehicles equipped with a floor mounted shift, connect the cable to the shift lever and install the routing bracket attaching bolt.

36. Connect the kickdown rod to the transmission lever.

37. Connect the neutral start switch harness.

38. Install the speedometer and the clamp bolt. Tighten the clamp bolt to 35–54 inch lbs. (4–6 Nm).

39. Install the catalytic converts using new seal(s) at the pipe(s) to exhaust manifold connection(s).

40. Install the pipe(s) to exhaust manifold attaching nuts. Do not tighten the attaching nuts.

41. Remove the wire supporting the muffler/pipe assembly and connect the pipe to the converter outlet. Do not tighten the attaching nuts.

42. Align the exhaust system and tighten the manifold and converter outlet attaching nuts.

43. Install the driveshaft.

44. Check and adjust the shift linkage, if necessary.

45. Lower the vehicle.

46. On models equipped with a 6–232 engine, install the two transmission–to–engine attaching bolts located at the top of the transmission bellhousing.

47. On models equipped with a 6–232 engine, connect the Thermactor® air injection hose to the converter check valve.

48. Position the fan shroud and install the attaching bolts.

49. On models equipped with a 6–232 engine, install the air cleaner assembly.

50. Connect the battery negative cable.

51. Start the engine. Make sure the engine cranks only when the selector lever is positioned in the neutral (N) or Park (P) detent.

52. Fill the transmission with type H fluid.

53. Raise the vehicle and inspect for fluid leaks.

Automatic Overdrive (AOD) Transmission

1. Raise and safely support the vehicle.

2. Place the drain pan under the transmission fluid pan. Starting at the rear of the pan and working toward the front, loosen the attaching bolts and allow the fluid to drain. Finally, remove all of the pan attaching bolts except two at the front, to allow the fluid to further drain. With the fluid drained, install two bolts on the rear side of the pan to temporarily hold it in place.

3. Remove the converter drain plug access cover from the lower end of the converter housing.

4. Remove the converter–to–flywheel attaching nuts. place a wrench on the crankshaft pulley attaching bolt to turn the converter to gain access to the nuts.

5. Place a drain pan under the converter to catch the fluid. With the wrench on the crankshaft pulley attaching bolts, turn the converter to gain access to the converter drain plug and remove the plug. After the fluid has been drained, reinstall the plug.

6. Disconnect the driveshaft from the rear axle and slide shaft rearward from the transmission. Install a seal installation tool in the extension housing to prevent fluid leakage.

7. Disconnect the cable from the terminal on the starter motor. Remove the three attaching bolts and remove the starter motor. Disconnect the neutral start switch wires at the plug connector.

8. Remove the rear mount–to–crossmember attaching bolts and the two crossmember–to–frame attaching bolts.

9. Remove the two engine rear support–to–extension housing attaching bolts.

10. Disconnect the TV linkage rod from the transmission TV lever. Disconnect the manual rod from the transmission manual lever at the transmission.

11. Remove the two bolts securing the bellcrank bracket to the converter housing.

12. Raise the transmission with a transmission jack to provide clearance to remove the crossmember. Remove the rear mount from the crossmember and remove the crossmember from the side supports.

13. Lower the transmission to gain access to the oil cooler lines.

14. Disconnect each oil line from the fittings on the transmission.

15. Disconnect the speedometer cable from the extension housing.

16. Remove the bolt that secures the transmission fluid filler tube to the cylinder block. Lift the filler tube and the dipstick from the transmission.

17. Secure the transmission to the jack with the chain.

18. Remove the converter housing–to–cylinder block attaching bolts.

19. Carefully move the transmission and converter assembly away from the engine and, at the same time, lower the jack to clear the underside of the vehicle.

20. Remove the converter and mount the transmission in a holding fixture.

To install:

21. Tighten the converter drain plug to 20–28 ft. lbs. (27–38 Nm).

22. Position the converter on the transmission, making sure the converter drive flats are fully engaged in the pump gear by rotating the converter.

23. With the converter properly installed, place the transmission on the jack. Secure the transmission to the jack with a chain.

24. Rotate the converter until the studs and drain plug are in alignment with the holes in the flywheel.

➡**Be sure to lubricate the pilot bushing.**

25. Align the yellow balancing marks on converter and flywheel on models with the 8–302 engine.

26. Move the converter and transmission assembly forward into position, using care not to damage the flywheel and the converter pilot. The converter must rest squarely against the flywheel. This indicates that the converter pilot is not binding in the engine crankshaft.

27. Install and tighten the converter housing–to–engine attaching bolts to 40–50 ft. lbs. (54–67 Nm). Make sure that the vacuum tube retaining clips are properly positioned.

28. Remove the safety chain from around the transmission.

29. Install a new O–ring on the lower end of the transmission filler tube. Insert the tube in the transmission case and secure the tube to the engine with the attaching bolts.

30. Connect the speedometer cable to the extension housing.

31. Connect the oil cooler lines to the right side of the transmission case.

32. Position the crossmember on the side supports. Position the rear mount on the crossmember and install the attaching bolt and nut.

33. Secure the engine rear support to the extension housing and tighten the bolts to 35–40 ft. lbs. (47–54 Nm).

34. Lower the transmission and remove the jack.

35. Secure the crossmember to the side supports with the attaching bolts and tighten them to 35–40 ft. lbs. (47–54 Nm).

36. Position the bellcrank to the converter housing and install the two attaching bolts.

37. Connect the TV linkage rod to the transmission TV lever. Connect the manual linkage rod to the manual lever at the transmission.

38. Secure the converter–to–flywheel attaching nuts and tighten them to 20–30 ft. lbs. (27–40 Nm).

39. Install the converter housing access cover and secure it with the attaching bolts.

40. Secure the starter motor in place with the attaching bolts. Connect the cable to the terminal on the starter. Connect the neutral start switch wires at the plug connector.

41. Connect the driveshaft to the rear axle.

42. Adjust the shift linkage as required.

43. Adjust throttle linkage.

44. Lower the vehicle.

45. Fill the transmission to the correct level with Dexron®II or Mercon® fluid. Start the engine and shift the transmission to all ranges, then recheck the fluid level.

DRIVELINE

Driveshaft and U–Joints

The driveshaft is the means by which the power from the engine and transmission (in the front of the car) is transferred to the differential and rear axles, and finally to the rear wheels.

The driveshaft assembly incorporates two universal joints, one at each end, and a slip yoke at the front end of the assembly, which fits into the rear of the transmission.

All driveshafts are balanced when installed in a car. It is therefore imperative that before applying undercoating to the chassis, the driveshaft and universal joint assembly be completely covered to prevent the accidental application of undercoating to the surfaces, and the subsequent loss of balance.

DRIVESHAFT REMOVAL

▶ **See Figures 37 and 38**

The procedure for removing the driveshaft assembly, complete with universal joint and slip yoke, is as follows:

1. Mark the relationship of the rear driveshaft yoke and the drive pinion flange of the axle. If the original yellow alignment marks are visible, there is not need for new marks. The purpose of this marking is to facilitate installation of the assembly in its exact original position, thereby maintaining proper balance.

2. Remove the four bolts which hold the rear universal joint to the pinion flange. Wrap tape around the loose bearing caps in order to prevent them from falling off the spider.

3. Pull the driveshaft toward the rear of the vehicle until the slip yoke clears the transmission housing and the seal. Plug the hole at the rear of the transmission housing or place a container under the opening to catch any fluid which might leak.

U–JOINT REPLACEMENT

▶ **See Figure 39**

1. Position the driveshaft assembly in a sturdy vise.

2. Remove the snaprings which retain the bearing cups in the slip yoke (front only) and in the driveshaft (front and rear).

3. Using a large vise or an arbor press and a socket smaller than the bearing cup on one side and a socket larger than the bearing cup on the other side, drive one of the bearings in toward the center of the universal joint, which will force the opposite bearing out.

4. As each bearing is forced far enough out of the universal joint assembly, grip it with a pair of pliers, and pull it from the driveshaft yoke. Drive the spider in the opposite direction in order to make the opposite bearing accessible, and pull it free with a pair of pliers. Use this procedure to remove all bearings from both universal joints.

5. After removing the bearings, lift the spider from the yoke.

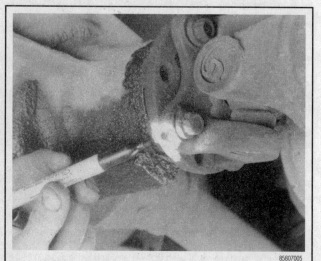

Fig. 37 Matchmark the rear driveshaft yoke and the axle's drive pinion companion flange

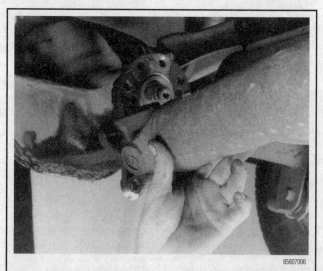

Fig. 38 Remove the attaching bolts and disconnect the driveshaft from the axle companion flange

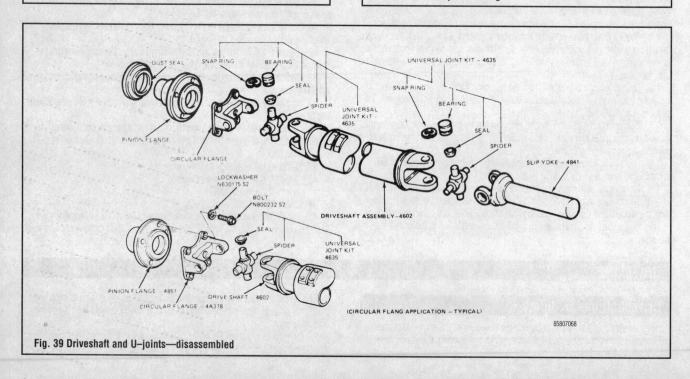

Fig. 39 Driveshaft and U–joints—disassembled

6. Thoroughly clean all dirt and foreign matter from the yokes on both ends of the driveshaft.

When installing new bearings in the yokes, it is advisable to use an arbor press. However, if this tool is not available, the bearings should be driven into position with extreme care, as a heavy jolt on the needle bearings can easily damage or misalign them, greatly shortening their life and hampering their efficiency.

7. Start a new bearing cup into the yoke at the rear of the driveshaft.

8. Position a new spider in the rear yoke and press the new bearing ¼ in. (6mm) below the outer surface of the yoke.

9. With the bearing in position, install a new snapring.

10. Start a new bearing cup into the opposite side of the yoke.

11. Press the bearing until the opposite bearing, which you have just installed, contacts the inner surface of the snapring.

12. Install a new snapring on the second bearing. It may be necessary to grind the surface of this second snapring.

13. Reposition the driveshaft in the vise, so that the front universal joint is accessible.

14. Install the new bearings, new spider, and new snaprings in the same manner as you did for the rear universal joint.

15. Position the slip yoke on the spider. Install new bearings, nylon thrust bearings, and snaprings.

REAR AXLE

Axle Shaft, Bearing and Seal

➡Both integral and removable carrier type axles are used. The axle type and ratio are stamped on a plate attached to a rear housing cover bolt. Axle types also indicate whether the axle shafts are retained by C–locks. To properly identify a C–lock axle, drain the lubricant, remove the rear cover and look for the C–lock on the end of the axle shaft in the differential side gear bore. If the axle has no cover (solid housing) it is not a C–lock. If the second letter of the axle model code is F, it is a Traction–Lok axle. Always refer to the axle tag code and ratio when ordering parts.

REMOVAL & INSTALLATION

➡Bearings must be pressed on and off the shaft with an arbor press. Unless you have access to one, it is inadvisable to attempt any repair work on the axle shaft bearing assemblies.

Flange Type

1. Jack up and safely support the rear of the car.

2. Remove the wheel, tire, and brake drum. On vehicles equipped with rear disc brakes, remove the caliper, retainer, nuts and rotor. New anchor plate bolts will be needed for reassembly.

3. Remove the nuts holding the retainer plate to the backing plate, or the axle shaft retainer bolts from the housing. Disconnect the brake line if equipped with drum brakes.

4. Remove the retainer and install nuts, finger–tight, to prevent the brake backing plate from being dislodged.

5. Pull out the axle shaft and bearing assembly, using a slide hammer. On models with a tapered roller bearing, the tapered cup will normally remain in the axle housing when the shaft is removed. The cup must be removed from the housing to prevent seal damage when the shaft is reinstalled. The cup can be removed with a slide hammer and an expanding puller.

If end–play is found to be excessive, the bearing should be replaced. Shimming the bearing is not recommended, as this ignores end–play of the bearing itself, and could result in improper bearing seating.

16. Check both reassembled joints for freedom of movement. If misalignment of any part is causing a bind, a sharp rap on the side of the yoke with a brass hammer should seat the bearing needle and provide the desired freedom of movement. Care should be exercised to firmly support the shaft end during this operation, as well as to prevent blows to the bearings themselves. Under no circumstances should the driveshaft be installed in a car if there is any binding in the universal joints.

DRIVESHAFT INSTALLATION

1. Carefully inspect the rubber seal on the output shaft and the seal in end of the transmission extension housing. Replace them if they are damaged.

2. Examine the lugs on the axle pinion flange and replace the flange if the lugs are shaved or distorted.

3. Coat the yoke spline with special–purpose lubricant. The Ford part number for this lubricant if B8A–19589–A.

4. Remove the plug from the rear of the transmission housing.

5. Insert the yoke into the transmission housing and onto the transmission output shaft. Make sure that the yoke assembly does not bottom on the output shaft with excessive force.

6. Locate the marks which you made on the rear driveshaft yoke and the pinion flange prior to removal of the driveshaft assembly. Install the driveshaft assembly with the marks properly aligned.

7. Install the U–bolts and nuts or bolts which attach the universal joint to the pinion flange. Torque the U–bolt nuts to 8–15 ft. lbs. (11–20 Nm) and the flange bolts to 70–95 ft. lbs. (95–128 Nm).

6. Using a chisel, nick the bearing retainer in 3 or 4 places. The retainer does not have to be cut, but merely collapsed sufficiently, to allow the bearing retainer to be slid from the shaft.

7. Press off the bearing.

To install:

8. Press the new bearing into position. With tapered bearings, place the lubricated seal and bearing on the axle shaft (cup rib ring facing the flange). Make sure that the seal is the correct length. Disc brake seal rims are black, and drum brake seal rims are gray. Press the bearing and seal onto the shaft.

9. Press on the new retainer.

➡Do not attempt to press the bearing and the retainer on at the same time.

10. On ball bearing–equipped models, replace the seal by removing the seal from the housing with an expanding cone type puller and a slide hammer. The seal must be replaced whenever the shaft is removed. Wipe a small amount of sealer onto the outer edge of the new seal before installation; do not put sealer on the sealing lip. Press the seal into the housing with a seal installation tool.

11. Assemble the shaft and bearing in the housing, being sure that the bearing is seated properly in the housing. On ball bearing models, be careful not to damage the seal with the shaft. With tapered bearings, first install the tapered cup on the bearing, and lubricate the outer diameter of the cup and the seal with axle lube. Then install the shaft and bearing assembly into the housing.

12. Install the retainer, drum or rotor and caliper, wheel and tire. Bleed the brakes.

13. Lower the vehicle.

C–Lock Type

▶ **See Figures 40 thru 54**

1. Jack up and safely support the rear of the car.

2. Remove the wheel and tire from the brake drum.

3. Place a drain pan under the housing and drain the lubricant by loosening the housing cover.

4. Remove the lock securing the brake drum to the axle shaft flange and remove the drum.

5. Remove the housing cover and gasket, if used.

6. Position jackstands under the rear frame member and lower the axle housing. This is done to give easy access to the inside of the differential.

7. Working through the opening in the differential case, remove the side gear pinion shaft lockbolt and the side gear pinion shaft.

8. Push the axle shaft inward and remove the C–lock from the inner end of the axle shaft. Temporarily replace the shaft and lockbolt to retain the differential gears in position.

9. Remove the axle shaft from the housing. Be sure the seal is not damaged by the splines on the axle shaft.

10. Using a Wheel Bearing and Seal Replacer (Tool T85L–1225–AH or equivalent) and a slide hammer, remove the bearing and oil seal as a unit from the housing. Position the tool behind the bearing, so that its tangs engage the bearing outer race, and dislodge the bearing and seal.

11. Separate the bearing from the seal, and inspect the bearing.

➡ Two types of bearings are used on some axles, one requiring a press fit and the other a loose fit. A loose fitting bearing does not necessarily indicate excessive wear.

12. Inspect the axle shaft housing and axle shaft for burrs or other irregularities. Replace any worn or damaged parts. A light yellow color on the bearing journal of the axle shaft is normal, and does not require replacement of the axle shaft. Slight pitting and wear is also normal.

To install:

13. Lightly coat the wheel bearing rollers with axle lubricant. Using Wheel Bearing Installer Tool T78P–1225–A or equivalent, lightly tap the wheel bearing into the housing bore, until the bearing seats firmly against the shoulder.

✳✳ WARNING

Installation of the bearing assembly without the proper tool may cause damage, and result in early bearing failure.

14. Wipe all lubricant from the oil seal bore, before installing the seal.

15. Inspect the original seals for wear. If necessary, these may be replaced with new seals, which are prepacked with lubricant and do not require soaking.

Fig. 40 Loosen the bolts which retain the axle housing cover

Fig. 41 Allow the gear lubricant to drain before removing the cover

Fig. 42 Move the brake line and mounting clip out of the way, if necessary

Fig. 43 Remove the axle housing cover

Fig. 44 A large ring gear is bolted to the differential case

Fig. 45 Loosen the side gear pinion shaft lockbolt

Fig. 46 Remove the side gear pinion shaft lockbolt

Fig. 47 Remove the differential pinion shaft

Fig. 48 Note the C–lock retaining the side gear to the axle shaft

➡Although the right and left side seals may be identical, there are many different types of seals which have been used on rear axle assembles. It is advisable, therefore, to have one or both of the old seals with you when you are purchasing new ones. If the seals are color coded for side identification, do not interchange them from side to side.

16. Using a Wheel Seal Installer (Tool T78P–1177–A or equivalent), gently tap the axle shaft seal into position. If this tool is not available, a wooden block may be substituted.

✲✲ WARNING

Installation of the seal without the proper tool can cause distortion and seal leakage. If the seal becomes cocked in the bore during installation, remove it and install a new one.

17. Remove the lockbolt and pinion shaft. Carefully slide the axle shaft into place. Be careful that you do not damage the seal with the splined end of the axle shaft. Engage the splined end of tne shaft with the differential side gears.

18. Install the axle shaft C–lock on the inner end of the axle shaft and seat the C–lock in the counterbore of the differential side gear.

19. Rotate the differential pinion gears until the differential pinion shaft can be installed. Install the differential pinion shaft lockbolt. Tighten to 15–22 ft. lbs. (20–30 Nm).

20. Install the brake drum on the axle shaft flange.

21. Install the wheel and tire on the brake drum and tighten the attaching nuts.

22. Clean the gasket surface of the rear housing and install a new cover gasket and the housing cover. Some models do not use a paper gasket. On these models, apply a bead of silicone sealer on the gasket surface. The bead should run inside the bolt holes. Tighten the bolts in a cross–wise pattern to ensure uniform draw against the cover.

23. Raise the rear axle so that it is in the running position. Remove the filler plug and add enough specified lubricant to bring the level to ½ in. (12.7mm) below the filler hole. Tighten the filler plug.

24. Lower the vehicle.

Pinion Seal

REMOVAL & INSTALLATION

◗ **See Figures 55 and 56**

➡**Special tools are needed for this job.**

1. Raise and support the vehicle and remove the rear wheels and brake drums, or calipers.

2. Mark the driveshaft end yoke and axle companion flange for reassembly reference. Disconnect the driveshaft from the rear axle companion flange, and remove the driveshaft from the transmission extension housing. Temporarily plug the extension housing to prevent oil leakage.

3. With a socket on the pinion nut and an inch lb. torque wrench, rotate the drive pinion several revolutions. Check and record the torque required to turn the drive pinion.

4. While using a flange holding tool to steady the companion flange, remove and discard the pinion nut.

5. Clean the area around the oil seal. Place a drain pan under the seal, or raise the front of the car higher than the rear.

6. Mark the companion flange and the drive pinion shaft for reassembly reference.

7. Remove the companion flange with Companion Flange Remover T65L–4851–B, or equivalent puller.

8. Lift out the pinion oil seal using grease seal remover TOOL–1175–AC and a slide hammer, or their equivalent. If necessary, pry the seal out of its housing.

Fig. 49 Push the flanged end of the axle shaft toward the center of the vehicle, and disengage the C–lock

Fig. 50 Remove the axle shaft assembly

Fig. 51 The axle shaft seal should be removed with the bearing as a unit. Use of a special seal and bearing removal tool is recommended.

Fig. 52 After bearing replacement, gently tap the seal into position

Fig. 53 Use a gasket scraper to remove traces of old sealant or cover gasket

Fig. 54 Gear lubricant is added to the rear axle housing through a removable filler plug

9. Clean and inspect the oil seal seating surface, and replace with a new one if the surface is pitted, grooved, or otherwise damaged.

To install:

10. Before installing the new seal, coat the lip of the seal with rear axle lubricant.

11. Install the seal, using Pinion Seal Replacer T79P–4676–A or equivalent, to drive it into place.

❋ WARNING

Installation without the proper tool may result in early seal failure. If the seal becomes cocked during installation, remove and replace with a new seal.

12. Install the companion flange on the pinion shaft. Align the marks made on the pinion shaft and flange during disassembly.

➡**The companion flange must not be hammered upon, or assembled with power tools.**

13. Install a new pinion nut. Tighten the nut until end-play is removed from the pinion bearing. Do not overtighten.

14. Check the torque required to turn the drive pinion. The pinion must be turned several revolutions to obtain an accurate reading.

15. Tighten the pinion nut to obtain the torque reading observed during disassembly (Step 3), plus 5 inch lbs. Tighten the nut minutely each time, to avoid overtightening. Do not loosen and then retighten the nut. Pinion preload should be 8–14 inch lbs. (1–2 Nm).

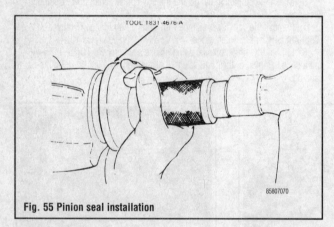

Fig. 55 Pinion seal installation

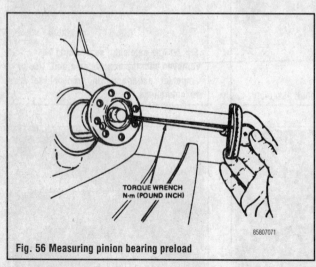

Fig. 56 Measuring pinion bearing preload

➡**If the desired torque is exceeded, a new collapsible pinion spacer sleeve must be installed and the pinion gear preload reset.**

16. Remove the plug from the extension housing, and install the front end of the driveshaft on the transmission output shaft. 17. Connect the rear end of the driveshaft to the axle companion flange, aligning the index marks made during disassembly. Tighten the four bolts to 70–95 ft. lbs. (95–128 Nm).

18. Add rear axle gear lubricant, if necessary, to bring the level to the bottom of the filler hole, and tighten the filler plug to 15–30 ft. lbs. (20–41 Nm). Remove the drain pan, if applicable.

19. Install the rear brake drums, or calipers, and wheels.

20. Lower the vehicle.

Axle Housing

REMOVAL & INSTALLATION

1. Raise the vehicle and support it on jackstands placed under the frame.
2. Remove the rear wheels.
3. Place an indexing mark on the rear yoke and driveshaft, and disconnect the shaft.
4. Disconnect the shock absorbers from the axle tubes. Disconnect the stabilizer bar at the axle bracket, on vehicles so equipped.
5. Disconnect the brake hose from the tee fitting on the axle housing. Disconnect the brake lines at the clips on the housing. Disconnect the vent tube at the axle.
6. Disconnect the parking brake cable at the frame mounting.
7. Support the rear axle with a jack.
8. Disconnect the lower control arms at the axle and swing them down out of the way.
9. Disconnect the upper control arms at the axle and swing them up out of the way.
10. Lower the axle slightly, and remove the coil springs and insulators.
11. Lower the axle housing.

To install:

12. Raise the axle into position and connect the lower arms. Do not tighten the bolts yet.
13. Lower the axle slightly, and install the coil springs and insulators.
14. Raise the axle and connect the upper control arms. Do not tighten the bolts yet.
15. Connect the parking brake cable at the frame mounting.
16. Connect the brake hose at the tee fitting on the axle housing.
17. Connect the vent tube at the axle. Apply thread locking compound to the threads.
18. Connect the stabilizer bar at the axle bracket, on vehicles so equipped.
19. Connect the shock absorbers from the axle tubes.
20. Connect the driveshaft.
21. Install the rear wheels.
22. Lower the vehicle.

Once the car is back on its wheels, observe the following torques:

Removable carrier axles:
- Lower control arm bolts — 90 ft. lbs. (122 Nm)
- Lower shock absorber nuts — 85 ft. lbs. (115 Nm)
- Upper control arm bolts — 120 ft. lbs. (163 Nm)

Integral carrier axles:
- Lower arm bolts — 100 ft. lbs. (135 Nm)
- Lower shock absorber nuts — 55 ft. lbs. (75 Nm)
- Upper arm bolts — 100 ft. lbs. (135 Nm)

❋ WARNING

Bleed and adjust the brakes accordingly, as detailed in Section 9.

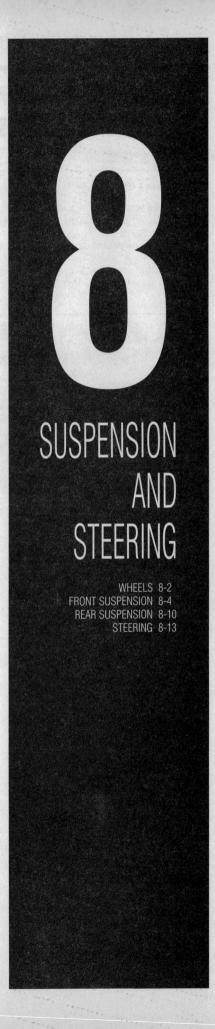

8

SUSPENSION AND STEERING

WHEELS

Wheel Assembly

REMOVAL & INSTALLATION

▶ **See Figures 1 thru 7**

1. Park the vehicle on a level surface.
2. Remove the jack, tire iron and, if necessary, the spare tire from their storage compartments.
3. Check the owner's manual or refer to Section 1 of this manual for the jacking points on your vehicle. Then, place the jack in the proper position.
4. If equipped with lug nut trim caps, remove them by either unscrewing or pulling them off the lug nuts, as appropriate. Consult the owner's manual, if necessary.

Fig. 1 Place the jack at the proper lifting point on your vehicle

TCCA8P00

5. If equipped with a wheel cover or hub cap, insert the tapered end of the tire iron in the groove and pry off the cover.
6. Apply the parking brake and block the diagonally opposite wheel with a wheel chock or two.

➡**Wheel chocks may be purchased at your local auto parts store, or a block of wood cut into wedges may be used. If possible, keep one or two of the chocks in your tire storage compartment, in case any of the tires has to be removed on the side of the road.**

7. If equipped with an automatic transmission/transaxle, place the selector lever in **P** or Park; with a manual transmission/transaxle, place the shifter in Reverse.
8. With the tires still on the ground, use the tire iron/wrench to break the lug nuts loose.

➡**If a nut is stuck, never use heat to loosen it or damage to the wheel and bearings may occur. If the nuts are seized, one or two heavy hammer blows directly on the end of the bolt usually loosens the rust. Be careful, as continued pounding will likely damage the brake drum or rotor.**

9. Using the jack, raise the vehicle until the tire is clear of the ground. Support the vehicle safely using jackstands.
10. Remove the lug nuts, then remove the tire and wheel assembly.

To install:
11. Make sure the wheel and hub mating surfaces, as well as the wheel lug studs, are clean and free of all foreign material. Always remove rust from the wheel mounting surface and the brake rotor or drum. Failure to do so may cause the lug nuts to loosen in service.
12. Install the tire and wheel assembly and hand-tighten the lug nuts.
13. Using the tire wrench, tighten all the lug nuts, in a crisscross pattern, until they are snug.
14. Raise the vehicle and withdraw the jackstand, then lower the vehicle.

TCCA8P01

Fig. 2 Before jacking the vehicle, block the diagonally opposite wheel with one or, preferably, two chocks

TCCA8P02

Fig. 3 With the vehicle still on the ground, break the lug nuts loose using the wrench end of the tire iron

TCCA8P03

Fig. 4 After the lug nuts have been loosened, raise the vehicle using the jack until the tire is clear of the ground

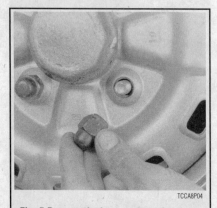

TCCA8P04

Fig. 5 Remove the lug nuts from the studs

TCCA8P05

Fig. 6 Remove the wheel and tire assembly from the vehicle

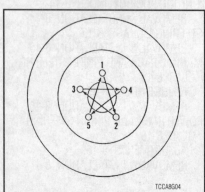

TCCA8G04

Fig. 7 Typical wheel lug tightening sequence

15. Using a torque wrench, tighten the lug nuts in a crisscross pattern to ft. lbs. (Nm). Check your owner's manual or refer to Section 1 of this manual for the proper tightening sequence.

✳ WARNING

Do not overtighten the lug nuts, as this may cause the wheel studs to stretch or the brake disc (rotor) to warp.

16. If so equipped, install the wheel cover or hub cap. Make sure the valve stem protrudes through the proper opening before tapping the wheel cover into position.

17. If equipped, install the lug nut trim caps by pushing them or screwing them on, as applicable.

18. Remove the jack from under the vehicle, and place the jack and tire iron/wrench in their storage compartments. Remove the wheel chock(s).

19. If you have removed a flat or damaged tire, place it in the storage compartment of the vehicle and take it to your local repair station to have it fixed or replaced as soon as possible.

INSPECTION

Inspect the tires for lacerations, puncture marks, nails and other sharp objects. Repair or replace as necessary. Also check the tires for treadwear and air pressure as outlined in Check the wheel assemblies for dents, cracks, rust and metal fatigue. Repair or replace as necessary.

Wheel Lug Studs

REMOVAL & INSTALLATION

With Disc Brakes

▶ **See Figures 8, 9 and 10**

1. Raise and support the appropriate end of the vehicle safely using jackstands, then remove the wheel.

2. Remove the brake pads and caliper. Support the caliper aside using wire or a coat hanger. For details, please refer to Section 9 of this manual.

3. Remove the outer wheel bearing and lift off the rotor. For details on wheel bearing removal, installation and adjustment, please refer to Section 1 of this manual.

4. Properly support the rotor using press bars, then drive the stud out using an arbor press.

➡**If a press is not available, CAREFULLY drive the old stud out using a blunt drift. MAKE SURE the rotor is properly and evenly supported or it may be damaged.**

To install:

5. Clean the stud hole with a wire brush and start the new stud with a hammer and drift pin. Do not use any lubricant or thread sealer.

6. Finish installing the stud with the press.

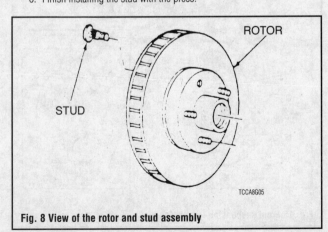

Fig. 8 View of the rotor and stud assembly

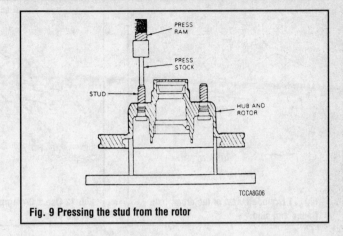

Fig. 9 Pressing the stud from the rotor

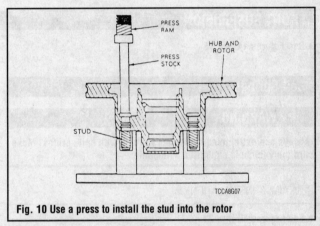

Fig. 10 Use a press to install the stud into the rotor

➡**If a press is not available, start the lug stud through the bore in the hub, then position about 4 flat washers over the stud and thread the lug nut. Hold the hub/rotor while tightening the lug nut, and the stud should be drawn into position. MAKE SURE THE STUD IS FULLY SEATED, then remove the lug nut and washers.**

7. Install the rotor and adjust the wheel bearings.

8. Install the brake caliper and pads.

9. Install the wheel, then remove the jackstands and carefully lower the vehicle.

10. Tighten the lug nuts to the proper torque.

With Drum Brakes

▶ **See Figures 11, 12 and 13**

1. Raise the vehicle and safely support it with jackstands, then remove the wheel.

2. Remove the brake drum.

3. If necessary to provide clearance, remove the brake shoes, as outlined in Section 9 of this manual.

4. Using a large C-clamp and socket, press the stud from the axle flange.

5. Coat the serrated part of the stud with liquid soap and place it into the hole.

To install:

6. Position about 4 flat washers over the stud and thread the lug nut. Hold the flange while tightening the lug nut, and the stud should be drawn into position. MAKE SURE THE STUD IS FULLY SEATED, then remove the lug nut and washers.

7. If applicable, install the brake shoes.

8. Install the brake drum.

9. Install the wheel, then remove the jackstands and carefully lower the vehicle.

10. Tighten the lug nuts to the proper torque.

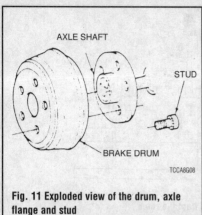

Fig. 11 Exploded view of the drum, axle flange and stud

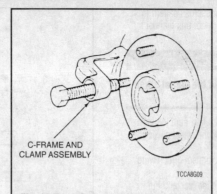

Fig. 12 Use a C-clamp and socket to press out the stud

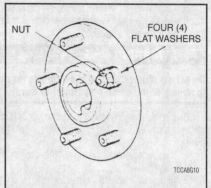

Fig. 13 Force the stud onto the axle flange using washers and a lug nut

FRONT SUSPENSION

♦ See Figures 14 and 15

Coil Springs

✳✳ WARNING

Always use extreme caution when working with coil springs. Make sure the vehicle is supported sufficiently.

REMOVAL & INSTALLATION

♦ See Figures 16 thru 21

1. Raise the front of the vehicle and place safety stands under both sides of the jack pads, just behind the lower arms.
2. Remove the wheel and tire assembly.
3. Disconnect the stabilizer bar link from the lower arm.
4. Remove the steering gear bolts, and move the steering gear out of the way.
5. Disconnect the tie rod end from the steering spindle, using tie rod end remover tool 3290-C, or equivalent.
6. Using spring compressor tool T82P-5310-A or equivalent, install one plate with the pivot ball seat down into the coils of the spring. Rotate the plate, so that it is fully seated into the lower suspension arm spring seat.
7. Install the other plate with the pivot ball seat up into the coils of the spring. Insert the ball nut through the coils of the spring. Insert the ball nut through the coils of the spring, so it rests in the upper plate.
8. Insert the compression rod into the opening in the lower arm through the lower and upper plate. Install the upper ball nut on the rod, and return the securing pin.

➡This pin can only be inserted one way into the upper ball nut because of a stepped hole design.

9. With the upper ball nut secured, turn the upper plate so that it walks up the coil, until it contacts the upper spring seat.
10. Install the lower ball nut, thrust bearing and forcing nut on the compression rod.
11. Rotate the nut until the spring is compressed enough so that it is free in its seat.
12. Remove the two lower control arm pivot bolts and nuts, and disengage the lower arm from the frame crossmember, then remove the spring assembly.
13. If a new spring is to be installed, mark the position of the upper and lower plates on the spring with chalk. Measure the compressed length of the

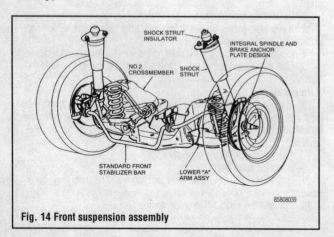

Fig. 14 Front suspension assembly

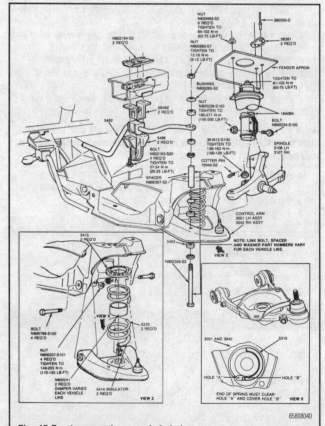

Fig. 15 Front suspension—exploded view

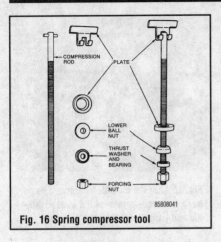

Fig. 16 Spring compressor tool

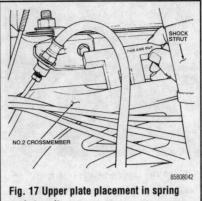

Fig. 17 Upper plate placement in spring pocket cavity

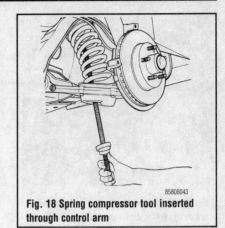

Fig. 18 Spring compressor tool inserted through control arm

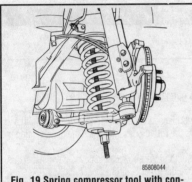

Fig. 19 Spring compressor tool with control arm and spring in position without tension

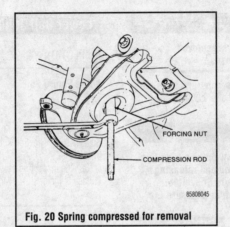

Fig. 20 Spring compressed for removal

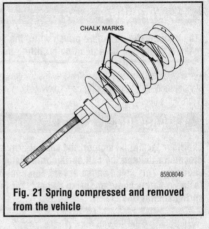

Fig. 21 Spring compressed and removed from the vehicle

spring as well as the amount of the spring curvature to assist in the compressing and installation of a new spring.

14. Carefully loosen the nut to relieve spring tension, and remove the tools from the spring.

To install:

15. Assemble the spring compressor tool, and locate it in the same position as indicted in Step 13 of the removal procedure.

✱✱ WARNING

Before compressing the coil spring, be sure the upper ball nut securing pin is inserted properly.

16. Compress the coil spring until the spring height reaches the dimension in Step 13.

17. Position the coil spring assembly into the lower arm.

✱✱ WARNING

Make sure that the lower end of the spring is properly positioned between the two holes in the lower arm spring pocket depression.

18. To finish installing the coil spring, reverse the removal procedure.

MacPherson Struts

The need for MacPherson strut replacement may or may not be indicated by the presence of oil on the strut body. A thin film of oil deposited on a new strut's outer tube is normal during a break-in period of 3,000–5,000 miles. If present, such weepage will not affect the strut's performance and will normally cease after the initial wetting of the strut body and seal break-in period. However, when oil leakage occurs beyond this period, or causes a constantly wet condition on the entire strut body (and possibly, the lower control arm) strut replacement is indicated.

→MacPherson struts are non-serviceable, and must be replaced as a unit. Although Ford deems it unnecessary to replace both struts if only one is defective, we suggest that you consider replacing struts in pairs, particularly after several years of service or extended mileage.

REMOVAL & INSTALLATION

▶ See Figures 22, 23, 24 and 25

1. Place the ignition key in the **UNLOCKED** position to permit free movement of the front wheels.

2. Working from the engine compartment, remove the large nut that attaches the strut to the upper mount. A screwdriver in the slot will hold the rod stationary while removing the nut. Loosen the smaller strut retaining nuts (usually 3), but do not remove at this time.

Fig. 22 Use a screwdriver and wrench to loosen the upper mounting nut

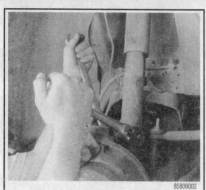

Fig. 23 Use two wrenches to remove the lower mounting bolts and nuts

Fig. 24 The lower portion of the strut assembly is secured by a bracket which fastens to the spindle

Fig. 25 After the mounting hardware has been removed, compress the strut assembly and withdraw it from the vehicle

❊❊ WARNING

The vehicle should not be driven while the nut is removed, so make sure the car is in position for lifting purposes.

3. Raise the front of the vehicle by the lower control arms, then place safety stands under the frame jacking pads, rearward of the wheels, but DO NOT remove the floor jack from the control arm.

❊❊ CAUTION

The floor jack must support the control arm at all times during this procedure to keep the coil spring from dislodging and releasing suddenly. This could cause severe personal injury. If available, install a safety chain or spring compressor in order to assure the spring cannot release.

4. Remove the tire and wheel assembly.

➡In order to provide sufficient clearance for strut removal and installation, it may be necessary to remove the brake caliper and brake pads.

5. Remove the brake caliper and pads, if necessary, without disconnecting the brake line. Suspend the caliper by a piece of wire or twine. (For further detail on caliper/brake pad removal and installation, refer to Section 9.)
6. Remove the small mounting nuts from the upper strut mount which were loosened earlier.
7. Remove the two lower nuts and bolts attaching the strut to the spindle.
8. Lift the strut up from the spindle to compress the rod, then pull down and remove the strut.

To install:
9. With the rod half extended, place the rod through the upper mount and hand start the mount as soon as possible.
10. Extend the strut and position it onto the spindle.
11. Install the two lower mounting bolts and hand start the nuts.
12. Loosely install the small upper mounting nuts.

➡Position a suitable tool in the slot to hold the rod stationary while the nut is being tightened.

13. Remove the suspension load from the lower control arm by lowering the jack, and tighten the lower mounting nuts to 150 ft. lbs. (203 Nm).
14. Raise the suspension control arm and tighten the nut that attaches the strut to the upper body mount to 60–75 ft. lbs. (81–102 Nm). This can be done from inside the engine compartment. Tighten the small upper mounting nuts which were loosely installed earlier.
15. If applicable, remove the wire or twine and install the brake caliper and pads.
16. Install the tire and wheel assembly.
17. Remove the safety stands and lower the vehicle.
18. Check and adjust the front wheel alignment, if necessary.

Lower Ball Joint

INSPECTION

◗ See Figure 26

1. Support the vehicle in its normal driving position with both ball joints loaded.
2. Wipe the grease fitting and inspection surface, so they are free of dirt and grease. The inspection surface is the round boss into which the grease fitting is threaded.
3. The inspection surface should project outside the cover. If the inspection surface is inside the cover, replace the lower control arm assembly.

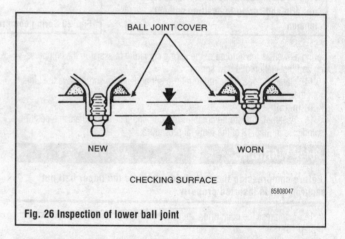

Fig. 26 Inspection of lower ball joint

REMOVAL & INSTALLATION

The lower ball joint is an integral part of the lower control arm. If the ball joint is defective, the entire lower control arm assembly must be replaced.

Sway Bar

REMOVAL & INSTALLATION

◗ See Figures 27 and 28

1. Raise and support the front end on jackstands.
2. Disconnect the stabilizer bar from the links, or the links from the lower arm.
3. Disconnect the bar from the retaining clamps.
4. Installation is the reverse of removal. Torque the stabilizer bar attaching

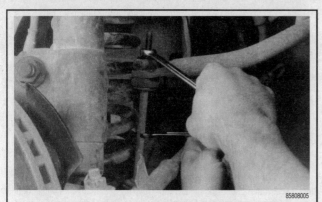

Fig. 27 Use a box wrench to remove the nut from the link bolt

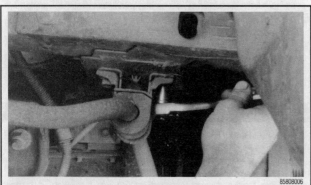

Fig. 28 The stabilizer bar is secured to the side rails by retaining clamps

link fasteners to 6–12 ft. lbs. (8–16 Nm) and the retaining clamp fasteners to 20–25 ft. lbs. (27–34 Nm).

Lower Control Arm

REMOVAL & INSTALLATION

1. Raise the front of the vehicle and position safety stands under both sides of the jack pads, just to the rear of the lower arms.
2. Remove the wheel and tire assembly.
3. Remove the disc brake caliper, and suspend it by wire or twine. Do not disconnect the brake hose. For further details, please refer to Section 9 of this manual.
4. Remove the brake rotor and dust shield, as described in Section 9.
5. If necessary, remove the steering gear bolts and position the gear so that the suspension arm bolt may be removed.
6. Disconnect the stabilizer bar link from the lower arm.
7. Remove the cotter pin from the ball joint stud nut, and loosen the ball joint nut one or two turns.
8. Tap the spindle sharply to relieve the stud pressure.

❊❊ CAUTION

Before proceeding, refer to the procedure earlier in this section regarding removal of coil springs.

9. Remove the tie rod end from the spindle. Place a floor jack under the lower arm, supporting the arm at both bushings. Properly install a spring compressor tool, then remove the coil spring as outlined earlier in this section.
10. Remove the ball joint nut and remove the arm assembly.
To install:
11. Place the new arm assembly into the spindle and tighten the ball joint nut to 100–120 ft. lbs. (136–163 Nm). Install the cotter pin.
12. Position the coil spring in the upper spring pocket. Make sure the insu-

lator is on top of the spring and the lower end is properly positioned between the two holes in the depression of the lower arm.
13. Carefully raise the lower arm with the floor jack until the bushings are properly positioned in the crossmember.
14. Install the lower arm bolts and nuts, finger-tight only.
15. Install and tighten the steering gear bolts.
16. Connect the tie rod end and tighten the nut to 35–47 ft. lbs. (47–64 Nm).
17. Connect the stabilizer link bolt and nut and tighten to 9–12 ft. lbs. (12–16 Nm).
18. Install the brake dust shield, rotor and caliper, as described in Section 9.
19. Install the wheel and tire assembly.
20. Remove the safety stands and lower the vehicle. After the vehicle has been lowered to the floor and is at curb height, tighten the lower arm nuts to 200–220 ft. lbs. (271–298 Nm) for 1979–82 cars, 150–180 ft. lbs. (203–244 Nm) for 1983–85 cars, or 110–150 ft. lbs. (149–203 Nm) for 1986–88 cars.

Knuckle and Spindle

REMOVAL & INSTALLATION

1. Raise and support the front end on jackstands positioned under the frame.
2. Remove the wheels.
3. Remove the calipers and suspend them out of the way.
4. Remove the hub and rotor assemblies.
5. Remove the rotor dust shields.
6. Unbolt the stabilizer links from the control arms.
7. Using a separator, disconnect the tie rod ends from the spindle.
8. Remove the cotter pin and loosen the ball joint stud nut a few turns. Do not remove it at this time!
9. Using a hammer, tap the spindle boss sharply to relieve stud pressure.
10. Support the lower control arm with a floor jack, compress the coil spring, using a spring compressor tool, and remove the stud nut.
11. Remove the two bolts and nuts attaching the spindle to the shock strut. Compress the shock strut until working clearance is obtained.
12. Remove the spindle.
To install:
13. Place the spindle on the ball joint stud, and install the stud nut, but do not tighten it yet.
14. Lower the shock strut until the attaching holes are aligned with the holes in the spindle. Install two new bolts and nuts.
15. Tighten the ball joint stud nut to 100–120 ft. lbs. (136–163 Nm) and install the cotter pin.
16. Torque the shock strut-to-spindle attaching nuts to 150–180 ft. lbs. (203–244 Nm) for 1979–85 cars, or 140–200 ft. lbs. (190–271 Nm) for 1986–88 cars.
17. Lower the floor jack.
18. Install the stabilizer links. Torque the nuts to 9–12 ft. lbs. (12–16 Nm).
19. Attach the tie rod ends and torque the nuts to 35–47 ft. lbs. (47–64 Nm).
20. The remainder of installation is the reverse of removal.

Front Wheel Bearings

ADJUSTMENT

1. Raise and safely support the front of the vehicle.
2. Remove the wheel cover and grease cap.
3. Remove the cotter pin and nut retainer.
4. Loosen the adjusting nut 3 turns, then rock the wheel back and forth a few times to release the brake pads from the rotor.
5. While rotating the wheel and hub assembly, tighten the adjusting nut to 17–25 ft. lbs. (23–34 Nm), to seat the bearings.
6. Back off the adjusting nut ½ turn, then retighten to 10–15 inch lbs. (1.1–1.7 Nm).
7. Install the nut retainer and a new cotter pin. Check the wheel rotation. If it is noisy or rough, the bearings either need to be cleaned and repacked or replaced. After adjustment is completed, install the grease cap and wheel cover.

8. Lower the vehicle. Before driving the vehicle, pump the brake pedal several times to restore normal brake pedal travel.

REMOVAL & INSTALLATION

▸ **See Figures 29 thru 41**

1. Raise and safely support the vehicle.
2. Remove the wheel and tire assembly, then remove the brake caliper. Suspend the caliper with a length of wire; do not let it hang from the brake hose.
3. Pry off the dust cap. Unbend, tap out and discard the cotter pin. Remove the nut retainer.
4. Remove the castellated nut and washer from the spindle.
5. Being careful not to drop the outer bearing, pull off the brake disc and wheel hub assembly.
6. Remove the inner grease seal using a small prytool. Remove the inner wheel bearing.

Fig. 29 Pry the dust cap from the hub, taking care not to distort or damage its flange

7. Clean the wheel bearings with solvent and inspect them for pits, scratches and excessive wear. Wipe all the old grease from the hub and inspect the bearing races. If either bearings or races are damaged, the races must be removed, then the bearings and races must be replaced as an assembly.
8. If the bearings are to be replaced, drive out the races from the hub using a brass drift.
9. Make sure the spindle, hub and bearing assemblies are clean prior to installation.

To install:

10. If the bearing races were removed, install new ones using a suitable bearing race installer. Grease the bearings with a bearing packer. If a packer is not available, work as much grease as possible between the rollers and cages.
11. Coat the inner surface of the hub and bearing races with grease.
12. Install the inner bearing in the hub. Being careful not to distort it, install the oil seal with its lip facing the bearing. Drive the seal in until its outer edge is even with the edge of the hub. Lubricate the lip of the seal with grease.
13. Install the hub/disc assembly on the spindle, being careful not to damage the oil seal.
14. Install the outer bearing, washer and spindle nut. Install the brake caliper along with the wheel and tire assembly.
15. Adjust the wheel bearings, as described earlier in this section. Be sure to install the nut retainer with a new cotter pin. After adjustment is completed, install the dust cap and wheel cover.
16. Lower the vehicle. Before driving, pump the brake pedal several times to restore normal brake pedal travel.

Wheel Alignment

If the tires are worn unevenly, if the vehicle is not stable on the highway or if the handling seems uneven in spirited driving, the wheel alignment should be checked. If an alignment problem is suspected, first check for improper tire inflation and other possible causes. These can be worn suspension or steering components, accident damage or even unmatched tires. If any worn or damaged components are found, they must be replaced before the wheels can be properly aligned. Wheel alignment requires very expensive equipment and involves

Fig. 30 The nut retainer is secured by a cotter pin

Fig. 31 Unbend or break off the ends of the cotter pin

Fig. 32 Remove the nut retainer after the cotter pin has been removed

Fig. 33 Loosen and remove the castellated nut from the spindle

Fig. 34 Remove the washer from the spindle

Fig. 35 With the nut and washer out of the way, the outer bearings may be removed from the hub

Fig. 36 Pull the hub and inner bearing assembly from the spindle

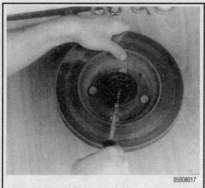

Fig. 37 Use a small prytool to remove the old inner bearing seal

Fig. 38 Clean the inner and outer wheel bearings with solvent, and inspect them for wear or damage

Fig. 39 Thoroughly pack the bearings with fresh, high temperature wheel bearing grease prior to installation

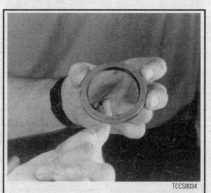

Fig. 40 Apply a thin coat of fresh grease to the new inner bearing seal lip

Fig. 41 Use a suitably sized driver to install the inner bearing seal to the hub

minute adjustments which must be accurate; it should only be performed by a trained technician. Take your vehicle to a properly equipped shop.

Following is a description of the alignment angles which are adjustable on most vehicles and how they affect vehicle handling. Although these angles can apply to both the front and rear wheels, usually only the front suspension is adjustable.

CASTER

▶ **See Figure 42**

Looking at a vehicle from the side, caster angle describes the steering axis rather than a wheel angle. The steering knuckle is attached to a control arm or strut at the top and a control arm at the bottom. The wheel pivots around the line between these points to steer the vehicle. When the upper point is tilted back, this is described as positive caster. Having a positive caster tends to make the wheels self-centering, increasing directional stability. Excessive positive

caster makes the wheels hard to steer, while an uneven caster will cause a pull to one side. Overloading the vehicle or sagging rear springs will affect caster, as will raising the rear of the vehicle. If the rear of the vehicle is lower than normal, the caster becomes more positive.

CAMBER

▶ **See Figure 43**

Looking from the front of the vehicle, camber is the inward or outward tilt of the top of wheels. When the tops of the wheels are tilted in, this is negative camber; if they are tilted out, it is positive. In a turn, a slight amount of negative camber helps maximize contact of the tire with the road. However, too much negative camber compromises straight-line stability, increases bump steer and torque steer.

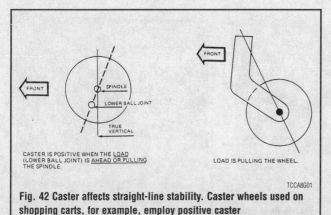

Fig. 42 Caster affects straight-line stability. Caster wheels used on shopping carts, for example, employ positive caster

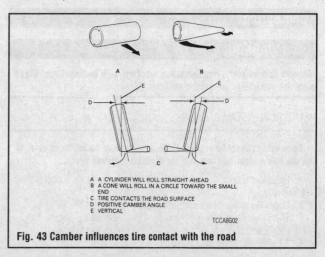

Fig. 43 Camber influences tire contact with the road

TOE

> See Figure 44

Looking down at the wheels from above the vehicle, toe angle is the distance between the front of the wheels, relative to the distance between the back of the wheels. If the wheels are closer at the front, they are said to be toed-in or to have negative toe. A small amount of negative toe enhances directional stability and provides a smoother ride on the highway.

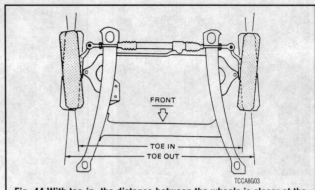

Fig. 44 With toe-in, the distance between the wheels is closer at the front than at the rear

WHEEL ALIGNMENT

Year	Model	Caster Range (deg.)	Caster Preferred Setting (deg.)	Camber Range (deg.)	Camber Preferred Setting (deg.)	Toe-in (in.)	Steering Axis Inclination (deg.)
1979	Mustang, Capri	①	7/8P	②	3/8P	3/16–7/16	15 1/4
1980	Mustang, Capri	1/4P–1 3/4P ①	1P	1/2N–1P ②	1/4P	1/16–5/16	15 1/4
1981	Mustang, Capri	1/4P–1 3/4P ①	1P	1/2N–1P ②	1/4P	1/16–5/16	15 1/4
1982	Mustang, Capri	3/8P–1 7/8P ①	1 1/8P	1/2N–1P ②	1/4P	1/16–5/16	15 1/4
1983	Mustang, Capri	1/2P–2P ①	1 1/4P	3/4N–3/4P	0	1/16–5/16	—
1984	Mustang, Capri	1/2P–2P ①	1 1/4P	3/4N–3/4P	0	1/16–5/16	—
1985	Mustang, Capri	1/4P–1 3/4P ①	1P	3/4N–3/4P	0	1/16–5/16	—
1986	Mustang, Capri	1/4P–1 3/4P ①	1P	3/4N–3/4P	0	1/16–5/16	—
1987	Mustang ③	3/32P–1 9/16P ①	13/16P	1/2N–1P	7/32P	1/16–5/16	—
	Mustang 5.0L-GT	1/2P–2P ①	1 9/32P	5/6N–29/32P	5/32P	1/16–5/16	—
1988	Mustang ③	0.40P–1.90P ①	1.15P	0.85N–0.65P	0.10N	1/16–5/16	—
	Mustang 5.0L-GT	1/2P–2P ①	1 1/4P	0.60N–0.90P	0.14P	1/16–5/16	—

N—Negative
P—Positive
① Caster is preset and non-adjustable
② Camber is preset and non-adjustable
③ Except 5.0L-GT

858080C1

REAR SUSPENSION

> See Figures 45 and 46

Coil Springs

✳✳ WARNING

Always use extreme caution when working with coil springs. Make sure the vehicle is supported sufficiently.

REMOVAL & INSTALLATION

➡ If one spring must be replaced, the other should be replaced also. If the car has a stabilizer bar, the bar must be removed first.

1. Raise and support the car at the rear crossmember, while supporting the axle with a jack.
2. Lower the axle until the shocks are fully extended.
3. Place a jack under the lower arm pivot bolt. Remove the pivot bolt and nut. Carefully and slowly lower the arm until the spring load is relieved.
4. Remove the spring and insulators.

5. To install, tape the insulator in place in the frame, and place the lower insulator in place on the arm. Install the internal damper in the spring.
6. Position the spring in place and slowly raise the jack under the lower

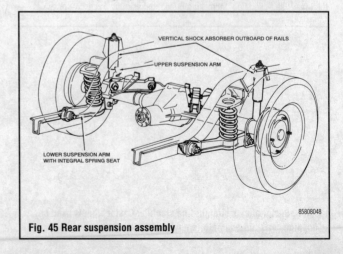

Fig. 45 Rear suspension assembly

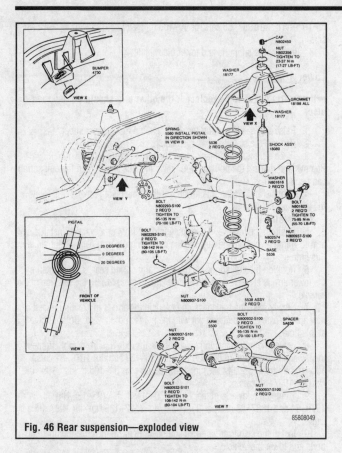

Fig. 46 Rear suspension—exploded view

85808049

arm. Install the pivot bolt and nut, with the nut facing outwards. Do not tighten the nut.

7. Raise the axle to curb height, and tighten the lower arm pivot bolt to 70–100 ft. lbs. (95–136 Nm) for 1979–81 cars, 90–100 ft. lbs. (122–136 Nm) for 1982–86 cars, or 70–100 ft. lbs. (95–136 Nm) for 1987–88 cars.

8. Install the stabilizer bar, if removed, and tighten the fasteners to 15–20 ft. lbs. (20–27 Nm) for 1979–81 cars, 45–50 ft. lbs. (61–68 Nm) for 1982–86 cars, or 33–51 ft. lbs. (45–69 Nm) for 1987–88 cars.

9. Remove the crossmember stands and lower the car.

Shock Absorber

TESTING

Bounce Test

Each shock absorber can be tested by bouncing the corner of the vehicle until maximum up and down movement is obtained. Let go of the vehicle. It should stop bouncing in 1–2 bounces. If not, the shock absorber should be inspected for damage and possibly replaced.

INSPECTION

Shock Absorber Mountings

Check the shock absorber mountings for worn or defective grommets, loose mounting nuts, interference or missing bump stops. If no apparent defects are noted, continue testing.

Fluid Leaks

Disconnect each shock absorber lower mount and pull down on the unit until it is fully extended. Inspect for leaks in the seal area. Shock absorber fluid is very thin and has a characteristic odor and dark brown color. Do not confuse the glossy paint on some shock absorbers with leaking fluid. A slight trace of fluid is a normal condition; shock absorbers are designed to seep a certain amount of fluid past the seals for lubrication. If you are in doubt as to whether the fluid is coming from the shock absorber itself or from some other source, wipe the seal area clean and manually operate the shock absorber, using the following procedure. Fluid will appear if the unit is leaking.

➡It may be necessary to fabricate a holding fixture for certain types of shock absorbers.

1. Grip the lower end of the shock absorber. Pull down (rebound stroke) and then push up (compression stroke). Compare the rebound resistance of both shock absorbers and compare the compression resistance. Usually, any shock absorber showing a noticeable difference will be the one at fault.

2. If the shock absorber has internal noises, extend it fully, then exert an extra pull. If a small additional movement is felt, this usually means a loose piston, and the shock absorber should be replaced. Other noises which indicate the need for replacement are a squeal after a full stroke in both directions, a clicking noise on fast reverse, and a lag at reversal near mid-stroke.

REMOVAL & INSTALLATION

▶ See Figures 47, 48, 49 and 50

➡It is recommended that shock absorbers be replaced in pairs, to maintain uniform handling.

1. Remove the upper attaching nut, washer, and insulator. Access is through the trunk on sedans and convertibles, or side panel trim covers on hatchbacks. The studs in sedans and convertibles are concealed by rubber caps.

2. Raise and safely support the rear of the car, including the rear axle.

3. Compress the shock absorber to clear the upper tower. Remove the lower nut and washer, then remove the shock absorber.

To install:

4. Purge the new shock absorber of air and compress it.

➡Purge a new shock absorber of air by repeatedly extending it in its normal position and compressing it while inverted.

85808025

Fig. 47 On hatchback models, the trim panel is retained by a screw

85808026

Fig. 48 Remove the trim panel inside a hatchback to access the shock absorber's upper stud mounting nut

85808027

Fig. 49 The shock absorber's lower mount is secured by a single bolt, washer and nut

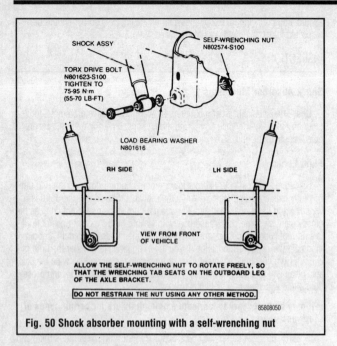

Fig. 50 Shock absorber mounting with a self-wrenching nut

5. Place the lower mounting eye over the lower stud, then install the washer and a new locking nut. Do not tighten the nut yet.

6. Place the inner washer and insulator on the upper stud. Extend the shock absorber and install the stud through the upper mounting hole.

7. Torque the lower mounting nut to 40–55 ft. lbs. (54–75 Nm) for 1979–81 cars, or 55–70 ft. lbs. (75–95 Nm) for 1982–88 cars. If equipped with a self-wrenching nut, be sure that the wrenching tab seats against the outboard leg of the axle bracket.

8. Remove the supports and lower the car.

9. Install the outer insulator and washer on the upper stud, and install a new nut. Tighten to 14–26 ft. lbs. (19–35 Nm) for 1979–81 cars, 24–26 ft. lbs. (33–35 Nm) for 1982 cars, 17–26 ft. lbs. (23–35 Nm) for 1983–86 cars, or 19–27 ft. lbs. (26–37 Nm) for 1987–88 cars.

10. Install the trim panel on hatchbacks, or the rubber cap on sedans and convertibles.

Control Arms

REMOVAL & INSTALLATION

Upper Arm

➡️**If one arm needs to be replaced, the other arm should be replaced also.**

1. Raise and safely support the vehicle at the rear crossmember.
2. Remove and discard the upper arm-to-axle pivot bolt and nut.
3. Remove and discard the upper arm-to-frame pivot bolt and nut. Remove the upper control arm.

To install:

4. Place the upper control arm into the bracket of the body side rail. Install a new arm-to-frame pivot bolt and nut with the nut facing outward. Do not tighten at this time.

5. Using a jack, raise the suspension until the upper arm-to-axle pivot hole is in position with the hole in the axle bushing. Install a new pivot bolt and nut with the nut facing inward. Do not tighten at this time.

6. Raise the suspension to curb height. Tighten the front upper control arm bolt to 85–120 ft. lbs. (115–163 Nm) for 1979–1981 cars, 100–105 ft. lbs. (135–142 Nm) for 1982–86 cars, or 80–105 ft. lbs. (108–142 Nm) for 1987–88 cars.

7. Tighten the rear upper control arm bolt to 70–100 ft. lbs. (95–135 Nm)

for 1979–81 and 1987–88 cars, or 90–100 ft. lbs. (122–135 Nm) for 1982–86 cars.

8. Remove the supports and lower the vehicle.

Lower Arm

➡️**If one arm needs to be replaced, the other arm should be replaced also.**

1. Raise and safely support the vehicle at the rear crossmember.
2. Remove the stabilizer bar, if so equipped.
3. Place a transmission jack under the lower arm-to-axle pivot bolt. Remove and discard the bolt and nut. Lower the jack slowly until the coil spring can be removed.
4. Remove and discard the lower arm-to-frame pivot bolt and nut. Remove the lower arm assembly.

To install:

5. Position the lower arm assembly into the front arm bracket. Install a new arm-to-frame pivot bolt and nut with the nut facing outward. Do not tighten at this time.

6. Position the coil spring on the lower arm spring seat, so the pigtail on the lower arm is at the rear of the vehicle and pointing toward the left side of the vehicle.

7. Slowly raise the transmission jack until the arm is in position. Insert a new arm-to-axle pivot bolt and nut with the nut facing outward. Do not tighten at this time.

8. Lower the transmission jack and raise the axle to curb height. Tighten the lower arm front bolt to 85–120 ft. lbs. (115–163 Nm) for 1979–81 cars, 100–105 ft. lbs. (135–142 Nm) for 1982–86 cars, or 80–105 ft. lbs. (108–142 Nm) for 1987–88 cars.

9. Tighten the lower arm rear bolt to 70–100 ft. lbs. (95–135 Nm) for 1979–81 and 1987–88 cars, or 90–100 ft. lbs. (122–135 Nm) for 1982–86 cars.

10. Install the stabilizer bar, if so equipped. Remove the crossmember supports and lower the vehicle.

Sway (Stabilizer) Bar

REMOVAL & INSTALLATION

▶ **See Figure 51**

1. Raise and safely support the rear end on jackstands.
2. Remove and discard the four stabilizer bar-to-lower control arm bolts.
3. Remove the stabilizer bar.
4. Installation is the reverse of removal. Torque the new bolts to 20 ft. lbs. (27 Nm) on 1979–81 cars; 45–50 ft. lbs. (61–67 Nm) on 1982–88 cars.

➡️**Be careful not to install the stabilizer bar upside down. A color code may be provided on the passenger side of the bar, as an aid for proper orientation.**

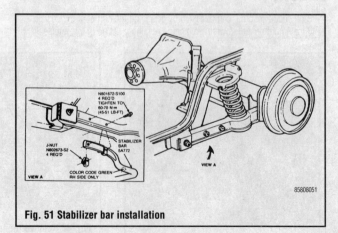

Fig. 51 Stabilizer bar installation

STEERING

Steering Wheel

REMOVAL & INSTALLATION

▶ **See Figures 52 thru 58**

1. Disconnect the negative battery cable.
2. On models with safety crash pads, remove the crash pad attaching screws from the underside of the steering wheel spoke and remove the pad. On all models equipped with a horn button or ring, remove the button or ring by pressing down evenly and turning it counterclockwise approximately 20 degrees, then lifting it from the steering wheel. On 1981 and later models, pull straight out on the hub cover. Disconnect the horn wires from the crash pad on models so equipped.

Fig. 52 Remove the horn button by pressing down and turning counterclockwise, before lifting from the steering wheel

3. Remove and discard the locknut from the end of the shaft, if so equipped. If the steering wheel is retained by a bolt, loosen the bolt 4–6 turns, but do not yet remove it. Install a steering wheel puller on the end of the shaft and remove the wheel.

❊❊ WARNING

The use of a knock-off type steering wheel puller or the use of a hammer on the steering shaft will damage the collapsible column.

4. Remove and discard the steering wheel retaining bolt, if so equipped.
To install:
5. Lubricate the upper surface of the steering shaft upper bushing with white grease. Transfer all serviceable parts to the new steering wheel.
6. Position the steering wheel on the shaft so that the alignment marks line up, and install and tighten a new bolt or locknut. On 1979–86 cars, torque the fastener to 30–40 ft. lbs. (41–54 Nm); on 1987–88 cars, torque the bolt to 21–33 ft. lbs. (31–45 Nm). Connect the horn wires.
7. Install the horn button or ring by turning it clockwise or install the crash pad.
8. Connect the negative battery cable.

Turn Signal Switch

REMOVAL & INSTALLATION

1. If equipped with a tilt column, remove the upper extension shroud by unsnapping the shroud from the retaining clip at the 9 o'clock position.
2. Remove the two trim shroud halves, after removing the attaching screws.
3. Remove the turn signal lever by grasping and pulling it straight out from the switch.

Fig. 53 Disconnect the electrical connector at the horn button

Fig. 54 Use the correct size socket to loosen the steering wheel bolt

Fig. 55 Attach a steering wheel puller and tighten the center bolt to press the wheel from the shaft

Fig. 56 Remove the bolt after using the steering wheel puller

Fig. 57 Lift the steering wheel from the shaft

Fig. 58 The inside of the steering column is exposed after the wheel is removed

4. Peel back the switch's foam sight shield. Disconnect the two electrical connectors.

5. Remove the two attaching screws and disengage the switch from the housing.

To install:

6. Position the switch to the housing and install the screws. Stick the foam shield to the switch.

7. Align the lever's key with the switch's keyway, then push the lever toward the switch until they fully engage.

8. Attach the two electrical connectors, test the switch, and install the trim shrouds.

Ignition Switch

REMOVAL & INSTALLATION

1979–81

1. Disconnect the negative battery cable.

2. On tilt columns, remove the upper extension shroud by unsnapping the shroud from the retaining clip at the 9 o'clock position.

3. Remove the trim shroud halves.

4. Disconnect the switch wiring.

5. Drill out the break-off head bolts attaching the switch to the lock cylinder with a ⅛ in. (3mm) drill bit.

6. Remove the remainder of the bolts with a screw extractor.

7. Disengage the switch from the actuator pin.

To install:

8. Slide the switch carrier to the switch lock position. Insert a ⁷⁄₁₆ in. (11mm) drill bit shank through the switch housing and into the carrier, thereby, preventing any movement. (New replacement switches already have a pin installed for this purpose.)

9. Turn the key to the **LOCK** position and remove the key.

10. Position the switch on the actuator pin.

11. Install new break-off bolts and hand-tighten them.

12. Push the switch towards the steering wheel, parallel with the column, to remove any slack between the bolts and the switch slots.

13. While holding the switch in this position, tighten the bolts until the heads break off.

14. Remove the drill bit or adjusting pin.

15. Connect the wiring.

16. The remainder of installation is the reverse of removal. Be sure to check the switch for proper function, including **START** and **ACCESSORY** positions. Also, check that the column is locked in the **LOCK** position.

1982–88

1. Disconnect the negative battery cable.

2. On tilt columns, remove the upper extension shroud by unsnapping the shroud from the retaining clip at the 9 o'clock position.

3. Remove the trim shroud halves, after unfastening the attaching screws.

4. Disconnect the switch wiring.

5. Turn the key to the **ON (RUN)** position.

6. On 1982–86 cars, drill out the break-off head bolts attaching the switch to the lock cylinder with a ⅛ in. (3mm) drill bit. Remove the remainder of the bolts with a screw extractor.

7. On 1987–88 cars, remove the bolts securing the switch to the lock cylinder housing.

8. Disengage the switch from the actuator pin.

To install:

9. Slide the switch carrier to the **ON (RUN)** position. New replacement switches will be in this position.

10. Turn the key to the **ON (RUN)** position.

11. Position the switch on the actuator pin. It may be necessary to move the switch slightly back and forth to align the switch mounting holes with the column lock housing threaded holes.

12. While holding the switch in position, install the retaining bolts. On 1982–86 cars, install new break-off bolts and tighten until the heads break off. On 1987–88 cars, install the bolts and tighten them to 50–60 inch lbs. (6–7 Nm).

13. Connect the wiring.

14. The remainder of installation is the reverse of removal. Be sure to check the switch for proper function, including **START** and **ACCESSORY** positions. Also, check that the column is locked in the **LOCK** position.

Ignition Lock Cylinder

REMOVAL & INSTALLATION

Functional Lock Cylinder

➡ **The following procedure pertains to vehicles with undamaged/unjammed lock cylinders. If an ignition key is unavailable, ignition key numbers must be known, so that the proper key can be made.**

1. Disconnect the negative battery cable.

2. On tilt columns, remove the upper extension shroud by unsnapping the shroud from the retaining clip at the 9 o'clock position.

3. Unfasten the trim shroud attaching screws, then remove the shroud halves.

4. Unplug the wire connector at the key warning switch.

5. Place the shift lever in PARK (column shift only) and turn the key to **RUN**.

6. Place a ⅛ in. (3mm) wire pin in the hole in the casting surrounding the lock cylinder and depress the retaining pin while pulling out on the cylinder.

To install:

7. Turn the lock cylinder to the **RUN** position and depress the retaining pin, then insert the lock cylinder into its housing in the flange casting. Assure that the cylinder is fully seated and aligned in the interlocking washer before turning the key to the **OFF** position. This will allow the cylinder retaining pin to extend into the cylinder cast housing hole.

8. Using the ignition key, rotate the lock cylinder to ensure correct mechanical operation in all positions. Install the electrical connector onto the key warning switch.

9. Check for proper starting action in PARK or NEUTRAL. Also check that the start circuit cannot be actuated in the DRIVE and REVERSE positions, and that the column is locked in the **LOCK** position.

10. Install the trim shroud onto the steering column.

11. Connect the negative battery cable.

Non-Functioning Lock Cylinder

➡ **The following procedure applies to vehicles in which the ignition lock is inoperative and the lock cylinder cannot be rotated due to a lost or broken ignition key, unknown key number, or lock cylinder cap which is damaged and/or broken.**

1. Disconnect the negative battery cable.

2. Remove the steering wheel, as described earlier in this section.

3. On tilt columns, remove the upper extension shroud by unsnapping the shroud from the retaining clip at the 9 o'clock position.

4. Remove the steering column trim shrouds.

5. Disconnect the wiring at the key warning switch.

6. Using a ⅛ in. (3mm) drill bit, mounted in a right angle drive drill adapter, drill out the retaining pin, going no deeper than ½ in. (12.7mm).

7. Tilt the column to the full down position. Place a chisel at the base of the ignition lock cylinder cap and, using a hammer, break away the cap from the lock cylinder.

8. Using a ⅜ in. (10mm) drill bit, drill down the center of the ignition lock cylinder key slot about 1¾ in. (44mm), until the lock cylinder breaks loose from the steering column cover casting.

9. Remove the lock cylinder and the drill shavings from the housing.

10. Remove the upper bearing snapring washer and steering column lock gear.

11. Carefully inspect the steering column housing for signs of damage from the previous operation. If any damage is apparent, the components should be replaced.

To install:

12. Install the ignition lock drive gear.

13. Install the ignition lock cylinder.

14. Install the shift lever detent plate that was retained from the housing with the damaged lock cylinder (column shift only). Install the new lock cylinder housing.

15. Adjust the ignition switch retained from the housing with the damaged lock cylinder, and install it onto the new lock cylinder housing.

16. Install the new lock cylinder housing assembly.

17. Install the shift cane assembly (column shift only) and upper bearing.

18. Install the steering column trim shroud.

19. Check for proper starting action in PARK or NEUTRAL. Also check that the start circuit cannot be actuated in the DRIVE and REVERSE positions, and that the column is locked in the **LOCK** position.

20. Install the steering wheel.

21. Connect the negative battery cable.

Steering Linkage

REMOVAL & INSTALLATION

Tie Rod Ends

▶ **See Figures 59, 60 and 61**

1. Remove the cotter pin and nut at the spindle.

2. Separate the tie rod end stud from the spindle with TOOL–3290–C, or an equivalent puller.

3. Matchmark the position of the locknut with paint on the tie rod. Unscrew the locknut. Unscrew the tie rod end, counting the number of turns required to remove.

To install:

4. Install the new end the same number of turns.

5. Attach the tie rod end stud to the spindle. Install the nut and torque to

Fig. 59 The cotter pin must be removed before the nut

Fig. 60 Use a puller to separate the tie rod end and spindle

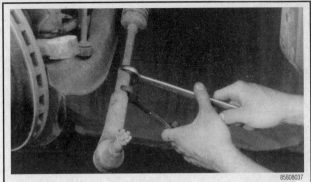

Fig. 61 Use one wrench on the tie rod end and another on the lock-nut

35–47 ft. lbs. (47–64 Nm), then continue to tighten until the cotter pin holes align. Install a new cotter pin.

6. Check the toe and adjust if necessary, then torque the tie rod end locknut to 35–50 ft. lbs. (47–68 Nm).

Manual Rack and Pinion Steering Gear

▶ **See Figure 62**

ADJUSTMENTS

The manual rack and pinion gear provides two means of service adjustment. The gear must be removed from the vehicle to perform both adjustments.

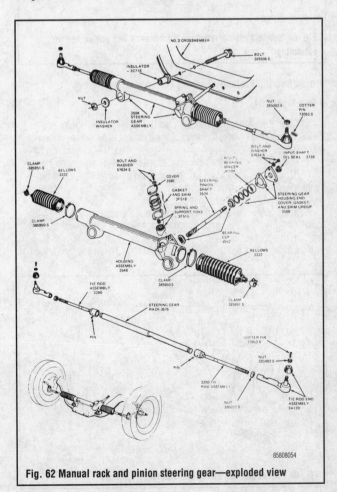

Fig. 62 Manual rack and pinion steering gear—exploded view

Support Yoke-to-Rack

▶ **See Figure 63**

1. Clean the exterior of the steering gear thoroughly and mount the gear by installing two long bolts and washers through the mounting boss bushings and attaching to a bench mounted holding fixture, tool T57L-500-B, or equivalent.
2. Remove the yoke cover, gasket, shims, and yoke spring.
3. Clean the cover and housing flange areas thoroughly.
4. Reinstall the yoke and cover, omitting the gasket, shims, and the spring.
5. Tighten the cover bolts lightly until the cover just touches the yoke.
6. Measure the gap between the cover and the housing flange. With the gasket, add selected shims to give a combined pack thickness 0.005–0.006 inches (0.13–0.15mm) greater than the measured gap.
7. Remove the cover.
8. Assemble the gasket next to the housing flange, then the selected shims, spring, and cover.
9. Install the cover bolts, sealing the threads with ESW-M46-132A or equivalent, and tighten.
10. Check to see that the gear operates smoothly without binding or slack.

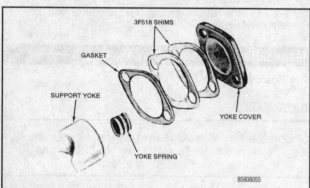

Fig. 63 Support yoke arrangement from rack and pinion housing assembly

Pinion Bearing Preload

▶ **See Figure 64**

1. Clean the exterior of the steering gear thoroughly and place the gear in the bench mounted holding fixture as outlined under Support Yoke-to-Rack Adjustment.
2. Loosen the bolts of the yoke cover to relieve spring pressure on the rack.
3. Remove the pinion cover and gasket. Clean the cover flange area thoroughly.
4. Remove the spacer and shims.
5. Install a new gasket, and fit shims between the upper bearing and the spacer until the top of the spacer is flush with the gasket. Check with a straight-edge, using light pressure.
6. Add one shim, 0.0025–0.0050 in. (0.0635–0.1270mm) to the pack in

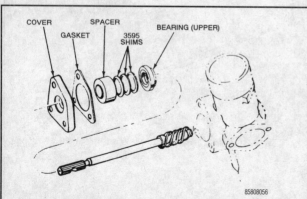

Fig. 64 Pinion bearing cover and shim arrangement

order to preload the bearings. The spacer must be assembled next to the pinion cover.
7. Install the cover and bolts.

REMOVAL & INSTALLATION

1. Disconnect the negative battery cable.
2. Remove the one bolt retaining the flexible coupling to the input shaft.
3. Leave the ignition key in the **ON** position, and raise the vehicle on a hoist.
4. Remove the two tie rod end retaining cotter pins and nuts. Separate the studs from the spindle arms, using the ball joint separator tool. Do not use a hammer or similar tool as this may damage spindle arms or rod studs.
5. Support the steering gear, and remove the two nuts, insulator washers, and bolts retaining the steering gear to the No. 2 crossmember.
6. Remove the steering gear assembly from the vehicle.
   To install:
7. Insert the input shaft into the flexible coupling, aligning the flats, and position the steering gear to the No. 2 crossmember. Install the two bolts and tighten them to 90–100 ft. lbs. (122–136 Nm).
8. Connect the tie rod ends to the spindle arms, and install the two retaining nuts. Tighten the nuts to 35–47 ft. lbs. (47–64 Nm) and install the two cotter pins.
9. Lower the vehicle, and install the one bolt retaining the flexible coupling to the input shaft. Tighten the bolt to 20–37 ft. lbs. (27–50 Nm).
10. Turn the ignition key to the **OFF** position
11. Connect the negative battery cable.
12. Check the toe, and reset if necessary.

Power Rack and Pinion Steering Gear

▶ **See Figure 65**

ADJUSTMENTS

The power rack and pinion gear provides for only one service adjustment. This adjustment can be performed with the gear in or out of the vehicle.

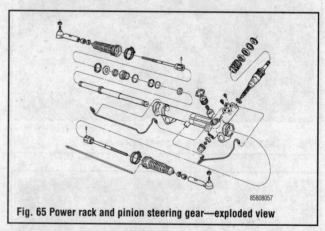

Fig. 65 Power rack and pinion steering gear—exploded view

Rack Yoke Plug Preload

▶ **See Figures 66 and 67**

IN VEHICLE

1. Position the steering wheel in a straight ahead position.
2. Clean the exterior of the steering gear in the area of the yoke plug thoroughly.
3. Loosen the yoke plug locknut with a pinion housing yoke locknut wrench, tool T78P-3504-H or equivalent. Back off at least one-quarter turn.
4. Loosen yoke plug with a ¾ in. socket wrench.
5. With the steering gear still at the center of travel, tighten the yoke plug to

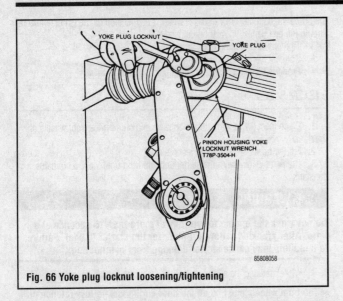

Fig. 66 Yoke plug locknut loosening/tightening

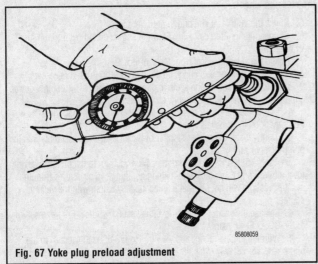

Fig. 67 Yoke plug preload adjustment

45–50 inch lbs. (5–5.6 Nm). Clean the threads of the yoke plug prior to tightening to prevent a false reading.

6. Back off the yoke plug approximately ⅛ turn (44 degrees minimum to 54 degrees maximum).

7. Place tool T78P-3504-H or equivalent on the yoke plug locknut. While holding the yoke plug, tighten the locknut to 44–66 ft. lbs. (60–89 Nm). Do not allow the yoke plug to move while tightening or the preload will be affected. Recheck input shaft torque after tightening the locknut.

OUT OF VEHICLE

1. Clean the exterior of the steering gear thoroughly.

2. Install two long bolts and washers through the bushing, and attach to the bench mounted holding fixture, Tool T57L-500-B or equivalent.

3. Do not remove the external pressure lines, unless they are leaking or damaged. If these lines are removed, they must be replaced with new lines.

4. Drain the power steering fluid by rotating the input shaft lock-to-lock twice using a pinion shaft torque adjuster, tool T74P-3504-R, or equivalent. Cover ports on the valve housing with shop cloth while draining the gear.

5. Insert an inch lb. torque wrench with a maximum capacity of 30–60 inch lbs. (3.4–6.8 Nm) into the pinion shaft torque adjuster. Position the adapter and wrench on the input shaft splines.

6. Loosen the yoke plug locknut with pinion housing yoke locknut wrench, tool T78P-3504-H or equivalent.

7. Loosen the yoke plug with a ¾ in. socket wrench.

8. With the rack at the center of travel, tighten the yoke plug to 45–50 inch lbs. (5–5.6 Nm). Clean the threads of the yoke plug prior to tightening, to prevent a false reading.

9. Back off the yoke plug approximately ⅛ turn (44 degrees minimum to 54 degrees maximum) until the torque required to initiate and sustain rotation of the input shaft is 7–18 inch lbs. (0.8–2.0 Nm).

10. Place Tool T78P-3504-H or equivalent on the yoke plug locknut. While holding the yoke plug, tighten the locknut to 44–66 ft. lbs. (60–90 Nm). Do not allow the yoke plug to move while tightening or the preload will be affected. Recheck input shaft torque after tightening the locknut.

11. If the external pressure lines were removed, they must be replaced with new service lines. Remove the plastic or copper seals from the housing ports prior to installation of new lines.

REMOVAL & INSTALLATION

▶ **See Figures 68 and 69**

1. Disconnect the negative battery cable. Leave the ignition key in the **ON** position.

2. Raise and safely support the vehicle. Position a drain pan to catch fluid from the power steering lines.

3. Remove the one bolt retaining the flexible coupling to the input shaft.

4. Remove the two tie rod end retaining cotter pins and nuts. Separate the studs from the spindle arms, using TOOL-3290-C or an equivalent puller.

5. Support the steering gear, and remove the two nuts, insulator, washers, and bolts retaining the steering gear to the No. 2 crossmember. Lower the gear slightly to permit access to the pressure and return line fittings.

6. Disconnect the pressure and return lines from the steering gear valve housing. Plug the lines and parts in the valve housing to prevent the entry of dirt.

7. Remove the steering gear assembly from the vehicle.

To install:

8. Support and position the steering gear, so that the pressure and return line fittings can be connected to the valve housing. Tighten the fittings to 10–15 ft. lbs. (14–20 Nm). The design allows the hoses to swivel when tightened properly. Do not attempt to eliminate looseness by overtightening, since this can cause damage to the fittings.

➡**The rubber insulators must be pushed completely inside the gear housing before the installation of the gear housing on the No. 2 crossmember.**

9. No gap is allowed between the insulator and the face of the gear boss. A rubber lubricant should be used to facilitate proper installation of the insulators in the gear housing. Insert the input shaft into the flexible coupling, and position the steering gear to the No. 2 crossmember. Install the two bolts, insulator washers, and nuts. Tighten the two nuts to 80–100 ft. lbs. (108–136 Nm) for 1979–84 cars, 90–100 ft. lbs. (122–136 Nm) for 1985 cars, or 30–40 ft. lbs. (41–54 Nm) for 1986–88 cars.

10. Install the one bolt retaining the flexible coupling to the input shaft. Tighten the bolt to 20–30 ft. lbs. (27–41 Nm).

11. Connect the tie rod ends to the spindle arms and install the two retaining nuts. Tighten the nuts to 35–47 ft. lbs. (47–64 Nm), then tighten the nuts to their nearest cotter pin castellation, and install two new cotter pins.

12. Remove the drain pan and lower the vehicle.

13. Turn the ignition key to the **OFF** position.

14. Connect the negative battery cable.

15. Remove the ignition coil wire.

16. Fill the power steering pump reservoir.

17. Engage the starter, and cycle the steering wheel to distribute the fluid. Check the fluid level and add as required.

18. Install the coil wire, start the engine, and cycle the steering wheel. Check for fluid leaks.

19. If the tie rod ends were loosened, check and adjust the wheel alignment, as required.

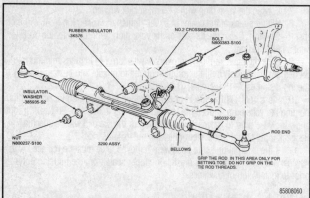

Fig. 68 Power rack and pinion steering gear installation

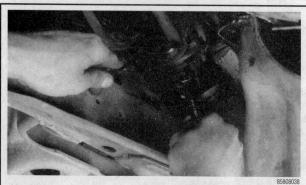

Fig. 69 Remove the one bolt retaining the flexible coupling to the input shaft

Power Steering Pump

REMOVAL & INSTALLATION

1. Drain the fluid from the pump reservoir by disconnecting the fluid return hose at the pump. Disconnect the pressure hose from the pump.
2. Remove the mounting bolts from the front of the pump.
3. Move the pump inward to loosen the belt tension and remove the belt from the pulley. Remove the pump from the car.

To install:

4. Position the pump on the mounting bracket and loosely install the mounting bolts and nuts. Put the drive belt over the pulley and move the pump outward against the belt until the proper belt tension is obtained. Do not pry against the pump body. Measure the belt tension with a belt tension gauge for the proper adjustment. Only in cases where a belt tension gauge is not available should the belt deflection method be used.

5. Tighten the mounting bolts and nuts.
6. Connect the hoses, then refill the reservoir.
7. Properly bleed the power steering pump system.

SYSTEM BLEEDING

1. Disconnect the ignition coil, then raise and support the front wheels off the floor.
2. Fill the power steering fluid reservoir.
3. Crank the engine with the starter and add fluid until the level remains constant.

> ✳✳ **WARNING**

Do not crank the engine for periods of more than 15 seconds at a time. After cranking, allow a minute for the starter to cool. Failure to heed this may cause starter damage from overheating.

4. While cranking the engine, rotate the steering wheel from lock-to-lock.

➡**The front wheels must be off the floor during lock-to-lock rotation of the steering wheel.**

5. Check the fluid level and add fluid, if necessary.
6. Connect the ignition coil wire. Start the engine and allow it to run for several minutes.
7. Rotate the steering wheel from lock-to-lock.
8. Shut off the engine and check the fluid level. Add fluid, if necessary.
9. If air is still present in the system, purge the system of air using a power steering pump air evacuator assembly, as follows:

   a. Make sure the power steering pump reservoir is filled to the COLD FULL mark on the dipstick.

   b. Tightly insert the rubber stopper of the air evacuator assembly into the pump reservoir fill neck.

   c. Apply 15 in. Hg (50.65 kpa) maximum vacuum to the pump reservoir for a minimum of 3 minutes with the engine idling. As air purges from the system, vacuum will fall off. Maintain adequate vacuum with the vacuum source.

   d. Release the vacuum and remove the vacuum source. Fill the reservoir to the COLD FULL mark.

   e. With the engine idling, apply 15 in. Hg (50.65 kpa) vacuum to the pump reservoir. Slowly cycle the steering wheel from lock-to-lock every 30 seconds for approximately 5 minutes. Do not hold the steering wheel on the stops while cycling. Maintain adequate vacuum with the vacuum source as the air purges.

   f. Release the vacuum and remove the vacuum source. Fill the reservoir to the COLD FULL mark.

   g. Start the engine and cycle the steering wheel. Check for oil leaks at all connections. In severe cases of aeration, it may be necessary to repeat Steps 9b–9f.

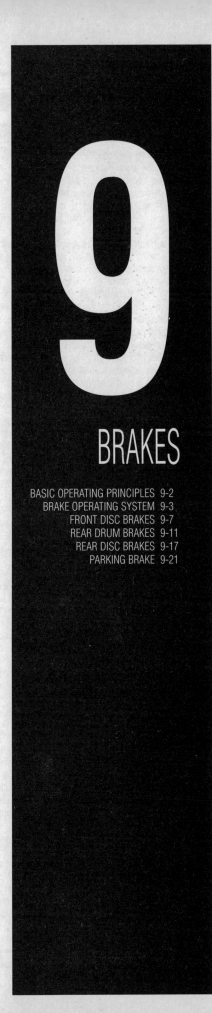

9

BRAKES

BASIC OPERATING PRINCIPLES

Hydraulic System

Hydraulic systems are used to actuate the brakes of all automobiles. The system transports the power required to force the frictional surfaces of the braking system together from the pedal to the individual brake units at each wheel. A hydraulic system is used for two reasons.

First, fluid under pressure can be carried to all parts of an automobile by small pipes and flexible hoses without taking up a significant amount of room or posing routing problems.

Second, a great mechanical advantage can be given to the brake pedal end of the system, and the foot pressure required to actuate the brakes can be reduced by making the surface area of the master cylinder pistons smaller than that of any of the pistons in the wheel cylinders or calipers.

The master cylinder consists of a fluid reservoir and a double cylinder and piston assembly. Double type master cylinders are designed to separate the front and rear braking systems hydraulically in case of a leak.

Steel lines carry the brake fluid to a point on the vehicle's frame near each of the vehicle's wheels. The fluid is then carried to the calipers and wheel cylinders by flexible tubes in order to allow for suspension and steering movements.

In drum brake systems, each wheel cylinder contains two pistons, one at either end, which push outward in opposite directions.

In disc brake systems, the cylinders are part of the calipers. One cylinder in each caliper is used to force the brake pads against the disc.

All pistons employ some type of seal, usually made of rubber, to minimize fluid leakage. A rubber dust boot seals the outer end of the cylinder against dust and dirt. The boot fits around the outer end of the piston on disc brake calipers, and around the brake actuating rod on wheel cylinders.

The hydraulic system operates as follows: When at rest, the entire system, from the piston(s) in the master cylinder to those in the wheel cylinders or calipers, is full of brake fluid. Upon application of the brake pedal, fluid trapped in front of the master cylinder piston(s) is forced through the lines to the wheel cylinders. Here, it forces the pistons outward, in the case of drum brakes, and inward toward the disc, in the case of disc brakes. The motion of the pistons is opposed by return springs mounted outside the cylinders in drum brakes, and by spring seals, in disc brakes.

Upon release of the brake pedal, a spring located inside the master cylinder immediately returns the master cylinder pistons to the normal position. The pistons contain check valves and the master cylinder has compensating ports drilled in it. These are uncovered as the pistons reach their normal position. The piston check valves allow fluid to flow toward the wheel cylinders or calipers as the pistons withdraw. Then, as the return springs force the brake pads or shoes into the released position, the excess fluid reservoir through the compensating ports. It is during the time the pedal is in the released position that any fluid that has leaked out of the system will be replaced through the compensating ports.

Dual circuit master cylinders employ two pistons, located one behind the other, in the same cylinder. The primary piston is actuated directly by mechanical linkage from the brake pedal through the power booster. The secondary piston is actuated by fluid trapped between the two pistons. If a leak develops in front of the secondary piston, it moves forward until it bottoms against the front of the master cylinder, and the fluid trapped between the pistons will operate the rear brakes. If the rear brakes develop a leak, the primary piston will move forward until direct contact with the secondary piston takes place, and it will force the secondary piston to actuate the front brakes. In either case, the brake pedal moves farther when the brakes are applied, and less braking power is available.

All dual circuit systems use a switch to warn the driver when only half of the brake system is operational. This switch is located in a valve body which is mounted on the firewall or the frame below the master cylinder. A hydraulic piston receives pressure from both circuits, each circuit's pressure being applied to one end of the piston. When the pressures are in balance, the piston remains stationary. When one circuit has a leak, however, the greater pressure in that circuit during application of the brakes will push the piston to one side, closing the switch and activating the brake warning light.

In disc brake systems, this valve body also contains a metering valve and, in some cases, a proportioning valve. The metering valve keeps pressure from traveling to the disc brakes on the front wheels until the brake shoes on the rear

wheels have contacted the drums, ensuring that the front brakes will never be used alone. The proportioning valve controls the pressure to the rear brakes to lessen the chance of rear wheel lock–up during very hard braking.

Warning lights may be tested by depressing the brake pedal and holding it while opening one of the wheel cylinder bleeder screws. If this does not cause the light to go on, substitute a new lamp, make continuity checks, and, finally, replace the switch as necessary.

The hydraulic system may be checked for leaks by applying pressure to the pedal gradually and steadily. If the pedal sinks very slowly to the floor, the system has a leak. This is not to be confused with a springy or spongy feel due to the compression of air within the lines. If the system leaks, there will be a gradual change in the position of the pedal with a constant pressure.

Check for leaks along all lines and at wheel cylinders. If no external leaks are apparent, the problem is inside the master cylinder.

Disc Brakes

Instead of the traditional expanding brakes that press outward against a circular drum, disc brake systems utilize a disc (rotor) with brake pads positioned on either side of it. Braking effect is achieved in a manner similar to the way you would squeeze a spinning phonograph record between your fingers. The disc (rotor) is a casting with cooling fins between the two braking surfaces. This enables air to circulate between the braking surfaces making them less sensitive to heat buildup and more resistant to fade. Dirt and water do not affect braking action since contaminants are thrown off by the centrifugal action of the rotor or scraped off the by the pads. Also, the equal clamping action of the two brake pads tends to ensure uniform, straight line stops. Disc brakes are inherently self–adjusting.There are three general types of disc brake:

1. A fixed caliper.
2. A floating caliper.
3. A sliding caliper.

The fixed caliper design uses two pistons mounted on either side of the rotor (in each side of the caliper). The caliper is mounted rigidly and does not move.

The sliding and floating designs are quite similar. In fact, these two types are often lumped together. In both designs, the pad on the inside of the rotor is moved into contact with the rotor by hydraulic force. The caliper, which is not held in a fixed position, moves slightly, bringing the outside pad into contact with the rotor. There are various methods of attaching floating calipers. Some pivot at the bottom or top, and some slide on mounting bolts. In any event, the end result is the same.

➡**All the cars covered in this book employ the sliding caliper design.**

Drum Brakes

Drum brakes employ two brake shoes mounted on a stationary backing plate. These shoes are positioned inside a circular drum which rotates with the wheel assembly. The shoes are held in place by springs. This allows them to slide toward the drums (when they are applied) while keeping the linings and drums in alignment. The shoes are actuated by a wheel cylinder which is mounted at the top of the backing plate. When the brakes are applied, hydraulic pressure forces the wheel cylinder's actuating links outward. Since these links bear directly against the top of the brake shoes, the tops of the shoes are then forced against the inner side of the drum. This action forces the bottoms of the two shoes to contact the brake drum by rotating the entire assembly slightly (known as servo action). When pressure within the wheel cylinder is relaxed, return springs pull the shoes back away from the drum.

Most modern drum brakes are designed to self–adjust themselves during application when the vehicle is moving in reverse. This motion causes both shoes to rotate very slightly with the drum, rocking an adjusting lever, thereby causing rotation of the adjusting screw.

Power Brakes

Power brakes operate just as non–power brake systems except in the actuation of the master cylinder pistons. A vacuum diaphragm is located on the front of the master cylinder and assists the driver in applying the brakes, reducing both the effort and travel he must put into moving the brake pedal.

The vacuum diaphragm housing is connected to the intake manifold by a vacuum hose. A check valve is placed at the point where the hose enters the diaphragm housing, so that during periods of low manifold vacuum brake assist vacuum will not be lost.

Depressing the brake pedal closes off the vacuum source and allows atmospheric pressure to enter on one side of the diaphragm. This causes the master cylinder pistons to move and apply the brakes. When the brake pedal is released, vacuum is applied to both sides of the diaphragm, and return springs return the diaphragm and master cylinder pistons to the released position. If the vacuum fails, the brake pedal rod will butt against the end of the master cylinder actuating rod, and direct mechanical application will occur as the pedal is depressed.

BRAKE OPERATING SYSTEM

ADJUSTMENTS

➡Disc brakes require no adjustments.

DRUM BRAKES

♦ See Figure 1

➡Drum brakes are self–adjusting and require a manual adjustment only after the brake shoes have been replaced, or when the length of the adjusting screw has been changed.

1. Raise and safely support the rear end on jackstands.
2. Remove the rubber plug from the adjusting slot in the brake backing plate.
3. Insert a brake adjusting spoon into the slot and engage the lowest possible tooth on the star wheel. Move the end of the brake spoon downward to move the star wheel upward and expand the adjusting screw. Repeat this operation until the brakes lock the wheel.
4. Insert a small screwdriver or piece of firm wire (coat–hanger wire) into the adjusting slot and push the automatic adjuster lever out and free of the star wheel on the adjusting screw.
5. Holding the adjusting lever out of the way, engage the topmost tooth possible on the star wheel with a brake adjusting spoon. Move the end of the adjusting spoon upward to move the adjusting screw star wheel downward and contact the adjusting screw. Back off the adjusting screw star wheel until the wheel spins freely with a minimum of drag. Keep track of the number of turns the star wheel is backed off.
6. Install the rubber plug in the adjusting slot of the brake backing plate.
7. Repeat this operation for the other side. When adjusting the brakes on the other side, the adjusting lever must be backed off the same number of turns to prevent side–to–side brake pull.
8. Remove the jackstands and lower the vehicle.
9. Prior to driving the vehicle, pump the brake pedal to obtain a firm, responsive pedal.
10. Complete the adjustment by applying the brakes with minimal pressure, while driving the vehicle in reverse. Move the vehicle forward after each stop, and repeat several times.

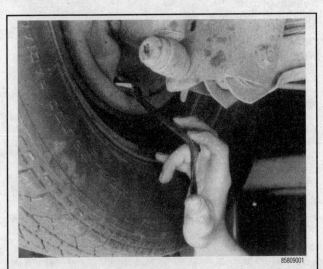

85809001

Fig. 1 Use a brake adjusting spoon to turn the star wheel

11. Road test the car. If new brake linings have been installed, allow a short break–in period before hard breaking, wherever possible.

Brake Light Switch

REMOVAL & INSTALLATION

1. Raise the locking tab and unplug the wiring harness at the switch.
2. Remove the hairpin clip from the stud and slide the switch up and down; remove the switch and washers from the pedal.

➡It is not necessary to remove the pushrod from the stud.

3. Installation is the reverse of removal. Position the U–shaped side nearest the pedal and directly over/under the pin. Slide the switch up and down, trapping the pushrod and bushing between the switch side plates.

Master Cylinder

➡1979–86 Mustang/Capri models were equipped with a metal master cylinder containing an integral body and reservoir. 1987–88 Mustangs were equipped with a metal master cylinder body and removable plastic reservoir.

REMOVAL & INSTALLATION

Manual Brakes

♦ See Figure 2

1. Disconnect the negative battery cable.
2. Disconnect the brake light switch wires at the connector, inside the vehicle.
3. Remove the spring retainer. Slide the brake light switch off the brake pedal pin just far enough to clear the end of the pin, and remove the switch. Be careful to avoid damage to the switch.
4. Disconnect the brake lines from the primary and secondary outlet ports of the master cylinder. Cap the lines and plug the ports.
5. Loosen the master cylinder attaching nuts or bolts from the inside of the engine compartment, and slide the master cylinder pushrod, nylon washers and bushings off the brake pedal pin.
6. Remove the attaching nuts that secure the master cylinder to the dash panel adapter.
7. Lift the cylinder forward and upward from the vehicle.
   To install:
8. Insert the master cylinder pushrod through the dash panel adapter opening, and position the master cylinder on the panel adapter.
9. Install, but do not tighten, the attaching nuts at the dash panel.
10. Coat the nylon bushings and washers with SAE 10W-40 motor oil.
11. Install the inner nylon washer, the master cylinder pushrod, and the brake light switch bushing on the brake pedal pin. Position the stop lamp switch so that it straddles the pushrod with the slot on the pedal pin, and the switch outer frame hole just clearing the pin. Slide the switch upward, onto the pin and pushrod. Slide the assembly inboard toward the brake pedal arm. Install the outer nylon washer and the pushrod retainer, then lock the retainer securely.
12. Attach the brake light switch electrical connector.
13. Tighten the master cylinder attaching nuts to 13–25 ft. lbs. (18–34 Nm).
14. Connect the brake lines to the master cylinder, and tighten to 10–18 ft. lbs. (14–24 Nm).
15. Refill the master cylinder with the specified brake fluid.

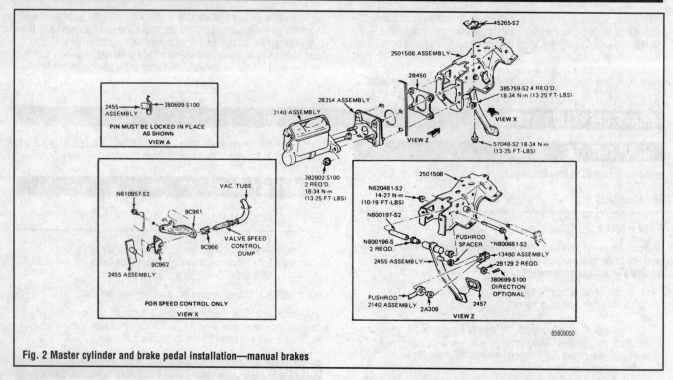

Fig. 2 Master cylinder and brake pedal installation—manual brakes

16. Bleed the master cylinder, as well as the primary and secondary brake systems.

17. Operate the brakes several times and check for external hydraulic leaks.

Power Brakes

▶ See Figures 3, 4 and 5

1. Disconnect the brake lines from the master cylinder. Cap the lines and plug the ports.

2. Remove the two nuts and lockwashers, if so equipped, that attach the master cylinder to the brake booster.

3. Disconnect the brake warning lamp connector, if so equipped.

4. Slide the master cylinder forward and upward from the booster.

To install:

5. Position the master cylinder assembly onto the two studs of the booster assembly.

6. Install the lockwashers, if so equipped, and the attaching nuts. Tighten the nuts to 13–25 ft. lbs. (18–34 Nm).

Fig. 3 Use an open end wrench to disconnect the brake lines at the master cylinder

7. Connect the front and rear brake tubes to the master cylinder outlet ports, and tighten to 10–18 ft. lbs. (14–24 Nm).

8. Attach the brake warning lamp connector, if so equipped.

9. Refill the master cylinder with the specified brake fluid.

10. Bleed the master cylinder, as well as the primary and secondary brake systems.

11. Operate the brakes several times and check for external hydraulic leaks.

Power Brake Booster

TESTING

The hydraulic and mechanical problems that apply to conventional brake systems also apply to power brakes, and should be checked for if the tests below do not reveal the problem.

Test for a system vacuum leak as described below:

1. Operate the engine at idle without touching the brake pedal for at least one minute.

2. Turn off the engine, and wait one minute.

3. Test for the presence of assist vacuum by depressing the brake pedal and releasing it several times. Light application will produce less and less pedal travel, if vacuum was present. If there is no vacuum, air is leaking into the system somewhere.

Test for system operation as follows:

4. Pump the brake pedal (with engine off) until the supply vacuum is entirely gone.

5. Put a light, steady pressure on the pedal.

6. Start the engine, and operate it at idle. If the system is operating, the brake pedal should fall toward the floor if constant pressure is maintained on the pedal.

Power brake systems may be tested for hydraulic leaks just as ordinary systems are tested.

REMOVAL & INSTALLATION

1. Working inside the car below the instrument panel, disconnect the booster valve operating rod from the brake pedal assembly.

2. Open the hood and disconnect the wires from the stop light switch at the brake master cylinder.

3. Disconnect the brake line at the master cylinder outlet fitting.

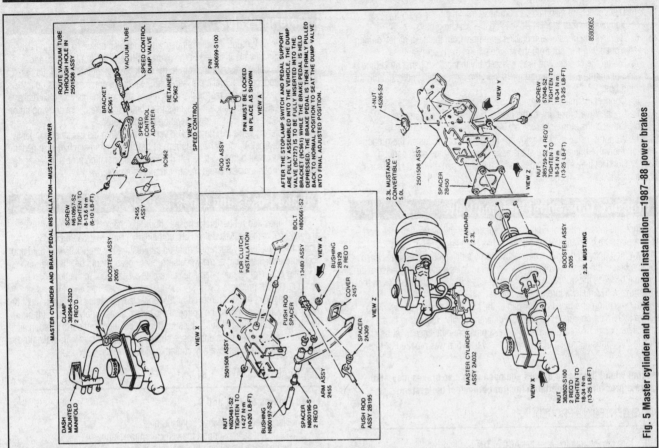

Fig. 5 Master cylinder and brake pedal installation—1987–88 power brakes

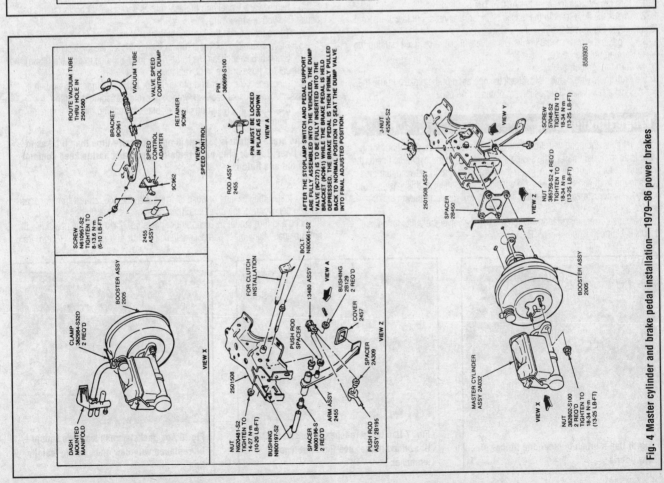

Fig. 4 Master cylinder and brake pedal installation—1979–86 power brakes

4. Disconnect the manifold vacuum hose from the booster unit.

5. Remove the four bracket–to–dash panel attaching bolts.

6. Remove the booster and bracket assembly from the dash panel, sliding the valve operating rod out from the engine side of the dash panel.

7. Mount the booster and bracket assembly to the dash panel by sliding the valve operating rod in through the hole in the dash panel, and installing the attaching bolts.

8. Connect the manifold vacuum hose to the booster.

9. Connect the brake line to the master cylinder outlet fitting.

10. Connect the stop light switch wires.

11. Working inside the car below the instrument panel, install the rubber boot on the valve operating rod at the passenger side of the dash panel.

12. Connect the valve operating rod to the brake pedal with the bushings, eccentric shoulder bolt, and nut.

Pressure Differential Warning Valve

Since the introduction of dual master cylinders to the hydraulic brake system, a pressure differential warning signal has been added. This signal consists of a warning light on the dashboard activated by a differential pressure switch located below the master cylinder. The signal indicates a hydraulic pressure differential between the front and rear brakes of 80–150 psi, and should warn the driver that a hydraulic failure has occurred.

After repairing and bleeding any part of the hydraulic system, the warning light may remain on due to the pressure differential valve remaining in the off–center position. To centralize the valve, a pressure difference must be created in the opposite branch of the hydraulic system that was repaired or bled last.

➡ **Front wheel balancing of cars equipped with disc brakes may also cause a pressure differential in the front branch of the system.**

VALVE CENTERING PROCEDURE

1. Turn the ignition to either the **ACC** or **ON** position.

2. Check the fluid level in the master cylinder reservoirs. Fill to within ¼ in. (6mm) of the top if necessary.

3. Depress the brake pedal firmly. The valve will centralize itself causing the brake warning light to go out.

4. Turn the ignition off.

5. Prior to driving the vehicle, check the operation of the brakes. Pump the brake pedal a few times, if necessary, to obtain a firm pedal.

Proportioning Valve

On vehicles equipped with front disc and rear drum brakes, a proportioning valve is an important part of the system. It is installed in the hydraulic line to the rear brakes. Its function is to maintain the correct proportion between line pressures to the front and rear brakes. No attempt at adjustment of this valve should be made, as adjustment is preset and tampering will result in uneven braking action.

To assure correct installation when replacing the valve, the outlet to the rear brakes is stamped with the letter **R**.

Metering Valve

On vehicles through 1980 equipped with front disc brakes, a metering valve is used. This valve is installed in the hydraulic line to the front brakes, and functions to delay pressure buildup to the front brakes on application. Its purpose is to reduce front brake pressure until rear brake pressure builds up adequately to overcome the rear brake shoe return springs. In this way disc brake pad lift is extended because it prevents the front disc brakes from carrying all or most of the braking load at low operating line pressures.

The metering valve can be checked very simply. With the car stopped, gently apply the brakes. At about 1 in. (25mm) of travel, a very small change in pedal effort (like a small bump) will be felt if the valve is operating properly. Metering valves are not serviceable and must be replaced if defective.

Brake Hoses and Lines

Metal lines and rubber brake hoses should be checked frequently for leaks and external damage. Metal lines are particularly prone to crushing and kinking under the vehicle. Any such deformation can restrict the proper flow of fluid and therefore impair braking at the wheels. Rubber hoses should be checked for cracking or scraping; such damage can create a weak spot in the hose and it could fail under pressure.

Any time the lines are removed or disconnected, extreme cleanliness must be observed. Clean all joints and connections before disassembly (use a stiff bristle brush and clean brake fluid); be sure to plug the lines and ports as soon as they are opened. New lines and hoses should be flushed clean with brake fluid before installation to remove any contamination.

REMOVAL & INSTALLATION

▶ **See Figures 6, 7, 8 and 9**

1. Disconnect the negative battery cable.

2. Raise and safely support the vehicle on jackstands.

3. Remove any wheel and tire assemblies necessary for access to the particular line you are removing.

4. Thoroughly clean the surrounding area at the joints to be disconnected.

5. Place a suitable catch pan under the joint to be disconnected.

6. Using two wrenches (one to hold the joint and one to turn the fitting), disconnect the hose or line to be replaced.

7. Disconnect the other end of the line or hose, moving the drain pan if necessary. Always use a back-up wrench to avoid damaging the fitting.

8. Disconnect any retaining clips or brackets holding the line and remove the line from the vehicle.

➡ **If the brake system is to remain open for more time than it takes to swap lines, tape or plug each remaining clip and port to keep contaminants out and fluid in.**

To install:

9. Install the new line or hose, starting with the end farthest from the master cylinder. Connect the other end, then confirm that both fittings are correctly threaded and turn smoothly using finger pressure. Make sure the new line will not rub against any other part. Brake lines must be at least 1/2 in. (13mm) from

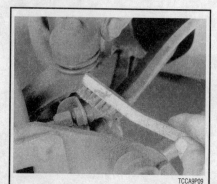

TCCA9P09

Fig. 6 Use a brush to clean the fittings of any debris

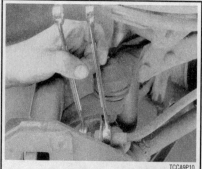

TCCA9P10

Fig. 7 Use two wrenches to loosen the fitting. If available, use flare nut type wrenches

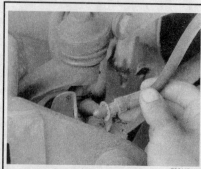

TCCA9P11

Fig. 8 Any gaskets/crush washers should be replaced with new ones during installation

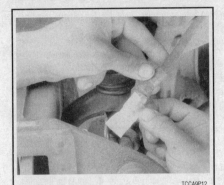

Fig. 9 Tape or plug the line to prevent contamination

TCCA9P12

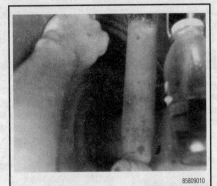

Fig. 10 On drum brakes, the bleeder screw is located just above the brake line fitting

85809010

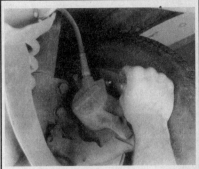

Fig. 11 If so equipped, remove the protective cap from the bleeder screw

85809011

Fig. 12 Attach the bleeder tubing and bottle of brake fluid, before opening the bleeder screw

85809012

the steering column and other moving parts. Any protective shielding or insulators must be reinstalled in the original location.

✳✳ WARNING

Make sure the hose is NOT kinked or touching any part of the frame or suspension after installation. These conditions may cause the hose to fail prematurely.

10. Using two wrenches as before, tighten each fitting.
11. Install any retaining clips or brackets on the lines.
12. If removed, install the wheel and tire assemblies, then carefully lower the vehicle to the ground.
13. Refill the brake master cylinder reservoir with clean, fresh brake fluid, meeting DOT 3 specifications. Properly bleed the brake system.
14. Connect the negative battery cable.

Bleeding Brake System

▶ See Figures 10, 11 and 12

➡The primary (front) and secondary (rear) hydraulic systems are independent of each other. If it is known that only one system has air in it, only that system has to be bled. Bleed the longest line first on the individual system being serviced.

1. Fill the master cylinder with brake fluid.
2. If the secondary system is to be bled, install a ⅜ in. box–end wrench on the bleeder screw of the right rear wheel cylinder. Be sure to first remove the screw's protective cap, if so equipped.
3. Push a piece of small diameter rubber or plastic tubing over the bleeder screw until it is flush against the wrench. Submerge the other end of the tubing in a glass jar partially filled with clean brake fluid. Make sure the tubing fits on the bleeder screw snugly.
4. Open the bleeder screw approximately ¾ turn and have an assistant apply pressure to the brake pedal. Observe the bottle of brake fluid. If bubbles appear in the glass jar, there is air in the system. When your assistant has pushed the pedal to the floor, immediately close the bleeder screw before he releases the pedal.
5. Repeat this operation until air bubbles cease to appear at the submerged end of the bleeder tubing.
6. When the fluid is completely free of air bubbles, tighten the bleeder screw and remove the bleeder tubing. Replace the protective cap on the bleeder screw, if so equipped.
7. Repeat this procedure at the left rear wheel cylinder. Refill the master cylinder reservoir after each wheel cylinder is bled. Do not allow the master cylinder to run dry.
8. If the primary system is to be bled, repeat steps 3–6, beginning with the right front caliper. (On disc brake systems, which do not use wheel cylinders, bleeder screws are located on the brake calipers.)
9. Repeat the bleeding procedure at the left front brake caliper.
10. Check the fluid level in the master cylinder and center the pressure differential warning valve, as described earlier in this section.

FRONT DISC BRAKES

✳✳ CAUTION

Brake shoes contain asbestos, which has been determined to be a cancer causing agent. Never clean the brake surfaces with compressed air! Avoid inhaling any dust from any brake surface! When cleaning brake surfaces, use a commercially available brake cleaning fluid.

Brake Pads

REMOVAL & INSTALLATION

▶ See Figures 13 thru 21

➡When installing new brake linings, replace the pads at both front wheels to avoid uneven braking.

1. Remove the master cylinder cap, and check the fluid level in the primary (large) reservoir. Remove brake fluid until the reservoir is half full. Discard this fluid.

2. Raise and safely support the vehicle. Remove the wheel covers.

3. Remove the wheel and tire assemblies from the hubs. Be careful to avoid damage to, or interference with, the caliper splash shield or bleeder screw fitting.

✳✳ WARNING

If you are not thoroughly familiar with the procedures involved in brake service, only disassemble and assemble one side at a time, leaving the other brake assembly intact as a reference.

4. Remove the caliper locating pins. If they have Torx® heads, use Caliper Pin Remover/Installer D79P–2100–T45, or equivalent.

5. Lift the caliper assembly from the integral spindle/anchor plate and rotor.

6. Suspend the caliper inside the fender housing with a wire hooked through the outer leg hole of the caliper. Be careful not to damage the caliper or stretch the brake hose.

7. Remove the outer shoe (pad) from the caliper assembly.

8. Remove the inner shoe (pad) from the caliper assembly.

9. Inspect both rotor braking surfaces. Minor scoring or buildup of lining material does not require machining or replacement of the rotor.

✳✳ CAUTION

Brake shoes contain asbestos, which has been determined to be a cancer causing agent. Never clean the brake surfaces with compressed air! Avoid inhaling any dust from any brake surface! When cleaning brake surfaces, use a commercially available brake cleaning fluid.

10. Remove and discard the plastic sleeves that are located inside the caliper locating pin insulators. These parts must not be reused.

11. Remove and discard the caliper locating insulator. These parts must not be reused.

12. Use a 4 in. (101mm) C–clamp and a block of wood 2 ¾ in. x 1 in. and approximately ¾ in. thick (70mm x 25mm x 19mm) to seat the caliper's hydraulic piston in its bore. This must be done to provide clearance for the caliper assembly to fit over the rotor when installed. Remove the C–clamp from the caliper (the caliper piston will remain seated in its bore).

13. Install new locating pin insulators and plastic sleeves in the caliper housing. Do not use a sharp edge tool to insert the insulators in the caliper housing. Check to see if both insulator flanges straddle the housing holes and if the plastic sleeves are bottomed in the insulators, as well as slipped under the upper lip.

14. Install the correct inner shoe and lining assembly in the caliper piston. All vehicles have a separate anti–rattle clip and insulator that must be installed to the inner shoe and lining prior to their assembly in the caliper. The inner shoes are marked LH or RH and must be installed in the proper caliper. Also, care should be taken not to bend the anti–rattle clips too far in the piston or distortion and rattles can result.

15. Install the correct outer brake shoe and lining assembly (RH/LH), making sure that the clip and/or buttons located on the shoe are properly seated. The outer shoe can be identified as right hand or left hand by the wear indicator (which must always be installed toward the front of the vehicle), or by a LH or RH mark.

✳✳ WARNING

Make certain that the two round torque buttons are seated solidly in the two holes of the outer caliper leg and that the shoe is held tightly against the housing by the spring clip. If the buttons are not seated, a temporary loss of brakes may occur!

16. Remove the caliper suspension wire or twine, and position the caliper and brake shoe assembly over the rotor.

Fig. 13 Removal of the wheel and tire assembly exposes the rotor, caliper and hub assemblies

Fig. 14 The caliper assembly straddles the upper, left portion of the rotor

Fig. 15 A Torx® bit and ratchet may be needed to loosen the caliper locating pins

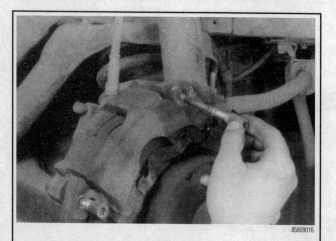

Fig. 16 Remove the partially threaded caliper locating pins

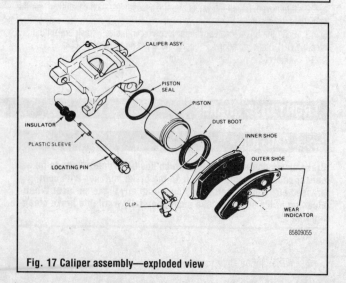

Fig. 17 Caliper assembly—exploded view

Fig. 18 Suspend the caliper inside the fender housing with a length of wire or twine

Fig. 19 Remove the outer shoe from the caliper assembly

Fig. 20 Remove the inner shoe from the caliper assembly

17. Insert new caliper locating pins through the outer shoe, and hand thread them into the spindle/anchor plate assembly, and through the insulators on the caliper assembly. (On Mustang SVO, the locating pins can be re–used.)

18. Tighten the locating pins to 30–40 ft. lbs. (41–54 Nm). On Mustang SVO, tighten the locating pins to 40–60 ft. lbs. (54–81 Nm). If the locating pins have Torx® heads, use Caliper Pin Remover/Installer D79P–2100–T45, or equivalent.

19. Repeat Steps 4–18 for the other side of the vehicle.

20. Install the wheel and tire assemblies, and tighten the wheel attaching nuts to 80–105 ft. lbs.

21. Lower the vehicle and install the wheel covers.

22. Pump the brake pedal prior to moving the vehicle to position the brake linings and obtain a firm pedal.

23. Refill the master cylinder with new brake fluid.

24. Road test the vehicle.

INSPECTION

1. Raise the vehicle until the wheel and tire clear the floor. Place safety stands under the vehicle.

2. Remove the wheel cover.

3. Remove the wheel and tire from the hub and disc.

✳✳ CAUTION

Brake shoes contain asbestos, which has been determined to be a cancer causing agent. Never clean the brake surfaces with compressed air! Avoid inhaling any dust from any brake surface! When cleaning brake surfaces, use a commercially available brake cleaning fluid.

4. Remove the brake pads as described above and visually inspect the shoe and lining assemblies. If the lining material has worn to a thickness of 0.125 in. (3.175mm) or less, or if the lining is contaminated with brake fluid, replace all pad assemblies on **both** front wheels. Make all thickness measurements across the thinnest section of the pad assembly. A slight taper on a used lining should be considered normal.

5. Reinstall or replace the brake pads and caliper assemblies, as described above.

➡ **When installing new brake linings, replace the pads at both front wheels to avoid uneven braking.**

6. Refill the master cylinder, if necessary.

7. Install the wheel and tire assembly and tighten the wheel lug nuts.

8. Install the wheel cover and lower the vehicle.

Brake Caliper

INSPECTION

1. Raise the vehicle until the wheel and tire clear the floor. Place safety stands under the vehicle.

2. Remove the wheel cover.

3. Remove the wheel and tire from the hub and disc.

✳✳ CAUTION

Brake shoes contain asbestos, which has been determined to be a cancer causing agent. Never clean the brake surfaces with compressed air! Avoid inhaling any dust from any brake surface! When

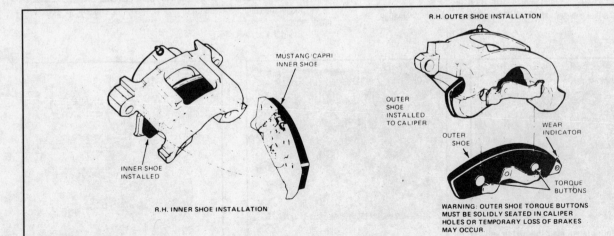

Fig. 21 Disc brake shoe installation

cleaning brake surfaces, use a commercially available brake cleaning fluid.

4. Visually check the caliper for signs of leakage. If leakage is evident, the caliper should be overhauled or replaced.

5. Install the wheel and tire assembly and tighten the wheel lug nuts. Install the wheel cover.

6. Remove the safety stands and lower the vehicle.

REMOVAL & INSTALLATION

♦ See Figures 15 and 16

1. Raise and safely support the vehicle. Remove the wheel cover.
2. Remove the wheel and tire assembly from the hub. Be careful to avoid damage to or interference with the caliper splash shield or bleeder screw fitting.
3. Disconnect the flexible brake hose from the caliper as follows:
   a. Disconnect the hose, and loosen the tube fitting that connects the hose to the brake tube at the bracket on the frame. Plug the brake tube.
   b. Remove the horseshoe shaped retaining clip from the hose and bracket.
   c. Disengage the hose from the bracket, and unscrew the entire hose assembly from the caliper.
4. Remove the caliper locating pins. If they have Torx® heads, use Caliper Pin Remover/Installer D79P–2100–T45, or equivalent.
5. Lift the caliper assembly from the integral spindle/anchor plate and rotor.

To install:

6. Install the caliper assembly over the rotor with the outer brake shoe against the rotor's braking surface.
7. Lubricate the rubber insulators with 4–8 grams of silicone dielectric compound or equivalent.
8. Install new locating pins (except for Mustang SVO, whose pins can be re–used), and hand thread them into the spindle/anchor plate assembly. Be sure that the pins are free from oil, grease and dirt.
9. Tighten the caliper locating pins to 30–40 ft. lbs. (40–60 ft. lbs. on Mustang SVO). If they have Torx® heads, use Caliper Pin Remover/Installer D79P–2100–T45 or equivalent.
10. For all vehicles except Mustang SVO, thread the flexible brake hose into its fitting on the caliper and tighten to 20–30 ft. lbs. This is a special self–sealing fitting that does not require a gasket.

➡When the hose is correctly tightened, there should be one or two threads of the fitting exposed. Do not overtighten.

11. On Mustang SVO, install the flexible brake hose to the caliper with a hollow bolt and two new sealing washers. Tighten the hose fitting to 17–25 ft. lbs.
12. Position the upper end of the flexible brake hose in its bracket, and install the retaining clip. Do not twist the hose.
13. Remove the plug from the brake tube. Connect the tube to the brake hose with the tube fitting nut, and tighten to 10–18 ft. lbs.
14. Bleed the brake system and centralize the brake pressure differential valve.

15. Top off the master cylinder to the specified level with new brake fluid.
16. Install the wheel and tire assembly and tighten the wheel lug nuts.
17. Install the wheel cover and lower the vehicle.
18. Apply the brake pedal several times to position the brake linings.
19. Road test the vehicle.

OVERHAUL

♦ See Figures 22 thru 27

✲✲ CAUTION

Brake shoes contain asbestos, which has been determined to be a cancer causing agent. Never clean the brake surfaces with compressed air! Avoid inhaling any dust from any brake surface! When cleaning brake surfaces, use a commercially available brake cleaning fluid.

1. Remove the caliper assembly from the vehicle as outlined above.
2. Place a cloth over the piston before applying air pressure to prevent damage to the piston.

➡Mustang SVO is equipped with a phenolic (plastic) piston. Before air pressure is applied, insert layers of shop towels to cushion the possible impact of the piston against the caliper iron. Do not use a screwdriver or similar tool to pry the piston out of its bore, since damage to the phenolic piston may result.

3. Apply air pressure to the fluid port in the caliper with a rubber tipped nozzle to remove the piston. If the piston is seized and cannot be forced from the caliper, tap lightly around the piston while applying air pressure. Use care, because the piston can develop considerable force from pressure buildup.
4. Remove the dust boot from the caliper assembly.
5. Remove the rubber piston seal from the cylinder, and discard it.
6. Clean all metal parts with isopropyl alcohol. Then, clean out and dry the grooves and passageways with compressed air. Make sure the caliper bore and component parts are thoroughly clean.
7. Check the cylinder and piston for damage or excessive wear. Replace the piston if it is pitted, scored, corroded, or the plating is worn off. Do not replace a phenolic piston for cosmetic surface irregularities or small chips between the piston boot groove and shoe face.
8. Apply a film of clean brake fluid to the new caliper piston seal, and install it in the cylinder. Be sure the seal does not become twisted but is firmly seated in the groove.
9. Install a new dust boot by seating the flange squarely in the outer groove of the caliper bore.
10. Coat the piston with brake fluid, and install the piston in the cylinder. Be sure to use a wood block or other flat stock when using a C–clamp to install the piston back into the cylinder. Never apply the C–clamp directly to a phenolic piston, and be sure the piston is not cocked. Spread the dust boot over the piston as it is installed. Seat the dust boot in the piston groove.
11. Install the caliper over the rotor and reconnect the brake hose, as outlined above.
12. Bleed the brake system.

Fig. 22 A cloth placed over the piston will help prevent damage when applying compressed air

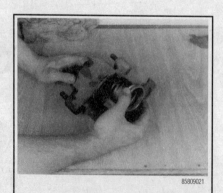

Fig. 23 Remove the piston from the cylinder

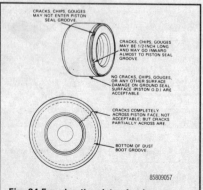

Fig. 24 Examine the piston for damage or excessive wear

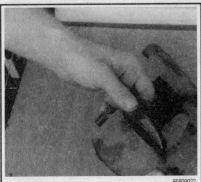

Fig. 25 Remove the dust boot from the caliper assembly

Fig. 26 Remove the piston seal from the cylinder

Fig. 27 Use a wood block and C–clamp to seat the piston in its bore

Brake Disc (Rotor)

REMOVAL & INSTALLATION

1. Raise and safely support the vehicle. Remove the wheel.

❄❄ CAUTION

Brake shoes contain asbestos, which has been determined to be a cancer causing agent. Never clean the brake surfaces with compressed air! Avoid inhaling any dust from any brake surface! When cleaning brake surfaces, use a commercially available brake cleaning fluid.

2. Remove the caliper. Slide the caliper assembly away from the disc and suspend it with a wire loop. It is not necessary to disconnect the brake line.
3. Remove the grease cap from the hub. Remove the cotter pin, nut lock, adjusting nut, and flat washer from the spindle.
4. Remove the outer wheel bearing cone and roller assembly from the hub.
5. Remove the hub and disc assembly from the spindle.

To install:

❄❄ WARNING

If a new disc is being installed, remove the protective coating with carburetor degreaser. If the original disc is being installed, make sure that the grease in the hub is clean and adequate, that the inner bearing and grease retainer are lubricated and in good condition, and that the disc breaking surfaces are clean.

6. Install the hub and disc assembly on the spindle.
7. Lubricate the outer bearing and install the thrust washer and adjusting nut.

REAR DRUM BRAKES

❄❄ CAUTION

Brake shoes contain asbestos, which has been determined to be a cancer causing agent. Never clean the brake surfaces with compressed air! Avoid inhaling any dust from any brake surface! When cleaning brake surfaces, use a commercially available brake cleaning fluid.

Brake Drums

REMOVAL & INSTALLATION

▶ **See Figures 28 and 29**

1. Raise the rear of the car and support the car with safety stands. Make sure the parking brake is not on.

8. Adjust the wheel bearing as outlined in the Wheel Bearing Adjustment section.
9. Install the nut lock, cotter pin, and grease cap.
10. Install the caliper assembly.
11. Install the wheel and tire assembly and torque the nuts to 75–110 ft. lbs.
12. Lower the vehicle and road test it.

INSPECTION

1. Raise the vehicle until the wheel and tire clear the floor. Place safety stands under the vehicle.
2. Remove the wheel cover.
3. Remove the wheel and tire from the hub and disc.

❄❄ CAUTION

Brake shoes contain asbestos, which has been determined to be a cancer causing agent. Never clean the brake surfaces with compressed air! Avoid inhaling any dust from any brake surface! When cleaning brake surfaces, use a commercially available brake cleaning fluid.

4. To check disc run-out, tighten the wheel bearing adjusting nut to eliminate end–play. Check to make sure the disc can still be rotated.
5. Hand spin the disc and visually check for run-out. If the disc appears to be out of round or if it wobbles, it needs to be machined or replaced. When the run-out check is finished, loosen the wheel bearing adjusting nut and retighten to specifications, in order to prevent bearing damage.
6. Visually check the disc for scoring. Minor scores can be removed with fine emery cloth. If it is excessively scored, it must be machined or replaced.
7. Install the wheel and tire assembly and tighten the wheel lug nuts.
8. Install the wheel cover. Remove the safety stands and lower the vehicle.

2. Remove the lug nuts that attach the wheels to the axle shaft and remove the tires and wheels from the car.

❄❄ CAUTION

Brake shoes contain asbestos, which has been determined to be a cancer causing agent. Never clean the brake surfaces with compressed air! Avoid inhaling any dust from any brake surface! When cleaning brake surfaces, use a commercially available brake cleaning fluid.

3. Remove the drum retainer nuts from the wheel studs, if so equipped. Pull the brake drum off the axle shaft. If the brakes are adjusted too tightly to remove the drum, see Step 4. If you can remove the drum, proceed to Step 5.
4. If the brakes are too tight to remove the drum, get under the car (make sure you have safety stands under the car to support it) and remove the rubber plug from the bottom of the brake backing plate. Shine a flashlight into the slot

Fig. 28 Removal of the tire and wheel assembly exposes the brake drum

Fig. 29 Pull the brake drum away from the backing plate and over the wheel lug studs

in the plate. You will see the top of the adjusting screw star wheel and the adjusting lever for the automatic brake adjusting mechanism. To back off on the adjusting screw, you must first insert a small, thin screwdriver or a piece of firm wire (coat hanger wire) into the adjusting slot and push the adjusting lever away from the adjusting screw. Then, insert a brake adjusting spoon into the slot and engage the top of the star wheel. Lift up on the bottom of the adjusting spoon to force the adjusting screw star wheel downward. Repeat this operation until the brake drum is free of the brake shoes and can be pulled off.

To install:

5. Line up the wheel studs with the holes in the brake drum. Push the drum over the studs until it seats fully against the hub.

➡**If the brake adjustment was altered in order to remove the drum, the brakes will need to be adjusted again. For a detailed description of drum brake adjustment, see the beginning of this section.**

6. Install the drum retainer nuts on the wheel studs, if so equipped, and tighten securely.

7. Install the tires and wheels, tightening the lug nuts securely.

INSPECTION

1. Remove the brake drum, as described above.

✳✳ CAUTION

Brake shoes contain asbestos, which has been determined to be a cancer causing agent. Never clean the brake surfaces with compressed air! Avoid inhaling any dust from any brake surface! When cleaning brake surfaces, use a commercially available brake cleaning fluid.

2. Examine the inside of the brake drum; it should have a smooth, dull finish. If excessive brake shoe wear caused grooves to wear in the drum it must be machined or replaced. If the inside of the drum is slightly glazed, but otherwise good, it can be cleaned up with medium grit sandpaper.

3. If no repairs are required, install the brake drum and wheel. If the brake adjustment was changed to remove the drum, adjust the brakes until the drum will just fit over the brakes. After the wheel is installed it will be necessary to complete the adjustment. See Brake Adjustment at the beginning of this section.

Brake Shoes

INSPECTION

1. Raise the rear of the car and support the car with safety stands. Make sure the parking brake is not on.

2. Remove the lug nuts that attach the wheels to the axle shaft and remove the tires and wheels from the car.

✳✳ WARNING

If you are not thoroughly familiar with the procedures involved in brake service, only disassemble and assemble one side at a time, leaving the other brake assembly intact as a reference.

3. Remove the drum retainer nuts from the wheel studs, if so equipped. Pull the brake drum off the axle shaft. If the brakes are adjusted too tightly to remove the drum, see Step 4. If you can remove the drum, proceed to Step 5.

4. If the brakes are too tight to remove the drum, get under the car (make sure you have safety stands under the car to support it) and remove the rubber plug from the bottom of the brake backing plate. Shine a flashlight into the slot in the plate. You will see the top of the adjusting screw star wheel and the adjusting lever for the automatic brake adjusting mechanism. To back off on the adjusting screw, you must first insert a small, thin screwdriver or a piece of firm wire (coat hanger wire) into the adjusting slot and push the adjusting lever away from the adjusting screw. Then, insert a brake adjusting spoon into the slot and engage the top of the star wheel. Lift up on the bottom of the adjusting spoon to force the adjusting screw star wheel downward. Repeat this operation until the brake drum is free of the brake shoes and can be pulled off.

✳✳ CAUTION

Brake shoes contain asbestos, which has been determined to be a cancer causing agent. Never clean the brake surfaces with compressed air! Avoid inhaling any dust from any brake surface! When cleaning brake surfaces, use a commercially available brake cleaning fluid.

5. Clean the brake shoes and the inside of the brake drum. There must be at least $\frac{1}{16}$ in. (1.6mm) of brake lining above the heads of the brake shoe attaching rivets. The lining should not be cracked or contaminated with grease or brake fluid. If there is grease or brake fluid on the lining, it must be replaced and the source of the leak must be found and corrected. Brake fluid on the lining means leaking wheel cylinders. Grease on the brake lining means a leaking grease retainer (front wheels) or axle seal (rear brakes). If the lining is slightly glazed but otherwise in good condition, it can be cleaned up with medium grit sandpaper. Lift up the bottom of the wheel cylinder boots and inspect the ends of the wheel cylinders. A small amount of fluid in the end of the cylinder should be considered normal. If fluid runs out of the cylinder when the boots are lifted, however, the wheel cylinder must be rebuilt or replaced.

6. If no repairs are required, install the brake drum and wheel. If the brake adjustment was changed to remove the drum, adjust the brakes until the drum

will just fit over the shoes. After the wheel is installed it will be necessary to complete the adjustment. See Brake Adjustment at the beginning of this section.

REMOVAL & INSTALLATION

▶ **See Figures 30 thru 44**

➡ **When installing new brake linings, replace the shoes at both rear wheels to avoid uneven braking.**

1. Remove the rear wheel covers.
2. Raise the rear of the car and support the car with safety stands. Make sure the parking brake is not on.
3. Remove the lug nuts that attach the wheels to the axle shaft and remove the tires and wheels from the car.

✳✳ WARNING

If you are not thoroughly familiar with the procedures involved in brake service, only disassemble and assemble one side at a time, leaving the other brake assembly intact as a reference.

4. Remove the brake drum, as described above.

✳✳ CAUTION

Brake shoes contain asbestos, which has been determined to be a cancer causing agent. Never clean the brake surfaces with compressed air! Avoid inhaling any dust from any brake surface! When cleaning brake surfaces, use a commercially available brake cleaning fluid.

5. Place the hollow end of the brake spring service tool (available at auto parts stores) on the brake shoe anchor pin and twist it to disengage one of the brake retracting springs. Repeat this operation to remove the other spring.

✳✳ CAUTION

Be careful that the springs do not slip off the tool during removal, as they could cause personal injury.

6. Reach behind the brake backing plate and place a finger on the end of one of the brake hold-down spring mounting pins. Using a pair of pliers or a specialty tool, grasp the washer on the top of the hold-down spring that corresponds to the pin that you are holding. Push down on the pliers or specialty tool, and turn 90 degrees to align the slot in the washer with the head on the spring mounting pin. Remove the spring and washer, and repeat this operation on the hold-down spring on the other brake shoe.
7. Place the tip of a screwdriver on top of the brake adjusting screw, and move the screwdriver upward to lift up on the brake adjusting lever. When there is enough slack in the automatic adjuster cable, disconnect the loop at the top of the cable from the anchor pin. Remove the automatic adjuster cable guide from the secondary brake shoe, and disconnect the cable hook from the adjuster lever.
8. Remove the shoe guide plate from the anchor pin.
9. Grasp the top of each brake shoe and move it outward, to disengage it from the wheel cylinder and parking brake link. When the brake shoes are clear, lift them from the backing plate. Twist the shoes slightly and the automatic adjuster assembly will disassemble itself.
10. Grasp the end of the brake cable spring with a pair of pliers and, using the brake lever as a fulcrum, pull the end of the spring away from the lever. Disengage the cable from the brake lever.

To install:

11. The brake cable must be connected to the secondary brake shoe before the shoe is installed on the backing plate. To do this, first transfer the parking brake lever from the old secondary shoe to the new one. This is accomplished by spreading the bottom of the horseshoe clip and disengaging the lever. Position the lever on the new secondary shoe and install the spring washer and the horseshoe clip. Close the bottom of the clip after installing it. Grasp the metal tip of the parking brake cable with a pair of pliers. Position a pair of side cutter

Fig. 30 Clean the brake assembly with spray solvent; never use compressed air

85809027

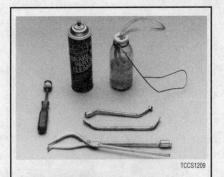

Fig. 31 Although not always necessary, using specialized brake tools will save time

TCCS1209

Fig. 32 Use a brake spring service tool to twist and disengage the brake retracting springs

85809029

Fig. 33 Remove the secondary shoe retracting spring

85809030

Fig. 34 Remove the primary shoe retracting spring

85809031

Fig. 35 A hold-down spring release tool simplifies removal of the spring and washer

85809032

Fig. 36 After rotating the slotted washer to align with the spring mounting pin, remove the spring and washer. If loose, the pin may also be removed.

Fig. 37 Lift up on the brake adjusting lever to create slack, and disconnect the cable loop from the anchor

Fig. 38 Remove the automatic adjuster cable guide from the secondary brake shoe

Fig. 39 Disconnect the cable hook from the adjuster lever

Fig. 40 Remove the shoe guide plate from the anchor pin

Fig. 41 Grasp the top of each brake shoe and move it outward

Fig. 42 With the brake shoes disengaged, remove the parking brake link and spring

Fig. 43 Pliers can be used to release the parking brake cable and return spring from the brake lever

Fig. 44 Drum brake shoes are connected by an array of parts

pliers on the end of the cable coil spring, and using the pliers as a fulcrum, pull the coil spring back with the side cutters. Position the cable in the parking brake lever.

12. Apply a light coating of high temperature grease to the brake shoe contact points on the backing plate. Position the primary brake shoe on the front side of the backing plate, and install the hold-down spring and washer over the mounting pin. Turn the washer 90 degrees with the pliers or specialty tool to secure the spring.

13. Install the secondary shoe on the rear side of the backing plate, and install the hold-down spring and washer over the mounting pin. Turn the washer 90 degrees with the pliers or specialty tool to secure the spring.

14. Install the parking brake link between the notch in the primary brake shoe and the notch in the parking brake lever.

15. Install the automatic adjuster cable loop end on the anchor pin. Make sure the crimped side of the loop faces the backing plate.

16. Install the return spring in the primary brake shoe and, using the tapered end of the brake spring service tool, slide the top of the spring onto the anchor pin.

✷✷ CAUTION

Be careful to make sure that the spring does not slip off the tool during installation, as it could cause injury.

17. Install the automatic adjuster cable guide in the secondary brake shoe, making sure the flared hole in the cable guide is inside the hole in the brake shoe. Fit the cable into the groove in the top of the cable guide.

18. Install the secondary shoe return spring through the hole in the cable guide and the brake shoe. Using the brake spring tool, slide the top of the spring onto the anchor pin.

19. Clean the threads on the adjusting screw and apply a light coating of

high temperature grease to the threads. Screw the adjuster closed, then open it ½ turn.

20. Install the adjusting screw between the brake shoes with the star wheel nearest to the secondary shoe. Make sure the star wheel is in a position that is accessible from the adjusting slot in the backing plate.

21. Install the short hooked end of the automatic adjuster spring in the proper hole in the primary brake shoe.

22. Connect the hooked end of the automatic adjuster cable and the free end of the automatic adjuster spring in the slot in the top of the automatic adjuster lever.

23. Pull the automatic adjuster lever (the lever will pull the cable and spring with it) downward and to the left and engage the pivot hook of the lever in the hole in the secondary brake shoe.

24. Check the entire brake assembly to make sure that everything is installed properly. Make sure that the shoes engage the wheel cylinder properly and are flush on the anchor pin. Make sure that the automatic adjuster cable is flush on the anchor pin and in the slot on the back of the cable guide. Make sure that the adjusting lever rests on the adjusting screw star wheel. Pull upward on the adjusting cable until the adjusting lever is free of the star wheel, then release the cable. The adjusting lever should snap back into place on the adjusting screw star wheel and turn the wheel one tooth.

25. Expand the brake adjusting screw until the brake drum will just fit over the brake shoes.

26. Install the brake drum and retainer nuts, if so equipped.

27. Repeat Steps 4–26 for the other side of the vehicle.

28. Install the wheel and tire assemblies and tighten the wheel lug nuts.

29. Lower the vehicle.

30. Complete the brake adjustment, as described at the beginning of this section.

31. Road test the vehicle. Allow a short break–in period before hard break-ing, if possible.

Wheel Cylinders

REMOVAL & INSTALLATION

▶ **See Figures 45, 46 and 47**

1. Remove the brake shoes, as described above.

2. Disconnect the brake line at the rear of the cylinder, but do not pull the line away from the cylinder, or it may bend.

3. Remove the bolts and lockwashers that attach the wheel cylinder to the backing plate and remove the cylinder.

To install:

4. Position the new or overhauled wheel cylinder on the backing plate, and install the cylinder attaching bolts and lockwashers.

5. Attach the metal brake line or rubber hose by reversing the procedure given in Step 2.

6. Install the brake shoes, as described above.

7. Bleed the brake system and centralize the pressure differential valve, as detailed earlier in this section.

OVERHAUL

▶ **See Figures 48 thru 57**

Wheel cylinder overhaul kits may be available, but often at little or no sav-ings over a reconditioned wheel cylinder. It often makes sense with these com-ponents to substitute a new or reconditioned part instead of attempting an overhaul.

If no replacement is available, or you would prefer to overhaul your wheel cylinders, the following procedure may be used. When rebuilding and

Fig. 45 Using a wrench, unscrew the brake line at the rear of the backing plate

Fig. 46 With a socket, unfasten the wheel cylinder retaining bolts

Fig. 47 Remove the wheel cylinder from the backing plate

Fig. 48 Remove the outer boots from the wheel cylinder

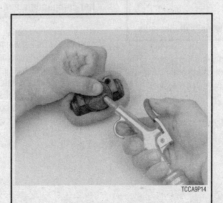

Fig. 49 Compressed air can be used to remove the pistons and seals

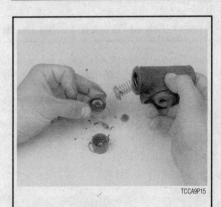

Fig. 50 Remove the pistons, cup seals and spring from the cylinder

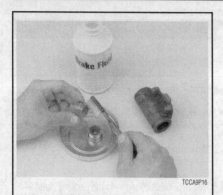

Fig. 51 Use brake fluid and a soft brush to clean the pistons . . .

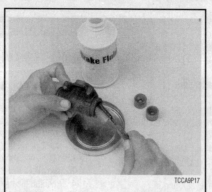

Fig. 52 . . . and the bore of the wheel cylinder

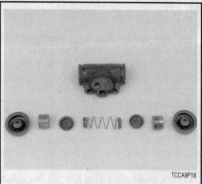

Fig. 53 Once cleaned and inspected, the wheel cylinder is ready for assembly

Fig. 54 Lubricate the cup seals with brake fluid

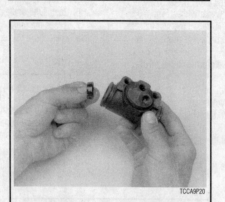

Fig. 55 Install the spring, then the cup seals in the bore

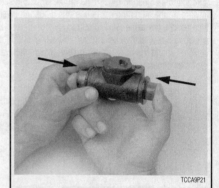

Fig. 56 Lightly lubricate the pistons, then install them

Fig. 57 The boots can now be installed over the wheel cylinder ends

installing wheel cylinders, avoid getting any contaminants into the system. Always use clean, new, high quality brake fluid. If dirty or improper fluid has been used, it will be necessary to drain the entire system, flush the system with proper brake fluid, replace all rubber components, then refill and bleed the system.

1. Remove the wheel cylinder from the vehicle and place on a clean workbench.

2. First remove and discard the old rubber boots, then withdraw the pistons. Piston cylinders are equipped with seals and a spring assembly, all located behind the pistons in the cylinder bore.

3. Remove the remaining inner components, seals and spring assembly. Compressed air may be useful in removing these components. If no compressed air is available, be VERY careful not to score the wheel cylinder bore when removing parts from it. Discard all components for which replacements were supplied in the rebuild kit.

4. Wash the cylinder and metal parts in denatured alcohol or clean brake fluid.

✴✴ WARNING

Never use a mineral-based solvent such as gasoline, kerosene or paint thinner for cleaning purposes. These solvents will swell rubber components and quickly deteriorate them.

5. Allow the parts to air dry or use compressed air. Do not use rags for cleaning, since lint will remain in the cylinder bore.
6. Inspect the piston and replace it if it shows scratches.
7. Lubricate the cylinder bore and seals using clean brake fluid.
8. Position the spring assembly.
9. Install the inner seals, then the pistons.
10. Insert the new boots into the counterbores by hand. Do not lubricate the boots.
11. Install the wheel cylinder.

REAR DISC BRAKES

Brake Pads

REMOVAL & INSTALLATION

▶ **See Figures 58 and 59**

➡**When installing new brake linings, replace the pads at both rear wheels to avoid uneven braking.**

1. Raise the vehicle and install safety stands. Block both front wheels if a jack is used.
2. Remove the rear wheel covers.
3. Remove the wheel and tire assemblies from the axle. Use care to avoid damage or interference with the splash shield.

✳✳ WARNING

If you are not thoroughly familiar with the procedures involved in brake service, only disassemble and assemble one side at a time, leaving the other brake assembly intact as a reference.

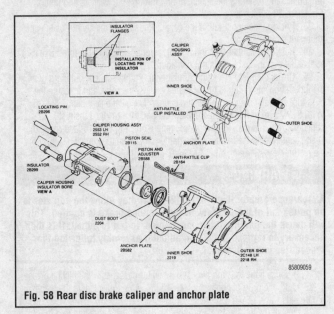

Fig. 58 Rear disc brake caliper and anchor plate

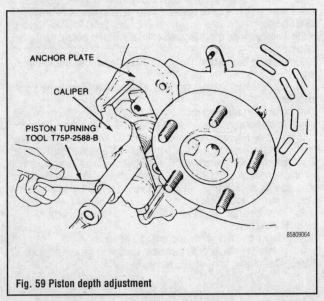

Fig. 59 Piston depth adjustment

4. Remove the caliper as outlined below. It is not necessary to disconnect the brake line. Simply wire the caliper to the frame to prevent the brake line from stretching or breaking.
5. Remove the pads and inspect them. If they are worn to within ⅛ in. (3mm) of the shoe surface, they must be replaced. Do not replace pads on just one side of the car, since uneven braking will result.

✳✳ CAUTION

Brake shoes contain asbestos, which has been determined to be a cancer causing agent. Never clean the brake surfaces with compressed air! Avoid inhaling any dust from any brake surface! When cleaning brake surfaces, use a commercially available brake cleaning fluid.

To install:

6. Remove the disc and install the caliper without the pads.
7. Adjust the piston depth, using Brake Piston Turning Tool T75P–2588–B or equivalent, as follows:
   a. Seat the turning tool firmly against the piston by holding the shaft and rotating the handle.
   b. Loosen the handle ¼ turn. Hold the handle and rotate the tool shaft clockwise until the caliper piston bottoms in its bore. The piston will continue to turn after it bottoms.
   c. Rotate the handle until the piston is firmly seated, then remove the tool.
8. Remove the caliper from the anchor plate.
9. Lubricate the anchor plate sliding ways with Disc Brake Caliper Grease D7AZ–019590–A or equivalent.

➡**Use only the specified grease, since a lower temperature type of lubricant may melt and contaminate the brake pads. Do not permit any lubricant to get on the braking surface!**

10. Install the anti–rattle clip on the lower rail of the anchor plate.
11. Place the inner brake shoe and lining assembly on the anchor plate with the lining toward the rotor.
12. Install the disc and retainer nuts.
13. Place the outer brake shoe and lining assembly on the anchor plate with the lining toward the rotor, and the wear indicator toward the top.
14. Reinstall the caliper, as outlined below.
15. Repeat Steps 4–14 for the other side of the vehicle.
16. Install the wheel and tire assemblies and tighten the wheel lug nuts. Install the wheel covers.
17. Remove the safety stands and lower the vehicle. Unblock the front wheels, if applicable.
18. Check the level of the brake fluid, and add new fluid if necessary.
19. Be sure a firm brake pedal application is obtained, and then road test for proper brake operation, including parking brakes.

Brake Caliper

REMOVAL & INSTALLATION

▶ **See Figure 60**

1. Raise the vehicle, and install safety stands. Block both front wheels if a jack is used.
2. Remove the rear wheel cover.
3. Remove the wheel and tire assembly from the axle. Use care to avoid damage or interference with the splash shield.
4. Disconnect the parking brake cable from the lever. Use care to avoid kinking or cutting the cable or return spring.

✳✳ CAUTION

Brake shoes contain asbestos, which has been determined to be a cancer causing agent. Never clean the brake surfaces with compressed air! Avoid inhaling any dust from any brake surface! When

cleaning brake surfaces, use a commercially available brake cleaning fluid.

5. Remove the caliper locating pins.

6. Lift the caliper assembly away from the anchor plate by pushing the caliper upward toward the anchor plate, and then rotate the lower end out of the anchor plate.

7. If insufficient clearance between the caliper and shoe/lining assemblies prevents removal of the caliper, it is necessary to loosen the caliper end retainer ½ turn, maximum, to allow the piston to be forced back into its bore. To loosen the end retainer, remove the parking brake lever, then mark or scribe the end retainer and caliper housing to be sure that the end retainer is not loosened more than ½ turn. Force the piston back into its bore, then remove the caliper.

✳✳ CAUTION

If the retainer must be loosened more than ½ turn, the seal between the thrust screw and the housing may be broken, and brake fluid may leak into the parking brake mechanism chamber. In this case, the end retainer must be removed, and the internal parts cleaned and lubricated; refer to Caliper Overhaul.

8. Remove the outer shoe and lining assembly from the anchor plate. Mark the shoe for identification, if it is to be reinstalled.

9. Remove the two rotor retainer nuts and the rotor from the axle shaft.

10. Remove the inner brake shoe and lining assembly from the anchor plate. Mark the shoe for identification, if it is to be reinstalled.

11. Remove the anti–rattle clip from the anchor plate.

12. Remove the flexible hose from the caliper by removing the hollow retaining bolt that connects the hose fitting to the caliper.

13. Clean the caliper, anchor plate, and rotor assemblies and inspect for signs of brake fluid leakage, excessive wear, or damage. The caliper must be inspected for leakage both in the piston boot area and at the operating shaft seal area. Lightly sand or wire brush any rust or corrosion from the caliper and anchor plate sliding surfaces, as well as the outer and inner brake shoe abutment surfaces. Inspect the brake shoes for wear. If either lining is worn to within ⅛ in. (3mm) of the shoe surface, both shoe and lining assemblies must be replaced using the shoe and lining removal procedures.

To install:

14. If the end retainer has been loosened only ½ turn, reinstall the caliper in the anchor plate without the shoe and lining assemblies. Tighten the end retainer to 75–96 ft. lbs. Install the parking brake lever on its keyed spline. The lever arm must point down and rearward. The parking brake cable will then pass freely under the axle. Tighten the retainer screw to 16–22 ft. lbs. The parking brake lever must rotate freely after tightening the retainer screw. Remove the caliper from the anchor plate.

15. If new shoe and lining assemblies are to be installed, the piston must be screwed back into the caliper bore, using Piston Turning Tool T75P–2588–B or

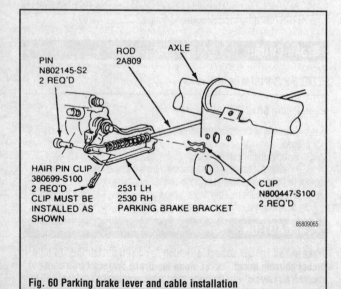

PIN
N802145-S2
2 REQ'D

ROD
2A809

AXLE

HAIR PIN CLIP
380699-S100
2 REQ'D
CLIP MUST BE
INSTALLED AS
SHOWN

2531 LH
2530 RH
PARKING BRAKE BRACKET

CLIP
N800447-S100
2 REQ'D

85809065

Fig. 60 Parking brake lever and cable installation

equivalent, to provide installation clearance. Remove the rotor, and install the caliper, without the shoe and lining assemblies, in the anchor plate. While holding the shaft, rotate the tool handle counterclockwise until the tool is seated firmly against the piston. Now, loosen the handle about ¼ turn. While holding the handle, rotate the tool shaft clockwise until the piston is fully bottomed in its bore; the piston will continue to turn even after it becomes bottomed. When there is no further inward movement of the piston, and the tool handle is rotated until there is a firm seating force, the piston is bottomed. Remove the tool and the caliper from the anchor plate.

16. Lubricate the anchor plate sliding ways with lithium or silicone grease. Use only specified grease because a lower temperature type of lubricant may melt and contaminate the brake pads. Use care to prevent any lubricant from getting on the braking surface.

17. Install the anti–rattle clip on the lower rail of the anchor plate.

18. Install the inner brake shoe and lining assembly on the anchor plate with the lining toward the rotor.

19. Be sure that the shoes are installed in their original positions, as marked for identification before removal.

20. Install the rotor and two retainer nuts.

21. Install the correct outer brake shoe and lining assembly on the anchor plate with the lining toward the rotor and wear indicator toward the upper portion of the brake.

22. Install the flexible hose by placing a new washer on each side of the fitting outlet, and inserting the attaching bolt through the washers and fitting. Tighten to 20–30 ft. lbs.

23. Position the upper tab of the caliper housing on the anchor plate upper abutment surface.

24. Rotate the caliper housing until it is completely over the rotor. Use care so that the piston dust boot is not damaged.

25. Check the Piston Position Adjustment: Pull the caliper outboard until the inner shoe and lining is firmly seated against the rotor, and measure the clearance between the outer shoe and caliper. The clearance must be ½₃₂–³⁄₃₂ in. (0.8–2.4mm). If it is not, remove the caliper, then readjust the piston to obtain the required gap. Follow the procedure given in Step 15, and rotate the shaft counterclockwise to narrow the gap or clockwise to widen it. (¼ turn of the piston moves it approximately ¹⁄₁₆ in. [1.6mm]).

✳✳ WARNING

A clearance greater than ³⁄₃₂ in. (2.4mm) may allow the adjuster to be pulled out of the piston when the service brake is applied. This will cause the parking brake mechanism to fail to adjust. It is then necessary to replace the piston/adjuster assembly following the procedures under Overhaul.

26. Lubricate the locating pins and insulator passages with silicone grease.

27. Add one drop of Loctite® E0AC–19554–A or equivalent to the locating pin threads.

28. Install the locating pins through the caliper insulators and into the anchor plate; the pins must be hand–inserted and hand–started. Tighten to 29–37 ft. lbs.

29. Connect the parking brake cable to the bracket and the lever on the caliper.

30. Bleed the brake system. Replace the rubber bleed screw cap after bleeding.

31. Fill the master cylinder as required to within ⅛ in. (3mm) of the top of the reservoir.

32. Check the Caliper Adjustment: With the engine running, pump the service brake lightly (approximately 14 lbs. pedal effort) about 40 times. Allow at least one second between pedal applications. As an alternative, with the engine Off, pump the service brake lightly (approximately 87 lbs. pedal effort) about 30 times. Now check the parking brake for excessive travel or very light effort. In either case, repeat pumping the service brake, or if necessary, check the parking brake cable for proper tension. The caliper levers must return to the Off position when the parking brake is released.

33. Install the wheel and tire assembly and tighten the wheel lug nuts. Install the wheel cover.

34. Remove the safety stands, and lower the vehicle.

35. Be sure a firm brake pedal application is obtained, then road test for proper brake operation, including the parking brakes.

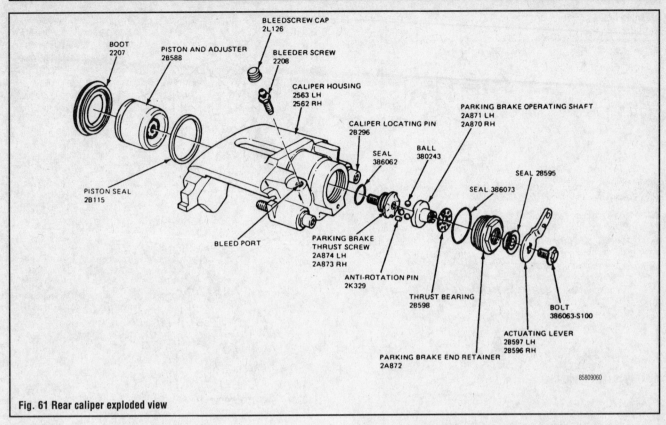

Fig. 61 Rear caliper exploded view

OVERHAUL

▶ **See Figures 61, 62, 63, 64 and 65**

1. Remove the caliper assembly from the vehicle, as outlined above.

✳✳ CAUTION

Brake shoes contain asbestos, which has been determined to be a cancer causing agent. Never clean the brake surfaces with compressed air! Avoid inhaling any dust from any brake surface! When cleaning brake surfaces, use a commercially available brake cleaning fluid.

2. Remove the parking brake cable bracket and caliper end retainer.
3. Lift out the operating shaft, thrust bearing, and balls.
4. Remove the thrust screw anti–rotation pin with a magnet or tweezers.

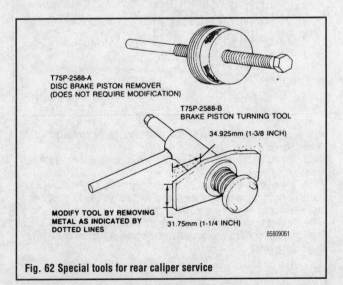

Fig. 62 Special tools for rear caliper service

➡**Some anti–rotation pins may be difficult to remove with a magnet or tweezers. In that case, use the following procedure.**

a. Adjust the piston out from the caliper bore using Piston Turning Tool T75P–2588–B or equivalent. The piston should protrude from the housing at least 1 in. (25mm).

b. Push the piston back into the caliper housing with the adjusting tool. With the tool in position on the caliper, hold the tool shaft in place, and rotate the handle counterclockwise until the thrust screw clears the anti–rotation pin. Remove the thrust screw and the anti–rotation pin.

5. Remove the thrust screw by rotating it counterclockwise with a ¼ in. allen wrench.

6. Remove the piston adjuster assembly by inserting Piston Removal Tool T75P–2588–A or equivalent through the back of the caliper housing and pushing the piston out.

✳✳ WARNING

Use care not to damage the polished surface in the thrust screw bore, and do not press or attempt to move the adjuster can. It is a press fit in the piston!

7. Remove and discard the piston seal, boot, thrust screw C–ring seal, end retainer O–ring seal, end retainer lip seal, and pin insulators.

8. Clean all metal parts with isopropyl alcohol. Use clean, dry, compressed air to clean out and dry the grooves and passages. Be sure the caliper bore and component parts are completely free of any foreign material.

9. Inspect the caliper bores for damage or excessive wear. The thrust screw bore must be smooth and free of pits. If the piston is pitted, scored, or the chrome plating is worn off, replace the piston/adjuster assembly.

10. The adjuster can must be bottomed in the piston to be properly seated and provide consistent brake function. If the adjuster can is loose in the piston, appears high in the piston, or is damaged, or if brake adjustment is regularly too tight, too loose, or non–functioning, replace the piston/adjuster assembly.

✳✳ WARNING

Do not attempt to service the adjuster at any time. When service is necessary, replace the piston/adjuster assembly.

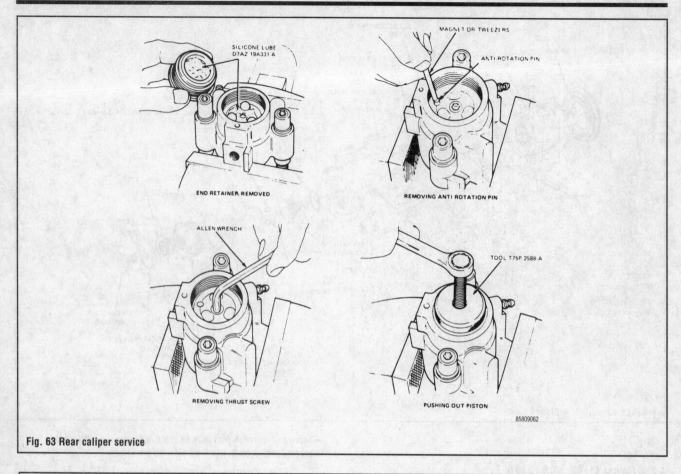

Fig. 63 Rear caliper service

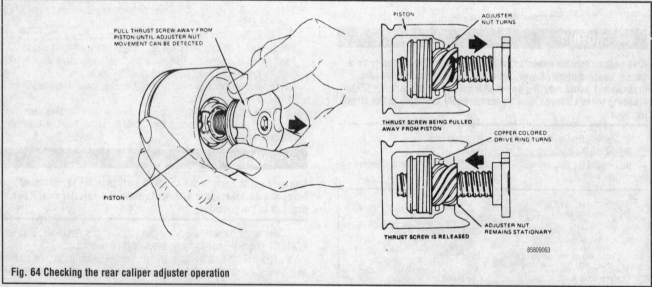

Fig. 64 Checking the rear caliper adjuster operation

11. Check adjuster operation by first assembling the thrust screw into the piston/adjuster assembly, pulling the two pieces apart by hand approximately ¼ in. (6mm), and then releasing them. When pulling on the two pieces, the brass drive ring must remain stationary, causing the nut to rotate. When releasing the two parts, the nut must remain stationary, and the drive ring must rotate. If the action of the components does not follow this pattern, replace the piston/adjuster assembly.

12. Inspect the ball pockets, threads, grooves, and bearing surfaces of the thrust screw and operating shaft for wear, pitting, or brinelling. Inspect the balls and anti–rotation pin for wear, brinelling, or pitting. Replace the operating shaft, balls, thrust screw, and anti–rotation pin if any of these parts are worn or dam-aged. A polished appearance on the ball paths is acceptable if there is no sign of wear into the surface.

13. Inspect the thrust bearing for corrosion, pitting, or wear. Replace if necessary.

14. Inspect the bearing surface of the end plug for wear or brinelling. Replace if necessary. A polished appearance on the bearing surface is acceptable if there is no sign of wear into the surface.

15. Inspect the lever for damage. Replace if necessary.

16. Lightly sand or wire brush any rust or corrosion from the caliper housing insulator bores.

To assemble:

17. Apply a coat of clean brake fluid to the new caliper piston seal, and install it in the cylinder bore. Be sure that the seal is not twisted and that it is seated fully in the groove.

18. Install a new dust boot by seating the flange squarely in the outer groove of the caliper bore.

19. Coat the piston/adjuster assembly with clean brake fluid, and install it in the cylinder bore. Spread the dust boot over the piston, as when it is installed. Seat the dust boot in the piston groove.

20. Install the caliper in a vise and fill the piston/adjuster assembly with clean brake fluid to the bottom edge of the thrust screw bore.

21. Coat a new thrust screw O–ring seal with clean brake fluid, and install it in the groove in the thrust screw.

22. Install the thrust screw by turning it into the piston/adjuster assembly with a ¼ in. allen wrench until the top surface of the thrust screw is flush with the bottom of the threaded bore. Use care to avoid cutting the O–ring seal. Index the thrust screw, so that the notches on the thrust screw and caliper housing are aligned. Then install the anti–rotation pin.

✳✳ WARNING

The thrust screw and operating shaft are not interchangeable from side to side because of the ramp direction in the ball pockets. The pocket surface of the operating shaft and the thrust screw are stamped with the proper letter (R or L), indicating part usage.

23. Place a ball in each of the three pockets of the thrust screw, and apply a liberal amount of silicone grease on all components in the parking brake mechanism.

24. Install the operating shaft on the balls.

25. Coat the thrust bearing with silicone grease and install it on the operating shaft.

26. Install a new lip seal and O–ring on the end retainer.

27. Coat the O–ring seal and lip seal with a light film of silicone grease, and install the end retainer in the caliper. Hold the operating shaft firmly seated against the internal mechanism while installing the end retainer to prevent mislocation of the balls. If the lip seal is pushed out of position, reseat the seal. Tighten the end retainer to 75–95 ft. lbs.

28. Install the parking brake lever on its keyed spline. The lever arm must point down and rearward. The parking brake cable will then pass freely under the axle. Tighten the lever retaining screw to 16–22 ft. lbs. The parking brake lever must rotate freely after tightening.

29. Secure the caliper in a vise, and bottom the piston with Piston Turning Tool T75P–2588–B or equivalent.

30. Install new pin insulators in the caliper housing. Check to see if both insulator flanges straddle the housing holes.

31. Install the caliper on the vehicle.

32. Check the Piston Position Adjustment, as described in Step 25 of Caliper Removal and Installation. Correct if necessary.

33. Install the parking brake cable brackets on the caliper housing. Before tightening the attaching bolts, apply the service brake lightly (approximately 14 lbs. pedal effort with the engine running, or approximately 87 lbs. pedal effort with the engine off). While the brakes are applied, rotate the parking brake bracket until the bracket lever stop contacts the actuating lever. Hold the bracket in this position while tightening the bolts to 30–44 ft. lbs.

34. Complete the caliper installation on the vehicle, as outlined above.

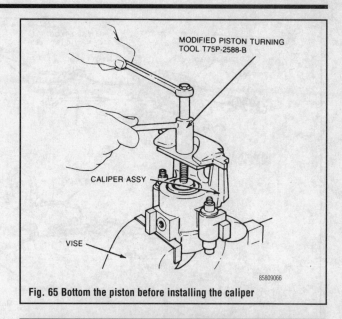

Fig. 65 Bottom the piston before installing the caliper

Brake Disc (Rotor)

REMOVAL & INSTALLATION

1. Raise the car and safely support it. Remove the wheel cover and the wheel and tire assembly.

✳✳ CAUTION

Brake shoes contain asbestos, which has been determined to be a cancer causing agent. Never clean the brake surfaces with compressed air! Avoid inhaling any dust from any brake surface! When cleaning brake surfaces, use a commercially available brake cleaning fluid.

2. Remove the caliper and brake pads, as outlined earlier.

3. Remove the retaining nuts and remove the disc from the axle.

4. Inspect the disc for excessive rust, scoring or pitting. A certain amount of rust on the edge of the disc is normal. Refer to the specifications chart and measure the thickness of the disc, using a micrometer. If the disc is below specifications, replace it.

5. Reinstall the disc, keeping in mind that the two sides are not interchangeable. The words **left** and **right** are cast into the inner surface of the raised section of the disc. Proper reinstallation of the disc is important, since the cooling vanes cast into the disc must face rearward.

6. Reinstall the caliper and brake pads, as outlined earlier.

7. Install the wheel and tire assembly and tighten the wheel lug nuts. Install the wheel cover.

8. Lower the car.

PARKING BRAKE

Cables

REMOVAL & INSTALLATION

▶ **See Figures 66 and 67**

✳✳ CAUTION

Brake shoes contain asbestos, which has been determined to be a cancer causing agent. Never clean the brake surfaces with compressed air! Avoid inhaling any dust from any brake surface! When cleaning brake surfaces, use a commercially available brake cleaning fluid.

1. Release the parking brake.

2. Remove the brake lever boot cover or console assembly, and loosen the cable adjusting nut.

3. Raise and support the rear end on jackstands.

4. Disconnect the cable ends from the equalizer.

5. Remove the cotter pin that attaches the conduit to the bracket and remove the retaining clip that attaches the cable to the underbody.

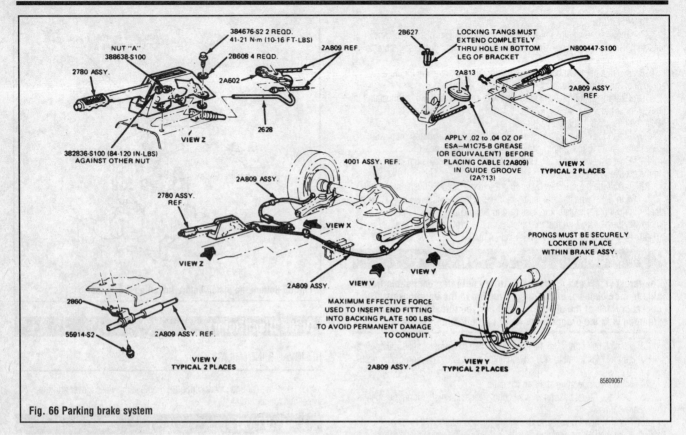

Fig. 66 Parking brake system

6. On cars with rear drum brakes:
  a. Remove the brake drums.
  b. Remove the brake shoes and disconnect the cable end from the self–adjusting lever.
  c. Compress the pronged retainers and remove the cable assembly from the backing plate.

7. On cars with rear disc brakes, remove the clevis pin securing the cable to the caliper actuating arm.

8. Installation is the reverse of removal. Adjust the parking brake, as described below.

ADJUSTMENT

▶ **See Figure 68**

With Rear Drum Brakes

The parking brake should be adjusted for proper operation every 12 months or 12,000 miles and adjusted whenever there is slack in the cables. A cable with too much slack will not hold a vehicle on an incline, thereby presenting a serious safety hazard. Usually, a rear drum brake adjustment will restore parking brake efficiency, but if the cables appear loose or stretched when the parking brake is released, adjust as necessary.

1. Fully release the parking brake.
2. Remove the brake lever boot cover or console assembly, to access the cable adjusting nut.
3. Place the transmission in Neutral. Raise and safely support the car using an axle hoist or a floor jack positioned beneath the differential. This is necessary so that the rear wheels are free to turn while the rear axle remains at curb attitude, without stretching the parking brake cables.

✳✳ CAUTION

If you are only raising the rear of the car, block the front wheels.

4. Tighten the adjusting nut against the cable equalizer until moderate drag is felt when turning the rear wheels. Then, loosen the adjusting nut until the rear brakes are fully released.

Fig. 67 The cable adjusting nut is located under the brake lever assembly

5. Lower the car and apply the parking brake. Under normal conditions, the third notch will hold the car if the brake is adjusted properly.
6. Install the brake lever boot cover or console assembly.

With Rear Disc Brakes

▶ **See Figure 68**

➡ If the caliper has been overhauled or the shoe linings have been changed, pump the brake pedal lightly, approximately 30 times, before adjusting the parking brake.

1. Fully release the parking brake.
2. Remove the brake lever boot cover or console assembly, to access the cable adjusting nut.

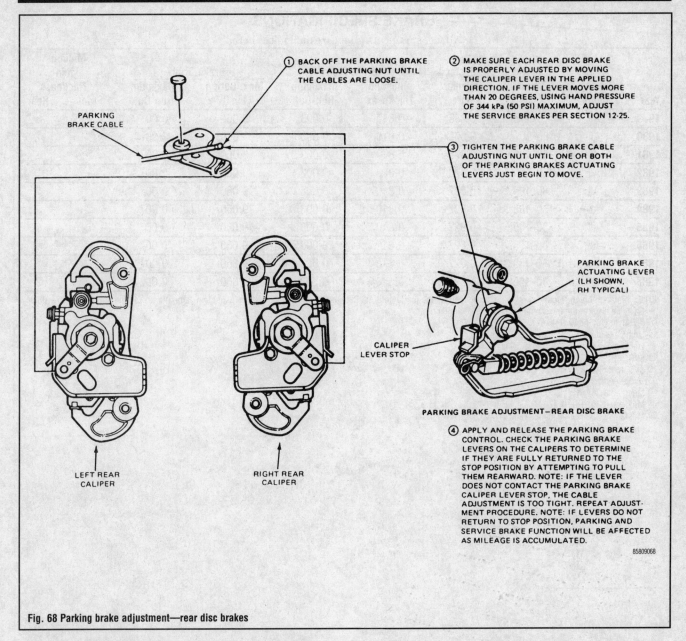

① BACK OFF THE PARKING BRAKE CABLE ADJUSTING NUT UNTIL THE CABLES ARE LOOSE.

② MAKE SURE EACH REAR DISC BRAKE IS PROPERLY ADJUSTED BY MOVING THE CALIPER LEVER IN THE APPLIED DIRECTION. IF THE LEVER MOVES MORE THAN 20 DEGREES, USING HAND PRESSURE OF 344 kPa (50 PSI) MAXIMUM, ADJUST THE SERVICE BRAKES PER SECTION 12-25.

③ TIGHTEN THE PARKING BRAKE CABLE ADJUSTING NUT UNTIL ONE OR BOTH OF THE PARKING BRAKES ACTUATING LEVERS JUST BEGIN TO MOVE.

PARKING BRAKE CABLE

PARKING BRAKE ACTUATING LEVER (LH SHOWN, RH TYPICAL)

CALIPER LEVER STOP

LEFT REAR CALIPER

RIGHT REAR CALIPER

PARKING BRAKE ADJUSTMENT—REAR DISC BRAKE

④ APPLY AND RELEASE THE PARKING BRAKE CONTROL. CHECK THE PARKING BRAKE LEVERS ON THE CALIPERS TO DETERMINE IF THEY ARE FULLY RETURNED TO THE STOP POSITION BY ATTEMPTING TO PULL THEM REARWARD. NOTE: IF THE LEVER DOES NOT CONTACT THE PARKING BRAKE CALIPER LEVER STOP, THE CABLE ADJUSTMENT IS TOO TIGHT. REPEAT ADJUSTMENT PROCEDURE. NOTE: IF LEVERS DO NOT RETURN TO STOP POSITION, PARKING AND SERVICE BRAKE FUNCTION WILL BE AFFECTED AS MILEAGE IS ACCUMULATED.

85809068

Fig. 68 Parking brake adjustment—rear disc brakes

3. In order to observe the parking brake levers, it may be necessary to elevate the vehicle. If so, raise and safely support the car using an axle hoist or a floor jack positioned beneath the differential, so that the rear axle remains at curb attitude, without stretching the parking brake cables.

✳✳ CAUTION

If you are only raising the rear of the car, block the front wheels.

4. Back off the cable adjusting nut until the cables are loose.
5. Make sure that each rear disc brake is properly adjusted by moving the caliper lever in the applied direction. If the lever moves more than 20 degrees while applying hand pressure of 50 psi or less, adjust the service brakes as detailed above.

6. Tighten the cable adjusting nut until one or both of the actuating levers just begin to move. Then, loosen the nut sufficiently for the lever(s) to fully return to the stop position. The levers are in the stop position when a ¼ in. (6mm) pin can be inserted past the side of the lever into the holes in the cast iron housing.
7. Check the operation of the parking brake. Make sure the actuating levers fully return to the stop position by attempting to pull them rearward. If the levers do not return to the stop position, the cable adjustment is too tight; this will cause a dragging rear brake and consequent brake overheating and fade. Repeat the adjustment procedure, if necessary.
8. Lower the car, if applicable, and install the brake lever boot cover or console assembly.

BRAKE SPECIFICATIONS
All measurements given are (in.) unless noted

Year	Model	Lug Nut Torque (ft. lbs.)	Master Cylinder Bore	Brake Disc Minimum Thickness	Brake Disc Maximum Run-Out	Brake Drum Max. Boring Limit	Brake Drum Maximum Run-Out	Minimum Lining Thickness Front	Minimum Lining Thickness Rear
1979	All	70–115	0.938	0.810	0.003	9.060	0.007	②	③
1980	All	80–105	0.875 ①	0.810	0.003	9.060	0.007	②	③
1981	All	80–105	0.875 ①	0.810	0.003	9.060	0.007	②	③
1982	All	80–105	0.875	0.810	0.003	9.060	0.007	②	③
1983	All	80–105	0.827	0.810	0.003	9.060	0.007	②	③
1984	All	80–105	0.827 ④	0.810 ⑤	0.003 ⑥	9.060	0.007	②	③
1985	All	80–105	0.827 ④	0.810 ⑤	0.003 ⑥	9.060	0.007	②	③
1986	All	80–105	0.827 ④	0.810 ⑤	0.003 ⑥	9.060	0.007	②	③
1987	All	80–105	0.827 ⑦	0.810 ⑧	0.003	9.060	0.007	②	③
1988	All	80–105	0.827 ⑦	0.810 ⑨	0.003	9.060	0.007	②	③

NOTE: Minimum lining thickness is as recommended by the manufacturer. Because of variations in state inspection regulations, the minimum allowable thickness may be different than recommended by the manufacturer.

① 0.750 in. with power brakes
② Lining measures 1/8 in. above metal shoe
③ Lining measures 1/16" in. above rivets
④ SVO: 1.125
⑤ SVO front disc: 0.972; SVO rear disc: 0.895
⑥ SVO rear disc: 0.004
⑦ Mustang 8-302: 1.125
⑧ Mustang 8-302 HO: 0.972
⑨ Mustang 8-302 HO (all models) and 4-140 convertible: 0.972

858090C1

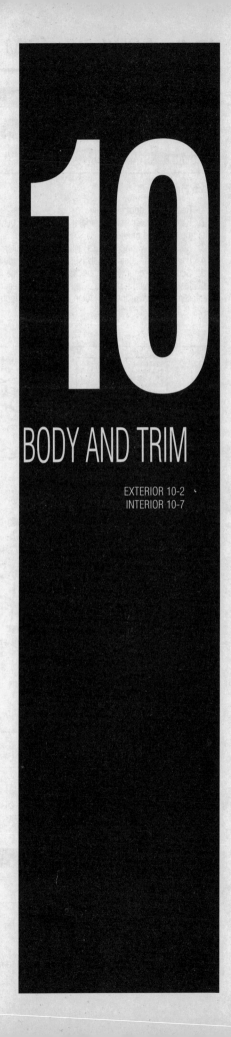

10

BODY AND TRIM

EXTERIOR

Doors

REMOVAL & INSTALLATION

▶ See Figure 1

1. Remove the door trim panel.
2. Remove the watershield, and, if a new door is being installed, save all the moulding clips and mouldings.
3. Remove the wiring harness, actuator and speakers.
4. If a new door is being installed, remove all window and lock components.
5. Support the door and unbolt the hinges from the door.
6. Installation is the reverse of removal. New holes may have to be drilled in a replacement door for the trim. Align the door and tighten the hinge bolts to 14–24 ft. lbs. (18–32 Nm).

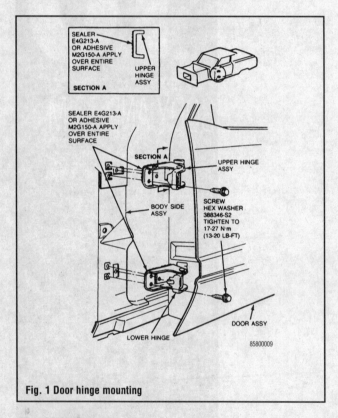

Fig. 1 Door hinge mounting

ADJUSTMENT

▶ See Figure 2

Door alignment is obtained by loosening the hinge-to-body bolts and moving the door as required to obtain a proper fit. Similarly, the latch striker must be loosened and repositioned for proper engagement with the latch.

Hood

REMOVAL & INSTALLATION

▶ See Figure 3

1. Open and support the hood.
2. Matchmark the hood-to-hinge positions.
3. Have an assistant support the hood while you remove the hinge-to-hood bolts from both sides.

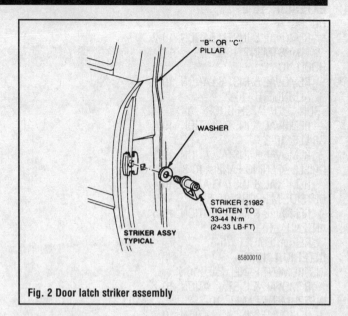

Fig. 2 Door latch striker assembly

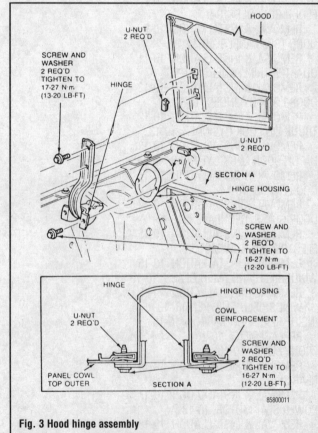

Fig. 3 Hood hinge assembly

4. Remove the hood.
5. Installation is the reverse of removal. Be sure to align the hood and hinge matchmarks, then tighten the attaching bolts to 13–20 ft. lbs. (17–27 Nm). Check the fit and adjust, if necessary.

ALIGNMENT

1. Side-to-side and fore-aft adjustments can be made by loosening the hood-to-hinge attachment bolts and positioning the hood as necessary.

2. Hood vertical fit can be adjusted by raising or lowering the hinge-to-fender reinforcement bolts.

3. To ensure a snug fit of the hood against the rear hood bumpers, it may be necessary to rotate the hinge around the attaching bolts.

Trunk Lid/Hatch Door

REMOVAL & INSTALLATION

Trunk Lid

1. Remove the hinge-to-trunk lid bolts and slide the trunk lid off of the hinges.
2. Installation is the reverse of removal.

Hatch Door

▶ **See Figure 4**

1. Open the hatch door and support with props.
2. Remove both lift assembly cylinders after disengaging the spring clips which secure the lift assemblies to the retainers.
3. Remove the upper rear interior center garnish moulding to expose the hinge bolts.
4. Remove the hinge bolts and remove the hatch door.
5. Installation is the reverse of removal

ALIGNMENT

Trunk Lid

1. Fore-and-aft and side-to-side fit may be adjusted by loosening the hinge-to-lid bolts and positioning the lid as necessary.
2. Vertical fit can be adjusted by adding or deleting shims located between the hinges and trunk lid.

Hatch Door

1. Fore-and-aft and side-to-side fit may be adjusted by loosening the hinge-to-roof panel attaching bolts and positioning the door as necessary.
2. The hatch door can be adjusted in-and-out by adding or deleting shims located between the hinges and roof panel.

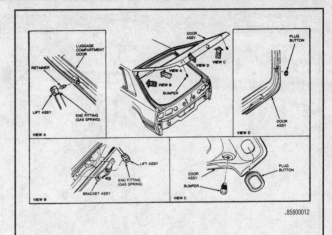

.85800012

Fig. 4 Hatch door assembly

Grille

➡ The Mustang grille is moulded integral with the grille opening panel, while the Capri is a separate moulded plastic part which is fastened to the grille opening panel reinforcement. As a result, removing the Mustang grille requires removal of the entire grille opening panel, while Capri grille removal can be accomplished without removing the entire grille opening panel.

REMOVAL & INSTALLATION

Capri

▶ **See Figure 5**

1. Remove the 5 grille retaining screws.
2. Disengage the locating lugs, if so equipped, and remove the grille.
3. Installation is the reverse of removal.

Grille Opening Panel

➡ The Mustang grille is moulded integral with the grille opening panel, while the Capri is a separate moulded plastic part which is fastened to

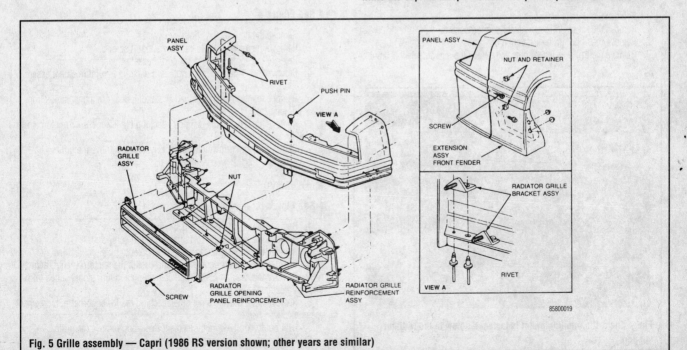

Fig. 5 Grille assembly — Capri (1986 RS version shown; other years are similar)

85800019

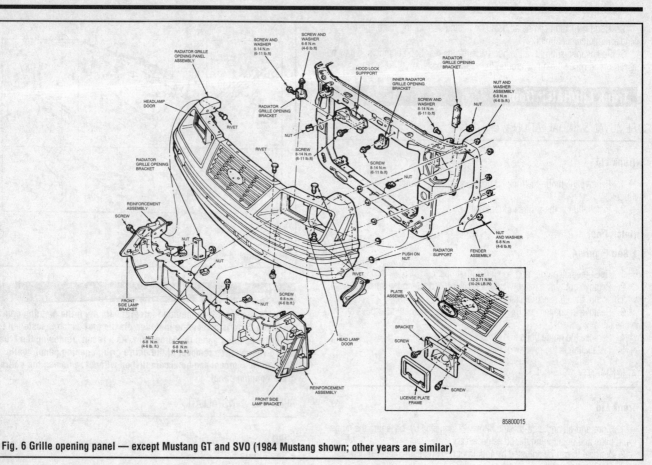

Fig. 6 Grille opening panel — except Mustang GT and SVO (1984 Mustang shown; other years are similar)

the grille opening panel reinforcement. As a result, removal of the Mustang grille requires removal of the entire grille opening panel.

REMOVAL & INSTALLATION

▶ See Figures 6 and 7

Except Mustang GT and SVO

1. Remove the license plate bolts or rivets.
2. Remove the lower grille-to-radiator support screws.
3. Remove the upper grille-to-support brackets.
4. Remove the grille-to-fender nuts and detach the reinforcement assembly.

Fig. 7 The grille opening panel is fastened below to the radiator support

5. Remove the headlamp, side marker, parking and turn signal lamps from the reinforcement.
6. Remove the 2 pushnuts per side attaching the lower corner reinforcement assembly.
7. Drill out the grille-to-reinforcement rivets and remove the grille.
8. Installation is the reverse of removal.

Mustang GT

▶ See Figure 8

1. Remove the license plate bolts or rivets.
2. Remove the lower grille-to-radiator support screws.
3. Remove the upper grille-to-support brackets.
4. Remove the grille-to-fender nuts and detach the reinforcement assembly.
5. Remove the headlamp side marker, parking and turn signal lamps from the reinforcement.
6. Remove the 2 pushnuts per side attaching the lower corner reinforcement assembly.
7. Drill out the grille-to-reinforcement rivets and remove the grille.
8. Installation is the reverse of removal.

Mustang SVO

▶ See Figure 9

1. Remove the license plate bolts or rivets.
2. Remove the lower grille-to-radiator support screws.
3. Remove the upper grille-to-support brackets.
4. Remove the grille-to-fender nuts and detach the reinforcement assembly.
5. Remove the headlamp side marker, parking and turn signal lamps from the reinforcement.
6. Remove the 2 pushnuts per side attaching the lower corner reinforcement assembly.
7. Drill out the grille-to-reinforcement rivets and remove the grille.
8. Installation is the reverse of removal.

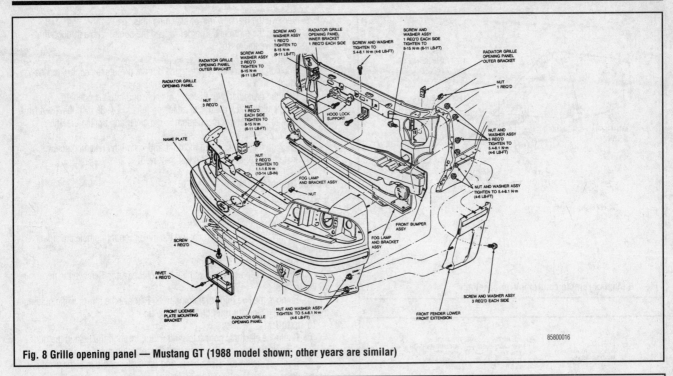

Fig. 8 Grille opening panel — Mustang GT (1988 model shown; other years are similar)

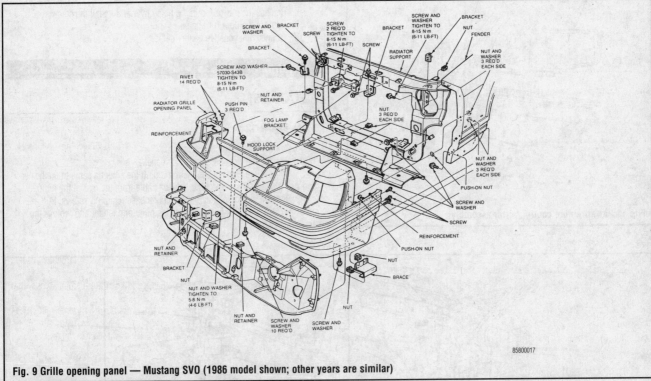

Fig. 9 Grille opening panel — Mustang SVO (1986 model shown; other years are similar)

Outside Mirrors

➡ Outside mirrors that are frozen must be thawed prior to adjustment. Do not attempt to free-up the mirror by pressing the glass assembly.

REMOVAL & INSTALLATION

Manual Type

1. Remove the inside sail trim cover.
2. Remove the nut and washer assemblies and lift the mirror off the door.

To install:

3. Position the mirror against the door.
4. Install and tighten the nut and washer assemblies.
5. Install the inside sail cover.

Manual Remote Control

♦ See Figure 10

1. Remove the trim cover retaining screw and loosen the Allen setscrew retaining the control mechanism to the cover.
2. Remove the control knob, if necessary and remove the cover.

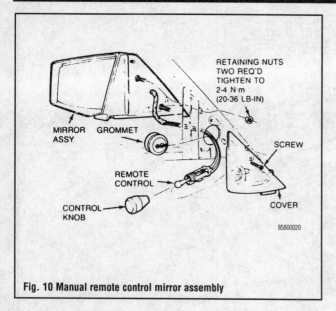

Fig. 10 Manual remote control mirror assembly

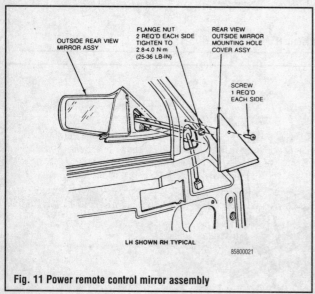

Fig. 11 Power remote control mirror assembly

3. Remove the rearview mirror attaching nuts.

4. Remove the grommet, in order to feed the control cable through the door, and remove the mirror.

To install:

5. Position the rearview mirror to the door and route the control mechanism through the opening.

6. Seat the grommet over the control cable and into the opening.

7. Install and tighten the mirror attaching nuts to 24–36 inch lbs. (3–4 Nm).

8. Position the control mechanism in the cover and tighten the Allen setscrew.

9. Position the trim cover to the door and install the retaining screw.

10. Install the control knob if it was removed.

Power Remote Control

♦ See Figure 11

1. Disconnect the negative battery cable.

2. Remove the one screw retaining the mirror mounting hole cover and remove the cover.

3. Remove the door trim panel.

4. Disconnect the mirror assembly wiring connector. Remove the necessary wiring guides.

5. Remove the two mirror retaining nuts. Remove the mirror while guiding the wiring and connector through hole in the door.

To install:

6. Route the electrical connector and wiring through the hole in the door and position the mirror. Install and tighten the retaining nuts.

7. Connect the mirror assembly wiring connector and install the wiring guides.

8. Replace the mirror mounting hole cover and install the screw.

9. Replace the door trim panel.

10. Connect the negative battery cable.

Antenna

REPLACEMENT

♦ See Figure 12

1. Remove the glove compartment.

2. Remove the right side cowl trim panel.

3. Remove the antenna cable clip holding the antenna cable to the heater and A/C plenum. Disconnect the antenna cable from the rear of the radio.

4. Remove the antenna cap and antenna base retaining screws. Pull the cable through the holes in the door hinge pillar and fender and remove the antenna assembly.

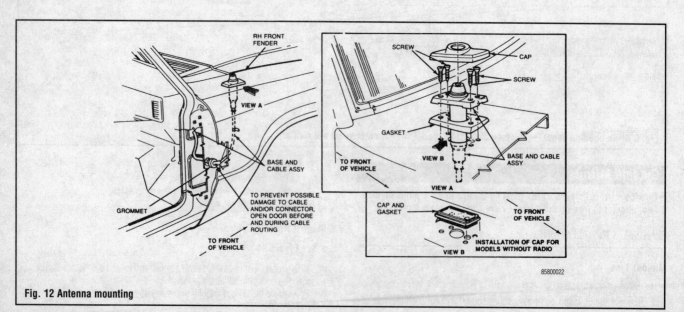

Fig. 12 Antenna mounting

To install:

5. With the front right door open, position the antenna assembly in the fender opening, put the gasket in position on the antenna and install the antenna base to the fender.

6. Pull the antenna lead through the door hinge pillar opening. Seat the grommet by pulling the cable through the hole from inside the vehicle.

INTERIOR

Instrument Panel Pad

REMOVAL & INSTALLATION

Except 1988 Mustang

▶ **See Figure 13**

1. Remove the instrument cluster and finish panel retaining screws.
2. Unfasten the instrument panel pad retaining screws in front, or on the ends of the panel.
3. Remove the instrument panel pad retaining screws in the top defroster openings, and remove the pad.
4. Installation is the reverse of removal.

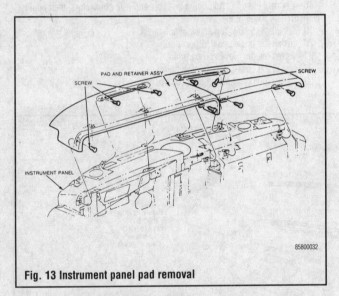

Fig. 13 Instrument panel pad removal

Instrument Panel

REMOVAL & INSTALLATION

Except 1987–88 Mustang

▶ **See Figure 14**

1. Disconnect the negative battery cable.
2. Remove the instrument panel pad, as described previously in this section.
3. Remove the two screws attaching the steering column opening lower cover to the instrument panel, and remove the cover.
4. Unfasten the screws on the underside of the steering column trim shrouds, and remove the shrouds.
5. Remove the four nuts attaching the steering column to the brake pedal support, then carefully lower the steering column just enough to rest it on the front seat.

➡ **On vehicles equipped with an automatic transmission, it may be necessary to lower the steering column for access to the transmission gear**

7. Route the cable behind the heater and A/C plenum and attach the locating clips. Connect the lead to the rear of the radio.
8. Install the right side cowl trim panel
9. Install the glove compartment.

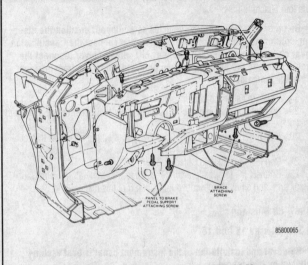

Fig. 14 Instrument panel installation—except 1987–88 Mustang

shift selector lever and cable assembly. Reach between the steering column and instrument panel and gently lift the selector lever cable off the shift selector lever. Remove the cable clamp from the steering column tube, then lay the steering column to rest on the front seat.

✳✳ WARNING

Do not lower the column further than necessary, or damage to the selector lever and/or cable may result.

6. Remove the screw attaching the instrument panel to the brake pedal support at the steering column opening.
7. Remove the screw attaching the lower brace to the lower edge of the instrument panel below the radio.
8. Remove the screw attaching the brace to the lower edge of the instrument panel below the glove compartment.
9. Disconnect the temperature control cable from the temperature blend door and the evaporator case bracket.
10. Disconnect the 7-port vacuum hose connector at the evaporator case.
11. Disconnect the blower resistor wire connector from the resistor on the evaporator housing, and the blower motor feed wire at the inline connector near the blower resistor wire connector.
12. Support the instrument panel and, using an angle Phillips screwdriver, remove three screws attaching the top of the instrument panel to the cowl.
13. Remove one screw attaching each end of the instrument panel to the cowl side panels.
14. Move the instrument panel rearward and disconnect the speedometer cable from the speedometer. Disconnect any wires that will not allow the instrument panel to lay on the front seat.

➡ **Be carefully not to scratch the instrument panel or the steering column during removal.**

To install:

15. Place the instrument panel near its installed position and engage any wires/connectors that were unplugged during removal.
16. Connect the speedometer cable to the speedometer.
17. Place the instrument panel in position and install one screw at each end.

18. Install three screws along the top front edge of the instrument panel with an angle Phillips screwdriver.

19. Connect the two support braces to the lower edge of the instrument panel with one screw each.

20. Connect the temperature control cable to the temperature blend door crank arm and the bracket.

21. Connect the vacuum hoses at the 7-port connector, and the blower motor wires at the resistor and inline connector near the resistor.

22. Install the screw attaching the instrument panel to the brake pedal support.

23. Position the steering column against the brake pedal support and install the four attaching nuts.

➡**On automatic transmission vehicles so equipped, position the steering column near the brake pedal support and connect the transmission gear shift selector lever cable to the shift selector lever. Connect the cable clamp to the steering column tube and adjust the transmission selector indicator.**

24. Install the steering column shrouds.

25. Position the steering column opening cover to the instrument panel and install the two attaching screws.

26. Install the instrument panel pad, as described previously in this section.

27. Connect the negative battery cable.

28. Connect the temperature control cable to the temperature blend door crank arm, and adjust as described in Section 6 of this manual.

1987–88 Mustang

◆ **See Figures 15 and 16**

➡**Removal and installation of the instrument panel is best accomplished by two people.**

1. Disconnect the negative battery cable.

2. In the engine compartment, disconnect all main wiring harness-to-instrument panel connectors.

3. Remove the rubber grommet from the firewall and feed all the wiring into the passenger compartment.

4. Remove the headlamp/fog lamp switch and disconnect the wiring.

5. Remove the steering column extension shroud.

6. Remove the steering column cover.

7. Remove the 6 steering column nuts (2 retaining the hood release mechanism and 4 retaining the steering column to the lower brake pedal support). Lower the steering column to the floor.

8. Remove the floor console.

9. Snap out the defroster grille.

10. Remove the screws from the speaker covers and snap them out.

11. Remove the 4 screws retaining the steering column reinforcement opening.

12. Remove the right and left side cowl panels.

13. Remove the cowl side retaining bolts.

14. Open the glove compartment door and bend the bin tabs inward. Let the door assembly drop.

15. Remove the brake pedal support nut.

16. Remove the 5 cowl top screw attachments.

17. Gently pull the instrument panel away from the cowl. Disconnect the air conditioning controls and wire connectors.

To install:

18. Connect the air conditioning controls and wire connectors, then position the instrument panel in the car.

19. Install the 5 cowl top screw attachments.

20. Install the brake pedal support nut.

21. Assemble the glove compartment.

22. Install the cowl side retaining bolts.

23. Install the right and left side cowl panels.

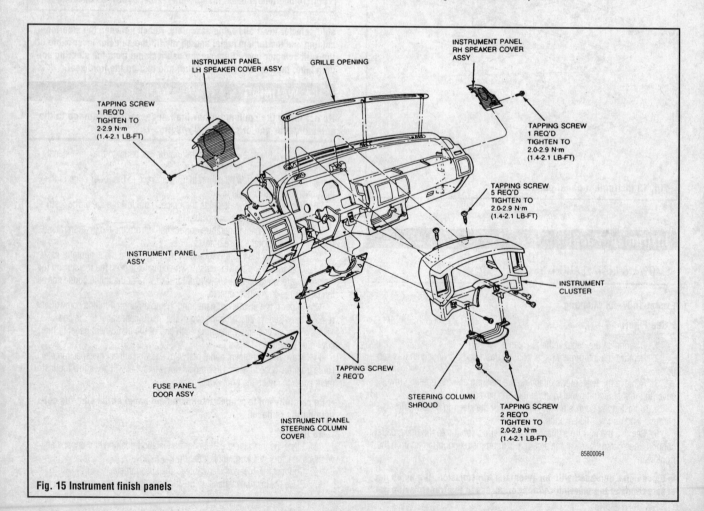

Fig. 15 Instrument finish panels

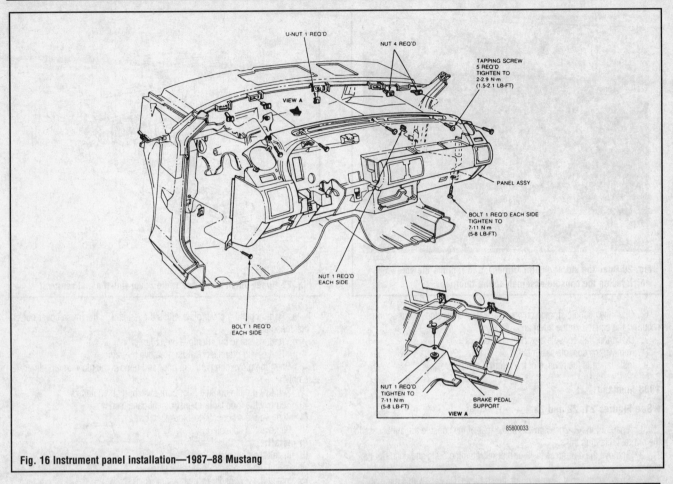

Fig. 16 Instrument panel installation—1987–88 Mustang

24. Install the 4 screws retaining the steering column reinforcement opening.
25. Install the speaker covers.
26. Install the defroster grille.
27. Install the floor console.
28. Install the steering column.
29. Install the steering column cover.
30. Install the steering column extension shroud.
31. Attach the electrical connector(s) and install the headlamp/fog lamp switch.
32. Install the wiring and rubber grommet in the firewall.
33. In the engine compartment, connect all main wiring harness-to-instrument panel connectors.
34. Connect the negative battery cable.

Floor Console

REMOVAL & INSTALLATION

Except 1988 Mustang

▶ See Figures 17, 18, 19 and 20

1. Pull up the gear shift lever opening plate at the front and remove from catch.
2. Push the gear shift lever opening plate forward and remove.
3. Remove two screws securing the console finish panel to the console assembly. Remove the finish panel.
4. Remove the front ash receptacle.
5. Remove two screws under the ash receptacle, securing the console assembly to the floorpan.

Fig. 17 The finish panel is fastened to the lip of the storage compartment

Fig. 18 Lift out the front ash receptacle

Fig. 19 Remove the screws beneath the ash receptacle which secure the console assembly to the floorpan

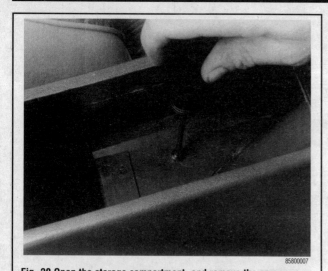

Fig. 20 Open the storage compartment, and remove the screws which fasten the console assembly to the floorpan

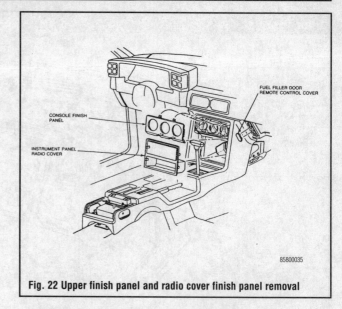

Fig. 22 Upper finish panel and radio cover finish panel removal

6. Open the console storage compartment door and remove four screws securing the console to the floorpan.

7. Disconnect all console electrical connectors.

8. Remove the console assembly.

9. Installation is the reverse of the removal procedure.

1988 Mustang

▶ See Figures 21, 22 and 23

1. Snap out the 2 access covers at the rear of the console to gain access to the armrest retaining bolts.

2. Remove the 4 armrest-to-floor bracket retaining bolts and snap out the armrest.

3. Snap out the shift lever opening finish panel. On cars with a manual transmission, the shift boot is attached to the bottom of the finish panel. Remove the shift knob, then slide the boot and finish panel up and over the shift lever.

4. To remove the top finish panel, position the emergency brake lever in the UP position. Remove the 4 retaining screws and lift the panel up. Disconnect the wiring.

5. Remove the 2 console-to-rear floor bracket retaining screws.

6. Insert a small screwdriver into the 2 notches at the bottom of the front upper finish panel and snap it out.

7. There are 3 combinations of radio cover finish panels:

   a. Radio opening cover plate with storage bin. Pry the finish cover out of the console.

   b. Radio storage bin. Remove the radio.

   c. Radio with graphic equalizer. Remove the radio.

8. Open the glove compartment door and remove the glove compartment assembly.

9. Remove the remote fuel filler door switch, if so equipped.

10. Remove the 2 console-to-instrument panel screws.

11. Remove the 4 console-to-bracket screws.

12. Remove the console.

To install:

13. Install the console.

14. Install the 4 console-to-bracket screws.

15. Install the 2 console-to-instrument panel screws.

16. Install the remote fuel filler door switch, if so equipped.

17. Install the glove compartment assembly.

18. Install the radio or cover panel.

19. Install the front upper finish panel.

20. Install the 2 console-to-rear floor bracket retaining screws.

21. Install the top finish panel. Connect the wiring.

22. Install the shift lever opening finish panel.

23. Install the shift knob and slide the boot and finish panel.

24. Install the armrest.

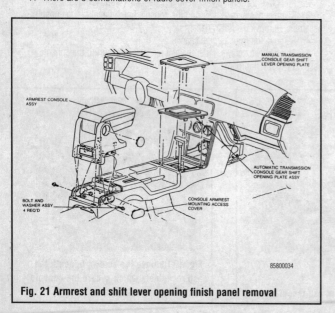

Fig. 21 Armrest and shift lever opening finish panel removal

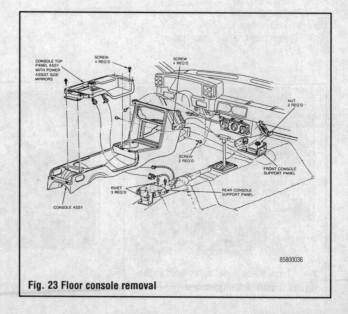

Fig. 23 Floor console removal

Door Trim Panels

REMOVAL & INSTALLATION

▶ **See Figures 24, 25, 26, 27 and 28**

1. Remove the window regulator handle retaining screw and remove the handle.
2. Remove the door latch handle retaining screw and remove the handle.
3. Remove the screws from the armrest door pull cup area.

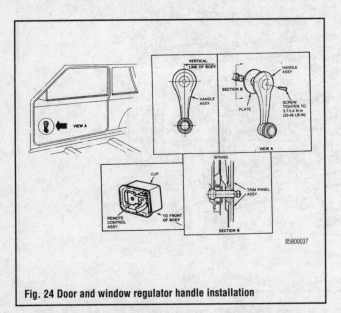

Fig. 24 Door and window regulator handle installation

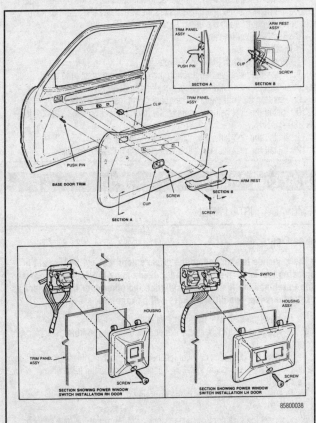

Fig. 25 Standard door trim panel — except 1988 Mustang

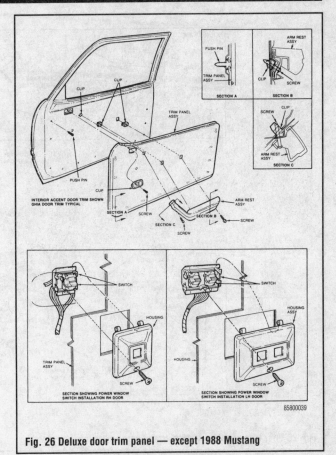

Fig. 26 Deluxe door trim panel — except 1988 Mustang

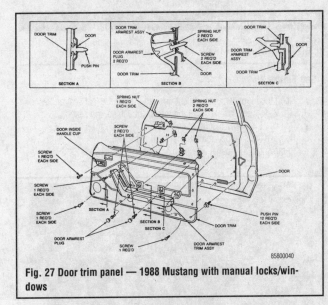

Fig. 27 Door trim panel — 1988 Mustang with manual locks/windows

4. Remove the retaining screws from the armrest.
5. On cars with power door locks and/or power windows, remove the retaining screws and power switch cover assembly. Remove the screws holding the switch housing.
6. Remove the mirror remote control bezel nut, if so equipped.
7. Remove the door trim panel retaining screws.
8. With a flat, wooden spatula, pry the trim retaining clips from the door panel. These clips can be easily torn from the trim panel, so be very careful to pry as closely as possible to the clips.
9. Pull the panel out slightly and disconnect all wiring.
10. If a new panel is being installed, transfer all necessary parts.
11. Installation is the reverse of removal.

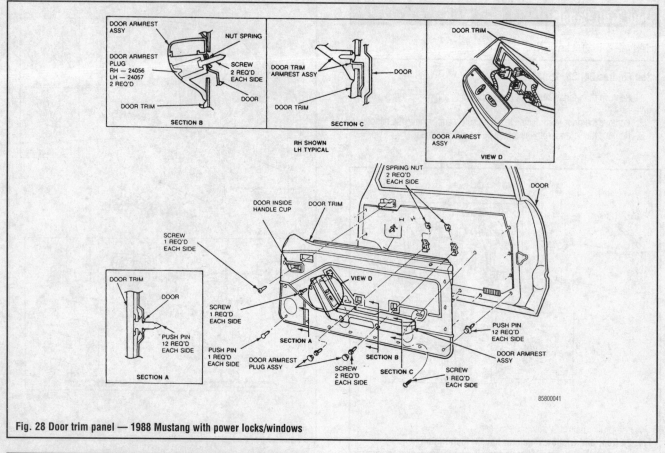

Fig. 28 Door trim panel — 1988 Mustang with power locks/windows

Quarter Trim Panels

REMOVAL & INSTALLATION

▶ **See Figure 29**

1. Open the luggage compartment door and lower the rear seat on 3-door models. On 2-door models, remove the rear seat cushion and seat back.
2. Remove the doorsill scuff plate.
3. Remove the seat belt retractors from the doorsill.
4. Remove the trim panel attaching screws.

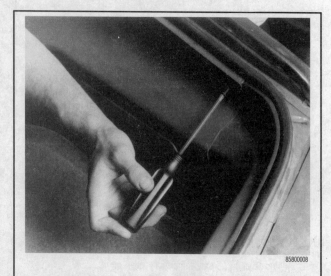

Fig. 29 Removing the rearmost quarter trim panel attaching screw

5. Remove the bezel from the rear seat belt opening in the trim panel, and remove the belt from the opening. Unsnap the shoulder belt lower bezel and slide the belt out through the upper bezel opening.
6. Remove the trim panel.

To install:

7. Position the trim panel in the vehicle.
8. Insert the rear seat belt through the opening and install the bezel. Slide the shoulder belt into the opening and install the bezel.
9. Position the trim panel to the quarter, and install the attaching screws.
10. Install the seat belt retractors in the doorsill, and tighten to 22–32 ft. lbs. (30–43 Nm).
11. Install the doorsill scuff plate.
12. Install the rear seat back and seat cushion on 2-door models.

Door Lock Cylinder

REMOVAL & INSTALLATION

▶ **See Figure 30**

➡ **The key code is stamped on the driver's door lock cylinder to aid in replacing lost keys. If a lock cylinder needs to be replaced, it is advisable to replace the ignition lock cylinder and other door lock cylinder as a set; otherwise, two different keys will be required.**

1. Remove the door trim panel and watershield.
2. Disconnect the lock control-to-door lock cylinder rod from the lock cylinder arm.
3. Remove the door lock cylinder retainer and slide the cylinder from the door. If a new lock cylinder is being installed, transfer the arm to the new cylinder.

To install:

4. Position the lock cylinder in the door and install the lock cylinder retainer.
5. Connect the lock control-to-door lock cylinder rod at the lock cylinder, and secure the retainer.
6. Position the watershield to the inner panel and install the trim panel.

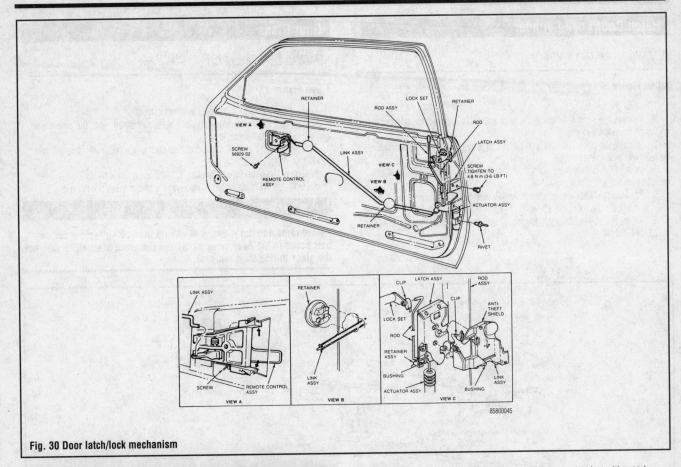

Fig. 30 Door latch/lock mechanism

Trunk Lid Lock Cylinder

REMOVAL & INSTALLATION

▶ **See Figure 31**

1. Open the trunk lid.
2. Unfasten the latch retaining screws and remove the latch.

3. Remove the lock cylinder retainer by drilling out the rivet with a ¼ in. (6mm) drill.
4. Remove the lock support and bracket.
5. Remove the lock cylinder retainer as you remove the lock cylinder and extension.
6. Installation is the reverse of the removal procedure. Use a new rivet or replace with a sheet metal screw. Torque the retaining screws 6–10 ft. lbs. (8–13 Nm).

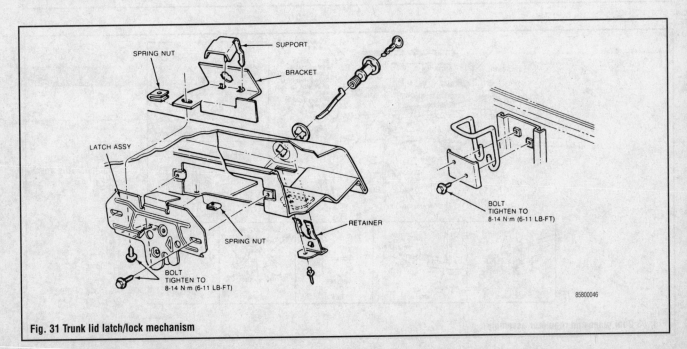

Fig. 31 Trunk lid latch/lock mechanism

Hatch Door Lock Cylinder

REMOVAL & INSTALLATION

▶ **See Figure 32**

1. Open the hatch door.
2. Remove the screws retaining the latch assembly. Remove the latch cover and latch bracket assembly.
3. Remove the pop-rivet and retainer. The lock cylinder and extension must be removed with the retainer.
4. Installation is the reverse of the removal procedure. Use a new rivet or replace with a sheet metal screw.
5. Position the latch and bracket assembly with the cover against the hatch door, and tighten the retaining screws to 7–10 ft. lbs. (10–13 Nm).
6. Adjust the striker assembly for proper seal and fit, and tighten to 20–28 ft. lbs. (14–38 Nm).

Door Glass

REMOVAL & INSTALLATION

▶ **See Figure 33**

1. Remove the door trim panel and watershield.
2. Remove the screw attaching each glass rear stabilizer to the inner panel, and remove the stabilizer.
3. Loosen the 2 screws that attach the door glass front run retainer to the inner door panel.
4. Lower the glass to gain access to the glass bracket rivets.
5. Drill out the glass bracket attaching rivets and push out the rivets.

❈❈ WARNING

Before removing the rivets, you should insert a suitable block support between the door outer panel and the glass bracket, to stabilize the glass during rivet removal.

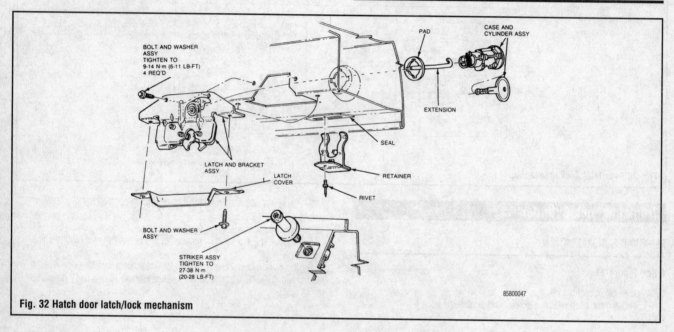

Fig. 32 Hatch door latch/lock mechanism

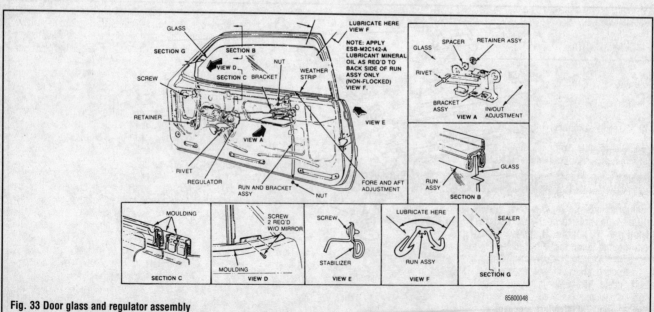

Fig. 33 Door glass and regulator assembly

6. Remove the glass.

7. Installation is the reverse of removal. Replace the rivets with ¼–20 X 1 in. nuts and bolts. When the glass is operating properly, tighten the bolts to 3–5 ft. lbs. (4–7 Nm).

Door Glass Regulator

REMOVAL & INSTALLATION

▶ See Figure 33

1979–83

1. Remove the door trim panel and watershield.
2. Support the glass in the full up position.
3. Drill out the motor bracket-to-inner panel attaching rivet and remove the rivet. Disconnect the motor wires at the connector. On the models with power windows, drill out the regulator attaching rivets and remove the rivets.
4. Disengage the regulator arm from the glass bracket and remove the regulator from the door.
5. If equipped with power windows, secure the regulator in a vise and drill a 5/16 in. hole through the regulator sector gear and the plate. Install a ¼ in. bolt and nut in the hole to prevent the sector gear from moving when the motor and drive assembly is removed.
6. Remove the motor assembly from the regulator and install it on a new regulator.
7. Installation is the reverse of removal. Replace the rivets with ¼–20 X ½ in. machine screws. Remove the regulator restraining bolt and nut if the old regulator was re-used.

1984–88

1. Remove the trim panel and watershield.
2. Prop the window glass in the full up position.
3. Disconnect the window motor wiring if so equipped.
4. Drill out the 3 rivets (manual windows) or 4 rivets (electric windows), attaching the regulator to the inner door panel.
5. Remove the upper screw and washer and the lower nut and washer, attaching the run and bracket to the inner door panel. Slide the run tube up between the door belt and glass. It's a good idea to cover the glass with a protective cloth.
6. Remove the regulator slide from the glass bracket and remove the regulator through the door access hole.
7. Installation is the reverse of removal. Replace the rivets with $FR1/4-20 X 1 in. bolts and nuts.

Electric Window Motor

REMOVAL & INSTALLATION

1979–83

1. Remove the trim panel and watershield.
2. Remove the speakers.
3. Disconnect the motor wires and the connector.

➡On 1980 models, sheet metal interference may obscure the upper motor mount screw. This interference may be removed by grinding.

✳✳ CAUTION

If equipped with power windows, secure the regulator in a vise and drill a 5/16 in. hole through the regulator sector gear and the plate. Install a ¼ in. bolt and nut in the hole to prevent the sector gear from moving when the motor and drive assembly is removed.

4. Working through the holes, remove the 3 motor and drive-to-regulator attaching bolts. Remove the motor and drive from the door.
5. Installation is the reverse of removal. When installing the motor and drive to the regulator, install the 3 screws just snugly enough to hold it. Remove the

regulator restraining bolt and nut if the old regulator was re-used. Connect the wires and cycle the glass through its run to ensure gear engagement. Then, tighten the attaching screws to 50–85 inch lbs. (6–9 Nm).

1984–88

1. Remove the trim panel and watershield.
2. Disconnect the battery ground.
3. Disconnect the motor wires and the connector.
4. Using the dimples located on the inner door panel, drill ¾ in. holes for access to the motor.

✳✳ WARNING

When drilling the holes, the glass must be in the up position. The hole saw pilot must not extend more than ¼ in. beyond the hole saw.

✳✳ CAUTION

Drill a 5/16 in. hole through the regulator sector gear and the plate. Install a ¼ in. bolt and nut in the hole to prevent the sector gear from moving when the motor and drive assembly is removed.

5. Working through the holes, remove the 3 motor and drive-to-regulator attaching bolts. Remove the motor and drive from the door.
6. Installation is the reverse of removal. When installing the motor and drive to the regulator, install the 3 screws just snugly enough to hold it. Remove the regulator restraining bolt and nut if the old regulator was re-used. Connect the wires and cycle the glass through its run to ensure gear engagement. Then, tighten the attaching screws to 50–85 inch lbs. (6–9 Nm).

Windshield and Fixed Glass

REMOVAL & INSTALLATION

If your windshield, or other fixed window, is cracked or chipped, you may decide to replace it with a new one yourself. However, there are two main reasons why replacement windshields and other window glass should be installed only by a professional automotive glass technician: safety and cost.

The most important reason a professional should install automotive glass is for safety. The glass in the vehicle, especially the windshield, is designed with safety in mind in case of a collision. The windshield is specially manufactured from two panes of specially-tempered glass with a thin layer of transparent plastic between them. This construction allows the glass to "give" in the event that a part of your body hits the windshield during the collision, and prevents the glass from shattering, which could cause lacerations, blinding and other harm to passengers of the vehicle. The other fixed windows are designed to be tempered so that if they break during a collision, they shatter in such a way that there are no large pointed glass pieces. The professional automotive glass technician knows how to install the glass in a vehicle so that it will function optimally during a collision. Without the proper experience, knowledge and tools, installing a piece of automotive glass yourself could lead to additional harm if an accident should ever occur.

Cost is also a factor when deciding to install automotive glass yourself. Performing this could cost you much more than a professional may charge for the same job. Since the windshield is designed to break under stress, an often life saving characteristic, windshields tend to break VERY easily when an inexperienced person attempts to install one. Do-it-yourselfers buying two, three or even four windshields from a salvage yard because they have broken them during installation are common stories. Also, since the automotive glass is designed to prevent the outside elements from entering your vehicle, improper installation can lead to water and air leaks. Annoying whining noises at highway speeds from air leaks or inside body panel rusting from water leaks can add to your stress level and subtract from your wallet. After buying two or three windshields, installing them and ending up with a leak that produces a noise while driving and water damage during rainstorms, the cost of having a professional do it correctly the first time may be much more alluring. We here at Chilton, therefore, advise that you have a professional automotive glass technician service any broken glass on your vehicle.

WINDSHIELD CHIP REPAIR

♦ **See Figures 34 and 35**

➥Check with your state and local authorities on the laws for state safety inspection. Some states or municipalities may not allow chip repair as a viable option for correcting stone damage to your windshield.

Although severely cracked or damaged windshields must be replaced, there is something that you can do to prolong or even prevent the need for replacement of a chipped windshield. There are many companies which offer windshield chip repair products, such as Loctite's® Bullseye™ windshield repair kit. These kits usually consist of a syringe, pedestal and a sealing adhesive. The syringe is mounted on the pedestal and is used to create a vacuum which pulls the plastic layer against the glass. This helps make the chip transparent. The adhesive is then injected which seals the chip and helps to prevent further stress cracks from developing

➥Always follow the specific manufacturer's instructions.

TCCA0P00

Fig. 34 Small chips on your windshield can be fixed with an after-market repair kit, such as the one from Loctite®

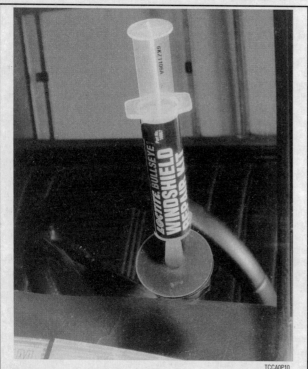

TCCA0P10

Fig. 35 Most kits use a self-stick applicator and syringe to inject the adhesive into the chip or crack

Inside Rear View Mirror

REPLACEMENT

♦ **See Figure 36**

1. Loosen the mirror assembly-to-mounting bracket setscrew.
2. Remove the mirror assembly by sliding it upward and away from the mounting bracket.
3. If the bracket vinyl pad remains on the windshield, apply low heat from an electric heat gun until the vinyl softens. Peel the vinyl off the windshield and discard.

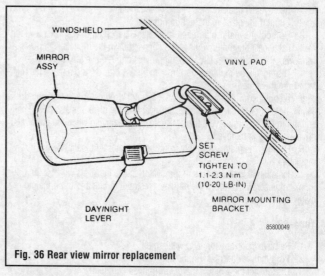

85800049

Fig. 36 Rear view mirror replacement

To install:

4. Make sure the glass, bracket and adhesive kit (Rear View Mirror Repair Kit D9AZ–19554–B or equivalent) are at a temperature of at least 65–75° F (18–24° C).
5. Locate and mark the mirror mounting bracket location on the outside surface of the windshield with a wax pencil.
6. Thoroughly clean the bonding surfaces of the glass and the bracket to remove the old adhesive. Use a mild abrasive cleaner on the glass and fine sandpaper on the bracket to lightly roughen the surface. Wipe clean with the alcohol-moistened cloth.
7. Crush the accelerator vial (part of Rear View Mirror Repair Kit D9AZ–19554–B or equivalent), and apply the accelerator to the bonding surface of the bracket and windshield. Let it dry for three minutes.
8. Apply two drops of adhesive (part of Rear View Mirror Repair Kit D9AZ–19554–B or equivalent) to the mounting surface of the bracket. Using a clean toothpick or wooden match, quickly spread the adhesive evenly over the mounting surface of the bracket.
9. Quickly position the mounting bracket on the windshield. The ⅜ in. (10mm) circular depression in the bracket must be toward the inside of the passenger compartment. Press the bracket firmly against the windshield for one minute.
10. Allow the bond to set for five minutes. Remove any excess bonding material from the windshield with an alcohol dampened cloth.
11. Attach the mirror to the mounting bracket and tighten the setscrew to 10–20 inch lbs. (1–2 Nm).

Front Seats

REMOVAL & INSTALLATION

♦ **See Figure 37**

1. Remove the seat track retaining screws, plastic shields, and nuts and washers from inside the vehicle.
2. Lift and remove the seat and track assembly from the vehicle. On power

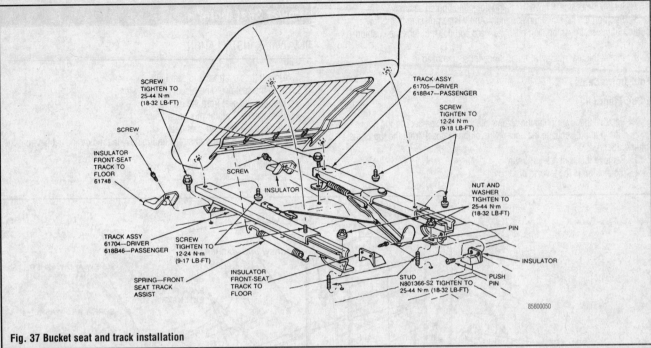

Fig. 37 Bucket seat and track installation

seats, tilt the seat backward and disconnect the motor wiring, before lifting the seat from the car.

3. In order to remove the seat track assemblies from the seat, proceed as follows:

a. Place the seat and seat track assemblies on a clean working area and disconnect the adjusting springs, if so equipped.

b. Remove the seat track-to-seat cushion attaching screws, and remove the seat cushion from the tracks.

c. Disconnect the latch tie rod from the seat tracks, if so equipped.

d. If the seat tracks are being replaced, transfer the spacers and seat side shields to the new track assemblies.

To install:

4. If the seat tracks were removed, proceed as follows:

a. Mount the seat tracks to the seat cushion. If applicable, connect the tie rod to the two tracks as they are positioned.

b. Install the seat track-to-seat cushion retaining screws and tighten to 9–17 ft. lbs. (12–24 Nm).

c. Connect the adjusting springs between the seat tracks and seat cushion, if so equipped.

5. Position the seat assembly in the vehicle.

6. Install the screws, plastic shields, and nuts and washers. Tighten the fasteners to 18–32 ft. lbs. (25–44 Nm).

Rear Seats

REMOVAL & INSTALLATION

Conventional Seats

▶ See Figures 38 and 39

1. Apply knee pressure to the lower portion of the rear seat cushion, and push rearward to disengage it from the retaining brackets.

2. Remove one of the rear quarter armrests, if so equipped, to remove the seatback assembly.

3. Remove the seatback lower retaining screws.

4. Grasp the seatback at the bottom and lift it up to disengage the hanger wire from the retaining brackets.

5. Remove the seatback assembly from the vehicle.

To install:

6. Position the seatback assembly into the vehicle so that the hanger wire is engaged with the retaining brackets.

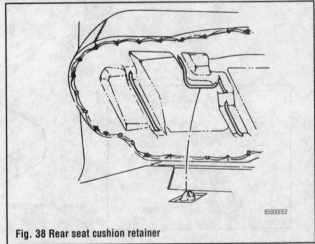

Fig. 38 Rear seat cushion retainer

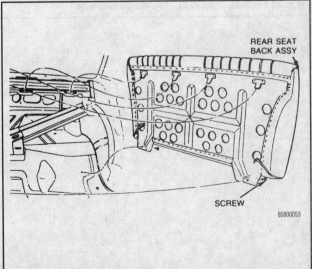

Fig. 39 Rear seatback installation

7. Install the seatback lower retaining bolts and tighten securely.

8. Position the seat cushion assembly. Apply knee pressure to the lower portion of the seat cushion, and push rearward and down to lock the cushion into position.

9. Install the rear quarter armrest, if previously removed.

Fold-Down Seats

▶ See Figure 40

1. Remove the lower retaining screws attaching the seatback to the floor.

2. Lift up and disengage the upper clips of the seatback from the top of the folding floor.

3. Remove the seatback assembly.

4. Installation is the reverse of removal.

Power Seat Motor

REMOVAL & INSTALLATION

1. Unbolt the seat track and seat belts.
2. Turn the seat over and disconnect the wiring.
3. Remove the seat from the car.
4. Remove the 3 motor mounting bolts.
5. Remove the cable-to-seat track clamps.
6. Open the wire retaining straps and remove the motor and cables from the seat.
7. Installation is the reverse of removal.

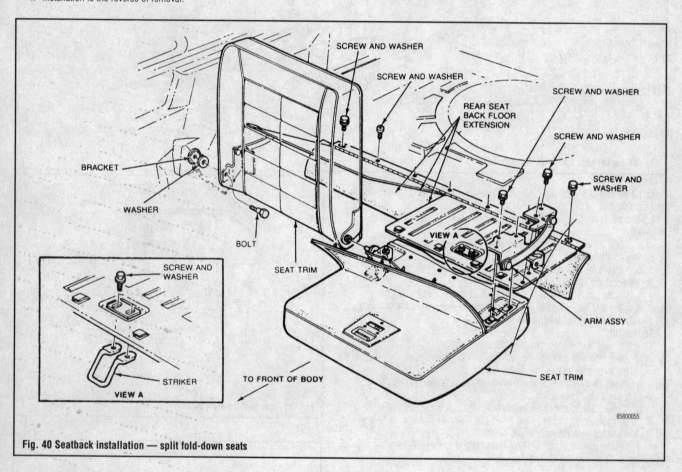

Fig. 40 Seatback installation — split fold-down seats

85800055

GLOSSARY

AIR/FUEL RATIO: The ratio of air-to-gasoline by weight in the fuel mixture drawn into the engine.

AIR INJECTION: One method of reducing harmful exhaust emissions by injecting air into each of the exhaust ports of an engine. The fresh air entering the hot exhaust manifold causes any remaining fuel to be burned before it can exit the tailpipe.

ALTERNATOR: A device used for converting mechanical energy into electrical energy.

AMMETER: An instrument, calibrated in amperes, used to measure the flow of an electrical current in a circuit. Ammeters are always connected in series with the circuit being tested.

AMPERE: The rate of flow of electrical current present when one volt of electrical pressure is applied against one ohm of electrical resistance.

ANALOG COMPUTER: Any microprocessor that uses similar (analogous) electrical signals to make its calculations.

ARMATURE: A laminated, soft iron core wrapped by a wire that converts electrical energy to mechanical energy as in a motor or relay. When rotated in a magnetic field, it changes mechanical energy into electrical energy as in a generator.

ATMOSPHERIC PRESSURE: The pressure on the Earth's surface caused by the weight of the air in the atmosphere. At sea level, this pressure is 14.7 psi at 32°F (101 kPa at 0°C).

ATOMIZATION: The breaking down of a liquid into a fine mist that can be suspended in air.

AXIAL PLAY: Movement parallel to a shaft or bearing bore.

BACKFIRE: The sudden combustion of gases in the intake or exhaust system that results in a loud explosion.

BACKLASH: The clearance or play between two parts, such as meshed gears.

BACKPRESSURE: Restrictions in the exhaust system that slow the exit of exhaust gases from the combustion chamber.

BAKELITE: A heat resistant, plastic insulator material commonly used in printed circuit boards and transistorized components.

BALL BEARING: A bearing made up of hardened inner and outer races between which hardened steel balls roll.

BALLAST RESISTOR: A resistor in the primary ignition circuit that lowers voltage after the engine is started to reduce wear on ignition components.

BEARING: A friction reducing, supportive device usually located between a stationary part and a moving part.

BIMETAL TEMPERATURE SENSOR: Any sensor or switch made of two dissimilar types of metal that bend when heated or cooled due to the different expansion rates of the alloys. These types of sensors usually function as an on/off switch.

BLOWBY: Combustion gases, composed of water vapor and unburned fuel, that leak past the piston rings into the crankcase during normal engine operation. These gases are removed by the PCV system to prevent the buildup of harmful acids in the crankcase.

BRAKE PAD: A brake shoe and lining assembly used with disc brakes.

BRAKE SHOE: The backing for the brake lining. The term is, however, usually applied to the assembly of the brake backing and lining.

BUSHING: A liner, usually removable, for a bearing; an anti-friction liner used in place of a bearing.

CALIPER: A hydraulically activated device in a disc brake system, which is mounted straddling the brake rotor (disc). The caliper contains at least one piston and two brake pads. Hydraulic pressure on the piston(s) forces the pads against the rotor.

CAMSHAFT: A shaft in the engine on which are the lobes (cams) which operate the valves. The camshaft is driven by the crankshaft, via a belt, chain or gears, at one half the crankshaft speed.

CAPACITOR: A device which stores an electrical charge.

CARBON MONOXIDE (CO): A colorless, odorless gas given off as a normal byproduct of combustion. It is poisonous and extremely dangerous in confined areas, building up slowly to toxic levels without warning if adequate ventilation is not available.

CARBURETOR: A device, usually mounted on the intake manifold of an engine, which mixes the air and fuel in the proper proportion to allow even combustion.

CATALYTIC CONVERTER: A device installed in the exhaust system, like a muffler, that converts harmful byproducts of combustion into carbon dioxide and water vapor by means of a heat-producing chemical reaction.

CENTRIFUGAL ADVANCE: A mechanical method of advancing the spark timing by using flyweights in the distributor that react to centrifugal force generated by the distributor shaft rotation.

CHECK VALVE: Any one-way valve installed to permit the flow of air, fuel or vacuum in one direction only.

CHOKE: A device, usually a moveable valve, placed in the intake path of a carburetor to restrict the flow of air.

CIRCUIT: Any unbroken path through which an electrical current can flow. Also used to describe fuel flow in some instances.

CIRCUIT BREAKER: A switch which protects an electrical circuit from overload by opening the circuit when the current flow exceeds a predetermined level. Some circuit breakers must be reset manually, while most reset automatically.

COIL (IGNITION): A transformer in the ignition circuit which steps up the voltage provided to the spark plugs.

COMBINATION MANIFOLD: An assembly which includes both the intake and exhaust manifolds in one casting.

COMBINATION VALVE: A device used in some fuel systems that routes fuel vapors to a charcoal storage canister instead of venting them into the atmosphere. The valve relieves fuel tank pressure and allows fresh air into the tank as the fuel level drops to prevent a vapor lock situation.

COMPRESSION RATIO: The comparison of the total volume of the cylinder and combustion chamber with the piston at BDC and the piston at TDC.

CONDENSER: 1. An electrical device which acts to store an electrical charge, preventing voltage surges. 2. A radiator-like device in the air conditioning system in which refrigerant gas condenses into a liquid, giving off heat.

CONDUCTOR: Any material through which an electrical current can be transmitted easily.

CONTINUITY: Continuous or complete circuit. Can be checked with an ohmmeter.

COUNTERSHAFT: An intermediate shaft which is rotated by a mainshaft and transmits, in turn, that rotation to a working part.

CRANKCASE: The lower part of an engine in which the crankshaft and related parts operate.

CRANKSHAFT: The main driving shaft of an engine which receives reciprocating motion from the pistons and converts it to rotary motion.

CYLINDER: In an engine, the round hole in the engine block in which the piston(s) ride.

CYLINDER BLOCK: The main structural member of an engine in which is found the cylinders, crankshaft and other principal parts.

CYLINDER HEAD: The detachable portion of the engine, usually fastened to the top of the cylinder block and containing all or most of the combustion chambers. On overhead valve engines, it contains the valves and their operating parts. On overhead cam engines, it contains the camshaft as well.

DEAD CENTER: The extreme top or bottom of the piston stroke.

DETONATION: An unwanted explosion of the air/fuel mixture in the combustion chamber caused by excess heat and compression, advanced timing, or an overly lean mixture. Also referred to as "ping".

DIAPHRAGM: A thin, flexible wall separating two cavities, such as in a vacuum advance unit.

DIESELING: A condition in which hot spots in the combustion chamber cause the engine to run on after the key is turned off.

DIFFERENTIAL: A geared assembly which allows the transmission of motion between drive axles, giving one axle the ability to turn faster than the other.

DIODE: An electrical device that will allow current to flow in one direction only.

DISC BRAKE: A hydraulic braking assembly consisting of a brake disc, or rotor, mounted on an axle, and a caliper assembly containing, usually two brake pads which are activated by hydraulic pressure. The pads are forced against the sides of the disc, creating friction which slows the vehicle.

DISTRIBUTOR: A mechanically driven device on an engine which is responsible for electrically firing the spark plug at a predetermined point of the piston stroke.

DOWEL PIN: A pin, inserted in mating holes in two different parts allowing those parts to maintain a fixed relationship.

DRUM BRAKE: A braking system which consists of two brake shoes and one or two wheel cylinders, mounted on a fixed backing plate, and a brake drum, mounted on an axle, which revolves around the assembly.

DWELL: The rate, measured in degrees of shaft rotation, at which an electrical circuit cycles on and off.

ELECTRONIC CONTROL UNIT (ECU): Ignition module, module, amplifier or igniter. See Module for definition.

ELECTRONIC IGNITION: A system in which the timing and firing of the spark plugs is controlled by an electronic control unit, usually called a module. These systems have no points or condenser.

END-PLAY: The measured amount of axial movement in a shaft.

ENGINE: A device that converts heat into mechanical energy.

EXHAUST MANIFOLD: A set of cast passages or pipes which conduct exhaust gases from the engine.

FEELER GAUGE: A blade, usually metal, or precisely predetermined thickness, used to measure the clearance between two parts.

FIRING ORDER: The order in which combustion occurs in the cylinders of an engine. Also the order in which spark is distributed to the plugs by the distributor.

FLOODING: The presence of too much fuel in the intake manifold and combustion chamber which prevents the air/fuel mixture from firing, thereby causing a no-start situation.

FLYWHEEL: A disc shaped part bolted to the rear end of the crankshaft. Around the outer perimeter is affixed the ring gear. The starter drive engages the ring gear, turning the flywheel, which rotates the crankshaft, imparting the initial starting motion to the engine.

FOOT POUND (ft. lbs. or sometimes, ft.lb.): The amount of energy or work needed to raise an item weighing one pound, a distance of one foot.

FUSE: A protective device in a circuit which prevents circuit overload by breaking the circuit when a specific amperage is present. The device is constructed around a strip or wire of a lower amperage rating than the circuit it is designed to protect. When an amperage higher than that stamped on the fuse is present in the circuit, the strip or wire melts, opening the circuit.

GEAR RATIO: The ratio between the number of teeth on meshing gears.

GENERATOR: A device which converts mechanical energy into electrical energy.

HEAT RANGE: The measure of a spark plug's ability to dissipate heat from its firing end. The higher the heat range, the hotter the plug fires.

HUB: The center part of a wheel or gear.

HYDROCARBON (HC): Any chemical compound made up of hydrogen and carbon. A major pollutant formed by the engine as a byproduct of combustion.

HYDROMETER: An instrument used to measure the specific gravity of a solution.

INCH POUND (inch lbs.; sometimes in.lb. or in. lbs.): One twelfth of a foot pound.

INDUCTION: A means of transferring electrical energy in the form of a magnetic field. Principle used in the ignition coil to increase voltage.

INJECTOR: A device which receives metered fuel under relatively low pressure and is activated to inject the fuel into the engine under relatively high pressure at a predetermined time.

INPUT SHAFT: The shaft to which torque is applied, usually carrying the driving gear or gears.

INTAKE MANIFOLD: A casting of passages or pipes used to conduct air or a fuel/air mixture to the cylinders.

JOURNAL: The bearing surface within which a shaft operates.

KEY: A small block usually fitted in a notch between a shaft and a hub to prevent slippage of the two parts.

MANIFOLD: A casting of passages or set of pipes which connect the cylinders to an inlet or outlet source.

MANIFOLD VACUUM: Low pressure in an engine intake manifold formed just below the throttle plates. Manifold vacuum is highest at idle and drops under acceleration.

MASTER CYLINDER: The primary fluid pressurizing device in a hydraulic system. In automotive use, it is found in brake and hydraulic clutch systems and is pedal activated, either directly or, in a power brake system, through the power booster.

MODULE: Electronic control unit, amplifier or igniter of solid state or integrated design which controls the current flow in the ignition primary circuit based on input from the pick-up coil. When the module opens the primary circuit, high secondary voltage is induced in the coil.

NEEDLE BEARING: A bearing which consists of a number (usually a large number) of long, thin rollers.

OHM: (Ω) The unit used to measure the resistance of conductor-to-electrical flow. One ohm is the amount of resistance that limits current flow to one ampere in a circuit with one volt of pressure.

OHMMETER: An instrument used for measuring the resistance, in ohms, in an electrical circuit.

OUTPUT SHAFT: The shaft which transmits torque from a device, such as a transmission.

OVERDRIVE: A gear assembly which produces more shaft revolutions than that transmitted to it.

OVERHEAD CAMSHAFT (OHC): An engine configuration in which the camshaft is mounted on top of the cylinder head and operates the valve either directly or by means of rocker arms.

OVERHEAD VALVE (OHV): An engine configuration in which all of the valves are located in the cylinder head and the camshaft is located in the cylinder block. The camshaft operates the valves via lifters and pushrods.

OXIDES OF NITROGEN (NOx): Chemical compounds of nitrogen produced as a byproduct of combustion. They combine with hydrocarbons to produce smog.

OXYGEN SENSOR: Use with the feedback system to sense the presence of oxygen in the exhaust gas and signal the computer which can reference the voltage signal to an air/fuel ratio.

PINION: The smaller of two meshing gears.

PISTON RING: An open-ended ring with fits into a groove on the outer diameter of the piston. Its chief function is to form a seal between the piston and cylinder wall. Most automotive pistons have three rings: two for compression sealing; one for oil sealing.

PRELOAD: A predetermined load placed on a bearing during assembly or by adjustment.

PRIMARY CIRCUIT: the low voltage side of the ignition system which consists of the ignition switch, ballast resistor or resistance wire, bypass, coil, electronic control unit and pick-up coil as well as the connecting wires and harnesses.

PRESS FIT: The mating of two parts under pressure, due to the inner diameter of one being smaller than the outer diameter of the other, or vice versa; an interference fit.

RACE: The surface on the inner or outer ring of a bearing on which the balls, needles or rollers move.

REGULATOR: A device which maintains the amperage and/or voltage levels of a circuit at predetermined values.

RELAY: A switch which automatically opens and/or closes a circuit.

RESISTANCE: The opposition to the flow of current through a circuit or electrical device, and is measured in ohms. Resistance is equal to the voltage divided by the amperage.

RESISTOR: A device, usually made of wire, which offers a preset amount of resistance in an electrical circuit.

RING GEAR: The name given to a ring-shaped gear attached to a differential case, or affixed to a flywheel or as part of a planetary gear set.

ROLLER BEARING: A bearing made up of hardened inner and outer races between which hardened steel rollers move.

ROTOR: 1. The disc-shaped part of a disc brake assembly, upon which the brake pads bear; also called, brake disc. 2. The device mounted atop the distributor shaft, which passes current to the distributor cap tower contacts.

SECONDARY CIRCUIT: The high voltage side of the ignition system, usually above 20,000 volts. The secondary includes the ignition coil, coil wire, distributor cap and rotor, spark plug wires and spark plugs.

SENDING UNIT: A mechanical, electrical, hydraulic or electro-magnetic device which transmits information to a gauge.

SENSOR: Any device designed to measure engine operating conditions or ambient pressures and temperatures. Usually electronic in nature and designed to send a voltage signal to an on-board computer, some sensors may operate as a simple on/off switch or they may provide a variable voltage signal (like a potentiometer) as conditions or measured parameters change.

SHIM: Spacers of precise, predetermined thickness used between parts to establish a proper working relationship.

SLAVE CYLINDER: In automotive use, a device in the hydraulic clutch system which is activated by hydraulic force, disengaging the clutch.

SOLENOID: A coil used to produce a magnetic field, the effect of which is to produce work.

SPARK PLUG: A device screwed into the combustion chamber of a spark ignition engine. The basic construction is a conductive core inside of a ceramic insulator, mounted in an outer conductive base. An electrical charge from the spark plug wire travels along the conductive core and jumps a preset air gap to a grounding point or points at the end of the conductive base. The resultant spark ignites the fuel/air mixture in the combustion chamber.

SPLINES: Ridges machined or cast onto the outer diameter of a shaft or inner diameter of a bore to enable parts to mate without rotation.

TACHOMETER: A device used to measure the rotary speed of an engine, shaft, gear, etc., usually in rotations per minute.

THERMOSTAT: A valve, located in the cooling system of an engine, which is closed when cold and opens gradually in response to engine heating, controlling the temperature of the coolant and rate of coolant flow.

TOP DEAD CENTER (TDC): The point at which the piston reaches the top of its travel on the compression stroke.

TORQUE: The twisting force applied to an object.

TORQUE CONVERTER: A turbine used to transmit power from a driving member to a driven member via hydraulic action, providing changes in drive ratio and torque. In automotive use, it links the driveplate at the rear of the engine to the automatic transmission.

TRANSDUCER: A device used to change a force into an electrical signal.

TRANSISTOR: A semi-conductor component which can be actuated by a small voltage to perform an electrical switching function.

TUNE-UP: A regular maintenance function, usually associated with the replacement and adjustment of parts and components in the electrical and fuel systems of a vehicle for the purpose of attaining optimum performance.

TURBOCHARGER: An exhaust driven pump which compresses intake air and forces it into the combustion chambers at higher than atmospheric pressures. The increased air pressure allows more fuel to be burned and results in increased horsepower being produced.

VACUUM ADVANCE: A device which advances the ignition timing in response to increased engine vacuum.

VACUUM GAUGE: An instrument used to measure the presence of vacuum in a chamber.

VALVE: A device which control the pressure, direction of flow or rate of flow of a liquid or gas.

VALVE CLEARANCE: The measured gap between the end of the valve stem and the rocker arm, cam lobe or follower that activates the valve.

VISCOSITY: The rating of a liquid's internal resistance to flow.

VOLTMETER: An instrument used for measuring electrical force in units called volts. Voltmeters are always connected parallel with the circuit being tested.

WHEEL CYLINDER: Found in the automotive drum brake assembly, it is a device, actuated by hydraulic pressure, which, through internal pistons, pushes the brake shoes outward against the drums.

MASTER
INDEX

10-24 MASTER INDEX